W9-ASK-260

EMPLOYEE SELECTION WITHIN THE LAW

EMPLOYEE SELECTION WITHIN THE LAW

Mary Green Miner
Consulting Editor and Director, BNA Surveys
The Bureau of National Affairs, Inc.

John B. Miner
Research Professor of Management
Georgia State University

The Bureau of National Affairs, Inc., Washington, D.C.

Library of Congress Cataloging in Publication Data

Miner, Mary Green.
Employee selection within the law.
Includes index.

1. Employee selection—Law and legislation— United States. 2. Discrimination in employment—Law and legislation—United States. 3. Employee selection—United States. I. Miner, John B., joint author. II. Title.
KF3457.M5 344'.73'01133 78-18889
ISBN 0-87179-264-8

Printed in the United States of America
International Standard Book Number: 0-87179-264-8

preface

Our purpose in preparing this book is to provide guidance for personnel practitioners in the increasingly uncertain area of employee selection, under the requirements of equal employment opportunity legislation. We have tried to bring together in one volume three diverse strands of background information which currently have major influence on selection procedures. The first is the legal aspect of selection; it is in this aspect that the greatest current uncertainty is found. The second is the influence of professional industrial psychology on selection techniques through validation research. The third is the area of personnel practice itself—the policies and practices employers are finding most effective in coping with the legal requirements for equal employment opportunity as they relate to employee selection.

The book is divided into six parts. The historical introductory chapter of Part 1 is followed by the three chapters of Part 2 which present the background and current status of the various laws, regulations, court decisions, and guidelines affecting selection. Part 3 covers the technical aspects of conducting workforce analyses to determine adverse impact and of conducting validation studies to determine the job-relatedness of selection procedures.

Parts 4 and 5 consist primarily of previously published examples of validation research along with commentary on how these studies might be or have been viewed by the government agencies enforcing the equal employment opportunity laws and regulations. The psychological literature in this field includes a multitude of validation studies that could be used to provide examples; the ones presented here have been chosen because the authors are familiar with the research and thus feel able to discuss the background and implications of the studies with some authority. Of the 12 articles included in Parts 4 and 5, six were written by the second author of this volume. Authors of the remaining six articles are listed in the Table of Contents and noted at the beginning of the text of each article.

Part 6 considers the types of programs employers have undertaken to achieve affirmative action goals in recruiting and selection and to show a "good faith effort" in complying with the requirements of the law. It is our hope that readers with a primarily legal background will benefit from the discussions and examples of validation research, that those with a psychological background will benefit from the discussions of the legal aspects, and that personnel generalists will find the meshing of the legal, psychological, and practical aspects of selection of value in overall policy formation and daily decision making.

The original intent was to publish this book as soon as possible after the various government agencies involved in equal employment opportunity agreed on a uniform set of guidelines governing selection procedures. For several years, there was anticipation that such agreement would be reached. In November 1976, with the publication of two sets of selection guidelines in the *Federal Register,* it became clear that the agencies were far from agreement on uniform guidelines. At that point, we decided to proceed on the basis of the two sets of guidelines currently in effect and to try to advise employers as best we could considering the situation. During the summer of 1977, a renewed effort on the part of the federal EEO agencies to produce a set of uniform guidelines influenced us to delay publication in the hope that such agreement was imminent. With the issuance of a set of proposed uniform guidelines—the first agreement among all the federal EEO agencies—in December 1978, we decided to push ahead with final publication.

It should be kept in mind that this book is based on the court decisions and regulations in effect as of early 1978. The reader should check the latest decisions concerning the legalities of the current situation beyond that date. The material on validation research and affirmative action programs, however, should change much more slowly; we expect our discussions in those areas to remain current for some time.

As is the case in any such endeavor, this book owes much to the support and assistance of many individuals other than ourselves. Although it is impossible to mention all of them by name, there are a few whose contributions deserve special acknowledgment. These include the first author's associates at The Bureau of National Affairs, Inc., who kept her informed of legal developments and in some cases provided her with advance reports of these developments; David Parker and Jean Linehan have been particularly helpful in this regard. We would like to thank Jean Linehan and Howard Anderson of BNA and Mary Tenopyr of AT&T for reading parts of the manuscript in draft form and Barbara Williams of Georgia State University for her usual expert and efficient processing of the manuscript. Finally, we express our appreciation to Donald Farwell, manager of BNA Books, for his encouragement and patience, and to Frances Reed and Mildred Cary for coping with the trials of the production process.

Atlanta, Georgia M.G.M.
April 1978 J.B.M.

table of contents

Part III. Techniques for Evaluating the Selection Process

Part IV. Comprehensive Validation of a Total Selection System in a Management Consulting Firm

Part V. Validation of Psychological Tests and Assessment Centers in Connection With the AT&T Case

Part VII. Exhibits

part 1

introduction

1

government pressures on employment practices

> An employer may set his qualifications as high as he likes, he may test to determine which applicants have these qualifications, and he may hire, assign, and promote on the basis of test performance.

These words were written by two United States senators as part of a memorandum interpreting various provisions of the Civil Rights Act of 1964 at the time it was passed.[1] The memorandum also includes this sentence: "There is no requirement in Title VII that employers abandon bona fide qualification tests where, because of differences in background and education, members of some groups are able to perform better on these tests than members of other groups."

As any person who has participated in, or observed, the practice of personnel administration over the past decade knows well, the impact of Title VII of the Civil Rights Act, which prohibits discrimination in employment based on race, color, religion, national origin, or sex, has been far greater than even opponents of some of its provisions envisaged when they raised what were then hypothetical questions such as the following:

> If the Negro labor force in a particular community constitutes 10 percent of the total labor force, will a company whose Negro employees constitute only 5 percent of the company payroll be guilty of discrimination?
>
> If the company has 100 executives and only four are Negro, would this constitute discrimination in promotions to executive pay levels if the

[1]Quoted in *The Civil Rights Act of 1964* (Washington, D.C.: The Bureau of National Affairs, Inc., 1964), p. 329.

> Negro work force in the rest of the company constitutes 10 percent of the total company work force?[2]

Today it is obvious that the answer to both these questions is likely to be yes in the absence of any special circumstances in the companies in question; furthermore, these questions no longer sound "far-fetched," as they were described in 1964.

The world of the personnel manager has changed dramatically as the Equal Employment Opportunity Commission (EEOC) and the courts have enforced and interpreted Title VII of the Civil Rights Act. Despite the disclaimer quoted at the beginning of this chapter, many employers have abandoned testing programs and other qualifications for employment in the wake of Title VII, with the result that selection procedures in some companies may be less scientific and effective than at any time in the last 50 years; in other cases, with validation, the reverse may be true. In addition, there has been a plethora of other laws and government regulations related to equal opportunity in the workplace which extend the list of protected groups beyond minorities and women to include the handicapped, disabled veterans, and Vietnam veterans.

This chapter will trace the steps leading from the enactment of the Civil Rights Act to the present time, with an emphasis on the courts' interpretation of "discrimination" in employment and on the approaches to enforcement taken by the EEOC.

Early approaches to EEO

Title VII became operative in July 1965. Before that time, the only major legal constraints on employer selection practices were the state and local Fair Employment Practice statutes dating back to 1945 and found in about one half of the states by the mid-1960s. As would be expected, the effectiveness of these FEP laws varied considerably from one jurisdiction to another depending on the political climate and funds available for enforcement. The number of cases actively pursued was relatively small and the overall impact on personnel practice almost nil except for the fact that certain questions on forms used for employment applications were eliminated.

[2] *Ibid.*, p. 244.

The Civil Rights Act was not the first federal law relating to discriminatory employment practices, however.[3] In 1963, Congress passed the Equal Pay Act in the form of an amendment to the wage-hour law; it requires all employers subject to the provisions of that law to pay equal wages to men and women for "equal work on jobs the performance of which requires equal skill, effort, and responsibility, and which are performed under similar working conditions." However, there are several exceptions, such as where the wages are paid pursuant to a seniority or merit system, and for a number of years it was difficult to tell what the law really meant. Since the Department of Labor was slow to bring suits under the Equal Pay Act, employers tended to ignore it.

Also predating the Civil Rights Act were a series of Executive orders that apply to any business doing a certain dollar amount of work under government contracts. Executive orders prohibiting discrimination in employment by government contractors date back to World War II. They are enforced by the Office of Federal Contract Compliance Programs (OFCCP) in the U.S. Department of Labor (for many years, the agency was called the OFCC; "Programs" was added to the designation in 1975). The OFCCP has authority to terminate government contracts and to debar companies from bidding on contracts in the future unless the employer takes steps to remedy discriminatory employment practices. Such actions have been rare, however.

At the time the Civil Rights Act was passed, hardly any employers viewed the employment provisions of Title VII with alarm. Because of rather lackadaisical enforcement of the existing federal regulations governing equal employment practices, there seemed little for the average company to be concerned about. Furthermore, the agency charged with enforcing Title VII, the EEOC, was given no power to bring suit where unlawful employment practices are alleged. Its power was limited to the investigation of complaints and to seeking voluntary compliance. If efforts at conciliation failed, individuals could bring suit in the federal courts and if it was found that an employer exhibited a "pattern or

[3]An 1886 federal law also has been interpreted as prohibiting racial discrimination in private employment, but it was not until after the Civil Rights Act was passed that this law was invoked in suits involving private employers.

practice" of discrimination in employment, the U.S. Attorney General could bring suit.

Based on enforcement of the state and local FEP laws that had existed for some time, most employers assumed that the enforcement process under Title VII would involve the conciliation of individual complaints of discrimination and that the person bringing the complaint would have the burden of proof. Furthermore, it was assumed that only companies with very obvious discriminatory employment practices would be called to task under the "pattern or practice" provisions. As one report on the enforcement of Title VII notes, "Certainly few businessmen anticipated that Title VII would ever be used to challenge their basic personnel policies and practices so long as they were evenhandedly administered."[4]

Title VII enforcement—the definition of "discrimination"

As with any federal legislation, the final impact is determined by the U.S. Supreme Court. Over the past decade, the courts have had numerous opportunities to rule on specific employment practices in specific situations, and accordingly, there are many conflicting lower court rulings. One crucial question that has evolved in EEO litigation has been—how does one define "discrimination" in employment practices?

Initially, the courts took the tack anticipated by most employers. They looked at the motives or intent behind the employment practice in question; if it was found that the employer had an *evil intent* not to hire persons because of their race, color, religion, national origin, or sex, then the employment practice was indeed discriminatory and a violation of the law. It soon became clear, however, that evil motive or evil intent is almost impossible to prove, and as a result there were few convictions in the first two or three years Title VII was in effect.

Soon the definition of discrimination was broadened to encompass what is known as the unjust-treatment, or *denial-of-equal-treatment,* theory. Under this approach, employers would not be found guilty of discrimination in employment if all job applicants or

[4]R.G. Shaeffer, *Nondiscrimination in Employment: Changing Perspectives, 1963-1972* (New York: The Conference Board, 1973), p. 7.

all employees were treated equally in matters of hiring, promotion, discipline, and so forth. As long as employment decisions are based on equal standards for whites and minorities, males and females, there is no discrimination. On the basis of this theory, some employers were proven guilty of discrimination, but change was very slow. Title VII still was having little impact, particularly in terms of the employment of blacks and other minorities.

The problem that became evident was that neither the evil-intent nor the denial-of-equal-treatment theories of discrimination took into account the effects of past discrimination. What this meant was that because of unequal training or educational opportunities in the past, separate seniority units, or lack of specific job experience, many minority persons would not qualify for certain jobs. Thus, even in the absence of proven evil intent or unjust treatment, there was little change in the employment picture for minorities or other protected groups.

The realization of this situation led to the *adverse-impact* theory, stated clearly by the U.S. Supreme Court in its landmark decision in *Griggs* v. *Duke Power Co.,*[5] handed down in 1971. The Court said:

> The objective of Congress in the enactment of Title VII is plain from the language of the statute. It was to achieve equality of employment opportunities and remove barriers that have operated in the past to favor an identifiable group of white employees over other employees. Under the Act, practices, procedures, or tests neutral on their face, and even neutral in terms of intent, cannot be maintained if they operate to "freeze" the status quo of prior discriminatory employment practices.

In this case, the Court agreed that the company had no evil motives in its employment practices and that the qualification requirements in question had been administered equally to blacks and whites, but the *consequences* of these employment practices resulted in an adverse impact on blacks. The Court pointed out, however, that if an employment practice can be shown to be a "business necessity" it would not be prohibited even though its use results in an adverse impact on a protected group. In the *Duke Power* case, the company

[5]401 U.S. 424 (1971), 3 FEP Cases 175. The full text of this decision appears at p. 373, *infra*.

failed to show that employment requirements were related to successful job performance or fulfilled any business need; therefore, the Court ruled, these employment practices were prohibited by Title VII.

The adverse-impact theory of discrimination has been the foundation for Title VII litigation since 1971. Once there is a clear case of adverse impact resulting from employment practices, it is up to the employer to prove such practices are job-related and thus involve a business necessity. The business-necessity requirement has been narrowly construed. Increasingly, employers have had to look at their employment practices in a different light. If a practice results in cutting off opportunities for certain groups, then the question is—does the practice in fact fulfill a legitimate business need?

The 1972 amendments

When the Civil Rights Act was passed in 1964, it was assumed by many people in the government that voluntary compliance and conciliation efforts by EEOC would take care of the majority of alleged violations of Title VII involving individual complaints. And only in the most blatant of circumstances would the Attorney General need to bring suits based on the pattern-or-practice-of-discrimination provisions. Both these assumptions turned out to be incorrect. As Senator Harrison Williams of New Jersey pointed out, "We did not anticipate the extent of discrimination which existed at the time we enacted the legislation, nor did we fully understand its nature."[6]

By 1972, the EEOC had a backlog of more than 30,000 complaints of Title VII violations, the Justice Department was being accused of dragging its feet in bringing Title VII suits, and civil rights advocates were extremely disappointed at the lack of progress in equal employment opportunity. Although a number of individual cases had been settled in the courts after EEOC conciliation efforts had failed and the definition of discrimination under Title VII had been broadened considerably, there was a general disenchantment with the overall results of Title VII enforcement.

The solution, according to equal opportunity proponents, was

[6]*The Equal Employment Opportunity Act of 1972* (Washington, D.C.: The Bureau of National Affairs, Inc., 1972), p. 360.

to give the EEOC direct enforcement powers, and this was accomplished by the Equal Employment Opportunity Act of 1972, which amended Title VII of the 1964 Act. In addition to extending coverage of the law to smaller employers and state and local governments, the amendments give EEOC the power to go to court for injunctions or other remedies against employers if conciliation efforts have failed to produce an acceptable disposition of a charge.

The new enforcement powers have had little noticeable effect on EEOC's case backlog; in fact, it has increased every year, and reached 125,000 in 1977. However, the potential for court action may very well have been a crucial factor in the final disposition of charges of discrimination against the nation's largest employer, the Bell System. These charges were settled in a consent decree entered into in January 1973 between AT&T and all associated Bell System companies, the EEOC, and the U.S. Department of Labor.[7] For employers throughout the nation, the estimated cost of the settlement ($38 million the first year and $25 to $35 million a year for the next five years) provided a warning that employment discrimination could indeed be costly. Since the Bell System consent decree, there have been several others involving sizable costs to employers.

The costly remedies: back pay and affirmative action

So far no personnel executive has been sent to jail for violation of equal employment opportunity laws, but it is conceivable. If a company should fail to live up to the requirements of a court-ordered affirmative action program or consent decree and cannot prove a good-faith effort to do so, there is the possibility a company official could be found in contempt of court and required to serve a sentence. While such a situation is unlikely, the remedies the courts have invoked can indeed be costly. This is particularly true where a class action suit is involved, and class actions are a favorite approach of the EEOC. What may begin as an individual complaint frequently becomes a class action on behalf of all persons adversely affected by the employment practices in question. In a 1975 decision the Supreme Court upheld EEOC's use of class action suits, saying that back pay as a remedy could be awarded to unnamed persons who did

[7]*Daily Labor Report,* No. 14, January 19, 1973, p. 1.

not themselves file charges if they are in the affected class.[8] In a more recent decision, however, the Court said that only "specifically identifiable" victims of unlawful discrimination should be entitled to back pay.[9] This ruling may serve to limit the large numbers of affected persons included in class action suits in the future, and thus reduce company liability for huge amounts of back pay.

A company's liability for back pay is limited to a period of two years preceding the filing of a charge, and in the case of an individual complaint the amount involved would be relatively small. However, the cases the government chooses to pursue are the ones involving multiple charges or class actions, and large back-pay awards in these cases are viewed as appropriate remedies for persons who have suffered because of unlawful employment discrimination. Furthermore, the Supreme Court has said that the use of back-pay awards is one way to achieve results in removing employment barriers. "If employers faced only the prospect of an injunctive order, they would have little incentive to shun practices of dubious legality."[10]

There are some cases where back pay is not an appropriate remedy, as when it is not possible to identify or find the individuals who have suffered from a company's discriminatory employment practices. In one such case, the court dismissed the individual charge as being without merit but decided the company's practices needed to be monitored to make sure its progress in equal employment opportunity continued. The remedy in such cases may involve court-ordered goals and hiring ratios similar to those called for in consent decrees. Such remedies involve what is known as *affirmative action* to achieve the goals specified.

The idea of requiring affirmative action to ensure equal employment opportunity began with an Executive order applying to government contractors issued in September 1965. This order was expanded in terms of coverage in 1968, and in 1970 Order No. 4 was issued, providing detailed requirements for affirmative action plans. All these orders predated the Supreme Court's *Duke Power* decision

[8] *Albemarle Paper Company* v. *Moody,* 422 U.S. 405 (1975), 10 FEP Cases 1181.

[9] *Teamsters* v. *U.S.,* 431 U.S. 324 (1977), 14 FEP Cases 1514.

[10] *Albemarle Paper Company* v. *Moody, supra* note 8.

based on the "adverse impact" theory of discrimination, but their intent was similar. In effect, they are based on the premise that it is not enough that an employer has no intent to discriminate and treats all individuals equally. If there is any evidence that the employment practices result in discrimination, then the employer is required to take affirmative action to eliminate the discriminatory results. Exactly what is required for affirmative action as it relates to selection will be discussed in the last part of this book; the important point here is that it is a concept that has been endorsed by both OFCCP and EEOC and upheld by the courts as an effective process for achieving equal employment opportunity.

Dealing with EEOC

What has turned out to be a major problem for many employers is trying to figure out how to deal with EEOC. It became apparent very quickly that the Commission views the investigation of an individual charge of employment discrimination as an opportunity to look into the whole range of an employer's personnel practices for evidence of barriers to equal opportunity. The result frequently is that instead of reaching a conciliation agreement with regard to the disposition of an individual situation, which a company may be very willing to do, the EEOC insists on an agreement calling for changes in the firm's basic employment practices. Furthermore, because of EEOC's case load there have been situations where an employer has found itself subject to court suit without any attempt at reaching a conciliation agreement first.

There has been a great deal of criticism of such tactics, and under streamlined procedures adopted by EEOC under pressure from the Carter Administration, there is some hope of change. These procedures call for more rapid processing of individual charges and more concentration of resources on systemic "pattern and practice" discrimination. The hope is that if employment practices are changed in large companies there will be a "trickle down" effect to smaller employers. The strategy is similar to that taken by the unions in collective bargaining for wages and fringe benefits, but it remains to be seen whether it will work for equal employment opportunity.

Employers may have anticipated that EEOC would operate on

the same model as the National Labor Relations Board, in a quasi-judicial relationship between the individuals charging discrimination in employment and the company charged. What has happened, however, is that EEOC has taken an adversary role, the same role played by the union in NLRB proceedings. Not only is EEOC taking an adversary role, but it also has adopted a missionary stance, with all the devotion and enthusiasm that entails. The EEOC staff includes many bright young people who are out to change the world, and often these people have little knowledge of or interest in how the business world operates; in fact, some observers charge that most EEOC investigators are "antibusiness," especially big business. Dealing with such individuals can be an exasperating experience for someone used to dealing with the ordinary civil servant.

The initial inkling that a company may have to deal with EEOC on a Title VII charge is a notice that such a charge has been filed, indicating who filed the charge and the general nature of the complaint. Because of EEOC's backlog, it may then be two or three years before any further notice about the complaint. Lawyers knowledgeable in Title VII litigation suggest that this time be used to good advantage so the company will be in the best position possible if the case should go to court. While it certainly is a good idea to consult with the company's legal counsel when a charge has been filed, it basically is up to the personnel administrator to develop the facts concerning a specific charge and to compile the statistics necessary to back up the company's action.

If there is a state or local FEP agency with jurisdiction, it will have first call on the complaint, since EEOC is required to defer to recognized state or local agencies before stepping in. It usually is to the employer's advantage to resolve the problem at this lower level if possible, because these agencies do not as a rule look at a company's overall employment practices, nor do they use the class action approach. Even with a settlement at this level, the filing of a complaint should be viewed as a red flag—an early warning that perhaps an assessment of the total record on equal employment opportunity is in order.

It is also suggested that all the facts relating to the complaint be documented as quickly as possible and made part of a permanent record. Since it may be three or four years before a case actually gets to court, it could easily happen that the supervisor making the final decision not to hire or not to promote the particular individual filing the charge is no longer available to testify as to his or her reasons. In making the investigation and compiling a record, the one thing to be sure to avoid is any discussion with the complaining party that could be construed as retaliation for filing a charge—that in itself is a violation of Title VII.

The most favorable outcome of such an investigation into a complaint would be a showing that there had been a lack of communication or a misunderstanding. Steps could then be taken to solve the problem, and the charge would be withdrawn. If the charge is pursued, it may be possible to conciliate a settlement even before EEOC sends its investigator; once the investigator does appear, however, one should be prepared for an examination of all relevant data and all personnel policies and practices.

To be optimistic, it may be that the investigator will decide the company's action was perfectly legal and all records are in order—this does happen. A recent BNA survey reported on the outcome of 93 investigations by EEOC or OFCCP; in 27 cases no cause for complaint was found and the charges were dropped, 21 were settled with a conciliation agreement, and 16 went to court. Of these 16, eight were decided in favor of the company, and eight went against the company.[11]

If there is evidence of discrimination and the company agrees that there is (by this time the legal staff should be working hand in hand with the personnel people), and if the company feels it is appropriate to take the steps required to remedy the situation, the next step is a conciliation agreement. With regard to specific issues or personnel practices, the courts make the final determination as to what constitutes discrimination, and EEOC takes this into account. For example, during the time when the Supreme Court was considering the problem of maternity benefits, the EEOC made a "temporary exception" and did not require the inclusion of any reference to such benefits in conciliation agreements. In late 1976, the Court resolved this issue with a ruling that employers are not required to

[11]*Equal Employment Opportunity: Programs and Results,* Personnel Policies Forum Survey No. 112, March 1976 (Washington, D.C.: The Bureau of National Affairs, Inc.), p. 15.

treat disability due to pregnancy the same as any other illness for purposes of disability insurance or sick leave benefits.[12]

A basic problem for the practice of personnel management is that under pressure from the legal staff or the financial officer, who have read about large back-pay awards, companies have agreed to change their practices under the terms of conciliation agreements or consent decrees without ever finding out how the courts actually would rule. This is one reason so many issues still are fuzzy in EEO litigation—they have not had a clear test in court. It obviously is going to be many more years before all the answers are in.

The scope of governmental regulation

Most of the discussion to this point has related to the interpretation and enforcement of Title VII of the Civil Rights Act. There are other federal statutes such as the Equal Pay Act and the Age Discrimination in Employment Act, as well as numerous regulations calling for affirmative action with reference to protected groups that apply to government contractors. The details of these laws and regulations are beyond the scope of this book, but it should be noted that what is said about selection procedures with regard to minorities and women may apply equally to other protected groups.

It also should be pointed out that the initial emphasis in EEOC litigation was primarily on charges of racial discrimination. By the early 1970s, an increasing number of charges of discrimination in employment on the basis of sex were being filed with EEOC. To the surprise of many, women were demanding an opportunity to work in the often dirty but higher paid craft jobs or to experience the extra stress and rewards of managerial responsibility. The issue of sex discrimination was a major factor in the AT&T consent decree and has become an important aspect of most affirmative action programs. As will be discussed in Chapters 21 through 23, however, affirmative action strategies with regard to women may be quite different from those that are most effective for minority groups.

Over the years it has become apparent that any area of personnel practice may be affected by the requirements for equal employment opportunity regardless of race, sex, and so forth. The

[12]*General Electric Co.* v. *Gilbert,* 429 U.S. 125 (1976). 13 FEP Cases 1657.

most obvious forms of employment discrimination, such as seniority units or job classifications limited to whites or males, have disappeared, at least on paper if not in fact. Employers are being asked to examine their policies with regard to compensation, benefits, training opportunities, discipline, and other aspects of employee relations that might have even a subtle discriminatory effect. If a company's statistics on employment of minorities or women are not good, any practice that might be contributing to the "adverse impact" should be examined with a view to justifying it in court as a "business necessity."

Until now many companies, while worried, have felt that they could ignore much of what the government has been doing in its efforts to enforce equal employment opportunity. EEOC primarily has charged large companies where there will be the greatest impact, and OFCCP, although it has issued many regulations and required much paperwork from government contractors, has rarely used its power actually to terminate a contract because of employment discrimination problems.

This era may be coming to an end, however. For one thing, the courts, particularly the U.S. Supreme Court, have made it very clear that equal employment opportunity is the law of the land and a matter of high priority. They have been supportive of EEOC's efforts, and they have made it expensive to be in violation. Second, the 1972 Equal Employment Opportunity Act provided an indication that Congress wants results—although there has been some progress, there certainly is a long way to go before it can be said that every American enjoys equal treatment in the job market or on the job. Finally, recent efforts aimed at reorganizing the federal government's EEOC structure over the next few years and consolidating all the enforcement programs under the EEOC indicate even stronger compliance efforts in years to come.

The importance of selection

The discussion in this book will concentrate on the effects of governmental pressures on selection in the broadest sense, including recruiting, hiring, testing, interviewing, promotion, and training in making selection decisions. It is our impression that in many other areas of personnel policy and procedure, such as wage and salary administration, the evidence for discrimination is fairly easy to find and the remedies obvious (although not necessarily easy to implement).

Selection is the first place to look for practices that result in adverse impact, and selection procedures have been the subject of detailed guidelines issued by the enforcement agencies. The courts have ruled on a number of specific selection policies with the result that there are certain qualifications that no longer should be used except in special situations where they can be justified. Selection procedures, particularly as they relate to recruiting, are the foundation of most affirmative action plans. These aspects of selection will be discussed in Part 6.

The question has been asked why companies should not abandon selection techniques as they have been used in traditional personnel practice, particularly if the use of such techniques results in adverse impact. One answer is that the selection technique per se does not result in discrimination but the way it is used may. Another answer is that there is a wide variety of selection procedures available and careful study can produce some that will eliminate or at least lessen the discriminatory effects. A third answer is that certain selection standards *are* based on business necessity and need to be adhered to for the company to survive and prosper.

A final reason for maintaining selection policies that are as effective as possible is that, without them, the problems of discrimination in employment will be compounded. A personnel executive may know his or her company is in a bad position in terms of statistics. If this is reported to other executives, their reaction could be something along these lines: "Rather than face the prospect of a class action, large amounts of back pay, or court-ordered hiring quotas, why not hire a few more blacks or a female manager or whatever is needed?" The questions then become, where would you find these people, what jobs would you give them, how would you know whether they can perform the work? And even more important, does such token compliance achieve its objectives in the long run?

There already is concern about turnover among the people companies have spent the most time and money recruiting as part of their affirmative action efforts. To put people in jobs where there is little likelihood of long-term success is an injustice to them and demoralizes the workforce as a whole; the net effect on the organization's goals is negative. It is our belief that a scientific selection program offers the best way of finding and maintaining an effective workforce within the requirements of equal employment opportunity.

part 2

the legal framework for selection

2

what the courts have ruled

In Chapter 1, the evolution of the definition of discrimination in employment was traced from the evil-motive concept to the idea of adverse impact. Under the adverse-impact doctrine, which has become the basic test for determination of discrimination by EEOC and the courts, any personnel procedure or policy that produces discriminatory results is unlawful unless it can be justified on the grounds of job-relatedness or business necessity. Furthermore, it is not relevant that an employer has no intention to discriminate and treats all groups equally in such matters as hiring, promotion, and firing; what counts are the results.

While the adverse-impact doctrine does provide a general framework for decisions relating to unlawful discrimination in employment, to date the courts have taken an ad hoc or situational approach to Title VII enforcement cases. The net effect is that the facts in each case are viewed quite independently, and an employment practice that is found to be unlawful as used in one company in one part of the country may not be unlawful in another company or in another locality. The basic questions that the courts have asked in each specific situation are these—

1. Is there proof of discrimination? Whether discrimination is defined as evil intent, unequal treatment, or adverse impact, this proof must be shown by the party charging a violation of Title VII.

2. What employment practices are causing the discrimination? If the court is convinced that there is in fact discrimination in employment, it has to be shown that certain practices are causing the discrimination.

3. Can the employment practices in question be justified on the

grounds of business necessity that is related to job performance? The burden of proof at this point is clearly on the employer to show a relationship between the practice in question and job performance.

In reaching their decisions in Title VII cases, the courts must answer two crucial questions—*what is adverse impact*? and *what constitutes job-relatedness or business necessity*?—in each situation they review. This chapter will provide examples of these definitions from court decisions and will discuss rulings on specific procedures used in the selection of employees for initial hiring and for promotion.

What is adverse impact?

There have been situations where it has been shown that an employer's employment practices are based on an evil intent to discriminate, or where protected groups have been denied equal treatment in employment opportunity, or both. In these cases, the costs to the company may reach extremely high figures because the courts can award damages as well as back pay and attorneys' fees. In recent years, however, most companies of any size have taken steps to eliminate these types of discrimination in employment. Thus, today the definition of discrimination used by EEOC and the courts is primarily that of adverse impact.

It should be emphasized that the party charging a violation of the law has to provide the proof of adverse impact, or proof of some other form of discrimination, before the court can rule on the employment practice in question. One court of appeals turned down a lower court decision, saying, "The missing ingredient in the proof here was the necessary showing of discrimination." This case involved nonvalidated tests and subjective hiring procedures, which the court says "are not violative of Title VII per se. Title VII comes into play when such practices result in discrimination."[1]

The proof of discrimination based on adverse impact involves statistics, and EEO litigation increasingly is characterized as "a numbers game." This statistical approach has been viewed by the courts as a matter of law in proving employment discrimination. In a relatively early Title VII case, a court ruled on this issue, saying,

[1]*Hester* v. *Southern Railway Co.*, 497 F.2d 1374 (1974), 8 FEP Cases 646.

"We hold as a matter of law that these statistics, which revealed an extraordinarily small number of black employees, except in the most part as menial laborers, established a violation of Title VII of the Civil Rights Act of 1964."[2]

To prove adverse impact, EEOC uses data from a variety of sources. To prove the adverse impact of requiring a high school diploma for entry-level jobs at Duke Power Company, for example, it was pointed out that according to the 1960 census data, in North Carolina only 12 percent of Negro males had graduated from high school compared to 34 percent of white males.[3] In this and other cases, evidence on certain test performance, showing that 58 percent of whites and only 6 percent of blacks obtained passing scores, was submitted as a factor contributing to adverse impact. In a more recent case, the statistics used were based on the company's own employment and payroll records. These figures indicated that black males with high school educations were making less money than white males with third grade educations and blacks with 10 years' seniority were making less than whites with two years' seniority.[4]

From these examples, it is obvious that EEOC looks at any data it can find to support a charge of adverse impact, and an employer faced with an EEOC charge of violation of Title VII is at a distinct disadvantage. One approach for the company is to submit statistics to refute a charge of adverse impact; the kinds of data that can be used as EEO statistics and their sources are discussed in greater detail in Chapter 5.

What is business necessity?

According to the courts, the only justification for an employer's continuing to use a personnel procedure that results in adverse impact is job-related business necessity. This requirement generally has been interpreted to mean that selection procedures must be related to job performance. This test has been applied to the entire range of

[2]*Parham* v. *Southwestern Bell Telephone Company,* 433 F.2d 421 (1970), 2 FEP Cases 1017.

[3]*Griggs* v. *Duke Power Company,* 401 U.S. 424 (1971), 3 FEP Cases 175.

[4]*Sledge* v. *J. P. Stevens & Co.,* No. 1201 (E.D.N.C. 1976), cited in *Daily Labor Report,* No. 133, July 9, 1976, p. A-4.

selection, including recruiting practices, initial hiring procedures, transfer and promotion decisions, policies for choosing employees for apprenticeship programs, and selecting employees for promotion to supervisory positions.

The test of business necessity was an important element in several of the early court decisions under Title VII involving company policies and seniority systems that served to restrict transfers and promotions and thus locked certain groups of employees into the less desirable jobs. In these cases, the courts made clear that inconvenience, additional expense, or a certain amount of disruption do not add up to business necessity. In one case, a court said, "avoidance of the expense of changing employment practices is not a business purpose that will validate the racially differential effects of an otherwise unlawful employment practice."[5] Another indication of the narrow interpretation of the business necessity exception is the following:

> Necessity connotes an irresistible demand. To be preserved, the seniority and transfer system must not only directly foster safety and efficiency of a plant, but also be essential to those goals. . . . If the legitimate ends of safety and efficiency can be served by a reasonably available alternative system with less discriminatory effects, then the present policies may not be continued.[6]

A classic case of selection standards being a business necessity involves the requirements for the job of flight officer or pilot hired by commercial airlines. In a situation involving a black applicant who lacked a college degree and had 204 hours of flight time compared to the 500 hours required by the airline, the court noted, "The risks involved in hiring an unqualified applicant are staggering." In upholding the airline's requirements, the court said:

> When a job requires a small amount of skill and training and the consequences of hiring an unqualified applicant are insignificant, the courts should examine closely any preemployment standard or criteria which discriminate against minorities. In such a case, the employer should have a heavy burden to demonstrate to the court's satisfaction that his employment criteria are job related. On the other hand, when

[5]*Robinson* v. *Lorillard Corporation,* 444 F.2d 791 (1971), 3 FEP Cases 653.

[6]*U.S.* v. *Bethlehem Steel Co.,* 446 F.2d 652 (1971), 3 FEP Cases 589.

the job clearly requires a high degree of skill and the economic and human risks involved in hiring an unqualified applicant are great, the employer bears a correspondingly lighter burden to show that his employment criteria are job-related.[7]

Rulings on specific selection procedures

It was emphasized in the beginning of this chapter that the courts have taken a situational approach in Title VII enforcement. Examples of rulings on selection procedures discussed below illustrate how the adverse-impact and business-necessity tests have been applied in ways that may result in a particular selection standard being unlawful in one situation and not in another. The discussion is not meant to provide a completely comprehensive coverage of court rulings regarding selection techniques; it is intended to provide a framework for reviewing the legality of certain practices in terms of the specific situation.

Recruiting. Where there is a racial imbalance in the company's present workforce, it has been found unlawful to rely on limited recruiting efforts such as word-of-mouth referrals from present employees or walk-in applicants. Employers also have been found guilty of discrimination where outside recruiting was conducted at only predominantly white educational institutions[8] and where workers were recruited through unions that barred blacks from membership.[9] Furthermore, a company with a previous policy of excluding minorities from certain job categories must make it known to the minority community that the discriminatory policies have been abandoned.[10]

The court rulings with regard to recruiting activities support the affirmative action approach to programs for eliminating discrimination in employment. In many instances, there was no overt discrimination in hiring because there were no applicants from the

[7]*Spurlock* v. *United Airlines,* 475 F.2d 216 (1972), 5 FEP Cases 17.

[8]*U.S.* v. *Georgia Power Co.,* 474 F.2d 906 (1973), 5 FEP Cases 587.

[9]*Ethridge* v. *Rhodes,* 268 F.Supp. 83 (1967), 1 FEP Cases 185.

[10]*U.S.* v. *Local 36, Sheet Metal Workers,* 416 F.2d 123 (1969), 2 FEP Cases 127.

protected groups and the recruitment system tended to perpetuate the same racial composition of the workforce. In effect, this type of recruiting created an adverse impact. More extensive recruiting programs may be more costly, but no employer has effectively argued that a limited recruiting approach constitutes a business necessity.

The extent of an employer's recruiting efforts, in terms of the geographical area to be included, is a matter of some controversy. In one case, however, a court upheld a company's policy of limiting its recruiting efforts to an area within a 15-mile radius of the plant.[11] In this particular case, the company was a government contractor and the OFCCP had issued a debarment order saying the firm's affirmative action plan was not based on a "realistic" recruitment area. In upholding the company, the court disagreed with the government's definition of the "local recruiting area." This definition, which is the standard for assessing the effectiveness of affirmative action efforts, will be discussed further in Chapter 5.

Hiring standards. Rigid hiring standards, such as minimum educational or physical requirements, for certain jobs have been scrutinized carefully by EEOC and the courts. The requirement of a high school education has been found unlawful in several cases where such a requirement resulted in an adverse impact and the employer did not show that it was sufficiently related to job performance. On the other hand, an educational requirement (graduation from high school, a certificate of high school equivalency, or an honorable discharge after three years of military service) was upheld in a case involving the Boston police department. The court found the requirement had a meaningful relationship to job performance ability on the basis of several studies showing that a high school education was viewed as the bare minimum for successful performance as a policeman.[12]

Policies that automatically exclude job applicants because of police arrest records or even convictions have been ruled illegal because of the adverse impact on minority employment; such policies disqualify a disproportionate number of blacks since they are

[11] *Timken Co.* v. *Vaughan,* 413 F.Supp. 1183 (1976), 12 FEP Cases 1140.

[12] *Castro* v. *Beecher,* 334 F.Supp. 930 (1971), 4 FEP Cases 37.

arrested more frequently than whites.[13] Where it has been shown that such a policy is justified on the basis of business necessity, the policy has been upheld. In the case of the job of hotel bellman, for example, an employer could require that applicants' records be reasonably free from convictions for serious property related crimes because bellmen have access to guests' rooms and belongings.[14]

Promotion and transfer policies. The tests of adverse impact and business necessity that apply to policies for hiring new employees also apply to policies for promotion and transfer. Some courts have required the complete revamping of seniority systems that tended to perpetuate the effects of past discrimination in matters of promotion and transfer.

Employers also have been found guilty of discrimination for what one court called "a casual approach" in selecting employees for promotion. In this case, vacancies were not posted and the managers were given no written guidelines for making promotion decisions with the result that the procedures were found to be biased.[15] In another case, the court ruled that a company could not rely solely on the recommendations of company foremen in selecting employees for promotion where the standards used by the foremen were vague and subjective.[16]

Promotion-from-within policies can result in employment discrimination by perpetuating an adverse impact, and as in the case of recruiting for entry-level jobs, affirmative action may be required to fill higher level positions. One company refused an accounting position to a black woman who responded to an advertisement for the job, and later promoted a less qualified employee into the job. In upholding the charge of discrimination, the court noted that the company had "few, if any Negro accountants or accounting clerks at the entry levels" and decided that affirmative action was required to "break the chain of discrimination."[17]

[13]*Gregory* v. *Litton Systems, Inc.,* 316 F.Supp. 401 (1970), 2 FEP Cases 842; *Green* v. *Missouri Pacific RR Co.,* 523 F.2d 1290 (1975), 10 FEP Cases 1409.

[14]*Richardson* v. *Hotel Corp. of America,* 332 F.Supp. 519, 3 FEP Cases 1031.

[15]*Hill* v. *Western Electric Co.,* 12 FEP Cases 1175.

[16]*Rowe* v. *General Motors Corp.,* 457 F.2d 348 (1972), 4 FEP Cases 445.

[17]*Gates* v. *Georgia-Pacific Corp.,* 326 F.Supp. 397 (1970), 2 FEP Cases 978.

The testing issue

What has emerged as the most troublesome aspect of selection in Title VII enforcement is the use of employment tests in making hiring and promotion decisions. As defined by EEOC, employment tests include "any paper-and-pencil or performance measure used as a basis for any employment decision and all formal, scored, quantified or standardized techniques of assessing job suitability."

Controversy over the testing issue already was evident in the enforcement of the state FEP statutes at the time the federal Civil Rights Act was passed. Consequently, an amendment to Title VII states explicitly that it is not an unlawful employment practice "for an employer to give and to act upon the results of any professionally developed ability test provided that such test, its administration or action upon the results is not designed, intended, or used to discriminate because of race, color, religion, sex, or national origin." Initially, it was anticipated that this amendment would be interpreted as protecting any test unless it could be shown that the employer had a specific intent to use it for discriminatory purposes.

Early in its enforcement efforts, the EEOC relied on statistics indicating that many of the tests commonly used for hiring purposes had an adverse impact on blacks. In one case, for example, "the evidence indicated that 37.3 percent of the whites as compared with 9.8 percent of the Negroes were passing the Wonderlic," and "on the Bennett, the passing rate was 64.9 percent of the whites and only 15.4 percent of the Negroes."[18] Furthermore, the government enforcement agencies, both EEOC and OFCC, were finding that many employers were using tests that had not been validated in terms of a relationship to subsequent job performance. It was this situation that prompted both enforcement agencies to issue "guidelines" for the use of employment tests and other selection procedures.

Basically, the guidelines required that any test used for employment decisions be related to the job sought by the applicant or the employee. In recent years, however, the guidelines themselves have been a matter of considerable controversy and there has been disagreement among various government agencies as to how stringent

[18] *Hicks v. Crown Zellerbach Corp.*, 319 F.Supp. 314 (1970), 2 FEP Cases 1059.

the validation requirements should be. The current guidelines in effect are discussed more fully in Chapter 4.

EEOC's position that any test which has an adverse impact on a protected group must be shown to be related to job performance, regardless of the employer's intent to discriminate, was upheld by the Supreme Court in the *Duke Power Company* case. In its decision, the Court also referred to the EEOC guidelines, saying they should be "entitled to great deference" as an administrative interpretation of Title VII. To date, three cases involving the use of tests have been ruled on by the Supreme Court,[19] and in two of them the employer has not shown to the Court's satisfaction that the tests are job-related.[20] In these cases, the employer has provided validation data to support the use of tests, but the Court has found the data lacking in some regard; in one case, the problem also involved the way in which job performance is measured.[21]

The one Supreme Court opinion that has upheld the use of a test, even where the test was shown to have an adverse impact on blacks, was not brought under Title VII, and neither the EEOC guidelines nor the *Duke Power* doctrine applied. The case involved the use of a verbal-skills test by the District of Columbia police department to screen applicants; blacks had a failure rate on the test four times that of whites. At the time the case was initiated, state and local government agencies were not covered by Title VII so the charge was a violation of constitutional rights rather than a violation of the Civil Rights Act. A lower court ruled that the use of the test was constitutional because it was shown to be directly related to the requirements of the police recruit training program. The appeals court disagreed, on the basis that the test had not been shown to be

[19]*Griggs* v. *Duke Power Co.,* 401 U.S. 424 (1971), 3 FEP Cases 175; *Albemarle Paper Co.* v. *Moody,* 422 U.S. 405 (1975), 10 FEP Cases 1181; and *Washington* v. *Davis,* 426 U.S. 229 (1976), 12 FEP Cases 1415.

While this volume was in press, the Supreme Court, without hearing any testimony or issuing a formal opinion, affirmed a lower court decision upholding the use of a test for teacher selection. (*U.S.* v. *South Carolina,* ____ U.S. ____ (1978), 16 FEP cases 501.) A significant aspect of the lower court's decision was that where the EEOC guidelines are in conflict with accepted professional standards, the guidelines need not be controlling.

[20]*Griggs* v. *Duke Power Co.* and *Albemarle Paper Co.* v. *Moody, supra* note 19.

[21]*Abemarle Paper Co.* v. *Moody, supra* note 19.

job-related under Title VII standards, but the Supreme Court reversed this decision, saying that these standards did not apply.[22]

The net effect of the court rulings involving the use of the tests is that the issue still is not resolved. It is clear that any test that can be shown to result in an adverse impact must be shown to be job-related, but not all the details of how job-relatedness must be proved have yet been specified by the courts.

Selection and sex discrimination

When the Civil Rights Act was passed, its major purpose was to deal with discrimination based on race, national origin, or religion. The ban on discrimination because of sex was not even taken seriously at the time the law was passed, and there was little perception of how pervasive was the discrimination against women in employment. The changes in employment practices as they relate to women have in many ways been more dramatic over the past decade than the changes in the employment of minorities.

An exception to the ban against discrimination based on sex is provided by Title VII. This is the *bona fide occupational qualification* (BFOQ) exception, which also applies to discrimination based on religion or national origin. Under EEOC regulations, jobs can no longer be classified as male or female, there can be no separate lines of progression or seniority lists based on sex, jobs cannot be advertised as male or female positions, and state laws originally aimed at "protecting" women in such matters as work and physical requirements have been superseded—unless there is a BFOQ.

Both EEOC and the courts have narrowly construed the BFOQ exception to the point that it rarely is applied today. Here are examples of some of the court decisions on this issue:

- The test of whether a BFOQ exists is whether it can be shown that the qualification is "demonstrably more relevant to job performance for a woman than a man," according to the Supreme Court. In a case involving a company rule against hiring women with preschool age children, the Court said that a lower court had erred in its interpretation that a com-

[22] *Washington* v. *Davis, supra* note 19.

pany could have one hiring policy for women and another for men in absence of proof of a BFOQ.[23]

- Two arguments related to the BFOQ exception were raised in a case where a woman was denied a job as a telephone company switch repairer. To the argument that strenuous lifting was involved, the court said the company failed to prove that few or no women could safely lift 30 pounds while all men could; to the argument that women should be denied jobs that involved late-hour call-outs, the court said: "Title VII rejects just this type of romantic paternalism as unduly Victorian and instead vests with individual women the power to decide whether or not to take on unromantic tasks."[24]
- Jobs as flight cabin attendants cannot be limited to females on the basis of a BFOQ, according to an appeals court, which said the test is whether the "essence of the business operation would be undermined by not hiring members of one sex exclusively."[25] Rules requiring stewardesses but not stewards to be unmarried are not valid on the basis of a BFOQ, either. As one court held, "The marital status of a stewardess cannot be said to affect the individual woman's ability to create the proper psychological climate of comfort, safety, and security for passengers. Nor does any passenger preference for single stewardesses provide a valid reason for invoking the rule."[26]

Interpretations such as these leave no doubt that there cannot be different standards applying to males and females in any matters relating to employment no matter what the preferences of the employees themselves or of customers may be. It seems clear that the only types of jobs where a BFOQ exemption will stand up are those involving what EEOC terms "authenticity or genuineness" such as actresses portraying females and those involving universally recognized standards such as female attendants in ladies' powder rooms. For purposes of selection, there no longer is any question that the

[23]*Phillips* v. *Martin Marietta Corp.,* 400 U.S. 542 (1971), 3 FEP Cases 40.

[24]*Weeks* v. *Southern Bell Telephone,* 408 F.2d 228 (1969), 1 FEP Cases 656.

[25]*Diaz* v. *Pan American World Airways,* 442 F.2d 385 (1971), 3 FEP Cases 337.

[26]*Sprogis* v. *United Air Lines,* 444 F.2d 1194, 3 FEP 621.

jobs existing in the typical American firm cannot be relegated to one sex or the other—men or women applying must be given consideration on the basis of the same standards.

While questions of sex discrimination in hiring for the most part have been resolved, there remain two areas of concern. The first is equal treatment between the sexes in compensation and benefits, and there is continuing litigation in this area both under Title VII and under the Equal Pay Act. The second major area of concern involves efforts to have more women work in supervisory and managerial positions; in many companies these efforts are required under consent decrees, conciliation agreements, or affirmative action plans submitted to government agencies. The effect of these programs and of court ordered goals and hiring ratios, as they apply to both women and minority groups are explored in the next chapter.

3

selection under government edict

The extent to which the government dictates a company's selection procedures varies widely. For the employer whose employment practices have not been the subject of any inquiry by a governmental EEO agency, it is simply a matter of caution, to minimize the extent to which the overall selection process results in an adverse impact on a protected class. Where there is such a result, it is a matter of making sure selection techniques are job-related.

In many cases where employers have been found guilty of discrimination in employment, remedies ordered by the courts (in addition to back-pay awards for the affected individuals or class of persons) frequently have taken the form of hiring goals or quotas for the job classifications in which the class in question is underrepresented. In most of these cases, procedures for achieving the goals are not specified by the court, with the result that the company still has a great deal of freedom to follow whatever selection procedures it feels are likely to contribute to the desired results.

The type of court action that calls for both the most specific goals and the most specific procedures for achieving those goals has been the *consent decree,* which is an agreement between a company and the EEOC (and perhaps other government agencies) filed in a federal court. *Conciliation agreements* between employers and government agencies, which are not enforceable through the courts, also frequently call for hiring goals for certain job classifications and outline selection procedures the company promises to follow. Similarly, *affirmative action plans* that are required of government contractors subject to OFCCP regulations may pinpoint areas of underutilization of minorities or women and suggest recruiting programs or selection methods aimed at improving the situation. This chapter will discuss and provide examples of these different types of government edicts with particular emphasis on their impact on selection.

Court-ordered goals and hiring ratios

The issue of hiring goals has been one of the thorniest aspects of the Civil Rights Act enforcement. Title VII states explicitly that the Act shall not be interpreted to require an employer "to grant preferential treatment" solely because of a racial imbalance in the workforce. What the courts have decided is that this provision of the law must be read in conjunction with the fundamental purpose of the Act—where a violation of Title VII has been established, the appropriate remedy may require the use of "mathematical ratios" to offset the effects of past discrimination. Furthermore, this type of remedy has not been limited to situations where the past discrimination had been intentional.

The nature of the goals specified by the courts has varied with the particular circumstances of the case involved. Goals have been expressed as specific numbers (for example, the employer is required to hire 30 to 35 applicants from minority groups), as percentages (minimum of 20 or 30 percent of all new hires to be blacks or other minorities), or as hiring ratios (one of every two or three persons hired must be a minority-group member). In most cases, the percentage or ratio of minority hires must be maintained until the employer has hired a specified number of minority persons, or until the percentage of minorities has reached a prescribed level. Such goals have been applied to the total workforce, to specific jobs or job classifications, and to admissions to apprenticeship or other kinds of training programs.

The courts ordering this type of remedy in discrimination cases have not viewed the hiring goals or ratios as permanent or inflexible. Rather, they serve as starting points in a process to correct the effects of past discrimination which has resulted in racial imbalance in the composition of a workforce. In many of these cases, the courts have not required changes in the procedures used for selection; the employer is permitted to continue to set certain standards for "qualified" applicants as long as enough qualified minority applicants can be found to fulfill the goals. In cases involving hiring goals where selection techniques have been found to be a cause of the unlawful discrimination, the problem generally has been the use of a test with adverse impact, and no evidence of business necessity. In those cases courts have ordered employers to stop using tests, to revise the test to eliminate the adverse impact, to use a different cutoff score, to find another test, or to demonstrate business necessity.

To date, most of the court decisions prescribing hiring goals have been in cases based on charges of racial discrimination, and they frequently have involved very specific job categories where the discrimination had been blatant and long-standing, such as in local police and fire departments and segregated school systems. A number of these cases also have related to union practices, rather than employer practices, in situations where the union has control over entry jobs through the requirement of union membership. For the majority of employers in the business world, the impact of court-ordered goals or hiring ratios on selection procedures has been minimal; they apply only in a few specific instances for a limited period of time.

Consent decrees

The consent decree as an approach to enforcement of equal employment opportunity involves a negotiated settlement that falls between voluntary compliance on the part of those facing discrimination charges and litigation ending with a court decision specifying remedies. The earliest consent decrees involved several governmental agencies working together on one side and representatives of many employers in the same industry or a very large employer on the other. They were a method for disposing of hundreds, and sometimes thousands, of individual charges of employment discrimination against a single employer or group of employers brought under Title VII, the Executive orders enforced by OFCCP, and the Equal Pay Act. In recent years, the number of EEOC consent decrees filed in the federal courts has grown (27 were filed in fiscal year 1974, 90 in 1975, and 123 in 1976) and many of them now involve single, relatively small employers.

A major provision of most consent decrees is for the payment of lump sums of money to individuals identified as having suffered from the effects of past discriminatory employment practices. The decree establishes procedures for allocating the amounts to be paid and for implementation of payment, and persons receiving payments generally must sign a release for any other claims of past employment discrimination. Thus, the consent decree provides a process for the settlement of many individual complaints without long, drawn-out litigation and liability for additional back-pay awards.

The cost to an employer of a consent decree begins with the lump sum payments made, but it certainly does not end with these payments. In many situations that have culminated in consent decrees, there has been an agreement for a complete overhaul of certain employment practices to comply with equal employment opportunity requirements. In the case of the steel industry, for example, it appeared, in view of the court decisions relating to seniority systems, that the departmental seniority systems permeating the industry had resulted in adverse impact and would have to be replaced by plantwide seniority. Decrees to accomplish this were signed in 1974 by most of the big steel producers, the Steelworkers Union, and the government. In addition to back pay amounting to $31 million for some 40,000 minority and female employees, the settlement established an audit and review committee to provide a continuing review of the progress of minorities and women with the goal of bringing both to their "rightful place" in the more desirable job classifications. (In light of a 1977 Supreme Court decision[1], it may not be necessary to abolish departmental seniority systems as long as they were not established with discriminatory motives, since Title VII includes a specific exception for the operation of "bona fide" seniority systems.)

Another feature of some consent decrees is the establishment of a special fund to be used in various ways for implementing the goals established by agreement. Thus, a consent decree in settlement of a class action suit against the Bank of America included the establishment of a $3.75 million trust fund to provide special training and development opportunities for minorities and women as an inducement to get them into bank management.

[1] *Teamsters* v. *U.S.*, 431 U.S. 324 (1977), 14 FEP Cases 1514.

From the selection standpoint, the most important aspects of the consent decrees are the long-term goals, intermediate targets, and timetables for achieving them that are established for job classifications where minorities and/or women have been underutilized in the past. The most comprehensive decree in this regard is the grandfather of consent decrees, signed with the nation's largest private employer, the Bell System (AT&T), in January 1973. This decree includes a model affirmative action plan to be implemented in all the Bell System companies and establishes goals and timetables for increasing the representation of women and minorities in craft and management-level jobs where they had been underutilized, and for increasing the representation of males in the telephone-operator and clerical jobs where they had been underutilized. In certain circumstances, an "affirmative action override" can be used to effect promotions outside the seniority system if a company is having difficulty meeting its targets. Recent Supreme Court decisions indicate there may be some problems in applying the affirmative action override, however.

To monitor the AT&T decree, a government coordinating committee (GCC) with representatives of four federal agencies works with AT&T's Human Resources Development Department, and all the Bell System companies are required to maintain and file detailed reports by sex and minority status on job applicants, placements, transfers, upgrades, promotions, resignations and dismissals, training classes, progress toward goals, and projections of job opportunities for the year. A special transfer bureau in each company is charged with undertaking programs to implement the decree and with keeping employees informed about job opportunities available.

After two years of experience under the consent decree, the GCC found that while there had been "a substantial accomplishment" in AT&T's performance, in many of the individual Bell System companies the targets were not being met. The result was a supplemental court agreement filed in May 1975 requiring preferential treatment for women, blacks, and Spanish-surnamed persons in hiring and promotion for job classifications still deficient with regard to these groups. The supplemental agreement makes note of what have turned out to be unanticipated difficulties in placing women in craft jobs and in transferring persons from nontechnical management jobs to technical management jobs. The agreement provides for the establishment of a special fund to finance studies in these areas, and research is under way by the Human Resources Development people at AT&T on changes in equipment used in craft jobs to make it easier for women to handle.

It is unlikely that many employers will have to cope with the extremely detailed requirements with regard to selection procedures and record keeping imposed on the Bell System companies; the government simply does not have the staff to monitor many such arrangements, and smaller employers could not stand the extra cost burden. The procedures and programs for recruiting, placement, orientation, and training for promotion suggested in the AT&T decrees, however, may be used as models by other employers. The government has indicated in the AT&T situation that companies will not be called to task for not meeting their targets if they have made "good-faith efforts" to achieve them; good-faith efforts are defined as "those efforts which a reasonably prudent manager would have foreseen and undertaken in furtherance of a legal obligation."[2]

Some of the programs provided by the AT&T settlement will be discussed further in connection with strategies for implementing EEO efforts in Chapters 21 to 23. With regard to the specifics of selection techniques, an important point to note is that one provision of the initial decree permits the telephone companies to continue to use their validated tests as long as they are not used to justify failure to meet targets. The supplemental agreement indicates that where test scores have contributed to a deficiency in meeting targets for a race or ethnic group, applicants not test-qualified but otherwise qualified should be offered job opportunities. These are of course provisions agreed to by the company. They have the force of law only for AT&T and do not constitute legal interpretations of existing federal legislation.

Conciliation agreements

The provisions of conciliation agreements negotiated between employers and government EEO agencies are very similar to the provi-

[2]*Daily Labor Report,* No. 94, May 13, 1975, p. D-5.

sions of consent decrees. There usually is a method established for identifying persons in the class or classes affected by past discriminatory practices and for payments to these individuals; there may be a list of jobs or job categories in which minorities and/or women are underrepresented with goals and timetables for achieving better representation; specific recruiting, selection, and training activities may be outlined as approaches to achieving the goals, or the agreement may merely incorporate an affirmative action plan already in effect; and the employer may agree to keep certain records and make periodic reports on progress under the agreement for a specific period of time.

The difference between a consent decree and a conciliation agreement is that a decree is filed in a federal court and is enforceable through the courts, whereas conciliation agreements are private agreements between employers and the EEOC. Conciliation agreements per se are not enforceable through the courts, although EEOC has been able to obtain consent decrees filed with the courts from employers who have failed to live up to the terms of conciliation agreements. They are not open to the public since they are exempt from the coverage of the Freedom of Information Act. The conciliation agreement is the most common approach to Title VII enforcement—in fiscal year 1975, for example, nearly 7,000 conciliation agreements were negotiated by the EEOC and state and local FEP agencies.

An example of a conciliation agreement is reproduced as Exhibit 2, page 381. The agreement, covering Gulf Oil Company's Port Arthur, Texas, refinery, was made public when it was submitted as evidence in a Title VII suit brought by some individual employees. It provides a typical example of what employers are asked to agree to in the settlement of EEOC charges, although the provisions vary widely depending on the nature of the charges. For the "target classifications," those for which minorities and/or women are "statistically underrepresented," the company agrees that one of every five vacancies will be filled by a Negro, a Spanish-surnamed American, or a woman; for the official/manager classification, the ratio called for is one out of every seven. The agreement specifies, however, that the ratios "shall not be fixed" but shall serve as a general measure of the company's progress. Furthermore, the company "will not be faulted if it fails to meet its goals and timetables in one or more classifications as long as its overall progress is satisfactory."

The major emphasis in the Gulf Oil conciliation agreement is on upgrading of present employees in lower jobs to the target classifications, and there is little mention of outside recruiting and selection procedures. The agreement does state explicitly that the company can insist that persons hired or placed have "the skill, ability, and qualifications to perform" the jobs in question. On one point—the matter of a battery of tests the company uses for employment and promotion purposes—the parties did not reach agreement. The final document signed by the parties notes this lack of agreement but permits the company to continue using test scores along with other selection criteria as long as the test scores are not used as justification for failure to meet its goals.

Affirmative action programs

As noted in Chapter 1, the concept of affirmative action as an approach for remedying discrimination in employment has been endorsed by the courts in the enforcement of Title VII of the Civil Rights Act. Most of the consent decrees and conciliation agreements entered into by EEOC contain some reference to affirmative action and many of the agreements incorporate formal affirmative action plans. Such formal written plans are not a requirement for being in compliance with Title VII. In its guidebook for employers, however, EEOC states that while the development of an affirmative action program cannot guarantee "immunity" from charges of discrimination, "the resulting employment system should provide equal opportunity as required by law."

Written affirmative action plans and periodic reports are required for government contractors with 50 or more employees and contracts of $50,000 or more. The plans are reviewed and monitored by the contracting agencies of the federal government under detailed guidelines and orders establishing standardized compliance reviews issued by the OFCCP. Because of the small staffs available to handle compliance matters in most government agencies, enforcement of plan requirements has not been stringent. To date, OFCCP has issued only a handful of debarment orders or notices of proposed debarment from future government contracts based on failure to meet affirmative action plan requirements. Furthermore, those debarment orders that have been issued have not always been upheld when challenged in the courts.

Requirements for an affirmative action program, under both the OFCCP guidelines and the EEOC suggestions, are comprehensive and rigorous. Exhibit 3, page 390, is a summary of the basic steps involved in the development of an affirmative action plan as set forth in the EEOC guidebook for employers. The basic steps called for are the commitment of management to the AAP and communication of this commitment both internally and externally; an analysis of workforce composition and development of goals and timetables to correct underutilization of protected groups; review of all personnel practices with action where needed to eliminate barriers to equal employment opportunity; establishment of auditing, reporting, and control systems; and the encouragement of support activities. As emphasized by EEOC, the heart of the AAP is the implementation of specific programs to achieve goals based on a review of current personnel procedures, particularly recruitment, selection, and upgrading.

An example of an affirmative action program from the company policy manual of a large oil company appears as Exhibit 4, page 392. This program was developed to comply with the requirements of OFCCP regulations applying to government contractors, and it sets forth steps that must be undertaken by the personnel staff and managers at every company facility to implement the program. Among the items listed as requiring "special corrective action" if they are found at any facilities are "tests and other selection techniques not validated" as required by governmental guidelines. The content and status of these selection guidelines issued by various federal agencies are discussed in Chapter 4.

In contrast to consent decrees and conciliation agreements, which are negotiated settlements of discrimination charges, affirmative action programs are voluntary programs aimed at heading off charges of discrimination. Although government agencies may influence employers by their "suggestions," "guidelines," and offers of "technical assistance" in developing affirmative action plans, the implementation of the program is entirely up to the individual employer unless it becomes incorporated into a legal agreement.

The problem of reverse discrimination

The differential impact of selection under a court order and selection under a voluntary affirmative action plan is highlighted by the problem of reverse discrimination. At present, the issue of reverse discrimination, resulting from preferential treatment rather than merely equal opportunity in employment matters for those in the classes protected by Title VII, has not been resolved. While a number of cases involving reverse discrimination have come before the federal courts, none involving equal employment opportunity under Title VII has been actually decided by the U.S. Supreme Court.[3] Thus definitive decisions are totally lacking; the existing lower court decisions may or may not come to hold as the law of the land.

Two recent cases illustrate the dilemma of reverse discrimination for employers. The first case involves a male employee who was deprived of a promotion at AT&T. Under the terms of the Bell System consent decree providing for an affirmative action seniority override to meet certain targets, the promotion was given to a less qualified, less experienced female employee. The court agreed that the company acted properly in promoting the female employee, but it ruled further that the male employee was entitled to monetary damages as compensation for pay lost as a result of not being promoted to the job he would have been entitled to were it not for the provisions of the consent decree.[4] The company claimed that the decision amounted to a ruling that it is "simultaneously in compliance and in violation of the same act by promoting the lesser qualified person." The company asked the court for a rehearing on the ruling, but before this hearing was held it agreed to an out-of-court settlement. The settlement gave the male employee $7,500 in damages plus payment of his attorney's fee (his original suit asked

[3]The most well-known case involving the question of reverse discrimination—*Bakke* v. *University of California (Davis)*—is expected to be decided by the Supreme Court momentarily. The effect of the Court's decision in the *Bakke* case may or may not be relevant for employment decisions under Title VII, however.

[4]*McAleer* v. *AT&T Co., 416 F. Supp. 435 (1976), 12 FEP Cases 1473.*

for $100,000 in damages) but did not say he was entitled to a promotion.

The second case was brought by a group of white employees who were passed over by the company in favor of blacks with less seniority in choosing employees for on-the-job training opportunities for craft positions. The blacks were chosen under the terms of a quota system provided for by the company's affirmative action plan; the plan had been developed voluntarily to remedy a discrepancy between a 40 percent minority representation in the local area population and 14.8 percent in the company's workforce. The court decided in favor of the white employees, noting that there was no evidence that the black employees involved had been discriminated against by the company in the past. Therefore, there was no reason for preferential treatment to remedy past discrimination.

The court made a distinction between quotas or affirmative action imposed on employers by court orders and those initiated voluntarily by employers, even though a voluntary plan may be intended to meet the requirements of governmental regulations. While a court may impose a quota system that results in preferential treatment, an individual employer may not, the court said. According to this decision, quotas should be imposed only in limited cases where necessary to cure the ill effects of past discrimination, and the courts alone are in a position to afford due process to all concerned.[5]

The net effect of these two decisions is to further complicate the problems of employers in effecting equal employment opportunity, and also perhaps to make EEOC's enforcement task more difficult. The ruling in the AT&T case, for example, may make employers even less willing than they have been in the past to sign a consent decree with EEOC. There may be some merit in signing such an agreement if it provides a lawful method for promotion of women or minorities outside the usual lines of seniority and if the decree can be used to convince managers and other employees that the employer has no choice but to fulfill the requirements of the decree or be liable for damages and other legal action. But no employer is knowingly

[5] *Weber* v. *Kaiser Aluminum & Chemical Corp., 415 F. Supp. 761 (1976), 12* FEP Cases 1615, *affirmed,* 563 F. 2d 216 (1977), 16 FEP Cases 1.

going to enter into an agreement that may result in liability for damages to other employees who may suffer in the future as a consequence of the targets established by the decree.

On the other hand, the ruling in the second case described seems to imply that employers also should be cautious in their efforts to comply voluntarily with EEOC or OFCCP regulations. It certainly says that there has to be some evidence of past discrimination against a protected group before any preferential treatment is accorded to members of that group. Employers could read this to mean that voluntary action should be limited to areas of personnel practice where preferential treatment does not come into play; in general this would mean concentrating affirmative action efforts on hiring for entry jobs at various levels in the organization where seniority is not ordinarily a factor. As the Supreme Court has made clear,[6] bona fide seniority systems can continue to be the basis for selection decisions despite an adverse impact resulting from discriminatory hiring practices that predate the Civil Rights Act.

In some types of organizations it may be feasible to hire people from the outside at all job levels. For the majority of companies, however, the emphasis at higher levels is on promotion from within and people enter the organization with the expectation of an opportunity to move upward. As far as the EEO enforcement agencies are concerned, it does not matter whether a job is filled from the outside or from within the company; the selection guidelines issued by the enforcement agencies apply to all selection decisions. These guidelines are discussed in the next chapter.

[6] *Teamsters* v. *U.S.*, *supra* note 1.

4

the selection guidelines

Governmental guidelines on employee selection procedures, initially limited to employment testing but later broadened to cover nearly all selection techniques, have been a major stumbling block to EEO enforcement and compliance. Over the past 10 years, various versions have been issued, which have been the subject not only of controversy among the different government agencies involved in their implementation but of much criticism and debate among psychologists and other professionals in the personnel field as well.

The basic requirement of all versions of the guidelines is that in any situation where the selection process results in an adverse impact with respect to groups protected by Title VII, the selection techniques must be validated and shown to be job-related. The major controversy revolves around what constitutes acceptable evidence of validity; as one federal court has pointed out, "standards for testing validity comprise a new and complicated area of the law."[1] Increasingly, the courts have been called upon to make judgments of a professional nature that previously were the exclusive province of industrial psychologists. While the industrial psychologists frequently are asked to provide expert testimony concerning validity studies, there rarely has been complete agreement among them. With expert witnesses on both sides of the question, the courts have been faced with the responsibility for making their own interpretations of what is required. The result is that at the present time the issue is still subject to influence by those who can bring effective arguments to bear. At least in the legal sense, and perhaps in the professional sense also, it is very much an open issue.

[1]*U.S.* v. *Georgia Power Company,* 474 F. 2d 906 (1973), 5 FEP Cases 587.

The early guidelines

The initial attempt by EEOC to provide some guidance to employers on practices to follow in the use of employment tests was entitled *Guidelines on Employment Testing Procedures;* it was issued in May 1966. The basic purpose of this set of guidelines apparently was to interpret the provisions of Title VII permitting the use of tests which are not "designed, intended or used to discriminate because of race." The 1966 guidelines were quite general in nature and called for sound psychological testing practices in accordance with the *Standards for Educational and Psychological Tests and Manuals* issued by the American Psychological Association (APA).

In September 1968, the OFCC issued a testing and selection order for government contractors. This order, which dealt with employment tests for lower level jobs, was much more specific than the earlier EEOC guidelines as regards what is acceptable evidence of validity.

The employee selection guidelines issued by EEOC in August 1970 were even more comprehensive than the OFCC order. These guidelines apply to jobs at all levels and to a much broader range of selection standards and techniques than did the 1966 version. A year later the OFCC issued a new order on employee testing and other selection procedures, which essentially imposed the same basic requirements for government contractors as those of EEOC for employers covered by Title VII.

With the passage of the 1972 amendments to the Civil Rights Act, the matter of selection guidelines became even more complicated, primarily because federal, state, and local government agencies were brought under Title VII coverage. Traditionally, selection for employment in government agencies has been based on the "merit" principle, which relies heavily on the use of written tests and other specific standards, most of which have not been validated in accordance with what appear to be the requirements of the EEOC guidelines. In the period preceding the 1972 amendments, there also had been a great deal of criticism of the different approaches and standards being used by the various federal agencies in the enforcement of EEO regulations. As a result the amendments established an Equal Employment Opportunity Coordinating Council (EEOCC) to "promote efficiency and avoid duplication of effort" by the government agencies involved in EEO enforcement.

The first proposed uniform guidelines

The first major effort by the EEO Coordinating Council, composed of the heads or deputies of the U.S. Civil Service Commission, Civil Rights Commission, EEOC, Department of Justice (Attorney General), and Department of Labor (OFCCP), was to prepare a set of uniform guidelines on employee selection procedures to standardize the position of the various agencies. The council issued a draft of such a set of uniform guidelines for preliminary comment in August 1973. The comments elicited by this initial draft were almost universally negative; the proposed guidelines were criticized as unworkable, unclear, and in some respects technically unsound.

A revised draft of the uniform guidelines was distributed by the council in June 1974 to selected individuals and groups for comment. A hearing for invited testing experts on the proposed draft was held in October. Again, the comments from representatives of industry, psychology and other professional groups, and from state and local governments were negative. At this point, an ad hoc industry group, formed for the primary purpose of reviewing the government's proposals for uniform selection guidelines, argued for the abandonment of specific, detailed guidelines on selection procedures and for the issuance of a set of "general principles" supplemented by interpretive material to replace the guidelines.

Over the next year, the council struggled with several drafts of the proposed uniform guidelines and finally circulated a draft dated September 24, 1975. This draft never became "official," however, because one of the agencies represented on the council, the EEOC, decided not to endorse it. The EEOC argued that the proposed guidelines were less stringent than its 1970 guidelines which it said had been upheld by the courts. The major point at issue was EEOC's preference for the types of validity studies that the Civil Service Commission said it could not afford. EEOC indicated it might be willing to make some revisions in its own guidelines to make them more acceptable to employers, but it would not go along with the uniform proposal.

In July 1976, despite opposition from EEOC, the council published another set of proposed uniform guidelines on selection procedures. Interested parties were asked for comments, and again the comments from industry and psychologists were critical, although substantial improvements over earlier versions were noted. In fact, they called this version of the proposed uniform guidelines "a workable document" that employers and professionals could support, provided "remaining problems can be resolved."[2]

Comments on the proposed guidelines from civil rights groups, on the other hand, indicated strong support for the position taken by EEOC—that the proposed uniform guidelines represented a weakening of the government's position. In general, the civil rights advocates said the proposed guidelines provided too many loopholes which would enable employers to avoid having to validate their selection procedures. This polarization of viewpoints, between the civil rights groups and the industrial psychology professionals, appeared to preclude the promulgation of uniform guidelines acceptable to all agencies represented on the coordinating council, despite four years of negotiations among the agencies.

The FEA guidelines

Finally, in November 1976, three of the five members of the Council—the Department of Labor, the Civil Service Commission, and the Justice Department—issued a new set of guidelines which essentially were the same as the proposed uniform guidelines. The "Federal Executive Agency Guidelines on Employee Selection Procedures" (or FEA Guidelines) apply to government contractors subject to OFCCP regulations and to federal, state, and local government agencies. The full text of these guidelines appears as Exhibit 5-A, p. 402.

EEOC, which together with the U.S. Commission on Civil Rights refused to endorse the new guidelines, then reissued its own selection guidelines. Originally issued in 1970, these guidelines were republished without any changes in the *Federal Register* the day after the guidelines of the other federal agencies were published to emphasize that they still apply to all employers subject to EEOC's

[2]*Daily Labor Report,* No. 183, September 20, 1976, p. A-5.

jurisdiction. The full text of the EEOC guidelines appears as Exhibit 5-B, p. 427.

As indicated earlier, the major reason that EEOC was not willing to go along with the federal uniform selection guidelines derives from the feeling that its own 1970 guidelines have been supported in the courts. In a decision handed down in June 1975, the U.S. Supreme Court agreed with a lower court that the EEOC guidelines are "entitled to great deference," and as measured against these guidelines found the company's validation study deficient.[3] However, two of the justices dissented on the guidelines issue, pointing out that the guidelines are not official federal regulations, in part because they were not submitted for public comment before being issued.

Many cases that have been decided at lower court levels have referred to the EEOC guidelines. In a number of instances, employers have argued successfully that their testing program was lawful by showing the tests are job-related in accordance with the requirements of the guidelines. Where an employer has used the guidelines as a defense, and the lower court decision has not been appealed by EEOC, it can be assumed that the employer has proven to the satisfaction of EEOC that the use of the selection technique in question constitutes a business necessity.

To date, cases where the EEOC guidelines have been the basis for decisions against an employer generally have involved situations where the evidence of validity has been clearly deficient. Experts in the field of employment testing are in agreement that the evidence presented in two cases involving the guidelines that have reached the Supreme Court did not measure up even to minimum professional standards. In one lower court ruling, later affirmed by the Supreme Court, it was decided that the EEOC guidelines need not be controlling where they are in conflict with professional standards.[4] However, there has not yet been a case that has tested the legality of the EEOC guidelines per se in terms of their specific requirements, especially the requirements for the most costly type of validity studies involving jobs at all levels and applying to all kinds of selection standards and techniques.

[3]*Albemarle Paper Co.* v. *Moody,* 422 U.S. 405 (1975), 10 FEP Cases 1181.
[4]*U.S.* v. *South Carolina,* ____ U.S. ____ (1978), 16 FEP Cases 501.

One reason for the lack of such a test case can be found by looking at the terms of many of the conciliation agreements and consent decrees negotiated between EEOC and employers. Frequently, there is a provision to the effect that the employer agrees to stop using employment tests or other selection standards that have not been validated in accordance with the EEOC guidelines. There is no indication of whether the selection techniques in question ever have been validated or whether the validation studies that have been conducted measure up to the stringent requirements of the EEOC guidelines. In effect, many employers have given in to EEOC's demands without pressing the issue.

The issues in conflict

The points of conflict between the EEOC and the other enforcement agencies with regard to selection guidelines can be viewed by summarizing the requirements of the two sets of guidelines. The major provisions of the 1970 EEOC guidelines are as follows:

1. "Tests" as defined by the guidelines include "any paper-and-pencil test or performance measure used as a basis for any employment decision." In addition to what are generally referred to as psychological tests, the definition specifically includes "all formal, scored, quantified or standardized techniques of assessing job suitability including . . . specific qualifying or disqualifying personal history or background requirements, specific educational or work history requirements, scored interviews, biographical information blanks, interviewers' rating scales, scored application forms, etc."
2. Where the use of a test has an adverse effect on the employment of members of the protected groups, the employer must (a) show that the test has been validated and "evidences a high degree of utility," and (b) demonstrate that alternative suitable selection procedures are not available.
3. Detailed requirements are specified for "evidence of validity" and "minimum standards for validation." These state that a test must be predictive of, or significantly related to, performance on the job for which the test is being

used, and that evidence of this validity should consist of empirical data based on criterion-related studies. (Criterion-related studies show the relationship between test performance and subsequent job performance.) If criterion-related studies *are not feasible,* evidence of content validity (the test measures actual work skills required for the job) or construct validity (the test measures an aptitude or characteristic that is needed for the job) may be used. Additional requirements include, among other things, that (a) tests be validated for each minority group for which it is used, "where technically feasible," and (b) the measures used for evaluating job performance be based on "careful job analyses."

The FEA guidelines, while somewhat longer and more detailed than the EEOC's, are less stringent. A summary of the major differences between the two sets of guidelines follows:

1. The FEA guidelines provide a definition of adverse impact in terms of the whole selection process with a specific rule of thumb for determining what amount of adverse impact is significant, and they suggest that government agencies take into account the employer's overall progress in providing equal employment opportunity. The EEOC guidelines do not define adverse impact; they require validation for virtually every selection procedure used, whereas the FEA guidelines recognize there are some procedures for which the validation techniques prescribed are not feasible or appropriate.
2. The FEA guidelines accept content or construct validity on an equal basis with criterion-related validity, depending on the nature of the selection procedure and the type of job for which it is used. The EEOC guidelines call for the much more costly and time-consuming criterion-related studies wherever feasible. The FEA guidelines permit test users to use validity evidence developed elsewhere and encourage cooperative validity studies; the EEOC guidelines require each user of a test to validate it separately.
3. Under the EEOC guidelines, the burden is on the employer

using a test with adverse impact to prove that there is no alternative selection procedure available that would not have an adverse impact. The FEA guidelines do not put the burden of proof on the test user, but they do say that test users "should make a reasonable effort to investigate suitable alternative selection procedures which have as little adverse impact as possible."

A summary of the differences between the EEOC guidelines and the FEA guidelines was provided by a spokesman for the Justice Department as follows:

> The EEOC Guidelines require validation of virtually all selection procedures and make it difficult for any employer or other user to show that any objective selection procedure is in fact valid. The Uniform Guidelines, while adhering to Federal Law as developed by the Supreme Court and other appellate courts and the standards of the psychological profession, provide some definitive standards which enable those employers and other users who wish to do so to bring themselves into compliance with Federal Law.[5]

Professional comment on the guidelines

Many of the difficulties with the EEOC selection guidelines involve technicalities of the validation process and of the concepts underlying the whole field of psychological measurement. These will be discussed in detail in later chapters. In essence, however, the basic argument of industry representatives and professional psychologists is that the guidelines go beyond the present state of the art and specify requirements and procedures beyond the capabilities of even the country's largest employers. Furthermore, the guidelines appear to endorse certain questionable premises, such as the notion of "differential validity" for different groups such as blacks and whites, which have not been supported consistently by research evidence.

The technical and theoretical problems presented by the guidelines have been pointed out repeatedly by such groups as the Ad Hoc Industry Group, APA's Division of Industrial and Organizational Psychology (Division 14), and the American Society for Personnel Administration (ASPA). These groups have viewed with increasing

[5]David L. Rose, Chief, Department of Justice Employment Section, *Daily Labor Report,* No. 121, June 22, 1976, p. AA-4.

alarm court decisions based on the EEOC guidelines, which, according to ASPA, "specify an overly rigid methodology for the acceptable validation of all employment tests in all contexts."[6] In general, the employer viewpoint is that without a workable framework for the use of some objective selection procedures, hiring would evolve into a quota system or a completely random process, with a consequent negative impact on workforce productivity.

The industry groups welcomed the efforts of the Coordinating Council to provide a new set of guidelines that would both be uniform for all government agencies involved in EEO matters and that might take into account some of the technical difficulties they had been pointing out. They also welcomed the opportunity provided to make comments on the proposed uniform guidelines, an opportunity that was not provided with regard to the EEOC guidelines. One of the strongest arguments raised by the industry groups against the EEOC guidelines is the fact that they were issued without going through the usual procedures for rulemaking. Thus, the argument continues, the courts should not treat the EEOC guidelines as "law." The attitude of the industry and professional groups, which clearly favored the FEA guidelines, was expressed in a letter to the EEOC urging the adoption of uniform guidelines. The letter stated that the proposed guidelines "are a far more accurate reflection of professional standards and the law than the unworkable and professionally unsound 1970 EEOC guidelines." This professional support of the proposed uniform guidelines was one reason for their adoption without the participation of EEOC.

The current uniform guidelines

The matter of uniform selection guidelines to be used by all federal enforcement agencies became a matter of highest priority with the advent of the Carter Administration in Washington. Considerable pressure was exerted on the agencies, EEOC in particular, to reach an agreement on a set of guidelines so that employers who are government contractors are not subject to conflicting rules concerning selection standards.

[6]"Test Justification and Title VII," *The Personnel Administrator,* Vol. 21, No. 1, January 1976, p. 46.

In mid-1977, the four agencies involved renewed their efforts to draft a set of guidelines acceptable to all of them; an agreement finally was achieved and on December 30, 1977 a new proposal on uniform guidelines was published in the *Federal Register* by EEOC, the Departments of Justice and Labor, and the U.S. Civil Service Commission. (The full text of these guidelines appears as Exhibit 6-A, p. 437.) Provision was made for interested parties to make comments and a public hearing on the proposed guidelines was held in April 1978. Once any changes have been made based on public comments, the uniform guidelines will be issued in final form and then will supersede both the 1970 EEOC guidelines and the 1976 FEA guidelines.

The current uniform guidelines represent a compromise between the two previous sets of guidelines. On the surface, the new guidelines appear to be more in line with the FEA version than with EEOC's. On the major points at issue noted above, the new uniform guidelines provide for the following:

1. Employers will be judged on the overall results of their selection process—or what is viewed as the "bottom line" concept. If the overall process does not result in adverse impact, using the FEA rule of thumb for measuring adverse impact, the individual steps of the selection process *generally* do not have to be evaluated for adverse impact or validated as job-related where there is evidence of adverse impact. The word *generally* was added at the insistence of EEOC.

2. Evidence of validity may be based on criterion-related studies, or on content or construct validity, although the requirements for construct validity are spelled out in more detail than in the FEA guidelines. Test users are permitted to use validity evidence developed elsewhere under special circumstances, and the provision of the FEA guidelines encouraging cooperative validity studies is included.

3. The requirement that employers search for suitable alternative selection procedures for ones that have an adverse impact is made more stringent than in the FEA guidelines. The new guidelines describe suitable alternatives as

ones with *substantially equal* validity; the previous uniform guidelines used the phrase *at least equal* validity.

The overall emphasis in this most recent set of guidelines is on the achievement of results through affirmative action rather than on validation of the various procedures of the selection process. Because of this shift in emphasis and because of the many revisions from the FEA guidelines, the professional and industry representatives offered detailed comments on the proposed uniform guidelines; the text of the comments submitted by the Ad Hoc Industry Group appears as Exhibit 6-B, p. 467.

The major concerns of the employer representatives involve the provisions noted above—in particular the requirement for searching suitable alternative selection procedures and the use of the ambiguous word "generally" with regard to the bottom line concept. The Ad Hoc Group's comments also note the lack of evidence for the existence of differential validity and recommend that all references to such validity and to test fairness be eliminated from the guidelines.

While applauding the efforts of the federal enforcement agencies to reach an agreement on uniform guidelines, the employer groups emphasized provisions of the proposed set of guidelines which are inconsistent with the accepted standards of the profession. It was anticipated that there was little likelihood of any substantial change from the proposed to the final version of the uniform guidelines; it had taken five years of work and negotiation among the four agencies involved to reach this agreement. Therefore, industry and professional representatives decided to establish clearly for the record what they viewed as inconsistencies between the guidelines and the professional standards. This goal was viewed as extremely important in view of the Supreme Court action affirming the *U.S.* v. *South Carolina* case in which the court accepted professional standards where there was a conflict between them and the EEOC guidelines.[7]

Coping with legal uncertainty in selection

Over the past decade, employers have been faced with increasing uncertainty as to what is and what is not legally required in the em-

[7] *U.S.* v. *South Carolina, supra,* note 4.

ployee selection process. Not surprisingly, since the use of paper-and-pencil pre-employment tests has been a major target of EEO agencies, many employers have taken the tack of abandoning their testing programs. A recent BNA survey of nearly 200 companies across the nation indicates that only 42 percent of the employers now give pre-employment tests, compared to 90 percent of the companies participating in a similar survey in 1963.[8]

For those employers who are using tests based on the general reputation of the test and/or test publisher without any evidence that the test is valid for the purpose at hand, it may be entirely appropriate to discontinue using tests. This is particularly true where it can be shown that the use of the test—or any other selection device—does have an adverse impact on a particular group of people. Furthermore, it cannot be denied that this type of situation did exist in many companies, even in some companies which otherwise had the most sophisticated selection practices, as the civil rights groups discovered soon after they became involved in equal employment litigation.

But what are the alternatives? It is apparent from the results of the BNA survey on selection procedures that as the use of tests has declined, the selection interview has become increasingly important. However, only 2 percent of the companies surveyed have attempted to validate their interview procedures. There already are court decisions pointing to the subjective and "casual" nature of selection interviews, and the uniform guidelines apply to "informal or casual interviews" as well as to tests. Sooner or later every aspect of selection will be under scrutiny.

Based on what has happened with the use of tests, employers faced with uncertainty about the legal aspects of other selection techniques may be tempted to abandon selection altogether. The result would be hiring on a random or quota basis, which is what many observers claim is EEOC's ultimate goal. For the large majority of jobs in American industry, however, hiring on a random basis is counterproductive. Without some objective clues—test results, educational record, past employment history—concerning an applicant's qualifi-

[8] *Selection Procedures and Personnel Records,* Personnel Policies Forum, Survey No. 114, September 1976 (Washington, D.C.: The Bureau of National Affairs, Inc.), page 7.

cations for a particular job, the probability of excessive and expensive turnover is extremely high. Neither the individual employer nor the economy as a whole can afford to undertake a strategy that would have such a negative impact on employee productivity. The consequences for individual employees, as they shift from job to job before finding an appropriate niche, are equally undesirable.

One positive result of the controversy over selection guidelines is that a number of companies have begun to take a closer look at their selection techniques and are conducting extensive validation studies. The long-term prospect is that because of EEOC pressures the selection procedures used for employment in American industry will be more scientific and less discriminatory. The technical problems associated with deciding what is or is not an acceptable validity study may turn out to be short-lived. The essential point may be that selection procedures are put to a test and are not adopted wholesale as they sometimes have been in the past.

While it is true that some specifics of the selection process may still be uncertain as far as the law is concerned, there are several basic issues that have been resolved, and these issues do provide a framework for selection within the law.

It is clear that any employer subject to federal EEO laws must

1. Determine whether the selection process overall results in an adverse impact on the employment of any group protected under the law.
2. Where there is an adverse impact, find out what specific step or technique used in the selection process is contributing to the adverse impact.
3. Prove that the selection technique resulting in an adverse impact is job-related and thus complies with the requirement of "business necessity." The proof must be in the form of acceptable evidence of validity.

The next section of this book will be devoted to outlining the steps to take and the types of data to use in determining adverse impact and in proving job-relatedness. It should be emphasized that these are studies that all employers can, and probably should, be doing on an ongoing basis whether or not faced with a Title VII complaint or contract-compliance review. When the government compliance officer already is knocking on the door, it may be too late. By pinpointing the problem areas and investigating solutions before complaints are filed, an employer will be in a much better position to defend existing selection procedures.

It also should be emphasized that the goal of Title VII of the Civil Rights Act is to end discrimination in employment, and the overriding mission of the EEOC is to achieve that goal. When it became apparent to those involved in EEO enforcement that many traditional industrial selection practices perpetuated what the Supreme Court called "built-in headwinds" against the employment of minorities and women, it is not surprising that stringent guidelines on selection procedures were issued. Such an approach is typical in an adversary situation. It is unfortunate that some employers reacted to events with the attitude of "you can't tell me who I can or cannot hire," without taking a good look at the situation within their workforce and at their methods of selection. Yet that too is not totally unexpected.

It is apparent that employers who can show goodfaith efforts at compliance do get consideration in the courts even if they are having difficulty meeting court-ordered goals for hiring. In the long run, however, EEOC's success or failure will be measured by statistics—national figures on improvements in the employment of minorities and women at various occupational levels. To date, there has been some change but the results are far from satisfactory to the civil rights advocates and women's rights activists. Thus, because it has failed to achieve better results, EEOC will inevitably increase its pressure on individual employers to achieve results.

part 3

techniques for evaluating the selection process

5

use of workforce data in defining discrimination

Just as discrimination in employment has come to be defined in terms of the results—rather than the intent—of a particular selection process, the proof of such discrimination increasingly takes the form of statistical data. As noted in Chapter 2, data submitted in court cases involving EEOC charges have come from a wide variety of sources, and the courts have agreed that a "prima facie case of discrimination may be established solely through the use of statistics." In general, the type of statistical evidence used against employers has involved a comparison of the makeup of the company workforce, or particular components of the workforce, with figures on the composition of some relevant population. What often becomes the basic issue in EEO litigation is the decision as to which population *is* most relevant for comparison; this issue will be discussed in greater detail later in this chapter.

Another type of statistical evidence that is of major concern with regard to selection involves appropriate documentary data on the validation of standards and techniques used in hiring and promotion. These are the statistics required by the various governmental guidelines for selection procedures discussed in the last chapter, which become necessary once discrimination is proved. The steps involved in gathering and analyzing data for purposes of validation of selection procedures will be outlined in Chapters 6, 7, and 8.

The type and extent of statistical data an employer needs to collect may differ considerably from one situation to another. It can be a relatively simple task to put together the figures necessary to determine whether a company's overall employment practices have resulted in an adverse impact, or discrimination, with respect to a protected group. For companies operating under a required affirmative action plan, a conciliation agreement, or a consent decree with hiring goals and targets, the data collection effort will be much more comprehensive. And when firms become involved with EEO litigation, the legal counsel may hunt extensively for any statistical data that might support the employer's case or rebut the data submitted by the complaining party. No matter how extensive the data search required, however, the initial step is the same—to make an analysis of the company's current workforce.

The workforce analysis

For most companies, the starting point for the workforce analysis is the EEO-1 Report Form, which must be filed annually by all employers with 100 or more employees and by government contractors. This form calls for employment data based on the following nine broad job categories: officers and managers, professionals, technicians, sales workers, office and clerical, craftsmen (skilled), operatives (semi-skilled), laborers (unskilled), and service workers. The figures are broken down for male and female employees, for total minority employees, and for four minority groups: Black, Hispanic, Asian or Pacific Islander, American Indian or Alaskan native. An EEO-1 Form with accompanying instructions including definitions of each minority group appears as Exhibit 7, p. 486.

As "suggested" by EEOC in its guidebook for employers, and required of government contractors subject to OFCCP regulations, the workforce analysis requires that a detailed listing be made of all classifications within each of the broad EEO job categories. According to the OFCCP regulations, the listing should include each job title (as it appears in any collective bargaining agreement or on the payroll records) from the lowest paid to the highest paid within each department or division. For each job title, the list should show the total number of male and female incumbents and the number of males and females in each of four minority groups. An example of a form used for this purpose appears as Exhibit 8, p. 496. The list should include the wage rate or salary range for each job title, and all job titles including those at the managerial level must be listed.

Utilization analysis

The data of the workforce analysis are used to help identify job classifications, departments, or work units in which minorities, females, or males are either *underutilized* or *concentrated.* This is the utilization analysis, which must be conducted separately for race and sex. According to EEO, *underutilization* is defined as having fewer minorities or women in a particular job category than would reasonably be expected by their presence in the relevant labor market; it also includes the employment of persons in jobs that do not make adequate use of their skills and training. *Concentration* is indicated when more of a particular group (males, females, blacks, etc.) are found in a job category or department than would reasonably be expected by their presence in the workforce. If the figures show significant underutilization or concentration, says EEOC, "there is a strong probability that discriminatory practices are operating in some aspects of your employment system."[1]

The difficult part of the utilization analysis involves trying to determine what can "reasonably be expected" in the way of employment of men, women, and minorities in each job classification. In defining the presence of a particular group in the relevant labor market, the following factors must be taken into consideration:

- The percentage of each minority group in the total population of the labor market area; for female employment the factor to consider is the availability of women seeking employment in the area.

- The percentage of each minority group and of women in the company workforce as compared with the total workforce in the area.

- The extent of unemployment of minority group members and women in the area.

- The general availability in the relevant recruiting area of minorities and women having the required skills.

- The availability of promotable or transferable minority group members and women currently employed within the company.

- The existence of training institutions in the community capable of training people in the needed skills.

[1]Equal Employment Opportunity Commission, *Affirmative Action and Equal Employment: A Guidebook for Employers* (Washington, D.C.: U.S. Government Printing Office, 1974), p. 24.

•The company's own capability for training minorities and women in the skills needed for all job classifications.

Examples of forms used for presenting these data appear as Exhibit 9, pp. 499-500.

Defining the relevant recruiting area. As noted in the beginning of this chapter, one of the thorniest problems to arise in EEO litigation is the definition of a relevant population with which to compare the makeup of an employer's workforce. The first question to be asked is what is the relevant recruiting area for the workforce as a whole or for particular job categories. Recruiting areas generally are considered to be national, regional, statewide, or local. Within a local area, there may be further breakdowns by city, county, or major urban areas on the basis of the Standard Metropolitan Statistical Areas (SMSA). Because the percentages of minorities and of women seeking employment may vary greatly from one recruiting area to another, the selection of a particular area for purposes of data analysis amounts to a crucial decision.

The case of the Timken Company in northern Ohio, mentioned in Chapter 2, illustrates one of the factors—commuting patterns—that can be taken into account in defining the recruiting area. As a government contractor, Timken was taken to court by the OFCCP because its affirmative action plan was not based on a "realistic recruitment area." The company's policy was to limit recruiting to persons within 15 miles of the plant, an area with a 0.6 percent minority group representation. The government argued that the recruiting area should be extended to include the city of Mansfield, which is 25 miles from the plant and has a minority group population of 15 percent. The court upheld Timken's recruiting policy on the basis of evidence that only an "infinitesimal" number of Mansfield residents commute to the area of the Timken plant to work.[2] Thus, existing commuting patterns can serve to define the relevant recruiting area.

It can reasonably be assumed that in situations such as Timken's where there are two possible relevant recruiting areas, the government will argue that the area with the highest percentage of

[2]*Timken Co.* v. *Vaughan,* 413 F. Supp. 1183, 12 FEP 1140.

minority group members is the appropriate one to use for analysis. And unless the employer has strong supporting evidence to the contrary, as Timken did, the courts generally have agreed that the area with the highest percentage of minorities is the one to use for measuring utilization of minorities and for establishing affirmative action goals.

It also should be noted that it is not necessarily the larger of two possible recruiting areas that may be most appropriate. In the case of a Western Electric plant located in the northern Virginia suburbs of Washington, D.C., the company relied on data for the Washington SMSA and noted that its employment figures at the plant compared favorably with the female and minority percentages in the SMSA. The court decided this area was too large to be considered the relevant labor market for the entry-level job openings in question.[3] In this case, the court based its finding of discrimination on figures comparing the percentages of black and female applicants hired to the white and male applicants, or what is known as the "applicant flow" data.

Sources of data. The major sources of data on minority group members and women in the relevant labor market or recruiting areas are various government agencies, particularly the U.S. Bureau of the Census and the state employment service offices under the Department of Labor. Standardized packets of local workforce statistics are now available at many employment service offices throughout the country, and these figures can be used with regard to jobs filled from statewide or local areas and for which no special skills are required.

When it comes to jobs for which recruiting is done on a regional or national level or for which special skills or training are required, the data-location task becomes more difficult. There are some government figures, particularly census data, that are helpful for certain types of jobs, but there are many types of jobs for which figures on the availability of women and minorities have been virtually nonexistent. Under the pressures of EEO enforcement requirements, these data are now being collected and made widely available. A number of companies that have made detailed analyses of the com-

[3]*Hill* v. *Western Electric,* 12 FEP Cases 1175.

position of the local labor market by race and sex, including such factors as occupational and educational levels, have provided their figures to other employers in the area.

A comprehensive list of sources of labor market data, prepared by the EEOC, is reproduced as Exhibit 10, pp. 501-505.

Putting the data together. The final step in the utilization analysis is to determine what percentages of women and minorities there should be in each of the company's major job families (jobs requiring similar skills) or job groupings based on other factors. Because these percentages are based on the availability of persons with appropriate skills in the relevant labor market, they will vary from one job family to another and perhaps from one level to another within the same job family.

While many employers rely on census data for the SMSA in which they are located to provide the relevant percentages for this analysis, some employers have developed other approaches. One example is an analysis of the "true employment market" devised by a research center in California. The analysis is based on concentric circles of 10, 20, and 30 miles from the office location, and statistics on the labor force are provided for each circle. The EEO percentages for each job classification are then developed on the theory that the higher the job levels and salaries, the greater the distances people are willing to travel to their work. Others have developed even finer categories based on geography and transportation availability.

No matter what the source or justification for the percentages used, their purpose is to indicate whether an employment discrimination problem exists in the current workforce, and if there is a problem, where it exists. Comparing these percentages with the figures from the company workforce analysis, it will be evident where minorities or females are being underutilized or concentrated. Any job groupings where there is a disparity between the relevant labor market percentage and the company workforce analysis are viewed as "focus job titles" by EEO enforcement agencies, and employers are expected to concentrate their affirmative action efforts on these jobs. Experience with EEO enforcement indicates that the greatest areas of underutilization of both women and minorities tend to occur in the EEO-1 categories of officials and managers, professionals, technicians, and skilled craft workers. Minorities tend to be underutilized also in the sales-worker and office and clerical categories. Thus, these are the categories in which the focus job titles are most likely to be found. They also may occur in the unskilled-laborer and service-worker categories if there is an indication of concentration of women or minorities.

A sample form for a utilization analysis and for setting goals and timetables, the next step in the process, appears as Exhibit 11, pp. 506-510.

Goals and timetables

Under the regulations applying to government contractors and under the terms of consent decrees and conciliation agreements with EEOC, employers are required to set certain goals and develop timetables for achieving these goals. For any employee groups in which there is a problem of concentration or underutilization, a long-range goal is established to achieve a reasonable representation of the underutilized sex or minority, based on availability in the relevant labor market. For each long-range goal, usually viewed as a five-year goal, intermediate annual targets are set. These targets specify the number of females or minorities to be hired or promoted into the affected job categories, or focus job titles.

The EEO enforcement agencies emphasize that the goals should not be viewed as rigid, inflexible quotas. Both the long-range goals and annual targets should be based on anticipated job openings and the availability of appropriate applicants, but they cannot be based upon completely predictable data. What is essential, according to OFCCP, is that the targets be reasonably attainable by the employer's putting forth "every good faith effort to make his overall affirmative action program work."[4]

The initial utilization analysis that an employer conducts will indicate where there may be a problem caused by past discrimination in employment practices. Although deficiencies of minorities or women in certain job categories are not always clear proof of past discrimination, the courts generally have viewed them as such unless the employer offers evidence to the contrary. After setting goals to

[4]OFCCP Affirmative Action Guidelines, as amended February 17, 1977 (published in BNA's *Fair Employment Practices*, p. 401:731).

offset the effects of past discrimination and taking steps to achieve the goals, an employer is in a better position to determine whether discriminatory employment practices have in effect been eliminated. The most crucial aspect of any affirmative action program is a periodic monitoring of results. Are the overall targets being met? How are individual departments doing? Are there certain job categories that continue to show deficiencies? Answers to questions such as these may indicate trouble spots where a company might be vulnerable to charges of discrimination.

In situations where there appears to be some difficulty in achieving affirmative action goals, or where there is evidence of past discrimination that is not being corrected, the government compliance agencies will look for some aspect of the selection process that may be resulting in an "adverse impact" on the employment of minorities or females. As the courts have decreed, it is the adverse effect of employment practices that constitutes illegal discrimination. If the company workforce statistics and affirmative action results indicate a continuing EEO problem, a detailed analysis of the entire selection process is called for to determine whether there is an adverse impact problem at some step of the process.

Determination of adverse impact

As used in EEO litigation, adverse impact refers to a selection process that results in a substantially higher percentage of a protected group's members being rejected for hiring, promotion, or other employment decisions than the percentage of nonprotected persons rejected. Under the uniform guidelines, if it is determined that the total selection process for a particular job has an adverse impact, then the individual steps of the selection process should be evaluated for adverse impact. EEOC's position, however, has been and continues to be that it may be appropriate to examine individual components of the selection process for adverse impact even in situations where the total selection process has no adverse impact.

Another difference between the EEOC and FEA guidelines in this area is that EEOC's guidelines did not provide an exact definition of adverse impact whereas the FEA guidelines do, and this definition is included in the uniform guidelines. The latter guidelines state: "A selection rate for any racial, ethnic or sex group which is less than four-fifths (4/5) (or eighty percent) of the rate for the group with the highest rate will generally be regarded by the Federal enforcement agencies as evidence of adverse impact."[5] This has been called "the 4/5 rule of thumb for guidance and operational use" by the enforcement agencies. According to staff personnel at the EEOC, that agency generally uses a 4/5 rule of thumb for determining adverse impact; however, it did not wish to be limited to such a specific definition in all cases. This is one of the major reasons the EEOC would not agree to accept the first proposed uniform guidelines.

In most situations it appears likely that employers can use the 4/5 rule with some confidence; that is, if the selection rate for a protected group is above 80 percent of the rate for the applicant group with the highest selection rate, enforcement agencies will not consider adverse impact to exist. A series of questions and answers published by the three agencies that adopted the FEA guidelines includes the following illustration of how adverse impact can be shown:

> *Adverse impact:* Over a six month period, there are 120 applicants, 80 white and 40 black, of whom 60 were hired—48 whites and 12 blacks. The selection rate for white applicants was thus 48/80 = 60%; while that for black applicants was 12/40 = 30%. In this example, the selection process adversely affected the employment opportunities of blacks because their selection rate (30%) was only 1/2 or 50% that of whites (60)%.

> *No adverse impact:* If, on the other hand, there were 120 applicants, of which 80 were white and 40 black, and 42 whites and 18 blacks were selected, the selection rate for blacks would be 18/40, or 45%, while that for whites would be 42/80, or 52.5%. Because the selection rate for blacks as compared to that for whites is 45/52.5, or 85.4% (i.e., more than 80% or 4/5), the difference in impact would not be regarded as substantial in the absence of additional information.[6]

[5]See Exhibit 6-A, p. 437.

[6]*Daily Labor Report,* No. 13, January 19, 1977, p. E-1.

To obtain the figures needed to determine the existence of adverse impact in the selection process, employers have had to set up detailed information systems on job applicants and to analyze the data on the basis of sex, race, type of job applied for, and so forth. (See Exhibit 12, p. 511 for a sample form for this purpose.) This type of information must be submitted to compliance officers by government contractors; it must be submitted on a periodic basis to EEOC under the terms of most consent decrees and conciliation agreements; and it frequently provides the basis of EEOC litigation.

Data on the applicant flow will indicate problems in the overall selection process, but even more detailed information is required to pinpoint possible sources of the problem. One of the most important questions involves the specific reason for rejection of a minority or female applicant. Are a high proportion of these applicants failing to pass required tests, or do they fail to meet minimum educational or physical requirements? By analyzing the reasons for rejection and the point in the selection process where the rejection occurs (e.g., at the initial screening in the employment office, at the personnel department interview, at the supervisory or department head level), it will be possible to find out if a single step in the process accounts for a preponderance of rejections. That step is the most likely source of any adverse impact that has been indicated, and it is that procedure which the government compliance people will attack. The attack takes the form of requiring proof that the procedure in question is based on business necessity. The proof of business necessity for selection procedures has been interpreted to require evidence that the procedure is job-related as demonstrated by the type of validity studies specified in the selection guidelines. Thus, a finding of adverse impact triggers the need for validation, a process which will be described in Chapters 6, 7, and 8.

Cautions on the use of population statistics

The heavy reliance on statistics introduced by EEO enforcement agencies, though endorsed by the courts, has been subject to frequent criticism. From an employer's viewpoint, the most difficult problem is that the data called for in making a utilization analysis may not be the same data that the government attempts to use in arguing a discrimination case before the courts. In fact, statistics presented to show a prima facie case of discrimination may not relate to a specific company's employment experience at all. In the landmark *Duke Power* case, for example, the company's high school education requirement was found discriminatory based on educational statistics for the state of North Carolina. It was the fact that statistically blacks were less likely to possess a high school diploma than whites that made the application of a seemingly neutral employment practice amount to unlawful discrimination.

In cases where the government does rely on the employer's workforce data for either the workforce as a whole or for specific jobs, there is no way to predict what "relevant" geographical area will be used to define the appropriate labor market for comparison. In *Duke Power* it was the entire state of North Carolina. In other instances, the entire southeastern section of the United States has been defined as the relevant recruiting area, but there also have been many cases where the labor market area was much smaller and based on city limits or the SMSA. This is why employers are advised, in making their own utilization analyses, to use the labor market area with the largest percentages of available minorities and women.

Even where there is little question as to the relevant recruiting area, statistics on the availability of persons in the protected groups with specific skills frequently are totally lacking or extremely inadequate. Even census data are quickly outdated, and there is no way statistics can take into account the desires of different groups of people for specific jobs or certain kinds of work. One of the problems encountered by an AT&T company, for example, was that Spanish-speaking persons in a large city refused to take jobs requiring them to work at night. The result was that the company had an extremely difficult time meeting its targets for hiring more Spanish-surnamed persons as telephone operators; many of the openings involved working at night.

The applicant-flow issue. One statistical approach involves a comparison of the percentages of minority and female applicants actually hired with the percentages of white and male applicants hired. This analysis of the "applicant flow" is what is required in determining whether the selection process as a whole, or certain components of the process, result in an adverse impact with regard to a protected group. As noted earlier, applicant-flow data also has been used in a number of cases before the courts, and in many instances the courts have held that a disparate applicant flow is evidence of discrimination. In several cases where applicant-flow data suggested a higher rejection rate for minorities or females, even though the workforce data did not indicate underutilization as compared with the relevant labor market, the courts have gone along with the applicant-flow argument.

As a number of employers have pointed out, the applicant-flow-data approach to defining discrimination in effect penalizes the companies that have been the most effective in their efforts to recruit minorities and women; the more applicants recruited from these groups for a particular job opening, the higher the percentage who will not be hired. Another problem with using figures based on applicant flow, it has been argued, is that frequently there is no way to determine the extent to which the applicants rejected have even the basic skills to perform jobs for which the company has openings. Some employers have charged that activist civil rights groups have flooded them with applicants, many of whom are not sincerely looking for work, and then insisted on using applicant flow as proof of discrimination. The final determinant of a company's "fair share" of minority and female employees, according to the employer's viewpoint, should be the proportion indicated by the workforce data of the relevant recruiting area. In recognition of this type of situation, the uniform guidelines state that differences in selection rates greater than the four-fifths rule would indicate may not constitute adverse impact "where special recruiting or other programs cause the pool of minority or female applicants to be atypical of the normal pool of applicants from that group."[7]

The data dilemma. Companies that have been involved in EEO litigation or that have had to deal with government contract compliance officers are well aware of what is required in terms of data collection, record keeping, and reporting. Consent decrees and conciliation agreements usually call for detailed reports on a quarterly and annual basis for periods of several years, and companies operating under such agreements frequently set up sophisticated computerized information systems to provide the necessary data.

[7]See Exhibit 6-A, p. 437.

But what about the employer who has not yet been faced with a charge of discrimination in employment and who wants to find out whether he might be vulnerable to any such charge? Because it no longer is deliberate or intentional discrimination that is the major issue, the only way to determine whether there is a discrimination problem is through the use of statistics in the ways described throughout this chapter. The dilemma arises if the data do indicate some problem areas, and if the government files charges before the employer has an opportunity to take steps to be in compliance with the law. At this point, any data that the employer has collected in good faith can be used against him. In the *J.P. Stevens* case[8] mentioned in Chapter 2, the plaintiffs were able to obtain the statistics showing the difference in pay between blacks and whites with the same educational backgrounds and seniority from the company payroll records. According to one EEOC attorney, getting the employer's statistics is "vital," because the "numbers game is the only game in town" in prosecuting Title VII cases. His advice to EEO lawyers is to become familiar with data processing, to find out what kind of information the employer has and how it is maintained, and then to request machine-readable material such as computer cards, tapes, and discs, as well as processed data.

With this approach to data collection on the part of EEOC, it is clear that any data the employer has may turn up as evidence for the complainant in court. This is why one management lawyer has advised employers to keep their personnel records off the computer; individual complaints of discrimination sometimes have turned into class actions when computerized personnel data were readily available for large groups of employees. However, this does not appear to be a very realistic approach in view of the advantages of some computerized employee information systems.

The decision as to how extensive an EEO analysis should be for an individual company is similar to the decision as to what data should be used in making the analysis. It depends on a variety of circumstances that differ from one company to another. At the very least, however, an employer needs to analyze the company workforce at some point in time and at periodic intervals thereafter—first

[8] *Sledge* v. *J.P. Stevens & Co.,* No. 1201 (E.D.N.C. 1976), cited in *Daily Labor Report,* No. 133, July 9, 1976, p. A-4.

to determine whether the company is vulnerable to charges of discrimination and then to monitor change. Any company that can show some change in the right direction in its employment picture is likely to fare better in court than a company that cannot demonstrate any such results. And even if the employment picture is slow to change and affirmative action results are negligible at first, the employer who has taken the trouble to analyze the situation and has made some good faith efforts to remedy the effects of past discrimination is in a far better position than the employer who simply has ignored the whole issue.

The chapters that follow discuss the second type of statistics involved in EEO litigation—statistics relating to the validation of selection procedures. Under the governmental selection guidelines, such validation is legally required only in situations where it has been shown that the selection process has an adverse impact. It is our belief that all selection procedures used for hiring or promotion decisions should be validated by whatever method is most appropriate in terms of the types of jobs and numbers of hires involved. Thus, whether there is adverse impact or not, an employer should determine whether any selection procedure is job-related; otherwise, there is little if any justification for using the procedure. Random selection, frequently advocated by civil rights activists, may very well be as effective as *unvalidated* selection procedures. However, both these approaches involve costs in terms of unnecessary turnover, low employee productivity, and other detrimental effects that can be avoided with the use of validated selection techniques.

In a special notice published by the enforcement agencies concerning the public hearing on the uniform guidelines, the agencies themselves note that "Employers have many economic incentives even where not required by Federal equal employment opportunity law to conduct validity studies and use properly validated selection procedures."[9]

[9] *Daily Labor Report,* No. 55, March 21, 1978, p. E-2.

6

the design of validation research

The first step in conducting a criterion-related validation study is the design of the research. Inherent in this process is the development of suitable criterion measures of job performance. Subsequent to data collection various statistical analyses are carried out to determine, among other things, whether a significant or real relationship exists between a selection technique and the criterion. These topics—design, criterion development, and statistical analysis—are considered in this and the following two chapters.

Although statistical considerations are clearly involved in the design process and in criterion construction, the authors have repeatedly found that learning about statistical techniques in the abstract is very difficult for many people. On the other hand, when a person knows why it is important to learn and what can be done with the techniques, many of the problems tend to disappear. This is why we present the rationales behind statistical analyses before considering the techniques themselves in any detail. The reader may find the statement prepared by the Division of Industrial-Organizational Psychology of the American Psychological Association, entitled *Principles for the Validation and Use of Personnel Selection Procedures,* reproduced as Exhibit 13, p. 512, a valuable adjunct to the present discussion; the glossary at the end should be particularly useful.

The longitudinal design with a single predictor

The logic of validation research is best presented using the longitudinal model which yields an index of predictive validity. Although in personnel practice generally multiple predictors are used to select people for hiring, it is simpler to start our discussion with the single-predictor case. Such a single-predictor validation study might be needed, for instance, if an enforcement agency questioned a particular selection device, such as a test or a reference-checking process, on the grounds that it produced adverse impact.

In a situation of this type the initial step is to administer the predictor measure over time to as large a number of candidates for a given job, or very closely related group of jobs, as possible. Hiring should then occur from this candidate group without using the predictor data. The reason for this procedure is that whether evidence of validity is obtained is strongly dependent on the amount of variation in predictor scores present in the group under study (those hired). If all the scores are bunched up at the top of the distribution, it is very difficult to demonstrate validity, even if it is present.

An approach sometimes used is to wait until shortly after hiring and administer the predictor measure then. This prevents the predictor from being used in hiring decisions and is often more palatable within the organization. It has the distinct disadvantage, however, that the degree of variation in scores of those hired cannot be compared with the variation in the candidate pool to be sure some restriction of range has not occurred. There are statistical techniques that can be used to determine what effects any restriction of range in the predictor scores of those hired may have had on validity, but these can only be used when one knows the degree of variation in both the total candidate group and the hired group.

Another alternative is to try to get as wide a distribution of predictor scores as possible while recognizing that complete neglect of these scores in making hiring decisions is impractical. This is distinctly a second-best solution, but it may be all that can be done. This alternative can be illustrated as follows, contrasting it with the ideal case where the predictor data are not used at all and with the worst possible situation where predictor scores at a high level determine all hiring decisions:

	Number of People Hired		
Predictor Scores	Predictor Not Used	Predictor Used	Predictor Used Somewhat
9	10	28	14
8	10	29	15
7	15	43	21
6	30	0	30
5	15	0	12
4	10	0	7
3	5	0	1
2	3	0	0
1	2	0	0

It should be noted that there are some situations where it is relatively easy not to use the predictor being validated in actual selection decisions until after the study is over. One such situation is when labor market conditions are very tight; for a period of time everyone that can be found must be hired just to keep available positions filled and the work from lagging badly. Another case where it is easy not to use the predictor is when the selection technique is clearly viewed as experimental and there is no widespread conviction in the organization that it will prove particularly useful; at the point in time that the validity study is conducted there is no general feeling that a failure to use the approach would do the company a great harm.

When such optimum conditions for validation do not exist, the point that must be kept in mind is that without a good range of predictor scores in the study group validity may not be established and the business-necessity defense is then lost. The only things that might compensate for such a restriction of range are if the predictor is in fact *very* highly related to the criterion or if a huge sample of individuals is available. Where the validity is not likely to be very high anyway and large samples are out of the question, adding in considerable restriction of range will doom any validity study to failure, even though the validity may really be there.

The size of the group to be studied will depend on the rate at which hiring occurs and the length of time one waits before cutting off the research. From the point of view of establishing validity it is desirable to accumulate predictor data over as long a period as needed to get the sample size up. This is because lower validity coefficients turn out to be statistically significant, and thus acceptable as demonstrations of job-relatedness, when the sample is large. This argues strongly for obtaining groups of several hundred or more employees, if one wants to demonstrate validity. The enforcement agencies may well not challenge a sample of only 30, but the company should. If there is good reason to expect a high real validity, if restriction of range is not a problem, and if the criterion used is highly stable and reliable, then perhaps a sample size (N) as small as 30 could yield an acceptable validity coefficient, but the authors would prefer not to bet on it.

Once predictor data have been gathered, in whatever form, the longitudinal design calls for a wait until it is appropriate to collect criterion information. This may be at the end of a training period, a probationary period, or some acceptable period of job performance. It will vary from job to job depending on how long it takes to get to full proficiency. In any event there has to be time for performance to stabilize. The specific approaches to criterion measurement which are appropriate will be considered in the next chapter.

Having obtained predictor and criterion data, the next step is to determine the degree of relationship between the two. Generally a correlation coefficient is computed to characterize this relationship. This coefficient, which may be called a validity coefficient, can be computed in several different ways. In most cases it yields values which may range from a low of −1.00 through 0 to +1.00, with the larger values, both negative and positive, indicating a closer relation between predictor and criterion. The larger the value the greater the predictive validity.

The concept involved in a validity coefficient may be depicted using a chart of the predictor criterion relationship, or scatter plot. For the two persons scoring 1 (very low) on the predictor, which might be a test, subsequent performance, which might be measured by a rating, was 1 and 2 on a scale of 7, whereas among 10 persons with test scores of 9 (very high) subsequent performance for two was

Predictor Values	Criterion Values 1	2	3	4	5	6	7
9				2	1	5	2
8			1	1	4	2	2
7			2	4	7	2	0
6		2	6	6	5	0	1
5		1	6	6	1	1	
4	2	4	2	0	2		
3		2	3	0			
2	2	0		1			
1	1	1					

rated 4; for one, 5; for five, 6; and for two, 7. In this instance the relationship is a positive one—those who score high on the predictor are likely to be high on the criterion measure—and the validity is clearly quite good.

The longitudinal design with multiple predictors

The addition of a number of predictors to the validation process, as when several different selection techniques are being validated or when a measure such as a personality test yields many different scores, introduces two major new design considerations. One relates to the fact that when a number of validity coefficients are calculated some will be quite high merely because of random fluctuations and not because a real relationship exists. The second arises out of the need to combine predictors in some way to use them.

Cross-validation. When a larger number of predictors is involved in a study and none of them is really valid, there still will be some high validity coefficients in both a positive and negative direction simply because of chance fluctuations around zero. If one were to repeat the study using a new group of employees, much the same range and distribution of validity coefficients would emerge, but it is very unlikely that exactly the same predictors would yield the high values again—if there were really no valid predictors, only chance fluctuations would result. On the other hand, if one or more of the predictors really were valid, the validity coefficients should be high in both studies.

The only way to know whether chance or real validity is involved in many cases is to do two studies, thus carrying out a cross-validation. This step is particularly important when large numbers of predictor-criterion correlations are computed and only relatively few are high enough to suggest statistical validity. To take these few measures and use them for selection purposes is a very risky business; they may well not select the best people at all. This sort of situation almost invariably arises in the construction of weighted application blanks or biographical inventories where many items are tested out and only those few with high predictor-criterion relationships are used in the final measure. Under such circumstances it is absolutely essential to cross-validate to see if the final measure holds its validity in the new sample; not infrequently such measures do not.

If the wait between predictor-data collection and criterion-data collection is relatively short, one can cross-validate merely by taking the most promising predictors from the first study and applying them to a second group. In actual practice it is common to use another company location or another shift for cross-validation. An alternative to consecutive validations is to split the original sample into two random parts and use it to conduct two validity studies. Those predictors that yield high correlations in both groups can then be considered to be valid.

Combining predictors. A variety of procedures may be used to combine predictors, some of which are statistical in nature and some of which are not. Of the statistical approaches one of the most widely used is multiple correlation. In this procedure the correlations between the predictors are computed, in addition to the correlations between the predictors and criterion, and then a multiple correlation coefficient is computed to yield a maximum index of the predictor-criterion relationship. The separate predictors are automatically weighted in a combination that produces the best prediction of the criterion. This statistical procedure also yields regression weights which may be multiplied by the actual scores obtained by a person on the various predictors to get a single total score, which represents a maximum estimate of the individual's chances for job success.

A somewhat simpler approach involves merely adding the values obtained by the individual on the various predictors together (without first applying the regression weights) and then computing the correlation between this composite score and the criterion. Additive correlations of this kind often yield a close approximation to the results obtained from the multiple-correlation approach.

Both multiple and additive correlations produce a single score distribution which may then be entered to establish a cutting score or qualification point, above which candidates will be hired and below which they will not be. In contrast to the use of a single score, the multiple-cutoff procedure utilizes the predictors one at a time. The various predictor-criterion correlations are computed and then the predictor with the highest correlation is identified for the purpose of establishing a cutting score on that measure only. All candidates who fall below this score are screened out; all others are then passed on to the predictor with the second highest criterion correlation and a similar test is applied. This process of successive screening is continued until all predictors having a sizable relationship with the criterion are exhausted. Those candidates who are hired are the ones who are consistently above the cutting scores on all valid predictors. In actual practice three or four such hurdles are all that are required, since little predictive power is normally added beyond that point.

Another possibility, which has seen relatively little use, however, is to separate out those individuals in the validation sample whose scores on the criterion are at a level sufficient to justify calling them successful, and then average their scores on each valid predictor. The result is a profile in predictor terms of the typical successful performer. Candidates are then matched against this profile. The degree of match may be calculated by summing the absolute values of all deviations from the ideal values established using the successful performers. A cutting score is then established on this deviation index to screen out those who vary too much from the ideal.

A closely related procedure is the horizontal percent method. The validation sample is again divided into successful and unsuccessful groups using the criterion. Then groupings of scores on each valid predictor such as 1 to 5, 6 to 10, and so on are established. Those individuals whose scores on a predictor fall in the same grouping are then checked against the criterion to see what percentage of them are in the successful category. Obviously the more the scores are associated with success the higher this percentage will be. These percentages are then used as weights to develop a total score across all valid predictors. Thus on predictor 1 a score between 11 and 15 might have a weight of 36, and a score much further up the scale, say between 51 and 55, a weight of 63; on predictor 2 the comparable weights might be 40 and 58, and so on. An individual candidate's overall score is the sum of the percentages attached to the ranges within which his scores on all valid predictors fall. Cutting scores may then be established on this composite index to determine who will be hired.

All of the procedures discussed so far involve a statistical combining of predictor scores, often in a manner based on the degree of validity. In contrast to such statistical prediction, in clinical prediction the combining of predictors is accomplished by a personnel manager or psychologist entirely on the basis of personal experience. The result is a hiring decision that takes into account the available information but weights the different predictors on an intuitive basis. On the average, clinical approaches of this kind are not as effective as the statistical procedures, but certain individuals may well use them with a great deal of precision. If clinical prediction is used, it is important to validate the final recommendation so that *all* steps that will be used in the actual hiring situation are assessed.

The concurrent design

The concurrent design is identical to the longitudinal, with one very important exception: The predictor measures, whether single or multiple, and the criterion data are obtained at approximately the same time, characteristically on individuals who have been employed for some period on the job under study. Thus, the wait between the collection of predictor data and criterion measurement is not present. Any cross-validation is also done using current employees.

This approach is clearly a shortcut and it does have certain disadvantages. The enforcement agencies, and probably the courts also, may well question it as a final solution to charges of adverse impact. There sometimes are advantages to doing a concurrent study first, because if validity is not obtained there, one should not expect it from a predictive or longitudinal study. But if validity is substantiated in a concurrent investigation, then it is desirable to go on and initiate a predictive study. This timetable is likely to elicit a finding of good faith on the part of the enforcement agencies, and thus a delay in any direct prosecution. On the other hand the longitudinal study must be completed sometime, and if it proves ineffectual the delay may be of little value.

There are reasons why a longitudinal study may not produce evidence of validity, when a concurrent study has. Some measures yield results which are largely a consequence of job tenure and experience. Indexes of job knowledge and skill are of this kind. Validations done with existing employees may therefore have little relevance for inexperienced job applicants. Also there are some potential predictors which may be influenced by the experiences of success and failure that have occurred on the job. Thus scores on a measure of self-confidence can well be determined by whether a person had experienced positive or negative evaluations, rather than the feeling of self-confidence being a cause of the level of performance outcomes.

Considerations such as these argue strongly for conducting longitudinal research if one needs to predict performance, as is the case when selecting people for hiring and promotion. Concurrent designs do not get at causation at all, while longitudinal designs do permit certain causal inferences. Yet it is quicker, easier, and less expensive to use a concurrent approach. In an uncharted situation it provides the best starting point, but if successful, it should be followed by a more demanding longitudinal investigation.

Content and construct validity

In contrast to the foregoing criterion-related methods of demonstrating business necessity, there are several other approaches that at least ostensibly will prove acceptable to the enforcement agencies; OFCCP is more favorably disposed to them than EEOC, but these approaches have been supported by the courts.

Establishing content validity. Content validity involves a systematic study of the job to establish what knowledge, skills, and behaviors are required. Based on this job analysis, an appropriate selection procedure is then developed through a rational, judgmental process. Most of the tests of job knowledge utilized by the government in meeting civil service requirements rely on content validity. A typing test used to select people for jobs in a typing pool should also possess content validity. An example supported by the courts is a test case used to select lawyers. The case is a real one taken from the files of the organization and the candidate must write an opinion rendering a decision and setting forth supporting evidence, just as would be required on the job.[1] This written sample opinion is evaluated by those lawyers who would evaluate actual job performance after hiring.

Content validity of this kind should be clearly differentiated from face validity. The former involves a judgment by an expert that the selection procedure is in fact job-related and is based upon the operations used to develop the measure. The latter involves merely an impression of appropriateness on the part of the person completing the measure and in fact can vary from one such person to another. Face validity would be present, for instance, if a test for retail sales clerks contained numerical items written with reference to actual store products and prices. Yet the computations required by the test might be so much more complex than those actually required by the job as to be totally irrelevant. It is true that content-valid techniques would be expected to be also face-valid, but the reverse need not be true.

Clearly content validation is not a procedure which is feasible for all selection techniques. It is basically applicable to job simulations or samples corresponding closely to major or critical components of the job description as developed through job analysis. The test should not require knowledge or skills characteristically learned on the job. This means that the approach is not applicable to many entry-level jobs; it is applicable only in those instances where candidates can be expected to come to the job already possessing the capabilities or knowledge measured.

An example of the process involved in establishing content validity is provided by a reading test developed for the plant operations of a chemical manufacturing company.[2] Reading was established as

[1]*Coopersmith* v. *Roundebush,* 517 F. 2d 818 (1975), 11 FEP Cases 247.

[2]Schoenfeldt, Lyle F.; Barbara B. Schoenfeldt; Stanley R. Acker; and Michael R. Perlson, "Content Validity Revisited: The Development of a Content-Oriented Test of Industrial Reading," *Journal of Applied Psychology 61* (1976), 581-588.

a key skill based on formal job analyses and discussions with managers and operating personnel. It was in fact the one skill that could not be developed on the job in entry-level positions and it was needed to achieve adequate proficiency levels in other aspects of the work. The occurrence of numerous severe accidents could be tied directly to an inability to read and comprehend job-related instructions.

The starting point for developing the test was the various materials actually read by employees. These were evaluated by managers for their importance to the work and by a reading expert to determine the reading skills involved. Test items were then written to emphasize the most important subjects and reading skills. The initial pretesting of items was carried out first on a group of eighth graders enrolled in an industrial arts curriculum and then on a sample of current employees. Based on these results the final test items were selected and an appropriate cutting point for hiring established. The measure was then studied further in actual use with an applicant group to verify the cutting score and to investigate adverse impact. Comparisons were also made between test items and the actual reading materials on the job to determine whether differences in difficulty levels existed. The result was an effective content-valid measure of the reading found to be important in performing job duties.

Establishing construct validity. Construct validity refers to underlying characteristics of the job performer, such as verbal ability or achievement motivation, of the kind often measured by psychological tests. For construct validity to apply, the particular theoretical construct must be well defined, the selection procedure must be well established as a measure of the construct, and an important component of job behavior must involve the construct. Establishing this type of validity requires rational inference from a body of research involving the construct, usually a sizable body of research of a programmatic nature. For instance, a measure of numerical ability might be shown to have a close relationship with other measures of numerical ability and to be less closely related to measures of other mental abilities. In addition, however, the relevance of the construct, say numerical ability, to the work itself must be demonstrated, and it is at this point that practical difficulties arise.

In the past the general position taken by the enforcement agencies, as yet untested by the courts, has been that establishing construct validity requires a criterion-related study in the actual company context where the measure is to be used for selection. This interpretation makes the whole idea of construct validity as applied to EEO considerations meaningless. Construct validity of this kind equals criterion-related validity *plus* additional research to establish the identity of the construct. Many lawyers have accordingly dismissed the idea of construct validity as irrelevant in any practical sense.

On the other hand the meaning of construct validity in the psychological profession differs considerably from what has been its meaning to the enforcement agencies. Criterion-related validity is important to identify those jobs for which the construct is important and in which high levels of the construct are desirable. But once these studies have been done and the nature of the construct as well as its significance for job performance are understood, further study is not needed. Known measures of the construct can be used for selection for appropriate jobs once construct validity has been firmly established in the literature without doing a criterion-related study in every situation. Following this line of reasoning, measures of achievement motivation could be used in connection with entrepreneurial activities, measures of creativity in selection for creative research positions, measures of managerial motivation as a basis for identifying talent in hierarchic organizations, and so on. Construct validity would then assume the same stature that content validity now has. We believe that appropriate use of the construct validity concept along these lines would be upheld by the courts. To date, however, it has neither been upheld nor rejected.

Differential validity

The concept of differential validity is applicable to criterion related studies and the need to test for it exists only when a predictor has an adverse impact on some protected group. Thus the use of a measure of verbal ability with minorities or of aggressiveness with females might well elicit pressures for investigations of differential validity as between whites and minorities in the first case and between males and females in the second.

The approach used is to split the validation sample into the appropriate separate components and then to carry out the research on each group just as one would in any other criterion-related study. Differential validity may be said not to exist when a predictor yields validity coefficients exceeding accepted levels of statistical significance for both groups, and when the difference between the two validity coefficients is not so large as to lead one to conclude that somehow the predictor is working differently in the two groups (i.e., there is no statistically significant difference between the validity coefficients). If a predictor were to yield a criterion correlation of + .60 in the white sample, for instance and of only + .05 in the black sample, differential validity would be in evidence.

Although the term differential validity is often used in a general way to apply to all types of unfairness, this is not in the strictest sense technically correct. In some cases research has yielded a statistically significant predictor-criterion relationship for a white sample, but not in a black sample, without there being a significant difference *between* the validity coefficients. In such instances the term single group validity provides a more precise description of the results. However, unless this particular case requires separate attention, it is generally considered less cumbersome to describe instances of unfairness generally as involving differential validity, and we will follow this practice here.

The problem of sample sizes. There is a widely voiced professional opinion that true differential validity does not exist; that where it appears to be present, the finding is in fact merely an artifact of faulty research design. Some have even gone so far as to suggest that the concept was devised by the governmental enforcement agencies in order to pressure companies into hiring more minority group members and women into jobs where they were previously rare. The logic of this argument is that in order to conduct the required differential study, a large number of minorities and/or women must now be hired merely to carry out the research.

Whatever one's position on the matter, however, it is apparent that given the current state of the art and the existing stance of the courts, it is highly desirable to be able to rule out any differential validity wherever it is technically feasible to do so. Certainly some seemingly well-designed studies have reported the phenomenon and it is impossible to prove that differential validity *might* not exist in a particular situation without testing for it.

On the other hand, it is increasingly apparent that many reported instances of differential validity were direct consequences of the research design. The problem is that many companies have relatively few minority group members or women in certain jobs in comparison to the number of white males. As a result, when the validation sample is split along racial or sex lines, one of the subsamples is much larger than the other. Because of the requirements of statistical significance tests, one can have roughly equal-sized validity coefficients in the two groups and still find the correlation in the large (white male) group of an acceptable level and the correlation in the other group insufficient to *show* validity. Thus, there is differential validity, or more correctly single group validity, at least in the minds of many enforcement personnel.

The only way out of this situation is to return to data collection, perhaps wait somewhat longer for more people to be hired, and add to the smaller sample to bring it up closer to the size of the group where validity has already been established. Although there is always the possibility that the validity coefficients will shrink as the sample size goes up, and thus remain non-significant, this is not usually the case. Typically it stays roughly the same and achieves significance in the larger sample.

Dealing with differential validity. The major antidote to differential validity thus is to obtain large and roughly equal-sized samples for all groups studied. But what if, once this is done, it becomes apparent that for some reason a predictor really is worthless with one group, while doing a good job in another? Certainly this is a theoretical possibility, and at least occasionally it is a practical reality as well.

If the measure is producing adverse impact, a finding of no validity in the affected group means that one should not use the measure with that group. One can use the predictor with the group for which it is valid and simply hire from applicants in the other group in a manner calculated to bring one's employment statistics into line. Better still, however, is a strategy which identifies some predictor which will work for minorities or women. Perhaps the original measure can be modified so as to eliminate those components contributing to the differential validity, or a new, valid measure can be developed for the group where validity was previously lacking. A number of studies of weighted application blank items have come up with different items and weights for use with males and females or blacks and whites. In any event, it is not necessary to eliminate a predictor entirely once evidence of differential validity has been obtained; all that is needed is to curtail its use in an appropriate manner.

Validation in the face of deficient samples

The discussion to this point has repeatedly extolled the advantages of large samples in validation research. But what about the small company that hires few people for any job, or those jobs in large companies that see very little movement and involve relatively few people? In these instances large samples simply are not possible within a reasonable time span.

One approach is to forego any meaningful selection effort in these cases and thus to hire almost anyone who comes along—random hiring. Such an approach would almost certainly avoid adverse impact and guarantee an adequate representation of minorities and women in all positions. Yet there is no reason to believe it would contribute in any effective way to a company's need for competent workers. Thus, in spite of the fact that the enforcement agencies often seem to advocate such a random approach, it appears desirable to look for alternatives. The job of the government agencies is to secure better jobs for those who may have been discriminated against in the past, not to ensure corporate profits. Companies on the other hand may have to set somewhat different priorities simply out of deference to economic necessities.

It is true that jobs populated by small numbers of people are less likely to feel the brunt of the enforcement agencies' efforts. Historically these agencies have tended to focus largely, but by no means universally, on large firms, and within these firms on the major entry-job categories. Yet this fact is no guarantee of protection; in any event a company should do all it can to hire the best people possible.

One approach, given small sample sizes, is to focus heavily on job analysis and on selection techniques which can be supported in terms of content and construct validity. For most purposes this means a strong reliance on some kind of testing procedure. Differential validity is not likely to be a problem in such cases. With content validity it is not relevant, and with construct validity data from other sources should be available to address the problem (either in terms of a lack of adverse impact or no demonstrable differential criterion relationship).

If a predictor that requires criterion-related validation is involved, there are certain approaches that may be used. The first consideration should be to expand the sample beyond one location to similar jobs in other company plants or offices. Such geographical dispersion is in fact desirable in any validity study. If this will not achieve the needed sample size, job analyses should be conducted on similar positions and comparable major components identified, as within a family of clerical positions. Predictors may then be established for these major across-the-job components. If necessary this approach may be extended to identical or similar jobs in more than one company. Validation studies of this kind, sponsored by trade associations and the like, are now being conducted. Their legal status is uncertain, and the very fact of the inclusion of data from many companies in the criterion measure militates against obtaining validity. Yet such efforts cannot help but be viewed as representing good faith, and if sufficient validity is demonstrated the courts may well support them. Finally, there is evidence as the guidelines go through one revision after another that the enforcement agencies are becoming more willing to accept validity data derived from other users or test publishers, provided an internal job analysis demonstrates the comparability of the jobs involved. At present, however, it would seem unwise to rely entirely on this defense, unless no other alternatives are available.

Ultimately, the best strategy might be to conduct a continuing longitudinal study in process. To do this, predictor and criterion data are obtained on all persons employed in a position, and one simply waits and waits, until sample sizes become adequate for a study. Analyses can be conducted at periodic intervals as data become available. It is even possible to start with a concurrent study on present employees, extending it subsequently over time and adding in new hires as they join the firm. The study is not defined as complete until one is satisfied the sample is large enough to establish validity should such validity be truly present. In the meantime, one is making a good-faith effort to validate to the extent sample sizes permit doing so. In samples of this nature differential validity is not really a problem if appropriate numbers of protected groups are included in the validation sample. Hiring is not of sufficient magnitude to develop one sample very quickly, let alone the multiple samples required to test for differential validity.

Taken as a whole, the implications of the business-necessity position stand out clearly—and this is true whether one is talking about business necessity as a legal defense or simply as a contribution to profitability. Employers should engage in continuing efforts to establish criterion-related, content, or construct validity on as many potential predictors or selection techniques as possible, and they should use the best, most appropriate designs available. The costs of such studies may be high, but they are not nearly as high as certain advocates of random hiring have stated. The benefits, on the other hand, of establishing a truly valid selection process which is both judgment-proof in a legal sense and a major contributor to profits in an economic sense can far outweigh the costs involved. It is a truism that a company is only as good as its people, and people invariably come in through the hiring process.

7

establishing criterion measures

A key factor in designing any criterion-related validation study is establishing the nature of the criterion measures themselves, or, if only one measure is used, the criterion itself. This is a complex issue. First there is the role of job analysis in identifying appropriate criteria. Then it is necessary to evaluate the alternative kinds of criteria with a view to both their practical usefulness and their legal status. Finally, there is a variety of special problems that may hamper the development of criterion measures. Many of these problems also are closely tied to the adequacy of a business-necessity defense.

The role of job analysis

The enforcement agencies, and the courts as well, have placed a strong emphasis on job analysis in the development of validation studies. Job analysis is important in the selection of predictors and becomes essential when a content or construct validation strategy is projected. However, the major emphasis on job analysis has been with regard to the criterion component of the research design, when a criterion-related study is undertaken, because it is through job analysis that one can determine whether a criterion measure is job-related and deals with a major facet of the job.

Actually, there is nothing in either the predictive or concurrent validation designs as such to prevent the choice of a criterion measure which has little if any relation to job behavior and the development of predictors which correlate highly with the non-job-related measure. One could even establish by definition that all white males are high on the criterion and all minorities or females are low, and then proceed to develop predictors that relate to this discrimination criterion. To prevent this type of situation, the courts have required that under most circumstances criterion choices be embedded in a comprehensive job analysis.

Conducting the job analysis. There is no one best way to conduct the job analysis, and certainly no particular approach has been endorsed by the courts. What is important is that a comprehensive effort to identify essential knowledge, skills, and behaviors can be demonstrated. The approach used should be systematic in nature, should call upon the experience of job experts, and should result in some weighting of job elements in terms of frequency of occurrence or importance. In general, it appears desirable to draw on the expertise of a number of knowledgeable individuals and then to pool this information into the final statement and weighting of job elements.

In some companies job analyses of this kind are conducted on a regular basis at periodic intervals. In other cases job descriptions once developed are rarely revised and have a tendency to become outdated. In this latter instance it would be well to re-analyze the jobs prior to conducting validity studies involving them. It is important to demonstrate what the job really is at the present time.

Job analysis information is most frequently developed from observation of performance and from interview or questionnaire reports involving those who perform the work and those who supervise it. In the past few years there has been an emergence of several standardized and quantified job-analysis instruments applicable to a wide range of positions which permit the profiling of jobs in terms of a preestablished set of factors. This approach has the advantage of permitting direct comparisons across jobs within a given company, between locations, and also between companies. The matter of transportability becomes important where validation studies have utilized pooled samples from several organizations or where a construct-validity argument is invoked because it is essential to be able to show that jobs have essentially the same elements.

Using job-analysis data in criterion development. The key to using job-analysis data effectively in criterion development is that measures of the level of performance on the major job elements can be established. This may not be a simple matter. Often what is easy to measure and what is important in the job are not the same. It is not essential that every aspect of the job be reflected in the criteria, but those that are should be of major importance as indicated by the job analysis.

Typically the basic instrument which results will deal with a number of facets of job performance, as when supervisory ratings are obtained on several different factors in job performance. At this point there are several criteria which often, but not invariably, are correlated with each other. A question arises as to whether these criteria should be combined into a composite measure or treated separately. A related question involves the use of a single global measure, such as an overall performance rating.

One of the problems with using multiple criteria directly is that if there also are multiple predictors the number of correlations computed can become sizable—10 predictors and 10 criteria would yield a matrix of 100 validity coefficients. As the number of these coefficients increases so does the probability that some of them will be quite large merely as a result of random fluctuations. This is the situation that frequently requires cross-validation. Thus, if cross-validation presents major problems as a design component, it is better to combine the criteria into a single measure. Several of the approaches described in the last chapter for combining predictors are equally applicable to this matter of combining criteria. If a weighting of the various criteria is desired in constructing the composite, weights may be derived directly from the job analysis using either frequency or importance assessments for the various job facets.

Such composite measures have the distinct advantage that they can be traced back directly through their various component measures to major job elements established through job analysis; showing job-relatedness is relatively easy. In contrast, a single overall performance rating typically lacks this potential for establishing job-relatedness; it could be measuring almost anything. If single overall measures are to be used, there should be a detailed statement of the factors to be considered in making the evaluation, and these factors should derive from the job analysis. An alternative is to show that the overall measure is essentially the same as a composite criterion compounded out of measures of a number of different, important job elements. Often overall ratings do turn out to be highly correlated with such a composite criterion.

Criteria not based on job analysis

There are a number of different criteria which do not require a job analysis to substantiate their use, although it may be necessary to develop other kinds of supporting data to establish that they are appropriate. In most cases direct measures of individual production output, error rates, scrap or waste, and the like do not require a detailed job analysis as long as it can be shown that these measures relate to behaviors that job incumbents engage in much of the time. The problem with such measures, however, is that they are often quite unstable, varying considerably from one time to another. Thus it is necessary to combine data for extended time periods if one is to obtain the kind of criterion index that will actually yield evidence of validity.

Another type of criterion measure that may well prove appropriate includes absenteeism, turnover, tardiness, and injury rates. In all but the latter case, it would generally be desirable to develop as much information as possible to show that the measure really does make a difference in the conduct of the business. Thus a company that made heavy investments in training for entry-level jobs and experienced high turnover shortly after the completion of training could use these facts to argue that turnover was costly and an important criterion measure to predict. A company requiring very low levels of job skill which resorted to frequent layoffs, however, might have considerable difficulty in substantiating a turnover criterion. So too would a company with a very low rate of turnover.

It is apparent that criteria differ considerably in the degree to which their job-relatedness is self-evident. When job-relatedness, or business necessity, is not readily apparent, then it must be demonstrated in some manner. In a great many cases, and particularly where rating criteria are used, job analysis is the preferred means of demonstrating relevance.

Rating criteria

Although the potential for some assertion of bias or discrimination exists when performance ratings are used as criterion measures, and the enforcement agencies are well aware of this fact, this does not mean that the use of ratings should be avoided; for some jobs they are the only kind of criteria that can be used meaningfully. On the other hand, it is well to recognize that ratings may have to be defended, and this likelihood increases sharply if it emerges that on the average minorities or women are rated lower than whites or males.

The role of job analysis in demonstrating job-relatedness has already been noted. It also is desirable to train managers in the use of rating systems. Training of this kind can be very effective in reducing various sources of error and bias. Generally, the more care and attention given to the development of the rating procedure and its implementation the better. This is true not only in gaining acceptance from the enforcement agencies and if necessary the courts, but also because the better the ratings the greater the likelihood of showing validity. A hastily constructed graphic scale where managers simply put a check mark at some point along a line and where the rating factors are highly generalized traits of personality is not likely to obtain the same respect as a carefully developed paired-comparison procedure where each person is compared individually with a number of others who work at the same job in terms of precisely defined job behaviors.

An approach which appears to have considerable promise in meeting EEO requirements, if not necessarily in overcoming the difficulties that tend to plague rating procedures, is variously called the behavioral-retranslation, or scaled-expectation, or behaviorally anchored rating technique. This procedure has a number of characteristics which make it particularly valuable as an example for developing guidelines for rating-criteria construction, even if one does not wish to use the procedure in its entirety.

Although their implementation and ordering may vary somewhat from situation to situation, the following steps are typical of the behavioral-retranslation approach:

1. Individuals with knowledge of the work to be rated identify and define a number of dimensions or aspects of the job.
2. The same individuals develop sets of statements illustrative of both effective and ineffective behaviors along each of these dimensions.
3. Another group of individuals equally knowledgeable about the work are given the dimensions with their definitions and the critical incidents of good and poor performance separately, and asked to assign each incident to the appropriate dimension. If the original incident-dimension fit is not maintained the incident is dropped from further consideration.
4. The second group of individuals places each remaining incident along a 7- or 9-point scale in terms of the degree of effectiveness/ineffectiveness of the behavior. If disagreement on scale position is pronounced, the incident is dropped from further consideration.
5. The final rating system contains a series of scales which may vary in number and content depending on the job considered, anchored by certain behavior-specific incidents placed along each scale according to the average scale value given in Step 4. The rater is to check the scale value which best describes the individual evaluated, considering what would be his or her expected behavior.

This approach involves a direct integration of the job analysis into rating-scale development. It also provides for the selection of scale descriptors according to whether knowledgeable people can agree on them and thus whether there is a consensus as to the definitions of good and poor performance. Any individual bias is neutralized in the totality. Finally, the emphasis is on specific behaviors in the job context, not on generalized statements; thus there is a strong job-relatedness.

This approach was originally developed with a view to establishing a set of independent, unrelated job dimensions. The idea was that the tendency to evaluate a person in a similar manner, favorably or unfavorably, on all or most of the dimensions of a rating form because of a general overall impression would be eliminated. Elimination of this so-called halo error was supposed to produce a sharp drop in the typically high intercorrelation between scale dimensions. On balance it cannot be said that this has occurred; yet the behavioral-retranslation approach does appear to contain many of the elements that the enforcement agencies are seeking.

The interchangeability of predictors and criteria

It is important to recognize that what is a predictor and what is a criterion depends much more on how a measure is used than on what type of measure is involved. This has been a matter of some confusion throughout the legal history of the business-necessity concept. Certain *types* of measures, if not identical measures, can serve in either the predictor or criterion role. This fact obviously needs some explanation.

Job samples and simulations. Because of the many possible sources of bias and error that can distort ratings of performance in the actual workplace, a variety of work simulations have been developed for evaluation purposes. Many of these are practically identical with the predictors discussed in the previous chapter as illustrative of content-valid measures, yet here the same type of measure is considered as a criterion.

Although some simulations are essentially knowledge tests indicating how much a person knows about the job, others go far beyond this, providing an opportunity to perform most of the tasks that would be performed in the work setting. The difference is that performance occurs in a standardized situation established so as to facilitate accurate measurement. The inbasket exercise, for instance, which has been widely used as a criterion, presents a manager with a wide range of decision-making tasks through the medium of letters, memos, telephone slips, and other such items that would be contained in a typical in-basket. Scoring of responses is carried out in a highly standardized manner.

Advocates of this kind of approach to criterion development argue that day-to-day performance does not provide a true measure because it is influenced by such factors as the nature of supervision, peer pressures to control productivity, individual motivation, and the like. In a simulated situation such factors can be held constant and measures of true proficiency can be obtained. Arguments of this kind are advanced by the personnel researchers who conducted the AT&T validation studies described in Part 4 of this book.

Fortunately, it is possible to recognize the merits of the simulation approach while still not accepting the negative view of on-the-job measures put forth by many advocates of simulation criteria. It does seem clear that even the most sophisticated simulation characteristically measures something which is not identical with on-the-job performance. For one thing, simulations tend to be measures of maximal, highly motivated performance, while on-the-job measures deal with typical performance, which may or may not be highly motivated. Yet both types of measures seem entirely appropriate, and both appear to be justifiable as criterion measures in validation research. What one uses in a study will depend upon such considerations as cost, availability, time, and expertise.

Training criteria. Many criterion measures administered during and at the completion of training are in fact work samples or simulations. Knowledge tests are widely used to measure progress in training, just as they are to measure learning in the educational context. Many such measures are equally applicable as predictors when selection decisions are to be made among experienced or already trained candidates. However, this fact in no way mitigates their value as criteria.

The use of training criteria for validation purposes can be fully justified as long as the training is needed and clearly job-related and the training performance measures are appropriate. Where successful completion of a training program is a necessary condition for job entry, training criteria are in fact the most relevant. A company has to select individuals who will complete the training or it will not have sufficient employees with the needed competence levels. Furthermore, the use of training criteria has the double advantage that in many cases a predictive study can be conducted over a relatively short time span and the criterion measures often are already available, having been developed to evaluate success in training. On the other hand, it is widely recognized that measures of mental ability are more likely to predict training success and measures of personality, character, and motivation are more likely to predict on-the-job success. Thus the use of a training criterion must be considered in the light of what type of predictor one wishes to validate.

There is little doubt that the use of training criteria can be a source of discrimination. If women score lower than men, or minorities lower than whites, it may well be necessary to show that the training criteria are job-related. This becomes difficult if, for instance, the training content deals with subject matter that has nothing to do with subsequent job performance and/or is much more complex than needed. As with other types of criteria, the answer to such problems with a training criterion lies in a comprehensive job analysis. One has to be able to demonstrate that both the training content and the training measures are in fact job-related.

Performance appraisals. In one sense training criteria are as much predictors as criteria. Under this interpretation they operate to select some people for subsequent job placement and screen out others, either from continued employment entirely or from employment in the positions for which training occurred. In such a situation any disparity between groups on a training-criterion measure becomes evidence of adverse impact and the use of job-analysis data to justify the training and its measures is in fact a demonstration of content-validity.

This dual role as criterion for initial selection procedures and predictor of subsequent success is equally evident in the use of performance ratings or any other appraisal procedure to select employees for upgrading or promotions in management. In actual fact the courts have on occasion interpreted performance appraisals in this light. In most cases an adequately developed criterion measure based on a comprehensive job analysis and administered under standardized conditions will qualify as a content-valid predictor as well. However, there are instances, as when assessment-center appraisals are to be used to select people for managerial positions, where a criterion-related study appears to be needed to establish a business-necessity defense.

The problem of criterion contamination

The design used in conducting criterion-related validation studies calls for independent measurements of the predictors and the criteria. If such independence of measurement is not maintained, a spurious predictor-criterion relationship may appear, which would not operate in the actual selection situation. The result of this criterion contamination may be an assumption of validity, and a selection technique may be used with a view to employing those candidates most likely to succeed when no validity is present at all and the selection technique contributes nothing.

Criterion contamination occurs when the predictor results actually influence the criterion measurement. Thus a mental ability test might be used to select people for hiring, with the test scores placed in a personnel file available to all members of management. If this file is routinely checked before making promotion decisions and if management generally believes that high intelligence is desirable in higher level positions, then the use of a promotion-rate criterion to validate the mental ability test will yield a good correlation even if intelligence is actually irrelevant to performance. Clearly the same kind of contamination could influence a performance-rating criterion. All that is needed is for a manager to be convinced that bright people are better than not-so-bright people.

Criterion contamination is most likely to be a problem in longitudinal studies, merely because there is more time and there are more subtle ways for predictor information to get to those who conduct the criterion measurement. It is not necessary that the specific criterion score itself become known. If that score serves to determine other events, such as selection for certain training programs, spurious validity coefficients can also result. In the case of concurrent validation, the likelihood of contamination is less because there is little time for it to occur. Yet even here there is the possibility that knowledge of predictor scores coupled with a capacity to influence criteria, and either a belief in the existence of a relationship or a desire to demonstrate validity, can operate to produce a spurious result.

The ideal solution to the criterion-contamination problem is to maintain independence of measurement. In fact, if there is any reason to believe independence has been compromised, the value of a study to a business-necessity argument may be seriously jeopardized. Predictor scores should be kept confidential during the conduct of the study and should not be used for any purpose other than the research if at all possible.

In addition, certain kinds of criteria appear to be more contamination-proof than others. Superior ratings are clearly quite vulnerable, while such things as a manager's profit performance or an individual's injury rate are not. Turnover, absenteeism, direct productivity, and the like can be influenced by a supervisor and to that extent might be contaminated by predictor knowledge, but the probabilities are less than with ratings. Under most circumstances simulations are relatively contamination-resistant, unless a judgmental element is present in the scoring.

Unreliability in the criterion

In addition to contamination, there is another problem that continually plagues criterion measurement, which tends, however, to reduce the size of the validity coefficients, rather than inflate them. This is the problem of criterion unreliability.

Reliability means that if one makes the same measurement twice, the same result will be obtained both times. To the extent this is not true, the measure is said to be unreliable. Thus, if one uses a ruler made of wood or metal to measure a distance twice, it is probable that almost identical results will be obtained. But if one tries to do the same thing with a thin rubber ruler, the results will depend on the tension induced, and the two measures may not yield the same results at all. Unfortunately, criterion measurement often seems to be like the situation with the rubber ruler: consistency or stability of measurement may be quite low, making it very difficult to achieve successful prediction. Prediction with an unreliable criterion is like trying to hit a target that is in constant, erratic motion; with a reliable criterion the target becomes motionless and thus much easier to hit.

Test-retest measures. A variety of procedures have been developed to measure criterion reliability, although the typical outcome, a correlation coefficient, is the same in all cases. The various procedures do tend to yield somewhat different values for this reliability coefficient, but the results tend to be sufficiently close so that the procedures may be considered interchangeable for practical purposes. Thus the approach used in measuring criterion reliability is largely a matter of convenience.

The test-retest approach requires a second criterion measurement at some time subsequent to the first and then correlation of the scores obtained in the two time periods. Thus a manager might rate subordinates on two different occasions or individual production data might be collected over two different time periods. A major question relates to the interval between measurements. It is essential that the two measures be independent of one another in the sense that one does not directly determine the other. Thus the interval should be sufficient so that memory effects are unlikely to determine the results. This is a problem in the use of rating measures; it is not a problem with such measures as production and absenteeism statistics. On the other hand, too long an interval increasingly confounds true and valid change in people with unreliability of measurement; this makes the reliability seem less than it is. The answer to the interval question, then, is that the measures should be taken as close together as possible, without compromising independence.

The parallel-form approach. One way of avoiding the independence problem is to use two different measures of the same criterion. Thus two simulations or work samples of a job might be developed containing different items, but with both truly reflecting the work. Because the measures are actually different, memory effects cannot operate, and the two forms may be used with a relatively short time interval between them.

The problem, of course, with the parallel-form approach is that two criterion measures must be developed and shown to yield the same results before one can go on and do a reliability study. Precise statistical definitions establishing the requirements for a parallel form have been advanced. However, for working purposes, parallel forms are said to exist where 1) the number of items of each type is the same, so that the measures concentrate equally on the same aspects of performance; 2) the average scores tend to be essentially the same; and 3) the distributions of actual scores through the range of possible scores are roughly comparable. Whether these conditions can be met, and in fact whether a parallel criterion measure can be developed at all, depends largely on the nature of the criterion involved.

Split-half reliability. A widely used approximation to the parallel-form approach involves splitting up an existing measure into two equal parts and then correlating the scores on these parts to obtain an estimate of reliability. It is common to use the odd-numbered items as one measure and the even-numbered ones as another. An example would be where individual production data are calculated on a daily basis. The first day's data would go in one measure, the second day's in the other, the third day's back with those for the first day, and so on. At the end of six weeks one could compute the average or total production for each person in the sample using both measures separately. The correlation between these two measures is a reliability coefficient.

However, where split-half reliability is used, one additional step remains. It is a statistical fact that a measure becomes more reliable as one includes more individual measurements. A rating form can be made more reliable, for instance, by increasing the number of rating variables used in calculating a composite score from, say, 10 to 20. But when one uses the split-half method the number of measurements included in the reliability coefficient is actually cut in half. Thus, with the production data just mentioned, the reliability estimate is really based on three weeks of data, not six. If one intends using a six-week measure as a criterion in a validity study, it is the reliability of that measure that is desired; the three-week coefficient that has been calculated needs to be corrected to make it equal to what would have been obtained over six weeks. Such a correction may be made statistically by applying the Spearman-Brown prophecy formula to the reliability coefficient calculated from the two halves.[1] The resulting value is the best estimate of actual criterion reliability.

Interrater reliability. An approach to reliability measurement frequently used with rating procedures is to obtain independent ratings of each individual from two, or perhaps even more, sources. These ratings are then correlated across a sample of employees to obtain a reliability coefficient. For this approach to be used, of course, there need to be at least two individuals who have comprehensive, first-hand knowledge of those aspects of the employee's performance to be rated. In the case of interrater reliability the two measures used do not utilize different instruments as such, or measures taken at different points in time. The rating forms are identical

[1]See R.M. Guion, *Personnel Testing* (New York: McGraw-Hill, 1965), for a description of this formula.

and the timing can be identical also. However, the measuring instrument is varied in the sense that two different people complete it based on what may well be somewhat different samples of the employee's job behavior.

When two or more independent ratings of this kind are to be averaged or totaled to obtain the actual criterion values used in a validity study—and this should be done if at all possible to increase criterion reliability—a situation much like that existing with the split-half coefficient is created. The number of measures (people making ratings) is reduced in calculating the initial reliability coefficient. Although often neglected in practice, it is usually appropriate and in fact desirable to apply the Spearman-Brown prophecy formula to correct for the proportionate reduction in number of independent raters involved in calculating the interrater coefficient over the number of raters to be used in the actual criterion measurement.

Reliability and validity. Early in the preceding chapter it was noted that two factors may contribute to a failure to demonstrate validity when validity is in fact present. One factor is a restriction of range in the predictors, usually caused by the fact that the predictors are used to select the validation sample and thus scores below a given cutting point are few or nonexistent. This factor is best corrected by letting a full range of candidates go on to employment. If necessary there is a statistical correction for restriction of range that can be employed. This formula serves to adjust the validity coefficient to what it would be if the spread of scores on the predictor in the validation sample were as large as the spread in the candidate group.

The second factor noted as limiting validity is the size of the validation sample. If the sample is small even rather sizable coefficients may not reach acceptable levels of statistical significance. Furthermore, there is some tendency to look askance at the practice of using a correction for restriction of range to raise a validity coefficient over the line into statistical significance. Raising an already acceptable coefficient is fine, but raising one that is appreciably too low is certain to raise the hackles of the enforcement agencies. Thus, the best solution to problems created by too small a sample is to increase the sample size.

Additional factors contributing to a failure to show validity are associated with the criterion. One is a restriction of range in the criterion caused by predictor restriction. If validity really is present and predictor-score distributions are truncated by the use of the predictor in selection, then the criterion-score distribution will be restricted too. Normally this problem cannot be handled through a statistical correction for restriction of range in the criterion, because data on what the spread of scores on the criterion should be is lacking. The best answer is to have the full range of predictor scores in the validation sample, and then the full range of criterion scores should be present also.

However, the major criterion-related factor limiting a demonstration of validity is unreliability in the criterion. Unreliability in a predictor can of course be a problem, but any unreliability there will also extend into the subsequent selection process itself and thus predictor unreliability should rightfully be included in the validity coefficient. But unreliability in a criterion represents a defect of the measurement process, not of the practical result. When validity is established with a rather unreliable criterion and then the predictors are used, one actually gets a better result than one bargained for. The problem is that the unreliable criterion measure may not yield a validity coefficient large enough to be acceptable.

8

statistical techniques in validation research

The objective of this chapter is to familiarize the reader with the various statistical methods used in validation studies. The primary role played by these methods is in analyzing the predictor-criterion relationship, and the major emphasis here is on procedures that may be used for this purpose. Accordingly, our treatment of statistical techniques is a circumscribed and focused one; we do not attempt to cover the full range of statistical approaches. In particular, attention is focused on those procedures actually used in the studies described in Parts 4 and 5. Upon completion of this chapter the reader should be in a better position to interpret the validation research reports which follow.

The treatment of statistics in this volume is intended to provide an understanding of the various techniques and a guide to when and how they should be used. Computational procedures and formulas are not included, on the assumption that the reader can easily gain access to this information once it is apparent what technique should be applied. In most companies computer center personnel can either provide standard programs for calculating the various measures or do the necessary programming themselves. Additional assistance and information related to actual calculations may be obtained from mathematical or statistical experts, if they are available, or from statistics textbooks. Of the latter, those emphasizing psychological and educational applications are most likely to prove helpful.

Means and medians

The final output of data collection in the conduct of a validity study is a set or distribution of predictor scores and of criterion scores.

Such a distribution can be developed for each measure or variable employed in the study. The distributions may take a variety of forms, and, as we shall see, the nature of predictor and criterion score distributions is a major determinant of the particular statistical techniques that should be used in the analysis. However, the most common distribution, where the scores spread out over a range of values, is one where there is a sizable concentration of scores near the middle with gradually declining frequencies on both sides of the distribution to the point where at the extremes there may be only one person with a given score value. A study of the scores obtained by 84 college graduates on a short 20-item vocabulary test yielded the following distribution, which is characteristic:

Test Score	Number of College Graduates
0-6	None
7	1
8	None
9	3
10	5
11	3
12	4
13	7
14	13
15	12
16	13
17	10
18	9
19	1
20	3

In instances such as the above, one typically needs some kind of overall summary statistic to provide a general index of how well the subjects do. Usually this summary statistic is an average, or measure of central tendency. The most common procedure is to calculate a mean ($\overline{X}$) by totalling all the scores and dividing by the number of subjects (N). In the study of college graduates, the total of all scores is 1237; divided by 84 (the N for this study), the mean is 15.4.

Although the mean is the preferred measure, there are instances where it can be misleading. Say, for instance, that in the study of vocabulary test scores of college graduates a frequency of 3, not 0, had been observed for a score of 4. This would pull the mean score down sharply, providing a somewhat distorted picture. In such cases it may be better to use the middle score, or median, to summarize the data. The median is that point on the scale of scores where the frequency above or below is 50 percent of the total frequency. The mean and median are, of course, identical when the shape of the frequency distribution is perfectly symmetrical, but the median moves more slowly in either direction when scores begin to accumulate which are either extremely high or extremely low.

In any event, it is common practice to compute either the mean or the median for all predictor and criterion distributions obtained from a validity study. It is by comparing such indexes for male and female applicants, for instance, that the adverse impact of a predictor may be evaluated.

The standard deviation

The second measure used to describe distributions, in addition to a measure of central tendency, is a measure of the spread or variability of scores. One could use the range from the lowest to the highest score for this purpose, but in carrying out statistical analyses this is rarely done. The range is a very unstable measure in that it may change from one group of subjects to another with practically no change in the overall distribution. Thus among the 84 college graduates the range is 14 test score points, but in another separate sample of college graduates there is a good chance that the one low score of 7 would merge into the rest of the distribution, thus reducing the range by a full two points.

The most commonly used measure of the spread of scores is the standard deviation (SD or σ). A large SD means that the scores are widely spread around the mean or median; a small SD that they are closely clustered. Using a predictor to select among candidates results in a restriction of range in the employed group and thus a smaller SD for the predictor scores of that group. An often-used derivative of the SD is the variance (v or σ^2) which is the SD value multiplied by itself (thus squared).

In the case of the normal, bell-shaped score distribution which is approximated so frequently in validation research, 34 percent of all scores will fall between the mean and the score which is one standard deviation above it. Since this type of distribution is symmetrical, the same holds for the score range between one SD below the mean and the mean. Thus, 68 percent of the scores are + or − one SD from the mean. If one goes out another SD proportionately fewer additional scores are picked up even though the score range is doubled, because the frequencies decline as one moves to the extremes. Thus roughly 95 percent of the scores are between − and + two SDs, and well over 99 percent are between − and + three SDs.

It is not uncommon to express predictor or criterion scores in standard deviation terms. The result is a conversion of so-called raw scores to standard scores. One such standard score is the *z*-score which sets the mean equal to 0 and the standard deviation equal to 1. Using this approach almost all scores will fall between the standard scores of −3 and +3. Another similar concept is the *T*-score which sets the mean equal to 50 and the SD equal to 10; here the effective range is 20 to 80. Or one can establish the mean at 500 and the SD at 100, as is done with the familiar college entrance examination scores. Standard scores of this kind are often used in combining predictor or criterion scores. Thus the scores on two or more predictors might be converted to some kind of standard score using the means and standard deviations for each measure's distribution; then these standard scores would be added to get a total score. This procedure serves to weight each predictor equally in the composite.

Standard scores provide a stable frame of reference for interpreting predictor and criterion data which is lacking when raw scores only are used. Another method of achieving the same result is to set scores equal to percentiles. Thus one starts at 0 and attaches percentages to scores by determining what proportion of the sample has scores equal to or below each successively higher score value. Thus the median becomes the 50th percentile; very high scores are at the 90th percentile and above.

On occasion a 9-point stanine scale is used for this same purpose. The first stanine contains the lowest 4 percent of all subjects in the score distribution. Each successive stanine encompasses successively higher score intervals, taking in the next 7, 12, 17, 20, 17, 12,

7, and finally at the ninth stanine 4 percent of the normative or standardization sample.

Statistical significance

The enforcement agencies have characteristically specified the .05 level ($P < .05$) as the maximum acceptable for demonstrating validity. Below the .05 level the relationship is said to be statistically significant or reliable; above that level it is not. What does this mean?

The concept of significance level relates primarily to generalization. To what extent can one be certain that a relationship (such as that between predictor and criterion) found to exist in one sample of employees will also appear in other samples? This is an important consideration in validation research, because the value of the research depends on generalization of the results to new samples of candidates for the positions studied.

This potentiality for accurate generalization of a result is typically expressed in terms of the probability (P) that a relationship in the same direction as that found in the experimental sample will appear in successive samples drawn from the same population. Thus, a positive validity coefficient significant at the .05 level means that the chances of obtaining a sample r value that high or higher when the r in the whole population is in fact .00 are less than 5 in 100. Clearly a 19 out of 20 bet is a reasonably good one. On the other hand, if one is studying a large number of independent predictor-criterion relationships, chance alone will yield one "significant" relationship for every 20 studied. This is why cross-validation is so important in such multimeasure studies. It also points up the value of establishing even lower P values if possible, at the .01 level for instance, where reversals can be expected only one time in a hundred.

Establishing significance levels. The significance of the various statistical measures may be calculated directly using the appropriate formulas. Many of the standard statistical computer programs do this automatically and provide a P value for each statistic. However, P values for most commonly used measures also may be obtained from tables presented in most statistics texts.

One enters such tables with a number known as the degrees of freedom (df), which represents the number of values which are free to vary once other scores are fixed (usually N-1). The specific df figure depends on the analytic approach used. In any event the table then provides a value of the statistic above which significance may be assumed. Usually at least the .05 and the .01 levels are thus specified. If the value obtained in a study is above that tabled for the .05 level, the statistic is significant at $P < .05$; if it is in addition large enough to exceed the tabled value for the .01 level, it is significant at $P < .01$. Should the statistic's value be less than that required for the .05 level, it is generally considered not significant (n.s.).

One-tailed and two-tailed tests. Although the .05 level as specified by the enforcement agencies, and as generally accepted in professional practice, might appear to provide a solid basis for decision-making, this is not entirely true. There is one additional complication. If one is absolutely sure about the direction, positive or negative, of any predictor-criterion relationship found, then there is little problem. Thus, if a mental ability test were being validated, an a priori decision might be made that only a positive relationship would be acceptable and result in actually using the test for selection purposes. In this case a statistically significant negative relationship has the same meaning as any nonsignificant negative relationship. The company simply is not interested in hiring people of low ability, even if on the particular job studied such individuals tend to do better than those with higher ability. In this case the lower 95 percent of the distribution of values of the statistic will yield an n.s. judgment (all values below 0, and the 45 percent next above 0). The 5 percent used to define the .05 level is all on the positive end.

However, in many cases either a positive or a negative value would result in a decision to use the measure in selection, provided significance is obtained. Personality tests and biographical data, for instance, are often studied with such an intention in mind. In such a case a significant negative relationship is not the same as nonsignificance, but is in fact comparable to a significant positive one. Yet if one applies the same definition of significance as used in the preceding one-tailed example at both the positive and the negative ends of the distribution the result is that only a .10 significance level is being required (5 percent at each tail or extreme of the distribution). To obtain a true .05 significance, it is necessary to require larger values of the statistic, equal to the .025 level, when a two-tailed test is involved. This is because negative as well as positive values are to be accepted. The two-tailed test is clearly more conservative than the one-tailed, insofar as accepting the fact of a significant relationship is concerned. For this reason the enforcement agencies tend to favor it, and one must be prepared to justify a one-tailed significance test, if a decision is made to use one.

Chi square tests

The simplest of the statistics that may be used in the manner just described to determine the significance of a predictor-criterion relationship is chi-square (χ^2). The χ^2 test uses frequency data. An example of its use would be a situation where employee interviewers placed all hired candidates in one of two categories—recommended hire and recommended rejection—and where subsequent job performance was evaluated by supervisors as either satisfactory or not. The resulting fourfold table used to calculate χ^2 for 100 employees might look as follows:

	Job Performance	
Hiring Recommendation	Not Satisfactory	Satisfactory
Recommended Hire	10 (25)	40 (25)
Recommended Reject	40 (25)	10 (25)

In this instance it would appear to make considerable sense to follow the interviewer recommendations. The application of χ^2 is an appropriate way to confirm this impression statistically and to determine whether the distribution of frequencies is in fact significantly different from what would be expected by chance alone—indicated in parentheses above. If the frequencies expected by chance alone (those in parentheses in the example) get very low, certainly below 5 and conservatively below 10, many statisticians believe χ^2 is not an appropriate statistic. For this reason it is often desirable to combine categories to achieve higher frequencies. One can even take variables with a sizable range of scores and split the distributions at the medians to create a fourfold table for computing χ^2. This is a particularly appropriate procedure when the distributions depart sharply from the normal, bellshaped curve. On the other hand, it should be recognized that χ^2 yields only a P value indicating the degree of significance, not an estimate of the extent of the relationship, as in correlation.

The *t*-test and analysis of variance

Where it is feasible to compute means and where the data distributions approximate the normal form, with the larger frequencies in the middle and symmetrically smaller frequencies at the extremes, the statistics discussed in this section are most appropriate. The *t*-test is used to compare mean scores in two groups to see if the difference between the means is large enough to warrant a conclusion that the groups differ in a statistically significant manner.

This type of analysis might be used, for instance, to evaluate adverse impact of a selection instrument as between males and females or between whites and minorities; a statistically significant *t*-value would be indicative of a real differential. The *t*-test may also be used to compare the mean scores on predictors of those who do and do not complete training, or of those who do and do not perform satisfactorily, or of those who separate within a given period of time and those who remain employed. Like χ^2, such *t*-tests yield information on significance levels only, not on the extent of the relationship involved.

Although the *t*-test is the usual approach used in comparing two groups where the score distributions are continuous and normally shaped, there are some approaches which focus directly on the degree of overlap between the two distributions, such as Tilton's 0 statistic. In this case the extremes are: complete overlap where the two distributions are perfectly superimposed (n.s.) and complete separation such that all scores in one distribution are below the lowest score in the other (highly significant).

When the number of groups to be compared increases above two and/or multiple continuous measures are involved, it is common to employ the analysis-of-variance technique (ANOVA) to determine whether overall significance is present. Analysis of variance yields an F statistic which may be evaluated for significance using the appropriate table and df values. Although an extremely powerful statistical tool, ANOVA is not widely used in validation research, primarily because the nature of research designs is such as to make correlational statistics more suitable.

Correlation techniques

The essential nature of correlation was considered in Chapter 6. Here we will take up the various measures of correlation that may be used. In contrast to the techniques considered previously, these statistics provide an index of the degree of relationship present. This measure of degree may then be tested, using available tables for the statistic in many cases, to determine whether it is large enough to warrant the position that it is significantly different from 0. Thus correlation procedures can provide a measure both of the size of predictor-criterion relationships and their significance. It is also possible to determine through appropriate analyses whether one correlation coefficient is significantly different from another, not just different from 0 (this requires transforming the two correlation values to z-values using a conversion table). All of these considerations argue strongly for using correlational techniques in validation research wherever possible; it is the usual practice to do so.

Rank-order correlation. One of the simplest measures of correlation uses ranked data on both measures. It yields a coefficient known as rho (ρ). Since rankings are often used in developing criterion measures, as when a supervisor ranks his subordinates, the rank-order approach has had considerable application in validation research. If one variable, say the criterion, is of a rank-order nature the other must be converted to the rank form if it is not already so organized. When ties exist the ranks are split between the individuals who are in tie positions. For example, if the second and third highest ranking individuals have the same score, both are ranked as 2.5.

The rank-order approach becomes quite cumbersome when large samples are used. In addition it tends to yield slightly lower values than the more conventional product-moment correlation coefficient. In general the use of ρ should be restricted to those cases where the data for one or both measures are available only in the rank form.

Product-moment correlation. The product-moment or Pearson correlation coefficient (r) is the most widely used validity index.

It is appropriate when actual scores on predictor and criterion are available and are spread over a number of values. When *r* has been calculated it provides an index of the direct linear relationship between two variables. Thus the larger the value of *r* the more accurately one can predict criterion values from a knowledge of predictor scores.

Prediction of this kind is achieved through the use of regression equations which define the best fit or regression lines between the two variables being correlated. Actually there are two such equations which may be generated from any correlation relationship. One equation is for predicting criterion values from a knowledge of predictor scores—this is of most interest in validation research; the other equation yields best estimates of predictor values given a knowledge of criterion values. The accuracy with which such regression equations will predict in a particular situation may be stated in terms of a statistic known as the standard error of estimate. The smaller the value of this statistic the more accurate the prediction possible.

One occasionally sees the value of *r* interpreted directly in percentage terms. Thus an *r* of .40 is interpreted to mean that a predictor can account for or explain 40 percent of the variance of variability in a criterion. This interpretation is incorrect. The appropriate statistic for determining how much of the variance in a criterion may be predicted from a knowledge of predictor values is the correlation coefficient squared (r^2). Thus an *r* of .40 actually permits an explanation of only 16 percent of the criterion variance, not 40 percent. For a number of reasons, however, this percentage of variance accounted for is not a good indication of the overall value of a predictor.

Biserial correlation. Product-moment correlation requires a spread of scores over multiple values of both predictor and criterion. However, there are instances where this spread does not exist. The most common instances involve predictors and/or criteria which are dichotomous, thus falling in only two categories. A number of correlation techniques are available to handle these situations. Each is appropriate to a somewhat different combination of score distributions, and it is important to understand when each type of correlation is appropriate.

Biserial correlation (r_{bis}) is used in the situation where one variable is continuous, in the same manner as when the product-moment coefficient is calculated, and the other, although potentially continuous also, has been dichotomized for convenience or some other reason. A common application is where there is a range of scores on a predictor, but the criterion has been developed so as to yield only two categories, such as "effective" and "less effective," in some aspect of performance. Clearly such a criterion could be made continuous by specifying degrees of effectiveness; often, however, it is difficult to get supervisors to do this and a dichotomous measure is used instead.

Where there is reason to believe that a graduated scale underlies the dichotomy, r_{bis} is the appropriate statistic. Such is the case in much validation research. However, on occasion one is faced with a dichotomy where the two categories are truly discrete and assigning a 0 to one and a 1 to the other is an entirely arbitrary process. This would be true of the male-female dichotomy, for instance. Usually in such cases one would compute means on the continuous variable for the male and the female groups and then test for significance using the *t*-test. However, if a measure of degree of relationship is desired the appropriate statistic is the point biserial coefficient (r_{pbis}). Biserial r and point biserial r are calculated in much the same manner. However, r_{bis} more nearly approximates the product-moment coefficient in its interpretation and thus should be used if possible.

Tetrachoric correlation and the phi coefficient. In some cases both variables are artificially dichotomized in the same manner as one is when r_{bis} is used. This would be the case, for instance, if one wished to correlate the above- and below-average ratings given by an interviewer with subsequent effective/ineffective ratings by a supervisor. Here the appropriate measure is tetrachoric correlation (r_{tet}). Like performance effectiveness, the hiring recommendation can be differentiated into degrees of suitability and would be expected to yield a distribution approximating the normal shape.

Because r_{tet} is easily calculated from available tables and graphs, there is a temptation to apply it in cases where the data permit the use of the product-moment r. All that is needed is to split both variables at the median, thus forming artificial dichotomies. This procedure is not recommended except in obtaining a preliminary picture of results. The product-moment r is a much more accurate statistic when it can be calculated appropriately, simply because it utilizes the full range of data.

An alternative to r_{tet} in some cases is the phi coefficient (ϕ). When both variables are true dichotomies this is the appropriate measure; however this is not a frequent situation in validation research. Another situation where ϕ is appropriate is the case where there are very few instances of one category of a dichotomy. In cases such as this where there is a sizable imbalance between the categories of a dichotomy, neither the biserial nor tetrachoric coefficients are very accurate. Thus in one study ϕ was used to validate a telephone reference-checking procedure when it was found that over 98 percent of the applicants checked received favorable recommendations and less than 2 percent negative ones. Even with such an extreme imbalance, validity was established against a dichotomous termination criterion using the phi statistic in a very large sample. One disadvantage of using ϕ in such cases, however, is that the maximum values possible are not $+1.00$ and -1.00, but much smaller figures. Thus ϕ cannot be interpreted within the same frame of reference as r.

Correlation ratio. In most validation situations the primary concern is with linear relationships; as scores on the predictor get proportionately higher so do scores on the criterion. That is what the correlation measures discussed to this point measure. However, should the relationship be other than linear, these techniques will underestimate its size. Major departures from linearity are not common in validation research, but they do occur. It is well to be aware of this potential and of methods for dealing with such departures when they occur.

An example of a nonlinear, curvilinear relationship would be where employees who scored low on a personality-test measure of conformity were rated low on job performance, those in the midrange of conformity were rated high, and those with high levels (excessive conformity) were again rated low—where both nonconformists and conformists do less well. In such situations the correlation ratio, eta (η), more correctly reflects the size of the relationship, and r may severely underestimate it. Thus a truly significant relationship may not be identified as such.

The best way to determine whether a deviation from linearity may be present is to inspect a scatter-plot of the correlation data. If the data appear curvilinear this impression may be tested statistically to determine whether the deviation from linearity is significant. When it is, η is the preferred statistic. However, if a significant η is obtained, it is important to use the predictor in the manner the findings would indicate, not in a linear fashion. Thus, individuals scoring both low and high on the measure of conformity should be rejected, not just low scorers. It is generally recommended that when η is used this way, the relationship be established by cross-validation or with quite large samples.

Multiple correlation. The correlation techniques considered up to this point deal with one predictor and one criterion. However, as noted in Chapter 6, there are procedures for dealing with multiple measures in a single analysis. The use of these techniques has escalated considerably with the advent of computers and computer programs to facilitate calculations. The most common situation is one where there are a number of predictors to be related to a single composite criterion. Such a situation calls for multiple correlation (R) or multiple regression, and this is the technique that we will consider here. However, it should be recognized that the multiple-correlation approach can be extended to cases where a number of predictors *and* criteria are present through the use of canonical correlation.

R has the same basic characteristics and requires the same distribution types as r. It is interpreted in the same manner, except that it is always positive. R is an index of the maximum correlation between a set of predictors and the criterion, and it permits the development of a regression equation which combines the various predictors in a manner which maximizes the prediction of criterion values from a knowledge of the various predictor values. This regression equation weights the various predictors in terms of their relationship to the criterion. These weights, which maximize the overall criterion relationship, are known as beta (β) weights.

The ideal situation in multiple-correlation studies is to have a number of predictors which are significantly and sizably correlated with the criterion and which in addition are uncorrelated with each other. In this case each predictor contributes considerable unique criterion variance to the overall statistic, and multiple R goes up rapidly as new measures are added. Many computer programs provide for stepwise calculations so that the extent of the contribution made by each predictor may be determined; the best predictor is used first and the R is calculated at each step as predictors of decreasing value are added. In this process a predictor which is highly correlated with another and which relates to the criterion in roughly the same manner contributes very little to the R value, because the two predictors account for almost identical variance. To obtain a sizable R the validation research should be designed to include a wide range of quite dissimilar predictors.

A question arises in multiple correlation as to how many predictors should be combined. There are procedures, such as the Wherry-Doolittle test-selection technique, for answering this question. Basically the stepwise approach is used, along with a formula for calculating the shrinkage in R that might be expected if the multiple correlation were computed in a completely new sample. There comes a point at which the addition of another predictor yields a shrunken R value which is actually less than the value without that predictor; the increase in error contributed by the additional measure is greater than the increase in validity. At this point the predictor set is stabilized and only those predictors already identified are actually applied in selection and entered into a regression equation.

In general it is desirable to keep the number of predictors involved in computing R as low as possible. With a small number of subjects and a large number of predictors, one can almost always obtain an R value significant at the .05 level, but it may not hold up in a cross-validation sample because the underlying single predictor-criterion relationships themselves represent only chance fluctuations. For this reason good multiple-correlation research requires quite large samples; usually five or six predictors are all that are needed and little gain in validity is achieved with more.

Expectancy tables. The various statistics considered represent procedures for summarizing predictor-criterion relationships and determining their significance. As such these statistics should be calculated and utilized in presenting findings to enforcement agencies and the courts. On the other hand it often is also useful to present findings in some manner which is more meaningful to the statistically uninitiated. One procedure for doing this is the expectancy table or chart.

Such a table may be constructed as follows:

1. Where the criterion is not already a dichotomy, make one by identifying superior (effective, above average, successful) performers as appropriate.
2. Set up a frequency distribution with three columns: superior, other, and total frequency.
3. Divide the predictor distribution into roughly equal fifths in terms of number of subjects, not scores.
4. Count the total number of cases and the number of superior cases in each of the five predictor-score categories; then determine the percentage in each category that are superior.

The resulting expectancy table might look as follows:

Predictor Score Range	Chances in 100 of Being Superior
18-20	86
16-17	75
14-15	58
12-13	22
0-11	20

Such a table may easily be converted into a bar chart if a graphic presentation is desired. The expectancy approach is a useful method of showing what a correlation may mean in practice.

Factor analysis

Although there are a number of different mathematical procedures that may be used in carrying out a factor analysis, the objective in all cases is to isolate and identify dimensions inherent in a correlation matrix, thus simplifying the matrix to make the information easier to use. Such a matrix is obtained when *r* values are calculated relating a number of measures each to the other. Thus, 20 different predictors might be employed in a validation study and one might desire to reduce these 20 down to a few key dimensions before calculating criterion relationships. Factor analysis is a method of doing this, and the starting point is a matrix showing the correlation between each of the 20 predictors and each of the 19 others. The mathematical techniques extract a reduced set of factors, the number depending on the composition of the matrix and the technique, and indicate the relationship of each predictor with each factor extracted.

The usual practice is to describe each factor in verbal terms by abstracting out subjectively whatever the predictors with high loadings (relationships) appear to have in common. In addition factor scores may be computed indicating an individual's relative position on each factor. The value of such an approach is that an original 20 predictor scores might be distilled down to from three to five factor scores. Some predictors are usually discarded. The remaining measures would be used in the validity study and thus correlated with criteria, but only as they contribute to the composite factor scores.

Statistical definitions of test bias

In discussing the concept of differential validity in Chapter 6, emphasis was placed on the correlation coefficients obtained in different groups, on differences between these coefficients, and on their deviations from zero. However, the size of the correlation coefficients is not sufficient to account for all that has occurred in the area. Efforts are increasingly being made to establish definitions of discrimination, or the unfairness of predictors, in terms of the slopes and positions of regression lines, or lines of best fit between predictors and criteria, in various groups (black and white, male and female). These efforts take a variety of forms, but except in the more extreme cases they accept the idea that when the regression lines closely approximate each other there is no problem as long as both correlations are significant. The problems arise when the regression lines, for blacks and whites for instance, are not the same and when they cross each other at some point.

What this means is that predictor bias could be defined not only in terms of the magnitude of validity coefficients but also in terms of the functions of regression equations. This is a complex issue and to date it has been argued primarily in the professional psychological literature rather than in the courts. Within this professional literature there is no consensus. It is becoming increasingly evident that verbal disagreements as to what constitutes discrimination can easily be converted into mathematical terms, but that doing so provides no more of a resolution than existed at the verbal level.

Nevertheless, this matter of statistical definitions of test bias is beginning to find its way into the courts. The following excerpt from a lower court decision provides an example of what is involved:

> Failure, however, to reject the hypothesis that the correlation coefficients are the same for both groups is not by itself sufficient to demonstrate fairness. Where, as in the present case, test scores by two groups are used in the same manner for members of both groups, it is on the assumption that in general an individual's test score will appropriately predict his standing on the criterion whether he is a member of one group or the other. The predictive relationship between the test score and the criterion can be represented by a regression line formula for converting a test score into a predicted criterion score. While regression lines can be calculated separately for the two groups and will almost always be somewhat different, it is important to know whether the slopes or intercepts (or both) of the lines are sufficiently different to call for abandonment of a common line for the two groups. Otherwise the common regression line (which is the effect of using test scores in the same way for both groups) may systematically underpredict for members of one group (while overpredicting for the other) their criterion score from a particular test score.
>
> . . .
>
> Significantly different regression lines may have the same or similar correlation coefficients. In such a situation comparison of the coefficients will not reveal the inappropriateness of using a common regression line. Thus with the sample containing 76 white and 28 black police officers, comparison of the coefficients respecting [test] scores and either academy grades or efficiency ratings does not, as to any comparison, lead to rejection of the hypothesis of the coefficients being the same. Yet when the same data are reviewed by analysis of covariance, as the court has done, for the hypothesis that a common regression line fits both whites and blacks, the obtained F ratios are . . . significant at $p < .05$.
>
> . . .
>
> In view of the fact that covariance analysis suggests rejection of a common regression line for both racial groups, one is tempted—since

> the differences between white and black means appear to be far greater on test scores than on the criterion measures—to conclude that the performance of blacks is being underpredicted. . . . However, if the regression lines are computed separately for blacks and whites using the results of any of the studies where their test scores and criterion scores are reported separately, it will be found that the lines cross and that for test scores below that crossing point the criterion scores thereby predicted for blacks are less than for whites for the same test scores. Above that point there should be underprediction for blacks, but the intersections occur at such high test scores. . . that few blacks would actually be affected. If one looks to see where any overprediction or underprediction is statistically significant, it is found that the only significant range of scores is for lower scores, where blacks are being overpredicted by the [test].
>
> . . .
>
> . . . the [test] is not to be criticized on the basis of differential validity inquiries.[1]

The advent of this type of opinion in court decisions suggests the advisability of carrying out the kind of comparison of regression lines employed in this case. If underprediction of protected groups can be ruled out, the analysis provides further substantiation of any claimed lack of differential validity. On the other hand, the legal status of a finding that underprediction may occur is currently just as clouded as the professional status, given that validity is established for both groups. Statistics simply will not answer questions that have not as yet been answered in nonmathematical terms.

[1]*Ensley Branch, NAACP* v. *Seibels et al.* and related cases, 14 FEP 670 (N. D. Ala. 1977).

part 4

comprehensive validation of a total selection system in a management consulting firm

overview

Part 4 provides examples of validation techniques discussed previously. It describes a comprehensive evaluation of all components of a large international management consulting firm's selection process. This evaluation was carried out by one of the authors, who served as a special consultant to the firm during the period when the studies were conducted.

The investigations were initiated with the primary objective of improving the firm's selection process for new associates. Thus the intention was to weed out procedures that were not satisfactory in identifying the most promising candidates and to introduce new procedures that would do a better job. As the studies progressed EEO considerations also began to take on increasing significance. However, the firm had employed only relatively few women and minorities in a consulting capacity up to the time the validation project was carried out, and therefore it was not possible to study these groups separately in a differential design.

At the time the project was initiated the following procedures were being used regularly to select new consultants:

1. Psychological evaluations conducted by various outside psychological consulting organizations.
2. Multiple interviews conducted by members of the firm and recorded subsequently on a standard interview-evaluation form.
3. Application blanks and résumés focused primarily on educational background and employment experience.
4. A general mental ability test—Alpha 9.

The firm maintained extensive files on past as well as present employees so that it was possible to validate these procedures largely on a historical basis while still using a predictive design. In addition to the four procedures noted above, occasional use was made of reference checks and of field investigations by outside investigative agencies. However, these procedures were not employed on a regular basis, and even when they were used, they rarely exerted much influence on selection decisions. In fact, in many cases a decision to hire was made prior to the actual receipt of the reference letters or background reports. Thus, these additional procedures were not deemed appropriate for validation and no formal studies were made of them. Nevertheless, data from these sources were utilized, when available, in conjunction with the application forms and résumés to develop a new weighted application blank (see Chapter 12).

At the same time that the studies were undertaken to evaluate existing procedures, several new approaches were introduced, largely on an experimental basis, to investigate their possible usefulness for consultant selection. These were:

1. Two personality tests—the Tomkins-Horn Picture-Arrangement Test and the Miner Sentence-Completion Scale.
2. Two additional mental ability tests—the Terman Concept-Mastery Test and the Vocabularly Test G-T.

Thus, in all, the program of validation spanned a total of eight different selection procedures. The strategy utilized involved conducting studies on a number of these procedures initially in a single relatively small U.S. office. As it became apparent that these pilot investigations were producing useful results, and as the consultant became increasingly familiar with the organization and with available sources of data within it, the research was expanded to include all U.S. offices. In some cases studies were conducted with a view to validating selection procedures in offices outside the United States as well.

Our intent in presenting this comprehensive validation process in as much detail as we do is to provide a model for similar efforts in other companies. It is important to note that this validation program was by no means limited to psychological tests. Furthermore, each procedure was evaluated by at least one study which utilized a longitudinal or predictive design. Because historical data from the files were employed extensively it was possible to conduct the whole analysis in somewhat less than three years. It should be noted that the effort did not represent a full-time commitment; the consultant was occupied with numerous other activities both within this firm and outside it throughout the period of the investigation. Because of the need for the passage of time in the studies involving the personality tests and the two new mental ability tests, the period of study could not have been reduced below two and a half years in any event. This is probably typical for validation efforts of this type and scope.

Four of the following five chapters contain articles which have been published in the professional literature. Because these articles were written for a professional audience of personnel managers and psychologists they contain certain material and discussions that would not be included in a report intended for internal use by the firm or for transmittal to a federal or state agency. In general, the articles give more attention to the broader implications of the studies—extending beyond the particular firm—than would be the case in reporting for use within a given organization or by enforcement agencies.

We feel, however, that it is desirable to present the research in the form in which it was finally approved by journal editors and other professional referees. This matter of professional approval and expert endorsement clearly is an important consideration in dealing with the courts and with relevant governmental agencies, and it appears best to present the studies in the form in which this approval and endorsement was received. All of the journal articles went through an extensive review by several professional peers, and in some cases additional statistical analyses of the data were undertaken on the basis of these reviews.

In order to make it easier to read these articles for the particular purpose of gaining an understanding of the validation process, we precede each with a brief introduction highlighting important points and placing the research in context. The technical terms used and the statistical techniques employed are discussed in Chapters 6 through 8 of Part 3.

9

validation study of psychological evaluations

Introductory notes

Of the studies described in this chapter all were predictive in nature. Study 4 was in fact performed first and was conducted as a pilot analysis in the smaller U.S. office of the consulting firm. The finding of one significant *negative* criterion correlation in this office, suggesting that the firm might be rejecting its *best* potential candidates by following the psychologists' recommendations, triggered the other more comprehensive studies.

These studies of the psychological evaluations failed to produce any statistically significant predictor-criterion relationships of either a positive or a negative nature. Given the fact that the firm had had very few minority-group or female applicants for consulting jobs over the period covered by the research, it would be very hard to establish adverse impact for the psychological evaluation procedure per se. However, given the disparity between the firm's employment posture and existing labor force ratios, the possibility of arousing governmental attention was considerable. The obvious response to such a situation is to increase recruiting efforts for women and minority groups, and this is what the firm did. However, the clear evidence that business necessity could not be claimed for the psychological evaluations, if an increased applicant flow of women and minorities subsequently should yield evidence of adverse impact, argues strongly for abandoning the procedure or at the very least revising it drastically. This conclusion is reinforced of course by the fact that a considerable amount of money was being spent without any identifiable benefit.

Another reason that the psychological evaluation process might well cause concern to governmental compliance personnel, in addition to the lack of demonstrated validity, is inherent in the finding of sizable variations among the hiring recommendations of different psychologists. Such a situation, where one person is much more prone to reject a particular applicant than another person, obviously is one in which discrimination biases can operate quite easily. Past experience would suggest that EEOC in particular might well attack such a technique.

The studies reported in this article all utilized predictor data available in personnel files. Much of the criterion data was already available also. Only the performance ratings utilized in studies one, two, and four had to be obtained specifically for the purposes of validation. Thus, studies of this kind can be carried out quite rapidly.

PSYCHOLOGICAL EVALUATIONS AS PREDICTORS OF CONSULTING SUCCESS*

Recent literature reviews have painted a relatively favorable picture of psychological evaluations as they are typically carried out in the business setting (Korman, 1968; Miner, 1968b). A number of studies have produced predictive validities which, if not extremely high, are still well above the level that might be expected on the basis of the arguments of those who favor "statistical" as opposed to "clinical" prediction (Meehl, 1954).

Yet it would be premature to conclude that we have all the answers regarding psychological evaluations in the business world. Many psychological consulting firms and individual psychologists are providing services of this nature to business organizations. The volume of work suggests that conducting psychological evaluations may well be the largest single area of activity for industrial psychologists at the present time; certainly it is the basic, bread and butter activity of a number of consulting firms. Given the extent of this work and the great diversity of techniques used in carrying out the evalu-

* Reprinted with permission from *Personnel Psychology,* Vol. 23 (1970), 393-405.

tions, the half-dozen or so studies that have been published to date can hardly be considered an adequate basis for reaching conclusions. This is particularly true since some of the existing research is quite restricted in scope and some deals with evaluation procedures which are not actually in wide use in industrial psychological practice. The research program reported here is one of the few comprehensive, long-term prediction studies currently available in this area. In addition it deals with actual hiring recommendations made by consulting psychologists to clients on the basis of the psychologists' regular evaluation procedures.

Procedure

The *first* study involved 80 individuals hired for consulting positions in the major office of a very successful international management consulting firm offering services primarily to business clients. Psychological evaluations were carried out in all cases prior to hiring and specific recommendations regarding employment were made by the psychologists. The evaluations were made by six different psychological consulting firms, although one particular firm predominated with 61 percent. The exact number of psychologists represented is not known, but is at least ten. Although the words used in making employment recommendations tended to vary somewhat among the reports, it was possible to classify the statements with relatively little difficulty. The scale used follows:

5 A clearly outstanding candidate
4 A good candidate, but with some risk
3 Mixed, but positively recommended
2 Mixed, but negatively recommended
1 Definitely not recommended

The subjects were followed over their entire career with the organization. These were all individuals who did not achieve promotion into the management ranks. Some no doubt would have, if they had chosen to stay; more left because they did not anticipate promotion. The periods of employment involved ranged from less than a month to nine years; the median was three years and three months.

Three types of criteria were employed. The first was tenure with the organization—How long did the individual last? The second was the mean increase in compensation rate per year employed. The third was the value placed on the individual's work by the manager in charge of the office. Because only one rater was used, the reliability of this particular set of ratings cannot be specified. However, similar ratings used in the same organization have typically yielded reliability coefficients of approximately .75. The ratings were on a 5-point scale as follows:

5 Sorry to have the individual leave—there is good reason to believe he would have been promoted had he stayed.
4 Sorry to have the individual leave—not a top prospect, but a good worker.
3 Sorry to have the individual leave—there is reason to believe he might have developed further.
2 Not really sorry to have the individual leave, although his was not an involuntary separation.
1 Glad to have the individual leave—including involuntary separations.

The three criterion measures were all significantly related. The reward structure as reflected in the compensation measure and the value structure as reflected in the ratings were correlated .60. Tenure was correlated with the former .47 and the latter .55.

To determine the predictive validity of the psychological evaluations the recommendation scores were correlated with the three criteria. In addition the psychological evaluations for 16 individuals designated by the manager in charge of the office as clear selection errors were compared with those for the remaining 64.

The *second* study was similar in design, but used as subjects 53 consultants who had separated from smaller offices of the same organization in the United States and Great Britain. Six different offices were represented. The psychological evaluations were carried out by seven different psychological firms. One of these did 45 percent, but this is not the same firm that did the majority of the evaluations in the first study. The psychological firm that did the major proportion of the evaluations in this study tends to stress interviewing procedures, rather than tests, more than do most such firms. The period of employment over which these individuals were evaluated varied from two months to seven years ten months with the median at three years and four months. The correlation between compensation change and the ratings made by the various managers in charge of offices was .67. Tenure correlated with the compensation measure .46 and the ratings .44. In all respects other than those noted this study was a replication of the first.

A *third* study utilized as subjects not separatees, but currently employed consultants below the managerial level. There were 73 individuals involved, all from the major office. With this group only the compensation change measure was used as a criterion of success. Correlations between psychological evaluations and this criterion were computed for the group as a whole and separately for the 36 individuals with two years or more service and the 37 with from six months to two years. This was done to identify any effects attributable to instability of the compensation change measure when based on short time periods. The median period of employment for the over two year group was three years one month with a high of six years nine months. The median for the under two years group was one year.

In this instance the evaluations were made by five different psychological consulting firms and 14 psychologists. Two firms did roughly 40 percent of the work each; neither was a firm which had predominated in the two preceding studies.

A *fourth* study dealt with 24 currently employed consultants in a single office of the organization. These individuals had been employed for periods ranging from nine months to seven years three months at the time of follow-up; the median was two years. The psychological evaluations were made by four firms with one of these performing 63 percent. Again this firm was one which had not predominated in prior studies.

The success criteria used in this instance differed in several respects from those described previously. In addition to the compensation change measure, ratings of overall performance effectiveness and potential for advancement into management were obtained from managers in the office. Each individual was rated by an average of 2.5 managers on a 10-point scale. The reliabilities of the two ratings as established by correlating pairs of ratings were .88 for performance and .91 for potential. A final criterion was the professional grade level of the individual which ranged through four levels from the most junior consultants to the most senior. None, however, had been promoted to management.

Again the success criteria were closely related. The lowest value was .58 which was obtained in two instances involving the professional grade level measure (potential rating and compensation change). The highest correlation was .96, between the two ratings.

A *fifth* study extended the analysis to the managerial level. Comparisons were made between the psychological evaluations for two levels of management in the organization and three of the groups already considered—the 80 major office separatees, the 53 separatees from minor offices, and the 73 currently employed consultants in the major office. The assumption was that those who had been selected for management positions should have received more favorable psychological evaluations at the time of hiring than those who had separated without being promoted to managerial positions or those who currently were working at a sub-managerial level; also that those who had reached the upper levels of management should on the average have been evaluated more favorably than the larger junior management group.

The upper level management sample contained 14 individuals. Four different psychological consulting firms were involved in the evaluations, but 71 percent were done by a single firm. This particular firm did relatively few of the evaluations of studies one through four. The psychological recommendations were made from nine years three months to eighteen years two months prior to the conduct of the study; the median was fifteen years three months.

The lower level managers numbered 39 and were evaluated by eight different firms. However, one firm, the one that did the majority of the evaluations in the first study, carried out 59 percent. The evaluations were done from five years nine months to eighteen years six months prior to the conduct of this research, with the median period being eight years six months.

Two additional studies were carried out, not to establish the predictive validity of the psychological evaluations, but to identify correlates that might provide insights into factors which influence psychological recommendations. The first such study attempted to determine whether individual psychologists differ in their tendency to make favorable or unfavorable hiring recommendations. Evaluations made by two psychological consulting firms over an eleven month period on 172 candidates were considered. There were six psychologists who made ten or more evaluations in this period—two from one firm with 38 and 25 respectively and four from another with 32, 29, 20 and 12.

The hiring recommendations involved could be classified in terms of a 4-point scale:

4 Highly recommended

3 Recommended

2 Serious questions

1 Not recommended

The first two categories (three and four) were considered to be favorable recommendations, matching the categories 3, 4, and 5 used in previous studies. Categories one and two were considered unfavorable, matching the same categories used previously. Comparisons were made between the percentages of favorable recommendations for the six psychologists and for the two firms; also between the mean psychological evaluation scores for the psychologists. Since there was every reason to believe that candidates were assigned to psychologists on the basis of availability rather than capability, real differences between the candidates evaluated by each psychologist can be assumed to be minimal.

The second study dealing with correlates of the psychological evaluations utilized the two separate samples of studies one and two. Information on various background factors was obtained as of the time of hiring—the same time the psychological evaluations were made. The hypothesis considered was that these factors might influence the recommendations; in particular favorable recommendations might be associated with evidence of prior accomplishment or family status. Product-moment or bi-serial correlation coefficients were computed as appropriate to the data.

The background measures were:

Age when hired

Height

Weight

Number of siblings

Years of education completed by father
Number of children
Class standing at college graduation
Class standing in graduate school
Years of previous business experience
Possession of an advanced degree
Having managerial experience in business
Married when hired
Serving as an officer in the armed forces
Graduate of an Ivy League college
Graduate of a state university
Born in a city of over 300,000 population
Father worked as a manager in a large corporation
Father employed in the business world
Father worked as a non-business professional

Results

The findings from the first study are given in Table 1. There is no evidence of any predictive validity for the psychological evaluations. The mean recommendation score for the 16 individuals designated as definite selection errors was 3.00; that for the 64 not so designated was 3.09. The difference between these two values is too small to provide any support for the psychological evaluations as predictors.

The second study, which represents a partial replication of the first, also failed to produce any statistically reliable results. The data are presented in Table 2.

Table 1

Relationships between Psychological Evaluations and Criteria of Subsequent Success among Separatees— Major Office Study (N = 80)

Success Criteria	*r*	*P*
Compensation Change	.02	n.s.
Performance Rating	−.04	n.s.
Tenure	.06	n.s.

Table 2

Relationships between Psychological Evaluations and Criteria of Subsequent Success among Separatees— Minor Offices Study (N = 53)

Success Criteria	r	P
Compensation Change	.14	n.s.
Performance Rating	.05	n.s.
Tenure	.18	n.s.

The third study used as subjects 73 currently employed consultants rather than separated consultants as in the two previous studies. The findings are contained in Table 3. It is apparent that restricting the analysis to subjects whose longer employment permits compensation changes to stabilize makes no appreciable difference. Among both the short-term and long-term employees the predictive validities are not significant.

The fourth study, also conducted with a currently employed group, utilized value as well as reward criteria. In addition the reliability of the ratings is known and high. Yet once again as Table 4 indicates, positive support for the psychological evaluations is lacking. In fact the only significant finding is the negative correlation between consultant grade level and the hiring recommendation—those with unfavorable psychological evaluations are somewhat more likely to be in the higher grades.

The fifth study extends this grade level analysis into the management ranks. The results of comparisons between two levels of management and various non-management consultant groups are given in Table 5. Although the upper managers do have the highest psychological evaluation scores of any group as hypothesized, none

Table 3

Relationships between Psychological Evaluations and Compensation Change among Currently Employed— Major Office Study

Groups	N	r	P
Two years or more of service	36	.12	n.s.
Less than two years of service	37	.03	n.s.
All currently employed	73	.08	n.s.

Table 4

Relationships between Psychological Evaluations and Criteria of Subsequent Success among Currently Employed—Minor Office Study (N = 24)

Success Criteria	*r*	*P*
Compensation Change	−.11	n.s.
Performance Rating	−.14	n.s.
Potential Rating	−.05	n.s.
Professional Grade Level	−.46	< .05

of the differences even approximate significance; nor do the lower level managers have significantly higher scores than the non-managers. The comparison between the lower management and major office separatee samples is of particular interest because the same psychological consulting firm did the majority of the evaluations in both instances.

When the two managerial samples are combined the resulting mean psychological evaluation score is 3.26. This value is almost identical with that obtained in one sample of individuals who separated without ever being promoted into management and only slightly higher than that for the other separatee group.

The sixth study attempted to determine whether there are significant differences between psychologists in their tendency to recommend favorably or unfavorably on hiring. The results are presented in Table 6. The chi-square value obtained from a comparison of the six psychologists' favorable and unfavorable recommendation frequencies was 11.35 ($P =< .05$ for 5 df). Psychologist three tends

Table 5

Mean Psychological Evaluation Scores for Various Groups

			Comparisons			
			Upper Mgmt.		Lower Mgmt.	
Group	*N*	Mean	*t*	*P*	*t*	*P*
Upper Management	14	3.50				
Lower Management	39	3.18	.81	n.s.		
Separatees-Major Office	80	3.08	1.08	n.s.	.41	n.s.
Separatees-Minor Office	53	3.25	.91	n.s.	.27	n.s.
Employed-Major Office	73	3.21	.96	n.s.	.12	n.s.

to make a disproportionately large number of favorable recommendations while psychologists two and six tend to be unfavorable. This same pattern emerges in the *t*-tests of differences between means presented in Table 6.

Table 6

Mean Psychological Evaluation Scores and Recommendation Percentages for Various Psychologists

Psychologist	*N*	Mean Evaluation Score	Percent Favorable Recommendations (3 & 4)
Firm A			
Psychologist 1	38	2.26	53%
Psychologist 2	25	1.76	32%
Firm B			
Psychologist 3	32	2.88	69%
Psychologist 4	29	2.28	55%
Psychologist 5	20	2.40	55%
Psychologist 6	12	2.08	25%

Comparisons between Mean Evaluation Scores

Psychologist	2		3		4		5		6	
	t	*P*	*t*	*P*	*t*	*P*	*t*	*P*	*t*	*P*
1	2.04	<.05	2.57	<.05	.05	n.s.	.49	n.s.	.62	n.s.
2			4.00	<.01	1.78	<.10	1.95	<.10	1.00	n.s.
3					2.16	<.05	1.49	n.s.	2.38	<.05
4							.38	n.s.	.56	n.s.
5									.84	n.s.

A comparison of the two firms reveals that Firm A made a total of 67 evaluations, 45 percent of which were favorable; Firm B made 105 evaluations, 56 percent of which were favorable. The resulting chi-square of 2.16 is not significant. Firm A tends to stress interview data, while Firm B places greater reliance on tests. These results tend to support the conclusion that the primary source of variability is the individual psychologist rather than the specific procedures or standards of a particular firm. This assumes, of course, that the candidates assigned to different psychologists and firms were in fact of equal potential.

The correlations of Table 7 are in general unrevealing. None of the factors studied appear to be related to the psychological recommendations. Only one of the correlations, that for marriage, is

Table 7

Correlates of Psychological Evaluation Scores

Factors Correlated	Major Office Sample (N = 80) r	P	Minor Office Sample (N = 53) r	P
Age	.05	n.s.	.12	n.s.
Height	.04	n.s.	.00	n.s.
Weight	.09	n.s.	−.09	n.s.
Siblings	−.06	n.s.	.24	< .10
Father's education	.07	n.s.	.09	n.s.
Children	.02	n.s.	.02	n.s.
College grades	.08	n.s.	.11	n.s.
Graduate school grades	.13	n.s.	−.12	n.s.
Business experience	.06	n.s.	.10	n.s.
Graduate degree	−.15	n.s.	.12	n.s.
Managerial experience	.01	n.s.	−.05	n.s.
Married	.37	< .05	.12	n.s.
Officer in service	−.09	n.s.	.02	n.s.
Ivy league graduate	−.04	n.s.	.18	n.s.
State university graduate	.17	n.s.	−.13	n.s.
Born in large city	.03	n.s.	.10	n.s.
Father corporate manager	−.15	n.s.	−.03	n.s.
Father in business	−.04	n.s.	−.02	n.s.
Father professional	.31	< .10	.08	n.s.

clearly significant and it does not hold up in the second sample. Thus this seventh study was not successful in providing insights into the dynamics of the evaluation process. On the other hand these results do not preclude the possibility that other background factors not studied might be associated with the recommendations.

Taken as a whole these results provide absolutely no evidence for the predictive validity of psychological evaluations as they are currently conducted in the business world. A total of 20 comparisons were made involving separate samples and/or criterion measures. Only one statistically significant finding was obtained and that was in a direction opposite to the one hypothesized. Thirteen of the comparisons were in a positive direction and seven were negative. The median correlation coefficient was .03.

Discussion

Since the organization in question was in fact hiring something over 50 percent of those who received favorable psychological evaluations and only about 13 percent of those with unfavorable evaluations, some restriction of range was clearly present in the studies. In view of the distribution of validities there is no reason to believe that this restriction could account for the results. Nevertheless, there were a number of individuals in the various samples who were hired in spite of unfavorable psychological recommendations. Did these individuals tend to do poorly, and thus would the inclusion of more such subjects in the studies have changed the nature of the conclusions?

Among the currently employed consultants in the major office (study 3) 17 percent were hired with unfavorable psychological evaluations and in the other currently employed consultant sample (study 4) this figure was 13 percent. In the managerial samples (study 5) 13 percent were hired with equally negative evaluations. Thus, those with negative psychological hiring recommendations appear to be achieving promotions into management in essentially the same proportion as they exist in the organization, not less frequently as one might anticipate.

In another analysis, individuals with various psychological evaluation scores were compared in terms of the proportion achieving an acceptable success level as reflected in their ratings, compensation progress and tenure. The sample contained the 80 separatees of study one plus 13 individuals who were promoted to management positions in the same office during the period the 80 were leaving. Of those definitely not recommended for hiring (scale value one), 50 percent subsequently achieved the specified success level. Of those with a mixed report, but still not recommended (scale value two), 44 percent achieved the same success level. Of those with favorable recommendations (scale values three through five), 51 percent had the same degree of success. Clearly those with unfavorable psychological evaluations were no less likely to succeed than those with more favorable evaluations. All in all it appears very unlikely that the addition of a number of subjects with unfavorable evaluations would have produced any meaningful change in the conclusions from the research.

The question remains: Why has a selection procedure which has had such wide application and which appears to have demonstrated considerable predictive validity in other studies, failed so completely in this instance? Although the data to answer this question with certainty are not available, several hypotheses appear feasible. For one thing the studies reported here have dealt primarily with the prediction of consulting success whereas previous research has been concentrated almost exclusively on managers. It may well be that psychologists know considerably less about the requirements of general management consulting than they do about the requirements for successful managers.

Secondly, the psychological evaluations studied were all carried out without any systematic attempt to relate aspects of the evaluation process to the reward and value structures of the organization. Studies have repeatedly demonstrated that these structures may vary drastically from one organization to another and even within segments of the same organization (Miner, 1968a). These differences in organizational character make it essential that selection procedures be introduced in conjunction with studies of the organization involved, if predictions are to rise above the level established by the within-occupation variance. In the present instance the failure to obtain feedback on subsequent performance and to adjust recommendations accordingly, combined with the lack of analyses of organizational character, appear to have resulted in a failure to predict with regard to both the occupationally derived and the organizationally derived variance components.

This indictment is not specific to any one psychological consulting firm. Six different firms performed a sufficiently large number of the evaluations in a given study so that the use of highly effective procedures by that firm should have had a distinctly positive impact on the results of the study. Yet in no case did any relationships that could not easily be accounted for by chance emerge, except for one significant negative correlation.

Even more disturbing is the fact that certain psychologists appear to have consistent tendencies to say either "yes" or "no" when faced with the hiring question. Employment would seem to depend more on the particular psychologist to which a candidate happened to be assigned than on any other factor identified in this research. Certainly the decision to hire was influenced more by the characteristic positive or negative attitudes of the specific psychologist than by the actual potentialities for success possessed by the candidate. This same tendency to accept different proportions of applicants has been found among employment interviewers as well (Webster, 1964). In actual practice individual differences in the selectors may well have a greater influence on employment decisions than individual differences in the candidates.

In summary, this series of studies raises serious questions with regard to psychological evaluation procedures as they are currently used in their natural habitat.

References

Korman, A.K. "The Prediction of Managerial Performance: A Review." *Personnel Psychology,* XXI (1968), 295-322.

Meehl, P. *Clinical vs. Statistical Prediction.* Minneapolis, Minnesota: University of Minnesota Press, 1954.

Miner, J.B. "Bridging the Gulf in Organizational Performance." *Harvard Business Review,* XLVI (1968), No. 4, 102-110. (a)

Miner, J.B. "Management Appraisal." *Business Horizons,* XI (1968), No. 5, 83-96. (b)

Webster, E.C. *Decision Making in the Employment Interview.* Montreal: Industrial Relations Centre, McGill University, 1964.

10

validation study of executive and personnel interviews

Introductory notes

No pilot study of interview validity was conducted initially in the single smaller office of the firm largely because inspection of the interview forms in the files of that office indicated only intermittent use and incomplete response when the forms were used. Later it became apparent that the data from other offices were more suitable for analysis and that interview validity studies could be conducted. The samples employed overlap considerably with those used in the psychological evaluation studies and the same criterion data often were used for both analyses.

The finding of validity for the interviews rests entirely on the promotion criterion. Studies using other criteria were found to suffer so badly from disagreements among different interviewers that validity could not possibly be obtained (due to unreliability of the predictor); thus the results of these latter studies must be discounted. However, the promotion criterion appears to be an entirely appropriate index, from both the EEO and company viewpoints, in situations of this type. In the typical consulting firm, promotion into partnership is the ultimate measure of success, and only one in six beginning consultants hired is so rewarded. The remaining five ultimately leave the firm. Thus promotion is not only important as a criterion in its own right but also because it is the obverse of turnover.

The findings, based on predictive studies, indicate that the interview process does "work" in an overall sense, and that by focusing on certain kinds of questions and certain types of interviewers, it could be sharpened into a quite effective selection tool. Thus, a case for business necessity does appear feasible. Nevertheless, the possibility that adverse impact might result with increased recruiting of female and minority-group candidates must be recognized. This is because size (height and weight) is found to be positively related to interviewer judgments. Carrying these bases for judgment over into a more diversified mix of candidates will clearly yield a higher proportion of men than women evaluated favorably in the interview. On the other hand, with enough women in the study sample, size might well disappear as a factor in interview judgments. The finding that those who have served in the past as officers in the armed forces are evaluated more positively would also tend to increase selection ratios for white males over those for women and minority group members. Given these findings EEOC might well argue that another predictor with less potential for adverse impact should be identified and utilized. Given the clear support of the findings for job-relatedness, however, it is not at all clear that a court would agree with such a contention.

EXECUTIVE AND PERSONNEL INTERVIEWS AS PREDICTORS OF CONSULTING SUCCESS*

In consulting firms, as in other enterprises, interviews play a particularly significant role among the various selection techniques used. The interviews usually vary in the range of two to six per candidate and are conducted both by consultants who are firm members and by personnel administrators (Association of Consulting Management Engineers, 1964).

In spite of this extensive use of the interview, and the crucial role it has in selection decisions, there is no published research available regarding the effectiveness of the technique in predicting subsequent consulting success. This lack of validity information is particularly noteworthy in view of the costliness of the procedure. Executive interviews typically are conducted by partners, whose time is billed to clients at very high rates. Thus, a firm may well forego

* Reprinted with permission from *Personnel Psychology,* Vol. 23 (1970), 521-538.

considerable income every time an executive interview is conducted.

The studies reported here were undertaken to provide some of the needed validity information. They parallel those reported previously dealing with the predictive validity of psychological evaluations (Miner, 1970).

Procedure

The *first* study involved 78 individuals hired for consulting positions in the *major office* of a very successful international firm providing general management consulting services, primarily to business clients. Data were collected for each man over his entire career with the firm. All were individuals who did not achieve promotion into partnership with its concomitant managerial responsibilities. They left prior to promotion either for what appeared to be more attractive opportunities or, more frequently, because promotion seemed unlikely. Length of employment ranged from less than a month to nine years, with the median at three years and three months. The firm utilized an up or out policy which tended to foster a positive relationship between tenure and success. Once a man was clearly established as unpromotable his employment was terminated.

Interview evaluations were recorded on a standard form, filled out by each interviewer after the candidate left. This form then became a part of the permanent personnel file for each individual. The form contained questions on the following:

1. Personal impression
2. Effectiveness with people (client acceptance)
3. Firm acceptance
4. Mental ability for problem solving
5. Imagination
6. Initiative and sustained drive (motivation)
7. Practical judgment
8. Technical competence
9. Character and habits
10. Self-confidence, maturity, and emotional stability
11. Writing skill

12. Pattern of success
13. Flexibility
14. Oral skill
15. Potential as a clientele builder
16. Promotion potential (to management)
17. Employment recommendation
18. Special comments

In many instances not all of these questions were answered by a particular interviewer. Among the less frequently answered were numbers 11 through 14 (Writing skill, Pattern of success, Flexibility, and Oral skill).

The forms were completed either by writing out an answer or making a checkmark on a scale or both. Where no serious question was raised on an item a "+" was given; where there was a negative indication or some expression of doubt the item was scored "–". Because the forms differed in the number of items filled out, the Total Form score was computed by dividing the number of "+" responses by the total number of items completed; the Key Questions score, obtained from items 15 through 18, by dividing the number of "+" responses on these four items by the number within this item-grouping that were completed.

Average Total Form and Key Questions scores for each man studied were computed for three interview groups and for all combined. The interviewer groups were managers (partners), professionals (consultants below the partner level), and personnel administrators. Not all of those conducted interviews in all instances, and the number of interviews conducted by any given group of interviewers varied considerably. In those instances where a candidate was not interviewed by at least one person of a particular group no score was given in that interviewer category. The total number of interviews for a particular candidate varied from one to nine.

The reported length of the interviews with the major office candidates in the separatee group ranged from 15 minutes to two and one-half hours, with the median at one hour. Although a standard interview form was used, these were by no means structured interviews. Each man used his own approach, although all attempted to answer much the same questions in the end. Interviewers did not receive any formal training in interviewing skills, and employment criteria were very loosely defined.

The various interview scores were correlated with three success criteria. First was a performance rating by the manager in charge of the major office on the following scale:

5 Sorry to have the individual leave—there is good reason to believe he would have been promoted had he stayed
4 Sorry to have the individual leave—not a top prospect, but a good worker
3 Sorry to have the individual leave—there is reason to believe he might have developed further
2 Not really sorry to have the individual leave, although his was not an involuntary separation
1 Glad to have the individual leave—including involuntary separations

The second criterion measure was the mean increase in compensation rate per year employed. Compensation practices and standards remained much the same throughout the period of the study. The third criterion was the man's tenure of employment. The three measures are all intercorrelated to a relatively high degree—performance rating with compensation change .64, performance rating with tenure .56, and compensation change with tenure .44.

The *second* study was a replication of the first except that subjects were drawn from *smaller offices* of the same firm. Six different offices in the United States and Great Britain were represented, and 51 individuals were included. The median reported interview length was again one hour, with the range from 15 minutes to three hours. The duration of employment was from two months to seven years ten months, the median being three years and three months.

The ratings were made by the six different managers of offices for those consultants in their employ. These ratings correlated .67 with compensation change and .45 with tenure. Compensation change and tenure correlated .46.

A *third* study compared the 78 professionals of study one, who separated without being promoted to the managerial level, with 24 men who did achieve promotion in the same major office. For predictive validity to be demonstrated, those promoted would have to achieve significantly higher interview scores than those who were not. Significance was tested using the *t*-test for differences between means, but biserial correlations were computed as well.

At the time the study was carried out, six of the 24 had been promoted again and thus had reached the upper level of management within the firm; the remaining 18 were in a lower level of management. The interviews had been conducted from six years one month to sixteen years one month previously. The median follow-up period was nine years six months. The interviews covered much the same time span as with the professionals who separated—from a half-hour to two hours, with the median at one hour.

The *fourth* study replicated the third in most respects. The comparison groups were the 51 separatees of study two and 18 men who were promoted to management in minor offices. Only one of these was an upper level manager at the time of this analysis. The interviewing had been done from five years nine months to fifteen years six months before, with the median at seven years eleven months. The interviews essentially were of the same length as in the previous studies—a range of fifteen minutes to two hours and again a median of one hour.

The average number of interviewers of various types used to evaluate the subjects of studies one through four is presented in Table 1. These are the numbers on which the various interview scores are based. In general personnel administrators were used sparingly and if they were used, only one interviewed each candidate. Almost all subjects were seen by at least one manager—most were seen by

Table 1

Average Number of Interviewers Used in Computing Interview Scores

	Major Office Separatees		Minor Offices Separatees		Promoted to Management	
Type of Interviewer	N	$\overline{X}$	N	$\overline{X}$	N	$\overline{X}$
Managers	77	2.57	45	1.98	41	2.58
Professionals	47	1.40	45	2.29	18	1.61
Personnel Administrators	3	1.33	25	1.04	11	1.09
All Interviewers	78	3.44	51	4.27	42	3.50

two or three. Professionals below the managerial level also interviewed a sizable proportion, but (except for the minor office separatees) the number of such interviews per man was well below the number of manager interviews.

Two further analyses were made with a view to identifying correlates of interviewer judgments. The objective was to gain further insight into processes that might be operating with some consistency in the interviews. The first of these analyses related interview scores to hiring recommendations made by consulting psychologists (Miner, 1970). The psychological evaluations typically were made subsequent to the interviews, but prior to hiring. A number of different psychological consulting firms participated and an even greater number of individual psychologists. However, all recommendations could be classified on a five point scale as follows:

5 A clearly outstanding candidate
4 A good candidate, but with some risk
3 Mixed, but positively recommended
2 Mixed, but negatively recommended
1 Definitely not recommended

Correlations were computed using the score obtained for manager interviewers only, a score for professionals and personnel administrators combined, and the score for all interviewers. Independent analyses were carried out using the major office separatees of study one and the minor offices separatees of study two. Any evidence of a significant relationship between psychological evaluations and interviews would appear to indicate either that the interview judgments were influencing the psychologists or that similar factors were operating in both contexts. Because of the temporal sequence involved the psychological evaluations could not have determined the interview judgments.

Another analysis was conducted to determine whether certain biographical factors might have exerted a significant influence on the interviewers. This seemed particularly important because the interviewers had application blank data available to them before the interview and might well evaluate a candidate at least in part in terms of these data, rather than on the basis of the interview itself. Product-moment or biserial correlations were computed, as appropriate to the data, between the Total Form interview score for all interviewers and the following background measures:

Age when hired
Height
Weight
Number of siblings
Years of education completed by father
Number of children
Class standing at college graduation
Class standing in graduate school
Years of previous business experience
Possession of an advanced degree
Having managerial experience in business
Married when hired
Serving as an officer in the armed forces
Graduate of an Ivy League college
Graduate of a state university
Born in a city of over 300,000 population
Father worked as a manager in a large corporation
Father employed in the business world
Father worked as a non-business professional

Finally, analyses were carried out to establish the reliability of the interviewer judgments. Was there a reasonable amount of agreement among the various individuals who interviewed the same candidate? The procedure used to answer this question required that pairs of Total Form and Key Questions interview scores be correlated. Separate reliability analyses were conducted for major office separatees, minor office separatees and the group promoted to management taken as a whole. In each instance three pairs of interview scores were drawn for each candidate. In those instances where a large number of interviewers had been used these were random pairs, where there were three interviewers all combinations were used, in those few cases where there were only two interviews the same pair was used three times. The three reliability estimates for each measure in each group were averaged using z transformations. The resulting average correlation was taken as the estimate of overall reliability. In addition a correction for the number of interviewers whose evaluations were averaged to obtain the scores for a given candidate was made by inserting the All Interviewers frequencies of Table 1 into the Spearman-Brown prophecy formula (Guion, 1965).

Results

The results of study one are given in Table 2. There is no definite evidence of any relationship between the various interview scores and the criteria, although the submanagerial professionals do exhibit a negative trend. There is some tendency for these interviewers to judge favorably those who are least likely to succeed, while those whom they evaluate less favorably have a higher probability of success. Correlations were not computed for the personnel administrator interviewers separately because insufficient interviews were conducted by these nonconsultants in this particular office during the period studied.

The second study, as indicated in Table 3, was equally unrevealing. No clearly significant results were obtained. The only trend is toward a reversal of the previously noted negative trend for the

Table 2

Relationships between Interview Scores and Criteria of Subsequent Success among Separatees—Major Office Study

Type of Interviewer and Measure		Success Criteria					
		Performance Rating		Compensation Change		Tenure	
	N	*r*	*P*	*r*	*P*	*r*	*P*
Managers	77						
Key Questions		−.02	n.s.	.11	n.s.	−.04	n.s.
Total Form		−.02	n.s.	.16	n.s.	−.01	n.s.
Professionals	47						
Key Questions		−.25	<.10	−.28	<.10	−.12	n.s.
Total Form		−.24	<.10	−.23	n.s.	−.04	n.s.
Personnel Administrators	3						
Key Questions							
Total Form							
All Interviewers	78						
Key Questions		−.09	n.s.	.01	n.s.	−.04	n.s.
Total Form		−.07	n.s.	.04	n.s.	−.02	n.s.

Table 3

Relationships between Interview Scores and Criteria of Subsequent Success among Separatees—Minor Offices Study

Type of Interviewer and Measure		Success Criteria					
		Performance Rating		Compensation Change		Tenure	
	N	r	P	r	P	r	P
Managers	45						
Key Questions		.03	n.s.	.06	n.s.	.04	n.s.
Total Form		.00	n.s.	.00	n.s.	.12	n.s.
Professionals	45						
Key Questions		.25	<.10	.07	n.s.	−.01	n.s.
Total Form		.19	n.s.	−.02	n.s.	.14	n.s.
Personnel Administrators	25						
Key Questions		.02	n.s.	−.07	n.s.	.09	n.s.
Total Form		.17	n.s.	.05	n.s.	.06	n.s.
All Interviewers	51						
Key Questions		.15	n.s.	.02	n.s.	.16	n.s.
Total Form		.12	n.s.	.08	n.s.	.04	n.s.

Table 4

Relationships between Interview Scores and Criteria of Subsequent Success among Separatees—All Offices

Type of Interviewer and Measure		Success Criteria					
		Performance Rating		Compensation Change		Tenure	
	N	r	P	r	P	r	P
Managers	122						
Key Questions		.00	n.s.	.09	n.s.	−.01	n.s.
Total Form		−.01	n.s.	.10	n.s.	.04	n.s.
Professionals	92						
Key Questions		−.03	n.s.	−.07	n.s.	−.06	n.s.
Total Form		−.05	n.s.	−.09	n.s.	.04	n.s.
Personnel Administrators	28						
Key Questions		.07	n.s.	.12	n.s.	.24	n.s.
Total Form		.19	n.s.	.13	n.s.	.15	n.s.
All Interviewers	129						
Key Questions		.05	n.s.	.01	n.s.	.05	n.s.
Total Form		.01	n.s.	.05	n.s.	.00	n.s.

professionals. Thus, there is no support for the prior finding on replication. In this instance the personel administrator interviewers could be studied separately, but there is no evidence that would indicate any predictive efficiency for this group.

In Table 4 the data of the first two studies have been combined. Even with these larger *N* values, significance is not obtained.

In contrast to the disappointing results reported to this point study three, as indicated in Table 5, was successful in establishing certain statistically significant relationships. At least in the case of the Key Questions measure the manager interviewers did give more favorable evaluations to those who subsequently achieved promotion. A similar trend is present with the professionals also, although the *t* value does not attain the .05 level. In view of the fact that the correlational analysis yields identical figures for both manager and professional interviewers, it would probably be erroneous to reject the finding for the professionals as a mere chance fluctuation.

The results of the fourth study are presented in Table 6. The manager interviewers tend again to judge those who later become managers as superior to those who do not, but this time statistical

Table 5

Relationships between Interview Scores and the Promotion Criterion—Major Office

Type of Interviewer and Measure	Separated without Promotion		Promoted to Management				
	N	$\overline{X}$	N	$\overline{X}$	t	P	r_{bis}
Managers	77		24				
Key Questions		69.5		83.5	2.68	<.01	.36
Total Form		70.5		76.2	1.59	n.s.	.21
Professionals	47		9				
Key Questions		64.6		87.1	1.81	<.10	.36
Total Form		68.2		74.1	.77	n.s.	.15
Personnel Administrators	3		5				
Key Questions							
Total Form							
All Interviewers	78		24				
Key Questions		67.7		84.6	3.36	<.01	.44
Total Form		70.0		75.6	1.60	n.s.	.22

Table 6

Relationships between Interview Scores and the Promotion Criterion—Minor Offices

Type of Interviewer and Measure	Separated without Promotion		Promoted to Management				
	N	$\bar{X}$	N	$\bar{X}$	t	P	r_{bis}
Managers	45		17				
Key Questions		75.6		87.2	1.63	n.s.	.27
Total Form		71.9		79.0	1.45	n.s.	.24
Professionals	45		9				
Key Questions		83.7		65.4	2.48	<.05	−.48
Total Form		77.7		60.4	3.35	<.01	−.63
Personnel Administrators	25		6				
Key Questions		79.8		100.0	1.99	<.10	.49
Total Form		73.5		88.5	1.94	<.10	.48
All Interviewers	51		18				
Key Questions		80.7		84.8	.81	n.s.	.13
Total Form		74.7		76.5	.55	n.s.	.09

Table 7

Relationship between Interview Scores and the Promotion Criterion—All Offices

Type of Interviewer and Measure	Separated without Promotion		Promoted to Management				
	N	$\bar{X}$	N	$\bar{X}$	t	P	r_{bis}
Managers	122		41				
Key Questions		71.8		85.1	3.14	<.01	.32
Total Form		71.0		77.4	2.19	<.05	.23
Professionals	92		18				
Key Questions		74.0		76.2	.29	n.s.	.04
Total Form		72.8		67.2	1.17	n.s.	.16
Personnel Administrators	28		11				
Key Questions		77.1		100.0	2.72	<.01	.54
Total Form		72.6		87.4	2.60	<.05	.52
All Interviewers	129		42				
Key Questions		72.9		84.7	3.17	<.01	.32
Total Form		71.9		76.0	1.66	<.10	.17

significance is not attained. The results obtained with the professionals as interviewers are exactly the reverse of those in the preceding study. Outside the major office these interviewers below the managerial level gave low evaluations to men who subsequently were promoted. The personnel administrator data verge on significance in the case of the *t* tests and yield sizable correlations. Unfortunately, however, the sample is small.

The combined data of Table 7 serve to increase the personnel administrator sample to a size where clear significance is obtained. The manager interviewers, too, yield highly significant results, although somewhat lower correlations. The conflicting trends in the two professional samples cancel each other out, and as a result the combined data do not yield significance. Yet the scores for all interviewers are significantly and positively related to the promotion criterion, particularly the Key Questions measure.

From the data of Table 8 it appears clear that interviewers within the organization and the psychologists were not making their decisions on the same bases, nor were the interview judgments influencing the psychologists. The correlations are all below any accepted level of significance.

The analyses based on biographical data are more revealing. Weight is consistently related to positive interview evaluations and

Table 8

Relationships between Interview Scores and Psychological Evaluations

Type of Interviewer and Measures	Major Office Separatees			Minor Offices Separatees		
	N	*r*	*P*	*N*	*r*	*P*
Managers	77			45		
Key Questions		.11	n.s.		.15	n.s.
Total Form		.15	n.s.		.03	n.s.
Professionals and Personnel Administrators	48			47		
Key Questions		−.08	n.s.		.13	n.s.
Total Form		−.09	n.s.		.06	n.s.
All Interviewers	78			51		
Key Questions		.03	n.s.		.11	n.s.
Total Form		.09	n.s.		.10	n.s.

height shows a similar trend. Overall it appears that the bigger, more prepossessing individuals were judged more favorably. Also there is some evidence to indicate that those who served as officers in the services were rated higher in the interviews. Other than this the biographical data produce no clearly significant results.

One possibility that might account for the low interview validities obtained in the first two studies is that the reliability of the interview measure was so low that sizable correlations were impossible. Table 10 provides data related to this question. It is evident that the pairs of interviews in the two separatee groups were not closely related—none of the correlations are significantly different from zero, although all are positive. Even when a correction is applied for the number of interviews used in computing averages the results are singularly unimpressive. Reliabilities in the

Table 9

Relationships between All Interviewers, Total Form Interview Score and Biographical Factors

Biographical Factor	Major Office Separatees (*N* = 78)		Minor Offices Separatees (*N* = 51)		All Offices Separatees (*N* = 129)	
	r	*P*	*r*	*P*	*r*	*P*
Age	.03	n.s.	−.06	n.s.	−.02	n.s.
Height	.16	n.s.	.19	n.s.	.19	<.05
Weight	.31	<.01	.26	<.10	.29	<.01
Siblings	−.07	n.s.	−.26	<.10	−.14	n.s.
Father's education	.21	<.10	−.03	n.s.	.14	n.s.
Children	.03	n.s.	.15	n.s.	.07	n.s.
College grades	−.17	n.s.	.10	n.s.	−.04	n.s.
Graduate school grades	.05	n.s.	.12	n.s.	.10	n.s.
Business experience	−.06	n.s.	.08	n.s.	−.06	n.s.
Graduate degree	.15	n.s.	.20	n.s.	.18	n.s.
Managerial experience	−.07	n.s.	.08	n.s.	−.01	n.s.
Married	−.18	n.s.	.01	n.s.	−.09	n.s.
Officer in Service	.19	n.s.	.31	<.10	.24	<.05
Ivy league graduate	−.05	n.s.	−.24	n.s.	−.14	n.s.
State University graduate	.01	n.s.	−.01	n.s.	.05	n.s.
Born in large city	.11	n.s.	.01	n.s.	.10	n.s.
Father corporate manager	.17	n.s.	−.06	n.s.	.10	n.s.
Father in business	.17	n.s.	−.03	n.s.	.08	n.s.
Father professional	−.01	n.s.	−.03	n.s.	.00	n.s.

.30s and .40s are rarely considered acceptable. With such an unstable measurement process it is very difficult to predict future performance.

On the other hand those individuals who subsequently became managers were evaluated more reliably prior to hiring. Although the correlations remain low relative to what is normally desired of a reliability coefficient, they are significantly different from zero and when corrected they begin to approximate respectability. With such reliabilities some predictive validity can be obtained; in all probability this is why validity was obtained using the promotion criterion. It is also true that this is the most important criterion in an organization such as this, which utilizes an up or out approach.

In view of the differences in predictive efficiency between managers, professionals, and personnel administrators as interviewers it seemed appropriate to check on the reliabilities involved here as well. Unfortunately, there were not a sufficient number of cases, where pairs of interviewers considered the same man, to determine the reliability of the personnel administrator interviews. However, the data for managers and professionals were essentially the same and in both cases the correlations were similar to those reported for separatees in Table 10. Although consistently positive, these reliabilities remained very low.

Analyses also were carried out to determine which questions on the interview form were yielding valid results. Because only the man-

Table 10

Reliability of the Interview Scores

Type of Interviewee and Measure	Average Correlation Between Random Pairs of Interviewers	Correlation Between Pairs Corrected for Number of Interviewers
Major Office Separatees		
Key Questions	.04	.13
Total Form	.18	.43
Minor Offices Separatees		
Key Questions	.12	.37
Total Form	.09	.30
Promoted to Management		
Key Questions	.38	.68
Total Form	.27	.56

ager and personnel administrator interviews had produced anything approaching a consistently positive predictive pattern, only these were utilized. Subjects were drawn from all four basic studies. On each item for each individual the trend of the judgments was considered to be "+" if a majority of the responses given were positive. If "+" and "−" responses equaled each other or the latter predominated then an overall score of "−" was given to the individual on that item. The frequencies for "+" and "−" overall judgments in both separatee and promoted groups were then established. The resulting 2 × 2 tables were evaluated for significance by the x^2 method and tetrachoric correlations were also computed. A one-tailed test of significance was used in view of the fact that significance had been established for the total interview score of which the individual items were components. The results of these analyses are given in Table 11. Items dealing with Writing Skill, Pattern of Success, Flexibility and Oral Skill were dropped from the analysis because of insufficient cases.

The items dealing with comments, potential, self-confidence and judgment are without doubt significantly related to promotion;

Table 11

Relationships between Interview Form Items and Promotion Criterion (Manager and Personnel Administrator Interviewers)

Interview Item	N	Per cent Positive Evaluations	x^2	P	r_{tet}
Personal impression	165	57	—	n.s.	.13
Effectiveness with people	167	54	—	n.s.	.04
Firm acceptance	143	81	—	n.s.	−.03
Mental ability for problem solving	165	75	2.20	<.10	.23
Imagination	152	71	2.48	<.10	.27
Initiative and sustained drive	164	74	—	n.s.	.14
Practical judgment	155	74	4.95	<.05	.37
Technical competence	94	39	—	n.s.	−.10
Character and habits	92	82	—	n.s.	−.12
Self-confidence, maturity, and emotional stability	98	81	3.57	<.05	.40
Key Questions					
Potential as clientele builder	126	82	—	n.s.	.05
Promotion potential	154	68	4.36	<.05	.36
Employment recommendation	166	92	1.81	<.10	.28
Special comments	151	49	14.28	<.01	.54

a clear trend is evident on those concerned with employment, imagination, and mental ability. Three of the four Key Questions items are on this list while only four of the ten outside the Key Question category appear. This is consistent with the finding of a somewhat higher validity for the Key Questions measure (Table 7). It is interesting to note that the highest predictive validity coefficient came from the free response item calling for special comments and an indication of personal enthusiasm. The actual employment recommendation, which used a simple Yes-No format, was only marginally significant as a predictor.

When the seven items noted were combined into a single interview measure (for manager and personnel administrator interviewers) by the horizontal per cent method, the resulting score yielded biserial correlations with the promotion criterion of .52 and .47 in the samples of studies three and four respectively. For the two groups combined the value was .50. All three coefficients are significant well beyond the .01 level.

Discussion

Promotion was the only one of the four criterion measures studied that yielded evidence of the interview's predictive validity. Certainly a factor in this finding was the greater reliability of the interview judgments relating to those individuals who were subsequently promoted. When these more reliably evaluated subjects were included in the analysis, validity emerged where it had previously been lacking. It is not clear why these differences in reliability were present. Apparently interview length was not a factor, since the reports of time spent with candidates were essentially the same for all groups studied.

Although reliability differentials would appear to be the major factor in the pattern of results, one cannot entirely dismiss the possibility that the promotion criterion may have been contaminated to some degree. There is a possibility that the necessary independence of predictor and criterion measures was lacking in that managers may have attempted to obtain promotions for those men whom they evaluated favorably in the pre-employment interview. By doing this they could demonstrate the validity of their initial predictions, and their own omniscience, quite independent of an individual's actual performance level.

The evidence on this point is of two kinds. First, there is the differential in the predictive power of the various types of interviewers. The rank order of positive validities appears to be for personnel administrators to come first, managers in the major office second, managers in the minor offices and professionals in the major office tied for third, and professionals in the minor offices last—with this latter group completely out of tune with the others. This ranking probably is consistent with the degree of knowledgeability regarding the value system of the organization. But it is not consistent with the extent of opportunity to influence promotions. This is a professional organization and promotional decisions are made by the most influential professionals on a participative basis, i.e., by the existing partners. The manager interviewers might have created self-validating predictions, but neither the personnel administrators nor the professionals were in any position to do so. Thus, the personnel administrator findings cannot be explained on this basis.

The second line of evidence arises from the fact that nominations for promotion are initiated by the office where a consultant is working. Thus, for self-validating prediction to operate, a man would have to be promoted in an office where at least one manager who interviewed him originally was also employed. Any evidence that men who were promoted spent their submanagerial professional careers in offices with manager interviewers more frequently than men with equally high manager interview scores who were not promoted (separatees) would tend to support the criterion contamination hypothesis.

To test this hypothesis the 42 men who were promoted were paired with 42 separatees on the basis of initial interview scores and type of office (major or minor) from which promotion or separation occurred. The separatee group had an average performance rating of only 3.0 ("Sorry to have the individual leave—there is reason to believe he might have developed further") on the 5-point scale. A check was then made to see whether the first (promoted) group more frequently had a manager interviewer in the same office.

The data do not fit the hypothesis. Of those promoted, 69 per cent spent their submanagerial careers in offices with managers who interviewed them. Rather than being much lower, as the hypothesis would require, this proportion was actually higher in the nonpromotion, separatee group—76 per cent. Thus, differentials in *opportunity* to influence promotions cannot account for the differences in success. Furthermore, it is apparent that a high interview score is no guarantee of promotion.

Taken as a whole the available information does not *prove* that initial interview reactions did not influence subsequent promotions in certain selected cases, but a lack of predictor-criterion independence is inadequate to account for all the positive results. The possibility of interviewer influence on promotion may be practically eliminated by taking only cases where all personnel administrator and manager interviews were conducted by individuals outside the office from which separation or promotion occurred. When this is done the tendency for higher interview scores to be associated with promotion remains (although the groups involved are too small to permit statistical analysis).

Another question raised by the findings has to do with the correlates of interview judgments (Table 9). The nature of the three significant relationships identified suggests that physical impact and bearing may have had a considerable influence on the interviewers. There is some support for this interpretation in a study conducted by Carroll (1966). He found that campus recruiters responded more favorably, in terms of subsequent opportunities provided for company visits, to male business school seniors who were consistently judged to be more handsome. Although this aspect of physical appearance was not considered in the present study, the sum total of these results would suggest that special attention to the physical variables of appearance, bearing and size might provide useful insights into the nature of the decision-making process in the interview.

The data of Table 11 on the various items are important as they relate to the question of which traits or characteristics yield the greatest validity when interview estimates are made. Recent literature reviews have not been entirely consistent in this area. Ulrich and Trumbo (1965) conclude that motivation to work and personal (social) relations contribute the most to interviewer decisions and yield the highest validity. Mayfield (1964) states that only mental abilities can be judged satisfactorily. Miner (1969a, 1969b) finds evidence supporting not only the Mayfield conclusion regarding mental abilities, but also self-confidence, effectiveness of expression, certain types of attitudes, and sociability.

In the present instance the measures in the social area (Personal impression, Effectiveness with people, Firm acceptance) did not prove to be effective predictors; nor did motivation to work (Initiative and sustained drive). On the other hand, the items that seem to have some relation to mental ability were more valid (Mental ability for problem solving, Imagination, Practical judgment).

The most striking finding of all was the high validity of the free comments. Here the interviewer was giving what might be described as his "gut" reaction to the man. He was in fact making an estimate of the probable match between the character of the candidate and the character of the organization, as he understood it.

To summarize briefly—it appears that the interview can make a useful contribution in the selection of consultants, but that in many instances it does not achieve anything approaching its potential. Considering matters of cost and validity, it would be better to make extensive use of personnel administrators, rather than practicing consultants. The interview might best be concentrated in those areas where valid predictions can be made—mental ability, self-confidence, promotion potential, and fit with the organizational value system. Finally every effort should be made to maximize agreement between interviewers. Reliability may be attained by averaging multiple interviews, but this is only a partial solution. The introduction of some structuring, perhaps through interviewer training, and constant feedback on the extent of agreement between interviewers seem desirable.

References

Association of Consulting Management Engineers. *Interviewing and testing techniques used in selecting management consulting personnel.* New York: the Association, 1964.

Carroll, S. J. Relationship of various college graduate characteristics to recruiting decisions. *Journal of Applied Psychology,* 1966, 50, 421-423.

Guion, R. M. *Personnel testing*. New York: McGraw-Hill, 1965.

Mayfield, E. C. The selection interview—A re-evaluation of published research. *Personnel Psychology,* 1964, 17, 239-260.

Miner, J. B. *Personnel and industrial relations: A managerial approach.* New York: Macmillan, 1969. (a).

Miner, J. B. *Personnel psychology*. New York: Macmillan, 1969. (b).

Miner, J. B. Psychological evaluations as predictors of consulting success. *Personnel Psychology,* 1970, 23, 393-405.

Ulrich, L. and Trumbo, D. The Selection Interview Since 1949. *Psychological Bulletin,* 1965, 63, 100-116.

11

validation study of personality tests

Introductory notes

The first study reported here was of a pilot nature, was concurrent in design, and was carried out in the same smaller United States office of the consulting firm as the other pilot studies. The personality tests had not been used previously; in fact no personality tests had been used by the firm except as they may have been included in outside psychological evaluations. Thus, in this case it was not possible to utilize data in the files, and any predictive study had to start "from scratch." In cases of this kind, it is generally advisable to do a concurrent study first; then, if validity is not established, the time and expense of predictive research can be avoided. In the present case the concurrent study was successful and accordingly predictive research was initiated. The tests were administered during an orientation training program, since this provided a convenient opportunity to test all new hires over a given time span. In order to obtain sufficient data, several successive offerings of the training program spanning roughly a 10-month period were utilized.

In a job like the consultant's, it takes a considerable period of time for performance rating, compensation change, and per diem change to develop much meaning. The consultants do not work for a single superior, but for many, and each superior needs time to develop a reliable and appropriate opinion. This fact plus the need to accumulate the sample over a sufficient time period resulted in a relatively extended study in the present instance. Under some other circumstances such predictive research often can be carried out over a much shorter time span.

The results indicate good validity for one of the personality tests in the United States offices of the firm. Yet the pattern of scores contributing to this validity is quite different, and is to a large extent the antithesis of that producing a similar level of validity outside the U.S., primarily in Europe. Although these findings for foreign nationals working in other countries have little direct significance for EEO compliance under U.S. law, they do point up an important consideration. Where work is performed in a much different context (in this case in different cultures) utilizing quite different types of people, it often is necessary to validate in separate locations, even for the same job within a single company. Whether this is true depends on the degree of similarity of contexts and people.

In general the findings do support the use of the one personality test within the United States. Both concurrent and predictive studies yield similar results. EEOC probably would argue for further, differential validation, but this could be carried out as increasing numbers of women and minority-group members are recruited and hired. In all likelihood EEOC would view increased minority and female recruiting coupled with an "in process" differential validity study as evidence of good faith and would delay any further immediate action with regard to this particular test. The one consideration most likely to produce a more negative reaction from EEOC would be evidence of adverse impact associated with the test.

Data bearing on the matter of adverse impact are not available with reference to this specific firm, of course, but they are available for the population as a whole. Generally women and men differ very little in their responses to the test and thus no adverse impact should be anticipated. Minorities and whites do differ rather greatly on a number of the tests' measures, in fact on roughly half of them. However, when these particular differences are compared against the findings of the validation research, it appears that minorities are just as likely to score high (like successful consultants) on the measures that emerge as valid as to score low (like less successful consultants). Thus, again, adverse impact should not be anticipated from use of the test in selection. This evidence might even be used to argue that the personality test be given precedence over interviews in the selection process.

PERSONALITY TESTS AS PREDICTORS OF CONSULTING SUCCESS*

Two previous articles have discussed the effectiveness of psychological evaluations (Miner, 1970a) and executive and personnel interviews (Miner, 1970b) as selection procedures used by consulting firms in hiring people for positions as consultants. In general the evidence has been that, in the forms most typically used in the past, these procedures have contributed very little toward predictive efficiency.

The studies considered here extend the prior analyses within the personality sphere. The original objective was to identify procedures that might supplement the psychological evaluations in this respect. At least as important as the objective of establishing predictors for use in selection, however, is the goal of learning about consulting success. What kinds of people, with what personality characteristics, perform effectively within the role structure of a successful management consulting firm?

Procedure

The *first* study was concurrent in nature and utilized as subjects all 24 consultants below the managerial level who were employed in a single office of an international management consulting firm. The office was located in the United States, and all those studied were citizens of this country. On the average the subjects had been employed by the organization in a consulting capacity for 2.3 years at the time the research was carried out; the average age was 30.

Two measures were administered under controlled conditions during the regular work day. The first was the Tomkins-Horn Picture Arrangement Test (PAT), a general personality measure, (Tomkins and Miner, 1957); the second, the Miner Sentence Completion Scale (MSCS), a measure of managerial motivation, (Miner, 1965). The PAT was scored using a simplified approach-avoidance procedure which yields 37 continuous measures in the areas of work motivation (10), social motivation (10), inner-life (8), self-

*Reprinted with permission from *Personnel Psychology,* Vol. 24 (1971), 191-204.

confidence (3), dependence (3), conformity (2) and emotional instability (Miner, 1969). The MSCS with eight measures provides information on attitudes toward authority figures, competitive motivation (2), attitudes toward the masculine role, power motivation, attitudes toward a differentiated role, attitudes toward administrative responsibility, and a total score.

Four different criteria of consulting success were obtained at approximately the same time as the tests were administered. Ratings were made by managers in the same office, for whom the subjects had worked. On the average each consultant was rated 2.5 times on a form that contained items dealing with problem-solving skills, client relations, firm acceptance, managerial capability, overall effectiveness, and potential for advancement. The first four items were combined to yield an average rating, which had a reliability of .88 calculated by correlating pairs of ratings. The overall rating had a reliability of .84 and the potential rating .91. The other, more specific items produced considerably lower reliabilities (all below .65), and for that reason were not considered except as they contributed to the average rating. All three rating criteria were intercorrelated in the .90s.

A fourth success criterion was the individual's total annual compensation as of the time of the study. This reward index was reasonably well correlated with the three value indices—.67 with average rating, .59 with overall rating, and .58 with potential rating.

The *second* study was undertaken as a replication of the first, with two major additions. First, the 51 subjects were employed in six different United States offices of the firm rather than one (as in the first study all subjects were citizens of this country). In addition, the research was predictive rather than concurrent in design. Testing was carried out an average of four months after hiring, during a centralized orientation program. Success criteria were collected an average of one year and seven months later. At this time the consultants were approximately 29 and one-half years of age on the average.

The personality measures were correlated with success criteria which differed in several respects from those used in the initial study. The ratings were made by either two or three managers with whom the consultant had worked for an extended period of time. In general these managers were employed in the same office, but this was not always the case. Presumably because opportunities for a common value structure to develop among the raters were less, the correlations between raters were lower in this study than in the first. The overall rating had a reliability of .74 and the advancement potential rating .76; all others were below .70 and thus were excluded from further consideration. The two ratings used were correlated .94.

The compensation criteria were total annual compensation at the time of follow-up and compensation change per year from hiring to follow-up, both corrected for regional differences. These two were correlated .53 and correlations with the rating criteria ranged from .45 to .72. In addition, the per diem charge being made to clients for a consultant's services at the time of follow-up was also used as an index of success. This was most closely related to total compensation (.85), but none of the correlations with other criteria were below .50.

The *third* study was also predictive and used the same success criteria, but the subjects differed in a number of respects. All 30 were employed in six offices of the firm located outside the United States, most of them in Europe. None were United States citizens. Ten were from Great Britain, five from Germany, four from France, three from Switzerland, two from the Netherlands and the rest from places as diverse as South Africa and Argentina.

As in study two testing followed hiring by approximately four months, but the follow-up was later by some four months ($t = 2.91$, $p < .01$). Also these consultants employed in offices outside the United States tended to be older, 31 years and eight months as contrasted with 29 years and six months ($t = 3.09$, $p < .01$) for the United States group.

In general the correlations among criteria were similar in studies two and three. The two ratings correlated .95. The compensation measures correlated .60 with each other and in the range .56 to .69 with the ratings. The per diem charge to clients, which in this instance required correction for geographical variations, was again closely associated with total compensation with a value of .80. The correlations with ratings were much the same as in the prior study also—.47 and .60. But the correlation between the per diem charge and compensation change per year declined from .50 to .27.

Results

The correlations between PAT and MSCS measures of personality and the four success criteria of study one are contained in Table 1. Only correlations with $p < .10$ are reported.

Of the 37 PAT measures eight correlate with one or more of the criteria at the .01 level or better, seven are in the .01 to .05 range, and four in the .05 to .10 range. Thus, some degree of significance is obtained on over half the measures. The successful consultant tends to score low on measures of active work motivation, high on social motivation, high on negative feelings (and low on positive), and low on dependence. In contrast to the PAT, the MSCS produced only one correlation in the .05 to .10 range.

The data of Table 2 provide a check on the findings of study one, although because of its predictive nature and more extensive sampling, study two is not in the true sense a replication. Once again the PAT yields a number of significant correlations. The actual magnitude of the values is somewhat less (as one might expect with a predictive study), but significance levels are maintained—five at the .01 level or below, thirteen between .01 and .05, and six in the .05 to .10 range.

To a large extent this second study does support the first. Of the 19 PAT measures which attained the .10 level or better in study one, 15 do so in study two and 13 have $p < .05$ (using a two-tailed test). Failure to confirm is most pronounced in the case of the inner-life scores. The findings of low work motivation, high social motivation (except with peer groups), and low dependence among the more successful consultants are supported. In addition, marginally significant evidence is present to suggest a lack of self-confidence and high emotional stability. There are no reversals from study one to study two in the direction of the significant findings.

The MSCS correlations are once again generally low. The one trend to significance of study one is not supported. There is consistent evidence across a number of criteria that the imposing wishes measure of power motivation is related to success, but in view of the lack of results on this measure in the first study generalization is not warranted.

Separate analyses using the Vocabulary Test G-T indicate that

Table 1

Correlations between Test Variables and Criteria of Success
(N = 24)

	Success Criteria							
	Average Rating		Overall Rating		Potential Rating		Total Compensation	
Test Measures	*r*	*p*	*r*	*p*	*r*	*p*	*r*	*p*
Active Work Motivation (PAT)								
When passivity at work is possible	—	—	—	—	—	—	−.48	<.05
When passivity at work is not possible	—	—	—	—	—	—	−.42	<.05
When work problems are present	—	—	—	—	—	—	−.36	<.10
When distractions are present	—	—	—	—	—	—	−.40	<.05
Indirect approach to active work	—	—	—	—	—	—	−.43	<.05
Total active work motivation score	—	—	—	—	—	—	−.52	<.01
Social Motivation (PAT)								
In nonwork situations	.44	<.05	—	—	—	—	.43	<.05
With authority figures at work	—	—	—	—	—	—	.42	<.05
When close proximity is involved	.55	<.01	.45	<.05	.46	<.05	.39	<.10
When support is involved	—	—	—	—	—	—	.43	<.05
Direct approach to social interaction	.50	<.05	.38	<.10	.34	<.10	.54	<.01
Direct avoidance of social interaction	−.37	<.10	−.37	<.10	—	—	—	—
Total social motivation score	.49	<.05	.38	<.10	.35	<.10	.52	<.01
Inner Life (PAT)								
Positive feelings	−.60	<.01	−.67	<.01	−.67	<.01	−.36	<.10
Negative feelings	—	—	—	—	—	—	.51	<.01
Indirect approach to inner life	—	—	−.34	<.10	−.38	<.10	—	—
Indirect avoidance of inner life	.36	<.10	.36	<.10	.38	<.10	—	—
Dependence (PAT)								
Positive responses to support	—	—	—	—	—	—	−.51	<.01
Total dependence score	—	—	—	—	—	—	−.51	<.01
Managerial Motivation (MSCS)								
Standing out from group	.36	<.10	—	—	—	—	—	—

$p < .10$.

Table 2

Correlations between Test Variables and Criteria of Subsequent Success
(N = 51)

	Success Criteria									
	Overall Rating		Potential Rating		Total Compensation		Compensation Change		Per Diem Change	
Test Measures	*r*	*p*	*r*	*p*	*r*	*p*	*r*	*p*	*r*	*p*
Active Work Motivation (PAT)										
When passivity at work is possible	—	—	—	—	−.23	<.10	−.35	<.01	—	—
When passivity at work is not possible	—	—	—	—	−.37	<.01	—	—	−.31	<.05
When work problems are present	—	—	—	—	−.31	<.05	−.26	<.10	−.29	<.05
When distractions are present	—	—	—	—	−.42	<.01	—	—	−.27	<.05
Direct approach to active work	—	—	—	—	−.31	<.05	−.26	<.10	—	—
Indirect approach to active work	—	—	—	—	−.27	<.05	—	—	—	—
Direct avoidance of active work	—	—	—	—	—	—	.30	<.05	—	—
Indirect avoidance of active work	—	—	—	—	—	—	.26	<.10	—	—
Total active work motivation score	—	—	—	—	−.39	<.01	−.29	<.05	−.28	<.05
Social Motivation (PAT)										
In nonwork situations	—	—	—	—	—	—	−.33	<.05	—	—
With authority figures at work	—	—	—	—	.38	<.01	—	—	.26	<.10
With groups of people	—	—	—	—	—	—	—	—	−.28	<.05
When close proximity is involved	—	—	—	—	.24	<.10	—	—	.23	<.10
When support is involved	—	—	—	—	.28	<.05	.30	<.05	.25	<.10
Direct approach to social interaction	—	—	—	—	.25	<.10	—	—	—	—
Direct avoidance of social interaction	—	—	—	—	−.27	<.05	—	—	—	—
Total social motivation score	—	—	—	—	.32	<.05	—	—	.25	<.10
Inner Life (PAT)										
Direct avoidance of inner life	—	—	—	—	−.28	<.05	—	—	—	—
Indirect avoidance of inner life	—	—	—	—	.24	<.10	—	—	.31	<.05
Self-Confidence (PAT)										
Approach responses to success	—	—	—	—	—	—	−.24	<.10	—	—
Avoidance responses to success	—	—	—	—	—	—	.27	<.05	—	—

Table 2—*continued*

	Success Criteria									
	Overall Rating		Potential Rating		Total Compensation		Compensation Change		Per Diem Change	
Test Measures	*r*	*p*	*r*	*p*	*r*	*p*	*r*	*p*	*r*	*p*
Total self-confidence score	—	—	—	—	—	—	−.26	<.10	—	—
Dependence (PAT)										
Positive responses to support	—	—	—	—	−.27	<.05	—	—	—	—
Emotional Instability (PAT)	−.24	<.10	−.26	<.10	—	—	—	—	—	—
Managerial Motivation (MSCS)										
Competitive games	—	—	—	—	—	—	—	—	.23	<.10
Imposing wishes	.31	<.05	.30	<.05	.41	<.01	—	—	.36	<.01
Total score	—	—	—	—	.24	<.10	—	—	—	—

$p < .10$.

both the PAT and MSCS measures are independent of intelligence in the samples of studies one and two. Thus the personality test results cannot be accounted for on the basis of an association with intelligence.

The results presented in Table 3 on the consultants employed in offices outside the United States depart in a number of respects from those for the two previous studies. The PAT measures yield correlations which attain the .05 level in eight instances and which are in the .05 to .10 range in four more cases. Yet these findings rarely support those for the United States consultants and quite frequently directly contradict them.

In the case of social motivation in non-work situations the more successful consultants do tend to obtain higher scores in all three studies. But there are nine measures which produced some degree of significance in study two which yield significant correlations in the reverse direction in study three. The remaining 14 measures with significant coefficients from study two do not find any support in study three. The data make it clear that the personality factors making for

Table 3

Correlations between Test Variables and Criteria of Subsequent Success—Offices Outside U.S.
($N = 30$)

	Success Criteria									
	Overall Rating		Potential Rating		Total Compensation		Compensation Change		Per Diem Change	
Test Measures	*r*	*p*	*r*	*p*	*r*	*p*	*r*	*p*	*r*	*p*
Active Work Motivation (PAT)										
When leaving work is possible	.41	<.05	.42	<.05	—	—	—	—	—	—
When distractions are present	—	—	—	—	—	—	—	—	.39	<.05
Direct approach to active work	.38	<.05	.43	<.05	—	—	—	—	.37	<.05
Direct avoidance of active work	—	—	—	—	—	—	—	—	−.40	<.05
Indirect avoidance of active work	−.34	<.10	−.39	<.05	—	—	—	—	−.31	<.10
Total active work motivation score	.32	<.10	.34	<.10	—	—	—	—	.37	<.05
Social Motivation (PAT)										
In nonwork situations	—	—	—	—	.32	<.10	—	—	—	—
When support is involved	—	—	−.36	<.05	—	—	—	—	—	—
Indirect approach to social interaction	—	—	—	—	—	—	−.34	<.10	—	—
Direct avoidance of social interaction	—	—	—	—	—	—	.37	<.05	—	—
Inner Life (PAT)										
Direct avoidance of inner life	—	—	—	—	—	—	—	—	.33	<.10
Dependence (PAT)										
Positive responses to support	.33	<.10	—	—	—	—	—	—	—	—
Managerial Motivation (MSCS)										
Competitive games	—	—	—	—	—	—	—	—	.32	<.10
Standing out from group	—	—	—	—	—	—	−.34	<.10	—	—
Total score	—	—	—	—	—	—	—	—	.32	<.10

p <.10.

success among non-United States citizens working outside this country are not the same as those that produce success among United States citizens in United States offices. Although further study on additional samples is needed to fix the conclusions with certainty, it appears that success outside the United States often goes to those who have characteristics associated with failure in this country—those with strong work motivation, a tendency to avoid social interaction and perhaps a high level of dependence.

The MSCS data do not attain acceptable levels of significance. It is interesting to note, however, that the association between power motivation and success, which was so evident in study two, is not present outside the United States.

The composite scores

In order to obtain composite measures from the test, weights were assigned to different score levels on those PAT variables which had predictive validity, using the horizontal per cent method (Guion, 1965). Separate scores were developed for use in United States offices and for those outside the United States.

To use the horizontal per cent method the United States consultants were divided into more successful and less successful groups. The percentage split was 43—57 with the successful designation limited to those individuals who were consistently above average on the various criterion measures. The biserial correlations between this success dichotomy and the composite score for United States offices was .65 when PAT measures only were used and .68 when MSCS measures were added. These composite scores correlate —.11 and —.15 respectively with intelligence as measured by the Vocabulary Test G-T. Neither correlation approaches significance.

Further evidence of the value of the composite PAT score for United States offices comes from tests administered to a small sample of individuals promoted to managerial responsibility in the firm. Three of these men were at the senior level and the other five were junior managers. All were promoted and still employed in United States offices when tested. The average score for the senior managers places them at the 72d percentile among consultants below the managerial level (all were above the 50th percentile). The average score for the junior managers was at the 67th percentile, although in two instances their scores were below the 50 percentile point. In these two instances the individuals involved have had greater difficulty than the other six during their consulting careers and advancement has come slowly. One (the one with the lowest score) has since separated and taken a position outside consulting.

Because of the small number of subjects and the lack of cross-validation the results obtained with the composite scores for offices outside the United States must be considered tentative. Applying the same criteria as with the United States sample a success dichotomy was established with a percentage split of 47—53. The biserial correlation between the PAT score and this success index was .82. This increased to .83 when the MSCS was included. The correlations between these scores and the Vocabulary Test G-T are —.08 and —.09 respectively. However, there is reason to question the use of this measure as an index of intelligence in this instance since a majority of the subjects had learned English as a second language.

Analysis of verbal responses

Among the findings emerging from studies one and two by far the most unexpected, while at the same time the most pronounced, is the pattern of strong avoidance motivation with regard to active work that was found to characterize the more successful consultants. The evidence seems to indicate a strong desire to avoid working—either to be passive or to do something else. But there is no evidence to indicate a desire to actually leave the work environment. The successful consultant appears to be a person who wants to stay in the work context, while at the same time avoiding actually doing the work. He is anything but super-ego driven insofar as work is concerned; when distractions are present, he is distracted. He does not want to solve problems and overcome obstacles in order to get on with the job. In the problem-solving context he prefers to avoid a solution that will commit him to actually carrying out the work.

These conclusions, based on the approach-avoidance scoring scales, leave one question unanswered. Are the successful consultants really motivated to avoid work in all its aspects, or are they simply avoiding *active* work—the doing or implementing aspects? It seems entirely possible that in moving away from active work they are often moving toward thinking and feeling about work, and that when they are not working there is a good reason involved other than mere laziness.

The approach-avoidance scales in themselves are not adequate to answer this question. But the brief verbal statements each subject writes describing the pictures of the Picture Arrangement Test provide an additional source of information. From these it is possible to get a specific statement of what the subject thinks a person might be doing if he is not actually engaged in active work.

To test the hypothesis that the successful consultants were in fact exhibiting approach motivation to performance and work related thought, even if not to active work itself, three sub-hypotheses were formulated in terms of specific measurement operations:

1. Successful consultants, more frequently than less successful, will describe a person depicted in a work context, but not working, as engaged in thinking or feeling with regard to the performance of work.
2. Successful consultants, more frequently than less successful, will describe a person depicted in a work context, but not working, as waiting to perform a work task.
3. Successful consultants, more frequently than less successful, will describe a person depicted in a work context, but not working, as not expected to work rather than as engaging in a minor or major infraction of work rules.

Examples of responses in the various categories are given in Table 4. Scoring was restricted to the 14 of the 25 PAT plates that deal with the work context. On these plates only verbal responses to pictures portraying passivity or activities far removed from active work were considered. Verbal responses to non-work pictures could not be placed in any of the categories of analysis. Thus, subjects typically had far less than 14 verbal responses actually included in the analysis.

In order to test the hypothesis two groups of consultants employed in United States offices were compared. The successful sample contained the 20 individuals who consistently had the highest values on the various success criteria utilized in study two. The

Table 4

Examples of Verbal Response Scoring

Category	Verbal Response
Inner-life	
Performance related	1. Plans how to best do his work
	2. Concerned about his performance
	3. Analyzes the difficulty and solves the problem
Not performance related	1. Pursues his daydream
	2. Criticizes the boss to himself
	3. Has a personal problem and cannot work with concentration
Waiting	
Performance related	1. Stops work to simply wait for help
	2. Waits for the next job
	3. Waiting for the start of his shift
Not performance related	1. Waits for his friends at the end of the day
	2. Waiting for lunch
	3. Waits for the break
Not working	
Not expected	1. Idle time, no fault of his own
	2. There's not enough work
	3. Has to quit because he's sick
Minor infraction	1. Relaxes for a minute
	2. Remembers a joke and tells his buddies
	3. Taking a break before resuming his task
Major infraction	1. Loafing and talking about vacation
	2. Is bored, tired and doesn't work
	3. By careful goldbricking he ends up in the hospital

unsuccessful sample contained the 20 who consistently had the lowest values on these criteria. As indicated in Table 5 these two groups did differ significantly both on the PAT composite score for United States offices and in total active work motivation score. The successful consultants had higher composite scores and were distinctly more avoidant with regard to active work.

The evidence of Table 5 generally supports the hypothesis. The two groups do not differ in the total number of inner life, waiting, or not working verbal responses given, but within these three categories differences between types of responses are present. The successful give performance related inner life responses more frequently than the less successful, and they give inner life responses that are clearly not performance related less frequently. The data for waiting re-

Table 5

Comparisons of Various Picture Arrangement Test Measures for Successful and Unsuccessful U.S. Consultants

Picture Arrangement Test Measure	$\bar{X}$ for Successful (N = 20)	$\bar{X}$ for Unsuccessful (N = 20)	t	p
Composite score	45.90	34.75	4.40	<.01
Total active work motivation score	–14.30	5.35	2.41	<.05
Verbal Responses				
Inner life total	3.85	3.70	.24	n.s.
Performance related	2.35	1.00	2.67	<.05
Not performance related	1.50	2.70	2.56	<.05
Waiting total	2.40	2.45	.07	n.s.
Performance related	2.25	1.90	.61	n.s.
Not performance related	.15	.55	1.77	<.10
Not working total	2.15	1.65	1.34	n.s.
Not expected	.85	.15	2.60	<.05
Minor infraction	.50	.55	.19	n.s.
Major infraction	.80	.95	.53	n.s.
Performance related or not expected to work	5.45	3.05	3.57	<.01

sponses are less clear-cut, but there is a tendency for waiting which is not performance-related to be higher among the less successful. Among not working responses, the not expected category has a higher frequency for the successful than the unsuccessful. Finally, when the three appropriate categories are combined to provide an overall test of the hypothesis the results yield very strong support for it.

It appears that the more successful consultants, in spite of their greater avoidance motivation insofar as *active* work is concerned, are more involved with thoughts and feelings about work, and have very good task-related reasons when they are not working. The data suggest that in the United States the effective consultant tends to be patient and responsive to aspects of the environment rather than to inner work needs. He is concerned about work, he thinks about matters related to work performance, but he does not move readily into the position of actually doing things himself. Much more than his less successful colleagues he appears to be a planner rather than a doer. What evidence we have suggests, however, that this pattern is completely reversed outside the United States, particularly in Europe.

Discussion

The results obtained with the personality tests are consistent with the interview study findings (Miner, 1970b), while extending them in a number of respects. The stress on planning and thinking rather than doing, in particular, fits well with the interview findings indicating the importance of mental ability, imagination and practical judgment. In the social sphere the more successful consultants seem drawn to authority figures, they do not want to be alone when away from work, they prefer physically close relationships, and they move toward supportive relationships. But support is desired for its own sake, presumably in conjunction with the desire to be with authority figures, rather than as a means to getting "geared up" for action. These are people who are quite capable of acting independently even though they seek out close, approving relationships with those in positions of authority. In addition the successful consultants are not characterized by approach motivation insofar as groups of peers are concerned. They want to spend their time with those who are above them rather than with "the boys." Yet their attitudes toward these authority figures are not particularly positive.

These characteristics seem to make considerable sense in a group of people who spend their working hours, and many of their non-working hours as well, in social interaction with the leaders of large corporations. And whose role in these relationships is to plan and think rather than actually carry out and do.

These conclusions regarding the successful consultant apply only in the United States context and they derive almost entirely from the PAT, not the MSCS. The evidence that success in consulting work can derive from other personality patterns, based on the results obtained with the sample from offices outside the United States, suggests that different consulting organizations having different types of relationships with clients may require different personality characteristics. It seems likely that these types of client relationships are particularly likely to vary from culture to culture.

In view of the trend of recent research findings with the MSCS it does not now appear surprising that this measure failed to predict in the consulting context. It has become increasingly clear that the

MSCS variables are of particular significance for relatively large administrative or bureaucratic organizations. They are of much less importance in relation to the value and reward structures of professional organizations, such as consulting firms (Miner, 1971).

References

Guion, R.M. *Personnel testing*. New York: McGraw-Hill, 1965.

Miner, J.B. *Studies in management education*. New York: Springer, 1965.

Miner, J.B. *Simplified scoring procedure—Tomkins-Horn Picture Arrangement Test*. [Atlanta, Ga.: Organizational Measurement Systems Press, 1969.]

Miner, J.B. Psychological evaluations as predictors of consulting success. *Personnel Psychology,* 1970, 23, 393-405. (a)

Miner, J.B. Executive and personnel interviews as predictors of consulting success. *Personnel Psychology,* 1970, 23, 521-538. (b)

Miner, J.B. *Management theory*. New York: Macmillan, 1971.

Tomkins, S.S. and Miner, J.B. *The Tomkins-Horn Picture Arrangement Test*. New York:Springer, 1957.

12

validation study of biographical data

Introductory notes

This research on biographical information was initiated in the small office of the consulting firm used in the other pilot studies. However, because the identification of individual items that might prove predictive requires good-sized samples, no formal study was carried out there. Certain trends in the data did suggest that a biographical approach might yield useful results, and consequently more comprehensive research was undertaken using samples which overlapped in large part with those of the psychological evaluation and interview studies. Subsequently, the current consultants in the same smaller office were employed in the cross-validation study for the composite biographical index noted in this chapter.

The predictor data for this research were all developed from various file sources, primarily but not exclusively application forms and résumés. All of the criterion information was used in validation studies of other selection techniques as well. The outcome of this research was a brief application blank entitled "Biographical Information—Consulting Staff," as given in the appendix to this chapter. This form could be scored in terms of weights assigned to different responses, the greater number of points being given to responses which had been found to be more predictive of consulting success.

A brief overview of this scoring process as applied to the nine predictive items is given below:

1. Extent of prior business experience
   Less than 1½ years—3 points

1½ to 5½ years—0 points
More than 5½ years—2 points

2. Type of prior business experience
   No business experience—3 points
   Business experience without managerial responsibility—0 points
   Business experience with managerial responsibility—3 points
3. Branch of service
   No active duty service—1 point
   Service in the Army, Air Force, or Coast Guard—1 point
   Service in the Navy or Marines—3 points
4. Type of military experience
   No active duty service—1 point
   Active duty without commissioned rank—0 points
   Active duty with commissioned rank—3 points
5. Type of secondary schooling
   Public or Catholic high school—1 point
   Private preparatory school—3 points
6. Type of college graduated from
   State college or university—0 points
   Small college—3 points
   Large private or municipal college or university—2 points
7. Graduate education
   No advanced degree—1 point
   Business or law degree from a recruiting priority school—2 points
   Harvard Business School degree—3 points
   Advanced degree other than those noted above—0 points
8. Extent of father's education
   Did not graduate from high school—3 points
   High school graduate or some college—1 point
   College degree—0 points
9. Father's highest occupational attainment
   Small businessman or corporate manager below middle level—3 points
   Non-professional, outside business—2 points
   Professional, outside business—1 point
   Middle or upper level corporate manager—0 points

It should be emphasized that merely because biographical information could be grouped and scored in this way does not mean that it had been so used prior to the validation research. In fact a comparison of the composite biographical scores for a group of individuals hired in one office of the firm with another group of candidates who were not hired during the same time period indicated practically no difference. Thus, it appears that although the firm had the needed biographical data, these data were not being employed effectively for lack of adequate validation information.

On the other hand, with the development of the composite biographical information index this situation changed, bringing with that change the possibility of easily demonstrating any subsequent adverse impact. With accelerated recruiting of women and minorities several of the items in the index could well serve to reduce the probability of actually hiring those who were recruited. Certainly the validity of this type of selection instrument should be studied in all groups separately. It may well be that items and weights different from those developed for white men are needed for women and for minorities. In addition measures of this kind have a tendency to lose their predictive power over time. Thus, the validity should be checked frequently and changes introduced in items and weights as needed. It would be rare indeed for a biographical index to retain its predictive capabilities intact for a period as long as five years, simply because societies, and the types of experiences people have within them, tend to change.

SUCCESS IN MANAGEMENT CONSULTING AND THE CONCEPT OF ELITENESS MOTIVATION*

Since biographical inventories first came into general use about 30 years ago, there have been a wide variety of studies relating various background factors to indexes of occupational success. A major focus of this research has been on management positions in business organizations. Although efforts to relate biographical data to managerial performance have not always produced meaningful results,

*Reprinted with permission from *Academy of Management Journal,* Vol. 14 (1971), 367-378.

those studies that have been successful have often identified very similar patterns in the life histories of the more effective managers. This common element has been variously described as a "life-style of success" [1, p. 196] or a "total life pattern of successful endeavor" [7, p. 112].

One of the hypotheses investigated in the present study relates to this "pattern-of-success" finding. More specifically, an attempt is made to determine whether the results obtained with managerial samples in business organizations could be extended to practitioners in professional organizations. The data derive from the various offices of a very successful and prestigious international management consulting firm. This organization appears particularly well suited to the investigation of the particular hypothesis, because it is a widely accepted belief among the partners that a history of outstanding accomplishment prior to joining the firm is prognostic of future success in consulting. The standard selection interview reporting form, for example, contained an item labelled, "pattern of success." (Over his lifetime—and particularly in recent years—has this man a record of excelling? Is he, in terms of responsibility, accomplishment, and financial progress "ahead of his class"?)

The second hypothesis considered was also a part of the lore of this particular firm. This hypothesis holds that successful consultants to business management typically come from socioeconomic, educational, and occupation backgrounds that provide maximum exposure to the corporate top management "culture." Such exposure is assumed to yield not only greater personal effectiveness in dealing with people in top management positions, but also greater access to future clients for the firm. Thus, the interview reporting form asks—Does this man appear to have qualities that would enable him to become a clientele builder?

The particular organization involved seemed as ideally suited to testing the "top management culture" hypothesis as the "pattern of success" hypothesis. In view of the basic assumptions held widely in the firm, it seemed unlikely, if the hypotheses did not receive considerable support here, that they would be supported in other professional organizations. Thus, the research strategy involved an initial testing of the hypotheses in a "high probability" context. Then, if they were confirmed, subsequent testing in other professional organizations would take place to establish the boundaries of generalization. It is this initial testing that is described in the present paper.

Method

The major office study

The organization studied has an "up or out" policy which guarantees that if a consultant is not elected to partnership by his ninth year, at the very latest, he will leave the firm. This situation provided an opportunity to obtain an evaluation of the individual based on his entire career there. For those who were promoted, election to partnership provided a similar evaluation over an initial period of employment which averaged 6¼ years.

The consultants' work itself is primarily carried out in large business organizations and at the top management level. Consultants work in teams and, during the period prior to promotion, are in large part interchangeable among assignments. Consequently, the great majority of consultants develop as generalists rather than specialists, although the nature of the firm's work is such that financial affairs are involved to a much greater extent than questions of human or material resources. The firm relies on an extensive research staff to provide specialized information to the consultants, but these research personnel were not included in the present analyses.

The initial study was conducted using consultants who had been either separated or promoted from the firm's headquarters office, which also is the largest. There were 76 individuals who had separated over a 6-year span and 28 who had been promoted. Since most of the subjects already had left the firm, biographical information was obtained from the personnel files. In one sense this operated as a constraint, in that many items of information that might ideally have been used to test the hypotheses simply were not available. On the other hand, this approach had the advantage of permitting a predictive study covering a sizeable time span for all subjects (with the exception of five who separated in the first year after employment). The median period covered for the 76 individuals who separated was 3 years, 3 months.

Although the major sources of data were application blanks and resumes, psychological evaluation reports, physical examination forms, credit bureau investigation reports, and letters of reference also produced useful information on occasion. Although data on some 40 items were obtained from the files, only 15 of these were viewed as having any relevance for the hypotheses under investigation; thus, they are considered here. The five items used to test the first hypothesis (pattern of success) were as follows:

(1) Class standing in college,
(2) Class standing in graduate work,
(3) Advanced degree (including law) vs no advanced degree,
(4) Commissioned officer in service vs a lower rank or no service, and
(5) Experience in a managerial capacity in business vs experience in a nonmanagerial capacity.

These five types of items are often found to be associated with *managerial* success. Grades and educational level have been studied the most frequently and have yielded the largest number of significant relationships. The 10 items used to test the second hypothesis (top management culture) are:

(1) Father's educational level (years completed),
(2) Father held a high level position in a corporation vs only lower level positions or a position as a small businessman,
(3) Graduate of a private preparatory school vs high school graduate,
(4) Undergraduate degree from an ivy league school vs another type,
(5) Undergraduate degree from a small, private college vs another type,
(6) Harvard Business School graduate vs advanced degree from elsewhere,
(7) Advanced degree from a school given priority in the firm's recruiting efforts (Harvard, Columbia, Pennsylvania, Chicago, MIT, and Stanford Business, Yale Administrative Science, Harvard Law, and Cambridge) vs advanced degree from elsewhere,
(8) Service in the Navy (Marines) or Air Force vs service in the Army,

(9) Years of prior business experience (for those with business experience), and

(10) At least one officer of a business corporation listed as a reference vs no corporate officers.

The rationale behind the choice of these items requires explanation. It was thought that fathers with more education who had held positions either in top management or close to it would be more likely to provide their children with exposure to top management culture. Prep school and ivy league schools as well as small colleges such as Williams and Amherst provide upper socioeconomic associations. The graduate schools noted have the same quality, while at the same time bringing their students closer to present top level managers themselves. In general, these are considered to be prestige schools, and this particular consulting firm hires a number of their graduates. On this count, however, the list is not meant to be exhaustive. There are other prestige schools that the firm does not stress in its recruiting and which have not been included in the list.

The Navy and Air Force are included and set against the Army because the latter has historically relied more heavily on the draft and set lower selection standards of an intellectual nature, thus producing a socio-economic differential [3]. In all probability, the Navy attracts the highest socio-economic level. More years of business experience should provide greater opportunity for exposure to top management culture. The use of a company officer as a reference is predicated on the assumption that if an applicant knows a member of top management who might speak favorably of him, he will list his name in applying to a firm which does consulting with the upper echelons of business organizations.

These background factors were considered in relation to three types of success criteria. One was a performance rating by the manager in charge of the office:

(1) Sorry to have the individual leave—there is good reason to believe that he would have been promoted had he stayed,

(2) Sorry to have the individual leave—not a top prospect, but a good worker,

(3) Sorry to have the individual leave—there is reason to believe that he might have developed further,

(4) Not really sorry to have the individual leave, although his was not an involuntary separation,

(5) Glad to have the individual leave—including involuntary separations.

In addition, data were obtained on compensation changes and the mean increase per year was computed. The performance rating and compensation change measures were used with the 76 separatees only. The third success criterion was the fact of promotion vs separation short of promotion. In this case the 76 separatees were compared with the 28 elected to partnership.

Product-moment, biserial, or tetrachoric correlations were computed as appropriate to the data. With dichotomized variables, tests for differences between means or χ^2 were used to establish significance levels. The number of cases varied somewhat for different analyses depending on the group utilized and the availability of information. The lowest *N* for any analysis was 54, and the highest was 104.

The minor offices study

The second study was much the same as the first, but utilized consultants who were either separated or promoted from six smaller offices located in other parts of the United States and in Great Britain. The work performed in these offices is essentially the same as in the major office. Initial assignments to offices are largely a matter of personal preference and the individual's geographic location prior to hiring. Although individual minor offices do develop some variations in the type of work undertaken, all of these variants exist also in the major office. Thus, the two studies deal with comparable groups.

The separatee sample contained 51 individuals, 5 of whom left before one year. The longest employment period was 7 years, 10 months, and the median was, again, 3 years, 3 months. In the analyses involving promotion, the 51 who separated were compared with 25 who were elected to partnership from the same 6 offices. Because of differences in the availability of information and in the groups considered, the number of cases used in different analyses varied from 27 to 76, although very few analyses were based on an N of less than 35.

Cross-validation study

The objective of the research was to conduct a test of the two hypotheses in the firm as a whole, thus attaining the maximum generalization for analyses conducted within a single organization. The concern was not to predict for consultants hired recently or in times past; for those in one office, or another; or for those with various special areas of expertise. Rather, the concern was to identify factors that operated independently of these differences, and which might therefore emerge with some consistency in a variety of professional organizations. Such an approach does not maximize the size of correlations, but it does permit more extensive generalization.

Accordingly, among the 15 factors, those that showed some predictive consistency across the two studies (major and minor offices) were combined to yield a composite score using the horizontal percent method [4, pp. 385-387]. This score was then applied to all 24 currently employed consultants in a single minor office of the firm. The composite score based on the positive findings from the previous two studies was correlated with ratings of the performance of the 24 consultants in the office who had not been promoted, made by the existing partners in the office. This study permitted an application of the findings to the most current generation of consultants.

Relationships among success criteria

Data on the correlations between two of the success criteria are given in Table 1. The value structure, as reflected in the performance ratings, and the reward structure, as reflected in compensation change, are unusually closely related in all three samples.[1] Furthermore, it is clear, as the presence of an up-or-out policy would suggest, that the more effective consultants, by either definition, continue with the firm longer.

[1]For comparison data, see John B. Miner, "Bridging the Gulf in Organizational Performance," *Harvard Business Review,* 46, No. 4 (1968), pp. 102-110.

Table 1

Correlations between Value and Reward Indexes and of Each to Tenure

		Factors Correlated		
Group Studied	*N*	Ratings vs Compensation Change	Ratings vs Tenure	Compensation Change vs Tenure
Major office	76	0.65	0.55	0.44
Minor offices	51	0.67	0.45	0.46
Cross-validation	24	0.68	0.68	0.58

The third success measure, promotion, is also known to be closely related to the other two. At least at the time they were promoted, those elected to partnership were invariably rated very high, and their compensation progress had been superior to that of most of those who separated. Obviously also, those who had been promoted have longer tenure with the firm. At the time the study was carried out, the 28 men promoted in the major office had been with the firm from 6 years, 1 month to 16 years, 8 months; the 25 from the minor offices from 5 years, 9 months to 18 years, 2 months. This compared to an average of 3 years, 3 months for those who separated.

As these data on employment duration suggest, the promoted groups represent a rather different generation of consultants from the separatees, and, accordingly, the findings obtained with the first two success criteria may not be entirely comparable to those obtained with the third. Approximately 70 percent of those promoted were elected to partnership during the same 6 years that those who left the firm separated. However, on the average, promotions occurred at 35.8 years of age, while the separations occurred at 32.7 years. The 35 percent of the promoted group who had been elected to partnership more than 6 years previously were to a much greater extent a product of an earlier generation.

Results

The findings related to the first hypothesis are given in Table 2. Prior experience at the management level is consistently related to success, and similar experience in the armed forces is related to the promotion criterion. On the other hand, grades and educational level, which in studies of corporate managers have yielded positive results with some consistency, fail completely in this instance.

Findings from the tests of the second hypothesis also fail of confirmation. Contrary to expectations, fathers of the more successful consultants are *less* well educated and in *lower* level positions. On the other hand, graduation from Harvard Business School and the other prestige schools considered has consistently yielded success. Graduation from private prep schools and small private colleges is a plus among those who eventually separate, as is service in the Navy or Air Force. (Correlations for the Navy alone are higher than those given in Table 2 when the promotion measure of success is used—major office, $r = 0.37, p < 0.05$; minor office, $r = 0.18$, n.s.; all of-

Table 2

Relationships between Biographical Factors and Criteria of Subsequent Success—Test of the First Hypothesis

	Success Criteria					
	Performance Rating		Compensation Change		Promotion	
Biographical Factors	r	P	r	P	r	P
Class standing in college						
Major office	0.17	n.s.	0.13	n.s.	0.15	n.s.
Minor offices	0.14	n.s.	0.07	n.s.	0.09	n.s.
All offices	0.16	<0.10	0.13	n.s.	0.14	n.s.
Class standing in graduate work						
Major office	0.25	<0.10	0.22	<0.10	0.11	n.s.
Minor offices	0.12	n.s.	0.08	n.s.	−0.05	n.s.
All offices	0.18	<0.10	0.16	n.s.	0.05	n.s.
Earned an advanced degree						
Major office	0.03	n.s.	0.37	<0.05	0.11	n.s.
Minor offices	−0.23	n.s.	−0.21	n.s.	0.00	n.s.
All offices	−0.06	n.s.	0.14	n.s.	0.03	n.s.
Commissioned officer in service						
Major office	−0.16	n.s.	−0.08	n.s.	0.28	<0.10
Minor offices	−0.09	n.s.	0.13	n.s.	0.59	<0.01
All offices	−0.13	n.s.	0.01	n.s.	0.43	<0.01
Management position in business						
Major office	0.27	<0.10	0.17	n.s.	0.48	<0.01
Minor offices	0.51	<0.01	0.66	<0.01	0.20	n.s.
All offices	0.37	<0.01	0.37	<0.01	0.33	<0.01

Table 3

Relationships between Biographical Factors and Criteria of Subsequent Success—Test of the Second Hypothesis

	Success Criteria					
	Performance Rating		Compensation Change		Promotion	
Biographical Factors	*r*	*P*	*r*	*P*	*r*	*P*
Father's educational level						
Major office	−0.25	<0.05	−0.21	<0.10	0.09	n.s.
Minor offices	−0.15	n.s.	0.01	n.s.	−0.46	<0.05
All offices	−0.21	<0.05	−0.11	n.s.	−0.11	n.s.
Father held a high level position in a corporation						
Major office	−0.63	<0.01	−0.36	<0.05	−0.03	n.s.
Minor offices	−0.30	n.s.	−0.18	n.s.	−0.48	<0.10
All offices	−0.52	<0.01	−0.27	<0.05	−0.23	n.s.
Graduate of a private prep school						
Major office	0.27	<0.10	0.20	n.s.	0.25	n.s.
Minor offices	0.26	n.s.	0.32	n.s.	0.05	n.s.
All offices	0.26	<0.05	0.22	<0.10	0.12	n.s.
Graduate of an ivy league college						
Major office	−0.17	n.s.	−0.06	n.s.	0.04	n.s.
Minor offices	−0.05	n.s.	0.22	n.s.	0.13	n.s.
All offices	−0.13	n.s.	0.01	n.s.	0.08	n.s.
Graduate of a small private college						
Major office	0.17	n.s.	0.37	<0.05	−0.02	n.s.
Minor offices	0.51	<0.01	0.57	<0.01	0.12	n.s.
All offices	0.30	<0.05	0.44	<0.01	0.01	n.s.
Harvard Business School graduate						
Major office	0.26	n.s.	−0.06	n.s.	0.62	<0.01
Minor offices	0.43	<0.05	0.23	n.s.	0.13	n.s.
All offices	0.33	<0.01	0.06	n.s.	0.37	<0.01
Graduate degree from school given priority in recruiting						
Major office	0.29	n.s.	0.10	n.s.	0.24	n.s.
Minor offices	0.61	<0.01	0.41	<0.05	0.33	n.s.
All offices	0.44	<0.01	0.24	<0.10	0.29	<0.10
Service in the Navy or Air Force						
Major office	0.36	<0.05	0.11	n.s.	0.33	n.s.
Minor offices	0.10	n.s.	0.03	n.s.	0.01	n.s.
All offices	0.25	<0.05	0.09	n.s.	0.16	n.s.
Amount of prior business experience						
Major office	−0.10	n.s.	−0.29	<0.05	−0.09	n.s.
Minor offices	0.11	n.s.	0.23	n.s.	0.46	<0.01
All offices	−0.04	n.s.	−0.14	n.s.	0.11	n.s.
Company officer as reference						
Major office	0.03	n.s.	0.02	n.s.	0.05	n.s.
Minor offices	0.20	n.s.	0.18	n.s.	−0.07	n.s.
All offices	0.10	n.s.	0.10	n.s.	−0.07	n.s.

fices, $r = 0.29$, $p < 0.05$.) Of the 10 factors hypothesized to be related to success in connection with the testing of the second hypothesis, only 3 (ivy league college, prior business experience, and officer references) yield no clear evidence of a consistent relationship with consulting success.

The hypotheses cannot be considered fully supported; however, 9 of the 15 biographical factors yield significant correlations with one or more success criteria in the all offices analyses. Furthermore, the cross-validation analysis using current consultants in a single office produced a correlation of 0.58 between performance ratings, and the biographical composite developed on the basis of the results presented in Tables 2 and 3. This same composite produced comparable correlations of 0.65 in the major office sample and 0.73 in the minor offices. It is apparent, therefore, that in spite of the failure to confirm the hypotheses, a number of the background factors considered are consistently and meaningfully related to success in management consulting.

Discussion

The concept of eliteness motivation

The results do identify a number of variables that are related to consulting success, even though these variables do not fit the categories provided by the hypotheses. There appears to be something operating here to produce the correlations, but the hypotheses offer little help in determining what it is. Under such circumstances, the next step in research is to attempt to establish a concept or abstraction that will subsume most or all of the variables correlated with success. The approach is similar to that in factor analysis, in which variables which have high loadings on a given factor are studied to abstract out a label or title for the factor. In the present case, however, the concern is with variables that are highly correlated with success.

In factor analysis, the ideal procedure, once a factor has been labelled, is to create a new measure of this construct, to operationalize it, and then to determine through subsequent research whether it behaves and relates to other variables as hypothesized—thus, to establish construct validity. Similarly in the present instance, if an underlying construct can be identified for the consultant groups, the next step in research is to create a measure of this construct and then to apply it to additional samples drawn from other professional organizations—not only to consulting firms, but also to those in accounting, law, architecture, and perhaps even to universities. If the theory underlying the construct is correct, this measure should show consistent relations with success, at both the individual and organizational levels.

Inspection of the nine significant findings and a comparison with the six that are not statistically significant suggests that an underlying construct can be identified. There appears to be a consistent pattern of prior identification with and membership in prestige organizations and groups among the more successful consultants—private prep schools, small private colleges, prestige business schools, the Navy and Air Force rather than the Army, the commissioned officer group in service, and the management group in business. Coupled with this is the evidence of upward mobility relative to their fathers which suggests a positive striving to achieve these elite associations. All these variables combine to define the eliteness motivation construct.

If one contrasts these variables with the remaining six, a qualitative difference does emerge. Grades in school represent individual accomplishments within organizations. Obtaining more education does not necessarily mean a prestige association. Considered independently of the particular school attended, it, too, is an individual accomplishment. Years of business experience per se do not mean a longer *prestige* association. Only in the case of the ivy league schools are the results inconsistent with the eliteness interpretation. Yet, successful consultants do attend ivy league graduate schools and small private colleges. Furthermore, although going to an ivy league college is not related to success one way or the other, graduation from a state university is associated with a lack of success (for all offices $r = 0.02$, n.s. with performance rating; $r = -0.26$, $p < 0.05$ with compensation change; $r = -0.34$, $p < 0.10$ with promotion). One hypothesis is that in their upward striving for elite associations, many of the successful consultants made it only as far as the small private colleges and then moved on to ivy league associations at the graduate level.

There is one further finding which supports the eliteness motivation hypothesis. As Table 1 indicates, those who are rated higher and paid more stay longer with the firm. Those who are promoted stay longer also (in fact, partners only very rarely leave under their own volition). The particular firm studied would qualify by almost any definition as a prestige association. Thus, by achieving success in this particular organization, consultants are able to prolong a prestige association. This result should be highly satisfying to anyone strongly motivated by a desire for eliteness. There is good evidence from other sources that this kind of conditioning of other strong motives to yield achievement-related behavior can occur [13, pp. 523-532].

Evidence from other studies

There is other evidence bearing on the eliteness motivation hypothesis, some of it derived from studies conducted in the same consulting organization. These studies suggest that the types of motives which are often associated with success in administrative organizations within the business sector are not equally important in professional organizations. Thus, motives such as those for achievement, power, and competition are frequently important for success in administrative organizations, but not in professional organizations [2, pp. 78-81; 6; 11, pp. 86-93]. The same psychological evaluation procedures which have proved quite effective in predicting managerial success consistently fail to predict satisfactory results in the consulting firm utilized in the present research [8, pp. 393-405]. Although strong work motivation has often been found positively associated with corporate success [1, p. 195], the reverse is true in the consulting firm [10, pp. 191-204]. Clearly, other constructs are needed to explain success within professional organizations—constructs other than those that have been applied with some success to corporate organizations.

In an analysis of relationships between ratings made by selection interviewers and the promotion index of subsequent success in this same consulting firm, such factors as initiative and sustained drive, potential as a clientele builder, and pattern of success did *not* predict [9, pp. 521-538]. Consultants initially rated high on these factors in the selection interview were no more likely to be elected to partnership than those who were rated low. This is consistent with the findings of the present study. Yet, selection interview ratings of practical judgment (Has he shown good judgment in job changes and otherwise?) and promotion potential (Does this man appear to have qualities that would enable him to become a management group member?) were predictive of promotion. It would appear that the interviewers were identifying some quality, perhaps related to past job changes, which would later serve to "make a difference" in the firm.

Further insight into the possible nature of this quality comes from research involving the use of personality tests in the same firm [10, pp. 191-204]. There was no evidence that consultants in the United States offices were more likely to succeed if they were characterized by strong work motivation; however, social motivation was positively related to success. Those who gave strong evidence of approach motivation when there was an opportunity to be with people were more likely to succeed. This was true in nonwork situations, with authority figures at work, when support was involved, and when close proximity was involved, but it was not true for peer groups ("being with the boys"). The data indicate clearly that a desire for certain types of associations with others, often those at higher levels, and not individualized accomplishment, represents a driving force among the better consultants. As with the findings presented in the present study, those obtained with the personality tests do not provide a direct test of the eliteness motivation hypothesis, but they are entirely consistent with it. Eliteness derives from association with groups of people who are viewed as elite or prestigious by oneself and by others.

Conclusions

The findings considered here indicate that further investigation of the role of eliteness motivation might well serve to fill the void that currently exists in our knowledge of motivational factors contributing to success within and among professional organizations. Yet, the very suggestion that eliteness motivation may be a crucial variable in professional organizations poses an interesting paradox.

Just as traditional management theory had its origins in manufacturing and appears primarily applicable there [5], the concepts of participative or democratic management had their origins in professional organizations (primarily universities) and appear particularly relevant to the professional context [12]. But, eliteness motivation would appear to be anything but a democratic concept. The words associated with it such as prep school, ivy league, officer class, management, and perhaps others such as private club, society, debutante, and country day school have anything but a democratic ring. Why then should eliteness motivation be a significant factor contributing to success within the very organizational form that produced participative management and within which it has prospered? Perhaps eliteness motivation is not as important as the present findings suggest; perhaps it is relevant only in professional organizations with up-or-out policies; perhaps the paradox can be resolved on other grounds. That is a research challenge for the future.

References

1. Campbell, John P., *et al., Managerial Behavior, Performance, and Effectiveness* (New York: McGraw-Hill, 1970).
2. Cummin, Pearson C., "TAT Correlates of Executive Performance," *Journal of Applied Psychology,* 51 (1967).
3. Ginzberg, Eli, *et al., The Lost Divisions* (New York: Columbia University Press, 1959).
4. Guion, Robert M., *Personnel Testing* (New York: McGraw-Hill, 1965).
5. Lawrence, Paul R., and Lorsch, Jay W., *Organization and Environment: Managing Differentiation and Integration* (Boston: Division of Research, Harvard Business School, 1967).
6. Litwin, George H., and Stringer, Robert A., *Motivation and Organizational Climate* (Boston: Division of Research, Harvard Business School, 1968).
7. Lopez, Felix M., *The Making of a Manager* (New York: American Management Association, 1970).
8. Miner, John B., "Psychological Evaluations as Predictors of Consulting Success," *Personnel Psychology,* 23 (1970).
9. ———, "Executive and Personnel Interviews as Predictors of Consulting Success," *Personnel Psychology,* 23 (1970).
10. ———, "Personality Tests as Predictors of Consulting Success," *Personnel Psychology,* 24 (1971).

11. _______________, *Management Theory* (New York: Macmillan, 1971).
12. Price, James L., *Organizational Effectiveness: An Inventory of Propositions* (Homewood, Ill.: Irwin, 1968).
13. Smith, C.P., "Relationships Between Achievement-Related Motives and Intelligence, Performance Level, and Persistence." *Journal of Abnormal and Social Psychology,* 68 (1964).

Appendix

Biographical Information—Consulting Staff
(Brief Form)

Name ____________________ Date ____________________

Address ______________________________________

Telephone ______________________________________

Date of Birth ____________________ Nationality ____________________

Work Experience. Please note all regular, full-time employment (not summer) starting with the most recent position.

1. Name and nature of organization ____________________
   Dates of employment (month & year) ____________________
   Titles of positions held ____________________
   Duties (highest level position) ____________________
2. Name and nature of organization ____________________
   Dates of employment (month & year) ____________________
   Titles of positions held ____________________
   Duties (highest level position) ____________________

   (Note additional positions on the back of this sheet using the same format.)

Military Experience. Please note active duty service only.

Nation __________ Branch (Army, Navy, Air Force, etc.) __________

Dates of service (month & year) ____________________

Rank at separation ____________________

Education.

Type of School	**Name and Location**	**From**	**To**	**Degree**	**Major**
High School					
Prep. School					
College					
Grad. School					

Early Background.

Place where spent childhood (longest residence) ____________________

Father's education (level and type) ____________________

Father's highest position ____________________

Name and nature of organization ____________________

Other positions held by father ____________________

Mother's education (level and type) ____________________

13

validation study of mental ability tests

Mental ability tests have been widely used in selection for many years. They have caught the brunt of EEOC's attack because they tend to produce adverse impact. Minorities score lower on the average and thus are rejected in disproportionate numbers if the same qualifying score is used for all applicants. Thus, almost all court cases involving testing have focused on the use of mental ability tests. The AT&T case considered in Part 5 is typical in this regard.

The consulting firm discussed in the foregoing chapters was using such a mental ability test along with the various procedures already discussed. Validation research involving this measure and other alternative measures considered subsequently is discussed in this chapter. Published versions of these studies are not available, and accordingly this chapter has been written specifically for this volume. Although we believe the research is of good quality, the findings were not of sufficient general importance to warrant journal publication.

The Alpha 9 test

The test in general use throughout the firm at the time the comprehensive validation was undertaken was Alpha 9, an updated version of the instrument originally developed for use in military selection and placement during World War I. This test was evaluated initially in the firm's smaller U.S. office as part of the overall pilot validation effort in that office.

The study was conducted using data in the files on 33 consultants. Tests administered at the time of hiring were compared with such subsequent performance records as were available. Only 18 of these consultants were still employed by the firm at the time of the study. The Alpha 9 test yields both numerical and verbal ability scores and a total score. The 33 consultants had a mean total score which placed them at the 92nd percentile among adult males applying for executive positions.

Criteria

The most comprehensive criterion measure used drew upon a variety of data sources and classified the consultants as successful ($N=15$) and less successful ($N=18$). Success was defined as meeting all of the following requirements which were appropriate, with a lack of success being indicated by a failure to meet one or more:

1. If separated, not fired and would be rehired.
2. If performance ratings were available, average was at least "up to standard."
3. If employed three years or more had an average yearly salary increase of at least $2,400.
4. If employed less than three years had an average yearly salary increase of at least $1,200.

Separate analyses were also made comparing the test scores of those who had separated (60 percent of whom had left involuntarily) and those still employed (some of whom could be expected to be elected to partnership), as well as the scores of those who had experienced compensation increases above and below average.

Results

No statistically significant differences were found using the comprehensive criterion of success. However, those who were still employed had higher verbal ability scores than those who had separated ($\chi^2 = 5.32, p < .05$) and those with above-average compensation increases tended to have higher verbal ability scores also ($\chi^2 = 3.81$, p almost .05). No significant differences were found involving numerical ability or the total test score. Further investigation revealed that test items of the verbal analogies type were particularly likely to differentiate those who were high or low on the criteria.

These findings give only very limited support for the continued use of Alpha 9 as a selection instrument. However, they do suggest that a test which emphasized verbal analogies might well yield much higher levels of validity.

The Terman Concept Mastery Test

In line with the results of the pilot study of Alpha 9, the Terman Concept Mastery Test, a quite difficult, primarily verbal measure made up of analogies and synonym-antonyms, was selected for further study. This test was administered to 34 individuals in the firm's major office constituted as follows (mean scores in parentheses):

6 recently promoted partners (133.8)
9 "hot" consultants, not yet promoted (135.4)
12 average consultants (125.9)
7 consultants viewed as "slow starters" (121.7)

When the two upper and two lower groups were combined the difference between the means was not statistically significant ($t = 1.39$, $p < .20$). However, the trend of the data was clearly in the expected direction and it seemed likely that with a larger sample significance would be obtained. Accordingly, a decision was made to introduce the Concept Mastery Test on a firmwide basis, replacing Alpha 9, and to conduct a more comprehensive validity study as soon as sufficient data became available.

The firmwide study

Test scores were obtained on 59 consultants from a variety of offices whose primary language was English. These individuals were tested at the time of hiring or shortly thereafter.

Criterion data were collected when these consultants had been with the firm an average of approximately one and one half years. The major source of criterion information was a performance rating made by the firm's director of personnel on a five-point scale. The personnel director was well informed regarding the work of 45 of the 59 consultants, having either worked with them or obtained detailed verbal evaluations from partners who had. In the remaining 14 cases the personnel director considered himself less knowledgeable and the ratings were assigned based on a combination of his judgment and the consultants' compensation histories. The mean scale rating was 2.8 and the mean Concept Mastery Test score 123 (slightly above the average score reported for graduate students in the United States).

The correlation between test and criterion for the total group of 59 consultants was .03—a figure far from statistically significant. However, when the analysis focused on the 16 consultants in the major office, where the earlier results had been at least suggestive of validity, a correlation of .50 ($p < .05$) was obtained. No significant correlations were found in any other offices, although sample sizes were so low that significance would have been difficult to obtain.

Vocabulary Test G-T

The Concept Mastery Test study, although predictive in design, suffered from the fact that the criterion was global in nature and of unknown reliability. A second study initiated at the same time and also utilizing a verbal ability measure was able to circumvent these criterion problems. This study employed the Vocabulary Test G-T which correlates .79 with the Concept Mastery Test. Thus the study provides a further check on the results previously reported.

Sample and criteria

The study utilized the same 51 U.S. consultants who were used in the second personality test study (Chapter 11). These consultants were tested during the orientation training program and criterion information was collected an average of one year and seven months later. Of the 51, a total of 23 were employed in the firm's major office, while the remainder were spread over five other U.S. offices. Thus, it was possible to look at the major office data separately to determine whether the significant results obtained with the Concept Mastery Test were present when the Vocabulary Test G-T was used.

The criteria included ratings on eight-point scales dealing with various aspects of the consulting job. The ratings on each person represented the average value given by either two or three partners for whom the individual had worked. The rating variables and the average inter-rater agreement (reliability) values are given in Table 1. In addition various compensation measures and per diem charges to clients were used. All of these criterion measures were positively correlated, with the median value being .60.

Results

For the total sample of 51 consultants the general trend of the data is negative—consultants of higher verbal ability tend to do less well. Several of the correlations are significant at the .05 level, although only minimally so.

On the other hand, this pattern is completely reversed in the major office. There verbal ability is consistently positively related to the success index. This pattern replicates that obtained with the Concept Mastery Test.

Table 1

Predictor-Criterion Correlations for Vocabulary Test G-T and Reliability Coefficients for Rating Criteria

		Criterion correlations			
		All offices (N = 51)		Major office (N = 23)	
Criteria	Reliability	r	p	r	p
Ratings					
Problem solving	.70	−.19	—	.50	<.05
Client relations	.60	−.07	—	.58	<.01
Work output	.58	−.28	<.05	.53	<.01
Firm relations	.45	−.28	<.05	.68	<.01
Total of four above	.68	−.23	—	.61	<.01
Overall evaluation	.74	−.18	—	.48	<.05
Advancement potential	.76	−.20	—	.43	<.05
Compensation					
Total		−.12	—	.65	<.01
Total change		−.30	<.05	.33	—
Change/year		−.18	—	.37	<.10
Per diem charge					
Total		−.17	—	.78	<.01
Total change		−.31	<.05	.55	<.01
Change/year		−.09	—	.55	<.01

Discussion

Based on the mental ability test validation research as a whole, a case can be made for job-relatedness only in the firm's major office. In the other offices, it might be argued that less intelligent candidates should be selected, but it is extremely unlikely that the firm would want to follow such a strategy. The consultants considered are all toward the upper end of the population mental ability distribution, and even the negative correlation reported might very well disappear were the firm to dip deeper down into the distribution of mental ability scores. On the Concept Mastery Test, for instance, the score of the average candidate was 105, that of the average person hired 123. Thus, the firm was hiring people of high mental ability even though in some offices the most intelligent individuals hired were not the most successful.

The data support the use of a verbal ability test, either the Concept Mastery Test or the Vocabulary Test G-T, in the major office. In the other offices the use of such tests could not withstand an attack from the enforcement agencies. Perhaps a person with a Concept Mastery Test score of 100 or less does have a high probability of failure, but given the relatively small number of such people hired there is no way of proving it, except in the major office.

The reason for recommending against the use of the mental ability measures in the minor offices is that adverse impact is so likely. On the Vocabulary Test G-T (Form A) the mean score for whites in the population has been found to be 11.06 and for minorities 8.08 ($t = 12.41, p < .001$). Although similar data for the Concept Mastery Test are not available, it seems probable it would yield similar results. Since job-relatedness for high-scoring individuals has not been demonstrated in the minor offices, using a verbal ability test to select such people based on a constant qualification score for whites and minorities would almost certainly be interpreted as discriminatory. On the other hand, setting a lower qualifying score for minorities, so that equal proportions of whites and minorities were hired, thus eliminating the adverse impact, would not be likely to draw the ire of EEOC or OFCCP. It would, however, result in hiring more people of relatively low mental ability than the firm is now hiring.

part 5

validation of psychological tests and assessment centers in connection with the AT&T case

overview

The most extensive enforcement effort yet mounted by EEOC involved AT&T and the operating Bell System telephone companies. The case was initiated in December 1970, based on over 2,000 charges of alleged discrimination, and was ultimately resolved through a series of consent decrees, as noted in Chapter 3. The first of these, dated January 18, 1973, represents the primary agreement; it cost the company $45 million in its first year of implementation alone. A subsequent consent decree dated May 31, 1974, deals specifically with management compensation, and a supplemental agreement dated May 13, 1975, modifies the 1973 decree to provide new procedures for the priority hiring and promotion of women and minority-group members. These modifications appeared necessary because the company was unable to meet the original affirmative action goals for the year 1973, although it was held to be in compliance for 1974.

Details of the events leading up to the 1973 agreement are given in Chapter 14. The scope of the case is evident in the fact that almost 60 days of public hearings plus numerous meetings between the parties were involved. The hearings produced 8,000 pages of transcripts, and 150 witnesses testified. The EEOC created a special task force to deal with the case in April 1971, and from then until the first consent decree was signed had a large portion of its personnel assigned to this one effort. During this period EEOC enforcement against other firms was severely curtailed as a result of the time and manpower requirements of the AT&T proceedings. In addition to the internal staff assigned, EEOC utilized a number of outside social scientists as special consultants on various aspects of the case.

One of the authors became involved in this effort at the time the special EEOC task force was established, serving as a consultant in the area of psychological testing. In this capacity he reviewed the various reports of validation research submitted by AT&T and prepared a memorandum evaluating these studies in terms of their professional soundness and implications for fair employment. This memorandum provides the basis for the article in Chapter 14. Although the author's assignment with EEOC was completed upon submission of the memorandum, he has continued to keep up with developments in the case and has held numerous discussions with the psychologists involved. Thus his knowledge of events extends considerably beyond published reports and public documents.

After the review of the case in Chapter 14, Chapters 15-20 focus on four validation studies carried out by the corporate personnel research unit of AT&T and on two studies initiated some time later dealing with the use of assessment centers in upgrading women into and within management. The introductory chapter provides a general overview of the scope and nature of validation efforts within the Bell System as a whole.

The four studies described in Chapters 15-18 were initiated subsequent to a determination that the mental abilities tests in use by the company were having an adverse impact. Nine operating companies supplied test data on 6,500 job applicants. Review of these data indicated that on the average minorities had lower scores, and fewer minority applicants proved to be test-qualified for hiring. The other major component of the selection process was an employment interview. In this case evidence on possible adverse impact was not available to the company because appropriate records had not been maintained; employment interviews were generally quite loosely structured. Accordingly, a decision was made to focus validation efforts on the psychological testing program where adverse impact was known to exist. In retrospect this decision can be questioned; it would have been well to have evaluated the interviews also. However, in the following chapters the concern is entirely with the matter of establishing job-relatedness for the use of the tests and assessment centers, because the research was done on these techniques.

The four studies of Chapters 15-18 arose out of a validation strategy which emphasized highly controlled, multicompany studies utilizing standardized criteria obtained subsequent to initial training.

The studies deal with four occupational groups—installation and repair personnel, service representatives, operators, and clerical personnel. These are the major entry-level occupations in the telephone companies for which tests are used. Because these are the jobs for which the largest number of people are hired, it was anticipated that governmental enforcement efforts would focus on them; this subsequently proved to be correct. All four studies have appeared in a highly reputable professional publication, the *Journal of Applied Psychology* of the American Psychological Association, and in this sense can be said to have passed a professional peer review. All were submitted in evidence in the case, although in several instances in a preliminary form. These are the only studies of the 31 submitted that have been so published. The others, although often of good quality, were not of sufficient general import to justify publication.

The remaining two studies, in Chapters 19 and 20, were undertaken in large part because the original consent decree called for the use of assessment centers to evaluate female college graduates for promotion up the management ladder. It thus became important to determine how effective these centers were in identifying managerial talent among women. Prior research had focused almost entirely on men, and thus evidence on differential validity was not available. Like the preceding articles included in this part, the two dealing with assessment centers have met the professional standards for publication in reputable journals. They can therefore be presumed to provide appropriate models for those who may wish to design their own validation efforts.

14

psychological testing and fair employment practices

Introductory notes

The AT&T case is of particular importance to those concerned with personnel selection because the company's testing program did survive, and it survived because comprehensive validation research had been conducted which supported continued use of the tests. This article reviews that research, including the four studies reported in greater detail in the chapters which follow. The review presented here was available to the EEOC lawyers prior to the hearings before the FCC and during the period when the agreement with the company was being negotiated. There is good reason to believe it exerted an influence on the stance that EEOC took on testing during this period.

It is important to note that, although a court might well not have required it, AT&T agreed in the consent decree not to permit the use of tests to create an adverse impact and thus to interfere with achieving hiring targets for women and minorities. This consideration is made even more specific in the section on testing in the May 13, 1975, supplemental agreement:

> . . . deficiencies in meeting intermediate targets shall be determined quarterly. In any job classification in any establishment where a deficiency or part of a deficiency in any quarter is a result of the Company having disqualified otherwise qualified applicants because of their test scores, the Company shall, in the following quarter, retrieve all applicants of the corresponding race or ethnic group who were not test qualified but were otherwise qualified, and offer them future opportunities in the job classification (unless better qualified applicants from their group are now available) until the test-related deficiency has been made up.

This type of procedure implies the use of differential selection with different cutting scores for differing groups if affirmative action targets are not met. The tests remain useful because the best people *within* groups may still be hired, but they are not as useful as they might be. The only way to avoid adverse impact and not reduce cutting scores is to resort to differential recruiting where disproportionate numbers of the potentially injured group are brought into the applicant population. Of these two approaches it appears that the Bell System subsequently has been making somewhat greater use of differential selection by dipping below the established cutting scores when goals are not being met.

A final point relates to the historical development of this case. At the time it was initiated in late 1970, EEOC could not proceed directly to court against a company on its own. That is the reason for the somewhat circuitous process of intervening in an FCC rate-increase hearing. Now, with the passage of the 1972 law, EEOC no longer faces this type of constraint. Accordingly, under similar circumstances a company should anticipate that court action would be initiated directly rather than that pressure by some federal regulatory body would be invoked.

PSYCHOLOGICAL TESTING AND FAIR EMPLOYMENT PRACTICES: A TESTING PROGRAM THAT DOES NOT DISCRIMINATE*

In the past few years a number of employing organizations have discontinued psychological testing programs or failed to initiate planned programs as a result of fair employment practices legislation and enforcement efforts by the Equal Employment Opportunity Commission (EEOC) and by the Office of Federal Contract Compliance (OFCC) (Bureau of National Affairs, 1971a). Given the uncertainties of the current situation these employers have decided that testing for purposes of hiring and promotion is not worth the risk involved. Although this kind of reasoning has been applied

*Reprinted with permission from *Personnel Psychology,* Vol. 27 (1974), 49-62.

primarily to the testing aspects of the selection process, it is being extended to application blanks and interviews as well. The result appears to be that some organizations are moving precipitously close to random hiring, with all the implications for subsequent performance failure that such an approach involves (Miner and Brewer, 1976).

Increasingly psychologists, lawyers, and personnel specialists are being asked to provide opinions as to whether testing programs will be acceptable to EEOC and/or OFCC. Both of these federal organizations have published guidelines and other documents in an effort to reduce uncertainty and assist employers to comply with legislation and executive orders bearing on testing. Yet, nothing has been published to date that would provide a sure guide to employer action; many uncertainties and ambiguities remain. Faced with the prospects of terminated federal contracts, sizable awards for damages, and restrictions on earnings by regulatory bodies it is not surprising that some companies have decided to forego further testing until the present situation clears.

Such a strategy may require a long wait. The reason is that both EEOC and OFCC have taken the position that they will not approve individual testing programs as being fair and nondiscriminatory. They argue in part that they lack the manpower to carry out the many investigations this would require. Even more important, however, is the government's position that under existing law it is up to the employer to establish that employment practices do not discriminate, and that government certification of testing programs would be wholly inconsistent with this particular legal strategy.

If there is a sizable disparity between the distribution of women or minorities in the labor force of the geographical area as compared with any major job category of an employer, this is in and of itself sufficient basis to warrant a charge of discrimination. It is then up to the organization involved to show that the disparity exists for some reason other than outright discrimination, if it can. To certify testing programs or any other selection procedures in advance would serve to undermine the government's legal position in such cases. As a result it seems clear that a full interpretation of fair employment practices legislation will emerge only after a series of court tests and hearings before the semi-judicial federal regulatory bodies.

Decisions of this kind such as *Griggs* vs. *Duke Power Company, United States* vs. *Georgia Power Company, et al.*, and *Moody, et al.* vs. *Albemarle Paper Company* have had a great deal more to say regarding types of procedures that are not acceptable, than about what is fair employment practice; the testing programs questioned in these cases have not emerged from the judicial process unscathed. Yet what is needed if adequate guides for action are to be developed are examples of testing programs which have been subjected to intensive federal scrutiny, and have survived intact. The first instance of this kind occurred recently in the case of charges brought by EEOC and certain civil rights groups against the American Telephone and Telegraph Company before the Federal Communications Commission.

It is particularly important that psychologists and others concerned with testing be fully aware of the details of this case because, in view of the nature and monetary value of the final settlement, the exoneration of AT&T testing procedures could easily be overlooked. The discussion which follows provides a brief historical overview of the case as a whole, an analysis of the evidence presented to EEOC regarding AT&T testing, and an attempt to draw implications for future testing strategies and practice in the employment context from this experience.

Historical overview

The initial action by EEOC occurred in the form of a petition to intervene in opposition to a rate increase for long distance telephone calls requested by AT&T from the Federal Communications Commission. This petition was filed December 10, 1970 and charged AT&T with violation of the Federal Communications Act, the Civil Rights Acts of 1866 and 1964, the Equal Pay Act of 1963, various Executive Orders, legislation passed by certain states and large cities, and the Fifth Amendment to the U.S. Constitution. More specifically the company was accused of discriminating in employment against women, blacks, Spanish-surnamed Americans and other minorities. EEOC argued that approval of the rate increase not only would be in violation of the FCC's statutory obligation, but also would deprive those discriminated against of due process of law. With regard to AT&T's testing practices specifically, EEOC alleged that these operated to systematically exclude blacks from high-paying craft jobs, and frequently from any jobs; the tests were described as unfair (Bureau of National Affairs, 1973a).

Subsequently, several civil rights organizations filed intervention petitions and the U.S. Court of Appeals for the District of Columbia granted a petition to review. As a result the FCC agreed to an adjudicatory hearing on the charges of discrimination in employment, while at the same time separating the rate increase issue from the discrimination charges and granting an interim rate increase.

Although originally AT&T objected to providing the detailed information on its employment practices requested by EEOC so that it might document its charges, these difficulties were ultimately overcome and the company provided some 3,000 documents for inspection and evaluation (Bureau of National Affairs, 1971b). Included were various internal memoranda and published reports dealing with AT&T test validation studies, which were reviewed in detail by the psychologists for the EEOC.

Three psychologists subsequently testified for EEOC based on their analyses of aspects of these reports; they were Felix M. Lopez (Felix M. Lopez & Associates), William H. Enneis (EEOC), and Philip Ash (University of Illinois at Chicago Circle). Psychologists testifying for AT&T considered some of these reports, primarily those prepared by AT&T personnel research, and in addition had certain updated validity information that did not become available until shortly before the hearing, and thus was not previously available to the EEOC psychologists. None of the seven psychologists involved based his testimony on a complete file of AT&T validation studies, although the Lopez analysis was considerably more comprehensive than the others. The four psychologists testifying on behalf of AT&T were Brent N. Baxter (American Institutes for Research), Douglas W. Bray (AT&T), Donald L. Grant (AT&T), and Robert M. Guion (Bowling Green State University).

The final resolution of the case came as a result of an agreement reached between AT&T, EEOC, and the Department of Labor which was entered in the form of a consent decree in the U.S. District Court for the Eastern District of Pennsylvania on January

18, 1973. The company agreed to compensate women and minority employees with payments which are estimated to run between $12- and $15-million. This settlement is based on alleged violations of the Equal Pay Act of 1963 and of Title VII of the Civil Rights Act of 1964. The payments are intended as retroactive compensation to those who in the past may have been victims of discrimination in promotions, transfers and salary administration (Bureau of National Affairs, 1973a). In addition AT&T agreed to undertake a variety of steps aimed at achieving a balance between the proportions of women and minorities in its various occupations and proportions existing in relevant labor forces.

Although the form in which the case was resolved precludes either an admission of guilt by AT&T or a finding of legal violations by the courts and the FCC, it is evident that where employment practices are not proscribed or drastically modified by the settlement, they have in effect been accepted as nondiscriminatory by the EEOC and the Department of Labor. It is in this light that it is particularly important to consider those aspects of the consent order which bear on psychological testing (Bureau of National Affairs, 1973b).

The most relevant statement reads as follows:

> Each Bell Company may continue to utilize test scores on validated tests along with other job-related considerations in assessing individual qualifications. However, no Bell Company shall rely upon the minimum scores required or preferred on its preemployment aptitude test batteries as justification for its failure to meet its intermediate targets for any job classification.

The only other statement directly concerned with testing appears in a model affirmative action program appended to the consent order. This is basically a restatement of the above in terms suitable for implementation:

> The . . . employee selection process is based on the concept that tests are only one of the many criteria. Both in the selection of applicants and employees for filling job vacancies, our company does not rely upon the minimum scores required or preferred on tests as justification for failure to meet intermediate targets for any job classification. Our company does utilize tests scores on validated tests along with other job related considerations in assessing individual qualifica-

> tions. Our company hires people as regular employees who do not pass pre-employment tests and these individuals may participate in one or more of our company's special intake-programs. All tests are only one predictor in selecting new employees. It is the basic objective in the EEOC program to have all tests and their uses conform with the OFCC Guidelines on Employee Testing and Other Selection Procedures and Company policy. The validation studies are made by the Personnel Research Section at The American Telephone and Telegraph Company in accordance with the OFCC Guidelines on Employee Testing and Other Section Procedures. Copies of validation studies are on file with that Company.

There is one further aspect of the settlement which bears on testing indirectly, and in a particularly positive manner. This has to do with the AT&T assessment centers which utilize psychological tests as one aspect of a procedure for identifying managerial potential (Bray and Grant, 1966). The statement runs as follows:

> Four-year college graduate female employees . . . will be surveyed to determine their interest in promotion to District level (third level) and above management positions. . . . Those employees . . . who are found to be interested will be scheduled for a two-to-three day assessment at a management center to evaluate their potential for promotion to District level. This assessment process will be conducted under procedures outlined by AT&T . . . the foregoing assessment procedure may not be relied upon as a defense by an individual Bell Company for its failure to reach the intermediate targets for those job classifications for which such procedures are used. Those employees evaluated . . . who do not receive a satisfactory rating will return to their current assignments and their assessment rating will not be entered into their permanent personnel file.

No other references are made to testing or test-based procedures.

The AT&T testing program

What, then, are the characteristics of the testing program which has elicited this degree of approval, or at least lack of disapproval, in the final analysis from governmental agencies concerned with fair employment practices and equal opportunity? What is the specific nature of the model thus presented to other employing organizations?[1]

A total of 31 validity studies were submitted to EEOC and reviewed by the author. Of these eight were multi-company studies utilizing data from widely dispersed geographical locations, 12 were conducted within the Pacific Telephone and Telegraph Company, six within the Southern and/or South Central Bell Companies,three within the New Jersey company, and two within the Michigan company. All the multi-company studies and one each from the Pacific Coast and the South were carried out by AT&T's personnel research unit; the remainder were conducted by the individual operating companies. Although the magnitude of this research may seem overwhelming, it should be remembered that AT&T is a very large, nationwide employer with many occupational groups.

Of the 10 studies by AT&T's personnel research unit seven reported results for training criteria only and no subsequent job performance relationships. These studies involved primarily those employee groups which were of greatest concern to EEOC—operators, clerks, plant craft employees, and service representatives. The remaining three studies which did utilize subsequent job performance criteria had salesmen and managers as subjects, jobs which were less focal for the EEOC investigation. In six of the seven cases where only training criteria were used the measures were specially devised job simulations and were not standard training evaluation procedures. Examples are described by Grant and Bray (1970) and Gael and Grant (1972). Only in one study involving computer programmers did the AT&T personnel researchers use standard training criteria based on instructor's ratings. Thus, it is clear that the basic validation strategy was to use indexes such as

[1] The following discussion draws primarily on a memorandum written by the author for the EEOC on October 31, 1971. This memorandum contains a review of all validity information which had been provided to EEOC by AT&T up to that time. It was prepared while the author was serving as a consultant to EEOC, but was not submitted in evidence before the FCC. Permission to publish this material has been given by David Copus of EEOC and Douglas W. Bray of AT&T. The contributions of both of these individuals to this article are gratefully acknowledged.

In additional to the above mentioned memorandum, the following discussion also draws upon updating information provided in the testimony of Donald L. Grant and Douglas W. Bray of AT&T before the FCC (dated August 1, 1972).

simulations, work samples, and specially developed job knowledge measures with those occupational groups which were of greatest concern to EEOC.

A question arises as to whether such special post-training criteria might not have been devised for the specific purpose of yielding high correlations with the predictors, irrespective of their relation either to actual training success or to subsequent job performance. These criteria place strong emphasis on intellectual or scholastic ability (learning ability) and the measures are obtained under conditions of maximal rather than typical motivation. Both of these conditions are inherent in the initial testing situation as well (the most consistently used predictor was the School and College Ability Test published by Educational Testing Service).

One approach to testing this hypothesis involves a comparison of results obtained with regular training criteria such as course grades, instructor's ratings, pass-fail decisions, performance on quizzes, and retention-separation during training with results obtained when the special post-training criteria are used. Of the nine analyses using regular criteria, three were conducted by AT&T personnel research (two of these used job performance criteria as well) and six by individual operating companies. Of the eight studies using specialized criteria, six were conducted by AT&T personnel research and two by operating companies. Data on the extent to which statistically significant validity coefficients ($p < .05$) were obtained using the two types of training criteria are given in Table 1.

On the record it appears that the specially devised post-training criteria have no particular proclivity for yielding validity; thus the hypothesis of biased selection of criterion measures is not supported. In subsequent analyses the two types of training criteria are treated as a single class.

From the data of Table 1 it would appear that the training criteria used in all 17 studies are closely related to the actual content of training. It remains to be demonstrated, however, that the training (and the training criteria) are associated with subsequent job performance. How, for instance, does the incidence of validity vary as between training criteria and job performance criteria such as supervisory ratings, field review ratings, promotion rates, and hard measures of productivity. Data are given in Table 2.

Table 1

Findings from Validation Studies Conducted Using Various Types of Training Criteria

Type of Criterion Measure	Valid (p<.05)	Not Valid (p>.05)	Validity Level Not Indicated
Regular Training Criteria	7 (78%)	1 (11%)	1 (11%)
Special Post-Training Criteria	8 (100%)	0	0
	(χ^2 = .44, N.S.; df = 1)		

Although there is a tendency for the incidence of nonvalid results to increase as one moves from training to later job performance, the shift is not sufficient to yield anything approaching statistical significance. Thus, it cannot be said that validity is obtained less frequently when actual job performance criteria are used. Given the fact that the validity analyses using performance data are based on predictions over longer periods of time (and thus permit greater opportunities for real changes in the individuals to intervene) than those based on training data, the comparisons of Table 2 might even be viewed as overstating the criterion differences.

There are three studies in which both training criteria and job performance criteria are used. In one instance the relationship between the two is not reported, in another it is not significant, and in the third it is a highly significant +.75. Where the two are negatively correlated, one could argue that the training is detrimental to ultimate objectives, and thus validation against training criteria is unwarranted. Where the two are uncorrelated, the use of training criteria must be justified in its own right—effective selection saves

Table 2

Findings from Validation Studies Conducted Using Training and Performance Criteria

Type of Criterion Measure	Valid (p<.05)	Not Valid (p>.05)	Validity Level Not Indicated
Training Criteria	15 (88%)	1 (6%)	1 (6%)
Job Performance Criteria	11 (65%)	5 (29%)	1 (6%)
	(χ^2 = 1.46, N.S.; df = 1)		

Note—Three studies utilized both types of criterion measures.

the cost of training. Where the two are positively correlated, validation using training criteria can be justified both in its own right and as it contributes to the prediction of a less than ultimate index of job performance. Based on these interpretations there is nothing in the data reported by AT&T that would lead one to reject the findings obtained using training criteria; there are no negative correlations between training and performance measures.

On the other hand it is entirely possible that in selecting those who will succeed in training, the company contributes to a higher turnover rate (and thus is burdened with greater replacement costs). The only data available related to this point derive from an incompletely described 1970 force loss study conducted in New York. In this instance, the separation rate was reported to be 24.7% per year for those with high test scores and 26.6% for those with lower scores. The difference is described as not significant, but tends to favor those with higher scores. Thus, again there is nothing to indicate that the findings obtained with training criteria should be rejected.

Taken as a whole this line of analysis tends to support the various criteria used in the AT&T studies. On the other hand, there are points at which the data become uncomfortably sparse. More information on relationships between various training criteria and indexes of subsequent job performance, especially retention, would make it easier to interpret the results that are reported. In many locations turnover appears to be quite high in the entry level jobs; yet little evidence is provided relating predictors to this criterion.

Another approach to criterion analysis involves consideration of minority group members separately. If, for instance, a criterion relationship is statistically significant for whites, but not blacks, there is a possibility that the mere fact that an individual is black may have had an impact on the criterion measurement process such as to eliminate any possibility of validity. This effect seems most likely when ratings are used, but it can occur with other criteria as well.

There are nine studies in which validities were calculated separately for blacks and whites. The results are given in Table 3.

Generally, significant correlations occur somewhat less fre-

Table 3

Findings from Validation Studies Using Both Black and White Subjects

Type of Criterion Measure	Valid ($p<.05$) for Both	Valid ($p<.05$) for Whites Only
Special Post-Training Criteria	6 (100%)	0
Job Performance Criteria	2 (67%)	1(33%)

quently among blacks than whites, but they do occur in both groups for all studies except one. In this one instance the criterion measure used was a direct index of output or productivity, and thus least vulnerable to any bias which would tend to obliterate validity; yet the validity coefficients were + .32 for whites and − .04 for blacks.

Inspection of the scatter plots given in Table 4 indicates a restriction of range at the lower end of the test score distributions in both the black and white samples; 25 has been used as a cutting score in both instances. The source of the differential validity, however, appears to be the similar limitation at the upper end of the test score distribution for blacks. This compression does not occur among the whites, and in fact it is the relationship demonstrated in cells where there are practically no blacks represented at all that accounts in large part for the significant correlation among whites. This analysis suggests that the failure to obtain validity for blacks in this instance is a function of the *test score* distribution in the sample much more than of the *criterion* distribution.

There is only one study where validities were computed separately for males and females and significance was obtained for both groups. In addition there are three studies utilizing Spanish surname subjects, although only two of these are reported in sufficient detail to determine whether statistical significance was obtained. In these latter instances validity was in fact established, using supervisory ratings and a post-training simulation as criteria.

Taken as a whole the studies of minority group members do not provide a basis for concluding that the criterion measures used introduce any special bias against minorities. Where the minority samples are lower on the criterion they tend to have lower test scores as well.

With only a few exceptions the 31 studies are predictive, rather than concurrent, in nature; also there is a heavy reliance on ability

Table 4

Relationships between Test Scores and Criterion Performance for Blacks and Whites

	Blacks			
	Criterion Performance			
Test Scores	Low	Medium	High	Totals
40 and over	0	0	1	1
35-39	2	3	1	6
30-34	3	0	1	4
25-29	6	5	4	15
				$N = 26$

	Whites			
	Criterion Performance			
Test Scores	Low	Medium	High	Totals
40 and over	1	5	11	17
35-39	11	4	14	29
30-34	13	9	9	31
25-29	13	13	10	36
				$N = 113$

tests, primarily mental ability. There are only four instances where validities are reported for other types of measures—a standardized interview including role playing, an assessment center evaluation covering many aspects of the individual, a stenographic test, and a typing test. A comparison of validities obtained with these measures as against those obtained with the mental ability tests is given in Table 5. On the evidence it would appear that wider use of tests other than those of mental ability could have been made without any sacrifice in validity.

Table 5

Findings from Validation Studies Using Various Types of Tests as Predictors

Type of Test	Valid ($p < .05$)	Not Valid ($p > .05$)	Validity Level Not Indicated
Mental Ability	23 (82%)	3 (11%)	2 (7%)
Other	3 (75%)	1 (25%)	0
	($X^2 = .11$, N.S.; $df = 1$)		

Note—One study utilized both types of tests.

Overall, in spite of the deficiencies of individual analyses, the results obtained from this series of 31 studies are very impressive in terms of the extent to which validity has been demonstrated.

Implications and conclusions

In the final analysis when all the evidence was in, EEOC did not continue to press on the matter of psychological testing, and accepted a settlement which left AT&T's existing testing program intact. This represented a major change in position from the one taken by EEOC at the time when the initial charges were filed. With full access to validity information, which they did not have in December, 1970, the government lawyers concluded that their case against AT&T's testing practices was not sufficiently strong to warrant pursuing this particular aspect of the case further.

On the other hand AT&T did agree not to "rely upon the minimum scores required or preferred on its pre-employment aptitude test batteries as justification for its failure to meet its intermediate targets for any job classification." What does this mean?

In agreeing to this provision, AT&T committed itself to one, or both, of two possible strategies, assuming that lower average test scores continue to characterize minority applicants as they have in the past. One approach involves a differential investment in recruiting such that a greater proportion of minority group members are induced to apply for jobs. Under this strategy the minimum test scores are held at the same level for all, and targets for hiring are met by locating more qualified minority group members and inducing them to join the company by offering attractive salaries, benefits and working conditions. In this instance the tests remain just as useful in identifying future effective performers among minorities as among whites.

An alternative to differential recruiting is differential selection. This involves establishing different minimum scores for different groups as required to meet the hiring targets. In the case of blacks at the present time, for instance, it would require a lower cutting score than for whites.

This approach does produce lower recruiting costs, but the savings may well be dissipated over time by increased training expenditures; further, there is greater risk of performance failure, assuming constant performance standards, and perhaps also certain problems, when it comes time for upgrading and promotion. Yet, even with the difficulties inherent in this approach tests continue to be useful; there is no basis for concluding that testing would make no contribution and, therefore, should be suspended for minority applicants. Tests can still be used to select those with the *highest* probability of effective performance *within* each group—white male, black, white female, Spanish surname, or whatever—even though differential cutting scores are used. Minimum scores need be set only as low as required to meet hiring targets. Furthermore, the test scores can prove useful in making post-hiring assignments and placement decisions.

Whatever strategy AT&T adopts, it will be able to retain many, if not the full, benefits of its testing program. On the other hand it is not entirely clear that the law does in fact require that hiring targets be given priority over the use of validated performance-related tests in making selection decisions. The AT&T case was settled by consent decree and AT&T agreed to this provision; no court required it. There is some feeling among lawyers who are active in the fair employment practices area that employing organizations have yielded on points that might have been decided in their favor had they been considered by the courts; and that there have been far too many consent decrees (Bureau of National Affairs, 1972). It is entirely possible the AT&T settlement represents a case in point.

In any event the clear implication of the final settlement is that testing programs can survive close government scrutiny and that psychological testing need not be abandoned in these times of increased governmental surveillance of all aspects of employment. In fact to follow the route of abandonment, as some personnel managers have advocated, may be an invitation to disaster. There are two reasons for this conclusion.

If some employing organizations, such as AT&T, continue to use valid tests these organizations are in a position to skim the top of a local labor force—male and female, black and white. Those who abandon testing will tend to abandon other selection procedures also as pressure for validation increases there too; inevitably they will move eventually to random hiring. But random hiring where everyone is employing randomly is one thing; random hiring in a labor market where a number of employers are actively selecting on a scientific basis is quite different. Under the latter conditions there may well be so little of the type of talent needed, remaining in a local labor force, that performance and productivity are seriously hampered. The situation is not unlike that occurring with the use of advertising, where if some companies invest, others in the industry are under strong pressure to follow suit, merely to remain in competition.

Another consideration in any decision regarding abandoning testing relates to the basic position taken by EEOC and other government enforcement agencies—"if an employer doesn't have a proper distribution of minorities in its workforce, he is guilty unless he can prove the imbalance is job related," (Bureau of National Affairs, 1972). The way to show that an imbalance is job related is to demonstrate that qualities needed for effective job performance are lacking in a segment of the labor force with which fair employment laws are concerned—a sex, racial, color, national origin, or religious group. If a psychological test can be shown to be valid (performance related), and the quality measured is not in balance as between men and women, blacks and whites, or whatever, then the imbalance in an employer's workforce can be said to be job related. With the use of psychological tests (plus acceptable validation and normative research) this response to a charge of discrimination can be readily advanced. Thus, discontinuing testing rather than providing protection against charges may well serve to eliminate the possibility of an effective and entirely justified defense; a charge of discrimination may accordingly be upheld for lack of test data.

It should be emphasized that AT&T, although apparently in a position to make this defense with regard to many of its installations and local labor markets, did not do so; rather it accepted the indicated hiring targets. The reasoning behind this outcome is not known to the author. In any event there is every indication from statements by EEOC lawyers and psychologists that such a line of defense could be sustained through proper psychological research; thus, that psychological testing can be used to show that a workforce imbalance is a function of job requirements rather than either intentional or unintentional discrimination.

References

Bray, D. W. and Grant, D. L. The assessment center in the measurement of potential for business management. *Psychological Monographs,* 1966, 80, 1-27.

Bureau of National Affairs, Inc. ASPA-BNA survey: Personnel testing. *Bulletin to Management,* September 9, 1971, 1-8 (a).

Bureau of National Affairs, Inc. EEOC's massive discrimination material from AT&T will go to FCC on December 1. *Daily Labor Report,* September 16, 1971, A6-7, (b).

Bureau of National Affairs, Inc. EEOC urges employers use job-related tests. *Daily Labor Report,* November 7, 1972, A9-10.

Bureau of National Affairs, Inc. District court approves AT&T agreement granting $15-million in job inequities. *Daily Labor Report,* January 19, 1973, 1, A6-7, E1-6 (a).

Bureau of National Affairs, Inc. *Fair Employment Practices.* Washington, D.C.: BNA, Inc., 1973 (b).

Gael, S. and Grant, D. L. Employment test validation for minority and nonminority telephone company service representatives. *Journal of Applied Psychology,* 1972, 56, 135-139.

Grant, D. L. and Bray, D. W. Validation of employment tests for telephone company installation and repair occupations. *Journal of Applied Psychology,* 1970, 54, 7-14.

Miner, J. B. and Brewer, J. F. The management of ineffective performance. In M. D. Dunnette (ed.), *Handbook of Industrial and Organizational Psychology.* Chicago: Rand McNally, 1976, 995-1029.

15

validation study of tests for installers and repairers

Introductory notes

This study was viewed as the weakest link in the AT&T validation effort by EEOC lawyers and psychologists and accordingly was subjected to considerable criticism during the hearings. In fact two of the psychologists devoted practically all of their testimony to the installation and repair occupations research.

One factor brought out in the hearings was that the actual use of the tests in selection would yield an adverse impact, if a constant qualification score were utilized with all groups. The reason no adverse impact was in evidence in the research samples was that a deliberate effort was made to include equal proportions of non-test-qualified individuals in both minority and nonminority groups, thus eliminating any restriction of range on the predictor variables. This process of not using a predictor to select when its validity is under study typically yields higher correlations with criteria, and is characteristic of what are considered the more elegant research designs. Thus, the intent in using this approach was not to obscure adverse impact, but to conduct the research in a manner most likely to reveal validity, if validity were in fact present. The very fact that the validity study was conducted is indicative of an expectation on the part of AT&T psychologists and personnel people that the actual use of these mental ability tests in selection would yield adverse impact and that therefore validity in both white and minority samples needed to be demonstrated as a basis for supporting a defense based on job-relatedness.

In spite of the fact that this validity was established, and no differential validity was found, EEOC took strong exception to the study. The basic argument was that the criterion used, the Learning Assessment Program (LAP) was not acceptable; thus the tests had not been validated and any adverse impact on hiring had to be viewed prima facie as discriminatory. It was said that the LAP had not been shown to be job-related based on a competent job analysis, that no evidence of the LAP's relationship to either training or job performance had been provided, and that this criterion had apparently been selected deliberately because of its high intellectual content, which would almost guarantee a good correlation with any mental ability test. Thus, the validity was viewed as a spurious consequence of using a criterion which was not really job-related at all. In fact the LAP was described as basically a test itself; thus the study was not of test-criterion relationships, but of test-test relationships, something that had nothing to do with job-relatedness.

As the published article indicates, the AT&T researchers appear to have anticipated as early as 1970 that the LAP might come under attack as a criterion measure. They argued at the hearings that the LAP had in fact emerged from an extensive job analysis, that it was really a work sample, and that anyone who actually observed it in use could readily see that it was content-valid for the occupations involved. They reiterated the view that the LAP is a pure measure of task proficiency. They also presented the results of the longitudinal research noted in the last paragraph of the article.

This follow-up analysis turned out to be of only limited value in clarifying the issues raised. Because of unexpectedly high turnover the sample shrank drastically between the data collection in 1967 and the last follow-up in 1969, and the shrinkage was most pronounced among those who had done poorly on LAP, thus producing a distinct restriction of range. Furthermore, the supervisory performance ratings obtained turned out to be severely lacking in reliability and therefore could not be used. The results obtained with the criteria that could be used are given in the following table:

Correlation of Test Composite Score and LAP Level Passed with Various Indexes of Subsequent Performance—1969 Data

Performance Indexes	Minority Sample			Nonminority Sample			Total Sample		
	N	Test	LAP	N	Test	LAP	N	Test	LAP
Number of days in plant schools	50	−.20	.11	74	.26*	.39*	124	.22*	.30*
Number of courses in plant schools completed	50	−.25	.09	74	.09	.22	124	−.01	.17
Level of performance in plant schools	30	−.17	.46*	45	.13	.18	75	.04	.28*
Number of times absent	52	−.01	−.32*	76	.08	−.14	128	.03	−.22*
Number of accidents	52	−.03	.06	75	−.04	−.37*	127	−.03	−.23*
Number of disciplinary actions	52	.02	−.02	75	.10	−.17	127	.02	−.09
Level of position attained	52	−.09	.14	77	−.21	.09	129	−.12	.11

*$p < .05$

In general the LAP does show a positive relation to the various training criteria and it does tend to predict who will be absent most and who will have the most accidents. There is some indication of differential validity for individual performance indexes, but there are two significant correlations in both samples. The data are not strong, but the overall trend is to back up the AT&T contention that the LAP is job-related; it appears to be training related in particular. On the other hand, the validity of the mental ability tests obtained using the LAP criterion is nowhere in evidence. It could be argued that validity has already been demonstrated with the LAP and that further evidence is not needed, especially since the LAP has now been shown to be relevant as a criterion. Yet one could certainly hope for more solid data.

Given the nature of the evidence adduced to date, it seems unlikely that EEOC will be any less critical of short programmed learning criteria such as the LAP in the future than it was in the AT&T case. In fact to use such a criterion now would almost invite attack. This is not to say what a court would decide, but it does suggest the advisability of using other criteria as well in validation research.

VALIDATION OF EMPLOYMENT TESTS FOR TELEPHONE COMPANY INSTALLATION AND REPAIR OCCUPATIONS*

Donald L. Grant[1] and Douglas W. Bray
American Telephone and Telegraph Company

Many thousands of applicants are screened each year for employment in the Plant departments of Bell System telephone companies. In 1968, for example, over 40,000 new employees were added. Of these, the great majority are employed for installation and repair work.

Telephone company Plant Department craft occupations are covered by those classified in the *Dictionary of Occupational Titles* (DOT, United States Department of Labor, 1965) under electrical assembling, installing, and repairing. They include such DOT codes and titles as: 822.281 (Central Office Repairman, Installer Repairman, Private-Branch-Exchange Repairman, Station Repairman), 822.381 (Lineman, PBX Installer, Station Installer, Test Deskman, Transmission Man), 822.884 (Frameman), 829.381 (Cable Splicer), and 829.887 (Cable Splicer Helper).

Some applicants for Plant jobs have had training or experience fitting them for the more complex occupations, such as Cable Splicer or Central Office Repairman. These are far outweighed, however, by those without relevant background who are employed for less complex starting jobs, such as cable splicer helper or frameman. All, however, are expected to be able to progress to the more complex work. Persons employed for craft work are not hired for a specific occupation but for a class of occupations.

The quality of telephone service is dependent on the functioning of a vast network of equipment which, in turn, reflects the performance of those installing and maintaining that equipment. Because of the specialized nature of the work and the expectation that employees will progress through various jobs to high skill levels, the

*From *Journal of Applied Psychology,* Vol. 54 (1970), 7-14. Copyright 1970 by the American Psychological Association. Reprinted by permission.

[1][Footnote omitted.—Ed.]

telephone companies provide extensive training. It is essential, therefore, that employees have the ability to profit from such training.

In order to select such employees the Bell System telephone companies have for many years used aptitude tests as aids in the employment process. Various validation studies of such tests have been made over the years and the selection battery has been revised from time to time. The present study represents an attempt to improve significantly on previous efforts by including a geographically spread sample, by developing more rigorous criterion measures, and by including Negroes as an identified portion of the sample.

Criterion

Aptitude tests are used in the expectation that they measure the capacity of the individual to acquire particular knowledge and/or skill. The most relevant criterion for such tests is, therefore, the degree to which the individual has acquired the knowledge or skill after an opportunity for learning has occurred. Day-to-day job performance is not usually a good measure of such task proficiency since it is a function not only of developed ability to do the job but of the nature of supervision, peer pressures to control output, individual motivation, etc. Much better would be a direct measure of task proficiency after training has occurred.

There are difficulties even with this type of criterion. Training is sometimes not standardized. Variability in the opportunity to learn will reduce the observed relationship between aptitude and developed skill.

In the present case another problem was presented. Telephone craftsmen, as was noted above, are employed with the expectation that they will progress upward through jobs of increasing complexity. This means that they may not be receiving training for advanced craft jobs until several years after employment. If a longitudinal study of employment selection tests had been conducted it would not only have taken years but many contaminating factors would have been impossible to control.

For the above reasons it was decided that the desired study design would be one in which new inexperienced employees would undergo standardized training and their development of task proficiency measured as they underwent that training. The training, furthermore, would include material normally taught later in an employee's career in addition to that usually given to new men.

Such a standardized training experience was available in the Plant Department Learning Assessment Program (LAP) developed by the Michigan Bell Telephone Co. This program had been developed in response to a recommendation by the authors that performance in training for a job for which an employee is a candidate would be a pertinent and palatable method of final selection for that job. The program is, thus, a program for screening candidates for upgrading.

One frequent objection to the use of training for screening is its cost. Training for the range of telephone installation and repair occupations would, for example, take many weeks. The further suggestion was made, therefore, that representative samples of the training might be taken, thus allowing a determination of the degree to which the individual could learn representative skills without the prohibitive cost of putting him through complete training. The LAP was developed to fill these requirements by C. Glenn Valentine.[2]

The program consists of key segments of training courses for Station Installer and Repairman occupations and for more complex occupations such as Central Office Repairman, PBX Installer, PBX Repairman, and Test Deskman. The program is organized into seven levels of training ranging from the more elementary to the more complex, including basic electricity, basic telephone, Bell System Practices, station circuits, advanced circuits, and trouble location. Levels 1-4 sample training for the Station Installer and Repairman occupations, Levels 5-7 for the more complex, "top craft," occupations.

The *S* is tested preceding each level on the content of that level. If he passes the pretest, he goes directly to the pretest for the next level. If he fails to pass the pretest, he goes through the training for that level and, when ready, takes a posttest. For any given level the proficiency tests, pre- and post-, have been designed to be equivalent

[2]Formerly with the Michigan Bell Telephone Company and currently Vice President of Learning Sciences, Inc. C. Glenn Valentine was assisted on problems of test construction by Ira Cisin, George Washington University.

in content and difficulty. Standards on the tests are based on the performance of experienced craftsmen.

All of the training has been programmed. The candidate is given the materials he needs by the administrator of the program and proceeds through the sequence at his own pace. Other than help in getting started, the candidate receives no instructional assistance. The tests are administered and scored (objectively) by the program administrator or his assistant.

Much of the training and testing involves performance with normal tools and especially adapted telephone equipment. A relatively small proportion of the program is verbal in content. The primary objective of the program is to assess a candidate's ability to perform, after adequate training, a sample of tasks regularly performed by Plant Department craftsmen.

Because of the self-paced nature of this program, the time required to complete it varies from candidate to candidate. On the average, candidates for Station Installer-Repairman positions take approximately 4 days to complete Levels 1-4 while those for "top craft" take approximately 6 days. For both groups the time required is, of course, considerably less than the full training programs for the occupations involved yet gives ample time to demonstrate ability to learn the work.

Method

The telephone companies agreeing to participate in the study were, in addition to the Michigan Bell Telephone Company, Bell Telephone Company of Pennsylvania, Chesapeake and Potomac Telephone Company, Illinois Bell Telephone Company, and Pacific Telephone and Telegraph Company. Each participating company selected a large-city location, a primary source of employment, in which to select a sample of applicants for the study. The locations were Detroit, Philadelphia, Washington, Chicago, and San Francisco.

Each company agreed to employ 100 men of which half would be Negroes. Agreement was reached, also, to insure an adequate range of test scores by employing half of the applicants in each group from those failing to meet the then recommended employment test standards and, as far as possible, to equate the two groups for range of tested ability. Persons employed for the study were to meet normal employment requirements (i.e., interviews, reference checks, medical examination). Applicants having special background for the work (e.g., graduates of 2-year technical institutes and those with experience in radio, television, radar, or other work of a similar nature) would not be assigned to the study. Such persons are not representative of typical applicants and might well have confounded the results of the study.

Those assigned to the study were informed at the time of employment that they were to participate in the study. A brief description of the study and of the LAP, to which they were sent immediately, was given them. They were informed that continued employment in Plant Craft work depended upon satisfactory performance in the LAP. For administrative purposes satisfactory performance was denoted by meeting the requirements, using Michigan Bell Telephone Company standards, for Levels 1-4 of the program.

The tests in use for Bell System Plant Department employment at the time of this study were the School and College Ability Test, Level 2, (published by Educational Testing Service) and the Test of Mechanical Comprehension, Form BB (published by the Psychological Corporation). In addition, three tests which, it was conjectured, might also cover relevant aptitudes were given. They were: (*a*) Bell System Qualification Test III,[3] (*b*) Abstract Reasoning, Form A (a nonverbal logical reasoning test in the Differential Aptitude Test series published by the Psychological Corporation) and (*c*) Crawford Small Parts Dexterity Test (also published by the Psychological Corporation). All tests were administered to *S*s prior to their entering the LAP.

[3]This test was originally developed in the New York Telephone Company for placement of Plant Department craftsmen in training for central office repair work. It consists essentially of a set of rules to be memorized and then applied to drawing a line through a series of symbols. The task required is similar, conceptually, to tracing trouble in a complex electrical circuit. Persons taking the test are first given a set of instructions and a practice problem. They are then given a set of rules to memorize. The rules are taken away after 10 min. and a sheet with symbols on it provided. The examinee has 5 min. to draw a line through the symbols in accordance with the rules memorized. A second set of rules is then provided and the process repeated. The score is the total right (lines drawn through appropriate symbols) minus ½ total wrong (lines drawn through inappropriate symbols).

Persons assigned to the study were expected to undertake all seven levels of the LAP. Those dropping out of the program prior to completing Levels 1-4 were not included in the study sample, though they were replaced by persons judged equivalent in tested ability. For administrative reasons those failing to meet the requirement on Levels 1-4, though completing them, were informed that they must pass Level 5 in order to proceed further. In addition, a generous time limit for completing each level of the program was allowed (up to 21 days for all 7 levels). Those taking excessive time on a level were asked to stop and take the posttest for the level, then to proceed to the next level.

A complete record of all data collected was made. Test scores were retained by employment office personnel as confidential information. The administrator of the LAP recorded scores on all performance tests (pre- and post-), information on meeting or failing to meet the requirements of the program (using Michigan Bell Company standards), highest level completed, highest level passed, and time taken to complete the program.

After all 100 *S*s in a participating company sample had been processed, the data were forwarded to the Personnel Research Section of the AT&T Co. Analyses were made for each company sample and for the combined company samples, separately for minority and nonminority groups and for both combined. Means and standard deviations for each variable (predictor and criteria) were computed as were the intercorrelations among all variables. Following inspection of the data, multiple correlation coefficients between selected predictor variables and a selected criterion variable were computed. Expectancy tables were determined and finally, after the most predictive tests had been identified and scores on them combined, the regression equations for the minority and nonminority groups were compared.

Results

By the end of 1967, complete data on 430 *S*s had been obtained (all of the data expected from four participating companies and partial data from the fifth). Average age of the *S*s was 21, with 54% being less than 21 and only 12% being over 25. Most (94%) of the *S*s were high school graduates and one-fifth had had some education beyond high school.

Scores of the nonminority and minority *S*s on the five aptitude tests given prior to the LAP were close both in mean and standard deviation, as Table 1 shows. The closeness of these values reflects the procedures in assigning applicants to the study.

Table 1

Means and Standard Deviations

Variable	Combined samples		Minority sample		Nonminority sample	
	$\bar{X}$	*SD*	$\bar{X}$	*SD*	$\bar{X}$	*SD*
SCAT Total	292	10	291	10	294	10
SCAT Quantitative	293	15	290	15	296	16
SCAT Verbal	290	14	289	12	291	15
Mechanical Comprehension	23	10	21	9	25	10
BS Qualification Test III	31	24	28	23	33	24
Abstract Reasoning	32	8	31	9	34	7
Small Parts Dexterity (Part I)	24[a]	5	23	4	24	5
Small Parts Dexterity (Part II)	26[b]	5	25	5	27	5
Highest Level Passed	4.4	1.8	4.1	1.8	4.6	1.8

Note—For the Combined samples, $N = 430$; for the Minority sample, $n = 211$; for the Nonminority sample, $n = 219$.
[a]Number of pins and collars completed in 3 minutes.
[b]Number of screws completed in 5 minutes.

Two-thirds of the *S*s (59% of the minority *S*s; 75% of the nonminority *S*s) met the requirements of the Learning Assessment Program for Levels 1-4 (Station Installer-Repairman) while only 10% (6% of the minority *S*s; 15% of the nonminority *S*s) met the requirements for Levels 5-7 (top craft). Evidently, the requirements of Levels 1-4 were within the competence of a majority of *S*s while those for Levels 5-7 were too difficult for most.

The data show, however, that nearly half, 46%, of the *S*s (38% minority *S*s and 53% nonminority *S*s) had met the requirements for Levels 1-4 of the LAP and also passed one or more of the higher levels (5, 6, or 7). It was decided, therefore, to use highest level passed, scored simply 0-7, as the single, most representative indicator of performance in the program. The correlation coefficients of aptitude test scores with highest level passed for minority

*S*s, nonminority *S*s, and total are presented in Table 2. The coefficients are not corrected for restrictions in range of test scores.

Table 2

Correlations with Highest Level Passed

Variable	Combined samples	Minority sample	Nonminority sample
	r	*r*	*r*
SCAT Total	.39	.41	.36
SCAT Quantitative	.40	.41	.37
SCAT Verbal	.27	.32	.24
Mechanical Comprehension	.34	.31	.32
BS Qualification Test III	.38	.38	.38
Abstract Reasoning	.44	.38	.50
Small Parts Dexterity (Part I)	.24	.25	.19
Small Parts Dexterity (Part II)	.19	.16	.17

Note.—For the Combined sample, $N = 430$; for the Minority sample, $n = 211$; for the Nonminority sample, $n = 219$.

The correlation coefficients, it will be noted, are quite similar for the two groups of *S*s. None of the differences between coefficients is statistically significant at the .05 level. All of the coefficients with highest level of LAP passed are significant at the .01 level except for Part II of the Small Parts Dexterity Test. The latter are significant at the .01 level for the entire sample and at the .05 level for each subsample.

Because of the reasonable comparability of the results for the two samples, the data for the combined samples were used in carrying out the next step of the analyses, that is, comparing the correlations of combinations of test scores with highest level passed in the LAP. Inspection of the coefficients with highest level passed (Table 2) and of the intercorrelations between the test scores (shown in Table 3) suggested that the Small Parts Dexterity Test would contribute little to a battery of employment tests for these occupations. Consequently, the coefficients for this test were omitted from the computations of multiple correlation coefficients. In addition, inspection of the data indicated that total scores on the School and College Ability Test were about as predictive as the quantitative scores and were more predictive than the verbal scores. Therefore,

Table 3

Intercorrelations of the Test Score for the Combined Samples

Variable	1	2	3	4	5	6	7	8
SCAT Total (1)		73	81	35	40	45	10	08
SCAT Quantitative (2)	73		32	34	44	47	14	14
SCAT Verbal (3)	81	32		28	22	28	08	03
Mechanical Comprehension (4)	35	34	28		29	37	21	33
BS Qualification Test III (5)	40	44	22	29		47	07	13
Abstract Reasoning (6)	45	47	28	37	47		23	19
Small Parts Dexterity (Part I) (7)	10	14	08	21	07	23		42
Small Parts Dexterity (Part II) (8)	08	14	03	33	13	19	42	

Note.—Decimals omitted.

looking ahead to possible future use of the test, it was decided to use the correlations for the total rather than for the part scores in computing multiple correlations.

The multiple correlations between all possible combinations of the School and College Ability Test (SCAT), Test of Mechanical Comprehension (MC), Bell System Qualification Test III (BSQT III) and Abstract Reasoning (AR) are shown in Table 4. From the results shown it is apparent, as would be expected, that a combination of all four tests yields the highest prediction but that the differences between the various combinations are relatively small. Because the highest predicting combination of two tests (SCAT and AR) yielded

Table 4

Multiple Correlations with Highest Level Passed for the Combined Samples

Test combination	R
SCAT + MC + BSQT III + AR	.53
SCAT + MC + BSQT III	.49
SCAT + MC + AR	.51
SCAT + BSQT III + AR	.51
SCAT + MC	.45
SCAT + BSQT III	.46
SCAT + AR	.49
MC + BSQT III	.45
MC + AR	.48
BSQT III + AR	.48

Note.—Abbreviations: SCAT = School and College Ability Test; MC = Mechanical Comprehension; BSQT III = Bell System Qualification Test III; AR = Abstract Reasoning.

a multiple correlation only slightly lower than for combinations of three and four tests, it was decided to carry out further analyses using this combination. It should be added that practical considerations of test administration in employment offices influenced this decision. Both the tests chosen are relatively easy to administer and total testing time is approximately 2 hr.

Scores on SCAT and Abstract Reasoning, then, were combined simply by summing, thus ignoring their respective beta weights, in order to develop expectancy tables for the separate and combined samples. Again, future administrative considerations, that is, scoring tests in many employment offices for literally thousands of applicants, influenced this decision. When correlated with highest level passed in the LAP, incidentally, the composite scores yielded correlations of .48 for minority *S*s, .46 for nonminority *S*s and .48 for the combined samples. The latter compares favorably with a .49 multiple correlation coefficient (Table 4) for the two tests.

In order to generalize from the results, expectancy tables for the separate and combined samples were developed. Stanines for the composite scores on the two tests were estimated from published norms for high school seniors. The resulting tables are summarized in Table 5, which groups stanines 1-4 (scores less than 314) and 6-9 (324 and above). It is estimated that 20% of the high school senior population would obtain Stanine 5 scores (314-323), while 40% would obtain higher and 40% lower scores.

As would be expected, the data in Table 5 reflect the correlational results, that is, in general, the higher the test score the greater are the percentages of *S*s meeting the requirements of the LAP. In addition, the percentages meeting the requirements tend to decline sharply from the least stringent (qualifying on Levels 1-4) to the most stringent (qualifying on Levels 5-7). Furthermore, at most test score intervals the percentages of nonminority *S*s meeting the requirements tend to exceed those of minority *S*s.

The final step in the analyses was to compare the regression equations (composite test scores on highest level passed in the LAP) for minority and nonminority *S*s. The method used is one outlined by Potthoff (1966, pp. 17-23). The results are presented in Table 6 and are illustrated in Figure 1. It can be seen from the table that the

Table 5

Expectancy Tables

Composite scores (SCAT + AR)	Number in each sample			Percentage qualifying on LAP Levels 1-4		
	Combined	Minority	Nonminority	Combined	Minority	Nonminority
324 & above	218	97	121	78	72	82
314-323	118	61	57	65	52	79
Less than 314	94	53	41	45	42	49
Total	430	211	219	67	59	75

slopes of the regression lines are practically identical but that there is a difference in the intercepts. As a consequence, the regression lines for the two samples are parallel.

Discussion

The two purposes of this study were to evaluate the relevance of certain preemployment tests for telephone company installation and repair work and to evaluate their applicability to minority as well as nonminority applicants. In respect to the first objective, the results show that the two tests in use at the time of the study were good indicators of ability to learn telephone craft work and that two other tests yielded approximately the same results. Any combination of these tests would be of advantage in employment decisions.

There are no significant differences between the correlation coefficients of each test with the criterion for minority and nonminority *S*s. These findings are similar to those reported by Cleary (1966) for predicting the scholastic performance of white and Negro students in integrated colleges and by Tenopyr (1967) for predicting machine-shop training success of minority and nonminority employees in the aircraft industry. In their studies the tests involved proved equally valid for the groups studied. The differences in the slopes of the regression lines are not statistically significant, though in some of the comparisons made the intercepts of the regression lines are significantly different.

The differences in the intercepts of the regression lines for the two groups of *S*s in the Plant craft study raises a question regarding

Table 5—*continued*

Composite scores (SCAT + AR)	Percentage qualifying on 1-4 and passing one or more higher levels			Percentage qualifying on LAP Levels 5-7		
	Combined	Minority	Nonminority	Combined	Minority	Nonminority
324 & above	59	48	67	17	10	22
314-323	42	41	44	4	2	7
Less than 314	19	17	22	2	2	2
Total	46	38	53	10	6	15

the "fairness" of using the tests for employment purposes. Application of a common regression line for the two groups in making predictions of performance tends to underestimate performance for the group having the higher intercept while overestimating performance for the group having the lower intercept. As can be readily determined from Table 6, a combined test score of 324 yields a prediction for highest level passed of 4.31 from the common regression equation, 4.17 from the minority regression equation and 4.46 from the nonminority regression equation. Similar findings are reported by Cleary (1966) and Tenopyr (1967) from their data. In such instances applying the common regression line biases the use of the tests for making predictions somewhat in favor of minority group

Table 6

Comparison of Regression Equations

Sample	Composite test scores		Highest LAP level passed			Regression equation	Significance tests	
	$\bar{X}$	*SD*	$\bar{Y}$	*SD*	r_{xy}		Slope *F*	Intercept *F*
Combined	325	15.6	4.4	1.8	.48	$\hat{Y} = .056X - 13.83$	.04	5.55*
Minority	322	15.9	4.1	1.8	.48	$\hat{Y} = .056X - 13.97$		
Nonminority	327	15.0	4.6	1.8	.46	$\hat{Y} = .054X - 13.04$		

$^*p < .05$.

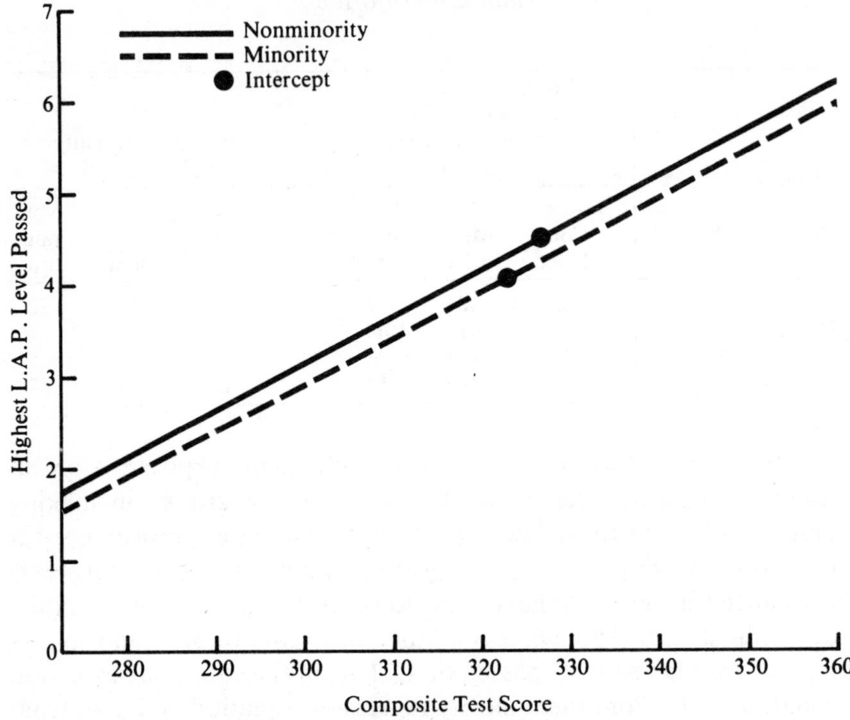

Figure 1. *Comparison of regression lines.*

applicants. For employment purposes, however, the effects are not of sufficient magnitude to warrant using different regression lines.

The performance measures derived from the Learning Assessment Program provide rather unique and novel criteria for evaluating aptitude tests. The LAP is an ingenious innovation. Its primary use, of course, is that of screening candidates being considered for upgrading. As a criterion instrument it makes it possible to ascertain in a relatively short time the proficiencies of new employees in performing representative Plant craft tasks. It should be added that it also made it possible to design and carry out a relatively well-controlled test validation study.

The present study is to be extended longitudinally by the yearly collection of data on the participants. The data will include carefully controlled supervisory ratings, retention in the Plant craft, occupations to which assigned, promotions, performance in training programs, absences, tardiness, disciplinary actions, and so forth. Though predicting the results of such a study would be presumptuous, it is hoped that it will yield relevant data regarding the efficacy of the LAP in identifying persons with high career potential in telephone company installation and repair occupations. Such follow-up information will serve to illuminate the relationships between task proficiency and overall worth as an employee and focus attention on motivational and situational determinants of job performance.

References

Cleary, T. A. Test bias: Validity of the Scholastic Aptitude Test for Negro and white students in integrated colleges (Research Bulletin 66-31). Princeton, N.J.: Educational Testing Service, 1966.

Potthoff, R. F. Statistical aspects of the problem of biases in psychological tests (Institute of Statistics Mimeo Service No. 479). Chapel Hill, N.C.: University of North Carolina, 1966.

Tenopyr, M. L. Race and socioeconomic status as moderators in predicting machine-shop training success. Paper presented at the meeting of the American Psychological Association, Washington, D.C., September 1967.

United States Department of Labor. *Dictionary of occupational titles.* Washington, D.C.: United States Government Printing Office, 1965.

16

validation study of tests for service representatives

Introductory notes

Two points about this study are important for our purposes. One is that adverse impact was in evidence even though an attempt was made to obtain a broad range of scores on the predictors. On most of the tests the mean score in the minority sample was significantly below that for the nonminority group. This decrease was matched by a lower level of minority performance on the criteria, and most tests proved to be valid in both white and minority samples. However, this kind of lower criterion performance is not a *necessary* condition for obtaining evidence of validity which is not differential.

The second important aspect relates to the criterion. In this case, as in the study in Chapter 15, the criterion measure is a work sample (or job sample, or simulation), but the measure was administered at the completion of training and covers both knowledge and skills included in that training. In this respect it differs from the LAP which was given before actual training and which attempts to sample the training and then measure learning of the sampled content. The FEA guidelines and the new uniform guidelines accept training criteria of the kind utilized in the service representative study; in its guidelines EEOC was mute on the point. Yet there is no evidence that EEOC considered the criterion used in this study vulnerable, at least to the extent the LAP was considered vulnerable. The Composite Performance Index used was not attacked in the hearings. Since training costs money, in most cases must be completed successfully before a person becomes eligible to perform the job, and can be assumed to represent the company's best efforts to prepare people for actual job performance, there are strong arguments for accepting training criteria as appropriate. This line of thinking appears to have been accepted by the Supreme Court also.[1] Thus, the overall evidence clearly indicates that the type of criterion used in this study can be justified.

EMPLOYMENT TEST VALIDATION FOR MINORITY AND NONMINORITY TELEPHONE COMPANY SERVICE REPRESENTATIVES*

Sidney Gael and Donald L. Grant
American Telephone and Telegraph Company

Employment test bias, as is the case with test utility, cannot be gauged unless the tests are related to meaningful job standards. The position that employment tests are biased against minority group members because they usually score lower than white applicants is untenable unless accompanied by a statement regarding job performance. Invariably, definitions and discussions of employment test bias or unfair discrimination refer to the important relationship between tests and job performance (e.g., Guion, 1966).

Unfortunately, studies of test bias have not paved the way for clear cut conclusions. In most cases white applicants averaged better on employment tests than their minority counterparts, but the ethnic groups did not necessarily attain different criterion levels (e.g., Kirkpatrick, Ewen, Barrett, & Katzell, 1968). Differential validity was obtained in several studies (O'Leary, Farr, & Bartlett, 1970) and equal validity in others (Gael & Grant, 1971; Grant & Bray, 1970). Bray and Moses (1972) point out ". . . as a general rule most studies showing lack of differential validity have used better than average

[1] *Washington* v. *Davis,* 426 U.S. 229 (1976), 12 FEP Cases 1415.

*From *Journal of Applied Psychology,* Vol. 56 (1972), 135-139.

A large number of employees at the Chesapeake and Potomac Telephone Company cooperated to develop the criterion instruments, but Marie Beeching and June Olsson, the JPR administrators, and Ruth Pyles and James McHenry deserve special mention for their participation in the development and administration of the criteria and the general conduct of the study.

criterion measures, while most of the studies supporting differential validity rely on subjective, poorly determined rating criteria [p. 554]."

The objectives of the present test validation study were to (*a*) determine which combination of tests already in use contribute significantly to the selection of job applicants with appropriate service representative (SR) potential, (*b*) ascertain the fairness of the selected tests to minority (black) as well as nonminority job applicants, and (*c*) formulate employment test standards for SRs that will be used nationwide.

Method

Job

A brief description of the SR job is contained in the *Dictionary of Occupational Titles* (United States Department of Labor, 1965) under Code 249.368. The SR is required to integrate a wide variety of customer contact, clerical, computational, and filing activities under the pace imposed by a steady influx of calls. Examples of the work performed are (*a*) taking orders for new telephone services, (*b*) explaining and adjusting telephone bills, (*c*) recording the details associated with equipment malfunctions and reporting problems to the maintenance organization, and (*d*) notifying customers that their payments are due and making payment arrangements. Throughout, the SR prepares, handles, and files a large amount of paperwork.

Sample

Applicants were first screened for the study in April 1968, and data collection continued until December 1969. Performance evaluations were obtained upon the conclusion of training for 107 minority and 193 nonminority SRs. The age range for the total sample was 18-47 yr., the average being 23 yr. Only 1% of the sample did not graduate from high school, while most had some education beyond high school, and 10% were college graduates. Two percent of the sample had no prior work experience, whereas the majority had worked for 2 or more yr. prior to accepting the SR job. Incidentally, the biographical items mentioned above were not related to performance as measured.

Predictors

A general learning ability test, five clerical aptitude tests, and a specially developed role-play interview were administered to study participants during the employment process. Specifically the tests were:

1. Bell System Qualification Test I (BSQT 1) Short Form—an adaptation of the School and College Ability Test, Level 2, published by Educational Testing Service;
2. Spelling—40 multiple-choice items with one of three spellings correct;
3. Number Comparison—100 pairs of four- to nine-digit numbers;
4. Arithmetic—100 simple addition and subtraction examples;
5. Number Transcription—25 randomly arranged numbers and 25 names to be paired with the numbers;
6. Filing—15 randomly listed names to be interfiled with 44 alphabetically arranged names; and
7. SR Aptitude (SRAT)—a role-playing interview modeled after tasks performed by SRs in telephone contacts with customers.

Unlike the BSQT I and the SRAT which require 30 and 45 min., respectively, the clerical tests are highly speeded with time limits ranging from 1½ min. for the Spelling test to 3½ min. for the Number Transcription test. Exclusive of directions, 87.5 min. were required to test each job applicant.

Employment offices were requested regarding the assignment of applicants to the study to obtain broad and comparable BSQT I score ranges for both ethnic groups.

Criteria

The guidelines followed in designing and developing the criterion instruments were to (*a*) measure both the acquisition and application of job knowledge as objectively as possible, and (*b*) obtain direct measures of task proficiency in a standardized situation. Accordingly, a pencil and paper achievement test, the Job Knowledge Review (JKR) and an individually administered work sample test, the Job Performance Review (JPR) were developed specifically for the study by a team of SR supervisors, SR trainers, and a psychologist. The JKR was composed of approximately 70 completion and 40 multiple-choice items covering every major aspect of the 8 wk. of training and was aimed at determining comprehension and retention of company policies and job procedures and practices. The JPR required about 75-90 min. for each administration and was composed of typical calls in which SRs engage, plus the concomitant clerical work.

When a class of SRs completed the JKR, one SR at a time was oriented to the JPR, a replica of the SR work position. The scene was set by a specially trained administrator who reviewed instructions and encouraged questions about the expected performance. Prior to leaving the SR on her own, the administrator set the wall clock at 8:55 A.M., and told the SR to get ready to begin a typical work day (the starting time, the date, and several other conditions were constant throughout to agree with the available records, etc.). The administrator then proceeded to an adjoining room where telephone calls to the SR originated. One administrator initiated the calls and acted as a customer while a second specially trained administrator listened to each customer contact and evaluated the SR's oral performance on a specially prepared rating form. Examples of oral behavior rated are the way the SR opened the contact with the customer, determined the primary reason the customer called, sold new equipment and services, quoted charges for different types of equipment, obtained credit information, and closed the contact.

Proficiency measures resulting from the JPR were (*a*) record preparation (RP), the sum of the points accorded each part of a record prepared or completed (points were determined by comparing the records to a model set with points already assigned); (*b*) verbal contact (VC), the sum of the ratings of the verbal interaction with the "customer"; and (*c*) filing (F), the number of records *not* in the designated location when the JPR was terminated.

Criterion scores were standardized by city, and standard scores were combined to form a composite performance index (CPI) by the formula

$$CPI = Z_{\mathrm{JKR}} + Z_{\mathrm{RP}} + 2Z_{\mathrm{VC}} - Z_{\mathrm{F}}.$$

The Z_{VC} was doubled because of its judged importance to overall performance, and the Z_{F} was subtracted because the raw score was an error score.

Separate analyses were conducted for the black, white, and combined samples by city and across cities. Means and standard deviations were computed for each variable. All variables intercorrelated, and statistics for the ethnic groups compared. A multiple correlation between the employment tests and the CPI was calculated in accordance with the Wherry test selection method (Stead, Shartle, Otis, Ward, Osborne, Endler, Dvorak, Cooper, Bellows, & Colbe, 1940). The two most predictive tests were combined by simply adding the raw scores. Regression equations were obtained for the combined white and black samples, and the regression equations compared using a procedure outlined by Potthoff (1966). Finally, expectancy tables were prepared and employment standards derived.

Table 1

Employment Test and Criteria Means and Standard Deviations

Variable	Nonminority sample			Minority sample			Minority vs. nonminority
	$\overline{X}$	*SD*	*N*	$\overline{X}$	*SD*	*N*	*t*
Employment tests							
BSQT I	307.3	11.3	193	299.4	11.0	106	5.88***
Arithmetic	57.3	18.1	186	53.1	15.7	103	2.06*
No. Comparison	49.7	17.2	186	51.2	11.0	103	.90
Filing	12.3	2.6	186	11.0	2.9	103	3.79***
No. Transcription	29.1	6.0	184	27.2	6.1	97	2.50*
Spelling	37.5	7.0	186	38.8	6.8	103	1.54
SR Aptitude	2.0	.51	184	2.0	.44	101	—
Composite	336.4	13.52	184	326.6	13.15	97	5.88***
Criteria							
JKR	.14	1.02	193	−.24	.91	107	3.33***
JPR							
F	−.08	1.02	193	.17	.93	107	2.17*
VC	.07	1.02	193	−.12	.94	107	1.63
RP	.08	1.02	193	−.13	1.07	107	1.66
CPI	.44	3.64	193	−.78	3.32	107	2.95**

Note.—Abbreviations: BSQT = Bell System Qualification Test, SR = service representative, JKR = Job Knowledge Review, JPR = Job Performance Review, F = filing, VC = verbal contact, RP = record preparation, CPI = composite performance index.

*$p < .05$.

**$p < .01$.

***$p < .001$.

Table 2

Validity Coefficients

Employment tests	JKR			JPR-F		
	Total	Non-minority	Minority	Total	Non-minority	Minority
BSQT I	40**	39**	31**	11	11	02
Arithmetic	18**	18*	11	08	13	−09
No. Comparison	02	03	01	04	03	08
Filing	23**	22**	15	12	09	10
No. Transcription	09	04	11	19**	19**	15
Spelling	13*	24*	−04	16**	26**	00
SR Aptitude	13*	13	14	09	05	20*

Note.—The sample size for each correlation is a smaller n in Table 1 for the pair. Decimal System Qualification Test, SR = service representative, JKR = Job Knowledge Review, JPR CPI = composite performance index. $^*p<.05$. $^{**}p<.01$.

Results

The predictor and criterion means; standard deviations; sample sizes for the combined, nonminority, and the minority samples; and the results of the comparisons between the nonminority and minority sample means are presented in Table 1. It was not possible within the data collection period to obtain the desired correspondence between the nonminority and minority sample BSQT I distributions. Though the BSQT I score ranges for the ethnic groups are comparable, the difference between the means is statistically significant, as are the differences between the arithmetic, filing, and number transcription test means. Criterion mean differences are significant for the JKR and the JPR-F but not for the RP and the VC. The difference in overall performance as represented by the CPI is significant with the nonminority sample attaining higher scores than the minority sample.

Validity coefficients are shown in Table 2. Six of the seven employment tests are significantly related to the CPI for the total and the nonminority samples, and three tests are significantly related for the minority sample. The BSQT I, Number Transcription, and SRAT are significantly related to the CPI for both ethnic samples. The differences between the validity coefficients for the minority and nonminority samples, except for the Spelling test, are not statistically significant.

Table 2—*continued*

JPR-RP			JPR-VC			CPI		
Total	Non-minority	Minority	Total	Non-minority	Minority	Total	Non-minority	Minority
23**	18**	28**	22**	27**	09	33*	33**	23*
11	10	10	17**	17*	16	19**	20**	13
05	02	16	01	02	08	04	02	13
10	09	07	10	09	06	18*	16*	13
21**	22**	16	17**	18*	12	23**	22**	20*
09	12	05	12*	18*	03	17**	27**	02
13*	19**	00	18*	15*	22*	20**	18*	24*

points have been omitted, and the JPR-F score was reflected. Abbreviations: BSQT = Bell
= Job Performance Review, F = filing, VC = verbal contact, RP = record preparation,

The best single predictor of overall performance for the total sample is the BSQT I. The Number Transcription and the SRAT were identified by the Wherry test selection method as the second and third tests to combine with the BSQT I. The respective shrunken multiple correlations are .37 and .40. None of the remaining tests contribute to the multiple correlation despite the fact that three of the four tests are individually predictive. The three employment tests selected by the Wherry method are the same three tests that are significantly related to the CPI for the total, minority, and nonminority samples. The SRAT, however, was not recommended for employment office use because its contribution to test variance and predictability was outweighed by practical administering and scoring considerations.

Test fairness or bias, a primary concern, was examined by comparing the slopes and intercepts of the minority and nonminority sample regression lines (Potthoff, 1966). The results of the comparisons, along with the composite test and criterion statistics, and the regression equations appear in Table 3. Regression line slopes and intercepts for the nonminority and minority samples are not significantly different, indicating that the composite predictor is unbiased.

Test standards were established by first selecting a proficiency level that distinguished the more from the less effective performers. Several managers responsible for SR performance concluded that

Table 3

Composite Predictor and Criterion Means and Standard Deviations, Regression Equations, and Comparison of Regression Lines

Sample	Composite test		Composite criterion			Regression equation	Significance test	
	$\bar{X}$	S_x	$\bar{Y}$	S_y	r		Slope F	Intercept F
Total	333.0	14.08	.00	3.57	.375	$\hat{Y} = .0950X - 31.6350$		
Nonminority	336.4	13.52	.44	3.64	.386	$\hat{Y} = .1039X - 34.5119$	1.04	1.67
Minority	326.6	13.15	−.78	3.32	.283	$\hat{Y} = .0714X - 24.0992$		

the total sample CPI average was a reasonable point at which to make the distinction. Composite predictor distributions were plotted separately for the more effective and less effective SRs, and the intersection of the distributions was used to determine the test cutting score that would minimize employment decision errors (Blum & Naylor, 1968).

Inasmuch as the lower limit of the second quarter coincided with the previously determined cutting score, the top two composite test score quarters were combined to form a test qualified category. The third quarter is offered as an intermediate range from which applicants can be selected only under extended tight labor market conditions. Finally, the bottom quarter is the test unqualified range. Table 4 contains the test standards recommended for employment office use and the associated expectancies.

Though the validity coefficients with the CPI range from zero to moderate (.02-.33) and the shrunken multiple correlation (.37) is not especially high, the expectancies indicate that the composite predictor differentiated the more from the less effective performers for the minority, nonminority, and total samples. As expected, the largest percentages of more effective performers are found in the test qualified range, and as the test score ranges decline so do the percentages, except for a slight reversal for the minority sample. Additionally, the percentages of more effective performers in the test qualified range differ sharply from those in the intermediate and test unqualified ranges. Nearly two-thirds of the test qualified SRs for the total sample were more effective performers, but only a little more than one-third of the SRs in the intermediate and unqualified ranges were more effective performers. Of the 140 SRs obtaining

Table 4
Expectancy Table for the Composite Predictor and Composite Criterion

Test category	Total sample[a]		Minority sample[b]	Non-minority sample[c]
	Predictor composite range	% Average & above	% Average & above	% Average & above
Qualified	332 & above	63	59	64
Intermediate	323—331	40	25	48
Unqualified	322 & below	32	29	36
Total		50	38	56

[a] $N = 281$.
[b] $N = 97$.
[c] $N = 184$.

average and above average CPIs, 26% are minority SRs and 74% are nonminority SRs. Below average CPIs were obtained by 43% minority and 57% nonminority SRs. When minority and nonminority samples are considered separately, the percentages obtaining average and above average CPIs are 38% and 56%, respectively.

Discussion

Tests, singly or in combination, can be said to be biased with respect to a population (specified by ethnic background, sex, age, etc.) if they are not predictive of performance for the population or inaccurately estimate performance of its members. The purpose of designing a test validation study in which the results are separately determined for identified populations is, therefore, to determine whether the tests involved are biased with respect to the populations studied.

The study described resulted in the selection of a combination of two tests which are reasonably free of the undesired bias for two ethnic populations, that is, minority (black) and nonminority applicants for SR positions in Bell System telephone companies. For both populations, scores on the combined tests are predictive of performance, as measured, and estimate performance with relatively the same degree of accuracy. Generalizing the results to other populations (e.g., Spanish-surnamed Americans), to other performance criteria (e.g., supervisory ratings), and to other occupations would, of course, be questionable. The results, however, do correspond with those achieved for other telephone company occupations (i.e., installation and repair [Grant & Bray, 1970] and toll operators [Gael & Grant, 1971]).

A major effort was devoted to the development of instruments that provide measures of directly relevant job proficiency. Although the overall correlations with performance are not as high as might be desired, probably due to restrictions in range on the predictors and on the criterion, it was shown that the selected test combination identifies SRs who, on the average, will be able to learn and perform the work.

References

Blum, M. L., & Naylor, J. C. *Industrial psychology: Its theoretical and social foundations.* New York: Harper, 1968.

Bray, D. W., & Moses, J. L. Personnel selection. *Annual Review of Psychology,* 1972, 23, 545-576.

Gael, S., & Grant, D. L. Validation of a general learning ability test for selecting telephone operators. *Experimental Publication System, 1971, Issue No. 10.* (Preprint).

Grant, D. L., & Bray, D. W. Validation of employment tests for telephone company installation and repair occupations. *Journal of Applied Psychology,* 1970, 54, 7-14.

Guion, R. M. Employment tests and discriminatory hiring. *Industrial Relations,* 1966, 5, 20-37.

Kirkpatrick, J. J., Ewen, R. B., Barrett, R. S., & Katzell, R. A. *Testing and fair employment.* New York: New York University Press, 1968.

O'Leary, B. S., Farr, J. L., Bartlett, C. J. *Ethnic group membership as a moderator of job performance.* Washington, D.C.: American Institutes for Research, 1970.

Potthoff, R. F. Statistical aspects of the problem of biases in psychological tests. *Institute of Statistics Mimeo Service No. 479,* Chapel Hill, N.C.: University of North Carolina, 1966.

Stead, W. H., Shartle, C. L., Otis, J. L., Ward, R. S., Osborne, H. F., Endler, O. L., Dvorak, B. J., Cooper, J. H., Bellows, R. M., & Colbe,

L. E. *Occupational counseling techniques.* New York: American Book, 1940.

United States Department of Labor. *Dictionary of occupational titles.* Washington, D.C.: United States Government Printing Office, 1965.

17

validation study of tests for telephone operators

Introductory notes

The research described here was not published until 1975, but the study was used in evidence much earlier; as indicated in the footnote on the first page, it was completed in 1971. As in the service representative research the attempt to obtain broad score ranges was not sufficient to eliminate adverse impact on most of the tests, especially in the case of blacks. But once again validity was demonstrated for both whites and blacks.

The criterion measure used is again a post-training simulation, and it too emerged unscathed from the EEOC evaluation. However, the attention given to job analysis in the write-up of this article is important to note. By 1975 the matter of job analysis had clearly become a major consideration in evaluating the adequacy of test selection and criterion development. In contrast to the articles of 1970 and 1972, the subject of job analysis is now given major attention. The discussion presented in the article could well serve as a model for those preparing a description of their research for enforcement agencies.

The validation data for the Spanish-surnamed sample require special attention. In sharp contrast with the findings for whites and blacks, only two of the 12 validity coefficients are statistically significant and even these might have occurred by chance. The multiple-correlation value is significant but only half as large as the other values, and it is based on the inclusion of two tests that were not in themselves significant predictors. These findings in the Spanish-surnamed sample are attributed to sample selection in the two locations involved and thus to restriction of range.

From the viewpoint of company practice the restriction-of-range argument seems sensible, and given the logic of the situation the use of the tests to select Spanish-surnamed employees appears appropriate. But it remains true that the demonstration of validity for this group is extremely tenuous. The current data show no adverse impact for the Spanish-surnamed group, but this is not a cross-section of hires. Should the tests subsequently prove to yield a disproportionately low number of Spanish-surnamed employees, it is almost certain that the use of the tests would be questioned for this group, given the pattern of the validation results. The data argue strongly for further research in this area.

EMPLOYMENT TEST VALIDATION FOR MINORITY TELEPHONE OPERATORS*

Sidney Gael, Donald L. Grant, and Richard J. Ritchie
American Telephone and Telegraph Company

Anyone even remotely interested in employment testing need scarcely be reminded of the controversy surrounding the use of tests for selecting minority-group job applicants. The major issue, in addition to whether or not tests should be included in the employment process at all, appears to be whether the same or different tests and test standards (cutoffs) can or should be used for minority and nonminority job applicants. Many of the pertinent issues have been addressed in general discussions of employment test fairness (APA Task Force on Employment Testing of Minority Groups, 1969; Guion, 1966), in presentations and critiques of models for assessing test fairness (Bartlett & O'Leary, 1969; Cleary, 1968; Cole, 1973;[1] Darlington, 1971; Einhorn & Bass, 1971; Humphreys, 1973; Thorndike, 1971; Petersen & Novick, Note 1; Potthoff, Note 2), in numerous test validation studies (e.g., see Bray & Moses, 1972), and in reviews of test validation research with respect to differential

*From *Journal of Applied Psychology,* Vol. 60 (1975), 411-419.

[1]The research reported herein was completed in 1971, but more recent publications have been cited.

validity or test bias or fairness (Boehm, 1972; Cooper & Sobol, 1969; Schmidt, Berner, & Hunter, 1973; Schmidt & Hunter, 1974; Ruch, Note 3).

Despite the surge of research and interest in test validation during the past several years, a number of perplexing problems will remain. What is clear, however, is that to emerge from the morass, considerably more thought and effort than have previously been the case should be devoted to the ingredients of test validation research; otherwise, the stream of excuses usually associated with unrewarding outcomes will continue. Bray and Moses (1972), for example, suggested that the few times differential validity has been observed are probably due to poorly determined, subjective criteria.

The strategy and objectives adopted for the telephone operator test validation studies described herein were to (a) conduct predictive, criterion-related research; (b) include sufficient minority group members in the sample so that data could be analyzed separately by ethnic group; (c) validate tests against objective, standardized proficiency criteria reflecting key job requirements; (d) identify tests, singly and in combination, that will enable the selection of applicants with the potential to learn telephone operator work; and (e) recommend test procedures for use in telephone operator selection that are appropriate for minority as well as nonminority applicants. In line with the research strategy and objectives, several job sample predictors were developed to measure skills required to perform telephone operator work. Further, high fidelity job simulations specifically designed or adapted for the validation research served as the criterion instruments (Gael, 1974). To the extent that the jobs were accurately simulated and the scoring appropriately reflected the quantity and quality of output, the simulations probably measured proficiency in a more effective, objective, and standardized manner than is usually obtained with other types of criteria.

The potential importance of this validation research from a test fairness standpoint should be immediately apparent, solely because of the sheer number of telephone operator applicants involved. These studies gain in significance when it is considered that all newly hired workers are inexperienced and are trained to perform telephone operator job activities.

Method

Jobs

The present study covers three Bell System telephone operator jobs, namely, Directory Assistance (DA), Toll, and Traffic Service Position (TSP) operators. DA operators process customer requests for telephone numbers by interpreting the request, searching the appropriate reference material for the information, and reporting the information to the customer. Toll and TSP operators help customers complete calls that were not dialed for some reason or could not be dialed directly, such as person-to-person calls, some long-distance calls, credit-card calls, and collect calls. Though the telephone operator population is extremely large, it is the hiring rate that affords the opportunity to meet the sample design features mentioned above—about 100,000 operators are hired yearly to fill new positions or replace those who leave.

Sample

Nationwide samples were obtained by 11 Bell System telephone companies in 12 major metropolitan areas. Each participating company agreed to hire 50 operators per job type and to evaluate their proficiency upon the completion of formal training in a prescribed manner. They further agreed that the samples would contain at least 30% minority group members (black and Spanish-surnamed Americans) and that the minority and nonminority samples would have comparably broad score ranges on the Bell System Qualification Test (BSQT I), 1 of 10 pencil-and-paper tests studied. The BSQT I, in other words, was used in a limited way to determine whether a job applicant would be included in the study; the remaining nine tests did not enter into any selection decisions involving the study participants.

Upon completion of data collection, the total sample was composed of 1,091 operators. The distributions across jobs and ethnic groups are displayed in Table 1. The black and white samples were comparable in age (approximately 21 years) and education (high school graduate), whereas the Spanish-surnamed American sample was somewhat younger (around 20 years), slightly more educated, and was also more homogeneous with respect to both age and education than were either the black or white samples.

Table 1

Distribution of Sample by Job and Ethnic Affiliation

	Job			
Ethnic affiliation	Directory Assistance	Traffic Service Position	Toll	Total
Black	175	84	242	501
Spanish-surnamed	52	—	74	126
White	185	98	181	464
Total	412	182	497	1091

Note. It was not possible to include a sufficient number of Spanish-surnamed Traffic Service Position (TSP) operators in the study because, when the study was initiated, there were very few locations where TSP operators were employed.

Job analysis

Detailed task and job analyses (e.g., Peterson, Note 4) were conducted prior to the study to support operator training. Within each of the three operator jobs studied, the equipment, procedures, and the kinds of calls processed are almost exactly the same regardless of geographical location. It follows that the skills required are also the same within jobs no matter where the work is performed; accordingly, standardized telephone operator training, including procedures for evaluating proficiency or skill acquisition, is developed centrally and distributed throughout the country. Analysis of the training information already at hand plus direct observation of the work; interviews with supervisors, instructors, and incumbents; and the authors' personal experience in performing the work served to identify the skills required to perform the work and thus as the foundation for selecting or developing aptitude tests and proficiency measurement methods.

The job activities performed by the three kinds of operators differ, but there is a degree of overlap in the skills required. Toll and TSP operators, for instance, handle the same kinds of calls and engage in some highly similar tasks; when their activities differ it is mainly due to differences in the equipment used to process calls.

Test selection and development

Ten tests were administered to the operators assigned to the study either during the employment process or prior to the start of formal training. Six of the 10 tests studied (1-6 following) were in use when the study was initiated and are described elsewhere (Gael & Grant, 1971); 4 tests (7-10 following) were developed specifically for the operator jobs. The 10 tests are:

1. Bell System Qualification Test I—Short Form (BSQT I).
2. Spelling.
3. Number comparison.
4. Arithmetic.
5. Number transcription.
6. Filing.
7. Perceptual speed. This test is a 40×25 matrix of randomly arranged single digits, in which pairs of like numbers appearing together in a row are to be circled.
8. Area codes. In this test a table of cities within states and associated area codes is presented along with a randomly arranged list of 84 cities and states; the task is to associate correct area codes with the randomly listed cities.
9. Marking. Sixteen 10-digit "telephone" numbers are presented directly above a representation of a mark sense card, and the task is to mark the numbered boxes that correspond to the 10-digit number presented above the "card."
10. Coding. One hundred sets of three letters are presented on a page, and the task is to associate one of three symbols with each set, depending on whether the three letters are the same, whether two are the same, or whether all are different.

Except for the BSQT I, for which 30 min are allowed, the remaining nine tests are highly speeded with time limits ranging from 1½ min for the coding test to 6 min for the area codes test.

Proficiency evaluation

Operator proficiency was evaluated during the standardized 1-hour job simulations administered individually upon the completion of formal training. Since the tests studied were to be used to identify applicants who were more likely to acquire the requisite knowledge and skill through training, the logical point in time to determine the degree of learning attributable to training appeared to be at the completion of training. Assessing proficiency at the end of training also provided an additional advantage of ruling out uncontrollable, probably unequal influences on proficiency such as office climate, output restriction, and nature of supervision.

Each job simulation was highly structured so that evaluations could be conducted in the same way for each operator job regardless of location. Sufficient material was contained in the simulations to keep the operators fully occupied for the evaluation period. Call contents, such as addresses, included in the simulations necessarily differed from location to location, but the same sets of call conditions or specifications (e.g., person-to-person, credit card) guided the development of the proficiency evaluations. It was therefore possible to keep call sequences and difficulty levels essentially the same within jobs across locations.

The proficiency evaluations were administered by supervisors who had been oriented to the special evaluation technique. According to instructions, trainers acting as customers initiated calls at a steady pace in the same way for each operator. Each activity to be performed on each call was listed on an evaluation form. Supervisors directly observed and assessed the effectiveness with which operators using actual equipment processed each call during the 1-hour simulation. All activities performed incorrectly, or not in accordance with operator training, or for which assistance was required were underlined on the evaluation form by the supervisor. The overall effectiveness with which each call was processed was also rated on a 5-point scale by the supervisor as soon as the call was completed. The ratings accounted for the severity of mistakes or deviations from accepted practices. The number of deviations or mistakes only partially indicates the effectiveness with which calls were processed; for example, a call in which one major mistake occurred might be rated lower than one in which two or three minor deviations were committed. The rating also indicated the operator's manner while processing a call.

Three call-handling proficiency measures were thus obtained and combined into a Composite Proficiency Index (CPI) to represent overall operator proficiency. The Composite Proficiency Index, computed in the same way for each operator, was comprised of the following scores:

1. Proportion of Activities Correct (PAC)—a call-handling quality index determined from the ratio of the total number of activities completed correctly to the total number completed.

2. Cumulative Work Units (CWU)—a productivity measure reflecting the number of calls completed and the complexity of the call-associated activities.

3. Average Rating per Call ($\overline{R/C}$)—a quality measure obtained by averaging the ratings assigned to each call processed.

As expected, the correlations between quality measures were quite high, and quantity and quality measures were not independent. Average correlations between criterion components were .63 between $\overline{R/C}$ and PAC, .33 between $\overline{R/C}$ and CWU, and .43 between PAC and CWU.[2]

A composite criterion was developed for each operator by first standardizing proficiency scores ($\overline{X} = 50$, $SD = 10$) and then weighting them in accordance with the emphasis devoted to quality and quantity of work during training. The formula used was:

$$\text{CPI} = 3T_{\text{PAC}} + 2T_{\text{CWU}} + T_{\overline{\text{R/C}}}$$

where quality (PAC and $\overline{R/C}$) is assigned twice the weight given to quantity (CWU). The major contribution to quality is based on directly observed activities, and the remainder is obtained from the observers' average call-handling rating. Quality of output continues to receive a great deal of attention on the job, but the emphasis on quantity of output increases considerably with time.

Results

The apparently atypical Spanish-surnamed sample must be commented upon here, because their results, though presented, cannot be discussed meaningfully in terms of substantive issues. The Spanish-surnamed samples were obtained at only two locations and evidently were screened too carefully; compared with other ethnic samples, very few Spanish-surnamed operators had low BSQT I

[2]All means, mean comparisons, and intercorrelations are available upon request. Further, there are three BSQT I scores—verbal, quantitative, and total—and each has been included in the analyses.

scores. They also were less variable on most predictors and criteria, as well as on biographical items, and these restricted ranges undoubtedly limited the magnitude of their validity coefficients. This contention regarding the Spanish-surnamed sample is supported by a subsequent test-validation study for clerical jobs (Gael, Grant, & Ritchie, 1975) in which characteristic results were obtained for black, white, and Spanish-surnamed samples. For these reasons, the results obtained for the Spanish-surnamed samples played a minor role in the selection of tests for the battery and in reaching the conclusion regarding differential validity and test fairness.

Comparisons between ethnic group means within jobs showed that most of the differences between the black and white sample test means and all of the differences between their proficiency means are statistically significant, with the white sample obtaining the higher mean in each case. Five comparisons between the Spanish-surnamed and white test means resulted in statistically significant differences, with the Spanish-surnamed sample obtaining the higher mean in each case; however, in the two proficiency mean comparisons which proved to be significantly different, the white sample obtained the higher mean. The Spanish-surnamed samples obtained significantly higher test and proficiency means than the corresponding black samples in 27 of 32 comparisons.

Validity coefficients were calculated separately for ethnic samples and combined samples within jobs, and many (387 out of 528) are statistically significant—315 validity coefficients are significant at the .01 level. Most of the tests are valid predictors of the Composite Proficiency Index for the black and white samples within jobs, but only two tests (filing and marking) correlate significantly with the composite criterion for the Spanish-surnamed sample. The smaller variation obtained by the Spanish-surnamed sample than by the white or black samples on several predictors and criteria accounts, to some degree, for their smaller validity coefficients.

The possibility of differential validity was investigated preliminarily by comparing ethnic sample test-Composite Proficiency Index correlations within jobs. Significantly different validity coefficients were obtained in 13 of the 84 comparisons—four of the significant differences involved black–white comparisons, three involved Spanish-surnamed–white comparisons, and six involved black–Spanish-surnamed comparisons. In three of the four black–white comparisons resulting in significantly different validity coefficients, the test proved to be more predictive for the black sample, and in two of those cases, both pairs of coefficients were significant. In all comparisons in which significant differences were obtained between a Spanish-surnamed sample and either a black sample or a white sample validity coefficient, the test was less predictive for the Spanish-surnamed sample. The validity coefficients for the Spanish-surnamed samples were practically zero in every comparison that resulted in a statistically significant difference, which, of course, was considered in terms of the range restriction previously mentioned.

It appeared reasonable to combine data across jobs for two reasons. First, the job studies indicated that the jobs were similar in some respects. Second, the patterns of validity coefficients with the Composite Proficiency Index were similar for each telephone operator job. Apparently, the tests are tapping behavioral dimensions common to all three jobs despite differences in particular job activities.

Table 2 presents test and proficiency data for each ethnic sample along with the results of comparisons between the ethnic sample means. All differences between the black and white sample means except one (filing test) are statistically significant, and in each comparison the white sample obtained the higher mean. Only two differences between the black and the Spanish-surnamed sample means were not significant (filing test and $\overline{R/C}$), and in every instance the Spanish-surnamed sample obtained the higher mean. Four differences between the Spanish-surnamed and white sample test means and two differences between their proficiency means were statistically significant, with the Spanish-surnamed sample obtaining the higher test mean in three of the four comparisons, and the white sample obtaining the higher proficiency mean in the two comparisons.

Validity coefficients with the Composite Proficiency Index for the ethnic samples across jobs and for the total sample are presented in Table 3. Every predictor is significantly related ($p < .01$) with the Composite Proficiency Index for the black, white, and total samples, but for the Spanish-surnamed sample only the filing and marking tests are significantly related.

Table 2

Means, Standard Deviations, and Comparison of Means for Combined Jobs

Test or proficiency measure	White (n = 464)		Black (n = 501)		Spanish-surnamed (n = 126)		t: White versus black	t: White versus Spanish-surnamed	t: Black versus Spanish-surnamed
	$\overline{X}$	*SD*	$\overline{X}$	*SD*	$\overline{X}$	*SD*			
Tests									
BSQT I-verbal	19.45	5.70	15.34	5.90	18.25	4.97	11.00**	2.33*	5.65**
BSQT I-quantitative	12.81	4.89	10.83	4.54	13.27	4.42	6.51**	1.01	5.51**
BSQT I-total	292.31	13.10	282.83	11.95	291.63	10.54	11.68**	.53	7.52**
Arithmetic	46.35	15.55	40.72	15.80	44.13	13.19	5.58**	1.46	2.24*
Spelling	34.19	7.52	33.03	7.84	36.20	7.07	2.32*	2.70**	4.13**
Filing	9.67	3.35	7.99	3.76	9.41	3.71	.18	.75	.16
Number comparison	52.08	10.23	49.23	11.96	56.46	11.14	3.96**	4.18**	6.15**
Number transcription	25.27	6.00	23.27	6.21	25.89	5.92	5.09**	1.03	4.28**
Perceptual speed	57.73	12.34	55.46	12.51	62.69	10.80	2.84**	4.10**	4.90**
Area codes	49.26	11.16	42.99	11.83	49.40	10.40	8.45**	.12	5.56**
Marking	110.69	25.94	93.20	27.01	114.54	25.88	10.21**	1.48	7.99**
Coding	79.18	15.80	73.47	18.58	82.02	14.37	5.12**	1.83	4.81**
Proficiency measures									
PAC	52.43	8.33	47.51	11.13	50.34	8.53	7.73**	2.49*	2.66**
$\overline{R/C}$	52.30	9.07	47.96	10.69	49.73	8.70	6.78**	2.84**	1.72
CWU	52.43	9.47	46.94	9.85	52.91	9.29	8.83**	.51	6.16**
CPI	314.48	41.16	284.38	54.12	306.61	39.84	9.68**	1.92	4.32**

Note. Abbreviations: BSQT I = Bell System Qualification Test I; PAC = proportion of activities correct; R/C = average rating per call; CWU = cumulative work units; CPI = composite proficiency index. *$p<.05$. **$p<.01$.

Table 3

Validity Coefficients with the Composite Proficiency Index for Combined Jobs

Predictor	Total (N = 1,091)	White (n = 464)	Black (n = 501)	Spanish-surnamed (n = 126)
BSQT I-verbal	33**	18**	37**	00
BSQT I-quantitative	32**	24**	37**	05
BSQT I-total	40**	29**	41**	04
Arithmetic	30**	25**	31**	01
Spelling	26**	27**	27**	04
Filing	36**	36**	32**	21*
Number comparison	26**	24**	25**	16
Number transcription	30**	27**	30**	14
Perceptual speed	18**	23**	16**	−09
Area codes	41**	36**	40**	16
Marking	32**	20**	30**	25**
Coding	26**	24**	24**	09

Note. Decimals omitted. BSQT I = Bell System Qualification Test I.
*$p<.05$.
**$p<.01$.

Stepwise multiple regression analyses for each ethnic sample and for the total sample showed that four tests (area codes, BSQT I, filing, and marking) were sufficient to maximize predictions of operator proficiency ($R = .51$ for the total sample). The beta weights were not intended for use in the employment process; instead, composite predictors were formed by converting test scores to stanines and simply summing the unit weighted stanines (see Lawshe, 1969), a procedure adopted to simplify test battery computations in employment offices throughout the country.

Composite predictor and criterion statistics, regression equations, and regression equation comparisons are presented in Table 4. The white and Spanish-surnamed sample means are larger than the black sample means on both composites. The validity coefficients for each ethnic sample are statistically significant. That the battery is more predictive for the black and white samples than for the Spanish-surnamed sample is probably due to the sampling procedure rather than any real population characteristic differences. Regression equation comparisons in accordance with a method described by Potthoff (Note 2) showed that the ethnic sample regression-line

Table 4

Comparison of Regression Equations

Sample	Composite test score $\bar{X}$	Composite test score SD	Composite proficiency index $\bar{Y}$	Composite proficiency index SD	r_{XY}	Regression equation	Standard error of estimate
Total	20.0	6.1	300	50	.51*	$\bar{Y} = 4.12\bar{X} + 217$	42.7
White	22.2	5.5	314	41	.43*	$\bar{Y} = 3.21\bar{X} + 243$	37.1
Black	17.5	5.8	284	54	.50*	$\bar{Y} = 4.66\bar{X} + 203$	46.9
Spanish-surnamed	22.5	5.1	307	40	.24*	$\bar{Y} = 1.90\bar{X} + 264$	38.8

Note. Regression equation comparisons: F = 8.85* for combined, 8.25* for slope, and 9.29* for intercept.
*$p < .01$.

slopes and intercepts differ significantly. Figure 1 shows the regression lines for each ethnic sample and for the total sample. At the low end of the test score range, the Spanish-surnamed and white sample regression lines are close together above the total sample regression line, and the black sample regression line is below the total sample regression line. As higher test scores are considered, the regression lines tend to converge, and at scores slightly above the total sample composite test mean (20) the regression lines practically coincide. At the high end of the composite test range the black and white sample regression lines are quite close, with the total sample regression line between them. The white sample regression line, however, is not below the total sample regression line as is the Spanish-surnamed sample regression line. It should be noted that the smaller Spanish-surnamed sample has much less of an impact on the common regression line than do the larger black and white samples.

The common regression equation, it appears, overpredicts black operator proficiency and underpredicts white and Spanish-surnamed operator proficiency at scores below the total sample composite predictor mean. Predicted criterion values using sample specific regression equations with composite test scores of 15, 20, 25, and 30 are shown in Table 5. When a score of 20 is entered into each equation, the predicted criterion values are almost the same for each sample and very close to the satisfactory proficiency level (a composite of at least 300). At scores above 20, the predicted criterion values for the white and black samples are almost equal to the values predicted with the total sample regression equation, but the total sample

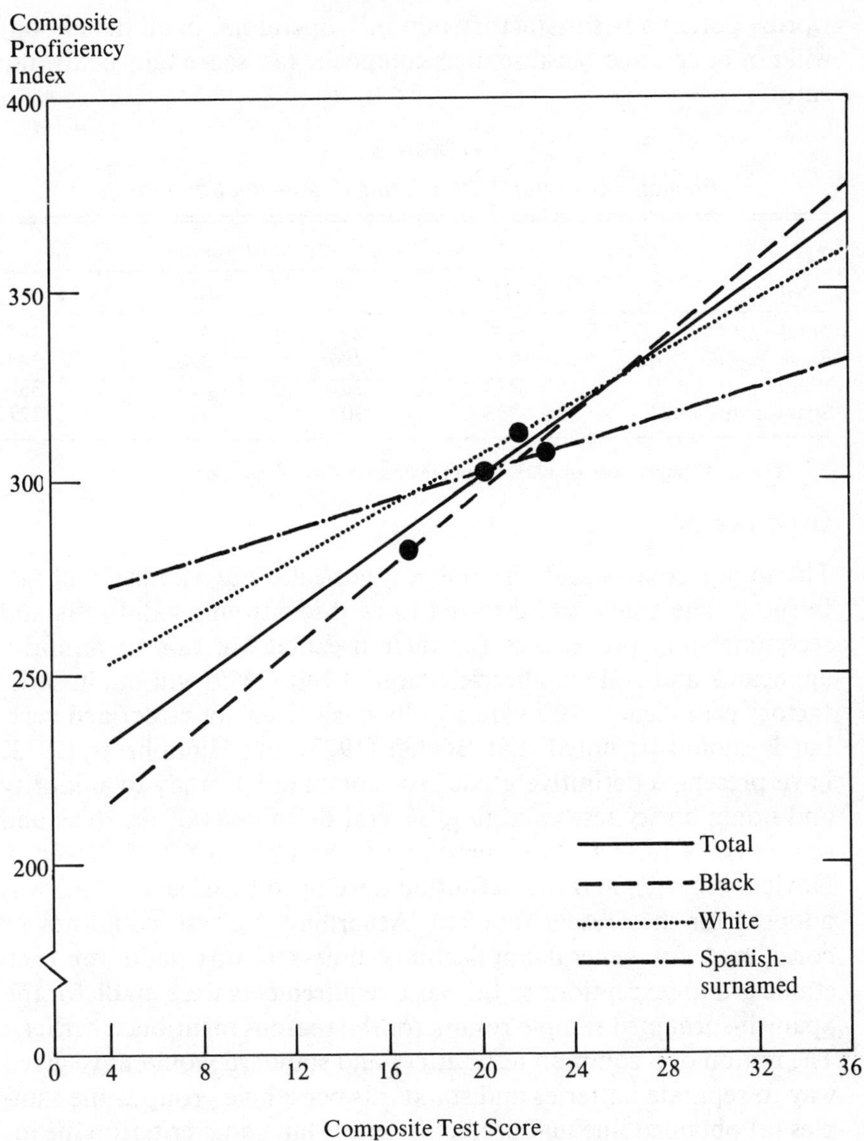

Figure 1. *Ethnic sample and total sample regression lines.*

regression equation tends to overpredict Spanish-surnamed sample proficiency. Operators attaining satisfactory proficiency generally do not obtain composite test scores below 20, and in this regard, a composite test score of 20 was recommended as a cutoff. In other words, potentially satisfactory minority operators, in all likelihood, will not be rejected because their composite test score falls below the cutoff.

Table 5

Predicted Criterion Values Using Regression Equations

Sample	Composite test score			
	15	20	25	30
Total	279	299[a]	320	341
Black	273	296	320	343
White	292	307	323	399
Spanish-surnamed	293	302	312	321

[a]The total sample mean of 300 was not predicted due to rounding error.

Discussion

The major concerns of the present work are test validity and test fairness. The study was directed toward identifying valid tests and recommending procedures for their use that are fair to minority applicants and will enhance selection of those who will attain satisfactory proficiency. Test validity obviously need not be defined here, but it should be noted that Boehm (1972) and Humphreys (1973) have presented definitive guides for comparative study of minority and nonminority test validities. Several definitions of test bias and test fairness have been offered (e.g., see Cole, 1973; Petersen & Novick, Note 1), and the definition developed by Cleary (1968) was adopted for the present research. Accordingly, a test would not be considered for general applicability unless it was valid for each ethnic group (exceptions to the basic requirements were made for the Spanish-surnamed sample results for the reasons mentioned earlier). The notion of a common test battery and standard would have given way to separate batteries and standards per ethnic group if the samples (a) obtained unequal predictor means but equal criterion means or (b) obtained predictor and criterion means that were in relatively opposite positions. Applicants represented by the sample with the lower predictor mean have a smaller chance of being hired, but, given the opportunity, they might equal or better the performance level attained by the ethnic group with the greater chance of being hired.

The results obtained parallel those of other test validation research conducted for Bell System occupations (Gael & Grant, 1971, 1972; Gael et al., 1975; Grant & Bray, 1970), in which single and composite predictors were formulated that are valid for each ethnic group, and test standards were recommended that are fair for minority job applicants and applicable for nonminority job applicants as well. The composite test battery and the standards are regarded as fair in the present case because the relative positions of the black and white sample predictor and criterion means are the same, and the composite battery score is highly valid ($p<.01$) for each ethnic sample. Minority applicants who stand to achieve satisfactory proficiency generally will not be rejected because of their test scores. The possibility of an adverse impact is more likely for white applicants, because a composite test score of 18 is sufficient to predict satisfactory proficiency for white applicants. In any case, the recommended battery and standard should further the selection of operators with the potential to become satisfactorily proficient, regardless of ethnic group, and do so in a fair manner.

The regularity of the Bell System test study results probably is due to the special attention devoted to the predictors and criteria used. Though most of the tests studied are predictive of operator proficiency, two of the four specially developed job behavior sample tests, area codes and marking, plus the filing test are sufficiently predictive for each job and ethnic sample to warrant their inclusion in the test battery. The criteria also directly represent the work in which incumbents frequently search for information arranged numerically or alphabetically in tables or books and keep track of telephone calls by filling in mark sense cards. The contribution of the specially developed job behavior sample predictors to the highly significant validities obtained clearly supports the utility of customizing job behavior sample predictors.

The possibility that the composite test validity coefficients are somewhat inflated is mentioned because the data on which the validities are based also served to identify the tests included in the battery. Cross-validation, a commonly recommended means for assessing the degree of chance capitalization that may arise in such cases, was not incorporated into the design for the following reasons: (a) The data were obtained as a result of three independent studies; (b) the regression equation weights were not used; (c) the large sample size tends to minimize the chance effect; and (d) the validities are no doubt conservative due to range restrictions which compensate to some degree for any chance capitalization.

One result which the present work shares with most reported research (e.g., see Bartlett & O'Leary, 1969; Boehm, 1972; Bray & Moses, 1972; Schmidt & Hunter, 1974; Ruch, Note 3) is that the ethnic samples obtained unequal predictor and criterion means. The attained predictor score levels may reflect existing unequal societal conditions that also affect the attainment of job proficiency similarly. The Bell System job proficiency measures on the whole have been found to be unbiased against minority group members (Miner, 1974). Whatever reasons underlie the fact that minority job applicants score lower on the average on tests and on job proficiency criteria than their nonminority counterparts, the use of aptitude and ability tests that are valid for minority job applicants certainly does not contribute to, but may alleviate, some of the problems associated with discriminatory employment practices.

Reference notes

1. Petersen, N. S., & Novick, M. R. *An evaluation of some models for test bias.* Unpublished manuscript, University of Iowa, 1974.
2. Potthoff, R. F. *Statistical aspects of the problem of biases in psychological tests* (Institute of Statistics Mimeo Service No. 479). Chapel Hill, N.C.: University of North Carolina, 1966.
3. Ruch, W. W. *A reanalysis of published differential validity studies.* Paper presented at the 80th Annual Convention of the American Psychological Association, Honolulu, September 1972.
4. Peterson, R. O. Outward operator training. In Human Resources Laboratory & Training Research Group (Eds.), *Proceedings of the Conference on Uses of Task Analysis in the Bell System.* New York: American Telephone & Telegraph, 1973.

References

American Psychological Association Task Force On Employment Testing of Minority Groups. Job testing and the disadvantaged. *American Psychologist,* 1969, *24,* 637-650.

Bartlett, C. J., & O'Leary, B. S. A differential prediction model to moderate the effects of heterogeneous groups in personnel selection and classification. *Personnel Psychology,* 1969, *22,* 1-18.

Boehm, V. R. Negro-white differences in validity of employment research and training selection procedures: Summary of research evidence. *Journal of Applied Psychology,* 1972, *56,* 33-39.

Bray, D. W., & Moses, J. L. Personnel selection. *Annual Review of Psychology,* 1972, *23,* 545-576.

Cleary, T. A. Test bias: Prediction of grades of Negro and white students in integrated colleges. *Journal of Educational Measurement,* 1968, *5,* 115-124.

Cole, N. S. Bias in selection. *Journal of Educational Measurement,* 1973, *10,* 237-255.

Cooper, G., & Sobol, R. B. Seniority and testing under fair employment laws: A general approach to objective criteria of hiring and promotion. *Harvard Law Review,* 1969, *82,* 1598-1679.

Darlington, R. B. Another look at "cultural fairness." *Journal of Educational Measurement,* 1971, *8,* 71-82.

Einhorn, H. J., & Bass, A. R. Methodological considerations relevant to discrimination in employment testing. *Psychological Bulletin,* 1971, *75,* 261-269.

Gael, S. Employment test validation studies. *JSAS Catalog of Selected Documents in Psychology,* 1974, *4,* 95. (Ms. No. 711)

Gael, S., & Grant, D. L. Validation of a general learning ability test for selecting telephone operators. *Experimental Publication System,* Feb. 1971, *10,* Ms. No. 351-2.

Gael, S., & Grant, D. L. Employment test validation for minority and nonminority telephone company service representatives. *Journal of Applied Psychology,* 1972, *56,* 135-139.

Gael, S., Grant, D. L., & Ritchie, R. J. Employment test validation for minority and nonminority clerks with work sample criteria. *Journal of Applied Psychology,* 1975, *60,* 420-426.

Grant, D. L., & Bray, D. W. Validation of employment tests for telephone company installation and repair occupations. *Journal of Applied Psychology,* 1970, *54,* 7-14.

Guion, R. M. Employment tests and discriminatory hiring. *Industrial Relations,* 1966, *5,* 20-37.

Humphreys, L. G. Statistical definitions of test validity for minority groups. *Journal of Applied Psychology,* 1973, *58,* 1-4.

Lawshe, C. H. Statistical theory and practice in applied psychology. *Personnel Psychology,* 1969, *22,* 117-124.

Miner, J. B. Psychological testing and fair employment practices: A testing program that does not discriminate. *Personnel Psychology,* 1974, *27,* 49-62.

Schmidt, F. L., Berner, J. C., & Hunter, J. E. Racial differences in validity of employment tests: Reality or illusion? *Journal of Applied Psychology,* 1973, *58,* 5-9.

Schmidt, F. L., & Hunter, J. E. Racial and ethnic bias in psychological tests: Divergent implications of two definitions of test bias. *American Psychologist,* 1974, *29,* 1-8.

Thorndike, R. L. Concepts of culture fairness. *Journal of Educational Measurement,* 1971, *8,* 63-70.

18

validation study of tests for clerks

Introductory notes

This article presents a picture that is by now becoming quite familiar: an occupational group of major size, a predictive study extending far enough into employment to allow learning, a reliance on job analysis in predictor selection and criterion development, a work sample or simulation criterion, subjects from multiple settings to facilitate generalization, mental ability test predictors, differential validity analysis, an attempt to obtain broad score ranges in the predictors, and a study of regression equations in relation to discrimination effects. Although not all of these characteristics are essential to an effective validation effort, many can be recognized by now as responsive to guidelines, agency pressures, and court decisions.

The findings presented here for Spanish-surnamed employees are particularly important in the context of the study described in Chapter 17. In this sample adverse impact is in evidence in that on a number of tests the Spanish-surnamed group scores below the whites. Furthermore when the score ranges are thus extended validities comparable to those for whites and blacks are obtained. In view of the comparability of the telephone operator and clerical jobs, there is every reason to expect that had a more representative applicant group of Spanish-surnamed subjects been obtained in the earlier study, comparable validity coefficients would have resulted. Thus, the present data argue even more strongly for further research focused on Spanish-surnamed telephone operators.

EMPLOYMENT TEST VALIDATION FOR MINORITY AND NONMINORITY CLERKS WITH WORK SAMPLE CRITERIA*

Sidney Gael, Donald L. Grant, and Richard J. Ritchie
American Telephone and Telegraph Company

Discriminatory employment practices are illegal and immoral, and can be extremely costly. Though the cost of erroneous employment decisions due to unfair employment practices is inestimable, financial restitutions to "affected" people have run into the millions. It is not surprising, therefore, that rather than incur possible penalties for past or future discriminatory practices, a number of organizations have chosen to discontinue or not to initiate employment testing programs.

Employment tests will not be beneficial unless employers can demonstrate that the tests measure job-related skills or aptitudes and are applicable for minority as well as nonminority applicants—test validity and fairness should be considered necessities. Test users who are not disproportionately rejecting protected group members, however, are seemingly on safe ground regardless of the relevance of their selection instruments, because the evidence will favor the employer should a complaint arise.

One problem employers face is that minority applicants typically score lower on employment tests than do their white counterparts (e.g., see Bartlett & O'Leary, 1969; Boehm, 1972; Bray & Moses, 1972; Schmidt & Hunter, 1974; Ruch, Note 1). Given the same test standards, minority applicants probably will be disproportionately rejected, and if the tests have not been validated the employer is liable for utilizing illegal employment procedures.

The objectives of the clerical job test validation research described herein were (a) to identify a combination of tests that would enhance the selection from among a large pool of applicants of those who would suitably perform clerical work, and (b) to recommend tests and test standards for employment office use that are applicable for minority as well as nonminority applicants. To fulfill

*From *Journal of Applied Psychology,* Vol. 60 (1975), 420-426. Copyright 1975 by the American Psychological Association. Reprinted by permission.

these objectives, a predictive, criterion-related study was designed in which tests would be validated against objective, standardized work sample criteria. Further, sufficient minority group members were involved so that data could be analyzed separately by ethnic sample.

Method

Jobs

The Bell System telephone companies employ about 120,000 people in clerical job classifications. Clerical jobs are performed in all departments, and several, such as keypunch operator, have many incumbents, while most have relatively few incumbents. The clerical rubric encompasses a wide variety of assignments ranging from messenger to computer console operator, and some clerks are primarily involved in recording and filing activities, some in computational activities, and some use mechanical devices to help carry out their work. The same clerical jobs across companies, however, are performed in an almost identical manner. For example, voucher audit clerks and payroll allotment clerks perform the same work regardless of geographic location.

Sample

Nine Bell System telephone companies and the American Telephone & Telegraph Company participated in the study which was conducted in 14 major metropolitan areas across the country. Participating companies agreed that at least 30% of those hired in each ethnic group (black, Spanish-surnamed, and white) would have scores below the median score for job applicants on the Bell System Qualifications Test I (BSQT I). They further agreed to obtain minority and nonminority samples with comparably broad BSQT I score ranges. The BSQT I, therefore, was used in a limited way to determine whether an applicant would be included in the study. Nine other pencil-and-paper tests, administered either during or shortly after employment, had no bearing on the decision to include a newly hired employee in the study.

The sample was composed of 143 black, 74 Spanish-surnamed, and 185 white newly hired clerical employees who met the additional requirements of less than 2 years of college credit, less than 1 year of previous clerical work experience, and/or less than 1 month of Bell System service. The black, Spanish-surnamed, and white samples were, on the average, rather close in age (20.2 years, 19.7 years, and 19.1 years, respectively) and educational level (12.0 grades, 11.9 grades, and 12.1 grades, respectively), though some of the age and educational level comparisons resulted in statistically significant differences.

Job analysis

The telephone company clerical jobs were analyzed in order to specify the behavioral requirements of clerical work. A job description content analysis method was employed to analyze the large variety of heterogeneous telephone company clerical jobs. In essence, the method consisted of extracting categories of clerical activity from the research literature and categorizing job activities mentioned in approximately 400 clerical job descriptions available in one telephone company into these extracted categories. The percentage of clerical jobs in which the various activities were found to occur was as follows:

Clerical activity category	Percentage of occurrence
Posting, recording, record preparation and maintenance	70
Computing, machine calculation (primarily adding and subtracting)	67
Checking	58
Filing	50
Classifying and sorting	35
Coding	24
Counting	13
Reviewing, analysis, and decision making	41

The clerical jobs were studied to identify the skills and abilities required, which, in turn, were used to select the predictors and to design and develop the desired work sample criteria.

Predictors

Ten pencil-and-paper tests were selected since they were predominantly tests of clerical aptitude and were already under study as predictors of telephone operator proficiency (Gael, Grant, & Ritchie, 1975). Briefly, the tests were: (a) the BSQT I, (b) number comparison, (c) arithmetic, (d) number transcription, (e) filing, (f) spelling, (g) perceptual speed, (h) area codes, (i) marking, and (j) coding. More complete descriptions appear in Gael et al. (1975). Except for the BSQT I, for which 30 min are allowed, each test is highly speeded with time limits ranging from 1½ min for coding to 6 min for area codes.

Criteria

The multitude of telephone company clerical jobs in conjunction with the job analysis results indicated the advisability of developing work samples to represent clerical activities, such as posting, computing, and checking performed across jobs. Samples of materials with which telephone company clerks work were configured to provide specific measures of proficiency in the major clerical activities identified by the job analysis, and incorporated in a Clerical Performance Measurement (CPM) package. This package was administered to each study participant within a month after employment. Participants were tested in a quiet room at separate tables.

The CPM is composed of eight separate exercises or units that require approximately 2 days to administer by a specially trained administrator. A manual and associated material were prepared to train and to assist CPM administrators in the administration and scoring of the CPM units. Completed CPM packages were scored independently by the administrator and an assistant, and all differences in the scoring were reconciled.

The eight CPM units can be categorized as either timed clerical tasks or self-paced programmed materials.

Timed clerical units. These included a variety of forms to be processed in accordance with specific instructions.

1. Filing—a set of 30 service orders is to be interfiled with a large set of 150 service orders. The orders are to be filed in ac-

cordance with a number that may appear in one of several locations on the form. The time limit is 10 min, and the score is the number of orders correctly filed.

2. Classifying—a special form used to adjust customer accounts is to be sent to one of several offices depending on the information contained on the form. The correct office can be found by checking reference material. The office, when determined, is to be written on a designated line on the reverse side of the form, and the form is to be placed on a 3 × 5 inch card that represents the location. There are 25 forms to be completed and classified within a 10-min limit. The total score is the sum of the points scored for forms correctly completed and classified.

3. Posting—a computer printout is checked to identify orders on which there are errors. The order in error must then be located, and four separate items associated with that order on the printout are to be posted on the order. Each of 111 items correctly posted within a 15-min limit is credited 1 point, and the total score is the sum of the points.

4. Checking—telephone bills with errors on them are compared with newly prepared, corrected bills to make certain that all the errors have been corrected. Errors discovered on the corrected bills are to be circled. There are 22 errors on 17 of the 27 corrected bills, and the total score is the number of errors detected within the 15-min time limit.

5. Coding—forty orders are to be examined to determine the kind of telephone equipment and service a customer has (already in code). The clerk then refers to a conversion table, locates the code number along with an associated code number, and writes the new code number in the appropriate space on another special form used for automatic billing purposes. The total score is the number of correctly posted codes within a 10-min limit.

Self-paced programmed materials. These were programmed instruction booklets and examinations used in training courses for certain clerks.

1. Toll fundamentals—a short programmed instruction booklet dealing with basic information needed by telephone operators to process telephone calls is presented. Usually, about 30 min are re-

quired to complete the booklet, after which a short, 11-item completion examination is given. One point is scored for each correct answer.

2. Punched card fundamentals—a short programmed instruction booklet designed to teach the basics about punched cards used in data processing is presented. Approximately 45 min are required to complete the booklet after which a 25-item fill-in examination is given. One point is scored for each fully correct answer.

3. Plant repair service—a part of a programmed instruction course designed to teach clerks how to process a repair call and fill out the appropriate associated forms is presented. Three to four hours are required to complete a programmed text and audio tapes after which a 94-item examination is given. The examination combines audio tape and pencil-and-paper material. One point is scored for each correct item.

Administration of the five timed clerical units is somewhat analogous to on-the-job instruction. The administrator reviews the materials with the participants to insure that they understand the instructions. Participants then work through an example provided with each unit under the guidance of the CPM administrator. The self-paced CPM units, on the other hand, are more like formal training given for certain clerical jobs. Though the clerks were oriented to the CPM units by the administrator, they were required to learn the programmed materials on their own.

Proficiency in clerical tasks was evaluated in the same way for each study participant, that is, the same administration and scoring instructions were used at all study sites. One score per CPM unit was obtained for each participant, and overall proficiency was calculated by standardizing ($\overline{X} = 50$, $SD = 10$) each CPM score and summing the eight-unit weighted standard scores. An initial plan to weight each CPM score in accordance with the percentage of occurrence in clerical jobs as determined with the job analysis was not followed because it was not possible to include each identified activity in the CPM.

Results

Predictor and criterion means, standard deviations, and compari-

Table 1

Predictor and Criterion Means, Standard Deviations, and Ethnic Sample Mean Comparisons

Predictors and criteria	Total		Black		Spanish-surnamed		White				
	$\overline{X}$	*SD*	$\overline{X}$	*SD*	$\overline{X}$	*SD*	$\overline{X}$	*SD*	t^a	t^b	t^c
Predictors											
BSQT I-verbal	17.3	5.5	15.8	5.2	15.9	4.8	19.1	5.5	5.56***	4.64***	.14
BSQT I-quantitative	12.5	4.6	11.1	4.4	12.2	4.1	13.7	4.6	5.21***	2.57**	1.83
BSQT I-total	288.8	12.7	284.0	11.7	286.2	9.1	293.6	13.2	6.97***	5.15***	1.53
Arithmetic	47.2	17.8	44.9	18.6	45.3	17.2	49.7	17.1	2.40*	1.86	.16
Spelling	33.8	7.3	33.1	8.2	33.0	6.8	34.7	6.6	1.90	1.83	.06
Filing	9.4	3.7	8.2	3.9	9.3	3.5	10.4	3.4	5.36***	2.30*	2.11*
Number comparison	47.7	17.0	43.9	17.2	51.2	16.0	49.3	16.8	2.85**	.85	3.10**
Number transcription	25.6	6.3	24.1	6.8	25.2	6.0	26.8	5.7	3.82**	1.97*	1.22
Perceptual speed	57.4	11.8	54.4	13.8	57.9	10.9	59.5	9.9	3.74***	1.09	2.04*
Area codes	47.6	11.2	44.5	12.8	45.9	10.2	50.6	9.3	4.80***	3.43***	.88
Marking	109.7	22.9	101.8	26.5	109.3	21.7	116.0	18.0	5.50***	2.35*	2.23*
Coding	77.9	16.0	75.0	17.4	75.7	15.0	81.1	14.6	3.37***	2.64**	.31
Criteria											
Filing	22.6	5.7	20.7	6.4	22.6	5.8	24.0	4.4	5.28***	1.87	2.21*
Classifying	46.1	5.2	44.5	6.4	45.7	5.1	47.5	3.4	5.08***	2.80**	1.50
Posting	80.1	25.1	73.0	26.5	73.6	22.8	88.3	22.4	5.54***	4.71***	.17
Checking	14.3	3.7	13.2	3.8	13.6	3.4	15.4	3.3	5.51***	3.88***	.79
Coding	36.3	6.6	35.6	7.1	36.6	5.3	36.7	6.6	1.43	.13	1.17
Toll fundamentals	10.1	2.3	9.8	2.5	10.1	2.4	10.4	2.1	2.31*	.94	.86
Punched card fundamentals	16.1	6.1	13.9	5.8	15.7	6.1	17.8	5.7	6.09***	2.55*	2.10*
Plant repair service	70.9	16.4	65.0	18.3	69.8	17.4	75.9	12.5	6.11***	2.75**	1.89
Composite proficiency	400.0	52.8	378.2	57.1	393.9	52.4	419.3	41.2	7.27***	3.73***	2.03*

[a]Black-white comparisons. [b]Spanish-surnamed—white comparisons. [c]Black—Spanish-surnamed comparisons. $*p<.05$. $**p<.01$. $***p<.001$.

sons of ethnic sample means are presented in Table 1. Practically all (19 out of 21) differences between the white and black sample predictor and criterion means are statistically significant, with most (15) of the ratios attaining the .001 significance level. The higher mean in each comparison was obtained by the white sample. Many (14 out of 21) of the differences between the white and Spanish-surnamed predictor and criterion means are also statistically significant, and in each comparison resulting in a statistically significant difference, the white sample had the higher mean. In one third of the comparisons between the black and Spanish-surnamed samples, the predictor or criterion means are significantly different, with the Spanish-surnamed sample obtaining the higher mean in those comparisons.

Most of the validity coefficients (334 out of 432) are statistically significant with a preponderance reaching the .01 level.[1] Validity coefficients with the composite criterion are shown in Table 2. Of the 48 validity coefficients with the composite, all but 4 are significant at the .01 level.

Differences between ethnic group validity coefficients with the composite criterion were examined for preliminary indications of differential validity (see Humphreys, 1973). In only 2 of 36 comparisons did statistically significant differences arise, and both instances indicate that marking is a more valid predictor for black than for white or Spanish-surnamed clerks.

Inspection of the validity coefficients with the composite criterion indicates that the most predictive tests across ethnic groups are area codes, filing, BSQT I, marking, and number transcription. Stepwise multiple regression analyses showed that four tests (BSQT I, filing, area codes, and marking) were sufficient to maximize predictions (R = .75). Since these four tests are the same tests found to be predictive of telephone operator proficiency (Gael et al., 1975), their potential as screening instruments was investigated further. Apparently, some of the aptitudes for learning to perform both clerical and telephone operator work are comparable.

The beta weights, it should be noted, were not intended for use in the employment process. Instead, composite predictor scores were

[1]Complete intercorrelation tables can be obtained from the first author upon request.

formed by converting test scores to stanines and simply summing the stanines (see Lawshe, 1969), a procedure adopted to simplify test battery computations in employment offices throughout the country. The stanines were formed on the basis of data obtained for a much larger, telephone operator sample (*N* = 1,091; Gael et al., 1975), thereby utilizing a range of test scores that was more representative of the applicant population—clerks and telephone operators are selected from the same applicant population.

Composite predictors were correlated with composite criteria, and ethnic sample regression equations were determined. The equations were compared for possible bias with a method described by Potthoff (Note 2), and the results of the comparisons are shown in Table 3. The intercepts are significantly different but the regression slopes are not.

Table 2

Validity Coefficients with the Composite Criterion

Predictor	Total	Black	Spanish-surnamed	White
BSQT I-verbal	44*	40*	34*	40*
BSQT I-quantitative	47*	44*	40*	40*
BSQT I-total	57*	54*	54*	50*
Arithmetic	27*	24*	16	30*
Spelling	35*	39*	30*	30*
Filing	59*	57*	51*	55*
Number comparison	24*	32*	16	12
Number transcription	45*	43*	42*	39*
Perceptual speed	32*	28*	21	29*
Area codes	61*	64*	55*	50*
Marking	56*	64*	42*	37*
Coding	42*	45*	41*	31*

Note. Decimal points omitted. *N* = 402; for black, *n* = 143; for Spanish-surnamed, *n* = 74; for white, *n* = 185.
$^*p < .01$.

The regression lines presented in Figure 1 illustrate that the total sample regression equation does not underpredict prospective proficiency levels for minority clerks. The total sample regression line falls between the white sample regression line and those for the minority samples at composite test scores below 20. The regression

Table 3

Composite Predictor and Criterion Means, Standard Deviations, Validities and Regression Equation Comparisons

Sample	N	Composite predictor $\overline{X}$	SD	Composite criterion $\overline{Y}$	SD	r_{XY}	Regression equation	Standard error of estimate
Total	402	21.6	5.6	400	53	.74**	$\overline{Y} = 7.00\overline{X} + 249$	35.4
White	185	23.7	5.0	419	41	.66**	$\overline{Y} = 5.68\overline{X} + 285$	30.2
Black	143	19.2	5.9	378	57	.75**	$\overline{Y} = 7.31\overline{X} + 238$	37.7
Spanish-surnamed	74	20.9	4.8	394	52	.67**	$\overline{Y} = 7.37\overline{X} + 240$	39.1

Note. Regression equation comparisons: F = 3.16** for combined, 3.01 for slope, and 3.27* for intercept.
*p<.05.
**p<.01.

lines converge as test scores increase, and at scores slightly above 20, all four regression lines just about coincide.

Discussion

The results of the present study agree with two general research outcomes. First, they correspond with other test validation research conducted for Bell System occupations (Gael & Grant, 1971, 1972; Grant & Bray, 1970; Gael et al., 1975) in that aptitude tests were found to be fair, in terms of Cleary's (1968) definition of test fairness, for selecting minority applicants. White and minority samples differ significantly on almost all of the tests in the composite predictor; they differ significantly on the criteria; and their relative positions on the predictors and criteria are the same. Further, the composite predictor is highly valid for all samples. Second, the results agree with those generally obtained in clerical test validation research (Ghiselli, 1966), namely, that success in clerical work is predictable with tests of intellectual ability and perceptual speed and accuracy. Evidently, tests very similar to those historically predictive of clerical proficiency are predictive regardless of ethnic group membership. The findings thus support those summarized by Schmidt, Berner, and Hunter (1973).

The similarities between the predictors and criteria are more than nominal and deserve to be mentioned briefly. Both the predictors and the CPM units were either selected or structured to

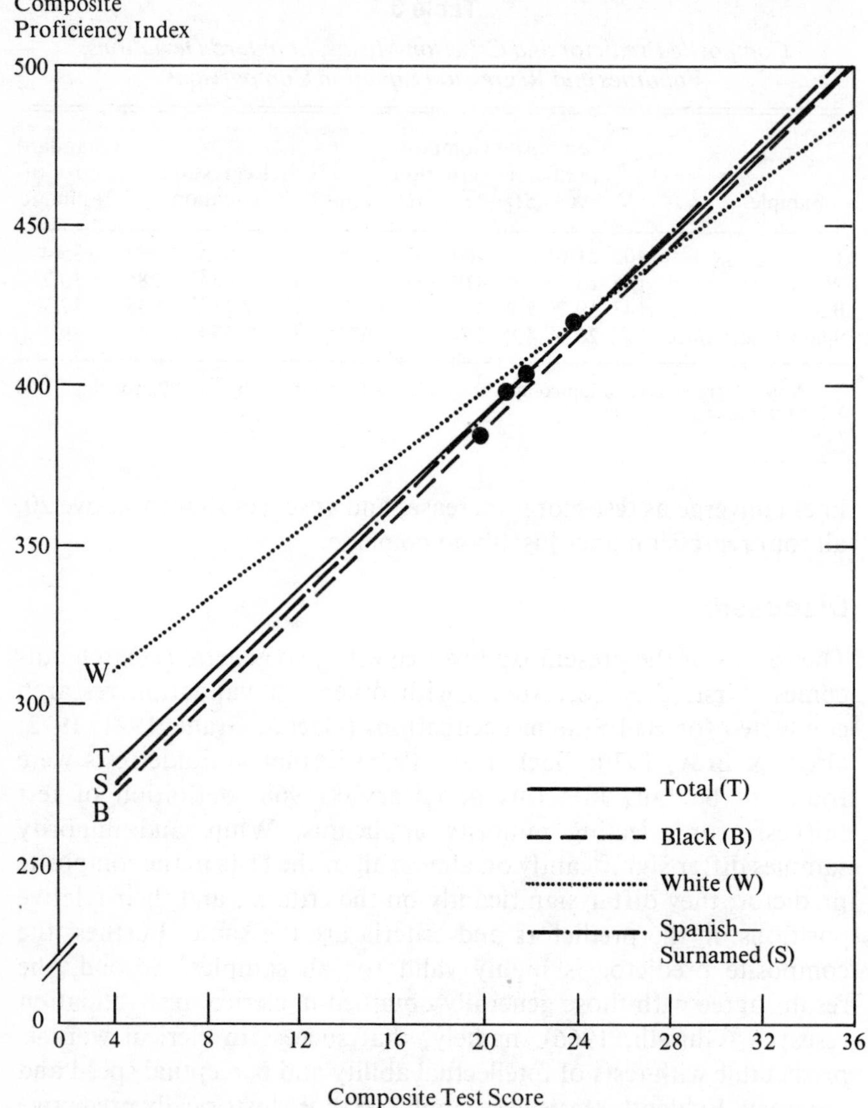

Figure 1. *Ethnic sample and total sample regression lines.*

reflect the job analysis results, and a high degree of cognitive correspondence or behavioral consistency between them was intended, as suggested by Wernimont and Campbell (1968). Apparently, the desired behavioral consistency was attained despite operational differences between the pencil-and-paper perceptual speed, accuracy, and general learning achievement (BSQT I) tests and the work sample and programmed learning criteria.

Criterion development proved to be quite a substantial undertaking, underscoring Viteles's contention (Horrocks, 1964) that one factor contributing to the decline of clerical employment test validation research was the difficulty associated with developing adequate criteria. Criterion development, in the present case, appears to have had a twofold payoff. CPM units are potentially useful as predictors of future clerical job performance when work samples are desired. More importantly, the obtained validities are sharply higher than those generally reported (Ghiselli, 1966) in clerical test validation research, attesting to the value derived from the endeavor.

Reference Notes

1. Ruch, W. W. *A reanalysis of published differential validity studies.* Paper presented at the 80th Annual Convention of the American Psychological Association, Honolulu, September 1972.
2. Potthoff, R. F. *Statistical aspects of the problem of biases in psychological tests* (Institute of Statistics Mimeo Service No. 479). Chapel Hill: University of North Carolina, 1966.

References

Bartlett, C. J., & O'Leary, B. S. A differential prediction model to moderate the effects of heterogeneous groups in personnel selection and classification. *Personnel Psychology,* 1969, *22,* 1-18.

Boehm, V. R. Negro-white differences in validity of employment research and training selection procedures: Summary of research evidence. *Journal of Applied Psychology,* 1972, *56,* 33-39.

Bray, D. W., & Moses, J. L. Personnel selection. In P. H. Mussen & M. R. Rosenzweig (Eds.), *Annual Review of Psychology,* 1972, *23,* 545-576.

Cleary, T. A. Test bias: Prediction of grades of Negro and white students in integrated colleges. *Journal of Educational Measurement,* 1968, *5,* 115-124.

Gael, S., & Grant, D. L. Validation of a general learning test for selecting telephone operators. *Experimental Publication System,* Feb. 1971, *10,* Ms. No. 351-2.

Gael, S., & Grant, D. L. Employment test validation for minority and nonminority telephone company service representatives. *Journal of Applied Psychology,* 1972, *56,* 135-139.

Gael, S., Grant, D. L., & Ritchie, R. J. Employment test validation for minority and nonminority telephone operators. *Journal of Applied Psychology,* 1975, *60,* 411-419.

Ghiselli, E. E. *The validity of occupational aptitude tests.* New York: Wiley, 1966.

Grant, D. L., & Bray, D. W. Validation of employment tests for telephone company installation and repair occupations. *Journal of Applied Psychology,* 1970, *54,* 7-14.

Horrocks, J. E. *Assessment of behavior.* Columbus: Merrill, 1964.

Humphreys, L. G. Statistical definitions of test validity for minority groups. *Journal of Applied Psychology,* 1973, *58,* 1-4.

Lawshe, C. H. Statistical theory and practice in applied psychology. *Personnel Psychology,* 1969, *22,* 117-124.

Schmidt, F. L., Berner, J. C., & Hunter, J. E. Racial difference in validity of employment tests: Reality or illusion? *Journal of Applied Psychology,* 1973, *58,* 5-9.

Schmidt, F. L., & Hunter, J. E. Racial and ethnic bias in psychological tests: Divergent implications of two definitions of test bias. *American Psychologist,* 1974, *29,* 1-8.

Wernimont, P. F., & Campbell, J. P. Signs, samples, and criteria. *Journal of Applied Psychology,* 1968, *52,* 372-376.

19

validation study of assessment centers for women

Introductory notes

In Chapter 14 the wording of the 1973 consent decree with reference to the selection of females for promotion in management is given. The decree called for the use of assessment centers to determine qualifications for promotion. Accordingly, AT&T established three special assessment centers and in a 15-month period 1634 women who otherwise might well not have been considered for promotion up the managerial ranks were assessed. Of those, 42 percent were evaluated as having the potential to move up to middle management positions and were put on promotion lists for advancement as soon as openings occurred.

The advent of this kind of use of the assessment-center method put AT&T under pressure to investigate differential validities. In the case of the nonmanagerial job studies described in the preceding four chapters the white-minority differential was the important one, since mental ability tests are known to be likely to produce adverse impact for minority applicants. In the case of the assessment centers, because of the use mandated in the consent decree, differential validity as between men and women became the key concern. The study described here represents an attempt to draw upon existing data within the company to obtain information on the question of differential validity.

The research indicates that the assessment-center approach is equally valid in the promotion of both men and women; it also appears to yield no adverse impact insofar as women are concerned. However, the study cannot be viewed as completely free from potential attack by enforcement agencies. There is a problem of criterion contamination, in that the assessment center results caused promotions and as a result predictor and criterion are not independent. In the early AT&T research on assessment centers with males the assessment center results were hidden away by the research staff, and management had no knowledge of them at all. As the authors of the article recognize, it would have been desirable to do the same thing here. However, that was not possible.

The authors argue that contamination did not occur when a woman was promoted a second time, that only the first promotion could have been influenced by the assessment-center results. Yet it would be difficult to convince the enforcement agencies that the timing and circumstances of the first promotion could not have had some influence on a second promotion or even a third. To expect some indirect effect of this kind stemming from the earlier assessment-center results seems only realistic. Thus, although this study is significant as part of a body of evidence related to differential validity, it cannot be viewed as definitive on this score. From a legal viewpoint the most important finding actually is that the assessment-center method as used in AT&T does not yield an adverse impact on women; they score just as high as do men.

RELATIONSHIP OF ASSESSMENT-CENTER PERFORMANCE TO MANAGEMENT PROGRESS OF WOMEN*

Joseph L. Moses and Virginia R. Boehm
American Telephone and Telegraph Company

Since its adaptation to civilian business use in the mid-1950s, the assessment-center method has grown increasingly popular as a method of identifying managerial talent. One key reason for its popularity is that the method has been shown to possess a considerable degree of validity when subsequent promotion into and

*From *Journal of Applied Psychology,* Vol. 60 (1975), 527-529. Copyright 1975 by the American Psychological Association. Reprinted by permission.

The authors wish to thank Richard J. Ritchie who provided data analysis service.

advancement within managerial ranks is used as a criterion measure (Bray, Campbell, & Grant, 1974; Bray & Grant, 1966; Kraut & Scott, 1972; Moses, 1972; Cohen, Moses, & Byham, Note 1).

Not surprisingly, the majority of participants assessed until recent years were male, and the validity data reported were based on male populations. Bray (1971) pointed out the feasibility of using assessment centers as a method for identifying management potential among women and as a vehicle for providing advancement opportunities for high-potential women. Two previous studies (Huck, 1974; Moses, 1973) indicated that overall levels of performance of men and women assessees do not differ.

Within the Bell System, women have been assessed since the early 1960s, initially in all-woman groups, and, starting in the later years of the decade, in integrated groups with men. Even when assessed separately, the techniques and procedures used were the same as those used for men.

That data regarding the validity of assessment for women should lag behind data regarding their performance is the inevitable result of the longitudinal criterion used. The present study reports on the relationship between assessment and subsequent progress in management for women in the Bell System.

Method

The method used follows that of Moses (1972). Assessment-center data were obtained on 4,846 women employed by the Bell System who had been evaluated in a Personnel Assessment Center from 1963 to 1971. These centers are designed to evaluate nonmanagement employees for promotion to supervisory management. These women had been evaluated in assessment centers in seven different Bell System telephone companies by the same techniques used by Moses (1972) for men. Of the staff members who evaluated the women, 30-40% were female managers. Each woman attended the center for 2 days, during which time she was observed and evaluated by a specially trained team of company managers who served as assessors.

The activities at the assessment center included: (a) participation in a leaderless group exercise in which each member is asked to sponsor a subordinate for promotion, utilizing materials supplied concerning the subordinate; (b) participation in a business game in which the group purchases materials and manufactures and markets a finished product; (c) participation in an in-basket exercise in which the assessee takes the role of manager in a new job and deals with the accumulated paperwork; (d) an interview with an assessment-center staff member; and (e) participation in a variety of tests and written exercises.

Each participant was observed and evaluated by the assessment-center staff. The participant was rated on a number of abilities or dimensions that had previously been shown to be related to management potential for males, including leadership, decision making, organizing and planning, perception, oral-communication skills, and written-communication skills. Test data on the School and College Ability Test (SCAT)—a verbal score, a quantitative score, and a total score—were also collected for each assessed individual. The assessment staff then gave each individual an overall rating in terms of advancement potential. The overall assessment rating could be one of four possible outcomes: more than acceptable, acceptable, questionable, or not acceptable in terms of potential to perform in a supervisory management assignment.

Management level at the end of 1973 was used as the criterion measure. The entire sample had been assessed at least 2 years previously, and some individuals had been assessed as long ago as 10 years prior to the study. The criterion was not adjusted for elapsed time since assessment. The number of women assessed increased sharply in the late 1960s, and the median year of assessment for the sample was 1969.

By using current management level as a criterion, rather than just the receipt of a single promotion following assessment, the problem of criterion contamination was circumvented to some degree. Since the assessment program is an operational one, with feedback of results to participants and their managers, receipt of one promotion could partially be a function of a favorable assessment outcome. Further advancement, however, would not be based on the assessment results, but on performance in the initial management assignment, as assessment results are not normally retained in an individual's file for more than a 2-3-year period, and assignment changes make it unlikely that a new supervisor would be aware of his or her subordinate's assessment performance.

Results and discussion

The distribution of final assessment ratings for all the participants, the corresponding distribution for men reported by Moses (1972), and the distribution of subsequent promotions for each assessment rating are shown in Table 1. The distributions of ratings for men and women are quite similar. The two top rating categories, "more than acceptable" and "acceptable" were obtained by about one third of all assessees, a figure quite consistent with other studies.

Table 1

Distributions of Final Assessment Ratings and Corresponding Subsequent Promotions

	Assessment performance				Subsequent promotions (women)			
	Women		Men (Moses, 1972)		Promoted once		Promoted twice or more	
Performance criteria	*N*	%	*N*	%	*N*	%	*N*	%
More than acceptable	294	6.1	638	7.2	208	71.4	20	6.9
Acceptable	1,364	28.1	2,279	25.6	954	70.4	82	6.1
Questionable	1,403	29.0	2,902	32.7	736	52.6	39	2.8
Not acceptable	1,785	36.8	3,066	34.5	552	30.9	11	0.6
Total	4,846		8,885		2,450		152	

Due to the relatively recent assessment of most of the women in the sample, the percentage of those who have received two or more promotions is still small; however, the differences in terms of assessment ratings are striking. An individual rated "more than acceptable" was about 10 times as likely to have received two or more promotions than one rated "not acceptable." While the percentages are considerably smaller than those reported by Moses (1972), the 10:1 ratio is identical.

Another comparison between the women's and men's performance and subsequent progress in management involved examining the extent to which the various measures taken during the assessment correlated with management level. These data are presented in Table 2.

Table 2

Correlations Between Each Assessment Measure and Management Level of Men and Women

Assessment measure	Management level: Women (N = 4,846)	Men (Moses, 1972; N = 8,885)
Overall assessment rating	.37	.44
Organizing and planning	.30	.34
Decision making	.28	.34
Leadership	.26	.38
SCAT (total score)	.25	.21
Oral communications	.24	.27
SCAT (verbal score)	.23	.20
Perception	.20	.31
SCAT (quantitative score)	.20	.18
Written communications	.20	.25

Note. SCAT = School and College Ability Test.

The four predictors that correlated most highly with management level for the women (overall rating, leadership, decision making, and organizing and planning) are also the same four with the strongest predictive power for the men. As has been found in other studies, the overall assessment rating is the best predictor of management level for both women and men. The rank order correlation between the men's and women's results in Table 2 is .75 ($p < .01$).

On the whole, the major conclusion that can be drawn from these findings is that the assessment process predicts the future performance of women as accurately as it does that of men. Consequently, use of this method enables managers to identify management talent among women as well as men. This kind of identification process has been successfully implemented for a large group of women college graduates in management positions (Moses & Hoyle, Note 2) and has been combined with subsequent developmental activities to further enhance the advancement of high-potential women (Boehm, Note 3).

Since the proportions of males and females who do well in assessment centers are nearly identical, the assessment-center method appears to be a logical means for providing equal opportunity to women for promotion into management positions and advancement within managerial levels.

Reference notes

1. Cohen, B. M., Moses, J. L., & Byham, W. C. *The validity of assessment centers* (Monograph 2). Pittsburgh: Development Dimensions, 1972.
2. Moses, J. L., & Hoyle, D. F. *The AT&T Management Assessment Center for College Graduate Women.* Paper presented at the meeting of the Second International Congress on the Assessment Center Method, West Point, New York, May, 1974.
3. Boehm, V. R. Changing career patterns for women in the Bell System. In L.D. Eyde (Chair), *Employment status of women in academia, business, government, and the military.* Symposium presented at the 82nd Annual Convention of the American Psychological Association, New Orleans, 1974.

References

Bray, D. W. The assessment center: Opportunities for women. *Personnel Magazine,* 1971, *48,* 30-34.

Bray, D. W., Campbell, R. J., & Grant, D. L., *Formative years in business.* New York: Wiley, 1974.

Bray, D. W., & Grant, D. L. The assessment center in the measurement of potential for business management. *Psychological Monographs,* 1966, *80* (17, Whole No. 625).

Huck, J. R. *Determinants of assessment center ratings for white and black females and the relationship of the dimensions to subsequent performance effectiveness.* Unpublished doctoral dissertation, Wayne State University, 1974.

Kraut, A. I., & Scott, G. J. Validity of an operational management assessment program. *Journal of Applied Psychology,* 1972, *56,* 124-129.

Moses, J. L. Assessment center performance and management progress. *Studies in Personnel Psychology,* 1972, *4*(1), 7-12.

Moses, J. L. The development of an assessment center for the early identification of supervisory potential. *Personnel Psychology,* 1973, *26,* 569-580.

20

validation study of assessment centers for blacks

Introductory notes

The first author of this article, although no longer employed in the Bell System, worked for Michigan Bell Telephone, where the study was conducted, prior to his present association. This research, like the studies described previously, was part of the overall company validation effort and was intended to provide answers to the assessment-center differential-validity question. In particular, the matter of differential validity as between black and white women was at issue.

The study does demonstrate comparable validity in both groups. It is an important study because the focus is on the upgrading of women into the first management position, a matter of particular concern to EEOC. Furthermore, the matter of criterion contamination is handled effectively, something that is much easier to accomplish when ratings rather than promotions are used as criteria.

Although the previous study did not indicate any adverse impact for assessment centers generally when applied to women rather than men, the present research does indicate that adverse impact within the female group can be expected for blacks, as opposed to whites. It is interesting to note that in spite of the less favorable assessments of black women, their actual promotion rate was somewhat higher than for white women. The situation appears to be analogous to that of differential selection, where different cutting scores are used in one group than in another so that a potential for adverse impact is not actually permitted to manifest itself in employment decisions. Certainly the pattern of promotions is consistent with the agreement in the consent decree that test data will not be used "as justification for failure to meet intermediate targets." Under such circumstances, where an affirmative action program is in effect, promotions and increases in compensation may not provide appropriate criterion measures.

MANAGEMENT ASSESSMENT CENTER EVALUATIONS AND SUBSEQUENT JOB PERFORMANCE OF WHITE AND BLACK FEMALES*

James R. Huck[1]
The Wickes Corporation
Douglas W. Bray
American Telephone and Telegraph Company

The assessment center method has become more and more widely used in the evaluation of management ability and potential. Since their first operational use in the Bell System in 1958 (Bray, 1964), assessment centers have spread into hundreds of other businesses, government agencies, and educational institutions. The method is in use not only in the United States but in Canada, Australia, Japan, Brazil, South Africa and elsewhere, and several International Congresses on the assessment center method have already been held.

Studies have consistently demonstrated that assessment center results predict later job performance (Huck, 1973; Cohen, Moses, and Byham, 1974). A variety of criteria have been used in such studies. They include advancement upward through one or more layers of management (Bray, Grant, and Campbell, 1972), observations of on-the-job behavior (Bray and Campbell, 1968), special ratings of job performance and further potential once the individual is promoted (Campbell and Bray, 1967), and absence of demotion in organizations in which demotion is common enough to make this a feasible criterion (Kraut and Scott, 1972). Considering the relatively

*Reprinted with permission from *Personnel Psychology,* Vol.29 (1976), 13-20.

[1]The authors wish to express their appreciation to Alan R. Bass for his valuable suggestions throughout this investigation and to the Michigan Bell Telephone Company for its support of the research.

Based on a dissertation submitted to Wayne State University in partial fulfillment of the requirements for the degree of Doctor of Philosophy, 1974.

short time management assessment centers have been used operationally, the number of predictive studies completed and the consistency of positive results are impressive.

The widespread use of the method and the regularity of predictive results have produced interest in the components of the assessment process. In nearly all centers the assessment staff rates each participant on a number of variables or dimensions after reviewing reports on the participant's behavior during the assessment period. One area of research has been the study of the interrelationships among these variables to determine the nature of the underlying factors being rated and their relationships to the overall assessment result and later criteria. The first such analyses, based on the Bell System's Management Progress Study, were published in 1966 (Bray and Grant, 1966) and reported more completely in 1974 (Bray, Campbell, and Grant, 1974). Some 25 variables were rated in the assessment centers included in these analyses. Factor analysis of these ratings produced a number of group factors which were labeled administrative skills, interpersonal skills, intellectual ability, stability of performance, work motivation, career orientation, and independence of others. These results were based on a sample composed entirely of college graduate males assessed by professional psychologists.

The appeal of the assessment center method as a selection technique has been enhanced since its offers an alternative to paper-and-pencil testing. Such testing has, of course, been under heavy legal fire because of a lack of sound validity studies and the suspicion that such tests may be unfair to minority groups. The assessment center has the advantage of basing judgments directly on observed behavior rather than inferring likely behavior from correlates such as test scores or biographical information. In addition, the assessment center offers a varied and lengthy view of the individual, often two days, and thus fits the "whole person" model often held up as highly desirable. Although the existence of differential validity in well-conducted studies has been brought into question (Bray and Moses, 1972), it is still important to examine the possibility particularly in connection with a method which is so attractive from an affirmative action point of view.

The present study, also conducted in the Bell System (Michigan

Bell Telephone), offers data relevant to the above questions on a population quite different from that of the Management Progress Study. The subjects in this study were assessed a decade later and were female. Few of them were college graduates, and a sizable percentage were black. The assessors, moreover, were specially trained line managers and not professional psychologists. A substantial number of the assessors were female and a small proportion were black. This study examines the power of such an assessment center to predict job performance, analyzes the structure of the assessment ratings that enter into that prediction, and provides separate analyses for white and black subjects.

Method

Samples

The primary sample consisted of 126 nonmanagement women who attended an assessment center during the years 1966-1971 and who were later promoted into one of two supervisory management jobs, group chief operator or business office supervisor. A further condition was that the women must have been in the position to which they were promoted for at least one year at the time of the study. The sample contains 91 white women and 35 black women.

In order to provide a larger number of cases for internal analyses of the assessment center processes, a supplementary sample of 479 women was drawn from women who had attended the same assessment center as the primary sample but who had not been promoted into one of the two management positions above. The sample of 479 was made up of 238 black women and 241 white women. This represented all the black women who met the above criteria and one-third of the white women (selected by taking every third name). The supplementary sample thus includes women who had been assessed but not promoted by the time of the study and those promoted into jobs other than group chief operator or business office supervisor.

Personnel assessment program

The purpose of the assessment center at which the subjects of this study were evaluated was to aid in the selection of nonmanagement employees for advancement to the first level of supervisory management. The subjects were, therefore, nonmanagement employees at the time they were assessed. Their average age was 29.6 years and, again on the average, they had been with the company just under seven years. Mean schooling was 12-½ years. None of these data are significantly different for the white and black groups. The women had reached the assessment center either because their supervisor had recommended them or they had nominated themselves to attend.

The assessment process occupied two full days of each candidate's time. The assessment techniques included a business game, a leaderless group discussion with assigned role, an in-basket and related interview, a personal interview preceeded by a background questionnaire, a written exercise, a *Q*-Sort, and two paper-and-pencil tests—the School and College Ability Test and a General Information Test. The assessors were second-level managers who had been specially trained to conduct the assessment center operation. Nearly 35% of the assessors were female and 5% were black. The center procedures called for staff members to write comprehensive reports on the behavior observed in each assessment technique for each of the subjects. These reports were then read to the full assessment staff. Following this, the assessment staff rated the candidate on eighteen variables and then gave an Overall Assessment Rating. The assessment variables were these:

Energy
Resistance to Stress
Inner Work Standards
Self-Objectivity
Managerial Identification
Forcefulness
Likeability
Range of Interests
Scholastic Aptitude
Awareness of Social Environment
Behavior Flexibility
Leadership
Need for Superior Approval
Need for Peer Approval
Organizing and Planning
Decision Making
Oral Communication Skill
Written Communication Skill

The Overall Assessment Rating scale was as follows:

5 Above the norm

Overall performance at the Assessment Center was rated above the norm by the staff. The assessee demonstrated management skills that exceeded first-level supervision requirements.

4 Met the norm

Overall performance at the Assessment Center was rated at the norm by the staff. The assessee demonstrated management skills that met first-level supervision requirements.

3 Moderate

Overall performance at the Assessment Center was rated below the norm by the staff. The assessee demonstrated strengths in some management skills that indicated moderate potential to meet first-level supervision requirements.

2 Limited

Overall performance at the Assessment Center was rated below the norm by the staff. The assessee demonstrated weaknesses in management skills that indicated limited potential to meet first-level supervision requirements.

1 Low

Overall performance at the Assessment Center was rated below the norm by the staff. The assessee demonstrated weaknesses in management skills that indicated significantly limited potential to meet first-level supervision requirements.

Summary reports of the performance of each subject at the assessment center were prepared and sent to middle-level management in the employee's district organization. This information was then used locally, in combination with appraisals of on-the-job performance, in later selection for promotion decisions.

Performance effectiveness measure

Behavioral rating scales were developed for each of the two jobs involved in this study using the behavioral retranslation method developed by Smith and Kendall (1963). The procedure was carried out separately for the two jobs. In each case a one-day workshop was conducted with seven second-level managers which led to defining the major dimensions in first-level management effectiveness. The managers then worked individually recording critical incidents. Later each participant sorted the incidents independently (their own plus three other sets) into the dimensional categories previously defined. The participants also scaled each incident on a 7-point effectiveness continuum ranging from highly effective to highly ineffective. Incidents showing low consensus among the managers in

Table 1

Varimax Rotated Factor Matrix, Variance of the Factor Loadings, and Commonalities of the Assessment Variables for Whites and Blacks

Assessment Variables	Whites (N = 241)					Blacks (N = 238)				
	I	II	III	IV	h^2	I	II	III	IV	h^2
Energy	.80	.30	.19	.13	.78	.77	.36	.22	.11	.79
Resistance to Stress	.68	.18	.10	.13	.52	.70	.21	.11	.08	.55
Inner Work Standards	.57	.25	.33	.21	.54	.53	.27	.31	.19	.48
Self Objectivity	.33	.25	.58	.10	.52	.33	.15	.66	.16	.58
Managerial Ident.	.22	.09	.63	.22	.51	.11	.14	.55	.28	.41
Forcefulness	.84	.23	.12	.08	.78	.77	.24	.21	.07	.69
Likability	.37	.20	.59	.09	.52	.46	.19	.28	.09	.33
Range of Interest	.13	.11	.16	.68	.52	.14	.24	.14	.61	.46
Scholastic Aptitude	.07	.18	.02	.78	.64	.14	.19	.17	.66	.52
Awareness of Soc. Env.	.44	.37	.59	.05	.68	.26	.24	.72	.17	.68
Behavior Flexibility	.68	.27	.45	.00	.75	.54	.16	.61	.04	.69
Leadership	.83	.24	.22	.05	.80	.70	.23	.41	.06	.71
Organizing and Planning	.26	.85	.20	.17	.86	.19	.88	.15	.13	.85
Decision Making	.30	.88	.08	.10	.87	.26	.87	.13	.11	.85
Oral Communication	.50	.15	.28	.21	.39	.58	−.08	.03	.31	.46
Written Communication	.14	.28	.21	.52	.41	.07	.20	.17	.63	.47
Variance	4.23	2.24	2.06	1.57		3.61	2.19	2.19	1.53	
Percentage of variance accounted for	26.4	14.0	12.9	9.8	63.1	22.6	13.7	13.7	9.55	59.5

I Interpersonal Effectiveness. II Administrative Skills. III Sensitivity. IV Effective Intelligence.

terms of the category to which they were assigned or in the scale values given were eliminated. The remaining incidents were presented to a second sample of second-level managers who had not participated in the original workshop. Those incidents showing consensus across all sorts were retained. Six job elements were found to be common to the two management jobs:

Initiative	Development of Subordinates
Interpersonal Skills	Communication Skills
Administrative Skills	Job Knowledge

After the scales had been developed, a member of Michigan Bell's research staff visited the subject's immediate supervisor. The supervisor was asked to fill out a rating booklet on each subject containing the behavioral dimensions, and to rate and rank all first-level supervisors who reported to him or her on their overall effectiveness. The supervisor then rated each subject's potential for advancement compared to other first-level supervisors in the company. In order to guard against criterion contamination no mention was made of assessment. The raters were assured of the confidentiality of their appraisals. After all rating scales had been completed, the supervisor was asked if he or she was aware whether the individual rated had ever attended an assessment center and, if so, whether her overall assessment rating was known. At the conclusion of the interview the staff member explained the nature of the study and why it had been necessary to conceal it until the ratings were made. The time interval between assessment and criterion ratings ranged from 1.2 to 5.8 years.

Results

Results for the supplementary sample will be reported first, since some of the analyses of the primary sample are dependent upon the factors derived from the larger supplementary sample.

As a first step the intercorrelations among sixteen assessment dimensions were computed separately for the white and black subjects and the resulting matrices factor analyzed. (Two assessment dimensions, Need Approval of Superiors and Need Approval of Peers, were not included since they had been redefined and rated in various ways during the years in which the subjects were assessed.) Both factorial solutions yielded four clearly distinguishable factors accounting for 63.1% of the total variance in the ratings for whites and 59.5% of the total rating variance for blacks. Table 1 presents the varimax rotated factor matrices, the factor variances, and the commonalities of the assessment variables. An examination of the table reveals a close correspondence in the loadings of the assessment variables on the factors for the two samples. In respect to Factor I, for example, the five variables which load highest for whites also load highest for blacks. These variables, with the two loadings, are as follows: Energy (.80 and .77), Resistance to Stress (.68 and .70), Forcefulness (.84 and .77), Behavior Flexibility (.68 and .54), and Leadership (.83 and .70). Comparable degrees of correspondence are found for the other three factors.

Factor I is labeled Interpersonal Effectiveness. The variables which load on this factor suggest an individual who is effective in interpersonal and group problem solving situations. The person is assertive and has definite personal impact. Work activity and performance are not hampered by unusual pressures.

Factor II is called Administrative Skills. Only the variables of Organizing and Planning and Decision Making load heavily on this factor. A person scoring high on this factor would be one having the ability to organize present work and to plan for the future. She can identify priorities and formulate corrective plans where problems exist. She would not hesitate to make decisions and her decisions would be of good quality.

Sensitivity is the label given to the third factor. A person scoring high on this factor would be one sensitive to the social environment, to her own strengths and limitations, and to the assets and liabilities of the company. She would also be sensitive to subtle cues in the behavior of others toward her.

The final factor, called Effective Intelligence, loads on Scholastic Aptitude (as determined by a paper-and-pencil test of general mental ability), Range of Interests (determined in part by a paper-and-pencil general information test), and Written Communication (rated mainly on the basis of a short autobiographical essay). The factor suggests an individual with good academic aptitude and skills.

As the next step in the analysis the subjects were given scores on each of the four factors. Exact factor scores were not utilized; composite scores were derived by summing the ratings of the variables selected for each factor. In order to eliminate as much overlapping factor variance as possible, stringent criteria were employed for inclusion of a variable in the factor score. The variable was required to load .60 or greater on the factor in either sample but no greater than .40 on any other factor. The variable Range of Interests was not included since data were not available for about one-sixth of the subjects. Table 2 shows the correlations of these factor scores with the Overall Assessment Rating separately for whites and blacks in the supplementary sample. There is a high degree of correspondence between the results for the two racial subsamples.

Table 2

Correlations of Factor Scores with Overall Assessment Rating for Supplementary and Primary Samples

	Supplementary Sample		Primary Sample	
	Whites (N = 241)	Blacks (N = 238)	Whites (N = 91)	Blacks (N = 35)
Assessment Factors				
Interpersonal Effectiveness	.85	.84	.87	.87
Administrative Skills	.74	.73	.80	.75
Sensitivity	.74	.67	.68	.70
Effective Intelligence	.46	.50	.52	.41

A matter of interest is whether whites and blacks received different ratings on the assessment variables or in their Overall Assessment Rating. Presentation of data on this point will, however, be deferred until it can be compared with that from the primary sample, to which we now turn.

Factor scores were assigned to the 126 subjects in the primary sample using the additive method described above. These factor scores were then correlated with the Overall Assessment Rating with these results also shown in Table 2. Once again, parallel results for the two racial subsamples can be observed, although the more cognitive factors of Administrative Skills and Effective Intelligence are less heavily weighted in the case of the blacks. The results for the two groups also correspond quite closely to those shown for the supplementary sample.

The primary sample, it will be recalled, was made up of 126 women who had been promoted into one of two supervisory management jobs. They represented 11.7% of the women who had been assessed. The promotion rate into these jobs for black women was slightly higher than for white women, 12.8% as compared to 11.3%.

Table 3 shows the average rating on each assessment variable, the four assessment factor scores, and the Overall Assessment Rating for the supplementary sample (those not promoted into one of the two jobs) and the primary sample (those promoted into one of the two jobs). Since assessment ratings were taken into consideration in promotion decisions, it is to be expected that the average ratings of those promoted would be higher than those not promoted. The table shows this to be the case; the average rating on the 16 assessment variables for whites was 3.0 for those not promoted and 3.3 for those promoted. The comparable figures for blacks were 2.8 and 3.0. The average Overall Assessment Rating for whites not promoted was 2.8 as compared to 3.4 for those who were promoted. The figures for blacks are 2.4 and 3.0.

Table 3 shows also that white assessees in the supplementary samples were rated significantly higher than blacks on many of the assessment variables. These differences are paralleled quite closely in the group of subjects that had been promoted (the primary sample). As far as the assessment factors are concerned, there were significant differences in favor of the whites on three of the four factors in both the promoted and not promoted groups. These differences were in the factors of Administrative Skills, Sensitivity, and Effective Intelligence. There were no significant differences between blacks and whites in either the promoted or nonpromoted groups in Interpersonal Effectiveness. Although the difference in the Overall Assessment Rating did not reach statistical significance, due to smaller sample size, the difference of .4 in the rating (3.4 as compared to 3.0) is actually of the same magnitude as the difference which was significant in the nonpromoted group.

The results to this point indicate that the nature of assessment judgments, the process of variable ratings, and the relationship of the variable ratings to the Overall Assessment Rating are quite uni-

Table 3

Mean Assessment Variable Ratings, Assessment Factor Scores, and Overall Assessment Ratings for Supplementary and Primary Samples

	Supplementary Sample		Primary Sample	
	Whites ($N = 241$)	Blacks ($N = 238$)	Whites ($N = 91$)	Blacks ($N = 35$)
Energy	3.5	3.4	3.9	3.5
Resistance to Stress	3.3	3.3	3.7	3.5
Inner Work Standards	3.6	3.5	3.8	3.7
Self-Objectivity	3.2	2.9**	3.5	3.1*
Managerial Identification	3.0	2.9	3.6	3.5
Forcefulness	2.7	2.8	3.2	3.0
Likability	3.4	3.5	3.7	3.7
Range of Interests	2.9	2.5**	2.8	2.6
Scholastic Aptitude	3.0	2.1*	3.1	2.1**
Awareness of Social Environment	2.9	2.6**	3.2	2.8*
Behavior Flexibility	2.7	2.4**	3.2	2.8*
Leadership	2.5	2.2**	2.8	2.6
Organizing and Planning	2.7	2.4**	3.2	2.8*
Decision Making	2.5	2.3**	2.9	2.5*
Oral Communication	2.7	2.6	3.1	3.1
Written Communication	3.3	3.0**	3.5	3.4
Mean	3.0	2.8	3.3	3.0
Interpersonal Effectiveness	12.0	11.7	13.5	12.7
Administrative Skills	5.2	4.6*	6.1	5.3*
Sensitivity	9.2	8.5**	10.2	9.5*
Effective Intelligence	6.3	5.1**	6.6	5.5**
Overall Assessment Rating	2.8	2.4**	3.4	3.0

*$p < .05$.
**$p < .01$.

form for those promoted and not promoted and for whites and blacks. There are the expected differences in ratings between those promoted and not promoted. In addition, there are consistent differences between white and black subjects in respect to a number of the assessment variable ratings and in the Overall Assessment Rating. In those cases reaching statistical significance, the differences are in favor of the white subjects.

Relationships with criteria

Table 4 gives the average rating on the six behavioral rating scales common to the two jobs under consideration in this study, the average rating assigned by the supervisor on Overall Job Performance and Potential for Advancement, and the intercorrelation among those criterion measures. The six behavioral scales utilized a 7-point system, and thus the theoretical average rating would be 4.0. The table shows that the average rating of both the white and black samples was above this theoretical average on all six scales. It will also be observed that the white group received a higher average rating on all of the scales than the black women. In only one case, however, did this difference reach statistical significance ($p < .01$). This was in respect to the Administrative Skills dimension where the whites were rated .9 above the blacks.

Table 4

Mean Ratings and Intercorrelations Among Criteria Measures for Whites and Blacks in Primary Sample

	1	2	3	4	5	6	7	8	Mean Rating	Standard Deviation
1. Initative	—	42	66	63	52	52	74	66	5.2	1.3
2. Interpersonal Skills	50	—	44	49	52	34	51	46	5.2	1.3
3. Administrative Skills	63	59	—	65	59	55	70	61	5.1	1.2
4. Development of Subordinates	74	50	63	—	64	48	74	61	4.7	1.3
5. Communication	47	56	56	46	—	39	64	58	5.1	1.2
6. Job Knowledge	46	37	48	56	51	—	43	46	5.0	1.3
7. Overall Job Performance	67	72	72	64	42	39	—	79	22.6	5.9
8. Potential For Advancement	66	78	66	66	55	42	87	—	5.8	2.0
Mean Rating	4.8	4.8	4.2	4.3	4.6	4.7	19.6	5.2		
Standard Deviation	1.5	1.6	1.5	1.3	1.5	1.4	6.6	2.0		

Note—Decimals in matrix omitted. Above diagonal—Whites ($N = 91$): below diagonal—Blacks ($N = 35$).

The whites were also rated significantly higher than the blacks on Overall Job Performance ($p < .05$). The difference was 3.0 on a 35-point rating scale. Potential for Advancement was rated on a 9-point scale. Here the difference between the whites and blacks was .6, which was not statistically significant. The degree of overlap coefficient (Dunnette, 1967), was 81% for Overall Job Performance and 88% for Potential for Advancement. The corresponding degree of overlap on the Overall Assessment Rating was 84%.

The relationships of most interest are those between the Overall Assessment Rating and the two global criterion ratings of Overall Job Performance and Potential for Advancement. For whites the Overall Assessment Rating correlated .41 ($p < .01$) with Overall Job

Performance, while the figure for the smaller black sample was .35 ($p < .05$). The relationships with rated Potential for Advancement were considerably higher, .59 for whites and .54 for blacks, and significant for both groups at the .01 level.

Before proceeding further with the presentation of data showing the relationship of other predictors to the criteria, the question of possible criterion contamination should be explored. It will be recalled that the criterion measures were gathered in interviews which made no initial mention of assessment and which were represented as part of research toward developing new performance appraisal devices. After all ratings had been made, the supervisor was asked if he or she was aware whether the individual rated had ever attended the assessment center. Forty-six percent of the supervisors reported that they were aware of the subordinate's prior attendance at the assessment center, 19% said that their subordinate had not attended, and 35% were not certain. The latter two groups were combined and compared to the 46% that definitely knew the subordinate had attended such a program. Table 5 shows the average rating of Overall Job Performance and Potential for Advancement given by the supervisors. The differences in both the means and the

Table 5

Job Performance, Potential and Overall Assessment Ratings of Subjects Whose Supervisors Knew and Did Not Know of Subject's Assessment

	Knowledge of Assessment (N = 58)	No Knowledge of Assessment (N = 68)
Overall Job Performance		
Mean	21.5	22.1
Standard Deviation	6.8	5.8
Potential for Advancement		
Mean	5.7	5.6
Standard Deviation	1.9	2.0
Overall Assessment Ratings		
Mean	3.3	3.2
Standard Deviation	1.1	1.0
Correlation of Overall Assessment Rating with:		
Overall Job Performance	.40	.44
Potential for Advancement	.52	.64

standard deviations are negligible. In addition, equivalent means and distributions on the Overall Assessment Rating are also evidenced for individuals in the two groups, indicating that the supervisors were not likely to remember only the unusually good and the unusually poor assessment performers. The table also shows the correlation of the Overall Assessment Rating with the overall ratings of Job Performance and Potential for Advancement for the two groups. The differences observed could easily be accounted for by chance. Criterion contamination does not appear to be a factor in the supervisory ratings obtained in this study.

The Overall Assessment Rating was, as seen above, predictive of Overall Job Performance and Potential for Advancement for both white and black subjects. These relationships will now be examined in more detail by comparing scores on the four assessment factors with ratings of the six aspects of job performance. Table 6 shows these relationships for white and black subjects separately; the relationship of each of the four assessment factors to Overall Job Performance and Potential for Advancement is also given. The likelihood of rater response bias was suggested previously in Table 4 by the moderate to high intercorrelations among the criterion scales. Further evidence of halo error can be seen in Table 6 by the lack of differences in the correlations of the assessment factors with the job performance variables. The pattern of correlations for each assessment predictor across the criterion measures is very similar. Some differences, however, are apparent in the pattern of correlations for white and black subjects. Assessment ratings of Administrative Skills and Effective Intelligence have generally higher relationships with job performance ratings for the whites than for the blacks. On the other hand, Sensitivity shows generally higher correlations for the blacks. One additional observation is that the correlation of the predictors with Overall Job Performance parallels to the correlations of each predictor with the six aspects of job performance. This is, of course, quite reasonable, but it adds to the probability that supervisors were not differentiating sharply among the various aspects of job performance.

Two observations are in order about the relationship of the four assessment factors to the Potential for Advancement rating. In all cases the predictors are more highly related to the rating of advance-

Table 6

Relationship of Assessment Factors to Job Performance and Potential Ratings

	Assessment Dimensions				Overall Assessment Rating
	I	II	III	IV	
Whites (N = 91)					
Initiative	29**	30**	14	35**	35**
Interpersonal Skills	30**	28**	04	18	29**
Administrative Skills	32**	39**	15	28**	38**
Development of Subordinates	30**	37**	11	20	35**
Communication Skills	28**	33**	12	27**	28**
Job Knowledge	31**	46**	25*	17	39**
Overall Job Performance	35**	37**	10	26*	41**
Potential for Advancement	51**	49**	27**	38**	59**
Blacks (N = 35)					
Initiative	28	13	33*	13	37*
Interpersonal Skills	18	05	09	−02	21
Administrative Skills	36*	17	24	10	37*
Development of Subordinates	29	21	24	17	34*
Communication Skills	18	18	21	12	33*
Job Knowledge	12	14	20	25	18
Overall Job Performance	40*	17	27	03	35*
Potential for Advancement	49**	34*	37*	25	54**

Note—Decimals omitted.
*$p < .05$.
**$p < .01$.
I Interpersonal Effectiveness.
II Administrative Skills.
III Sensitivity.
IV Effective Intelligence.

ment potential than to the rating of performance on the present job. Secondly, some of the notably low correlations with Overall Job Performance rise to more respectable levels when the comparison is with Potential for Advancement. This is true of Administrative Skills and Effective Intelligence for the black subjects and Sensitivity for the white subjects. The authors note, however, that since the performance criteria are more behaviorally-oriented than the Potential for Advancement measure, this latter rating may be more subject to reputational bias.

The data presented earlier showed that there were negligible, and certainly not significant, differences between the white and black samples in the correlations of the Overall Assessment Rating with the two global criterion ratings of Overall Job Performance and Potential for Advancement. It will be recalled that the prediction of Overall Job Performance resulted in correlations of .41 for whites and .35 for blacks, and of Potential for Advancement .59 and .54, respectively. As an additional check for possible differences between the races, the regression equations for the two groups and the performance criteria were compared by the method outlined by Potthoff (1972). Differences between the two slopes (F = .03) and between the two intercepts (F = .001) do not even approach statistical significance. Consequently, a common regression line can be applied to the two groups.

Since there were no significant differences, the black and white samples were combined to produce expectancy tables showing Overall Job Performance ratings and Potential for Advancement ratings achieved by those receiving different Overall Assessment Ratings (Table 7). It will be observed that most of the subjects received a satisfactory or better Overall Job Performance Rating; only 10% were rated less than satisfactory. This is possibly because the subjects had been selected for first-level management on the basis of assessment and were being compared to a less highly-selected group of first-level peers.

Table 7

Relationship Between Overall Assessment Rating and Ratings of Job Performance and Potential for Advancement

Overall Assessment Rating	Overall Job Performance			Potential for Advancement			
	Less Than Satisfactory	Satisfactory	Better Than Satisfactory	Less Than Satisfactory	Satisfactory	Better Than Satisfactory	Total
High	2%	22%	76%	3%	31%	66%	100%
	(1)	(13)	(44)	(2)	(18)	(38)	(58)
Moderate	12%	50%	38%	17%	55%	28%	100%
	(5)	(20)	(15)	(7)	(22)	(11)	(40)
Low	25%	57%	18%	46%	39%	14%	100%
	(7)	(16)	(5)	(13)	(11)	(4)	(28)
Total	10%	39%	51%	17%	41%	42%	100%
	(13)	(49)	(64)	(22)	(51)	(53)	(126)

Table 7 reveals a substantial relationship between the Overall Assessment Rating and rated job performance. Over three quarters (76%) of those who had been rated high at the assessment center were rated as better than satisfactory on the job as compared to only 18% of those who had achieved a low assessment rating. On the other hand, some 25% of those who had received a low assessment rating were seen as performing less than satisfactorily in first-level management as compared to only 2% of those who had been rated high at assessment.

Parallel data comparing the Overall Assessment Rating with Potential for Advancement are also shown. This latter rating was, of course, given by the supervisor. The subjects were rated quite highly; only 17% were seen to have low Potential for Advancement. The Overall Assessment Rating is once again highly predictive. Of those rated high at assessment some 66% were seen as having high Potential for Advancement as compared to only 14% of those who had been given low assessment ratings. Conversely, almost half (46%) of those who received a low Overall Assessment Rating were seen as having low Potential for Advancement, compared to only 3% of those who had been rated high by the assessment staff.

Discussion

The present research adds to the already considerable evidence that judgments made by assessment center staffs are good predictors of later performance. The substantial relationships shown in this study would most likely have been even larger had a less-restricted sample been used. The sample consisted of those who had, in fact, been promoted to one of two supervisory jobs rather than a random sample of all assessed. The study supports most previous research also in that the Overall Assessment Rating is the best single predictor of the various ratings and measures available at assessment (Bray and Grant, 1966; Bray and Campbell, 1968; Moses, 1971; Wollowick and McNamara, 1969), and that the assessment results are even more predictive of potential for further advancement than for performance on the current job (Campbell and Bray, 1967; Carleton, 1970; Finley, 1970; Jaffee, Bender, and Calvert, 1970; Michigan Bell, 1962).

The attempt to study the relationship between different assessment predictors and different aspects of job performance by providing behavioral rating scales of facets of job performance was not particularly successful. The assessment predictors generally correlated about the same with the various ratings of job performance, even though the aspects of job performance would not logically be presumed to be that highly interrelated. This remains, therefore, one of the areas where assessment center research is scanty. There are few data showing the relationship between particular kinds of behavior at the assessment center and good measures of the same types of behavior on the job.

Three of the four factors underlying the ratings of the 16 variables made by the assessment staff are comparable to those found in the Management Progress Study (Bray, Campbell, and Grant, 1974). These are Interpersonal Effectiveness, Administrative Skills, and Effective Intelligence. The fourth factor, Sensitivity, has not emerged in previous Bell System studies. In addition, three strong factors found by Bray, Campbell, and Grant did not appear in the present research. They are Stability of Performance, Work Motivation, and Career Orientation. A likely explanation for the absence of these factors here is that the Management Progress Study assessment centers used many more assessment techniques, including projective tests, personality questionnaires and more clinical interviews by staff psychologists. The more lengthy assessment approach and the use of professional psychologists would have been expected to produce more motivational information than a two-day center conducted by line managers which deliberately avoided personality testing and psychological probing.

The present study afforded an unusual opportunity to compare assessment center results for white and black subjects. It was quite clear that the black subjects did somewhat less well at assessment than the white subjects. (They also received somewhat lower criterion ratings.) This was true on three of the four assessment factors and on the Overall Assessment Rating. The factors were those of Administrative Skills, Sensitivity, and Effective Intelligence. It is noteworthy, however, that the blacks were not significantly lower in the most important assessment factor of Interpersonal Effectiveness.

There was very little difference, and certainly no significant difference, between the white and black subjects in the correlations of the Overall Assessment Ratings with Overall Job Performance or Potential for Advancement. In addition, tests of the regressions for the two groups showed no significant difference. This research, therefore, supports other predictive studies which show that when the study is carefully controlled and when the criteria are appropriate to the predictors, the hypothetical phenomenon of differential validity is not found.

There are, nevertheless, some interesting aspects of the present data having to do with white-black differences and ratings of such subjects in assessment. Although the number of cases does not allow for making these observations on the basis of statistical significance, it appears that Administrative Skills and Effective Intelligence are important components of rated job performance for whites. These two factors are not particularly related to job performance for blacks, but here Sensitivity seems to play a greater role. The change in such phenomena when one asks supervisors to rate potential for further advancement rather than current job performance is interesting. Here the correlations for all four factors for both groups rise, in some cases appreciably. It is as though supervisors are saying, "This person can perform well at her current job level in spite of some weaknesses, but those who are to be promoted further ought to be strong in all four factors."

In addition to its strong appeal for general selection purposes, the assessment center method is especially attractive for affirmative action such as the accelerated advancement of minority groups and women. A major attraction is the validity of the method which substantially increases the likelihood that those advanced will do well on the job, thus enhancing further affirmative action. A second attraction is that the assessment center bases judgments on overt behavior paralleling that required on the job and avoids excessive reliance on paper-and-pencil and biographical methods. Subjects in this study, both white and black, who were rated high at assessment showed excellent job performance and high potential for advancement with almost four times the frequency of those rated low. The assessment center method appears to be highly useful in providing opportunity to the most capable in an unbiased manner.

References

Bray, D. W. The management progress study. *American Psychologist,* 1964, 19, 419-420.

Bray, D. W. and Campbell, R. J. Selection of salesmen by means of an assessment center. *Journal of Applied Psychology,* 1968, 52, 36-41.

Bray, D. W., Campbell, R. J. and Grant D. L. *Formative years in business: A long-term AT&T study of managerial lives.* New York: Wiley-Interscience, 1974.

Bray, D. W. and Grant, D. L. The assessment center in the measurement of potential for business management. *Psychological Monographs,* 1966, 80 (17, Whole No. 625).

Bray, D. W., Grant, D. L. and Campbell, R. J. The study of management careers and the assessment of management ability. In A. J. Marrow (Ed.), *The failure of success.* New York: AMACOM, 1972.

Bray, D. W. and Moses, J. L. Personnel selection. *Annual Review of Psychology,* 1972, 23, 545-576.

Campbell, R. J. and Bray, D. W. Assessment centers: An aid in management selection. *Personnel Administration,* 1967, 30, 6-13.

Carleton, F. O. Relationships between follow-up evaluations and information developed in a management assessment center. Paper presented at the 78th annual meeting of the American Psychological Association, Miami Beach, Florida, 1970.

Cohen, B. M., Moses, J. L., and Byham, W. C. *The validity of assessment centers: A literature review.* Monograph 11. Pittsburgh, Pennsylvania: Development Dimensions Press, 1974.

Dunnette, M. D. *Personnel selection and placement.* Belmont, California: Wadsworth Publishing Company, 1966.

Finley, R. M., Jr. Evaluation of behavior predictions from projective tests given in a management assessment center. Paper presented at the 78th annual meeting of the American Psychological Association, Miami Beach, Florida, 1970.

Huck, J. R. Assessment centers: A review of the external and internal validities. *Personnel Psychology,* 1973, 26, 191-212.

Huck, J. R. Determinants of assessment center ratings for white and black females and the relationship of these dimensions to subsequent performance effectiveness. Unpublished doctoral dissertation, Wayne State University, Detroit, Michigan, 1974.

Jaffee, C., Bender, J., and Calvert, D. The assessment center technique: A validation study. *Management of Personnel Quarterly,* Fall, 1970, 9-14.

Kraut, A. A. and Scott, G. J. Validity of an operational management assessment program. *Journal of Applied Psychology,* 1972, 56, 124-129.

Michigan Bell Telephone. *Personnel assessment program: Evaluation study.* Plant Department, 1962.

Moses, J. L. Assessment center performance and management progress. Paper presented at the 79th annual meeting of the American Psychological Association, Washington, D.C., 1971.

Potthoff, R. F. Statistical aspects of the problem of biases in psychological tests. Institute of Statistics. Mimeo Series No. 479. Department of Statistics, University of North Carolina, Chapel Hill, N.C., 1972.

Smith, P. C. and Kendall, L. M. Retranslation of expectations: An approach to the construction of unambiguous anchors for rating scales. *Journal of Applied Psychology,* 1963, 47, 149-155.

Wollowick, H. B. and McNamara, W. J. Relationship of the components of an assessment center to management success. *Journal of Applied Psychology,* 1969, 53, 348-352.

part 6

organizational strategies for effective selection within the law

21

affirmative action recruiting and hiring

Theoretically, there are three groups of employers who should have no concern about the legal requirements of the equal opportunity laws as they apply to selection. The first group would include companies with minimal hiring needs or those hiring only people with very narrow qualifications. It may be that a firm has a very stable workforce with practically no turnover, or that because of retrenchment almost all vacancies are filled by employees already on the payroll, or that the people hired need such specialized skills that they are recruited from a very limited number of sources, or that the organization is so small that not more than one or two people are hired in the course of a year. The likelihood of EEO selection problems in these situations is nearly nonexistent.

The second group with few legal concerns would include companies with the "right" workforce statistics—the appropriate percentages of minorities and women in all job classifications at all organizational levels. Such companies would show no indication of adverse impact, and it would be difficult to make a case for unlawful discrimination in selection against them. However, it is doubtful that many, if any, such companies exist in the United States today. While a large number of employers have been able to show increases for the protected groups in the lower level job categories, nearly all companies still evidence underutilization of these groups in the skilled and managerial categories.

The third group of employers who should be relatively confident that they are in compliance with the law are those who can prove to the satisfaction of EEOC or OFCCP that any selection procedures they use are job-related and thus constitute a business necessity. It would appear that there are not many companies that fall into this group either, at least at the present time, although the number appears to be increasing. Industrial psychologists have been urging employers to validate their selection procedures since long before the question of adverse impact became relevant, but many companies have only recently begun validation studies and in many cases it is too soon for the results to be of much use in EEO litigation.

It seems clear, then, that except for very small or very specialized firms, the majority of employers do not qualify for membership in any of the "safe" groups and are liable for charges of noncompliance with EEO laws and regulations. It is our belief that, where possible, employers should take the approach of validating their selection procedures as the best way of staying within the law; as noted, however, this cannot be accomplished instantaneously. And unfortunately, under EEOC enforcement the existence of evidence of validity has not always deterred the filing of charges of discrimination. The evidence of validity may be the key to a favorable ruling in court, but employers who have won their cases on this basis have had to spend large amounts of time and money in the litigation process.

Unless EEOC should change its approach, it is difficult to predict when a complaint will result in prolonged litigation. The most effective deterrent to charges of discrimination based on proof of adverse impact appears to be a showing of good-faith efforts, or affirmative action, on the part of the employer to offset the adverse impact. As noted in Chapter 3, affirmative action is required under the terms of conciliation agreements, consent decrees, and court orders affecting hundreds of employers. And hundreds of thousands of employers are covered by the executive orders regulating government contractors, which also call for affirmative action. Any employer fortunate enough not to have had to submit the detailed data and reports required under most affirmative action plans can benefit from taking a look at what they typically provide.

In this final section of the book we will examine specific aspects of the selection process with particular reference to programs and procedures that have proved effective in offsetting problems of adverse impact. Requirements of affirmative action plans as they relate to specific practices will be discussed, and practices that have become "red flags" in EEO enforcement will be noted.

It should be pointed out again that there are few, if any, categorical rights and wrongs in selection, either legally or professionally. Every company, every job, sometimes every location, has to be evaluated individually to determine what selection standards are valid and/or legal. No one can tell an employer a certain procedure should or should not be used in employee selection without some knowledge of the specific situation. However, there are certain questions that can be asked, certain variables that need to be taken into account, and certain mitigating factors that may be relevant in evaluating a selection technique for a particular job. With a knowledge of these, any personnel executive should be able to assess the effectiveness—and the legality—of his or her organization's selection processes.

In this chapter, we are concerned with procedures involved in hiring people into the organization from the outside. Chapter 22 will emphasize programs for upgrading and promoting employees already in the organization, and Chapter 23 will discuss ways of detecting and removing organizational barriers to the implementation of EEO selection policies.

Looking at the jobs to be filled

One of the requirements for the validation of selection techniques, under enforcement agency guidelines, is that "careful job analyses" be the basis for determining the critical work behaviors used as criteria for measuring employee performance. In essence, what this means is that whatever measure is used must actually be related to an important aspect of the job being studied. In the case of a work-sample type of test, such as a typing measure, it is relatively simple to tell which jobs require typing skills and how important typing is for these jobs, and it also is relatively easy to measure subsequent typing performance on the job. Such factors as personality characteristics present a more difficult problem than skills or knowledge. For example, it may be that for a particular type of work, the performance evaluation includes a rating of the employee's initiative; and in hiring people for this work, personnel representatives are asked to include an assessment of the applicant's initiative based on results of a personality test, background information, and/or specific interview questions. What the guidelines require is that a job analysis with regard to such jobs indicate clearly that the work does in fact require a certain level of initiative and that persons lacking initiative would very likely fail in the job.

Whether or not job analyses are carried out with validation studies in mind, job analysis is an approach that is recommended for any job or group of jobs for which an employer hires any sizable number of people. The important part of the job analysis for selection is the job specification—the part that identifies the skills, knowledge, and abilities needed to perform the job. In reviewing the job specification with EEO in mind, there are several factors to consider. One is to make sure that the job analysts, supervisors, or job incumbents providing the input for the job analysis do so on the basis of what is required for satisfactory performance for a *beginner* in the job; job descriptions frequently are written in terms of what is being done by someone who has been on the job for five or 10 years and/or who is viewed as being "exceptional" in that type of work. Using standards based on such performance clearly would have the effect of disqualifying the majority of applicants, who are unlikely to be experienced as yet.

Another important consideration, emphasized by a multitude of court decisions, is that *every* standard specified must be proven to be a valid requirement for the job. EEOC and the courts scrutinize very carefully specifications such as the following:

- *Physical standards*—are minimum height or weight limits, which have an adverse impact on the employment of women and some minority groups, essential for performance of the type of work involved?
- *Experience requirements*—can you prove that a person needs five years of prior experience to perform the job measurably more effectively than someone with only two or three years experience?
- *Skill requirements*—if a required skill is one that can be acquired quickly, is there opportunity to learn on the job?
- *Educational requirements*—can the requirements be stated in terms of ability, such as eighth-grade reading ability, rather than in terms of a specific diploma or degree?

Another issue involving job specifications is that they can be written in terms of skills or abilities necessary for higher level positions in the same job family, but only if there is strong evidence that most people hired for the job in question are in fact later promoted to the higher level jobs. Unless an employer can point to a policy of automatic upward progression from entry-level jobs and has data to show this policy actually has been followed in the past, enforcement agencies will not look kindly on excessively high requirements for the beginning jobs.

Basically what EEOC would like employers to do is to evaluate all the qualifications for all jobs to make sure there are no excessive or unnecessary requirements that might have the effect of disqualifying a disproportionate number of minorities or women. This approach should apply whether the concern is with large numbers of hires in jobs for which a formal job analysis has been prepared or with jobs that are filled from the outside infrequently. The usual procedure for filling individual vacancies is for the supervisor or department head to send the employment office a job requisition form that lists the requirements for the position open. The person filling out the requisition form should be cautioned against listing any requirements that cannot be proven to be job-related; what can often happen is that the supervisor pulls an old job description out of the file to use as the basis for the requisition without checking it against the realities of the current situation.

It should be obvious to any personnel person that one of the first things to be done in checking for compliance with EEO regulations is to take a hard look at existing job descriptions and specifications for any clearly discriminatory requirements. This is especially important in cases where results of validity studies are submitted to government agencies for review, because the job specifications need to be included in the documentary evidence. In at least one situation we know of, a government contractor submitted old job descriptions calling for "males only" in certain classifications that clearly had no BFOQ. As a result the OFCCP psychologist examining the evidence in the case, a woman, sent it back without even looking at the results of the validity studies.

Job redesign. In certain types of business, such as professional firms, nearly all the jobs require college or professional training or advanced skills of the type that minority group members and women are less likely to possess, at least at the present time and for some time to come. Under current EEO enforcement, most professional firms have little to be concerned about because there is no proof of adverse impact where there are so few minorities or women with the necessary qualifications.

As part of their affirmative action programs and also as a result of programs emphasizing the employment of the disadvantaged, however, a number of employers have taken the approach of job redesign. This approach involves restructuring existing jobs by taking out certain tasks that could be performed by people with less skill or experience and making them into a separate job. This also permits the more highly skilled person to use his or her work time to better advantage. A number of programs of this nature have been undertaken in the legal and medical professions, where paralegal and paramedical jobs are becoming common. One example is the "clinic assistant" position created by the Kaiser Medical Foundation in California. The job gives unskilled people a starting point and relieves nurses of routine chores such as weighing patients and taking temperatures.

In manufacturing companies and in other essentially nonprofessional industries, there also are many jobs that can be restructured to increase the number of positions available to persons with little skill or experience. In the skilled crafts, for example, "helper" jobs have been created for beginners. A large-scale program with an approach similar to that of job redesign is the human engineering effort undertaken by the Bell System with a view to making jobs in the traditionally male plant departments more attractive to women. For most employers, job redesign or human engineering programs certainly are not required for compliance with the law, but these are approaches with some merit if there are presently few positions in a company for which many minorities or women qualify—and the qualifications clearly are based on business necessity.

The objective of this first step—looking at the jobs to be filled, checking qualifications for job-relatedness, and perhaps restructuring some jobs—is to determine what jobs or groups of jobs there are that might be filled by minorities or women. The company workforce analysis should indicate which jobs and which protected groups to concentrate on, and the data on the relevant labor market should indicate the general availability of the types of people the company needs. The next step is to find these people.

Finding the people to fill the jobs

The recruitment process is an aspect of the personnel function that has been affected directly by governmental pressures for EEO. In the past, there were companies that took pride in the fact that they rarely had to recruit for new employees on the outside. Because they were viewed as such good places to work, all that had to be done was to spread the word that a vacancy existed and there would be plenty of qualified applicants among friends and relatives of employees already on the payroll. As noted in Chapter 2, one of the first things to be made clear by EEO agencies was that this type of recruiting is unlawful, where the current workforce is predominantly white or male, because it tends to perpetuate the present composition of the workforce.

On the other hand, once a company has some experienced and effective minority-group employees, they may be excellent sources of new recruits. The problem is where to begin. According to employers responding to a recent BNA survey, the most effective outside recruiting sources for minority-group applicants are community agencies, while advertising is the most effective way to recruit women, particularly for professional or managerial positions. Recruiting at predominantly minority or female colleges also is considered an effective approach by the survey respondents.[1] A list of recruitment resources prepared by EEOC, including community action agencies and rosters of appropriate colleges and universities, is reproduced as Exhibit 13, p. 512.

While each employer must look at his own situation in terms of the types of applicants needed and the relevant minority or female population, a number of suggestions have been offered as aids in recruiting with EEO in mind. For example:

[1]*Equal Employment Opportunity: Programs and Results,* Personnel Policies Forum Survey No. 112, March 1976 (Washington, D.C.: The Bureau of National Affairs, Inc.).

- Find out who the minority-group and women leaders are in the community and enlist their cooperation. In black communities, for example, ministers frequently have the greatest influence on young people, and barber shops and beauty parlors often are the social centers. One telephone company gave a group of black beauticians a tour to show them the kinds of jobs it had and asked them to let their customers know what jobs were available.
- Wherever possible use minority-group employees to recruit and interview minority applicants and female employees for female applicants.
- Participate in job fairs and other special recruiting centers set up in areas of high minority population.
- Work through the U.S. Employment Service offices; in some areas the USES has set up offices in predominantly black or Spanish-speaking neighborhoods.
- Establish contact with the schools and colleges that train people with the skills needed, and work with both vocational guidance counselors and teachers or professors in the subject areas relevant to the types of jobs to be filled. Some companies have cooperated with local schools in setting up special courses or training programs to teach students specific skills, and many employers have found work-study programs or summer employment to be effective ways of recruiting minority employees.
- Focus advertising for job openings in ethnically oriented newspapers and magazines or radio and television stations. For technical, professional, or managerial recruiting use trade or professional publications known to have readership among minority groups or women.

The approaches suggested for EEO recruiting are based on the same premises as those applying to any recruiting effort, and many of the sources might be used for any type of recruitment program. The difference is that in addition to looking for people with specific qualifications, the goal of these approaches is to find as many people as possible from the groups underrepresented in the company work force who have these qualifications. Furthermore, EEO recruiting efforts need to be evaluated in the same way that any recruiting program should be. Records should be kept of the results of each approach used to show how many minority or female applicants were recruited from each source, how many of these applicants were qualified for the type of work available; and, of the applicants offered jobs, how many accepted, how long they stayed with the company, and what the level of their performance was. Over a period of time, these records will provide a good indication of where an employer can expect to get the most for the EEO recruiting dollar.

One of EEOC's recommendations is that employers maintain an affirmative-action file of all qualified minority-group and female applicants who have been considered for employment but not hired for a particular opening. The more successful a company is in recruiting minority-group and female candidates, the bigger this file will be; presumably its application forms and resumes will be a fruitful source to begin the search when a future opening occurs. Unless the file is kept up to date, however, it will frequently turn out that few—if any—of the people on file are still in the job market. And the more qualified an applicant, the greater the likelihood that he or she will have been employed by another company interested in fulfilling its affirmative action goals. Obviously, an affirmative action file needs to be kept current by contacting the potential candidates on a regular basis to check on their availability. As the file dwindles, more recruitment may be necessary to ensure adequate numbers of applications from the EEO focus group.

Getting through the selection process

No matter how successful recruiters are in locating qualified minority and female applicants, a company still can have adverse-impact problems if not enough applicants make it through the selection process and get on the payroll. As suggested in Chapter 5, each step of the selection process should be monitored to determine if that step is a stumbling block to the employment of minorities or women. By looking at the applicant-flow figures, it should be possible to determine where problems may exist. In the typical organization, the processing of candidates for employment includes the initial application and screening, preemployment testing, reference checking, and one or more interviews.

Initial application and screening. Basically, information included on application forms or asked in an initial interview must be job-related, particularly when it involves such matters as educational background or experience which may have the effect of screening out disproportionate numbers of minorities or women. Among the questions sometimes included in preemployment inquiries that have been found unlawful, *in particular situations*, are those relating to arrest and conviction records, credit ratings and other financial matters, marital status, and child-care arrangements (for female applicants). As pointed out by the various enforcement agencies, inquiries on these matters as well as questions about applicants' race, national origin, or religion are not violations of the law per se; it is only when such information is used as the basis for a selection decision that it may be unlawful. In fact, certain information along these lines is necessary to comply with EEOC reporting requirements, and employers operating with affirmative action plans have to find some way of providing detailed figures on the applicant population by race, sex, and so forth.

As a practical matter, most companies use the same application form for the majority of job openings. Thus, if there are any jobs for which information on arrests or convictions constitutes a business necessity, the application form for all jobs may well include such questions. At this point the importance of the job specification for the individual position under consideration becomes manifest. With a knowledge of the qualifications for a particular job, the person doing the initial screening can indicate that certain questions on the application form need not be answered, or these questions can simply be ignored in evaluating the applicant.

One problem for employers is that some information on such matters as marital status and date of birth is necessary for compliance with laws other than those of EEO. However, this information is needed only for employees actually on the payroll; a number of employers have eliminated these questions from the preemployment application form and have new hires fill out an additional information sheet after they have been selected. This approach also can be used for employers who want to validate items to be used on a weighted application form or biographical data of the type used in the study discussed in Chapter 12. During the period the study is being made, selection decisions should be made without taking into account the items being studied; thus the information can best be gathered after hiring. If the information in question proves to be a valid predictor of subsequent performance and thus job-related, it can then be included on the preemployment application form.

Preemployment testing. It has been emphasized throughout this book that employers using preemployment tests must determine whether the use of a test results in an adverse impact, and, if so, to make sure the use of the test can be proven to be job-related. The enforcement agencies and the courts require this, and good personnel practice necessitates that the test be validated in any event.

At the present time, many companies still are using unvalidated tests, while others have discontinued testing altogether. According to a 1976 BNA survey on selection procedures in nearly 200 companies, about two fifths were using tests and only about one half of these had done any validity studies.[2] In a similar survey conducted in 1963, nine out of 10 employers were using tests. Even in the majority of cases where employers have submitted evidence of validity to EEOC, their studies have been judged deficient. One estimate is that only about 2 percent of the validation studies submitted have been found to fully satisfy EEOC standards, while another 18 percent have been given conditional approval until results of additional studies are available. However, this says nothing about how the courts would judge these same studies. As it has developed, EEOC has become very much an advocacy type of agency.

Some suggestions for approaches to use while validation studies are in progress were mentioned in Chapter 6. Where the use of the test clearly has an adverse impact, it may be necessary to try to find an alternative selection technique until the validation studies have been completed. Some companies have substituted work-sample tests for intelligence or aptitude tests, and others have used lower scores as the minimum for hiring on certain tests. A number of Federal Government agencies have stopped giving typing tests and are

[2]*Selection Procedures and Personnel Records,* Personnel Policies Forum Survey No. 114, September 1976 (Washington, D.C.: The Bureau of National Affairs, Inc.).

using a "self-certification" system under which applicants certify on the application that they can type a certain number of words per minute. According to the Civil Service Commission, three fourths of self-certified applicants hired during a trial period of the system were later rated as either "excellent" or "very good" employees.

The approach taken by the Civil Service Commission illustrates what may be required. In this case a test was eliminated but the alternative method used still had to be proven valid. In most situations, it is easier to conduct a validity study for a test that provides a numerical score, or passing grade, than it is to validate a more subjective selection technique, such as the supervisory interview. Thus, for the majority of jobs, some type of preemployment test probably is the best predictor that can be found that can be proven valid.

One type of preemployment test, the physical examination, has not been discussed to this point. The reason is that while a majority of companies do require physical examinations as part of the selection process, the examination often is given after the person has been hired. The results of the examination are used more for placement decisions than for selection decisions. In the relatively rare case where a candidate is rejected on the basis of a physical examination, the jobs involved clearly require certain physical standards. An example would be the eyesight and other physical requirements for truck drivers in jobs regulated by the Interstate Commerce Commission. As long as any employment decisions based on the physical examination are job-related, which is nearly always the case, and as long as all applicants for a particular type of work are given the same exam, regardless of color, sex, and so forth, there is little likelihood of any EEO problems. On the other hand, if an employer rejects a sizable number of protected applicants on the basis of physical examinations, there should be some proof of the validity of the examination.

Reference checking. Although the EEOC has gone on record as believing that the practice of reference checking has an adverse impact on minorities, this practice has been proven to provide a valid prediction of subsequent job performance on at least one occasion and has been supported by the courts.[3] Certainly checking with

[3]*EEOC* v. *National Academy of Sciences*, 12 FEP Cases 1690.

former employers, schools, and teachers who have known the job applicant in a work or study situation can provide valuable insight into such characteristics as honesty, dependability, and ability to work with others—any one of which may be an important aspect of a particular job. Where such characteristics are known to be important, they should be included in the qualifications listed in the job specification for the use of the person doing the reference check.

As long as the questions asked in a reference check are related to the applicant's previous performance and as long as the persons contacted are people who would have this knowledge, this practice should not be the source of EEO difficulty. In the majority of companies, this would appear to be the case. In the BNA survey of selection procedures, for example, it was found that nine out of 10 employers verified information on the applicant's previous employment record by checking with former employers, and slightly more than one half the companies checked schools or colleges listed on the application.[4] However, only one third checked personal references, one sixth checked police records, one eighth checked military service records, and one tenth checked credit records—all of which are less likely to be predictors of job performance than previous employment or education.

The effectiveness of the reference check as a selection device may have diminished in recent years as a result of concern with protection of privacy and other personal rights. There have been instances where a former employee brought suit against a company because his previous supervisor gave a prospective employer negative information which was used as the basis for rejecting his application. As a result of cases such as these, many companies now have special forms for checking with previous employers that include a statement signed by the applicant authorizing release of the information requested. Furthermore, employers often require that all requests for information on former employees be handled through the personnel department; contact with former supervisors, the ones who would be most knowledgeable about the applicant's job performance, is prohibited. One personnel executive responding to the BNA survey said his company "always tried to give positive infor-

[4]*Selection Procedures and Personnel Records, supra* note 2.

mation" on former employees; this type of information may not be very valid in making a selection decision.

In cases where a check with previous employers or schools does result in negative information on job applicants, it is wise to check as many sources as possible. This is particularly true if the applicant is a member of a minority group or a woman, if the job is one in which this group is underrepresented, and if the result of the reference check is the only basis for rejection. Care should be taken also to provide guidelines on the evaluation of information provided by previous employers to make sure that not only is the same information obtained for all, but that it is used in the same way. If a bad attendance record on a previous job is to be used as a standard for rejection, this standard should be applied to all applicants regardless of race, sex, and so forth.

Interviews. The interview, though perceived as more subjective and less scientific than other steps in the selection process, is undoubtedly the most important part of a great many hiring decisions. In recent years, as some employers have abandoned preemployment testing programs rather than undertake studies to validate them, the interview has become even more important. Among the personnel executives on BNA's Personnel Policies Forum, for example, 56 percent said the interview was the most important aspect of the selection procedure in 1976, compared to 44 percent in 1963.[5]

In the long run, it is unlikely that the interview as a selection technique will escape the long arm of EEOC, where there is any evidence that the use of the interview results in adverse impact. If the utilization analysis points to an EEO problem and selection decisions are based almost entirely on interviews, sooner or later the interviewing procedures will have to be validated. And the process of validation for interviews can be a much more complex task than that for a testing instrument. This may account for the fact that of the 200 companies responding to the BNA survey on selection, only four had conducted any validity studies of their interview process.[6] Such studies can be done, however, as illustrated by the article reported in Chapter 10.

[5]*Ibid.*
[6]*Ibid.*

For the majority of jobs in most companies, more than one interview is involved in the selection process; and for certain jobs, as many as five or six different interviews may be involved. The initial interview is sometimes called the "gate-keeper" interview, because its purpose frequently has been to cull out less desirable applicants and to accept application forms only from those who appear to be the best prospects. At some companies, this role is performed by a receptionist or secretary with no professional training or background as an interviewer. This approach is not recommended for employers with EEO problems, for obvious reasons.

In most large companies, the people doing the interviewing in the personnel office do receive special training, which currently usually emphasizes the aspects of the interview that might cause EEO problems. Two important reasons for conducting interviews at this early stage of the selection process are to obtain information that is not included in the application form and to clear up items on the form that may be difficult to understand. In order to know what items on the application form need to be clarified, the interviewer must be knowledgeable about the job or jobs for which the company is hiring, and the questions should be limited to those that clearly relate to the job requirements. Often the interviewers are trained to structure the interview so that the same questions are asked of each applicant for a particular job, and written interview forms are sometimes used which call for ratings of various qualifications and personality characteristics. Where such ratings are used, they can and should be validated.

For purposes of implementing affirmative action programs, the initial screening interview should be perceived not so much as gatekeeping as gate-opening. Among the suggestions from enforcement agencies is one that calls for interviewers to counsel job applicants. If the applicant is not qualified for the job opening at hand, are there other jobs available that might be suitable? Or, are there jobs for which the company will likely be hiring in the near future or at other locations? It also should be required that the interview be documented, whether a written interview form is used or not. In other words, there should at least be a piece of paper attached to the application form noting the date of the interview, the interviewer's name, and the result. Did the interviewer tell the applicant there were no jobs available for which he or she qualified, or was the application processed further?

The sequence of events in the selection process can vary from company to company and from job to job. In some cases, for example, applicants are required to take certain tests, particularly skill tests such as typing, before they are interviewed. This approach provides the interviewer with the test results as well as the background information on the application form, which then can be discussed with the applicant. Another approach is to conduct the interview before the application is filled out or without seeing the form; this has been used as a way to counteract any biases the interviewer may have that might be influenced by information on the form. The interviewer has to make a recommendation solely on the basis of what can be gleaned in the face-to-face situation.

Whatever the sequence of events in the early part of the selection process, the final or nearly final step is an interview by the supervisor of the work unit where the job vacancy exists, and sometimes one by the head of the department as well. The usual procedure is for the personnel department or employment office to try to find at least three, and perhaps more, candidates with the basic qualifications for the job to be filled. A major problem in most companies is that the supervisor often has had no training in interviewing and wants to devote as little time to it as possible because it takes him or her away from other duties. The higher the job level and the more crucial it is in the operation of the work unit or department, the more time the supervisor should be willing to spend, however. But for the most numerous entry-level job openings where many of the minority or female candidates will be involved, the typical supervisor would like to keep interviewing time to a minimum.

To make the job easier for supervisors, many companies do give them training in interviewing, but in a situation where a supervisor has a job opening only once every two or three years this type of training is hardly worthwhile. From the EEO viewpoint, the main thing is to caution supervisors to focus their interviews on job requirements. This does not necessarily mean the supervisor has to limit his consideration to such things as education, skills, and experience. There are jobs, for example, that involve considerable interaction with people and where cooperative efforts are essential to performing the work. The supervisor will want to use the interview to assess the applicant's social skills for this type of job. But such requirements should be indicated in the job specification, and the supervisor and personnel people should agree on some definition of the level of social skills needed. As has been noted in the discussion of every aspect of the selection process, accurate knowledge of the job requirements is the basic essential ingredient.

The hiring decision

Anything—and everything—about a job applicant that is uncovered in the selection process may be crucial to the final decision to hire the person. If there are three applicants and one job, two applicants are going to be rejected. While personnel people can reject applicants early in the selection process, it usually is the supervisor or department head who makes the final decision on which applicant actually gets the job. The rationale for this procedure is that the person closest to the job and the environment in which the work is performed should be the best judge of who is most likely to become an effective employee in that position.

The applicant-flow analysis will suggest problems that may exist with regard to the final selection decisions. If the personnel department has been successful over a period of time in recruiting qualified applicants among the groups being underutilized, but the workforce data do not show a change, there is a problem at the decision-making level. It should be possible to determine what specific individuals are contributing to this situation. Supervisors who consistently choose whites over blacks or vice versa, or who insist on maintaining an all-male or all-female unit irrespective of qualifications, are certainly not helping the company stay within the law.

It is a rare company currently that does not permit supervisors to make their own selection decisions, although a number of companies, including those in the Bell system, have recently eliminated supervisory decision-making interviews for nonmanagement positions. If it does it at all, the personnel department usually does the final hiring only for jobs at the lower levels or for jobs in which large numbers of people are needed for more than one work unit. Thus, in most companies the solution cannot be for the personnel department to make all the decisions based on the company's affirmative action commitments. Accordingly it must be made attractive, or even necessary, for supervisors to make their decisions with the company's EEO needs in mind. Ways of doing this will be suggested in the final chapter of this book.

22

upgrading and promotion policies

The affirmative action recruiting and hiring policies discussed in the previous chapter are the initial steps toward a good-faith effort in equal employment opportunity. These policies should result in the employment of larger numbers of qualified minorities and females in jobs which traditionally are filled by applicants from outside the organization. To ensure continuing positive EEO results, additional steps may be required with regard to upgrading and promotion policies. Many companies fill nearly all job openings at upper levels by promoting or transferring employees already on the payroll; what the law appears to require is that promotions and transfers not be denied to protected groups in disproportionate numbers unless there is proof of business necessity.

Essentially, employers need to look at the figures on transfers and promotions in the same way as the figures on new hires are assessed. For each job category, how many openings have been filled by promotions or transfers from within the company; and of these, what percentage were filled by persons in the underrepresented protected groups? If the company workforce utilization analysis indicates problems in job categories usually filled from within, and the figures show few, if any, minorities or females being promoted or transferred into these jobs, an investigation into possible causes of the situation is called for.

As is the case with selection from outside the company, the investigation with regard to selection from among internal candidates should begin by pinpointing the work units and job categories where there is evidence of adverse impact. Then the skills, qualifications, and other selection standards for these jobs need to be evaluated for their job-relatedness. Any tests or other scored instruments used should be studied to determine whether they are contributing to the adverse impact; and if so, steps should be taken to validate their use. These requirements are the same as those outlined in the last chapter.

The major area in which selection from within—promotion or transfer—differs from selection from the outside is in recruiting. Effective internal recruitment calls for a system for keeping track of employees' skills and abilities and matching these with appropriate jobs as well as some method of keeping employees informed about opportunities for transfer and promotion. For affirmative action purposes, additional procedures may be necessary or desirable. These procedures include the restructuring of seniority systems and lines of job progression to permit upward mobility, efforts to encourage minorities or females to apply for positions in what have been nontraditional occupations for them, training programs to provide the skills needed for upper level jobs, and reviewing performance evaluation systems used as the basis for promotion recommendations to make sure they are based on objective, job-related standards.

Employee information systems and skills inventories

A basic element for implementing recruitment from within policies is an information system to provide data on current employees. Information provided in such a system may include skills and special abilities (both those required for the employee's current job and those presently unused), educational background, training programs completed, prior experiences in other types of work, and any special skills such as knowledge of a foreign language. Some companies poll employees about their interest in possible transfer to other locations or other types of work, and this information is added to the system. Evaluations of the employee's performance with an indication of additional training he or she may need and an assessment of promotion potential also may be included.

The output from the information system is an inventory of the skills, interests, and capabilities of the present work force. In larger organizations, where such systems usually are computerized, they provide a method for determining whether there are employees already on the payroll at other locations who might qualify for and be interested in a job vacancy before going outside to recruit. Where the company has made forecasts of future human resource needs, the personnel skills inventory can indicate the need for more recruiting or training programs.

There are pros and cons in the whole concept of employee information systems and promotion-from-within policies; supervisors, for example, frequently are loathe to recommend good employees for promotions into other work units because of the problems of recruiting and training a new person to fill the vacancy created. However, these policies have been strongly urged by EEO agencies as providing the best method of upward mobility for classes of persons who were denied such opportunities in the past. Often, it has been found that minorities, especially, are locked into a particular job category and given no chance to move up.

Some companies, while not using a full-scale computerized information system covering all employees, do attempt to evaluate minorities and females in lower level jobs to determine whether people with potential for advancement are available. This evaluation may include testing for the aptitudes or abilities needed for higher level positions with a view to providing training in any specific skills or job knowledge also necessary for these positions. Economic factors led one firm to a program for evaluating women and minorities for their "promotability" or "qualifiability." During a slow period when there was no hiring for entry-level jobs, managers agreed to do no outside hiring for higher level jobs if there were any employee in the workforce who had been evaluated as promotable into that type of job or who could be trained to do the job. In this company, the employees who were evaluated were then told, on an individual basis, what they could anticipate. In particular, if the jobs they were in were dead-end jobs, they were told what the opportunities were for transferring out or getting into a training program to move up.

Structural barriers to upward mobility

One aspect of the program described in the preceding paragraph was a goal on the part of the employer to restructure the jobs in such a way as to eliminate those of a dead-end variety. As mentioned several times in Part 2 in connection with the discussion of the legal framework for selection, structural barriers, such as those perpetuated by seniority systems, have been a major target of the enforcement agencies. The result has been that many conciliation agreements and court orders contain detailed provisions requiring changes in seniority systems, outlining procedures for allowing minorities and women to assume their "rightful place" in the line of job progression, and frequently calling for retroactive pay to compensate for promotion opportunities denied in the past because of the operation of the seniority system.

In general, what has been required in these cases is the elimination of seniority lists segregated by sex or race by merging them, and seniority systems established on a departmental basis have been revised to permit and encourage plantwide transfers and promotions without loss of seniority. The mechanics of these agreements, such as the one affecting the steel industry, can become very complex, and it will take many years before all affected persons have been given an opportunity to progress. In the steel industry, as in any unionized situation, it was essential to have the union's cooperation before the barriers could be eliminated because the union contract usually covers seniority, promotion and transfer policies in detail. As noted in Part 2, however, "bona fide" seniority systems can continue to operate despite adverse impact on minorities and women because of a special provision of Title VII.

In nonunion companies without contractual requirements governing promotion and transfer policies, there often have been systems just as rigid as those in unionized firms. The dead-end job category at lower levels, into which people are hired with no skills and from which there is no way of moving up in the organization, has been common in many nonunion companies, as has been the practice of promoting those employees who have been with the company the longest period of time merely to avoid hard feelings among other employees desiring promotion. Furthermore, many companies have never established formal lines of job progression to indicate that a person hired at one level will have an opportunity to move up to higher levels within a reasonable period of time.

To implement affirmative action goals, employers are encouraged to study their current job structures for potential barriers to upward mobility and to take steps to overcome any barriers they identify. One suggested approach is to group jobs into job families.

Using information from the job analysis, jobs from different work units or even widely separated departments can be grouped on the basis of similarity of the tasks involved or of special skills or aptitudes required. The establishment of job families on this basis can facilitate promotion or transfer of employees across departments.

Another approach, designed specifically to encourage upward mobility and eliminate dead-end jobs, is the career ladder. Jobs are grouped vertically on the basis of similar skill requirements but with varying degrees of the required skills. Each job in the same family at a higher level on the ladder incorporates all the work activities of the jobs at lower levels. The assumption is that with a certain amount of experience at the lower level, and perhaps some extra training or outside education, an employee can be upgraded to higher level jobs in the same career ladder. Ideally, all the jobs in an organization could be fitted into one career ladder or another so that an opportunity for advancement would be present for any employee who wanted to take advantage of it.

The type of program necessary to overcome structural barriers takes a good deal of study and time to implement and usually results in a period of upheaval. For this reason, most companies prefer to move slowly when such a program is undertaken, and the program is not likely to produce very quick results in terms of changes in workforce statistics. As discussed below, there are some steps related to promotion and transfer policies that should produce faster results and that can be adopted while the need for structural change is being studied or while such changes are being effected.

Publicizing job openings and job counseling

A common feature of many EEO agreements and affirmative action plans is a commitment to publicize opportunities for promotion or transfer to jobs with better opportunities for advancement. In some cases, these efforts are required only for affected classes of persons; in others, there is a general requirement to publicize all job vacancies to all employees. The usual method used is posting of notices on bulletin boards throughout the company premises; union contracts often include provisions for posting of vacancies and procedures for employees to bid on the jobs. In the union situation, however, the notices are limited to jobs covered by the contract, and the notices are not required to be posted in departments not included in the union bargaining unit. Thus, there is little or no opportunity to transfer from jobs outside the bargaining unit to those in the unit, which often are better paid. Needless to say, this type of situation can spell trouble with the EEO agencies when the union-represented work units are mostly male and/or white. Compliance officers will try to get companies to adopt companywide posting wherever possible.

In addition to job posting, there are several other methods for publicizing vacancies, including announcements in regular employee publications and special memos to supervisors asking for names of potential candidates. A number of approaches, some of which have been required under court order, call for special efforts to acquaint persons in the affected classes with the types of jobs available outside their own unit. These efforts are not related to the filling of a specific vacancy but are aimed at encouraging minority and female workers to think about the possibility of transferring into what have been viewed as nontraditional jobs for them. According to EEOC, certain minority and female employees in the Bell System have never applied for better jobs because they have assumed it was AT&T's policy not to give them higher paying positions. This was the reason for the establishment of a transfer bureau in each Bell System company with requirements for extensive in-house recruiting and communication of job opportunities.

Some agreements call for the company to provide tours of plants or other facilities where better jobs might be available, and frequently individual job counseling programs are initiated to acquaint women and minorities with the possibilities for moving into better jobs. Often, however, despite extensive publicity and counseling efforts, persons in the affected classes are not motivated to apply for the higher level jobs. They may feel comfortable and competent in their present positions and not want to risk the possibility of failure, particularly in a situation where one would be very visible as the first black or the first woman promoted into a given job category. This is why in the Bell System, for example, in trying to achieve better female representation in the plant departments, an effort is made to assign women who apply for transfer to work locations where other women already are assigned. Some agreements even have included extra financial incentives to motivate people in the affected classes to try for higher paying jobs. A consent decree involving Braniff Airways includes a provision for the payment of $1,500 to each black incumbent member of the affected class who transfers to the position of aircraft mechanic and successfully completes the probation period.

Providing training opportunities

Although motivation sometimes is a problem in encouraging upward mobility, an even more likely problem is lack of knowledge or lack of the skills required for higher level jobs. Information collected through a skills inventory or through individual counseling may point to deficiencies that can be alleviated through proper training. Under the impetus of affirmative action goals, employers have put renewed emphasis on existing training programs and have established innovative approaches to employee development. Enforcement agencies are particularly concerned about minority and female representation in apprenticeship and similar programs that are required for the better paying skilled jobs.

All the traditional training methods and techniques can be brought to bear; basically it is a matter of making sure those in the underutilized protected groups know about available training opportunities and encouraging them to take advantage of the opportunities. Many companies are making special efforts to publicize their tuition-aid plans. Counselors from local colleges sometimes are asked to participate in programs designed to provide employees with information on courses that might provide skills for higher level positions. In the field of higher education itself there currently is great interest in continuing education for adults, and local colleges or universities are providing more and more programs of this variety. Often instructors or professors will teach courses on company premises during lunch hours or after work if enough employees are interested.

The courses or training programs undertaken are primarily a function of the type of business the employer is in, but there are some courses that are useful in all kinds of organizations. These would include courses that might be viewed as preparing employees to move into supervisory or managerial positions, such as courses in communications skills and human relations. This type of program is offered by many educational institutions and by business and professional associations; minorities and women should be included in such programs wherever possible.

Whether a company can rely on its regular training programs and simply guide minorities and women to apply for them, or whether completely new programs are needed, depends on the circumstances of the particular business and the local area. In parts of the country where certain minorities have been deprived of suitable educational opportunities, the employer may have to enter the education business for a period of time. In some cases, companies have had to offer courses in reading and writing English to minority-group members where this knowledge is essential to job performance. And in the AT&T situation, a number of training programs have been established in efforts to prepare women for physically arduous jobs involving climbing telephone poles and so forth.

What is crucial in assessing training-program needs is much the same as what is crucial in assessing selection standards—a knowledge of the basic requirements of the jobs to be filled at all levels of the organization. If there is no opportunity outside the company for employees to acquire the skills or knowledge necessary to move into higher level positions, then the company may need to provide this opportunity.

Finding managerial talent

Of growing concern among the EEO agencies is the matter of moving minorities and women into managerial positions. Although the majority of EEO cases taken to court have dealt with lower level employees, there have been a few that involved denials of promotion to supervisory positions, and a number of the major consent decrees have addressed the problem of discrimination at management levels. As time goes on, it can be anticipated that the enforcement agencies will become even more concerned with this issue, since the greatest discrepancies between population figures and workforce data are in the professional and managerial occupational categories.

One difficulty encountered in these ranks is the question of demand. Top-level positions do not become vacant very frequently, and by and large they are filled by moving someone up from a middle-manager slot. If it takes an average of 15 to 20 years from the time of hiring to reach higher management, then these positions will now be filled by people hired in the early 1960s. This group is not likely to include many minorities in the average firm, and many women hired then were not thinking in terms of long-term managerial careers.

Fortunately, at the present time, the "manager" classification used by the government for the EEO-1 form includes all job levels from first-line supervisor up. In terms of the annual reports required to be filed, substantial progress can be indicated merely by concentrating on hiring or promoting minorities and women into the supervisory level. For purposes of affirmative action programs and under the terms of certain consent decrees, however, data must be reported for various levels of management. In establishing goals for the higher management levels, companies may be overoptimistic and not take a realistic look at how many vacancies can be anticipated over the next five years. Only in very large organizations will there be more than a handful of top-level positions that become open as a result of retirements or other terminations. In many companies that are no longer expanding as they were in the 1960s, the number of middle- and top-management positions may be declining, with the result that there is even less opportunity for women and minorities.

As long as companies set their goals realistically, and as long as the EEO agencies accept the realities of the demand situation, employers can begin to take steps that should result in the achievement of these goals over a period of years. Special recruiting programs for the positions that traditionally have led to upper management can be focused on minority and female sources. In one sense, the supply situation is favorable in that the enrollment of women and minorities in business, engineering, and other professional schools that are a major source of potential managers is increasing. Although change is slow, there will be a larger group of people in the protected classes prepared to undertake management careers in the future.

There are other factors that make finding potential managers among women and minorities a difficult task. Studies of successful managers over the years indicate that there are three essential ingredients contributing to managerial effectiveness. The first of these is basic knowledge relevant to the type of work involved and the organization itself. Much of this knowledge is acquired through experience in the company or in another company in the same industry, and some knowledge is acquired through training or education, such as a degree in business administration for jobs in financial institutions. There is no question that at the present time, there are relatively fewer women or minorities who have had the opportunity to acquire the level of experience and knowledge necessary for high level management positions. On the other hand, there is no reason they cannot acquire the relevant knowledge rapidly once they have the opportunity.

The second requirement for managerial effectiveness is a high level of mental ability, particularly verbal ability. In the vast majority of managerial jobs, verbal ability is essential; most of what managers do involves oral or written communications. This requirement presents no problem as far as the employment of women as managers is concerned. Most studies indicate that what small differences in verbal ability do exist as between males and females tend to favor the females. There is a problem for some minority groups, however, particularly in parts of the country where educational opportunities have been denied, and where they have not been exposed to the majority white culture. It may be unfortunate that the intelligence tests that are such good predictors of managerial success favor whites, but that is largely because most managerial careers occur in the predominant white culture. As minorities are provided with better education and have more opportunities to move into the business world, this may become less and less of a problem.

The third factor that needs to be taken into account, at least in large bureaucratic organizations such as our major corporations and government agencies, is what is known as motivation to manage, or will to manage. Basically, motivation to manage involves a person's feeling challenged by, or at least comfortable with, the requirements of the managerial role. A manager has to be willing to stand out from the group, be assertive and competitive, be willing to exercise power and to perform routine administrative duties, and must have a favorable attitude toward those in positions of higher authority.

Among persons actually in supervisory or managerial positions, there is no difference between men and women in their managerial motivation and any differences between white and minority men appear to favor the minorities. The more successful managers have higher levels of motivation to manage regardless of sex or race.

Among student groups, however, there are some differences that might affect the supply of potential managers. First, women students as a whole tend to have less motivation to manage than men. Second, over the past 15 to 20 years there has been a marked decline in managerial motivation among groups of college students, including those enrolled in schools of business administration. Thus, the level of managerial motivation among college graduates in the 20- to 30-year age range is lower than among older graduates. When these people are needed to assume middle- and upper-management positions, there will be fewer who have the motivation required to be effective. On the other hand, as more minorities and women are included in the potential pool of managers, the chances of finding enough people with the necessary motivation increases.

Women as managers. The question of promoting women into managerial levels is being raised more and more frequently with pressures both from the government and from women's rights activists. There is no doubt that women have not had their share of the top positions in business. Figures consistently show that even in industries where the workforce is predominantly female, the management component is predominantly male. Until fairly recently, however, there were few voices raised in protest; men and women alike generally viewed the situation as a reflection of woman's rightful place in our society.

Now this situation is changing rapidly. Management in many companies is committed to affirmative action goals with regard to promoting women into higher levels of responsibility, and more and more women are electing the career option rather than—or in addition to—the housewife role. However, many women are not interested in assuming a managerial role. The difficult aspect of the task is to find those women who do have a will to manage and to encourage them to take on the challenge.

In many companies, there are large numbers of women with high levels of intelligence and with college backgrounds working at jobs that do not use these capabilities. As part of their affirmative action efforts, some companies have undertaken special programs to identify these women and to counsel them about promotion opportunities. The activities included in such a program at one company are the following:

- All job openings below the director level are posted throughout the company.
- Recruiting committees in each division of the company interview and counsel women employees and applicants about job opportunities.
- All women employees are shown slide tapes of role models—"pioneer" women in jobs that were traditionally filled by men.
- Top and middle managers attend seminars to increase awareness of their responsibilities with regard to female affirmative action goals.

In this particular company, women also are encouraged to think in terms of long-term careers by a policy of treating pregnancy as a regular disability and by allowing women on maternity leave to accrue seniority. These are policies the enforcement agencies strongly advocate. The agencies also try to encourage companies to set up day-care centers as part of their affirmative action efforts; to date not many employers have done so, however, and it is unlikely EEOC would go to court over this issue.

Minority managers. Finding minority-group members for professional and managerial positions is a different story from finding females in most companies. There often are not enough minority-group members with the appropriate educational background, intellectual ability, and business experience to fill all the management positions that might be allocated to minorities under affirmative action goals. The result frequently has been that the more effective minority-group managers are pirated from one company to another. Another result is that the bidding for blacks and other minorities graduating from engineering schools or obtaining masters degrees in business is intense. Only companies willing and able to pay high salaries can hope to meet their goals through college recruiting.

Because the basic problem involves a lack of educational opportunity, one approach employers can take is to advise minority-group employees currently in lower level jobs to try to secure the required education. They should be made aware of any educational leave policies or tuition aid benefits that might be available and be shown the types of positions they might qualify for by taking certain college courses or other types of training. This obviously is a long-term approach to the problem. As was pointed out in the beginning of the discussion on managerial talent, however, any solution to the problem of women and minorities in management has to be a long-term one. The composition of American management cannot be turned around overnight.

The promotion recommendation

Whether an employee is being considered for promotion to a higher level skilled job, for promotion to a management position, or for participation in a training program that could lead to a promotion, there usually has to be a recommendation from the employee's current supervisor. Frequently, the regular performance evaluation form filled out by the supervisor includes a question about the employee's promotability and may ask for a list of jobs he or she is ready to be promoted into. Where this is the case, the information is readily available in the employee's personnel file. Where there is no formal performance appraisal system, the supervisor is called upon to make a recommendation at the time the employee is considered for promotion to a specific vacancy.

In either case, the potential for unlawful discrimination is great. As discussed in Chapter 7, performance appraisal systems need to be reviewed for the possibilities of bias of all kinds and for evidence of adverse impact. The courts frequently have found that reliance on supervisors' recommendations in making promotion decisions tends to perpetuate discrimination. This is especially true in situations where supervisors are not given instructions or guidelines indicating what standards should be used in assessing an employee's qualifications for the job in question. It should not be a question of how much the supervisor likes or dislikes the employee; it should be a question of whether or not the employee has the necessary qualifications. This question can be answered only if the supervisor knows what the job requires. Again, the essence of selection within the law, whether for hiring or for upgrading, is that the decision be based on job-related factors rather than on personal factors. The crux of this matter—how to ensure that supervisors, managers, and personnel people do make proper selection decisions—is discussed in the next and final chapter.

23

implementation of EEO policies

In the final analysis, a company's vulnerability to charges of discrimination in selection can be measured by results. Employers who can point to changes in the workforce figures in the direction desired by the EEO agencies are less likely to have to prove the validity of their selection processes according to the requirements currently in force. If companies are successful in recruiting enough people in the protected groups, or in providing suitable training opportunities for upgrading among those already employed, applicants for hiring or promotion can be selected on the basis of standards proven to be job-related to the satisfaction of the personnel profession rather than to the satisfaction of government lawyers.

The types of programs and techniques discussed in the previous two chapters all have a common goal—to offset the effects of adverse impact in selection by making a good-faith effort with regard to equal employment opportunity. Some of these programs involve the elimination of practices that are not job-related; others involve opening up opportunities to persons denied them in the past. By and large, the programs described in these two chapters come under the responsibility of the personnel function in most companies. The personnel executive frequently can and does take the initiative in such areas as recruiting, selection techniques, job analysis, skills inventories, promotion, and training.

To achieve meaningful, long-term results in the EEO area, however, it is generally agreed that not only the personnel department but managers throughout the organization need to be involved. It is important, in particular, that top management be committed to, and supportive of, the EEO objectives of the organization. As indicated in Exhibit 3, p. 390, the first three basic steps for an affirmative action program as outlined by EEOC relate to organizational commitment. The first step is to issue a written policy stating the commitment, the second step outlines the responsibility for directing and implementing the commitment, and the third step calls for publicizing the commitment both internally and externally.

The implementation of policy in the area of EEO is no different from the implementation of any organizational policy. While a well-publicized written statement may give credibility to what a company plans to achieve, more is required to guarantee the actual accomplishment of the stated objectives. The implementation of any new policy is likely to be impeded by that well-known phenomenon, resistance to change. In the case of EEO policy, the resistance to change may become intense because basic cultural beliefs, unconscious stereotypes, and generations-old prejudices are being challenged. The first step, then, for effective implementation of EEO policy is to try to determine what barriers are likely to occur and where in the organization; in other words, where is the resistance to change most likely to manifest itself?

Detecting barriers to implementation of EEO

A review of applicant-flow figures should provide the first clue as to where the barriers to effective affirmative action occur. The figures should indicate whether there is a problem in recruiting enough qualified applicants, or in getting a certain proportion of the qualified applicants accepted as employees. If it is the latter problem, the flow data also will indicate where the situation is the worst—the divisions or departments where EEO goals are not being met even though hiring is taking place.

Barriers at the recruiting level. If the barriers appear to exist at the recruiting level, despite extensive efforts, there may be little an employer can do. At the same time, however, if there are no minority or female applicants for entry jobs or for upgrading, there is little likelihood of charges of discrimination in selection. Many employers, when asked what is the most difficult aspect of their affirmative-action programs, point to recruiting. In areas where minority groups constitute a very small percentage of the population or are nonexistent, the insistence of government agencies on setting goals for minorities makes little sense. Although recruiting for engineering or managerial positions may be on a nationwide basis, companies located in small towns in predominantly rural states may have difficulty in convincing educated, urban minority-group members to relocate. As long as such persons are in short supply and in such great demand, they are in a position to begin their careers where they wish; this is likely to be in areas where they and their families feel comfortable, and have family ties and potential friendships.

Similar problems exist with regard to recruiting women for upper level positions. A midwest banking firm reports that its most difficult problem is recruiting female college graduates willing to settle in a small city of 50,000 population and stay long enough to reach a high level of responsibility. As noted in the previous chapter, many employers indicate that women are reluctant to apply for management positions because of sex-role stereotyping. Studies have shown that both men and women tend to view managerial jobs as basically masculine in nature. Furthermore, married women sometimes are afraid that if they move into a position where the needs of the career take precedence over the needs of maintaining a home, their marriages may be threatened. A few women also report they do not want to risk accepting a position that would make their income higher than that of their husbands, because it might jeopardize their marriages. Whether or not these fears are rational, they are real.

Various types of awareness and counseling programs have been suggested both for women and for minority-group members who are hesitant about moving upward to more responsible and better paying positions. A question could be raised as to how far employers should go in trying to encourage people to better themselves. It is one thing to make sure the persons involved are made aware of the opportunities available and to be supportive if they want to accept the challenge, but not all people desire the full-time career commitment and pressures that frequently accompany the challenge of managing. Under the stress of government influence, some companies appear to be trying to convince people to take risks they are not prepared for. On the other hand, because of the high "wash-out" rate among women applying for plant jobs, in some companies women have been encouraged to observe the work involved closely and to take physical conditioning training before applying.

Barriers at the selection decision level. For locations or types of jobs where recruiting is not a problem and large numbers of qualified minority-group and female applicants are available, any EEO selection problems that exist must be the result of the decisions made by the supervisors, department heads, or personnel people doing the hiring. It is a simple matter to detect those work units or departments where this type of barrier exists. But it is not always a simple matter to eliminate the barriers.

There are many reasons managers may prefer to choose a white person over a minority-group member. It may be the result of years of ingrained cultural training, as is the case in a small southern manufacturing company where the personnel executive reports his most difficult problem is that of "overcoming southern prejudice in old line managers in the 55 to 65 age bracket." It is not an easy task to ask these managers to hire people they always have believed are inferior in terms of intellect and ability. Even where prejudice is not overt, there are many managers who think both women and minority-group members lack the capability to perform certain kinds of work. In many cases, these managers have had very little experience working closely with women or minorities.

Supervisors may not have such prejudices themselves, but they may think some of the employees in their work units or their fellow managers do, and they would prefer not to create a difficult situation by bringing a woman or minority person into the group. An example is the supervisor who thinks his men would have to clean up their usual shop talk if a woman were hired. Another concern, in work that involves customer contact, is that a "nontraditional" person might cause alarm among customers and subsequent loss of business. There have been a few reports of housewives refusing to let female telephone installers perform their jobs because it involves getting dirty. On the other hand, a study of IBM's experience in hiring blacks as salesmen and repairmen found little difficulty in their being accepted by the public in jobs that previously had been held only by whites.

Sometimes, managers who pride themselves on being free of prejudice, liberal, open-minded, and so forth still make their selection decisions consistently in favor of majority candidates. This has been demonstrated when it comes to deciding between men and women for managerial positions. Studies involving hiring or promotion decisions for management jobs have been conducted using applications or work histories that are identical except for the fact that one bears a man's name and the other a woman's. The results typically indicate the existence of anti-female biases with regard to the ability to handle higher level responsibilities.

In the case of a few individual supervisors with outright prejudices or what have been labeled "hard-core assumptions," such as the one concerning the offensiveness of four-letter words in the presence of women, counseling on an individual basis may be the best solution. For the majority of managers making selection decisions, however, special training and continuing communication are the usual methods used.

Sensitizing managers to the problem

EEO training has become a regular component of the development program for supervisors and higher level managers in those companies that have established ongoing training programs of this type. Companies too small to have ongoing programs frequently send their managers to seminars on EEO and affirmative action presented by organizations at locations throughout the country. All of these training efforts have as their objectives educating supervisors and managers in what the law requires in general and in specific situations and making them aware of their own beliefs and of how negative attitudes can be overcome.

In programs conducted by an individual company, general legal requirements can be translated into the specific requirements of the particular company's situation. A government contractor will have an affirmative action plan specifying that company's goals, and companies operating under consent decrees will have certain target areas where EEO efforts need to be focused. These matters can be discussed in some detail with a view to convincing supervisors that compliance is serious business and that the ultimate responsibility in this area rests with those making hiring and promotion decisions.

Once supervisory responsibility has been spelled out, training sessions may emphasize the specific aspects of selection (and other personnel actions such as discipline) that should be scrutinized for possible discrimination. This is where supervisors are cautioned about questions asked in the interview, for example, to make sure they are job-related. They may be given guidelines for setting standards for job vacancies and for performance reviews. Emphasis on performance evaluation is perhaps one of the most crucial aspects of EEO training for managers, since performance evaluations may be used as criterion measures in validation studies and also are the basis for future promotions. There is some evidence that ratings of black managers on such factors as social and human relations skills may be influenced by racial attitudes and biases, with the result that they may not be moved up the managerial hierarchy when their performance warrants.

The most difficult part of EEO training for managers is "awareness" training, which attempts to sensitize managers to some of the barriers and stereotyped attitudes mentioned earlier in this chapter. Various approaches have been developed for awareness training, using role-playing, small discussion groups, films, and other audio-visual aids. Blue Shield of California has developed such a program, covering black Americans, native Americans, Mexican Americans, Chinese Americans, Japanese Americans, and those of Filipino ancestry. (An outline of the Blue Shield program appears as Exhibit 15, p. 545.)

The objective of awareness training is, as the name implies, to make managers aware of their own biases or prejudices. The goal is not necessarily to change these biases but rather to change managerial behavior so that decisions are made on the basis of affirmative action goals rather than being determined by the individual manager's personal preferences. Sensitizing managers to EEO problems is only half the battle, however; they must also be convinced that meeting EEO goals is crucial to their careers.

Making EEO goals matter

A basic problem with many kinds of management training is that what is learned in the training program is antithetical to the situation back on the job. This is just as true in the EEO area. Personnel managers and supervisors often are sent to EEO programs to find out "how far we need to go" to stay out of trouble with the law. If there is no real commitment on the part of top management, there is little likelihood of success in the achievement of affirmative action goals and little if any incentive for supervisors to contribute. In the current context, personnel executives can do everything in their power in the way of recruiting and eliminating structural barriers to the employment of women and minorities, yet this will be to no avail if the organizational climate is not supportive of EEO.

The commitment of upper level management to EEO and affirmative action goals can be demonstrated in several ways. Initially, the commitment may be communicated throughout the organization in letters from the company president, memos to department heads and managers, and feature items in employee publications. In some companies this proves to be as far as the effort goes, signifying a fairly weak organizational commitment.

Some companies have appointed a special EEO officer, often reporting directly to the chief executive officer, who has responsibility for promoting equal employment opportunity and for monitoring the company's results in this area. There is some disagreement, however, regarding the effectiveness of this approach, and it has not been adopted widely; fewer than one out of five companies participating in a recent BNA survey have such an officer.[1] However, the surveyed companies with a special executive in charge of affirmative action programs appear to have better EEO results than those companies without a separate EEO officer. What is cause and what is effect here is not clear.

An alternative approach that has been suggested is to assign responsibility for EEO to a high-level officer with other responsibilities as well. This person might lead a task force of several top managers to work with an experienced outside consultant on EEO matters. By involving officers from various organizational functions, the EEO commitment can be spread more widely throughout the company. The presence of an outside expert may make it easier to win acceptance of changes necessary to implement EEO policy; these

[1]*Equal Employment Opportunity: Programs and Results,* Personnel Policies Forum Survey No. 112, March 1976 (Washington, D.C.: The Bureau of National Affairs, Inc.).

changes might encounter more resistance and hostility if proposed by an insider.

Rewarding EEO achievements. Actions speak louder than words, and it is what top management does, not what it says, that matters most in EEO policy implementation. One way of ensuring that managers accept responsibility for the achievement of affirmative action goals is to include these goals in organizational reward systems—thus managers who do better in this area would expect to get bigger raises and more promotions. One of the earliest companies to include EEO results in managers' performance evaluations was General Electric. Over the years GE has been successful in implementing affirmative action policies by establishing specific goals for every manager in the company with responsibility for hiring and firing. Rewards and punishments are tied to these goals through management appraisal and compensation systems. At Sears, Roebuck, a policy called "Mandatory Achievement of Goals" calls for the filling of one out of every two openings with women or minority-group members. Allowance is made for situations where this is not feasible, but the managers are accountable for results.

The approach of including EEO results in performance evaluations appears to be effective; it is used in one third of the companies represented on BNA's Personnel Policies Forum.[2] Some organizations have institutionalized this practice by including a section in the position description of each manager's job specifying responsibility for achievement of affirmative action goals.

Another type of reward is recognition. Some companies make it a practice to publicize their EEO results on a regular basis, quarterly or annually, to provide individual plants or departments with a measure of how well they are doing compared to other units. Because EEO is viewed as a sensitive area, however, many companies prefer not to publicize their results, or they limit the distribution of such reports to the top levels of management. Unless the results are fairly positive, companies may fear that publicizing them is tantamount to asking for trouble with the enforcement agencies.

The ultimate test. As the saying goes, "money talks," and the ultimate test of a company's commitment to EEO is how much it is

[2]*Ibid.*

willing to spend to achieve affirmative action goals. A company may have an extensive program for recruiting minority college graduates, but it also must be willing and able to pay the salaries needed to bring them on to the payroll before meaningful results actually occur.

The types of training and support programs that may be required to keep minorities and women in jobs they have been recruited for also can be expensive. In many cases, where special programs have not been undertaken to provide a supportive environment, turnover has been a problem. However, it may be that these efforts will be needed only in the early years of a company's affirmative action program. Presumably, as the company is successful in bringing members of the protected classes into the work force, these people will provide models and a more supportive environment for those who follow. This is one reason it has been suggested that the EEO agencies would do well to concentrate their efforts on the upper job categories. If companies could be convinced they need to hire more women and minority-group members at the upper organizational levels, better results at the lower levels would be much easier to achieve. With a black or female top executive as a model, other blacks and women could be recruited for professional or lower level jobs much more easily.

At the present time, the matter of how much a company should spend on EEO is primarily a function of how much it might cost not to be in compliance with the law. No matter how liberal top management may be in the area of equal rights, if a company is operating in a competitive situation it cannot afford to spend unlimited amounts to implement EEO. For the typical business firm, there must be a balance between expenditures for affirmative action and the risks of expensive litigation, possible damages, and costly court-ordered decrees governing employment practices. As was pointed out in the beginning of this book, the costs of noncompliance can be extremely high, but so can the cost of headlong, unthinking compliance.

Fortunately, as far as selection is concerned, the costs of compliance with EEO regulations need not be extreme. As outlined in this book, the basic steps involved are (1) to analyze the current workforce for evidence of underutilization of protected groups, (2) to study current selection practices for indications of adverse impact, (3) to study current selection practices for job-relatedness (*i.e.,* to validate them), (4) to revise selection procedures that cannot be proven to be job-related, and (5) to take action to lessen the effects of any adverse impact that does exist while still not neglecting the requirements of business necessity. The latter would include recruiting, training, or any of the other approaches discussed in these final three chapters, which constitute a good-faith effort to provide equal employment opportunity.

Using outside professional help

Much of what is required to carry out the steps listed above can be done by the staff of the personnel department with no outside help, and in many companies everything can be handled internally. Certainly the first two steps can be done internally. The first is a matter of collecting figures on the makeup of the work force, and comparing them with the relevant groups available in the labor market. The second step involves monitoring applicant flows and in-house promotions and transfers at each stage of the selection process to pinpoint areas of potential discrimination or adverse impact. Relatively simple reporting procedures can be set up to provide the figures needed, and a periodic tally and review of the figures will highlight not only problems but also changes over time. It should be noted that this type of monitoring process may unearth selection problems that have nothing to do with equal employment opportunity and may indicate the most effective sources or procedures for selection in general.

Help with validation studies. The third step, validation of selection procedures to show job-relatedness, is an area where a company might benefit from the use of outside professional help, although this is not absolutely necessary. There are many organizations, particularly the nation's large corporations, that have an adequate professional staff of industrial psychologists to perform the necessary validity studies. However, a degree in industrial psychology is not a prerequisite to conducting validity studies, and personnel people without this background can do much of the work involved themselves. As suggested in Chapter 8, assistance with the statistical analyses required in validation research frequently can be obtained from the company's computer staff.

Some employers have a continuing arrangement with a psychological consulting firm or an individual consultant to help set up selection procedures and to conduct ongoing validation studies. If outside help is to be used, this is the recommended approach. The same consultant should be retained from the beginning of a validation research project in order to ensure full awareness of the situation; this is especially important if the consultant might be called upon to testify in court on the results of the studies. One of the major problems that has arisen in litigation involving validity studies to date is that consultants have been called in to conduct studies of selection techniques that they were not involved in installing initially. As was noted earlier, when a selection technique has already been questioned by a compliance officer, it may be too late to begin the validation research; predictive studies in particular may be difficult under such circumstances.

In general, we would recommend, in companies without a professional industrial psychologist on the staff, that the personnel department conduct some preliminary research on current selection techniques. The results of this research could very well indicate that there is such a strong relationship between the selection technique and subsequent job performance that there is no need for further research. If the results of the preliminary study are weak, inconclusive, or suggest a negative relationship, additional study is called for. At this point, it may be advisable to call in a consultant for guidance. If the studies should indicate that current selection techniques are not job-related, then a complete revamping of the selection process may be in order. In this case, a consultant may be able to offer suggestions for new techniques and might be helpful in setting up studies of the new procedures.

For any selection techniques or standards found to result in adverse impact, it is recommended that studies of job-relatedness be conducted. If preliminary investigation of a technique with an adverse impact suggests a problem with validity, outside help in conducting further studies certainly would be advisable. Even if it looks as though the technique in question is a valid predictor of performance, the corroboration of an outside expert is helpful to have on record for compliance officers.

When a consultant is called in to advise on selection procedures and to conduct validity studies, there should be an agreement that he or she would be willing to testify concerning the results of the studies if the company should ever become involved in EEO litigation. This should be sufficient to ensure that the consultant will not be tempted to come up with the result the employer desires. When the company's attitude is one of "let's get a consultant to *prove* the technique is valid," rather than "let's get a consultant to find out *whether* the technique is valid," conditions are not ideal for the conduct of court-proof research.

Help in implementing change. Unless an employer is extremely lucky, or has been conducting validity studies of selection procedures all along, the results of the validity studies can be expected to indicate changes. It may be that a study reveals a certain technique to have no validity whatsoever, as in the case of the psychological evaluations reported in Chapter 9. The company involved had been spending large amounts of money for the evaluations and was able to reduce its selection costs considerably by eliminating this procedure. Without substantial evidence from a study conducted by someone from outside the organization, however, it would have been difficult to convince management to go along with the change. Personnel executives frequently can make a much stronger case for introducing changes with supporting evidence from an outside "expert."

As noted earlier in this chapter, outside consultants may be useful not only with regard to validation research, but also in implementing affirmative action programs. A consultant may serve in a continuing EEO advisory capacity, helping to effect the changes necessary and monitoring results. Or consultants may be called in on a short-term basis to provide assistance in specific areas where problems are found to exist. Whatever types of programs are needed—from training employment interviewers to setting up employee information systems to briefing supervisors on their EEO responsibilities—there are consultants specializing in them. Most personnel consultants are frequent participants in local and national personnel conferences and write about their special areas in personnel periodicals (many of these articles are listed in the references section at the end of this book). Consultants in personnel management also may be found on the faculties of most universities with colleges of business administration. As is the case with consultants in any area of business, it is wise to check with other companies the consultant has worked for before making any final arrangement.

Whether or not to hire a consultant for help in establishing an effective selection system within the law is a decision the personnel executive must make on the basis of knowledge of the particular organization. There are some companies that absolutely refuse to use consultants at all, and others that use them only for tax and legal matters. We would urge that the personnel executive, wherever possible, review the company's selection process before lawyers become involved. Frequently, a lawyer's approach is to advise companies simply to abandon techniques that have even a possibility of adverse impact. Unless the personnel executive at the outset has figures to prove no adverse impact or results of validation research to prove job-relatedness, a perfectly effective selection tool may be eliminated under pressure from the legal counsel, thus moving the company one step closer to random hiring.

Although the improvement of personnel practice was not one of the goals of the Civil Rights Act, Title VII may well have that result. Certainly in the area of selection, the requirements for compliance with the law also can contribute to more effective hiring and promotion decisions. Decisions must be made on one basis or another, and it is unlikely that most organizations would be willing to make selection decisions on a completely random basis if they were aware that that is what they were doing. There is too much at stake in terms of organizational effectiveness and achievement of goals. As long as the techniques used for selection must be related to job performance, which really is all that the law requires, our selection processes should be more effective in the future than they often have been in the past. This is not only in the interest of society; it is in the interest of its component organizations as well.

part 7

exhibits

exhibit 1

Griggs v. *Duke Power Co.*

401 U.S. 424 (1971), 3 FEP Cases 175

MR. CHIEF JUSTICE BERGER delivered the opinion of the Court.

We granted the writ in this case to resolve the question whether an employer is prohibited by the Civil Rights Act of 1964, Title VII, from requiring a high school education or passing of a standardized general intelligence test as a condition of employment in or transfer to jobs when (a) neither standard is shown to be significantly related to successful job performance, (b) both requirements operate to disqualify Negroes at a substantially higher rate than white applicants, and (c) the jobs in question formerly had been filled only by white employees as part of a longstanding practice of giving preference to whites.[1]

Congress provided, in Title VII of the Civil Rights Act of 1964, for class actions for enforcement of provisions of the Act and this proceeding was brought by a group of incumbent Negro employees against Duke Power Company. All the petitioners are employed at the Company's Dan River Steam Station, a power generating facility located at Draper, North Carolina. At the time this action was instituted, the Company had 95 employees at the Dan River Station, 14 of whom were Negroes; 13 of these are petitioners here.

The District Court found that prior to July 2, 1965, the effective date of the Civil Rights Act of 1964, the Company openly discriminated on the basis of race in hiring and assigning of employees at its Dan River plant. The plant was organized into five operating departments: (1) Labor, (2)

[1]The Act provides:

"Sec. 703. (a) It shall be an unlawful employment practice for an employer—

"(2) to limit, segregate, or classify his employees in any way which would deprive or tend to deprive any individual of employment opportunities or otherwise adversely affect his status as an employee, because of such individual's race, color, religion, sex, or national origin.

"(h) Notwithstanding any other provision of this title, it shall not be an unlawful employment practice for an employer . . . to give and to act upon the results of any professionally developed ability test provided that such test, its administration or action upon the results is not designed, intended or used to discriminate because of race, color, religion, sex or national origin. . . ." 78 Stat. 255, 42 U.S.C. §2000e -2.

Coal Handling, (3) Operations, (4) Maintenance, and (5) Laboratory and Test. Negroes were employed only in the Labor Department where the highest paying jobs paid less than the lowest paying jobs in the other four "operating" departments in which only whites were employed.[2] Promotions were normally made within each department on the basis of job seniority. Transferees into a department usually began in the lowest position.

In 1955 the Company instituted a policy of requiring a high school education for initial assignment to any department except Labor, and for transfer from the Coal Handling to any "inside" department (Operations, Maintenance, or Laboratory). When the Company abandoned its policy of restricting Negroes to the Labor Department in 1965, completion of high school also was made a prerequisite to transfer from Labor to any other department. From the time the high school requirement was instituted to the time of trial, however, white employees hired before the time of the high school education requirement continued to perform satisfactorily and achieve promotions in the "operating" departments. Findings on this score are not challenged.

The Company added a further requirement for new employees on July 2, 1965, the date on which Title VII became effective. To qualify for placement in any but the Labor Department it became necessary to register satisfactory scores on two professionally prepared aptitude tests, as well as to have a high school education. Completion of high school alone continued to render employees eligible for transfer to the four desirable departments from which Negroes had been excluded if the incumbent had been employed prior to the time of the new requirement. In September 1965 the Company began to permit incumbent employees who lacked a high school education to qualify for transfer from Labor or Coal Handling to an "inside" job by passing two tests—The Wonderlic Personnel Test, which purports to measure general intelligence, and the Bennett Mechanical Comprehension Test. Neither was directed or intended to measure the ability to learn to perform a particular job or category of jobs. The requisite scores used for both initial hiring and transfer approximated the national median for high school graduates.[3]

The District Court had found that while the Company previously followed a policy of overt racial discrimination in a period prior to the Act,

[2]A Negro was first assigned to a job in an operating department in August, 1966, five months after charges had been filed with the Equal Employment Opportunity Commission. The employee, a high school graduate who had begun in the Labor Department in 1953, was promoted to a job in the Coal Handling Department.

[3]The test standards are thus more stringent than the high school requirement, since they would screen out approximately half of all high school graduates.

such conduct had ceased. The District Court also concluded that Title VII was intended to be prospective only and consequently, the impact of prior inequities was beyond the reach of corrective action authorized by the Act.

The Court of Appeals was confronted with a question of first impression as are we, concerning the meaning of Title VII. After careful analysis a majority of that court concluded that a subjective test of employer's intent should govern, particularly in a close case, and that in this case there was no showing of a discriminatory purpose in the adoption of the diploma and test requirements. On this basis, the Court of Appeals concluded there was no violation of the Act.

The Court of Appeals reversed the District Court in part, rejecting the holding that residual discrimination arising from prior employment practices was insulated from remedial action.[4] The Court of Appeals noted, however, that the District Court was correct in its conclusion that there was no showing of a racial purpose or invidious intent in the adoption of the high school diploma requirement or general intelligence test and that these standards had been applied fairly to whites and Negroes alike. It held that, in the absence of a discriminatory purpose, use of such requirements was permitted by the Act. In so doing, the Court of Appeals rejected the claim that because these two requirements operated to render ineligible a markedly disproportionate number of Negroes, they were unlawful under Title VII unless shown to be job related.[5] We granted the writ on these claims. 399 U.S. 926.

The objective of Congress in the enactment of Title VII is plain from the language of the statue. It was to achieve equality of employment opportunities and remove barriers that have operated in the past to favor an identifiable group of white employees over other employees. Under the Act, practices, procedures or tests neutral on their face, and even neutral in terms of intent, cannot be maintained if they operate to "freeze" the status quo of prior discriminatory employment practices.

[4]The Court of Appeals ruled that Negroes employed in the Labor Department at a time when there was no high school or test requirement for entrance into the higher paying departments could not now be made subject to those requirements, since whites hired contemporaneously into those departments were never subject to them. The Court of Appeals also required that the seniority rights of those Negroes be measured on a plantwide, rather than a departmental, basis. However, the Court of Appeals denied relief to the Negro employees without a high school education or its equivalent who were hired into the Labor Department after institution of the educational requirement.

[5]One member of that court disagreed with this aspect of the decision, maintaining, as do the petitioners in this Court, that Title VII prohibits the use of employment criteria that operate in a racially exclusionary fashion and do not measure skills or abilities necessary to performance of the jobs for which those criteria are used.

The Court of Appeals' opinion, and the partial dissent, agreed that, on the record in the present case, "whites register far better on the Company's alternate requirements" than Negroes.[6] 420 F. 2d 1225, 1239 n. 6. This consequence would appear to be directly traceable to race. Basic intelligence must have the means of articulation to manifest itself fairly in a testing process. Because they are Negroes, petitioners have long received inferior education in segregated schools and this Court expressly recognized these differences in *Gaston County* v. *United States,* 395 U.S. 285 (1969). There, because of the inferior education received by Negroes in North Carolina, this Court barred the institution of a literacy test for voter registration on the ground that the test would abridge the right to vote indirectly on account of race. Congress did not intend by Title VII, however, to guarantee a job to every person regardless of qualifications. In short, the Act does not command that any person be hired simply because he was formerly the subject of discrimination, or because he is a member of a minority group. Discriminatory preference for any group, minority or majority, is precisely and only what Congress has proscribed. What is required by Congress is the removal of artificial, arbitrary, and unnecessary barriers to employment when the barriers operate invidiously to discriminate on the basis of racial or other impermissible classification.

Congress has now provided that tests or criteria for employment or promotion may not provide equality of opportunity merely in the sense of the fabled offer of milk to the stork and the fox. On the contrary, Congress has now required that the posture and condition of the jobseeker be taken into account. It has—to resort again to the fable—provided that the vessel in which the milk is proffered be one all seekers can use. The Act proscribes not only overt discrimination but also practices that are fair in form, but discriminatory in operation. The touchstone is business necessity. If an employment practice which operates to exclude Negroes cannot be shown to be related to job performance, the practice is prohibited.

On the record before us, neither the high school completion requirement nor the general intelligence test is shown to bear a demonstrable relationship to successful performance of the jobs for which it was used. Both were adopted, as the Court of Appeals noted, without meaningful study of

[6]In North Carolina, 1960 census statistics show that, while 34% of white males had completed high school, only 12% of Negro males had done so. U.S. Bureau of the Census, U.S. Census of Population: 1960, Vol. 1, Characteristics of the Population, pt. 35, Table 47.

Similarly, with respect to standardized tests, the EEOC in one case found that use of a battery of tests, including the Wonderlic and Bennett tests used by the Company in the instant case, resulted in 58% of whites passing the tests, as compared with only 6% of the blacks. Decision of EEOC, CCH Empl. Prac. Guide ¶17, 304.53 (Dec. 2, 1966). See also Decision of EEOC 70-552, CCH Empl. Prac. Guide ¶6139 (Feb. 19, 1970).

their relationship to job-performance ability. Rather, a vice president of the Company testified, the requirements were instituted on the Company's judgment that they generally would improve the overall quality of the work force.

The evidence, however, shows that employees who have not completed high school or taken the tests have continued to perform satisfactorily and make progress in departments for which the high school and test criteria are now used.[7] The promotion record of present employees who would not be able to meet the new criteria thus suggests the possibility that the requirements may not be needed even for the limited purpose of preserving the avowed policy of advancement within the Company. In the context of this case, it is unnecessary to reach the question whether testing requirements that take into account capability for the next succeeding position or related future promotion might be utilized upon a showing that such long-range requirements fulfill a genuine business need. In the present case the Company has made no such showing.

The Court of Appeals held that the Company had adopted the diploma and test requirements without any "intention to discriminate against Negro employees." 420 F. 2d, at 1232. We do not suggest that either the District Court or the Court of Appeals erred in examining the employer's intent; but good intent or absence of discriminatory intent does not redeem employment procedures or testing mechanisms that operate as "built-in headwinds" for minority groups and are unrelated to measuring job capability.

The Company's lack of discriminatory intent is suggested by special efforts to help the undereducated employees through Company financing of two-thirds the cost of tuition for high school training. But Congress directed the thrust of the Act to the consequences of employment practices, not simply the motivation. More than that, Congress has placed on the employer the burden of showing that any given requirement must have a manifest relationship to the employment in question.

The facts of this case demonstrate the inadequacy of broad and general testing devices as well as the infirmity of using diplomas or degrees as fixed measures of capability. History is filled with examples of men and women who rendered highly effective performance without the conventional badges of accomplishment in terms of certificates, diplomas, or degrees. Diplomas and tests are useful servants, but Congress has mandated the commonsense proposition that they are not to become masters of reality.

[7]For example, between July 2, 1965, and November 14, 1966, the percentage of white employees who were promoted but who were not high school graduates was nearly identical to the percentage of nongraduates in the entire white work force.

The Company contends that its general intelligence tests are specifically permitted by § 703(h) of the Act.[8] That section authorizes the use of "any professionally developed ability test" that is not "designed, intended or *used* to discriminate because of race. . . " (Emphasis added.)

The Equal Employment Opportunity Commission, having enforcement responsibility, has issued guidelines interpreting §703(h) to permit only the use of job-related tests.[9] The administrative interpretation of the Act by the enforcing agency is entitled to great deference. See, e.g., United States v. City of Chicago, 400 U.S. 8 (1970); Udall v. Tallman, 380 U.S. 1 (1965); Power Reactor Co. v. Electricians, 367 U.S. 396 (1961). Since the Act and its legislative history support the Commission's construction, this affords good reason to treat the guidelines as expressing the will of Congress.

Section 703(h) was not contained in the House version of the Civil Rights Act but was added in the Senate during extended debate. For a period, debate revolved around claims that the bill as proposed would prohibit all testing and force employers to hire unqualified persons simply because they were part of a group formerly subject to job discrimination.[10] Proponents of Title VII sought throughout the debate to assure the critics that the Act would have no effect on job-related tests. Senators Case of New Jersey and Clark of Pennsylvania, comanagers of the bill on the Senate floor, issued a memorandum explaining that the proposed Title VII "ex-

[8]Section 703(h) applies only to tests. It has no applicability to the high school diploma requirement.

[9]EEOC Guidelines on Employment Testing Procedures, issued August 24, 1966, provide:

"The Commission accordingly interprets 'professionally developed ability test' to mean a test which fairly measures the knowledge or skills required by the particular job or class of jobs which the applicant seeks, or which fairly affords the employer a chance to measure the applicant's ability to perform a particular job or class of jobs. The fact that a test was prepared by an individual or organization claiming expertise in test preparation does not, without more, justify its use within the meaning of Title VII".

The EEOC position has been elaborated in the new Guidelines on Employee Selection Procedures, 29 CFR§1607, 35 Fed. Reg. 12333 (Aug. 1, 1970). These guidelines demand that employers using tests have available "data demonstrating that the test is predictive of or significantly correlated with important elements of work behavior which comprise or are relevant to the job or jobs for which candidates are being evaluated." Id., at §1607.4(c).

[10]The congressional discussion was prompted by the decision of a hearing examiner for the Illinois Fair Employment Commission in Myart v. Motorola Co. (The decision is reprinted at 110 Cong. Rec. 5662.) That case suggested that standardized tests on which whites performed better than Negroes could never be used. The decision was taken to mean that such tests could never be justified even if the needs of the business required them. A number of Senators feared that Title VII might produce a similar result. See remarks of Senators Ervin, 110 Cong. Rec. 5614-5616; Smathers, id., at 5999-6000; Holland, id., at 7012-7013; Hill, id., at 8447; Tower, id., at 9024; Talmadge, id., 9025-9026; Fulbright, id., at 9599-9600; and Ellender, id., at 9600.

pressly protects the employer's right to insist that any prospective applicant, Negro or white, *must meet the applicable job qualifications.* Indeed, the very purpose of Title VII is to promote hiring on the basis of job qualifications, rather than on the basis of race or color." 110 Cong. Rec. 7247.[11] (Emphasis added) Despite these assurances, Senator Tower of Texas introduced an amendment authorizing "professionally developed ability tests." Proponents of Title VII opposed the amendment because as written, it would permit an employer to give any test, "whether it was a good test or not, so long as it was professionally designed. Discrimination could actually exist under the guise of compliance with the statute." 110 Cong. Rec. 13504 (remarks of Sen. Case).

The amendment was defeated and two days later Senator Tower offered a substitute amendment which was adopted verbatim and is now the testing provision of §703(h). Speaking for the supporters of Title VII, Senator Humphrey, who had vigorously opposed the first amendment, endorsed the substitute amendment stating: "Senators on both sides of the aisle who were deeply interested in Title VII have examined the text of this amendment and have found it to be in accord with the intent and purpose of that title." 110 Cong. Rec. 13724. The amendment was then adopted.[12] From the sum of the legislative history relevant in this case, the conclusion

[11]The Court of Appeals majority, in finding no requirement in Title VII that employment tests be job related, relied in part on a quotation from an earlier Clark-Case interpretative memorandum addressed to the question of the constitutionality of Title VII. The Senators said in that memorandum:

"There is no requirement in Title VII that employers abandon bona fide qualification tests where, because of differences in background and education, members of some groups are able to perform better on these tests than members of other groups. An employer may set his qualifications as high as he likes, he may test to determine which applicants have these qualifications, and he may hire, assign and promote on the basis of test performance." 110 Cong. Rec. 7213.

However, nothing there stated conflicts with the later memorandum dealing specifically with the debate over employer testing, 110 Cong. Rec. 7247 (quoted from in the text above), in which Senators Clark and Case explained that tests which measure "applicable job qualifications" are permissible under Title VII. In the earlier memorandum Clark and Case assured the Senate that employers were not to be prohibited from using tests that determine *qualifications.* Certainly a reasonable interpretation of what the Senators meant, in light of the subsequent memorandum directed specifically at employer testing, was that nothing in the Act prevents employers from requiring that applicants be fit for the job.

[12]Senator Tower's original amendment provided in part that a test would be permissible "if . . . in the case of any individual who is seeking employment with such employer, such test is designed to determine or predict whether such individual is suitable or trainable with respect to his employment in the particular business or enterprise involved. . . ." 110 Cong. Rec. 13492. This language indicates that Senator Tower's aim was simply to make certain that job-related tests would be permitted. The opposition to the amendment was based on its loose wording which the proponents of Title VII feared would be susceptible of misinterpretation. The final amendment, which was acceptable to all sides, could hardly have required less of a job relation than the first.

is inescapable that the EEOC's construction of §703(h) to require that employment tests be job related comports with congressional intent.

Nothing in the Act precludes the use of testing or measuring procedures; obviously they are useful. What Congress has forbidden is giving these devices and mechanisms controlling force unless thay are demonstrably a reasonable measure of job performance. Congress has not commanded that the less qualified be preferred over the better qualified simply because of minority origins. Far from disparaging job qualifications as such, Congress has made such qualifications the controlling factor, so that race, religion, nationality and sex become irrelevant. What Congress has commanded is that any tests used must measure the person for the job and not the person in the abstract.

The judgment of the Court of Appeals is, as to that portion of the judgment appealed from, reversed.

MR. JUSTICE BRENNAN took no part in the consideration or decision of this case.

exhibit 2

EEO conciliation agreement between Gulf Oil Co. and Labor Dep't, EEOC

A charge having been filed under Title VII of the Civil Rights Act of 1964, as amended, by a Commissioner of the U.S. Equal Employment Opportunity Commission against the Respondent, the charge having been investigated and reasonable cause having been found, the parties do resolve and conciliate this matter as follows:

A. General Provisions

1. It is understood that this Agreement does not constitute an admission by the Respondent of any violation of Title VII of the Civil Rights Act of 1964, as amended.

2. The U.S. Equal Employment Opportunity Commission hereby waives and releases its cause of action against the Respondent under the instant charge and covenants not to sue the Respondent independently or on behalf of any individual including, but not necessarily limited to, persons listed on Attachments "A" and "B" hereto with respect to any matter alleged thereunder, subject to performance by the Respondent of the promises and representations contained herein.

3. The Respondent understands that the Commission, on its own motion, may review compliance with this Agreement. As a part of such review, the Commission may require written reports concerning compliance, may inspect the premises, examine witnesses, and examine and copy documents pertinent to such review. The Commission agrees that the Respondent reserves all rights and protection afforded by the Freedom of Information Act, as amended.

4. The Respondent reaffirms that all of its hiring, promotion practices, classification, assignments, layoffs and all other terms and conditions of employment shall be maintained and conducted in a manner which does not discriminate on the basis of race, color, religion, sex or national origin in violation of Title VII of the Civil Rights Act of 1964, as amended.

Source: *Daily Labor Report,* July 16, 1976, F-1 through F-4.

5. The Respondent agrees that it will not knowingly practice nor permit its supervisory or other personnel to practice discrimination or retaliation of any kind against any person because of his or her opposition to any practice declared unlawful under Title VII of the Civil Rights Act of 1964, as amended, or because of the filing of a charge, or giving of testimony or assistance, or participation in any manner in any investigation, proceeding, or hearing under Title VII of the Civil Rights Act of 1964, as amended.

6. Recognizing the exception with respect to sex as regards toilets, showers and the like, the Respondent reaffirms that all facilities on the premises or furnished its employees, including recreational opportunities and all other conveniences and services, are available for the use and enjoyment of any employee without regard to race, color, religion, sex or national origin; that there is no discrimination against any employee on said grounds with respect to the use of facilities; and that the notices required to be posted by Title VII of the Civil Rights Act of 1964, as amended, are posted.

B. Settlement Agreement—Back Pay

1. Appertaining to back pay, the Affected Class is hereby defined as all Negroes employed by the Respondent on July 2, 1965, whose seniority date antecedes January 1, 1957, and all hourly rated females employed by the respondent in its Package and Grease Department on July 2, 1965.

2. The Commission agrees that a thorough search has been made to identify all individuals potentially entitled to back pay under this Agreement, that the Respondent's personnel records since the effective date of Title VII of the Civil Rights Act of 1964 have been exhaustively analyzed and that, through examination of documents submitted by the Respondent, no persons potentially entitled other than those listed on Attachments "A" and "B" hereto could be found.

3. For the sake of convenience, the Affected Classes, as shown on Attachments "A" and "B", shall be designated and hereinafter referred to as Group "A" and "B" respectively.

4. The Respondent agrees that all individuals identified as belonging to Group "A" or "B" shall immediately be awarded upon notification of acceptance as described below, such back pay as is hereinafter provided:

a. The Respondent represents that it has set aside a sum for purposes of fulfilling all back pay obligations which are or might have been incurred as a result of employment practices complained of in the instant charge or which were treated in the Commission's Letters of Determination thereon, including matters found by the Commission to be like and related.

b. The United States Equal Employment Opportunity Commission concurs that the sum set aside is sufficient to meet the purposes of providing equitable relief to designated members of Group "A" or Group "B" and stipulates that $35,000.00 of said amount may be reserved and held in a special account by the Respondent for a period of five years. The Commission agrees that, insofar as matters encompassed by this Agreement are raised to issue in the future, the Respondent shall utilize its special account to dispose of contingent liabilities, and that any undispensed funds remaining, after passage of the account's established five year life, shall be returned to the Respondent's general control for unrestricted use.

c. In formulating the specific relief due each individual hereunder credits will be awarded as follows:

(1) To members of Group "A", $5.62 for each month of continuous service with the Respondent prior to January 1, 1957, and $2.81 for each month of continuous service thereafter until date of termination or until January 1, 1971, whichever occurs earlier.

(2) To members of Group "B", $5.62 for each month of continuous service with the Respondent until date of termination or until January 1, 1975, whichever occurs earlier.

d. Back pay awards previously tendered to members of Group "A" under the Respondent's Agreement dated May 7, 1971, with the Office for Equal Opportunity, United States Department of the Interior shall be deducted from amounts hereunder due those same individuals.

e. Back pay awards will be subject to standard deductions for F.I.C.A. and Federal Income Tax Withholding.

f. Upon accepting a back pay award, each Group "A" or Group "B" member will be required to execute a general release to the Respondent for any and all claims against the Respondent as a result of events arising from its employment practices occurring on or before the date of release, or which might arise as the result of the future effects of past or present employment practices.

g. Prior to tendering back pay awards, the Respondent agrees to notify in writing each member belonging to Group "A" or Group "B" that he or she has been so identified, and of the general formula used to calculate awards and of the conditions of waiver or release required in accepting back pay. Each member shall be furnished a form on which to notify the Respondent, within thirty days, whether such member desires to accept or decline back pay consideration. A failure on the part of any member to respond within thirty days shall be interpreted as acceptance of back pay. It is agreed that the form of notification to be utilized shall be reviewed and signed by a Commission representative prior to being implemented or disseminated.

h. In the event that a member of Group "A" or Group "B" is deceased, notice shall be given and payment made to his or her estate. Upon accepting a back pay award, the deceased member's heir or heirs shall be required to execute a general release as is provided in subsection (f) herein-above.

i. In the event that a member of Group "A" or Group "B" refuses his or her award, or cannot be located or, if deceased, his heir or heirs cannot be located through the exercise of reasonable effort, his or her back pay award shall be placed in the Respondent's special account, as provided in subsection (b) above, to be returned to the Respondent's general control, if unclaimed upon expiration of the account's life.

C. *Settlement Agreement—Goals and Time-tables*

1. a. For Affirmative Action purposes, the Affected Class is hereby defined as all hourly rated females presently employed in the Respondent's Package and Grease Department whose seniority date antecedes April 5, 1975 and all members of back pay Group "A" who are presently employed in the classification of Operator Helper No. 1, Boiler Washer "X", Brander "X", Operator Helper No. 2, Utility Helper or Laborer.

b. For the sake of convenience, the Affected Class for Affirmative Action purposes shall be designated and hereinafter referred to as Group "C".

2. The Respondent, firm in its commitment to act in good faith and compliance with Title VII of the Civil Rights Act of 1964, as amended, has conducted a thorough analysis of its work force and has, as of January 1, 1976, identified those classifications wherein Negroes, Spanish Surnamed Americans and/or females are statistically underrepresented. Said classifications, designated and hereinafter referred to as "Target Classifications," are as follows:

a. Analytical Tester
b. Area Storehouseman
c. Boiler Fireman
d. Boilermaker
e. Bricklayer
f. Carpenter
g. Clerical
h. Compounder No. 1
i. Craft Apprentice and Trainee
j. Dockman

k. Electrician
l. Garage mechanic
m. Gas Dispatcher
n. Greasemaker No. 1
o. Greasemaker No. 2
p. Instrument man
q. Insulator
r. Lineman
s. Machinist
t. Operator No. 1
u. Operator No. 2
v. Assistant Operator
w. Painter
x. Pipefitter
y. Power Plant Engineer No. 1
z. Power Plant Engineer No. 2
aa. Power Plant Operator
bb. Pumper No. 1
cc. Pumper No. 2
dd. Railroad Craft Group
ee. Receiving Room Man
ff. Treater No. 1
gg. Treater No. 2
hh. Tinner
ii. Treater Helper No. 1
jj. Troubleman
kk. Water Pumper No. 2
ll. Water Tender
mm. Water Treater No. 1
nn. Water Treating Plant Operator
oo. Welder
pp. EEO-1 Technician Category
qq. EEO-1 Professional Category
rr. EEO-1 Official and Manager Category

3. With respect to the Respondent implementing its Affirmative Action Program as provided herein, the Commission stipulates that:

a. Ratios shall not be fixed but shall serve solely as general measures of the Respondent's satisfactory progress hereunder.

b. Although it is assumed and expected that minority and female placement within the above listed "Target Classifications" will be evenly distributed, the Respondent will not be faulted if it fails to meet its goals and timetables in one or more classifications as long as its overall progress is satisfactory.

c. The Respondent shall not be restricted to selection of Group "C" Affected Class members in meeting its goals and timetables, but may, at its discretion, select other qualified Negro, Spanish Surnamed American or female employees, or recruit from outside its workforce, thereby equally satisfying Affirmative Action commitments.

d. Failure by the Respondent to meet its goals and timetables hereunder shall not serve as justification to increase or renegotiate backpay as provided in Section B.

4. Considering the above, the Respondent agrees to establish a goal to fill one of every five vacancies in "Target Classifications" other than its EEO-1 Official and Manager Category, wherein the ratio shall be one of every seven, with a Negro, a Spanish Surnamed American or a female until

such time as their respective representation jointly within said classifications equals or exceeds their joint representation throughout the Respondent's workforce.

5. On occasions when a vacancy is to be filled with a Group "C" member, the Respondent will fill it by selecting the bidder having greatest seniority, subject to relative skills, abilities, and qualifications, and provided that the Respondent's initial entry requirements are met.

6. Group "C" members upgrading hereunder shall be classified as provisional and shall be on trial for a period not to exceed 120 days. They will receive the same training and orientation given other employees, and, if qualifying according to normal company competency standards, the provisional title shall be dropped. The Respondent may make its determination prior to expiration of the full 120-day period. An employee determined by the Respondent not to be qualified for the job for which he or she has been on trial shall be returned to his or her former classification without loss of seniority. Determination that any employee has qualified hereunder shall not bind the Respondent to accept the employee for any other classification, but such employee shall be judged at each level in the same manner as other employees. An upgraded Group "C" member may disqualify himself or herself during the 120-day trial period and, in that event, shall be returned to his or her former classification with an uninterrupted seniority.

7. Each upgraded Group "C" member shall have his or her seniority date determined by applicable collective bargaining agreement provisions, with the exception that in the event of a reduction in force or layoff, any Group "C" member who has upgraded to a Clerical classification or to a classification represented by the United Transportation Union; the Bricklayer, Masons and Plasterers International Union Local No. 13; the International Association of Machinists and Aerospace Workers, Port Arthur Lodge No. 823; or the International Brotherhood of Electrical Workers, AFL-CIO, Local Union No. 390 shall have bumpback rights into the Operator Helper No. 2 pool or into the classification of Utility Helper or Laborer, according to his or her former seniority at the time upgraded. The Respondent shall retain the right to select into which of the above three classifications the affected Group "C" member shall be placed. Each Group "C" member so displaced shall continue to hold rights to recall into his or her craft position from which displaced, as though he or she had not bumped back.

8. The Respondent agrees that the rate of pay for each upgraded Group "C" member shall be the higher of his or her permanent rate at the time upgraded or the appropriate new rate. This provision shall not apply in

the event that a Group "C" member bids into a classification in which the top rate for the new line of progression is less than his or her former rate.

9. Each member of Group "C" who participates in this special program shall receive one bona fide opportunity to upgrade. Such opportunity shall be satisfied, and the employee's rights hereunder shall terminate, when the employee either (a) takes a job and qualifies therefor, (b) takes a job and fails to qualify or requests to return to his or her former job classification or (c) declines an offer to upgrade. Group "C" members who resign from employment with the Respondent shall have no further rights hereunder.

10. An upgraded employee's failure to qualify during the established trial period, or a declination of a job offer made to an employee by the Respondent, shall not satisfy that particular exercise of the Respondent's obligation under established ratios toward goals and timetables, and such opportunity shall be extended to another individual.

11. Notwithstanding any of the foregoing, the Respondent shall not be required to place or retain any person in a job who does not have the skill, ability and qualifications to perform said job.

12. The United States Equal Employment Opportunity Commission and the Respondent remain in disagreement as to the Respondent's continued use of test battery results for employment and promotion purposes. However, in order to provide a means to resolve those matters held in dispute, the Commission agrees that the Respondent reserves the right to utilize test scores along with other job related criteria in assessing individual qualifications. In consideration therefore, the Respondent represents that it shall not rely upon test scores as justification for its failure to meet goals and timetables in any job classification.

D. Affirmative Action

The Respondent agrees to refine and strengthen on a continuing basis positive and objective nondiscriminatory employment standards, procedures and practices and represents that in its business operations it exerts continuing effort to uniformly apply such standards, practices, and procedures in a manner which will assure equal employment opportunities in all aspects of its total work force and operations without regard to race, color, religion, sex, or national origin.

E. Commission Assertion and Reporting Requirements

1. The Equal Employment Opportunity Commission agrees that upon fulfillment of its obligations hereunder the Respondent will be in full compliance with all provisions of Title VII of the Civil Rights Act of 1964, as amended, at its Port Arthur, Texas Refinery.

2. Six months after the date of approval of this Agreement and every six months thereafter for its established life of five years, the Respondent shall send to the Commission a written report concerning all actions encompassed by the provisions hereinabove set forth.

Such reports shall accurately, fully and clearly describe the nature of the remedial and affirmative action undertaken and shall be submitted to the District Director, Equal Employment Opportunity Commission, 2320 LaBranch, Room 1101, Houston, Texas 77004 with a copy submitted to the Regional Manager, Office for Equal Opportunity, Department of the Interior, Denver Federal Center, Building 67, Room 880, Denver, Colorado 80225.

F. Signatures

I have read the foregoing Conciliation Agreement and I accept and agree to the provisions contained herein:

4/14/76 /s/ Merlin Breaux
Date Gulf Oil Company—U.S.
Port Arthur, Texas
Respondent

I recommend approval of this Conciliation Agreement:

April 14, 1976 /s/ James R. Anderson
Date Equal Opportunity Specialist (E)

I concur in the above recommendation for approval of this Conciliation Agreement:

4-14-76 /s/ Carl D. Hanley
Date Supervisory Equal Opportunity Specialist (E)

Approved on behalf of the Commission:

April 14, 1976 /s/ Herbert C. McClees
Date District Director

G. Certificate of Review and Approval

1. This is to certify on behalf of the Office of Equal Opportunity, United States Department of the Interior, review and approval of the foregoing conciliation agreement by and between the U.S. Equal Employment Opportunity Commission and Gulf Oil Company—U.S., Port Arthur, Texas.

2. It is agreed that the Respondent has complied with all of the provisions of the letter agreement between Edward E. Shelton, Director of Office for Equal Opportunity, United States Department of Interior and L.R.

Johnston, Vice President, Employee Relations, Gulf Oil Company—U.S. dated May 7, 1971 and all points have been resolved to the complete satisfaction of the Office for Equal Opportunity, United States Department of Interior with the single exception of a portion of paragaph 2e. "Free Bidding—Non-Related Jobs" in said agreement.

With regard to such paragraph, vacancies in the following jobs will be posted for bid to present employees in Group "B":

Checker	Was Packing House-Pump House 78 (Lubricating)
Checker	Drum Filling and Loading (Package and Grease)
Fire Assistant	Maintenance Division
Truck Driver	Maintenance Division
Bathhouse Attendant	Maintenance Division

3. Should a bidding employee in Group "B" be senior to the employee who would receive the job through normal promotional procedures, such employee should be awarded the job. In addition, should her present rate be greater than the posted job in question, she should retain her present rate and also should have the option of returning to her former position within a thirty-day period. Other members of the "affected class" shall not have such bidding rights.

4. The Office for Equal Opportunity, Department of Interior agrees that upon fulfillment of its obligations hereunder the Respondent will be in full compliance with all provisions of Executive Order 11246, as amended, at its Port Arthur, Texas Refinery.

5. The Respondent recognizes that it has a continuing obligation for Affirmative Action under Executive Order 11246, as amended, and the implementing regulations of the Department of Labor.

April 14, 1976 /s/ Gerald C. Williams
Date Western Regional Manager

Reviewed:

April 14, 1976 /s/ James R. Anderson
Date Equal Opportunity Specialist (E)

Approved on behalf of the United States Equal Employment Opportunity Commission:

April 14, 1976 /s/ Lorenzo D. Cole
Date Deputy Director

exhibit 3

basic steps to develop an effective affirmative action program

A. *Issue written equal employment policy and affirmative action commitment.*

B. *Appoint a top official with responsibility and authority to direct and implement your program.*

   1. Specify responsibilities of program manager.
   2. Specify responsibilities and accountability of all managers and supervisors.

C. *Publicize your policy and affirmative action commitment.*

   1. Internally: to managers, supervisors, all employees and unions;
   2. Externally: to sources and potential sources of recruitment, potential minority and female applicants, to those with whom you do business, and to the community at large.

D. *Survey present minority and female employment by department and job classification.*

   1. Identify present areas and levels of employment.
   2. Identify areas of concentration and underutilization.
   3. Determine extent of underutilization.

E. *Develop goals and timetables to improve utilization of minorities, males and females in each area where underutilization has been identified.*

F. *Develop and implement specific programs to achieve goals.*

   This is the heart of your program. Review your entire employment system to identify barriers to equal employment opportunity; make needed

Source: U.S. Equal Employment Opportunity Commission, *Affirmative Action and Equal Employment: A Guidebook for Employers* (Washington, D.C.: U.S. Government Printing Office, January 1974), pp. 16-17.

changes to increase employment and advancement opportunities of minorities and females. These areas need review and action:

1. Recruitment: all personnel procedures.
2. Selection process: job requirements; job descriptions, standards and procedures. Pre-employment inquiries; application forms; testing; interviewing.
3. Upward mobility system: assignments; job progressions; transfers; seniority; promotions; training.
4. Wage and salary structure.
5. Benefits and conditions of employment.
6. Layoff; recall; termination; demotion; discharge; disciplinary action.
7. Union contract provisions affecting above procedures.

G. *Establish internal audit and reporting system to monitor and evaluate progress in each aspect of the program.*

H. *Develop supportive in-house and community programs.*

exhibit 4

a sample affirmative action program (large nationwide oil company)

AFFIRMATIVE ACTION PROGRAM FOR EQUAL EMPLOYMENT OPPORTUNITY (Revised April 1975)

By policy and preference, ______________ Company reaffirms its continuing commitment to afford all individuals who have the necessary qualifications an equal opportunity to compete for employment and advancement with the Company. To assure equal employment opportunity, there shall be no discrimination and/or preferred treatment concerning any individual or group because of race, color, religion, sex, age or national origin. This philosophy is affirmed in the Company's Nondiscrimination and Equal Employment Opportunity Policy which is attached to and made a mandatory part of this Affirmative Action Program.

This Affirmative Action Program was initially developed and is reaffirmed to assure the effective application of the Company's Nondiscrimination and Equal Employment Opportunity Policy; to insure compliance with applicable government regulations and to serve as a guide for the development, revision and/or meaningful administration of Affirmative Action Programs at each of the Company's reporting establishments.

This Program includes mandatory steps to be taken at all Company locations to maintain the existence of equal employment opportunity and the continued absence of discrimination throughout the Company. Also included are steps which must be taken to encourage members of minority groups and women to seek employment with the Company.

Every member of management *is expected* to carry forward the Company's policy of nondiscrimination, equal employment opportunity and af-

Source: *Equal Employment Opportunity: Programs & Results,* Personnel Policies Forum, Survey No. 112, March 1976, (Washington, D.C.: The Bureau of National Affairs, Inc.), pp. 27-37.

firmative action within his or her assigned area of responsibility. To assist in this regard, the Manager of Labor Relations and Equal Opportunity Affairs is assigned to the overall responsibility for providing the necessary guidance and coordination in implementing and administering this Affirmative Action Program and any necessary or desired revisions thereto.

I. Policy and Plan Communication

A. Internal Dissemination:

1. A copy of this guide Affirmative Action Program, as revised, shall be distributed to all managerial personnel and a copy of the Nondiscrimination and Equal Employment Opportunity Policy shall be included in the Corporate Policy Manual.
2. A copy of this guide Affirmative Action Program shall be maintained at each of the Company's operating establishments in accordance with a list developed and maintained by the Manager of Labor Relations and Equal Opportunity Affairs.
3. It is expected that each Executive and Manager will comply wholeheartedly and will communicate to and assure proper administration of these program and policy provisions by those in his/her area of assigned responsibility to whom he/she designates authority; including, but not limited to:
   a. The holding of periodic meetings to explain and/or reemphasize the program and policy provisions to assure continued effective application of this Affirmative Action Program effort;
   b. The holding of special employee meetings to communicate and discuss the provisions of this Program and explanation of Company expectations and individual responsibilities;
   c. The inclusion of this Program and Policy in all employee orientation and management training programs.
4. The Company's Nondiscrimination and Equal Employment Opportunity Policy shall be expressed in appropriate Company publications.
5. The notice(s) required to be posted by Executive Order 11246, as amended, will continue to be posted on Company bulletin boards and/or in other conspicuous places available to employees and applicants for employment.
6. The Company will meet with and/or otherwise notify all labor unions who have bargaining agreements with the Company of the Company's policy of nondiscrimination and will request their co-

operation. The Company has and will continue to propose the inclusion of nondiscrimination clauses in collective bargaining agreements which do not presently contain such clauses. All contract clauses will continue to be reviewed to insure they are nondiscriminatory.

7. Whenever applicable, articles covering EEO progress, progress reports, promotions, etc., of minority and female employees will be published in Company publications. If employees are featured in product, consumer or recruitment advertising; employee handbooks or similar publications, both minority and non-minority men and women will be pictured.

B. External Dissemination:

1. The Company will communicate its employment policy in writing to all sources of recruitment, including minority and women's organizations, community agencies, community leaders, secondary schools and colleges, as may be appropriate. The Company will actively seek out new additional sources of recruitment if present sources fail to refer or yield qualified minority and female candidates for employment consideration.

2. All advertisements seeking applicants for employment will identify the Company as "An Equal Opportunity Employer". The stimulation of applications from minority groups and women will be considered when selecting the media utilized for employment advertisements.

3. The Company will communicate to prospective employees the existence of its Affirmative Action Program and will make job opportunity information equally available to minority and non-minority men and women applicants.

4. The Company may offer training and education programs to employees to assist them in their personal development as well as to fulfill the skill and ability requirements of this Company. The Company will continue to insure that all employees are given equal opportunity to participate in such programs without regard to race, religion, color, sex, age or national origin.

5. Qualified minority and female employees will be encouraged to take advantage of Company training and development opportunities.

6. When employees are pictured in consumer or help wanted advertisements, both minorities and non-minority men and women will be shown whenever appropriate.

7. The "Equal Opportunity Employer" Clause will be included in all purchase orders, leases, contracts, etc., covered by Executive Order 11246, as amended, and its applicable implementing regulations.
8. Written notification of Company policy regarding nondiscrimination, equal employment opportunity and affirmative action will be sent to all subcontractors, vendors and suppliers requesting appropriate action on their part.

II. Policy and Plan Implementation

A. Responsibility:

1. Mr.__________ of the Corporate Employee Relations Division is appointed to coordinate all Corporate activities involving Equal Opportunity Affairs. Mr.__________ has the unqualified support of top Management of__________Company in developing, revising, implementing and coordinating the overall Corporate program. His responsibilities include, but are not limited to:
   a. Development of policy statements, affirmative action programs, internal and external communication techniques;
   b. Assistance with the identification of problem areas;
   c. Assisting line management with problem solving;
   d. Designation and implementation of audit and reporting systems and/or methods to measure programs' effectiveness, to identify need for remedial action and to measure the degree to which goals and objectives have been attained;
   e. Serve as liaison between the Company and enforcement agencies;
   f. Keeping management informed of the latest developments in the entire area of equal opportunity;
   g. Active involvement as necessary with minority organizations, women's organizations, community action groups and community service programs;
   h. Periodic audit of program progress, compliance, training programs, hiring and promotion patterns to remove impediments and to assure compliance with Company and future requirements, and attainment of Corporate goals and objectives of equal opportunities for minorities and females;
   i. Regular discussions with facility coordinators, management and employees to assure Corporate policies are being followed;
   j. Delegation of basic line program responsibilities to representa-

tives of each reporting establishment for maximum functional control and effectiveness. Overall coordination responsibility and guidance supervision will remain with the Manager of Labor Relations and Equal Opportunity Affairs.

2. Executives of the various Groups, Divisions and/or Affiliates, working in conjunction with Corporate Equal Opportunity Affairs, shall insure that all supervisory employees understand that:
   a. Maintenance of equal employment opportunity is an integral part of their job duties and is a part of their performance evaluation;
   b. Appropriate corrective or preventive action is expected to stop and/or preclude any harassment of minorities or women because of the Company's Affirmative Action efforts.
3. It shall be the responsibility of the various Groups, Divisions and/or Affiliates of the Company to provide Corporate Equal Opportunity Affairs with such information and/or statistical data as may be necessary to measure progress toward attainment of goals and to assure good faith efforts to implement and sustain the Affirmative Action Program. Such information and/or statistical data shall be used to analyze and identify areas of minority group and female underutilization and in the revision of goals and timetables for the correction of any identifiable deficiencies. Records, goals and timetables shall be maintained at the appropriate operating facilities of the Company.

B. Implementation:

1. Analysis and identification of problem areas:
   a. An analysis of minority and female employees representation in major job categories by organizational units and job classifications and an evaluation of opportunities for the additional utilization of minority and female personnel will be made by the Operating Groups working in concert with Corporate Equal Opportunity Affairs. This work force analysis must be made separately for minorities and women, and should include the following with particular attention directed to trainees and major job categories 4-9 as listed on the annual EEO-1 Report (i.e. Officials and Managers, Professionals, Technicians, Sales Workers, Office and Clerical and Craftsmen-Skilled):
      (1) Composition of the work force by minority group status and sex;

(2) Composition of applicant flow by minority group status and sex;

(3) Position descriptions and titles, worker specifications, application forms, interview procedures, test administration and test validity, referral procedures and final selection process are included in the total selection process of hiring new employees;

(4) Transfer and promotion policies;

(5) Facilities, Company-sponsored recreation and social events and special programs such as educational assistance;

(6) Seniority practices and seniority provisions in union contracts;

(7) Apprenticeship programs;

(8) Formal and informal Company training programs;

(9) Work force attitude;

(10) Posters, notification to unions, retention of applications, notices to subcontractors.

b. In determining whether minorities and women are being underutilized in any job classification, the following factors must be considered:

For Minorities—

(1) The minority population of the labor area surrounding the facility;

(2) The size of the minority unemployment force in the labor area surrounding the facility;

(3) The percentage of the minority work force as compared with the total work force in the immediate labor area;

(4) The general availability of minorities having requisite skills in the immediate labor area;

(5) The availability of minorities having requisite skills in an area in which the Company can reasonably recruit;

(6) The availability of promotable and transferable minorities;

(7) The existence of training institutions capable of training persons in the requisite skills;

(8) The degree of training which the Company is reasonably able to undertake to help make all job classes available to minorities (location by location basis).

For Women—

(1) The size of the female unemployment force in the labor area surrounding the facility;

(2) The percentage of the female work force as compared with the total work force in the immediate labor area;

(3) The general availability of women having requisite skills in the immediate labor area;

(4) The availability of women having requisite skills in an area in which the Company can reasonably recruit;

(5) The availability of women seeking employment in the labor or recruitment area of the facility;

(6) The availability of promotable and transferable female employees at the facility;

(7) The existence of training institutions capable of training persons in the requisite skills;

(8) The degree of training which the facility can reasonably undertake as a means of making all job classes available to women.

c. Findings of analysis which require special corrective action include but are not limited to:

(1) An underutilization of minorities or women in specific work classifications;

(2) Lateral and/or vertical movement of minority or female employees occurring at a lesser rate (compared to work force mix) than that of nonminority or male employees;

(3) Elimination of a disproportionately higher percentage of minorities and women than nonminorities or men in the selection process;

(4) Pre-employment application and other forms which do not comply with federal legislation;

(5) Position descriptions which do not accurately reflect the true job duties;

(6) Tests and other selection techniques not validated, as required by OFCC Order on Employee Testing and other Selection Procedures;

(7) Existence of de facto segregation;

(8) A disparity by minority group status or sex exists when comparing length of service and types of jobs held.

2. Establishment of Goals and Timetables:
   a. On completion of work force analysis as outlined in II, B above, goals and timetables shall be established to remedy deficiencies, if any, which are found. These goals and timetables should be definite and precise and be attainable in terms of each facility's analysis of deficiencies and its entire Affirmative Action Program. In establishing these goals and timetables—where applicable—it is necessary to consider the results which can reasonably be expected by the application of every good faith effort to make the overall Affirmative Action Program work. In determining levels of goals, the factors outlined in Part II, B above should be considered.
   b. When establishing goals, the following should be involved wherever applicable:
      (1) Personnel relations staff;
      (2) Department and division heads;
      (3) Local and unit managers.
   c. Goals shall be significant, measurable and attainable.
   d. Goals shall be specific for planned results, with timetables for completion.
   e. Goals are not to be rigid and inflexible quotas which must be met, but must be targets reasonably attainable by means of applying every good faith effort.
   f. Any anticipated expansion and work force contraction and turnover must be considered in establishing goals and timetables.
   g. Where deficiencies are found to exist and where numbers or percentages are relevant in determining corrective action, specific goals and timetables shall be established separately for minorities and women.
   h. Goals and timetables, where applicable, with supporting documented data and resulting analysis shall be a part of the written Affirmative Action Program at each Company facility.
   i. Where goals and timetables are not established at a facility, the written Affirmative Action Program must specifically analyze the factors listed in Part II, B hereof and list in detail the reasons for not establishing a goal.
3. Supporting data for the required analysis and Affirmative Action Program shall be compiled and maintained as part of each Com-

pany's facility's Affirmative Action Program. This data shall include, but is not necessarily limited to the following, whenever applicable:

a. Progression line charts;
b. Seniority rosters;
c. Applicant flow data;
d. Applicant rejection ratios indicating minority and sex status.

4. Copies of Affirmative Action Programs and/or copies of supporting data shall be made available to the appropriate compliance agency or the Office of Federal Contract Compliance, at the request of either, for such purposes as may be appropriate to the fulfillment of their responsibilities under Executive Order 11246, as amended.

III. Internal Audit and Reporting

A. Each facility shall adopt and include in its Affirmative Action Program a system of periodic internal audit to measure the effectiveness of its program. A formal audit of the entire program at each facility shall be made at least quarterly, with spot checks on a weekly or monthly basis, as deemed appropriate. This audit should include monitoring records of referrals, placements, transfers, promotions and terminations; review of program results and notification to top management at the facility of the program effectiveness.

B. Each facility shall be required to report its program status and effectiveness to Corporate Equal Opportunity Affairs at least semi-annually in a form prescribed and developed at the Corporate level for such purposes.

C. Corporate Executive management shall be advised of program results, accomplishments and recommended improvements at least once yearly.

IV. Employee Status

A. It is a policy of the Company to promote from within where possible. Steps will be taken to insure that all qualified employees continue to receive equal consideration for promotion, transfer and upgrading. It is a Company objective to promote the best qualified employee without regard to race, religion, color, sex, age or national origin except for specific jobs where sex or age is a bona fide occupational qualification.

B. Any work force reductions and the recall of employees after such reductions will be applied without discrimination because of race, religion, color, sex, age or national origin.

C. All employees will be compensated on the principal of equal pay for equal work performed and the amount of compensation for any specific job will be based on standards in the industry, the nature of the work performed and the qualifications and experience of the employee. A continuing review of compensation is in effect on a Corporate-wide basis.

V. Facilities

A. The Company will not permit segregation based on race, religion, color or national origin in facilities under its control. The term "facilities" will include, but is not limited to, such items as waiting rooms, work areas, eating areas, parking lots, recreation areas and transportation facilities. Rest rooms, wash rooms and locker rooms will be provided on a separate, but comparable basis for both sexes, wherever applicable.

B. The Company will not sponsor, endorse or contribute to a social or recreational establishment that follows a policy of excluding minority groups or women.

VI. General

A. The Company will comply with the requirements of Executive Order 11246, as amended, and with other applicable regulations.

B. The objectives and performance of the Affirmative Action Program will be reviewed and amended, as necessary, to assure the continued implementation of the Company's policy of Nondiscrimination and Equal Employment Opportunity.

exhibit 5-A

"Federal Executive Agency Guidelines on Employee Selection Procedures" issued by Justice and Labor Departments, and Civil Service Commission*

Subpart A—General Principles

§ 60-3.1 Statement of purpose.

These guidelines are intended to be a set of principles which will assist employers, labor organizations, employment agencies, and licensing and certification boards in complying with equal employment opportunity requirements of Federal law with respect to race, color, religion, sex and national origin. They are designed to provide a framework for determining the proper use of tests and other selection procedures consistent with Federal law. These guidelines do not require a user to conduct validity studies of selection procedures where no adverse impact results. However, all users are encouraged to use selection procedures which are valid, especially users operating under merit principles. Nothing in these guidelines is intended or should be interpreted as discouraging the use of procedures which have been properly validated in accordance with these guidelines for the purpose of determining qualifications or selecting on the basis of relative qualifications. Nothing in these guidelines is intended to apply to persons not subject to the requirements of Title VII, Executive Order 11246, or other equal employment opportunity requirements of Federal law. These guidelines are not intended to apply to any responsibilities an employer, employment agency or labor organization may have under the Age Discrimination Act of 1975 not to discriminate on the basis of age, or under section 503 of the Rehabilitation Act of 1973 not to discriminate on the basis of handicap. Nothing contained in these guidelines is intended to interfere with any obligation

*Published in the *Federal Register,* November 23, 1976.

imposed or right granted by Federal law to users to extend a publicly announced preference in employment to Indians living on or near an Indian reservation in connection with employment opportunities on or near an Indian reservation.

§ 60-3.2 Scope.

(a) These guidelines will be applied by the Department of Labor to contractors and subcontractors subject to Executive Order 11246 as amended by Executive Order 11375 (hereinafter "Executive Order 11246"); and by the Civil Service Commission to Federal agencies subject to Sec. 717 of the Civil Rights Act of 1964, as amended by the Equal Employment Opportunity Act of 1972 (hereinafter "the Civil Rights Act of 1964") and to its responsibilities toward state and local governments under Section 208(b)(1) of the Intergovernmental Personnel Act; by the Department of Justice in exercising its responsibilities under Federal law; and by any other Federal agency which adopts them. The Department of Justice and the Civil Service Commission have codified these guidelines in 28 CFR Part 50 and Appendices to Federal Personnel Manual Supplements 271-1, 271-2, 335-1, and 990-1 (Book 3), Part 900, subpart F, respectively.

(b) These guidelines apply to selection procedures which are used as a basis for any employment decision. Employment decisions include but are not limited to hire, promotion, demotion, membership (for example in a labor organization), referral, retention, licensing and certification, to the extent that licensing and certification may be covered by Federal equal employment opportunity law. Selection for training is also considered an employment decision if it leads to any of the decisions listed above.

(c) These guidelines do not apply to the use of a bona fide seniority system within the meaning of Title VII of the Civil Rights Act of 1964, as amended, as defined by Federal appellate court decisions, for any employment decision. These guidelines do not call for the validation of such a seniority system used as a basis for such employment decisions, and the use of such a seniority system as a basis for such employment decisions is consistent with these guidelines.

(d) These guidelines do not apply to the entire range of Federal equal employment opportunity law, but only to selection procedures which are used as a basis for making employment decisions. For example, the use of recruiting procedures designed to attract racial, ethnic or sex groups which were previously denied employment opportunities or which are presently underutilized may be necessary to bring an employer into compliance with Federal law, and is frequently an essential element to any effective affirmative action program; but the subject of recruitment practices is not addressed by these guidelines because that subject concerns procedures other than selection procedures.

§ 60-3.3 Relationship between use of selection procedures and discrimination.

(a) The use of any selection procedure which has an adverse impact on the members of any racial, ethnic or sex group with respect to any employment decision will be considered to be discriminatory and inconsistent with these guidelines, unless the procedure is validated in accordance with the principles contained in these guidelines or unless use of the procedure is warranted under § 60-3.3b.

(b) There are circumstances in which it is not feasible or not appropriate to utilize the validation techniques contemplated by these guidelines. In such circumstances, the user would utilize selection procedures which are as job related as possible and which will minimize or eliminate adverse impact. (i) When an unstandardized, informal or unscored selection procedure which has an adverse impact is utilized, the user should seek insofar as possible to eliminate the adverse impact, or, if feasible, to modify the procedure to one which is a formal, scored or quantified measure or combination of measures and then to validate the procedure in accord with these guidelines, or otherwise to justify continued use of the procedure in accord with Federal law. (ii) When a standardized, formal or scored selection procedure is used for which it is not feasible or not appropriate to utilize the validation techniques contemplated by these guidelines, the user should either modify the procedure to eliminate the adverse impact or otherwise justify continued use of the procedure in accord with Federal law.

(c) Generally, where alternative selection procedures are available which have been shown to be equally valid for a given purpose, the user should use the procedure which has been demonstrated to have the lesser adverse impact. Accordingly, whenever a validity study is called for by these guidelines, the user should make a reasonable effort to investigate suitable alternative selection procedures which have as little adverse impact as possible, for the purpose of determining the appropriateness of using or validating them in accord with these guidelines. If a user has made a reasonable effort to become aware of such alternative procedures and a validity study for a job or group of jobs has been made in accord with these guidelines, the use of the selection procedure may continue until such time as it should reasonably be reviewed for currency. Whenever the user is shown a suitable alternative selection procedure with evidence of at least equal validity and less adverse impact, the user should investigate it for the purpose of determining the appropriateness of using or validating it in accord with these guidelines. This subsection is not intended to preclude the combination of procedures into a significantly more valid procedure, if such a combination has been properly validated.

§ 60-3.4 Information on impact.

(a) Each user should have available for inspection records or other information which will disclose the impact which its selection procedures have upon employment opportunities of persons by identifiable racial, ethnic or sex groups in order to determine compliance with the provisions of § 60-3.3 above. Where there are large numbers of applicants and procedures are administered frequently, such information may be retained on a sample basis, provided that the sample is appropriate in terms of the applicant population and adequate in size. The records called for by this section are to be maintained by sex, and by racial and ethnic groups as follows: blacks (Negroes), American Indians (including Alaskan Natives), Asians (including Pacific islanders), Hispanic (including persons of Mexican, Puerto Rican, Cuban, Central or South American, or other Spanish origin or culture regardless of race), whites (Caucasians) other than Hispanic and totals. The classifications called for by this section are intended to be consistent with the Employer Information (EEO-1 et seq.) series of reports. The user should adopt safeguards to insure that records of race, color, religion, sex, or national origin are used for appropriate purposes such as determining adverse impact, or (where required) for developing and monitoring affirmative action programs, and that such records are not used for making employment decisions.

(b) The information called for by this section should be examined for possible adverse impact. If the records called for by this section indicate that the total selection process for a job has no adverse impact, the individual components of the selection process need not be evaluated separately for adverse impact. If a total selection process does have adverse impact, the individual components of the selection process should be evaluated for adverse impact.

A selection rate for any racial, ethnic or sex group which is less than four-fifths (4/5) (or eighty percent) of the rate for the group with the highest rate will generally be regarded as evidence of adverse impact, while a greater than four-fifths rate will generally not be regarded as evidence of adverse impact. Smaller differences in selection rate may nevertheless be considered to constitute adverse impact, where they are significant in both statistical and practical terms. Greater differences in selection rate would not necessarily be regarded as constituting adverse impact where the differences are based on small numbers and are not statistically significant, or where special recruiting or other programs cause the pool of minority or female candidates to be atypical of the normal pool of applicants from that group.

(c) Federal agencies which adopt these guidelines for the purpose of the enforcement of the equal employment opportunity laws or which have responsibility for securing compliance with them (hereafter referred to as enforcement agencies) will consider in carrying out their obligations the general posture of the user with respect to equal employment opportunity for the job classification or group of classifications in question. Where a user has adopted an affirmative action program, the Federal enforcement agencies will consider the provisions of that program, including the goals and timetables which the employer has adopted and the progress which the employer has made in carrying out that program and in meeting the goals and timetables. These guidelines recognize that a user is prohibited by Federal law from the making of employment decisions on the basis of race and color and (except for bona fide occupational qualifications) on the basis of sex, religion and national origin; and nothing in this subsection or in these guidelines is intended to encourage or permit the granting of preferential treatment to any individual or to any group because of race, color, religion, sex or national origin of such individual or group.

§ 60-3.5 General standards for validity studies.

(a) For the purposes of satisfying these guidelines users may rely upon criterion-related validity studies, content validity studies or construct validity studies, in accordance with the standards set forth in Part II of these guidelines, § 60-3.12 *infra.*

(b) These guidelines are intended to be consistent with generally accepted professional standards for evaluating standardized tests and other assessment techniques, such as those described in the *Standards for Educational and Psychological Tests* prepared by a joint committee of the American Psychological Association, the American Educational Research Association, and the National Council on Measurement in Education (American Psychological Association, Washington, D.C. 1974) (hereinafter "APA *Standards*"), and standard text books and journals in the field of personnel selection.

(c) For any selection procedure which has an adverse impact each user should maintain and have available such documentation as is described in Subpart C of these guidelines, § 60-3.13 *infra.*

(d) Selection procedures subject to validity studies under § 60-3.3(a) above should be administered and scored under standardized conditions.

(e) In general, users should avoid making employment decisions on the basis of measures of knowledges, skills or abilities which are normally learned in a brief orientation period, and which have an adverse impact.

(f) Where cut-off scores are used, they should normally be set so as to be reasonable and consistent with normal expectations of acceptable proficiency with the work force. Where other factors are used in determining cut-off scores, such as the relationship between the number of vacancies and the number of applicants, the degree of adverse impact should be considered.

(g) Selection procedures may be used to predict the performance of candidates for a job which is at a higher level than the job for which the person is initially being selected if a majority of the individuals who remain employed will progress to the higher level within a reasonable period of time. A "reasonable period of time" will vary for different jobs and employment situations but will seldom be more than five years. Examining for a higher level job would not be appropriate (1) if the majority of those remaining employed do not progress to the higher level job, (2) if there is a reason to doubt that the higher level job will continue to require essentially similar skills during the progression period, or (3) if knowledges, skills or abilities required for advancement would be expected to develop principally from the training or experience on the job.

(h) Users may continue the use of a selection procedure which is not at the moment fully supported by the required evidence of validity, provided: (1) the user can cite substantial evidence of validity in accord with these guidelines and (2) the user has in progress, when technically feasible, studies which are designed to produce the additional data required within a reasonable time.

If the additional studies do not produce the data required to demonstrate validity, the user is not relieved of or protected against any obligations arising under Federal law.

(i) Whenever a validity study has been made in accord with these guidelines for the use of a particular selection procedure for a job or group of jobs, additional studies need not be performed until such time as the validity study is subject to review as provided in § 60-3.3(c) above. There are no absolutes in the area of determining the currency of a validity study. All circumstances concerning the study, including the validation strategy used, and changes in the relevant labor market and the job should be considered in the determination of when a validity study is outdated.

§ 60-3.6 Cooperative validity studies and use of other validity studies.

(a) It is the intent of the agencies issuing these guidelines to encourage and facilitate cooperative development and validation efforts by employers, labor organizations and employment agencies to achieve selection procedures which are consistent with these guidelines.

(b) Criterion-related validity studies conducted by one test user, or described in test manuals and the professional literature, will be considered acceptable for use by another user when: (1) the weight of the evidence from studies meeting the standards of § 60-3.12(b) below shows that the selection procedure is valid; (2) the studies pertain to a job which has substantially the same major job duties as shown by appropriate job analyses and (3) the studies include a study of test fairness for those racial, ethnic and sex subgroups which constitute significant factors in the borrowing user's relevant labor market for the job or jobs in question. If the studies relied upon satisfy (1) and (2) above but do not contain an investigation of test fairness, and it is not technically feasible for the borrowing user to conduct an internal study of test fairness, the borrowing user may utilize the study until studies conducted elsewhere show test unfairness, or until such time as it becomes technically feasible to conduct an internal study of test fairness and the results of that study can be acted upon.

If it is technically feasible for a borrowing user to conduct an internal validity study, and there are variables in the other studies which are likely to affect validity or fairness significantly, the user may rely upon such studies only on an interim basis in accord with § 60-3.5(h), and will be expected to conduct an internal validity study in accord with § 60-3.12(b) below. Otherwise the borrowing user may rely upon such acceptable studies for operational use without an internal study.

(c) Selection procedures shown by one user to be content valid in accord with § 60-3.12(c) will be considered acceptable for use by another user for a performance domain if the borrowing user's job analysis shows that the same performance domain is present in the borrowing user's job. The selection procedure may be used operationally if the conditions of § 60-3.12(c)(3) and § 60-3.12(c)(6) are satisfied by the borrowing user.

(d) The conditions under which findings of construct validity may be generalized are described in § 60-3.12(d)(4).

(c) If validity evidence from a multiunit or cooperative study satisfies the requirements of subparagraphs b, c or d above, evidence of validity specific to each unit or user usually will not be required unless there are variables in the units not studied which are likely to affect validity significantly.

§ 60-3.7 No assumption of validity.

(a) Under no circumstances will the general reputation of a selection procedure, its author or its publisher, or casual reports of its validity be accepted in lieu of evidence of validity. Specifically ruled out are: assumptions of validity based on a procedure's name or descriptive labels; all forms of promotional literature; data bearing on the frequency of a procedure's usage; testimonial statements and credentials of sellers, users, or consultants; and other non-empirical or anecdotal accounts of selection practices or selection outcomes.

(b) Professional supervision of selection activities is encouraged but is not a substitute for documented evidence of validity. The enforcement agencies will take into account the fact that a thorough job analysis and careful development of a selection procedure enhances the probability that the selection procedure is valid for the job.

§ 60-3.8 Employment agencies and employment services.

(a) An employment agency, including private employment agencies and State employment agencies, which agrees to a request by an employer or labor organization to devise and utilize a selection procedure should follow the standards for determining adverse impact and, if adverse impact is demonstrated, show validity as set forth in these guidelines. An employment agency is not relieved of its obligation herein because the user did not request such validation or has requested the use of some lesser standard of validation than is provided in these guidelines. The use of an employment agency does not relieve an employer or labor organization of its responsibilities under Federal law to provide equal employment opportunity or its obligations as a user under these guidelines.

(b) Where an employment agency or service is requested to administer a selection program which has been devised elsewhere and to make referrals pursuant to the results, the employment agency or service should obtain evidence of the absence of adverse impact, or of validity, as described in these guidelines, before it administers the selection program and makes referrals pursuant to the results. The employment agency must furnish on request such evidence of validity. An employment agency or service will be expected to refuse to make referrals based on the selection procedure where the employer or labor organization does not supply satisfactory evidence of validity or lack of adverse impact.

§ 60-3.9 Disparate treatment.

The principle of disparate or unequal treatment must be distinguished from the concepts of validation. A selection procedure—even though validated against job performance in accordance with the guidelines in this part—cannot be imposed upon members of a racial, sex or ethnic group where other employees, applicants, or members have not been subjected to that standard. Disparate treatment occurs where members of a racial, sex, or ethnic group have been denied the same employment, promotion, transfer or membership opportunities as have been made available to other employees or applicants. Those employees or applicants who have been denied equal treatment, because of prior discriminatory practices or policies, must at least be afforded the same opportunities as had existed for other employees or applicants during the period of discrimination. Thus, the persons who were in the class of persons discriminated against and were available in the relevant job market during the period the user followed the discriminatory practices should be allowed the opportunity to qualify under the less stringent selection procedures previously followed, unless the user demonstrates that the increased standards are required for the safety or efficiency of the operation. Nothing in this section is intended to prohibit a user who has not previously followed merit standards from adopting merit standards; nor does it preclude a user who has previously used invalid or unvalidated selection procedures from developing and using procedures which are validated in accord with these guidelines.

§ 60-3.10 Retesting.

Users should provide a reasonable opportunity for retesting and reconsideration. The user may however take reasonable steps to preserve the security of its procedures. Where examinations are administered periodically with public notice, such reasonable opportunity exists, unless persons who have previously been tested are precluded from retesting.

§ 60-3.11 Affirmative action.

The use of selection procedures which have been validated pursuant to these guidelines does not relieve users of any obligations they may have to undertake affirmative action to assure equal employment opportunity. Nothing in these guidelines is intended to preclude the use of selection procedures (consistent with Federal law—see § 60-3.4(c)) which assist in the achievement of affirmative action objectives.

Subpart B—Technical Standards

§ 60-3.12 Technical standards for validity studies.

The following minimum standards, as applicable, should be met in conducting a validity study. Nothing in these guidelines is intended to preclude the development and use of other professionally acceptable techniques with respect to validation of selection procedures.

(a) Any validity study should be based upon a review of information about the job for which the selection procedure is to be used. The review should include a job analysis except as provided in § 60-3.12(b)(3) below with respect to criterion-related validity. Any method of job analysis may be used if it provides the information required for the specific validation strategy used.

(b) *Criterion-related validity.*

(1) Users choosing to validate a selection procedure by a criterion-related validity strategy should determine whether it is technically feasible (as defined in Subpart D) to conduct such a study in the particular employment context. The determination of the number of persons necessary to permit the conduct of a meaningful criterion-related study should be made by the user on the basis of all relevant information concerning the selection procedure, the potential sample and the employment situation. These guidelines do not require a user to hire or promote persons for the purpose of making it possible to conduct a criterion-related study; and do not require such a study on a sample of less than thirty (30) persons.

(2) There should be a review of job information to determine measures of work behaviors or performance that are relevant to the job in question. These measures or criteria are relevant to the extent that they represent critical or important job duties, work behaviors or work outcomes as developed from the review of job information. The possibility of bias should be considered both in selection of the measures and their application. In view of the possibility of bias in subjective evaluations, supervisory rating techniques should be carefully developed. All criteria need to be examined for freedom from factors which would unfairly alter scores of members of any group. The relevance of criteria and their freedom from bias are of particular concern when there are significant differences in measures of job performance for different groups.

(3) Proper safeguards should be taken to insure that scores on selection procedures do not enter into any judgments of employee adequacy that are to be used as criterion measures. Criteria may consist of measures other than work proficiency including, but not limited to length of service, regularity of attendance, training time or properly measured success in job relevant training. Measures of training success based upon pencil and paper tests will be closely reviewed for job relevance. Whatever criteria are used should represent important or critical work behaviors or work outcomes. Job behaviors including but not limited to production rate, error rate, tardiness, absenteeism and turnover, may be used as criteria without a full job analysis if the user can show the importance of the criterion to the particular employment context. A standardized rating of overall work performance may be utilized where a study of the job shows that it is an appropriate criterion.

(4) The sample subjects should insofar as feasible be representa-

tive of the candidates normally available in the relevant labor market for the job or jobs in question, and should insofar as feasible include the racial, ethnic and sex groups normally available in the relevant job market. Where samples are combined or compared, attention should be given to see that such samples are comparable in terms of the actual job they perform, the length of time on the job where time on the job is likely to affect performance and other relevant factors likely to affect validity differences; or that these factors are included in the design of the study and their effects identified.

(5) The degree of relationship between selection procedure scores and criterion measures should be examined and computed, using professionally acceptable statistical procedures. Generally, a selection procedure is considered related to the criterion, for the purpose of these guidelines, when the relationship between performance on the procedure and performance on the criterion measure is statistically significant at the .05 level of significance, which means that it is sufficiently high as to have a probability of no more than one (1) in twenty (20) to have occurred by chance. Absence of a statistically significant relationship between a selection procedure and job performance should not necessarily discourage other investigations of the validity of that selection procedure.

Users should evaluate each selection procedure to assure that it is appropriate for operational use. Generally, if other factors remain the same, the greater the magnitude of the relationship (e.g., correlation coefficient) between performance on a selection procedure and one or more criteria of performance on the job, and the greater the importance or number of aspects of job performance covered by the criteria, the more likely it is that the procedure will be appropriate for use. Reliance upon a selection procedure which is significantly related to a criterion measure, but which is based upon a study involving a large number of subjects and has a low correlation coefficient will be subject to close review if it has a large adverse impact. Sole reliance upon a single selection instrument which is related to only one of many job duties or aspects of job performance will also be subject to close review. The appropriateness of a selection procedure is best evaluated in each particular situation and there are no minimum correlation coefficients applicable to all employment situations. In determining whether a selection procedure is appropriate for operational use the following considerations should also be taken into account: the degree of adverse impact of the procedure, the availability of other selection procedures of greater or substantially equal validity; and the need of an employer, required by law or regulation to follow merit principles, to have an objective system of selection.

(6) Users should avoid reliance upon techniques which tend to overestimate validity findings as a result of capitalization on chance unless an appropriate safeguard is taken. Reliance upon a few selection procedures or criteria of successful job performance, when many selection procedures or criteria of performance have been studied, or the use of optimal statistical weights for selection procedures computed in one sample, are techniques which tend to inflate validity estimates as a result of chance. Use of a large sample is one safeguard; cross-validation is another.

(7) *Fairness of the selection procedure.*

(i) When members of one racial, ethnic, or sex group characteristically obtain lower scores on a selection procedure than members of another group, and the differences are not reflected in differences in measures of job performance, use of the selection procedure may unfairly deny opportuities to members of the group that obtains the lower scores.

(ii) Where a selection procedure results in an adverse impact on a racial, ethnic or sex group identified in accordance with the classifications set forth in § 60-3.4 above and that group is a significant factor in the relevant labor market, the user generally should investigate the possible existence of unfairness for that group if it is technically feasible to do so.

The greater the severity of the adverse impact on a group, the greater the need to investigate the possible existence of unfairness. Where the weight of evidence from other studies shows that the selection procedure is a fair predictor for the group in question and for the same or similar jobs, such evidence may be relied on in connection with the selection procedure at issue and may be combined with data from the present study; however, where the severity of adverse impact on a group is significantly greater than in the other studies referred to, a user may not rely on such other studies.

(iii) Users conducting a study of fairness should review the APA *Standards* regarding investigation of possible bias in testing. An investigation of fairness of a selection procedure depends on both evidence of validity and the manner in which the selection procedure is to be used in a particular employment context. Fairness of a selection procedure cannot necessarily be specified in advance without investigating these factors. Investigation of fairness of a selection procedure in samples where the range of scores on selection procedures or criterion measures is severely restricted for any subgroup sample (as compared to other subgroup samples) may produce misleading evidence of unfairness. That factor should accordingly be taken into account in conducting such studies and before reliance is placed on the results.

(iv) If unfairness is demonstrated through a showing that members of a particular group perform better or poorer on the job than their scores on the selection procedure would indicate through comparison with how members of other groups perform, the user may either revise or replace the selection instrument in accordance with these guidelines, or may continue to use the selection instrument operationally with appropriate revisions in its use to assure compatibility between the probability of successful job performance and the probability of being selected.

(v) In addition to the general conditions needed for technical feasibility for the conduct of a criterion-related study (see § 60-3.14(j), below) an investigation of fairness requires the following:

> (1) A sufficient number of persons in each group for findings of statistical significance. These guidelines do not require a user to hire or promote persons on the basis of group classifications for the purpose of making it possible to conduct a study of fairness; and do not require a user to conduct a study of fairness on a sample of less than thirty (30) persons for each group involved in the study.
>
> (2) The samples for each group should be comparable in terms of the actual job they perform, length of time on the job where time on the job is likely to affect performance, and other relevant factors likely to affect validity differences; or such factors should be included in the design of the study and their effects identified.

(vi) If a study of fairness should otherwise be performed, but is not technically feasible, the use of a selection procedure which has otherwise met the validity standards of these guidelines will be considered in accord with these guidelines, unless the technical infeasibility resulted from discriminatory employment practices which are demonstrated by facts other than past failure to conform with requirements for validation of selection procedures. However, when it becomes technically feasible for the user to perform a study of fairness and such a study is otherwise called for, the user should conduct the study of fairness.

(c) *Content validity.*

(1) There should be a definition of a performance domain or the performance domains with respect to the job in question. Performance domains may be defined through job analysis, analysis of the work behaviors or activities, or by the pooled judgments of persons having knowledge of the job. Performance domains should be defined on the basis of competent information about job tasks and responsibilities. Performance domains include critical or important work behaviors, work products, work activities, job duties, or the knowledges, skills or abilities shown to be necessary for performance of the duties, behaviors, activities or the production of work. Where a performance domain has been defined as a knowledge, skill or ability, that knowledge, skill or ability must be used in job behavior. A selection procedure based on inferences about psychological processes cannot be supported by content validity alone. Thus content validity by itself is not an appropriate validation strategy for intelligence, aptitude, personality or interest tests. Content validity is also not an appropriate strategy when the selection procedure involves knowledges, skills or abilities which an employee will be expected to learn on the job.

(2) If a higher score on a content valid selection procedure can be expected to result in better job performance the results may be used to rank persons who score above minimum levels. Where a selection procedure supported solely by content validity is used to rank job candidates, the performance domain should include those aspects of performance which differentiate among levels of job performance.

(3) A selection procedure which is a representative sample of a performance domain of the job as defined in accordance with subsection (1) above, is a content valid procedure for that domain. Where the domain or domains measured are critical to the job, or constitute a substantial proportion of the job, the selection procedure will be considered to be content valid for the job. The reliability of selection procedures justified on the basis of content validity should be a matter of concern to the user. Whenever it is feasible to do so, appropriate statistical estimates should be made of the reliability of the selection procedures.

(4) A demonstration of the relationship between the content of

the selection procedure and the performance domain of the job is critical to content validity. Content validity may be shown if the knowledges, skills or abilities demonstrated in and measured by the selection procedure are substantially the same as the knowledges, skills or abilities shown to be necessary for job performance. The closer the content of the selection procedure is to actual work samples, behaviors or activities, the stronger is the basis for showing content validity. The need for careful documentation of the relationship between the performance domain of the selection procedure and that of the job increases as the content of the selection procedure less resembles that of the job performance domain.

(5) A requirement for specific prior training or for work experience based on content validity, including a specification of level or amount of training or experience, should be justified on the basis of the relationship between the content of the training or experience and the performance domain of the job for which the training or experience is to be required.

(6) If a selection procedure is supported solely on the basis of content validity, it may be used operationally if it represents a critical performance domain or a substantial proportion of the performance domains of the job.

(d) *Construct validity.* Construct validity is a more complex strategy than either criterion-related or content validity. Accordingly, users choosing to validate a selection procedure by use of this strategy should be careful to follow professionally accepted standards, such as those contained in the APA *Standards* and the standard text books and journals.

(1) There should be a job analysis. This job analysis should result in a determination of the constructs that underlie successful performance of the important or critical duties of the job.

(2) A selection procedure should be selected or developed which measures the construct(s) identified in accord with subparagraph (1) above.

(3) A selection procedure may be used operationally if the standards of subparagraphs (1) and (2) are met and there is sufficient empirical research evidence showing that the procedure is validly related to performance of critical job duties. Normally, sufficient empirical research evidence would take the form of one or more criterion-related validity studies meeting the requirements of § 60-3.12(b). See also second sentence of § 60-3.12.

(4) Where a selection procedure satisfies the standards of subsec-

tions (1), (2) and (3) above, it may be used operationally for other jobs which are shown by an appropriate job analysis to include the same construct(s) as an essential element in job performance.

Subpart C
Documentation of Validity Evidence

§ 60-3.13 Documentation.

(a) For each selection procedure having an adverse impact (as set forth in § 60-3.4) the user should maintain and have available the data on which the adverse impact determination was made and one of the following types of documentation evidence:

(1) Documentation evidence showing criterion-related validity of the selection procedure (see § 60-3.13(b) *infra*).

(2) Documentation evidence showing content validity of the selection procedure (see § 60-3.13(c)*infra*).

(3) Documentation evidence showing construct validity of the selection procedure (ss § 60-3.13(d) *infra*).

(4) Documentation evidence from other studies showing validity of the selection procedure in the user's facility (see § 60-3.13(e) *infra*).

(5) Documentation evidence showing what steps were taken to reduce or eliminate adverse impact, why validation is not feasible or not appropriate and why continued use of the procedure is consistent with Federal law.

This evidence should be compiled in a reasonably complete and organized manner to permit direct evaluation of the validity of the selection procedure. Previously written employer or consultant reports of validity are acceptable if they are complete in regard to the following documentation requirements, or if they satisfied requirements of guidelines which were in effect when the study was completed. If they are not complete, the required additional documentation should be appended. If necessary information is not available the report of the validity study may still be used as documentation, but its adequacy will be evaluated in terms of compliance with the requirements of these guidelines.

In the event that evidence of validity is reviewed by an enforcement agency, the reports completed after the effective date of these guidelines are expected to use one of the formats set forth below.

Evidence denoted by use of the word "(ESSENTIAL)" is considered critical and reports not containing such information will be considered incomplete. Evidence not so denoted is desirable, but its absence will not be a basis for considering a report incomplete.

(b) *Criterion-related validity.* Reports of criterion-related validity of selection procedures are to contain the following information:

(1) *User(s), and location(s) and date(s) of study.* Dates of administration of selection procedures and collection of criterion data and, where appropriate, the time between collection of data on selection procedures and criterion measures should be shown (ESSENTIAL). If the study was conducted at several locations, the address of each location, including city and state, should be shown.

(2) *Problem and setting.* An explicit definition of the purpose(s) of the study and the circumstances in which the study was conducted should be provided. A description of existing selection procedures and cut-off scores, if any, should be provided.

(3) *Review of job information or job analysis.* Where a review of job information results in criteria which are measures other than work proficiency (see § 60-3.12(b)(3)), the basis for the selection of these criteria should be reported (ESSENTIAL). Where a job analysis is required, the report should include either: (a) the important duties performed on the job and the basis on which such duties were determined to be important, such as the proportion of time spent on the respective duties, their level of difficulty, their frequency of performance, the consequences of error, or other appropriate factors; or (b) the knowledges, skills, abilities and/or other worker characteristics and basis on which they were determined to be important for job performance (ESSENTIAL). Published descriptions from industry sources or Volume I of the *Dictionary of Occupational Titles* Third Edition, United States Government Printing Office, 1965, are satisfactory if they adequately and completely describe the job. If appropriate, a brief supplement to the published description should be provided.

If two or more jobs are grouped for a validity study, a justification for this grouping, as well as a description of each of the jobs, should be provided (ESSENTIAL).

(4) *Job titles and codes.* It is desirable to provide the user's job title(s) for the job(s) in question and the corresponding job title(s) and code(s) from United States Employment Service *Dictionary of Occupational Titles* Volumes I & II. Where standard titles and codes do not exist, a notation to that effect should be made.

(5) *Criteria.* A full description of all criteria on which data were collected, including a rationale for selection of the final criteria, and

means by which they were observed, recorded, evaluated and quantified, should be provided (ESSENTIAL). If rating techniques are used as criterion measures the appraisal form(s) and instructions to the rater(s) should be included as part of the validation evidence (ESSENTIAL).

(6) *Sample.* A description of how the research sample was selected should be included (ESSENTIAL). The racial, ethnic and sex composition of the sample should be described, including the size of each subgroup (ESSENTIAL). Racial and ethnic classifications should be those set forth in § 60-3.4a above. A description of how the research sample compares with the racial, ethnic and sex composition of the relevant labor market is also desirable. Where data are available, the racial, ethnic and sex composition of current applicants should also be described.

(7) *Selection procedure.* Any measure, combination of measures, or procedures used as a basis for employment decisions should be completely and explicitly described or attached (ESSENTIAL). If commercially available selection procedures are used, they should be described by title, form, and publisher (ESSENTIAL). Reports of reliability estimates and how they were established are desirable. A rationale for choosing the selection procedures investigated in the study should be included.

(8) *Techniques and results.* Methods used in analyzing data should be described (ESSENTIAL). Measures of central tendency (e.g., means) and measures of dispersion (e.g., standard deviations and ranges) for all selection procedures and all criteria should be reported for all relevant racial, ethnic and sex subgroups (ESSENTIAL). Statistical results should be organized and presented in tabular or graphical form, by racial, ethnic and/or sex subgroups (ESSENTIAL). All selection procedure-criterion relationships investigated should be reported, including their magnitudes and directions (ESSENTIAL). Statements regarding the statistical significance of results should be made (ESSENTIAL).

Any statistical adjustments, such as for less than perfect reliability or for restriction of score range in the selection procedure or criterion, or both, should be described; and uncorrected correlation coefficients should also be shown (ESSENTIAL). Where the statistical technique used categorizes continuous data, such as biserial correlation and the phi coefficient, the categories and the bases on which they were determined should be described (ESSENTIAL). Studies of test fairness should be included where called for by the requirements of

§ 60-3.12(b)(7) (ESSENTIAL). These studies should include the rationale by which a selection procedure was determined to be fair to the group(s) in question. Where test fairness has been demonstrated on the basis of other studies, a bibliography of the relevant studies should be included (ESSENTIAL). If the bibliography includes unpublished studies, copies of these studies, or adequate abstracts or summaries, should be attached (ESSENTIAL). Where revisions have been made in a selection procedure to assure compatibility between successful job performance and the probability of being selected, the studies underlying such revisions should be included (ESSENTIAL).

(9) *Uses and applications.* A description of the way in which each selection procedure is to be used (e.g., as a screening device with a cut-off score or combined with other procedures in a battery) and application of the procedure (e.g., selection, transfer, promotion) should be provided (ESSENTIAL). If weights are assigned to different parts of the selection procedure, these weights and the validity of the weighted composite should be reported (ESSENTIAL).

(10) *Cut-off scores.* Where cut-off scores are to be used, both the cut-off scores and the way in which they were determined should be described (ESSENTIAL).

(11) *Source data.* Each user should maintain records showing all pertinent information about individual sample members in studies involving the validation of selection procedures. These records (exclusive of names and social security number) should be made available upon request of a compliance agency. These data should include selection procedure scores, criterion scores, age, sex, minority group status, and experience on the specific job on which the validation study was conducted and may also include such things as education, training, and prior job experience. If the user chooses to include, along with a report on validation, a worksheet showing the pertinent information about the individual sample members, specific identifying information such as name and social security number should not be shown. Inclusion of the worksheet with the validity report is encouraged in order to avoid delays.

(12) *Contact person.* It is desirable for the user to set forth the name, mailing address, and telephone number of the individual who may be contacted for further information about the validity study.

(c) *Content validity.* Reports of content validity of selection procedures are to contain the following information:

(1) *Definition of performance domain.* A full description should

be provided for the basis on which a performance domain is defined (ESSENTIAL). A complete and comprehensive definition of the performance domain should also be provided (ESSENTIAL). The domain should be defined on the basis of competent information about job tasks and responsibilities (ESSENTIAL). Where the performance domain is defined in terms of knowledges, skills, or abilities, there should be an operational definition of each knowledge, skill or ability and complete description of its relationship to job duties, behaviors, activities, or work products (ESSENTIAL).

(2) *Job title and code.* It is desirable to provide the user's job title(s) and the corresponding job title(s) and code(s) from the United States Employment Service *Dictionary of Occupational Titles* Volumes I & II. Where standard titles and codes do not exist, a notation to that effect should be made.

(3) *Selection procedures.* Selection procedures including those constructed by or for the user, specific training requirements, composites of selection procedures, and any other procedure for which content validity is asserted should be completely and explicitly described or attached (ESSENTIAL). If commercially available selection procedures are used, they should be described by title, form, and publisher (ESSENTIAL). Where the performance domain is defined in terms of knowledges, skills or abilities, evidence that the selection procedure measures those knowledges, skills or abilities should be provided (ESSENTIAL).

(4) *Techniques and results.* The method by which the correspondence between the content of the selection procedure and the job performance domain(s) was established and the relative emphasis given to various aspects of the content of the selection procedure as derived from the performance domain(s) should be described (ESSENTIAL). If any steps were taken to reduce adverse racial, ethnic, or sex impact in the content of the procedure or in its administration, these steps should be described. Establishment of time limits, if any, and how these limits are related to the speed with which the duties must be performed on the job, should be explained. The adequacy of the sample coverage of the performance domain should be described as precisely as possible. Measures of central tendency (e.g., means) and measures of dispersion (e.g., standard deviations) should be reported for all selection procedures as appropriate. Such reports should be made for all relevant racial, ethnic, and sex subgroups, at least on a statistically reliable sample basis.

(5) *Uses and applications.* A description of the way in which each

selection procedure is to be used (e.g., as a screening device with a cut-off score or combined with other procedures in a battery) and the application of the procedure (e.g., selection, transfer, promotion) should be provided (ESSENTIAL).

(6) *Cut-off scores.* The rationale for minimum scores, if used, should be provided (ESSENTIAL). If the selection procedure is used to rank individuals above minimum levels, or if preference is given to individuals who score significantly above the minimum levels, a rationale for this procedure should be provided (ESSENTIAL).

(7) *Contact person.* It is desirable for the employer to set forth the name, mailing address and telephone number of the individual who may be contacted for further information about the validation study.

(d) *Construct validity.* Reports of construct validity of selection procedures are to contain the following information:

(1) *Construct definition.* A clear definition of the construct should be provided, explained in terms of empirically observable behavior, including levels of construct performance relevant to the job(s) for which the selection procedure is to be used (ESSENTIAL).

(2) *Job analysis.* The job analysis should show how the constructs underlying successful job performance of important or critical duties were determined (ESSENTIAL). The job analysis should provide evidence of the linkage between the construct and the important duties of the job and how this linkage was determined (ESSENTIAL).

(3) *Job titles and codes.* It is desirable to provide the selection procedure user's job title(s) for the job(s) in question and the corresponding job title(s) and code(s) from the United States employment Service *Dictionary of Occupational Titles,* Volumes I and II. Where standard titles and codes do not exist, a notation to that effect should be made.

(4) *Selection procedure.* The selection procedure used as a measure of the construct should be completely and explicitly described or attached (ESSENTIAL). If commercially available selection procedures are used, they should be identified by title, form and publisher (ESSENTIAL). The evidence demonstrating that the selection procedure is in fact a proper measure of the construct should be included (ESSENTIAL). Reports of reliability estimates and how they were established are desirable.

(5) *Anchoring.* The empirical evidence showing that performance on the selection procedure is validly related to performance of critical job duties should be included (ESSENTIAL).

(6) *Uses and applications.* A description of the way in which each selection procedure is to be used (e.g., as a screening device with a cut-off score or combined with other procedures in a battery) and application of the procedure (e.g., selection, transfer, promotion) should be provided (ESSENTIAL). If weights are assigned to different parts of the selection procedure, these weights (and the validity of the weighted composite) should be reported (ESSENTIAL).

(7) *Cut-off scores.* Where cut-off scores are to be used, both the cut-off scores and the way in which they were determined should be described (ESSENTIAL).

(8) *Source data.* Each user should maintain records showing all pertinent information about individual sample members in studies involving the validation of selection procedures. These records (exclusive of names and social security number) should be made available upon request of a compliance agency. These data should include selection procedure scores, criterion scores, age, sex, minority group status, and experience on the specific job on which the validation study was conducted and may also include such things as education, training, and prior job experience. If the user chooses to include, along with a report on validation, a worksheet showing the pertinent information about the individual sample members, specific identifying information such as name and social security number should not be shown. Inclusion of the worksheet with the validity report is encouraged in order to avoid delays.

(9) *Contact person.* It is desirable for the user to set forth the name, mailing address, and telephone number of the individual who may be contacted for further information about the validity study.

(e) *Evidence of validity from other studies.* When validity of a selection procedure is supported by studies not done by the user, the evidence from the original study or studies should be compiled in a manner similar to that required in the appropriate section of this § 60-3.13 above. In addition, the following evidence should be supplied:

(1) *Evidence from criterion-related validity studies*

(i) *Job information.* A description of the important duties of the user's job and the basis on which the duties were determined to be important should be provided (ESSENTIAL). A full description of the basis for determining that these important job duties are sufficiently similar to the duties of the job in the original study (or studies) to warrant use of the selection procedure in the new situation should be provided (ESSENTIAL).

(ii) *Relevance of criteria.* A full description of the basis on which the criteria used in the original studies are determined to be relevant for the user should be provided (ESSENTIAL).

(iii) *Other variables.* The similarity of important applicant pool/sample characteristics reported in the original studies to those of the user should be described (ESSENTIAL). A description of the comparison between the race and sex composition of the user's relevant labor market and the sample in the original validity studies should be provided (ESSENTIAL).

(iv) *Use of the selection procedure.* A full description should be provided showing that the use to be made of the selection procedure is consistent with the findings of the original validity studies (ESSENTIAL).

(v) *Bibliography.* A bibliography of reports of validity of the selection procedure for the job or jobs in question should be provided (ESSENTIAL). Where any of the studies included an investigation of test fairness, the results of this investigation should be provided (ESSENTIAL). Copies of reports published in journals that are not commonly available should be described in detail or attached (ESSENTIAL). Where a user is relying upon unpublished studies, a reasonable effort should be made to obtain these studies. If these unpublished studies are the sole source of validity evidence they should be described in detail or attached (ESSENTIAL). If these studies are not available, the name and address of the source, an adequate abstract or summary of the validity study and data, and a contact person in the source organization should be provided (ESSENTIAL).

(2) *Evidence from content validity studies*

(i) *Similarity of performance domains.* A full description should be provided of the similarity between the performance domain in the user's job and the performance domain measured by a selection procedure developed and shown to be content valid by another user (ESSENTIAL). The basis for determining this similarity should be explicitly described (ESSENTIAL).

(3) *Evidence from construct validity studies*

(i) *Uniformity of construct.* A full description should be provided of the basis for determining that the construct identified as underlying successful job performance by the user's job analysis is the same as the construct measured by the selection procedure (ESSENTIAL).

Subpart D—Definitions

§ 60-3.14 Definitions.

The following definitions shall apply throughout these guidelines:

(a) Ability: The present observable competence to perform a function.

(b) Adverse Impact: Defined in § 60-3.4 of these guidelines.

(c) Employer: Any employer subject to the provisions of the Civil Rights Act of 1964, as amended, including state or local governments and any Federal agency subject to the provisions of Sec. 717 of the Civil Rights Act of 1964, as amended, and any Federal contractor or subcontractor or federally assisted construction contractor or subcontractor covered by Executive Order 11246, as amended.

(d) Employment agency: Any employment agency subject to the provisions of the Civil Rights Act of 1964, as amended.

(e) Labor organization: Any labor organization subject to the provisions of the Civil Rights Act of 1964, as amended, and any committee controlling apprenticeship or other training.

(f) Enforcement agency: Any agency of the executive branch of the Federal Government which adopts these guidelines for purpose of the enforcement of the equal employment opportunity laws or which has responsibility for securing compliance with them.

(g) Labor organization: Any labor organization subject to the provisions of the Civil Rights Act of 1964, as amended, and any committee controlling apprenticeship or other training.

(h) Racial, sex or ethnic group: Any group of persons identifiable on the grounds of race, color, religion, sex or national origin.

(i) Selection procedure: Any measure, combination of measures, or procedure, other than a bona fide seniority system, used as a basis for any employment decision. Selection procedures include the full range of assessment techniques from traditional paper and pencil tests, performance tests, training programs or probationary periods and physical, educational and work experience requirements through informal or casual interviews and unscored application forms.

(j) Selection Rate: The proportion of applicants or candidates who are hired, promoted or otherwise selected.

(k) Technical feasibility: The existence of conditions permitting the conduct of meaningful criterion-related validity studies. These conditions include: (a) an adequate sample of persons available for the study to achieve findings of statistical significance; (b) having or being able to obtain a sufficient range of scores on the selection procedure and job performance measures to produce validity results which can be expected to be representative of the results if the ranges normally expected were utilized; and (c) having or being able to devise unbiased, reliable and relevant measures of job performance or other criteria of employee adequacy. See § 60-3.12(b)(1). With respect to investigation of possible unfairness, the same considerations are applicable to each group for which the study is made. See § 60-3.12(b)(7).

(l) Unfairness of Selection Procedure (differential prediction): A condition in which members of one racial, ethnic, or sex group characteristically obtain lower scores on a selection procedure than members of another group, and the differences are not reflected in differences in measures of job performance. See § 60-3.12(b)(7).

(m) User: Any employer, labor organization, employment agency, or licensing or certification board, to the extent it may be covered by Federal equal employment opportunity law which uses a selection procedure as a basis for any employment decision. Whenever an employer, labor organization, or employment agency is required by law to restrict recruitment for any occupation to those applicants who have met licensing or certification requirements, the licensing or certifying authority to the extent it may be covered by Federal equal employment opportunity law will be considered the user with respect to those licensing or certification requirements. Whenever a state employment agency or service does no more than administer or monitor a procedure as permitted by Department of Labor regulations, and does so without making referrals or taking any other action on the basis of the results, the state employment agency will not be deemed to be a user.

exhibit 5-B

republication of EEOC's 1970 guidelines on employee selection procedures*

Title 29—Labor

CHAPTER XIV—EQUAL EMPLOYMENT OPPORTUNITY COMMISSION

PART 1607—GUIDELINES ON EMPLOYEE SELECTION PROCEDURES

Republication of Guidelines

The Equal Employment Opportunity Commission hereby republishes its Guidelines on Employee Selection Procedures (originally published at 35 FR 12333, August 1, 1970). Notwithstanding the publication of "Federal Executive Agency Guidelines on Employee Selection Procedures," the Equal Employment Opportunity Commission Guidelines on Employee Selection Procedures remain applicable to all employers and other entities subject to the jurisdiction of this Commission under Title VII of the Civil Rights Act of 1964, as amended, 42 U.S.C. 2000e et seq.

Signed at Washington, D.C. this 19th day of November 1976.

ETHEL BENT WALSH,
Vice Chairman.

29 CFR Part 1607 is revised as set forth below:

Sec.

*Published in the *Federal Register,* November 24, 1976.

AUTHORITY: The provisions of this Part 1607 issued under Sec. 713, 78 Stat. 265, 42 U.S.C. sec. 2000e-12.

§ 1607.1 Statement of purpose.

(a) The guidelines in this part are based on the belief that properly validated and standardized employee selection procedures can significantly contribute to the implementation of nondiscriminatory personnel policies, as required by Title VII. It is also recognized that professionally developed tests, when used in conjunction with other tools of personnel assessment and complemented by sound programs of job design, may significantly aid in the development and maintenance of an efficient work force and, indeed, aid in the utilization and conservation of human resources generally.

(b) An examination of charges of discrimination filed with the Commission and an evaluation of the results of the Commission's compliance activities has revealed a decided increase in total test usage and a marked increase in doubtful testing practices which, based on our experience, tend to have discriminatory effects. In many cases, persons have come to rely almost exclusively on tests as the basis for making the decision to hire, transfer, promote, grant membership, train, refer or retain, with the result that candidates are selected or rejected on the basis of a single test score. Where tests are so used, minority candidates frequently experience disproportionately high rates of rejection by failing to attain score levels that have been established as minimum standards for qualification. It has also become clear that in many instances persons are using tests as the basis for employment decisions without evidence that they are valid predictors of employee job performance. Where evidence in support of presumed relationships between test performance and job behavior is lacking, the possibility of discrimination in the application of test results must be recognized. A test lacking demonstrated validity (i.e., having no known significant relationship to job behavior) and yielding lower scores for classes protected by Title VII may result in the rejection of many who have necessary qualifications for successful work performance.

(c) The guidelines in this part are designed to serve as a workable set of standards for employers, unions and employment agencies in determining whether their selection procedures conform with the obligations contained in Title VII of the Civil Rights Act of 1964. Section 703 of Title VII places an affirmative obligation upon employers, labor unions, and employment agencies, as defined in section 701 of the Act, not to discriminate because of race, color, religion, sex, or national origin. Subsection (h) of section 703 allows such persons ". . . to give and to act upon the results of any professionally developed ability test provided that such test, its administration or action upon the results is not designed, intended or used to discriminate because of race, color, religion, sex or national origin."

§ 1607.2 "Test" defined.

For the purpose of the guidelines in this part, the term "test" is defined as any paper-and-pencil or performance measure used as a basis for any employment decision. The guidelines in this part apply, for example, to ability tests which are designed to measure eligibility for hire, transfer, promotion, membership, training, referral or retention. This definition includes, but is not restricted to, measures of general intelligence, mental ability and learning ability; specific intellectual abilities; mechanical, clerical and other aptitudes; dexterity and coordination; knowledge and proficiency; occupational and other interests; and attitudes, personality or temperament. The term "test" includes all formal scored quantified or standardized techniques of assessing job suitability including, in addition to the above, specific qualifying or disqualifying personal history or background requirements, specific educational or work history requirements, scored interviews, biographical information blanks, interviewers' rating scales, scored application forms, etc.

§ 1607.3 Discrimination defined.

The use of any test which adversely affects hiring, promotion, transfer or any other employment or membership opportunity of classes protected by Title VII constitutes discrimination unless: (a) The test has been validated and evidences a high degree of utility as hereinafter described, and (b) The person giving or acting upon the results of the particular test can demonstrate that alternative suitable hiring, transfer or promotion procedures are unavailable for his use.

§ 1607.4 Evidence of validity.

(a) Each person using tests to select from among candidates for a position or for membership shall have available for inspection evidence that the tests are being used in a manner which does not violate § 1607.3. Such evidence shall be examined for indications of possible discrimination, such as instances of higher rejection rates for minority candidates than nonminority candidates. Furthermore, where technically feasible, a test should be validated for each minority group with which it is used; that is, any differential rejection rates that may exist, based on a test, must be relevant to performance on the jobs in question.

(b) The term "technically feasible" as used in these guidelines means having or obtaining a sufficient number of minority individuals to achieve findings of statistical and practical significance, the opportunity to obtain unbiased job performance criteria, etc. It is the responsibility of the person claiming absence of technical feasibility to positively demonstrate evidence of this absence.

(c) Evidence of a test's validity should consist of empirical data demonstrating that the test is predictive of or significantly correlated with important elements of work behavior which comprise or are relevant to the job or jobs for which candidates are being evaluated.

(1) If job progression structures and seniority provisions are so established that new employees will probably, within a reasonable period of time and in a great majority of cases, progress to a higher level, it may be considered that candidates are being evaluated for jobs at that higher level. However, where job progression is not so nearly automatic, or the time span is such that higher level jobs or employees' potential may be expected to change in significant ways, it shall be considered that candidates are being evaluated for a job at or near the entry level. This point is made to underscore the principle that attainment of or performance at a higher level job is a relevant criterion in validating employment tests only when there is a high probability that persons employed will in fact attain that higher level job within a reasonable period of time.

(2) Where a test is to be used in different units of a multiunit organization and no significant differences exist between units, jobs, and applicant populations, evidence obtained in one unit may suffice for the others. Similarly, where the validation process requires the collection of data throughout a multiunit organization, evidence of validity specific to each unit may not be required. There may also be instances where evidence of validity is appropriately obtained from more than one company in the same industry. Both in this instance and in the use of data collected throughout a multiunit organization, evidence of validity specific to each unit may not be required: *Provided,* That no significant differences exist between units, jobs, and applicant populations.

§ 1607.5 Minimum standards for validation.

(a) For the purpose of satisfying the requirements of this part, empirical evidence in support of a test's validity must be based on studies employing generally accepted procedures for determining criterion-related validity, such as those described in "Standards for Educational and Psychological Tests and Manuals" published by American Psychological Association, 1200 17th Street, NW., Washington, D.C. 20036. Evidence of content or construct validity, as defined in that publication, may also be appropriate where criterion-related validity is not feasible. However, evidence for content or construct validity should be accompanied by sufficient information from job analyses to demonstrate the relevance of the content (in the case of job knowledge or proficiency tests) or the construct (in the case of trait measures). Evidence of content validity alone may be acceptable for well-developed tests that consist of suitable samples of the essential knowledge, skills or behaviors composing the job in question. The types of knowledge, skills or behaviors contemplated here do not include those which can be acquired in a brief orientation to the job.

(b) Although any appropriate validation strategy may be used to develop such empirical evidence, the following minimum standards, as applicable, must be met in the research approach and in the presentation of results which consititute evidence of validity:

(1) Where a validity study is conducted in which tests are administered to applicants, with criterion data collected later, the sample of subjects must be representative of the normal or typical candidate group for the job or jobs in question. This further assumes that the applicant sample is representative of the minority population available for the job or jobs in question in the local labor market. Where a validity study is conducted in which tests are administered to present employees, the sample must be representative of the minority groups currently included in the applicant population. If it is not technically feasible to include minority employees in validation studies conducted on the present work force, the conduct of a validation study without minority candidates does not relieve any person of his subsequent obligation for validation when inclusion of minority candidates becomes technically feasible.

(2) Tests must be administered and scored under controlled and standardized conditions, with proper safeguards to protect the security of test scores and to insure that scores do not enter into any judgments of employee adequacy that are to be used as criterion measures. Copies of tests and test manuals, including instructions for administration, scoring, and interpretation of test results, that are privately developed and/or are not available through normal commercial channels must be included as a part of the validation evidence.

(3) The work behaviors or other criteria of employee adequacy which the test is intended to predict or identify must be fully described; and, additionally, in the case of rating techniques, the appraisal form(s) and instructions to the rater(s) must be included as a part of the validation evidence. Such criteria may include measures other than actual work proficiency, such as training time, supervisory ratings, regularity of attendance and ten-

ure. Whatever criteria are used they must represent major or critical work behaviors as revealed by careful job analyses.

(4) In view of the possibility of bias inherent in subjective evaluations, supervisory rating techniques should be carefully developed, and the ratings should be closely examined for evidence of bias. In addition, minorities might obtain unfairly low performance criterion scores for reasons other than supervisors' prejudice, as, when, as new employees, they have had less opportunity to learn job skills. The general point is that all criteria need to be examined to insure freedom from factors which would unfairly depress the scores of minority groups.

(5) Differential validity. Data must be generated and results separately reported for minority and nonminority groups wherever technically feasible. Where a minority group is sufficiently large to constitute an identifiable factor in the local labor market, but validation data have not been developed and presented separately for that group, evidence of satisfactory validity based on other groups will be regarded as only provisional compliance with these guidelines pending separate validation of the test for the minority group in question. (See § 1607.9). A test which is differentially valid may be used in groups for which it is valid, but not for those in which it is not valid. In this regard, where a test is valid for two groups but one group characteristically obtains higher test scores than the other without a corresponding difference in job performance, cut-off scores must be set so as to predict the same probability of job success in both groups.

(c) In assessing the utility of a test the following considerations will be applicable:

(1) The relationship between the test and at least one relevant criterion must be statistically significant. This ordinarily means that the relationship should be sufficiently high as to have a probability of no more than 1 to 20 to have occurred by chance. However, the use of a single test as the sole selection device will be scrutinized closely when that test is valid against only one component of job performance.

(2) In addition to statistical significance, the relationship between the test and criterion should have practical significance. The magnitude of the relationship needed for practical significance or usefulness is affected by several factors, including:

(i) The larger the proportion of applicants who are hired for or placed on the job, the higher the relationship needs to be in order to be practically useful. Conversely, a relatively low relationship may prove useful when proportionately few job vacancies are available;

(ii) The larger the proportion of applicants who become satisfactory employees when not selected on the basis of the test, the higher the relationship needs to be between the test and a criterion of job success for the test to be practically useful. Conversely, a relatively low relationship may prove useful when proportionally few applicants turn out to be satisfactory;

(iii) The smaller the economic and human risks involved in hiring an unqualified applicant relative to the risks entailed in rejecting a qualified applicant, the greater the relationship needs to be in order to be practically useful. Conversely, a relatively low relationship may prove useful when the former risks are relatively high.

§ 1607.6 Presentation of validity evidence.

The presentation of the results of a validation study must include graphical and statistical representations of the relationships between the test and the criteria, permitting judgments of the test's utility in making predictions of future work behavior. (See § 1607.5(c) concerning assessing utility of a test.) Average scores for all tests and criteria must be reported for all relevant subgroups, including minority and nonminority groups where differential validation is required. Whenever statistical adjustments are made in validity results for less than perfect reliability or for restriction of score range in the test or the criterion, or both, the supporting evidence from the validation study must be presented in detail. Furthermore, for each test that is to be established or continued as an operational employee selection instrument, as a result of the validation study, the minimum acceptable cutoff (passing) score on the test must be reported. It is expected that each operational cutoff score will be reasonable and consistent with normal expectations of proficiency within the work force or group on which the study was conducted.

§ 1607.7 Use of other validity studies.

In cases where the validity of a test cannot be determined pursuant to § 1607.4 and § 1607.5 (e.g., the number of subjects is less than that required for a technically adequate validation study, or an appropriate criterion measure cannot be developed), evidence from validity studies conducted in other organizations, such as that reported in test manuals and professional literature, may be considered acceptable when: (a) The studies pertain to jobs which are comparable (i.e., have basically the same task elements), and (b) There are no major differences in contextual variables or sample composition which are likely to significantly affect validity. Any person citing evidence from other validity studies as evidence of test validity for his own jobs must substantiate in detail job comparability and must demonstrate the absence of contextual or sample differences cited in paragraphs (a) and (b) of this section.

§ 1607.8 Assumption of validity.

(a) Under no circumstances will the general reputation of a test, its author or its publisher, or casual reports of test utility be accepted in lieu of evidence of validity. Specifically ruled out are: assumptions of validity based on test names or descriptive labels; all forms of promotional literature; data bearing on the frequency of a test's usage; testimonial statements of sellers, users, or consultants; and other nonempirical or anecdotal accounts of testing practices or testing outcomes.

(b) Although professional supervision of testing activities may help greatly to insure technically sound and nondiscriminatory test usage, such involvement alone shall not be regarded as constituting satisfactory evidence of test validity.

§ 1607.9 Continued use of tests.

Under certain conditions, a person may be permitted to continue the use of a test which is not at the moment fully supported by the required evidence of validity. If, for example, determination of criterion-related validity in a specific setting is practicable and required but not yet obtained, the use of the test may continue: *Provided:* (a) The person can cite substantial evidence of validity as described in § 1607.7(a) and (b); and (b) He has in progress validation procedures which are designed to produce, within a reasonable time, the additional data required. It is expected also that the person may have to alter or suspend test cutoff scores so that score ranges broad enough to permit the identification of criterion-related validity will be obtained.

§ 1607.10 Employment agencies and employment services.

(a) An employment service, including private employment agencies, State employment agencies, and the U.S. Training and Employment Service, as defined in section 701(c), shall not make applicant or employee appraisals or referrals based on the results obtained from any psychological test or other selection standard not validated in accordance with these guidelines.

(b) An employment agency or service which is requested by an employer or union to devise a testing program is required to follow the standards for test validation as set forth in these guidelines. An employment service is not relieved of its obligation herein because the test user did not request such validation or has requested the use of some lesser standard than is provided in these guidelines.

(c) Where an employment agency or service is requested only to administer a testing program which has been elsewhere devised, the employment agency or service shall request evidence of validation, as described in the guidelines in this part, before it administers the testing program and/or makes referral pursuant to the test results. The employment agency must furnish on request such evidence of validation. An employment agency or service will be expected to refuse to administer a test where the employer or union does not supply satisfactory evidence of validation. Reliance by the test user on the reputation of the test, its author, or the name of the test shall not be deemed sufficient evidence of validity (see § 1607.8(a)). An employment agency or service may administer a testing program where the evidence of validity comports with the standards provided in § 1607.7.

§ 1607.11 Disparate treatment.

The principle of disparate or unequal treatment must be distinguished from the concepts of test validation. A test or other employee selection standard—even though validated against job performance in accordance with the guidelines in this part—cannot be imposed upon any individual or class protected by Title VII where other employees, applicants or members have not been subjected to that standard. Disparate treatment, for example, occurs where members of a minority or sex group have been denied the same employment, promotion, transfer or membership opportunities as have been made available to other employees or applicants. Those employees or applicants who have been denied equal treatment, because of prior discriminatory practices or policies, must at least be afforded the same opportunities as had existed for other employees or applicants during the period of discrimination. Thus, no new test or other employee selection standard can be imposed upon a class of individuals protected by Title VII who, but for prior discrimination, would have been granted the opportunity to qualify under less stringent selection standards previously in force.

§ 1607.12 Retesting.

Employers, unions, and employment agencies should provide an opportunity for retesting and reconsideration to earlier "failure" candidates who have availed themselves of more training or experience. In particular, if any applicant or employee during the course of an interview or other employment procedure claims more education or experience, that individual should be retested.

§ 1607.13 Other selection techniques.

Selection techniques other than tests, as defined in § 1607.2, may be improperly used so as to have the effect of discriminating against minority groups. Such techniques include, but are not restricted to, unscored or casual interviews and unscored application forms. Where there are data suggesting employment discrimination, the person may be called upon to present evidence concerning the validity of his unscored procedures as well as of any tests which may be used, the evidence of validity being of the same types referred to in §§ 1607.4 and 1607.5. Data suggesting the possibility of discrimination exist, for example, when there are differential rates of applicant rejection from various minority and nonminority or sex groups for the same job or group of jobs or when there are disproportionate representations of minority and nonminority or sex groups among present employees in different types of jobs. If the person is unable or unwilling to perform such validation studies, he has the option of adjusting employment procedures so as to eliminate the conditions suggestive of employment discrimination.

§ 1607.14 Affirmative action.

Nothing in these guidelines shall be interpreted as diminishing a person's obligation under both Title VII and Executive Order 11246 as amended by Executive Order 11375 to undertake affirmative action to ensure that applicants or employees are treated without regard to race, color, religion, sex, or national origin. Specifically, the use of tests which have been validated pursuant to these guidelines does not relieve employers, unions or employment agencies of their obligations to take positive action in affording employment and training to members of classes protected by Title VII.

exhibit 6-A

uniform guidelines on employee selection procedures*

I. General Principles

§ 1 Statement of purpose.

A. The Federal government's need for a uniform set of principles on the question of the use of tests and other selection procedures has long been recognized. The Equal Employment Opportunity Commission, the Civil Service Commission, the Department of Labor, the Department of Justice, and the Department of the Treasury jointly have adopted these uniform guidelines to meet that need, and to apply the same principles to the Federal government as are applied to other employers.

B. These guidelines incorporate a single set of principles which are designed to assist employers, labor organizations, employment agencies, and licensing and certification boards to comply with requirements of Federal law prohibiting employment practices which discriminate on grounds of race, color, religion, sex, and national origin. They are designed to provide a framework for determining the proper use of tests and other selection procedures. These guidelines do not require a user to conduct validity studies of selection procedures where no adverse impact results. However, all users are encouraged to use selection procedures which are valid, especially users operating under merit principles.

C. These guidelines are based upon, combine, and supersede all previously issued guidelines on employee selection procedures. These guidelines have been built upon court decisions, the previously issued guidelines of the agencies, and the practical experience of the agencies, as well as the standards of the psychological profession. These guidelines are intended to be consistent with existing law.

* Published in the *Federal Register,* December 30, 1977.

§ 2 Scope.

A. These guidelines will be applied by the Equal Employment Opportunity Commission in the enforcement of Title VII of the Civil Rights Act of 1964, as amended by the Equal Employment Opportunity Act of 1972 (hereinafter "Title VII"); by the Department of Labor and the contract compliance agencies in the administration and enforcement of Executive Order 11246, as amended by Executive Order 11375 (hereinafter "Executive Order 11246"); by the Civil Service Commission and other Federal agencies subject to Sec. 717 of Title VII; by the Civil Service Commission in exercising its responsibilities toward state and local governments under Section 208 (b) (1) of the Intergovernmental Personnel Act; by the Department of Justice in exercising its responsibilities under Federal law; by the Office of Revenue Sharing of the Department of the Treasury under the State and Local Fiscal Assistance Act of 1972, as amended; and by any other Federal agency which adopts them.

B. These guidelines apply to tests and other selection procedures which are used as a basis for any employment decision. Employment decisions include but are not limited to hiring, promotion, demotion, membership (for example, in a labor organization), referral, retention, licensing, and certification, to the extent that licensing and certification may be covered by Federal equal employment opportunity law. Other selection decisions, such as selection for training or transfer, may also be considered employment decisions if they lead to any of the decisions listed above.

C. These guidelines apply only to selection procedures which are used as a basis for making employment decisions. For example, the use of recruiting procedures designed to attract racial, ethnic, or sex groups, which were previously denied employment opportunities or which are currently underutilized, may be necessary to bring an employer into compliance with Federal law, and is frequently an essential element of any effective affirmative action program; but the subject of recruitment practices is not addressed by these guidelines because that subject concerns procedures other than selection procedures. Similarly, these guidelines do not pertain to the question of the lawfulness of a seniority system within the meaning of § 703(h) of Title VII, or the question of the lawfulness of a seniority system under Executive Order 11246 or other provisions of Federal law or regulation, except to the extent that such systems utilize selection procedures to determine qualifications or abilities to perform the job. Nothing in these guidelines is intended or should be interpreted as discouraging the use of a selection procedure for the purpose of determining qualifications or for the purpose of selection on the basis of relative qualifications, if the selection procedure has been validated in accord with these guidelines for each such purpose for which it is to be used.

D. These guidelines apply only to persons subject to Title VII, Executive Order 11246, or other equal employment opportunity requirements of Federal law. These guidelines do not apply to responsibilities under the Age Discrimination Act of 1975, not to discriminate on the basis of age, or under section 504 of the Rehabilitation Act of 1973, not to discriminate on the basis of handicap.

E. These guidelines do not restrict any obligation imposed or right granted by Federal law to users to extend a preference in employment to Indians living in or near an Indian reservation in connection with employment opportunities on or near an Indian reservation.

§ 3 Discrimination defined: Relationship between use of selection procedures and discrimination.

A. The use of any selection procedure which has an adverse impact on the hiring, promotion, or other employment or membership opportunities of members of any racial, ethnic, or sex group will be considered to be discriminatory and inconsistent with these guidelines, unless the procedure has been validated in accordance with these guidelines, or the provisions of § 6 below are satisfied.

B. Where two or more selection procedures are available which are substantially equally valid for a given purpose, the user should use the procedure which has been demonstrated to have the lesser adverse impact. Accordingly, whenever a validity study is called for by these guidelines, the user should include an investigation of suitable alternative selection procedures and suitable alternative methods of using the selection procedure which have as little adverse impact as possible, to determine the appropriateness of using or validating them in accord with these guidelines. If a user has made a reasonable effort to become aware of such alternative procedures and validity has been demonstrated in accord with these guidelines, the use of the test or other selection procedure may continue until such time as it should reasonably be reviewed for currency. Whenever the user is shown an alternative selection procedure with evidence of less adverse impact and substantial evidence of validity for the same job in similar circumstances, the user should investigate it to determine the appropriateness of using or validating it in accord with these guidelines. This subsection is not intended to preclude the combination of procedures into a significantly more valid procedure, if the use of such a combination has been shown to be in compliance with the guidelines.

§ 4 Information on impact.

A. Each user should maintain and have available for inspection records or other information which will disclose the impact which its tests and other selection procedures have upon employment opportunities of persons by identifiable racial, ethnic, or sex groups as set forth in subparagraph B below in order to determine compliance with these guidelines. Where there are large numbers of applicants and procedures are administered frequently, such information may be retained on a sample basis, provided that the sample is appropriate in terms of the applicant population and adequate in size.

B. The records called for by this section are to be maintained by sex, and the following racial and ethnic groups: blacks (Negroes), American Indians (including Alaskan Natives), Asians (including Pacific Islanders), Hispanic (including persons of Mexican, Puerto Rican, Cuban, Central or South American, or other Spanish origin or culture, regardless of race), whites (Caucasians) other than Hispanic and totals. The classifications called for by this section are intended to be consistent with the Employer Information (EEO-1 et seq.) series of reports. The user should adopt safeguards to insure that the records required by this paragraph are used for appropriate purposes such as determining adverse impact, or (where required) for developing and monitoring affirmative action programs, and that such records are not used improperly. See § 4E and § 13B(4) below.

C. If the information called for by § 4 A and B above shows that the total selection process for a job has no adverse impact, the Federal enforcement agencies will not expect a user to evaluate the individual components for adverse impact, or to validate such individual components, and generally will not take enforcement action based upon adverse impact of any component of that process, including the separate parts of a multi-part selection procedure or any separate procedure that is used as an alternative method of selection. If a total selection process does have an adverse impact, the individual components of the selection process should be evaluated for adverse impact.

D. A selection rate for any racial ethnic or sex group which is less than four-fifths (4/5) (or eighty percent) of the rate for the group with the highest rate will generally be regarded by the Federal enforcement agencies as evidence of adverse impact, while a greater than four-fifths rate will generally not be regarded by Federal enforcement agencies as evidence of adverse impact. Smaller differences in selection rate may nevertheless constitute adverse impact, where they are significant in both statistical and practical terms or where a user's actions have discouraged applicants disproportionately on racial, sex, or ethnic grounds. Greater differences in selection rate may not constitute adverse impact where the differences are based on small numbers and are not statistically significant, or where special recruiting or other programs cause the pool of minority or female candidates to be atypical of the normal pool of applicants from that group. Where the user's evidence concerning the impact of a selection procedure indicates adverse impact but is based upon numbers which are too small to be reliable, evidence concerning the impact of the procedure over a longer period of time and/or evidence concerning the impact which the selection procedure had when used in the same manner in similar circumstances elsewhere may be considered in determining adverse impact. Where the user has not maintained data on adverse impact as called for by these guidelines, the Federal enforcement agencies may draw an inference of adverse impact of the selection process from the failure of the user to maintain such data, if the user has an underutilization of a group in the job category, as compared to the group's representation in the relevant labor market or, in the case of jobs filled from within, the applicable workforce.

E. In carrying out their obligations, the Federal enforcement agencies will consider the general posture of the user with respect to equal employment opportunity for the job or group of jobs in question. Where a user has adopted an affirmative action program the Federal enforcement agencies will consider the provisions of that program, including the goals and timetables which the user has adopted and the progress which the user has made in carrying out that program and in meeting the goals and timetables. While such affirmative action programs may in design and execution be race, color, sex, or ethnic conscious, selection procedures under such programs should be based upon the ability or relative ability to do the work as shown by properly validated selection procedures.

§ 5 General standards for validity studies.

A. For the purposes of satisfying these guidelines, users may rely upon criterion related validity studies, content validity studies or construct validity studies, in accordance with the standards set forth in Part II of these guidelines, § 14 below.

B. Evidence of the validity of a test or other selection procedure by a criterion related validity study should consist of empirical data demonstrating that the selection procedure is predictive of or significantly correlated with important elements of job performance. See § 14B, below. Evidence of the validity of a test or other selection procedure by a content validity study should consist of data showing that the selection procedure is a representative sample of important work behaviors to be performed on the job for which the candidates are to be evaluated. See § 14C, below. Evidence of the validity of a test or other selection procedure through a construct validity study should consist of data showing that the procedure measures the degree to which candidates have identifiable characteristics which have been determined to be important in successful performance in the job for which the candidates are to be evaluated. See § 14D below.

C. These guidelines are intended to be consistent with generally accepted professional standards for evaluating standardized tests and other selection procedures, such as those described in the Standards for Educational and Psychological Tests prepared by a joint committee of the American Psychological Association, the American Educational Research Association, and the National Council on Measurement in Education (American Psychological Association, Washington, D.C., 1974) (hereinafter "APA Standards"), and standard text books and journals in the field of personnel selection.

D. For any selection procedure which is part of a selection process which has an adverse impact and which selection procedure has an adverse impact, each user should maintain and have available such documentation as is described in Part III of these guidelines, § 15, below.

E. Selection procedures subject to validity studies under § 3A above should be administered and scored under standardized conditions.

F. In general, users should avoid making employment decisions on the basis of measures of knowledges, skills, or abilities which are normally learned in a brief orientation period, and which have an adverse impact.

G. Where cutoff scores are used, they should normally be set so as to be reasonable and consistent with normal expectations of acceptable proficiency within the work force. Where applicants are ranked on the basis of properly validated selection procedures and those applicants scoring below a higher cutoff score have little or no chance of being selected for employment, the higher cutoff score may be appropriate, but the degree of adverse impact should be considered.

H. If job progression structures are so established that employees will probably, within a reasonable period of time and in a majority of cases, progress to a higher level, it may be considered that the candidates are being evaluated for a job or jobs at the higher level. However, where job progression is not so nearly automatic, or the time span is such that higher level jobs or employees' potential may be expected to change in significant ways, it should be considered that employees are being evaluated for a job at or near the entry level. A "reasonable period of time" will vary for different jobs and employment situations but will seldom be more than five years. Evaluation for a higher level job would not be appropriate (1) if the majority of those remaining employed do not progress to the higher level job, or, in the case where the user's employment practices systematically screen out a disproportionate number of any racial, sex, or ethnic group, if the majority of those originally hired do not progress to the higher level job; (2) if there is a reason to doubt that the higher level job will continue to require essentially similar skills during the progression period; or (3) if knowledges, skills or abilities required for advancement would be expected to develop principally from the training or experience on the job.

I. Users may continue the use of a selection procedure which is not at the moment fully supported by the required evidence of validity, provided: (1) The user can cite substantial evidence of validity in accord with these guidelines and (2) the user has in progress, when technically feasible, studies which are designed to produce the additional data required within a reasonable time. If the additional studies do not demonstrate validity, this provision of these guidelines for interim use shall not constitute a defense in any action, nor shall it relieve the user of any obligations arising under Federal law.

J. Whenever validity has been shown in accord with these guidelines for the use of a particular selection procedure for a job or group of jobs, additional studies need not be performed until such time as the validity study is subject to review as provided in § 3B above. There are no absolutes in the area of determining the currency of a validity study. All circumstances concerning the study, including the validation strategy used, and changes in the relevant labor market and the job should be considered in the determination of when a validity study is outdated.

§ 6 Alternative Selection Procedures and Modification of Selection Procedures.

A. A user may choose to utilize alternative selection procedures in order to eliminate adverse impact or as part of an affirmative action program. Such alternative procedures may include but are not limited to: (1) Those measures set forth in the affirmative action provisions of § 13B below; (2) measures of superior scholarship; culture, language or experience factors; selected use of established registers; selection from a pool of disadvantaged persons who have demonstrated their general competency; use of registers limited to qualified persons who are economically disadvantaged.

B. There are circumstances in which a user cannot or need not utilize the validation techniques contemplated by these guidelines. In such circumstances, the user should utilize selection procedures which are as job related as possible and which will minimize or eliminate adverse impact, as set forth below. (i) When an unstandardized, informal or unscored selection procedure which has an adverse impact is utilized, the user should eliminate the adverse impact, or modify the procedure to one which is a formal, scored or quantified measure or combination of measures and then validate the procedure in accord with these guidelines, or otherwise justify continued use of the procedure in accord with Federal law. (ii) When a standardized, formal or scored selection procedure is used which has an adverse impact, the validation techniques contemplated by these guidelines usually should be followed if technically feasible. Where the user cannot or need not do so, the user should either modify the procedure to eliminate adverse impact or otherwise justify continued use of the procedure in accord with Federal law.

§ 7 Use of Other Validity Studies.

A. Users may, under certain circumstances, support the use of selection procedures by validity studies conducted by other users or conducted by test publishers or distributors and described in test manuals. While publishers of selection procedures have a professional obligation to provide evidence of validity which meets generally accepted professional standards (see, § 5C above), users are cautioned that they are responsible for compliance with these guidelines. Accordingly, users seeking to obtain selection procedures from publishers and distributors should be careful to determine that, in the event the user becomes subject to the validity requirements of these guidelines, the necessary information to support validity has been determined and will be made available to the user.

B. Criterion-related validity studies conducted by one test user, or described in test manuals and the professional literature, will be considered acceptable for use by another user when: (1) Evidence from the available studies meeting the standards of § 14B below clearly demonstrates that the selection procedure is valid; (2) the studies pertain to a job the incumbents of which perform substantially the same major work behaviors as shown by appropriate job analyses both on the job on which the validity study was performed and on the job on which the selection procedure is to be used; and (3) the studies include a study of test fairness for those racial, ethnic and sex subgroups which constitute significant factors in the borrowing user's relevant labor market for the job or jobs in question. If the studies under consideration satisfy (1) and (2) above but do not contain an investigation of test fairness, and it is not technically feasible for the borrowing user to conduct an internal study of test fairness, the borrowing user may utilize the study until studies conducted elsewhere show test unfairness, or until such time as it becomes technically feasible to conduct an internal study of test fairness and the results of that study can be acted upon. Users obtaining selection procedures from publishers should consider, as one factor in the decision to purchase a particular selection procedure, the availability of evidence concerning test fairness.

C. If validity evidence from a multi-unit study satisfies the requirements of § 7B above, evidence of validity specific to each unit will not be required, unless there are variables which are likely to affect validity significantly.

D. If there are variables in the other studies which are likely to affect validity significantly, the user may not rely upon such studies, but will be expected either to conduct an internal validity study or to comply with § 6 above.

§ 8 Cooperative Studies.

A. The agencies issuing these guidelines encourage employers, labor organizations and employment agencies to cooperate in research, development, search for alternatives, and validity studies in order to achieve procedures which are consistent with these guidelines.

B. If validity evidence from a cooperative study satisfied the requirements of § 7 above, evidence of validity specific to each user will not be required unless there are variables in the user's situation which are likely to affect validity significantly.

§ 9 No Assumption of Validity.

A. Under no circumstances will the general reputation of a test or other selection procedure, its author or its publisher, or casual reports of its validity be accepted in lieu of evidence of validity. Specifically ruled out are: assumptions of validity based on a procedure's name or descriptive labels; all forms of promotional literature; data bearing on the frequency of a procedure's usage; testimonial statements and credentials of sellers, users, or consultants; and other non-empirical or anecdotal accounts of selection practices or selection outcomes.

B. Professional supervision of selection activities is encouraged but is not a substitute for documented evidence of validity. The enforcement agencies will take into account the fact that a thorough job analysis was conducted and that careful development and use of a selection procedure in accordance with professional standards enhance the probability that the selection procedure is valid for the job.

§ 10 Employment agencies and employment services.

A. An employment agency, including private employment agencies and State employment agencies, which agrees to a request by an employer or labor organization to devise and utilize a selection procedure should follow the standards in these guidelines for determining adverse impact. If adverse impact exists the agency should comply with these guidelines. An employment agency is not relieved of its obligation herein because the user did not request such validation or has requested the use of some lesser standard of validation than is provided in these guidelines. The use of an employment agency does not relieve an employer or labor organization or other user of its responsibilities under Federal law to provide equal employment opportunity or its obligations as a user under these guidelines.

B. Where an employment agency or service is requested to administer a selection program which has been devised elsewhere and to make referrals pursuant to the results, the employment agency or service should obtain evidence of the absence of adverse impact, or of compliance with these guidelines, before it administers the selection program and makes referrals pursuant to the results. The employment agency must furnish on request such evidence of validity. An employment agency or service which makes referrals based on the selection procedure where the employer or labor organization does not supply satisfactory evidence of validity or lack of adverse impact is not in compliance with these guidelines.

§ 11 Disparate treatment.

The principle of disparate or unequal treatment must be distinguished from the concepts of validation. A selection procedure—even though validated against job performance in accordance with the guidelines in this part—cannot be imposed upon members of a racial, sex or ethnic group where other employees, applicants, or members have not been subjected to that standard. Disparate treatment occurs where members of a racial, sex, or ethnic group have been denied the same employment, promotion, membership or other employment opportunities as have been made available to other employees or applicants. Those employees or applicants who have been denied equal treatment, because of prior discriminatory practices or policies, must at least be afforded the same opportunities as had existed for other employees or applicants during the period of discrimination. Thus, the persons who were in the class of persons discriminated against during the period the user followed the discriminatory practices should be allowed the opportunity to qualify under the less stringent selection procedures previously followed, unless the user demonstrates that the increased standards are required by business necessity. This section does not prohibit a user who has not previously followed merit standards from adopting merit standards which are in compliance with these guidelines; nor does it preclude a user who has previously used invalid or unvalidated selection procedures from developing and using procedures which are in accord with these guidelines.

§ 12 Retesting.

Users should provide a reasonable opportunity for retesting and reconsideration. The user may however take reasonable steps to preserve the security of its procedures. Where examinations are administered periodically with public notice, such reasonable opportunity exists, unless persons who have previously been tested are precluded from retesting.

§ 13 Affirmative Action.

A. The use of selection procedures which have been validated pursuant to these guidelines does not relieve users of any obligations they may have to undertake affirmative action to assure equal employment opportunity. Nothing in these guidelines is intended to preclude the use of selection procedures which assist in remedying the effects of prior discriminatory practices, or the achievement of affirmative action objectives.

B. These guidelines are also intended to encourage the adoption and implementation of voluntary affirmative action programs by users who have no obligation under Federal law to adopt them; but are not intended to impose any new obligations in that regard. The agencies issuing and endorsing these guidelines endorse and reaffirm, both for private employers and governmental employers, the Equal Employment Opportunity Coordinating Council's "Policy Statement on Affirmative Action Programs for State and Local Government Agencies," (41 FR 38814, Sept. 13, 1976). That statement did not attempt to set either the minimum or maximum voluntary steps that employers may take nor did it attempt to deal with remedies imposed after a finding of discrimination. That statement also was not designed to supersede or replace existing or later developed affirmative action requirements imposed under E.O. 11246 or other provisions of Federal law.

The major sections of the Policy Statement include the following:

. . .

(2) Voluntary affirmative action to assure equal employment opportunity is appropriate at any stage of the employment process. The first step in the construction of any affirmative action plan should be an analysis of the employer's work force to determine whether percentages of sex, race or ethnic groups in individual job classifications are substantially similar to the percentages of those groups available in the relevant job market who possess the basic job related qualifications.

When substantial disparities are found through such analyses, each element of the overall selection process should be examined to determine which elements operate to exclude persons on the basis of sex, race, or ethnic group. Such elements include, but are not limited to, recruitment, testing, ranking certification, interview, recommendations for selection, hiring, promotion, etc. The examination of each element of the selection process should at a minimum include a determination of its validity in predicting job performance.

(3) When an employer has reason to believe that its selection procedures have the exclusionary effect described . . . of that statement above, it should initiate affirmative steps to remedy the situation. Such steps, which in design and execution may be race, color, sex or ethnic "conscious," include, but are not limited to, the following:

(a) The establishment of a long term goal, and short range, interim goals and timetables for the specific job classifications, all of which should take into account the availability of basically qualified persons in the relevant job market;

(b) A recruitment program designed to attract qualified members of the group in question;

(c) A systematic effort to organize work and re-design jobs in ways that provide opportunities for persons lacking "journeyman" level knowledge or skills to enter and, with appropriate training, to progress in a career field;

(d) Revamping selection instruments or procedures which have not yet been validated in order to reduce or eliminate exclusionary effects on particular groups in particular job classifications;

(e) The initiation of measures designed to assure that members of the affected group who are qualified to perform the job are included within the pool of persons from which the selecting official makes the selection;

(f) A systematic effort to provide career advancement training, both classroom and on-the-job, to employees locked into dead end jobs; and

(g) The establishment of a system for regularly monitoring the effectiveness of the particular affirmative action program, and procedures for making timely adjustments in this program where effectiveness is not demonstrated.

(4) The goal of any affirmative action plan should be achievement of genuine equal employment opportunity for all qualified persons. Selection under such plans should be based upon the ability of the applicant(s) to do the work. Such plans should not require the selection of the unqualified, or the unneeded, nor should they require the selection of persons on the basis of race, color, sex, religion or national origin.

Part II—Technical Standards

§ 14 Technical Standards for Validity Studies.

The following minimum standards, as applicable, should be met in conducting a validity study. Nothing in these guidelines is intended to preclude the development and use of other professionally acceptable techniques with respect to validation of selection procedures. Where it is not technically feasible for a user to conduct a validity study, the user has the obligation otherwise to comply with these guidelines. See §§ 6 and 7 above.

A. *Job Information.* (1) Any validity study should be based upon a review of information about the job for which the selection procedure is to be used. The review should include a job analysis except as provided in § 14B(3) below with respect to criterion related validity. Any method of job analysis may be used if it provides the information required for the specific validation strategy used.

B. *Criterion-Related Validity.* (1) Users choosing to validate a selection procedure by a criterion-related validity strategy should determine whether it is technically feasible (as defined in Part IV) to conduct such a study in the particular employment context. The determination of the number of persons necessary to permit the conduct of a meaningful criterion-related study should be made by the user on the basis of all relevant information concerning the selection procedure, the potential sample and the employment situation. Where appropriate, jobs with substantially the same major work behaviors may be grouped together for validity studies, in order to obtain an adequate sample. These guidelines do not require a user to hire or promote persons for the purpose of making it possible to conduct a criterion-related study.

(2) There should be a review of job information to determine measures of work behaviors or performance that are relevant to the job in question. These measures or criteria are relevant to the extent that they represent critical or important job duties, work behaviors or work outcomes as developed from the review of job information. The possibility of bias should be considered both in selection of the criterion measures and their application. In view of the possibility of bias in subjective evaluations, supervisory rating techniques and instructions to raters should be carefully developed; and the ratings should be examined for evidence of racial, ethnic or sex bias. All criteria need to be examined for freedom from factors which would unfairly alter scores of members of any group. The relevance of criteria and their freedom from bias are of particular concern when there are significant differences in measures of job performance for different groups.

(3) Proper safeguards should be taken to insure that scores on selection procedures do not enter into any judgments of employee adequacy that are to be used as criterion measures. Whatever criteria are used should represent important or critical work behaviors or work outcomes. Criteria also may consist of measures other than work proficiency including, but not limited to production rate, error rate, tardiness, absenteeism and length of service, which may be used without a full job analysis if the user can show

the importance of the criteria to the particular employment context. A standardized rating of overall work performance may be used where a study of the job shows that it is an appropriate criterion. Where performance in training is used as a criterion, success in training should be properly measured and the relevance of the training should be shown either through a comparison of the content of the training program with the critical or important work behaviors of the job(s), or through a demonstration of the relationship between measures of performance in training and measures of job performance. Measures of relative success in training include but are not limited to instructor evaluations, performance samples, or tests. Measures of training success based upon paper and pencil tests will be closely reviewed for job relevance.

(4) Whether the study is predictive or concurrent, the sample subjects should insofar as feasible be representative of the candidates normally available in the relevant labor market for the job or jobs in question, and should insofar as feasible include the racial, ethnic and sex groups normally available in the relevant job market. Where samples are combined or compared, attention should be given to see that such samples are comparable in terms of the actual job they perform, the length of time on the job where time on the job is likely to affect performance and other relevant factors likely to affect validity differences; or that these factors are included in the design of the study and their effects identified.

(5) The degree of relationship between selection procedure scores and criterion measures should be examined and computed, using professionally acceptable statistical procedures. Generally, a selection procedure is considered related to the criterion, for the purposes of these guidelines, when the relationship between performance on the procedure and performance on the criterion measure is statistically significant at the .05 level of significance, which means that it is sufficiently high as to have a probability of no more than one (1) in twenty (20) to have occurred by chance. Absence of a statistically significant relationship between a selection procedure and job performance should not necessarily discourage other investigations of the validity of that selection procedure.

(6) Users should evaluate each selection procedure to assure that it is appropriate for operational use, including establishment of cut off scores or rank ordering. Generally, if other factors remain the same, the greater the magnitude of the relationship (e.g., correlation coefficient) between performance on a selection procedure and one or more criteria of performance of the job, and the greater the importance and number of aspects of job performance covered by the criteria, the more likely it is that the procedure will be appropriate for use. Reliance upon a selection procedure which is signifi-

cantly related to a criterion measure, but which is based upon a study involving a large number of subjects and has a low correlation coefficient will be subject to close review if it has a large adverse impact. Sole reliance upon a single selection instrument which is related to only one of many job duties or aspects of job performance will also be subject to close review. The appropriateness of a selection procedure is best evaluated in each particular situation and there are no minimum correlation coefficients applicable to all employment situations. In determining whether a selection procedure is appropriate for operational use the following considerations should also be taken into account: The degree of adverse impact of the procedure, the availability of other selection procedures of greater or substantially equal validity.

(7) Users should avoid reliance upon techniques which tend to overestimate validity findings as a result of capitalization on chance unless an appropriate safeguard is taken. Reliance upon a few selection procedures or criteria of successful job performance, when many selection procedures or criteria of performance have been studied, or the use of optimal statistical weights for selection procedures computed in one sample, are techniques which tend to inflate validity estimates as a result of chance. Use of a large sample is one safeguard; cross-validation is another.

(8) *Fairness of the Selection Procedure.* This section generally calls for studies of unfairness where technically feasible. The concept of fairness or unfairness of selection procedures is a developing concept, however. In addition, fairness studies generally require substantial numbers of employees in the job or group of jobs being studied. For these reasons, the Federal enforcement agencies recognize that the obligation to conduct studies of unfairness imposed by the guidelines generally will be upon users or groups of users with a large number of persons in a job class, or test developers; and that small users utilizing their own selection procedures will generally not be obligated to conduct such studies because it will be technically infeasible for them to do so.

(a) When members of one racial, ethnic, or sex group characteristically obtain lower scores on a selection procedure than members of another group, and the differences are not reflected in differences in measures of job performance, use of the selection procedure may unfairly deny opportunities to members of the group that obtains the lower scores.

(b) Where a selection procedure results in an adverse impact on a racial, ethnic or sex group identified in accordance with the classifications set forth in § 4 above and that group is a significant factor in the relevant labor market, the user generally should investigate the possible existence of unfairness for that group if it is technically feasible to do so. The greater the severity of the adverse impact on a group, the greater the need to investigate the possible existence of unfairness. Where the weight of evidence from other studies shows that the selection procedure is a fair predictor for the group in question and for the same or similar jobs, such evidence may be relied on in connection with the selection procedure at issue and may be combined with data from the present study; however, where the severity of adverse impact on a group is significantly greater than in the other studies referred to, a user may not rely on such other studies.

(c) Users conducting a study of fairness should review the APA Standards regarding investigation of possible bias in testing. An investigation of fairness of a selection procedure depends on both evidence of validity and the manner in which the selection procedure is to be used in a particular employment context. Fairness of a selection procedure cannot necessarily be specified in advance without investigating these factors. Investigation of fairness of a selection procedure in samples where the range of scores on selection procedures or criterion measures is severely restricted for any subgroup sample (as compared to other subgroup samples) may produce misleading evidence of unfairness. That factor should accordingly be taken into account in conducting such studies and before reliance is placed on the results.

(d) If unfairness is demonstrated through a showing that members of a particular group perform better or poorer on the job than their scores on the selection procedure would indicate through comparison with how members of other groups perform, the user may either revise or replace the selection instrument in accordance with these guidelines, or may continue to use the selection instrument operationally with appropriate revisions in its use to assure compatibility between the probability of successful job performance and the probability of being selected.

(e) In addition to the general conditions needed for technical feasibility for the conduct of a criterion-related study (see § 16(J), below) an investigation of fairness requires the following:

(i) A sufficient number of persons in each group for findings of statistical significance. These guidelines do not require a user to hire or promote persons on the basis of group classifications for the purpose of making it possible to conduct a study of fairness; but the user has the obligation otherwise to comply with these guidelines.

(ii) The samples for each group should be comparable in terms of the actual job they perform, length of time on the job where time on the job is likely to affect performance, and other relevant factors likely to affect validity differences; or such factors should be included in the design of the study and their effects identified.

(f) If a study of fairness should otherwise be performed, but is not technically feasible, a selection procedure may be used which has otherwise met the validity standards of these guidelines, unless the technical infeasibility resulted from discriminatory employment practices which are demonstrated by facts other than past failure to conform with requirements for validation of selection procedures. However, when it becomes technically feasible for the user to perform a study of fairness and such a study is otherwise called for, the user should conduct the study of fairness.

C. *Content Validity*. (1) Users choosing to validate a selection procedure by a content validity strategy should determine whether it is appropriate to conduct such a study in the particular employment context. A selection procedure can be supported by content validity strategy only to the extent that it is a representative sample of the content of the job. Accordingly, a content validity strategy is only appropriate where it is feasible to devise a selection procedure which is a representative sample of one or more work behaviors of the job, or a representative work sample. A selection procedure which purports to measure a knowledge, skill or ability may only be used to the extent that the knowledge, skill or ability is used in a job behavior and the selection procedure replicates the level of complexity and difficulty of the knowledge, skill or ability as used in the job behavior. A selection procedure based upon inferences about mental processes cannot be supported solely or primarily on the basis of content validity. Thus, a content strategy is not appropriate for demonstrating the validity of selection procedures which purport to measure traits or constructs, such as intelligence, aptitude, personality, common sense, judgement, leadership, dexterity and spatial ability. Content validity is also not an appropriate strategy when the selection procedure involves knowledges, skills or abilities which an employee will be expected to learn on the job.

(2) There should be a job analysis which includes an analysis of the work behaviors required for successful performance and their relative importance (as defined in § 15C(3) below), and to the extent appropriate, an analysis of the work products. Any job analysis should focus on the work behaviors and the associated tasks of the job. If work behaviors are not observable, the job analysis should identify and analyze those aspects of the behaviors that can be observed and the observed work products. The work behaviors selected for measurement should be critical work behaviors and/or important work behaviors constituting most of the job.

(3) A selection procedure designed to measure the work behavior may be developed specifically from the job and job analysis in question, or may have been previously developed by the user, or by other users or by a test publisher.

(4) A selection procedure which is a representative sample of work product(s) or a representative sample of work behavior(s) is a content valid procedure for that work behavior if it is necessary for that work product or work behavior. The closer the content and the context of the selection procedure is to actual work samples or work behaviors, the stronger is the basis for showing content validity. As the content of the selection procedure less resembles a work behavior, or the setting and manner of the administration of the selection procedure less resemble the work situations or the result less resembles a work product, the less likely the selection procedure is to be content valid, and the greater the need for other evidence of validity.

(5) The reliability of selection procedures justified on the basis of content validity should be a matter of concern to the user. Whenever it is feasible, appropriate statistical estimates should be made of the reliability of the selection procedure.

(6) A requirement for specific prior training or for work experience based on content validity, including a specification of level or amount of training or experience, should be justified on the basis of the relationship between the content of the training or experience and the content of the job for which the training or experience is to be required.

(7) Where a training program is used as a selection procedure and the content of a training program is justified on the basis of content validity, it should be justified on the relationship between the content of the training program and the content of the job.

(8) A selection procedure which is supported on the basis of content validity may be used for a job if it represents a critical work behavior (i.e., a behavior which is necessary for performance of the job) or job behaviors which constitute most of the important parts of the job.

(9) If a user can show, by a job analysis or otherwise, that a higher score on a content valid selection procedure is likely to result in better job performance, the results may be used to rank persons who score above minimum levels. Where a selection procedure supported solely or primarily by content validity is used to rank job candidates, the selection procedure should measure those aspects of performance which differentiate among levels of job performance.

D. *Construct Validity.* (1) Construct validity is a more complex strategy than either criterion-related or content validity. Construct validation is a relatively new procedure in the employment field, and there is a lack of a substantial literature extending the concept to employment practices. The user should be aware that the effort to obtain sufficient empirical support for construct validity is both an extensive and arduous effort involving a series of research studies, including criterion related and/or content validity studies and a rigor of proof of at least the same level as in criterion related validation studies. Users choosing to justify use of a selection procedure by this strategy should therefore take particular care to assure that the validity study meets the standards set forth below.

a. There should be a job analysis. This job analysis should show the work behaviors required for successful performance of the job, or the groups of jobs being studied, the critical or important work behaviors in the job or group of jobs being studied, and an identification of the construct(s) believed to underlie successful performance of these critical or important work behaviors in the job or jobs in question. The construct should be named and defined, so as to distinguish it from other constructs. If a group of jobs is being studied the jobs should have in common one or more critical or important work behaviors at a comparable level of complexity.

b. A selection procedure should then be identified or developed which measures the construct identified in accord with subparagraph (a) above. The user should show by empirical evidence that the selection procedure is validly related to the construct and that the construct is validly related to the performance of critical or important job behaviors. The relationship between the construct measured by the selection procedure and the related work behavior(s) should be supported by empirical evidence from one or more criterion-related studies involving the job or jobs in question which satisfy the provisions of § 14B above.

(2) a. In view of the lack of a substantial literature extending the concept of construct validity to employment practices, the Federal agencies will evaluate any claim of construct validity generalization on a case-by-case basis. Until such time as the professional literature provides more guidance on the generalizability of construct validity, the Federal agencies will only accept a claim of construct validity generalization if it meets the standards for transportability of criterion related validity studies as set forth above in 7. However, if a study pertains to a group of jobs having common critical or important work behaviors at a comparable level of complexity, and the evidence satisfies subparagraphs § 14D(1) "a" and "b" above for that group of jobs, the selection procedure may be used for the jobs in the groups studied. If the construct validity is to be generalized to other jobs or groups of jobs, the Federal enforcement agencies will expect at a minimum additional empirical research evidence meeting the standards of subparagraphs § 14D(1) "a" and "b" above for the additional jobs or groups of jobs.

b. In determining whether two or more jobs have one or more work behaviors in common, the user should compare the observed work behaviors in each of the jobs and should compare the observed work products in each of the jobs. If neither the observed work behaviors in each of the jobs, nor the observed work products in each of the jobs are the same, the Federal enforcement agencies will presume that the work behaviors in each job are different. If the work behaviors are not observable, then evidence of similarity of work products and any other relevant research evidence will be considered in determining whether the work behavior in the two jobs is the same.

Part III—Documentation of Validity Evidence

§ 15A. Where a total selection process has an adverse impact (see § 4 above) the user should maintain and have available for each selection procedure in that process the data on which the adverse impact determination was made and, for each selection procedure in that process having an adverse impact (see § 4 above), one of the following types of documentation evidence:

(1) Documentation evidence showing criterion related validity of the selection procedure (see § 15B, below).

(2) Documentation evidence showing content validity of the selection procedure (see § 15C, below).

(3) Documentation evidence showing construct validity of the selection procedure (see § 15D, below).

(4) Documentation evidence from other studies showing validity of the selection procedure in the user's facility (see § 15E, below).

(5) Documentation evidence showing why a validity study cannot or need not be performed and why continued use of the procedure is consistent with Federal law.

This evidence should be compiled in a reasonably complete and organized manner to permit direct evaluation of the validity of the selection procedure. Previously written employer or consultant reports of validity are acceptable if they are complete in regard to the following documentation requirements, or if they satisfied requirements of guidelines which were in effect when the study was completed. If they are not complete, the required additional documentation should be appended. If necessary information is not available the report of the validity study may still be used as documentation, but its adequacy will be evaluated in terms of compliance with the requirements of these guidelines.

In the event that evidence of validity is reviewed by an enforcement agency, the reports completed after the effective date of these guidelines are expected to use one of the formats set forth below. Evidence denoted by use of the word "(Essential)" is considered critical and reports not containing such information will be considered incomplete. Evidence not so denoted is desirable, but its absence will not be a basis for considering a report incomplete.

B. *Criterion-related validity.* Reports of criterion-related validity of selection procedures are to contain the following information:

(1) *User(s), and Location(s) and Date(s) of Study.* Dates and location of administration of selection procedures and collection of criterion of data and, where appropriate, the time between collection of data on selection procedures and criterion measures should be shown (Essential). If the study was conducted at several locations, the address of each location, including city and state, should be shown.

(2) *Problem and Setting.* An explicit definition of the purpose(s) of the study and the circumstances in which the study was conducted should be provided. A description of existing selection procedures and cut-off scores, if any, should be provided.

(3) *Job Analysis or Review of Job Information.* A description of the procedure used to analyze the job, or to review the job information should be provided (Essential). Where a review of job information results in criteria which are measures other than work proficiency (see § 14B(3)), the basis for the selection of these criteria should be reported (Essential). Where a job analysis is required a complete description of the work behaviors or work outcomes, and measures of their criticality or importance should be provided (Essential). The report should describe the basis on which the behaviors or outcomes were determined to be critical or important, such as the proportion of time spent on the respective behaviors, their level of difficulty, their frequency of performance, the consequences of error, or other appropriate factors (Essential). Published descriptions from industry sources or Volume I of the Dictionary of Occupational Titles Third Edition, United States Government Printing Office, 1965, are satisfactory if they adequately and completely describe the job. If appropriate, a brief supplement to the published description should be provided. Where two or more jobs are grouped for a validity study, the information called for above should be provided for each of the jobs, and the justification for the groupings (see § 14B(1)) should be provided (Essential).

(4) *Job Titles and Codes.* It is desirable to provide the user's job title(s) for the job(s) and code(s) from United States Employment Service Dictionary of Occupational Titles Volumes I and II. Where standard titles and codes do not exist, a notation to that effect should be made.

(5) *Criteria.* A full description of all criteria on which data were collected, including a rationale for selection of the final criteria, and means by which they were observed, recorded, evaluated and quantified, should be provided (Essential). If rating techniques are used as criterion measures, the appraisal form(s) and instructions to the rater(s) should be included as part of the validation evidence (Essential). Any methods used to minimize the possibility of bias should be described.

(6) *Sample.* A description of how the research sample was selected should be included (Essential). The racial, ethnic and sex composition of the sample should be described, including the size of each subgroup (Essential). Racial and ethnic classifications should include those set forth in § 4A above. A description of how the research sample compares with the racial, ethnic and sex composition of the relevant labor market or work force is also desirable. Where data are available, the racial, ethnic and sex composition of current applicants should also be described. Descriptions of educational levels, length of service, and age are also desirable.

(7) *Selection Procedure.* Any measure, combination of measures, or procedure used as a basis for employment decisions should be completely and explicitly described or attached (Essential). If commercially available selection procedures are used, they should be described by title, form, and publisher (Essential). Reports of reliability estimates and how they were established are desirable. The various selection procedures investigated and their impacts should be described, and the rationale for choosing the selection procedure for operational use should be included (Essential).

(8) *Techniques and Results.* Methods used in analyzing data should be described (Essential). Measures of central tendency (e.g., means) and measures of dispersion (e.g., standard deviations and ranges) for all selection procedures and all criteria should be reported for all relevant racial, ethnic and sex subgroups (Essential). Statistical results should be organized and presented in tabular or graphical form, by racial, ethnic and/or sex subgroups (Essential). All selection procedure-criterion relationships investigated should be reported, including their magnitudes and directions (Essential). Statements regarding the statistical significance of results should be made (Essential). Any statistical adjustments, such as for less than perfect reliability or for restriction of score range in the selection procedure or criterion, or both, should be described; and uncorrected correlation coefficients should also be shown (Essential). Where the statistical technique used categories continuous data, such as biserial correlation and the phi coefficient, the categories and the bases on which they were determined should be described (Essential). Studies of test fairness should be included where called for by the requirements of § 14B(8) (Essential). These studies should

include the rationale by which a selection procedure was determined to be fair to the group(s) in question. Where test fairness has been demonstrated on the basis of other studies, a bibliography of the relevant studies should be included (Essential). If the bibliography includes unpublished studies, copies of these studies, or adequate abstracts or summaries, should be attached (Essential). Where revisions have been made in a selection procedure to assure compatibility between successful job performance and the probability of being selected, the studies underlying such revisions should be included (Essential).

(9) *Uses and Applications.* A description of the suitable alternative methods of using each selection procedure (e.g., as a screening device with a cutoff score or combined with other procedures in a battery) and the impacts thereof, and the rationale for choosing the method for operational use, and the intended application of the procedure (e.g., selection, transfer, promotion) should be provided (Essential). If weights are assigned to different parts of the selection procedure, these weights and the validity of the weighted composite should be reported (Essential).

(10) *Cut-off Scores.* Where cut-off scores are to be used, both the cut-off scores and the way in which they were determined should be described (Essential).

(11) *Source Data.* Each user should maintain records showing all pertinent information about individual sample members in studies involving the validation of selection procedures. These records (exclusive of names and social security number) should be made available upon request of a compliance agency. These data should include selection procedure scores, criterion scores, age, sex, minority group status, and experience on the specific job on which the validation study was conducted and may also include such things as education, training, and prior job experience. If the user chooses to include, along with a report on validation, a worksheet showing the pertinent information about the individual sample members, specific identifying information such as name and social security number should not be shown. Inclusion of the worksheet with the validity report is encouraged in order to avoid delays.

(12) *Contact Person.* It is desirable for the user to set forth the name, mailing address, and telephone number of the persons (a) who may be contacted for further information about the validity study, (b) who directed the job analysis or the review of job information, and (c) who directed the validity study.

C. *Content Validity.* Reports of content validity of selection procedures are to contain the following information:

(1) *User(s), and Location(s) and Date(s) of Study.* Date(s) and location(s) of the job analysis should be shown.

(2) *Problem and Setting.* An explicit definition of the purpose(s) of the study and the circumstances in which the study was conducted should be provided. A description of existing selection procedures and cut-off scores, if any, should be provided.

(3) *Job Analysis.* A description of the method used to analyze the job should be provided (Essential). The work behaviors, the associated tasks, and the work products should be completely described (Essential). Measures of criticality and/or importance of the work behavior and the method of determining these measures should be provided (Essential). Where the job analysis also identified the knowledges, skills, and abilities used in work behaviors, an operational definition for each knowledge, skill or ability and the relationship between each knowledge, skill or ability and each work behavior, as well as the method used to determine this relationship, should be provided (Essential). The work situation should be described including the setting in which work behaviors are performed, and where appropriate, the manner in which knowledge, skills and abilities are used, and the complexity and difficulty of knowledge, skill or ability as used in the job behavior.

(4) *Job Title and Code.* It is desirable to provide the user's job title(s) and the corresponding job title(s) and code(s) from the United States Employment Service Dictionary of Occupational Titles Volumes I and II. Where standard titles and codes do not exist, a notation to that effect should be made.

(5) *Selection Procedures.* Selection procedures including those constructed by or for the user, specific training requirements, composites of selection procedures, and any other procedure for which content validity is asserted should be completely and explicitly described or attached (Essential). If commercially available selection procedures are used, they should be described by title, form, and publisher (Essential). Where the selection procedure purports to measure terms of knowledges, skills, or abilities, evidence that the selection procedure measures those knowledges, skills or abilities should be provided (Essential).

(6) *Techniques and Results.* The evidence demonstrating that the selection procedure is a representative work sample, a representative sample of the work behavior, or a representative sample of a knowledge, skill or ability as used as a part of a work behavior and necessary for that behavior should be provided (Essential). If any steps were taken to reduce adverse racial, ethnic, or sex impact in the content of the procedure or in its administration, these steps should be described. Establishment of time limits, if any, and how these limits are related to the speed with which duties must be

performed on the job, should be explained. Measures of central tendency (e.g., means) and measures of dispersion (e.g., standard deviations) and estimates of reliability should be reported for all selection procedures as appropriate. Such reports should be made for all relevant racial, ethnic, and sex subgroups, at least on a statistically reliable sample basis.

(7) *Uses and Applications.* A description of the suitable alternative methods of using each selection procedure (e.g., as a screening device with a cutoff score or combined with other procedures in a battery) and the impacts thereof, and the evidence and rationale for choosing the method for operational use, and the intended application of the procedure (e.g., selection, transfer, promotion) should be provided (Essential).

(8) *Cut-Off Scores.* Where cut-off scores are to be used, both the cut-off scores and the way in which they were determined should be described (Essential).

(9) *Contact Person.* It is desirable for the user to set forth the name, mailing address, and telephone number of the persons (a) who may be contacted for further information about the validity study, (b) who directed the job analysis or the review of job information, and (c) who directed the validity study.

D. *Construct Validity.* Reports of construct validity of selection procedures are to contain the following information:

(1) *Problem and Setting.* An explicit definition of the purpose(s) of the study and the circumstances in which the study was conducted should be provided. A description of existing selection procedures and cut-off scores, if any, should be provided.

(2) *Construct Definition.* A clear definition of the construct should be provided, explained empirically in terms of observable behavior, including levels of construct performance relevant to the job(s) for which the selection procedure is to be used (Essential). There should be a summary of the position of the construct in the psychological literature or in the absence of such a position, a description of the way in which the definition and measurement of the construct was developed and the psychological theory underlying it.

(3) *Job Analysis.* A description of the method used to analyze the job should be provided (Essential) A complete description of the work behaviors, and to the extent appropriate, work outcomes and measures of their criticality and/or importance should be provided (Essential). The report should also describe the basis on which the behaviors or outcomes were determined to be important, such as their level of difficulty, their frequency of performance, the consequences of error or other appropriate factors (Es-

sential). Published descriptions from industry sources or Volume I of the Dictionary of Occupational Titles, Third Edition, United States Government Printing Office, 1965, are adequate if they completely and accurately describe the job. If appropriate, a brief supplement to the published description should be provided. Where two or more jobs are grouped together for a validity study, the information called for above for each job and the justification for the grouping (see § 14D a above) should be provided (Essential).

(4) *Job Titles and Codes.* It is desirable to provide the selection procedure user's job title(s) for the job(s) in question and the corresponding job title(s) and code(s) from the United States Employment Service Dictionary of Occupational Titles, Volumes I and II. Where standard titles and codes do not exist, a notation to that effect should be made.

(5) *Selection Procedure.* The selection procedure used as a measure of the construct should be completely and explicitly described or attached (Essential). If commercially available selection procedures are used, they should be identified by title, form and publisher (Essential). The research evidence of the relationship between the selection procedure and the construct should be included (Essential). Reports of reliability estimates and how they were established are desirable.

(6) *Anchoring.* The criterion related study(ies) and other empirical evidence of the relationship between the construct measured by the selection procedure and the related work behavior(s) for the job or jobs in question should be provided (Essential). Documentation of the criterion related study(ies) should satisfy the provisions of § 15B above, except for studies conducted prior to the effective date of these guidelines (Essential).

(7) *Uses and Applications.* A description of the suitable alternative methods of using each selection procedure (e.g., as a screening device with a cutoff score or combined with other procedures in a battery) and the impacts thereof, and the rationale for choosing the method for operational use, and the intended application of the procedure (e.g., selection, transfer, promotion) should be provided (Essential). If weights are assigned to different parts of the selection procedure, these weights and the validity of the weighted composite should be reported (Essential).

(8) *Cut-off Scores.* Where cut-off scores are to be used, both the cut-off scores and the way in which they were determined should be described (Essential).

(9) *Source Data.* Each user should maintain records showing all pertinent information about individual sample members in studies involving the validation of selection procedures. These records (exclusive of names and

social security number) should be made available upon request of a compliance agency. These data should include selection procedure scores, criterion scores, age, sex, minority group status, and experience on the specific job on which the validation study was conducted and may also include such things as education, training, and prior job experience. If the user chooses to include, along with a report on validation, a worksheet showing the pertinent information about the individual sample members, specific identifying information such as name and social security number should not be shown. Inclusion of the worksheet with the validity report is encouraged in order to avoid delays.

(10) *Contact Person.* It is desirable for the users to set forth the name, mailing address, and telephone number of the individual who may be contacted for further information about the validity study.

E. *Evidence of Validity from other Studies.* When validity of a selection procedure is supported by studies not done by the user, the evidence from the original study or studies should be compiled in a manner similar to that required in the appropriate section of this § 15 above. In addition, the following evidence should be supplied:

(1) *Evidence from Criterion-related Validity Studies.* a. *Job Information.* A description of the important job behaviors of the user's job and the basis on which the behaviors were determined to be important should be provided (Essential). A full description of the basis for determining that these important work behaviors are the same as those of the job in the original study (or studies) should be provided (Essential).

b. *Relevance of Criteria.* A full description of the basis on which the criteria used in the original studies are determined to be relevant for the user should be provided (Essential).

c. *Other Variables.* The similarity of important applicant pool/sample characteristics reported in the original studies to those of the user should be described (Essential). A description of the comparison between the race, sex and ethnic composition of the user's relevant labor market and the sample in the original validity studies should be provided (Essential).

d. *Use of the Selection Procedure.* A full description should be provided showing that the use to be made of the selection procedure is consistent with the findings of the original validity studies (Essential).

e. *Bibliography.* A bibliography of reports of validity of the selection procedure for the job or jobs in question should be provided (Essential). Where any of the studies included an investigation of test fairness, the results of this investigation should be provided (Essential). Copies of reports published in journals that are not commonly available should be described in detail or attached (Essential). Where a user is relying upon unpublished studies, a reasonable effort should be made to obtain these studies. If these unpublished studies are the sole source of validity evidence they should be described in detail or attached (Essential). If these studies are not available, the name and address of the source, an adequate abstract or summary of the validity study and data, and a contact person in the source organization should be provided (Essential).

(2) *Evidence from Content Validity Studies.* See § 14C(3) and § 15C above.

(3) *Evidence from Construct Validity Studies.*

a. Documentation satisfying the provision of § 15E(1) should be provided (Essential).

b. Where a study pertains to a group of jobs, and validity is asserted on the basis of the study to a job in the group, the observed work behaviors and the observed work products for each of the jobs should be described (Essential). Any other evidence used in determining whether the work behavior in each of the jobs is the same should be fully described (Essential).

Part IV—Definitions

§ 16 The following definitions shall apply throughout these guidelines:

A. *Ability:* The present observable competence to perform a function.

B. *Adverse Impact:* See § 4 of these guidelines.

C. *Compliance with these Guidelines:* Use of a selection procedure is in compliance with these guidelines if such use has been validated in accord with these guidelines (as defined in § 16P below), or if such use does not result in adverse impact on any racial, sex or ethnic group (see § 4, above), or, in unusual circumstances, if use of the procedure is otherwise justified in accord with Federal law (see § 6B, above).

D. *Content validity.* Demonstrated by data showing that a selection procedure is a representative sample of important work behaviors to be performed on the job. See § 5B and § 14C.

E. *Construct validity.* Demonstrated by data showing that the selection procedure measures the degree to which candidates have identifiable characteristics which have been determined to be important for successful job performance. See § 5B and § 14D.

F. *Criterion-related validity:* Demonstrated by empirical data showing that the selection procedure is predictive of or significantly correlated with important elements of work behavior. See § 5B and § 14B.

G. *Employer:* Any employer subject to the provisions of the Civil Rights Act of 1964, as amended, including state or local governments and any Federal agency subject to the provisions of Sec. 717 of the Civil Rights Act of 1964, as amended, and any Federal contractor or subcontractor or federally assisted construction contractor or subcontractor covered by Executive Order 11246, as amended.

H. *Employment agency:* Any employment agency subject to the provisions of the Civil Rights Act of 1964, as amended.

I. *Enforcement action:* A proceeding by a federal enforcement agency such as a lawsuit, or a formal administrative proceeding leading to debarment from or termination of government contracts, or the suspension or withholding of Federal funds; but not a finding of reasonable cause or a conciliation process by the Equal Employment Opportunity Commission or the isuance of right to sue letters under Title VII.

J. *Enforcement agency:* Any agency of the executive branch of the Federal Government which adopts these guidelines for purposes of the enforcement of the equal employment opportunity laws or which has responsibility for securing compliance with them.

K. *Labor organization:* Any labor organization subject to the provisions of the Civil Rights Act of 1964, as amended, and any committee subject thereto controlling apprenticeship or other training.

L. *Racial, sex or ethnic group:* Any group of persons identifiable on the grounds of race, color, religion, sex or national origin.

M. *Selection procedure:* Any measure, combination of measures, or procedure used as a basis for any employment decision. Selection procedures include the full range of assessment techniques from traditional paper and pencil tests, performance tests, training programs or probationary periods and physical, educational and work experience requirements through informal or casual interviews and unscored application forms.

N. *Selection Rate:* The proportion of applicants or candidates who are hired, promoted or otherwise selected.

O. *Technical feasibility:* The existence of conditions permitting the conduct of meaningful criterion related validity studies. These conditions include: (a) An adequate sample of persons available for the study to achieve findings of statistical significance; (b) having or being able to obtain a sufficient range of scores on the selection procedure and job performance measures to produce validity results which can be expected to be representative of the results if the ranges normally expected were utilized; and (c) having or being able to devise unbiased, reliable and relevant measures of job performance or other criteria of employee adequacy. See § 14B(2). With respect to investigation of possible unfairness, the same considerations are applicable to each group for which the study is made. See § 14B(8).

P. *Unfairness of Selection Procedure (differential prediction):* A condition in which members of one racial, ethnic, or sex group characteristically obtain lower scores on a selection procedure than members of another group, and the differences are not reflected in difference in measures of job performance. See § 14B(7).

Q. *Users:* Any employer, labor organization, employment agency, or licensing or certification board, to the extent it may be covered by Federal equal employment opportunity law which uses a selection procedure as a basis for any employment decision. Whenever an employer, labor organization, or employment agency is required by law to restrict recruitment for any occupation to those applicants who have met licensing or certification requirements, the licensing or certifying authority to the extent it may be covered by Federal equal employment opportunity law will be considered the user with respect to those licensing or certification requirements. Whenever a state employment agency or service does no more than administer or monitor a procedure as permitted by Department of Labor regulations, and does so without making referrals or taking any other action on the basis of the results, the state employment agency will not be deemed to be a user.

R. *Validated in accord with these Guidelines or properly validated:* One or more validity study(ies) meeting the standards of these guidelines has been conducted, including investigation and, where appropriate, use of suitable alternative selection procedures as contemplated by § 3B, and has produced evidence of validity sufficient to warrant use of the procedure for the intended purpose under the standards of these guidelines.

S. *Work behavior:* A goal directed mental or physical activity applied in performance of a job.

exhibit 6-B

comments of the Ad Hoc Group on the proposed uniform guidelines*

II. Major Policy/Legal Issues (Detailed Analysis)

Section 3B—Suitable Alternatives

When the FEA Guidelines were in the final stages of development, the Supreme Court had handed down the *Albemarle* doctrine on suitable alternatives. Specifically, the Court refused to adopt the 1970 EEOC Guideline section on the subject, and held that employers are required to show only that selection procedures are job-related; if such a showing is made, then it is the charging party's burden to show the availability of alternatives of *at least equal* validity with less adverse impact. While the final FEA Guidelines (3c) did not fully reflect the *Albemarle* language, the relevant section was sufficiently consistent to be acceptable.

The new Guidelines, however, are clearly inconsistent with and in fact propose to obliterate the *Albemarle* formulation. "At least equal" validity is now "substantially equal" validity. In addition, and contrary to professional standards, the user now is called upon to consider alternative methods of using a procedure, instead of validating it. Combinations of procedures are not precluded if they are "in compliance with these guidelines," as opposed to "properly validated." (FEA 3c.)

In summary, the Act, *Griggs* and *Albemarle* call only for a showing of the job-relatedness of procedures which adversely affect the opportunities of any group. Any suggestion to the contrary and any calls for deliberate changes in use to arrive at numerically satisfactory outcomes in lieu of validation and without supporting data violates the law's intent, as well as professional standards.

Recommendation:

Delete 3B in its entirety or restore FEA 3c, revised to include the stringent

*Dated February 17, 1978. [Preface and Part I—Need for Uniform Guidelines on Selection Procedures—omitted.]

transport requirements of 7B. Revise all related documentation requirements.

Section 4C—The Bottom Line Concept

An important foundation of any practical approach to sound guidelines is the "bottom line" concept—that employers will be judged on overall results and need not validate every procedure within a total selection process where overall results are satisfactory.

EEOC's 1970 Guidelines take the contrary view, requiring employers to validate any procedure having an adverse impact on any protected group, no matter what the overall result of the entire selection process is with respect to that group.

The new proposed uniform guidelines seem to represent a "compromise," although an unsatisfactory and ambiguous one.* In compromise, the new guidelines provide that the bottom line concept will "generally" be followed, but reserve the agencies' right to examine components.

A prior draft (October) stated:

> The federal enforcement agencies will not expect a user to evaluate the individual components for adverse impact, or to validate such individual components, and will not take enforcement action based upon adverse impact of any component of that process.

This language was similar to that of the 1976 FEA Guidelines issued by the Departments of Justice and Labor and the Civil Service Commission.** The section has now been changed to read: "The federal enforcement agencies . . . will *generally* not take enforcement . . ." [Emphasis added.] *A new*

*Thus, the Minutes of the EEOC Meeting of December 22, 1977, at which the draft Proposal was adopted for publication report:

> BLUMROSEN: . . . First, the guidelines clearly adopt a "bottom line" philosophy. . . . if the employer community secures the results of an improved equal employment opportunity, then the thesis of the guidelines is that the government will not inquire deeply into the details of the process by which it was done. . . . [T]he Commission commits itself not to take enforcement action on its own with respect to the individual component of a selection procedure where the overall selection procedure does not have an adverse impact.

But then Commissioner Leach is reported to have said: " 'That is not true. It is simply not true. . . . I want it on the record . . . that there are times when the Commission will indeed go after an employer whose bottom line may be pure, but who has a component of that selection process that is discriminatory.' "

**Note comments of Alfred W. Blumrosen, *Developments in Equal Employment Opportunity Law—1976,* 36 FED. BAR J. 55, 61-64 (1977). In analyzing *Washington* v. *Davis,* 426 *section in the definitions at the end of the guidelines defines* "enforcement action" as follows:

> *Enforcement action:* A proceeding by a federal enforcement agency such as a lawsuit, or a formal administrative proceeding leading to debarment from or termination of government contracts, or the suspension or withholding of federal funds; but *not a finding of reasonable cause or a conciliation process by the Equal Employment Opportunity Commission or the issuance of right to sue letters under Title VII.* [Emphasis added.]

First, the dilution of the agencies' commitment to the "bottom line" concept through the addition of the word "generally" is unfortunate. It can lead to uncertainty, to differential and inconsistent enforcement within an agency, and (once again) to differences among the agencies. Indeed, the EEOC Commissioners seem already to be emphasizing loopholes. Commissioner Walsh, in the December 22 meeting, declared with satisfaction: "We have not precluded the individual from filing a charge and cause being found, or conciliation being conducted, or . . . EEOC's option to go forward with the litigation under exceptional or appropriate circumstances." Vice Chair Leach went even further: "I don't feel at all inhibited as a Commissioner in exercising my 707 power [i.e., to bring a Commissioner's charge], which is really the only unique power that I have, in identifying a component of a selection process for . . . examination." Finally, Chair Norton produced a very broad reading of the term "generally":

> It is clear that in reserving its options through the use of the word "generally" this Commission has reserved its options if it wanted to sue in every case next year. . . . In other words, we're putting employers on notice without at the same time limiting ourselves.

If this is the spirit with which the EEOC approaches the "bottom line," employers may legitimately expect that they will again be presented with conflicting standards among and within the various federal EEO agencies.

The Ad Hoc Group recognizes, however, that the "bottom line" should not be an ironclad, inflexible concept, and that under unusual and aggravated circumstances (e.g., intentional use of a component to "weed out" members of a particular subgroup), inquiry into a component and en-

---

U.S. 229, 12 FEP 1415 (1976), he cited with approval the action of the District Court:

> District Judge Gesell wisely insisted on viewing the entire recruitment and hiring process as a whole. He concluded that since the process resulted in significant placements on the job, he would not apply the rigorous "validation standards" of the EEOC guidelines . . . since the judge found that there was no adverse effect from the *overall* recruitment, hiring, training and placement process, he chose not to apply the testing guidelines literally.

forcement proceedings based on its use may be appropriate, despite a "bottom line" that shows no adverse impact overall.

Second, the newly added definition of "enforcement action" (§ 16I) is far too limited in what it includes and too broad in what it excludes. It is recognized that there is a legitimate reason for the exclusion of the issuance of right to sue letters under Title VII, as an individual is entitled to bring suit if he/she chooses even where EEOC does not believe the circumstances would justify it.

The definition also omits several punitive actions that are available to the enforcement agencies and that should be eschewed as inconsistent with the "bottom line" principle. Thus not only formal, but informal penalties—such as OFCCP non-responsibility findings leading to contract pass-overs—should be included in the definition. Contract suspensions as provided for in OFCCP regulations also are enforcement actions which must be included. In short, the present language, without modification, renders the bottom line meaningless.

Recommendation:

1. Section 4C of final uniform guidelines should retain the clear "bottom line" commitment contained in the earlier October draft. If there are to be any exceptions to that commitment, they should be clearly and specifically defined in a series of questions and answers.
2. Revise 16I as follows:

> *Enforcement action:* A proceeding by a federal enforcement agency such as a lawsuit, or a formal *or informal* administrative proceeding leading to debarment from, *loss of* or termination of government contracts, or the suspension or withholding of federal *funds or contracts, or a finding of reasonable cause by the Equal Employment Opportunity Commission, or the conduct of conciliation proceedings* by any agency; but not *the investigation of a complaint or charge of discrimination by any federal agency having such investigative responsibility* or the issuance of right to sue letters under Title VII.

Section 6A—Alternative Procedures

According to *Griggs,* a showing of job-relatedness is required for any selection procedure that "adversely affects" any group. *Griggs* also holds (1) that if a selection procedure is properly validated, it is not to be considered discriminatory even though it may have an adverse impact, (2) that discriminatory preference for any group, minority or majority, is proscribed by the Act, and (3) that Congress has not commanded that the less qualified be preferred over the better qualified simply because of minority origins.

Section 6A suggests that as part of an affirmative action program or to avoid adverse impact, users "may" consciously select alternatives such as culture or language, selected use of established registers, selection from a pool of disadvantaged persons who have demonstrated their general competency, and use of registers limited to qualified persons who are economically disadvantaged. Nothing is said about the job-relatedness of these alternatives or how "general competency" or "qualified" is to be determined. Further, and whether mandatory or voluntary, the alternatives suggested are race and sex conscious devices which would govern employee selection decisions without proved or demonstrated past discrimination. Users who "choose" to follow these recommendations without such proof would thereby be violating the Act and the *Griggs* holdings cited above.

The concern raised by publication of Section 6A is intensified when one reviews reports of the EEOC position. The confusion as to the intent of Section 6A is compounded by concern that EEOC, at least, may intend to interpret these ambiguous regulations in order to discourage validation and encourage invalid race, ethnic and sex-conscious selection decisions. This possibility, perhaps inadvertently, is enhanced by remarks of EEOC Chair Norton at the December 22, 1977 meeting:

> There is not any way in which black people tomorrow as a group are going to, no matter what kind of test you give them, score the same way that white people score. . . . I can't live with that. I think employers can. And I think test validation gives them an A-1 out. Because if you validate your tests you don't have to worry about exclusion of minorities and women any longer, you have done what it seems to me is increasingly a fairly minimal thing to do . . . [u]nless somebody pushes employers to find other ways other than tests to find qualified people. . . . But I sincerely believe that tests do not tell us very much about who is qualified to do the job. . . . If I wanted really to find out whether or not you could do the job for me, I wouldn't give you the test. I'd call around and find out about you . . . the employer community has now caught on to a nice new thing, and . . . if they continue to rely as heavily on validation they could actually undercut the purposes of Title VII. . . . Thus, I think that by giving alternatives, we relieve especially minorities of the frustration they find inevitably in taking validated tests.

While Ms. Norton has consistently supported (in other statements) the right of public and private employers to hire the best qualified individual, this seeming encouragement of alternatives to validation is not easy to reconcile with that commitment.

It is unfortunate that this draft can be interpreted to contain broad hints that use of tests and other impartial selection procedures designed to operate on a non-discriminatory basis may be abandoned. It is unfortunate, too, that the draft contains overtones of repeated rejection of validity demonstrations in favor of emphasis on avoiding adverse impact only by resort to "the numbers game." Unless corrected, so as to recommend only what is lawful, the underlying practical and positive philosophy and approach of these Guidelines will be destroyed. It is counterproductive, as well as illegal, to say: "you must take a route other than valid selection procedures." It is nearly as dangerous to encourage the use of unvalidated selection procedures on a voluntary basis where the alternatives recommended are of doubtful legality if used other than to remedy proved past discrimination. The least that should be expected from government is to recommend and require only what is lawful.

Recommendation:

Since this section clearly emphasizes the use of invalid alternatives which would adversely affect groups not favored by such use, Section 6A must be removed.

At the same time, however, it should be noted that there is no disagreement with the objective of finding better ways to increase the number of employed minorities and females. While the suggestions contained in 6A are invalid, even illegal, and few, if any professionals would agree with the Chair's concept of validity, the insistence on the removal of 6A does not mean that a search for valid alternatives should be discarded. We believe that part of the answer lies in the "total assessment" concept expressed in the 1966 EEOC Guidelines. We also would be more than willing to convene a select group of professionals and practicioners from the public and private sectors to fully explore this issue and prepare recommendations for consideration by agency principals.

Section 13—Affirmative Action Policy

While § 11 of the FEA Guidelines is similar to § 13A of the Uniform Guidelines, there is one important distinction. Under the FEA Guidelines, employers are encouraged to use selection procedures to achieve affirmative action so long as those procedures are "consistent with Federal law." That phrase is deleted in the new draft.

The Alternative Procedures section, as presently written, endorses the "measures set forth in the affirmative action provisions of § 13B." Section 13B consists of a restatement of most of the Equal Employment Opportunity Coordinating Council's Policy Statement on Affirmative Action Programs for State and Local Government Agencies, issued in August, 1976.

While there is no desire to quarrel here with the concept or necessity of such a policy statement, the Ad Hoc Group questions the appropriateness of including it in guidelines on selection procedure validation. Since the purpose of guidelines is to guide employers to selection standards that will enable them to avoid violations of law, the guidelines must necessarily be a statement of *legal minima.* It is thus wholly inappropriate to use the guidelines to include provisions concerning actions that are unconcerned with testing and selection and more appropriately published elsewhere. Further, this section may be misleading by implying that the establishment of a voluntary affirmative action program such as that outlined in the Policy Statement would be a satisfactory defense to a charge growing out of the use of an unvalidated selection procedure that has an adverse impact on any group.

It also should be noted that the affirmative action statements in § 13B are cross-referenced in § 6A as providing an acceptable "alternative" procedure for employee selection. The only hint in § 13B of an alternative procedure is the declaration in paragraph (3)(d) that selection instruments that have not yet been validated may be revamped in order to reduce or eliminate their adverse impact. This may be saying no more than § 6B(ii) says, in that it may merely encourage employers to validate where possible and to minimize adverse effect where validation is not feasible. If it says more than § 6B(ii), and truly encourages the modification of selection techniques without validation (before or after the modification) then it conflicts with § 6B(ii) and makes for inconsistency. There are serious doubts about the legality of this provision if the second meaning is the one intended, since the deliberate use of unvalidated techniques in order to produce race, ethnic or sex conscious employment decisions may violate Title VII.

Finally, there are a number of instances in which the affirmative action statement is inconsistent with other sections of the draft:

1. The method for inferring disparities or adverse impact summarized in § 13B(2) involves an examination of workforce data relative to group representation in the relevant labor market. This method conflicts with the standard for determining evidence of adverse impact proposed in § 4; a standard concerned with differences in selection rates. Multiple operational definitions or standards of adverse impact can only lead to confusion with regard to enforcement actions as well as to confusion on the part of users attempting to bring their selection procedures into compliance with the guidelines.

2. Section 13B(2) requires that, when adverse impact is found, *each* element of the overall selection process be examined not only for adverse impact, but also for validity. This requirement goes beyond §§ 4C and 3A

which, taken together, suggest that if the total selection process has an adverse impact, the individual components must be investigated for adverse impact, and any component procedure found to have an adverse impact must be validated. Components of the process which do not have an adverse impact need not be validated.

3. Section 13B(2) requires that the individual elements of a total process having adverse impact be demonstrated to have "validity in *predicting* job performance [emphasis added]." This statement clearly suggests a preference for criterion-related validity, whereas § 5A supports the acceptability of each of the three validation strategies when used appropriately.

4. Section 13B(2) suggests that one element of the selection process which should be examined, if the total process has adverse impact, is "recruitment." Further, § 13B(3b) states that a user, faced with adverse impact, should consider instituting a recruitment program designed to attract qualified members of affected groups. These sections are inconsistent with § 2C which declares that "the subject of recruitment practices is not addressed" by the Uniform Guidelines.

5. References to the availability of "basically qualified person" (13B(3a)) and to "qualified persons" (13B(4)) suggest the exclusion of "well-qualified" and "best-qualified" applicants. Yet in §§ 2C and 4E, an analysis of "relative" qualifications is supported indicating that the employer has the right to select the individual most qualified to do the job. Section 13B(3e) recommends that employers initiate measures designed to assure that "qualified" members of affected groups are within the pool of persons from which the selecting official makes the selection. This is a confusion in terms and a clear invitation to violate merit systems, public or private, in which selection is made from among the "best-qualified" applicants.

Recommendation:

Delete § 13B in its entirety. Replace § 13A with FEA Guidelines § 11. Wherever else 13B is published, it should be made consistent with relevant guideline sections.

III. Major Technical Issues (Detailed Analysis)

Section 4D—The 80 Percent Rule—Use of Other Data

1. While there is a clear need for an operational standard to permit users and enforcement agency personnel to determine if adverse impact exists, the only true test of the meaning of differences is one of statistical

significance. Since the guidelines already apply that standard to smaller differences in selection rate, it also should apply to greater differences in selection rate.

The four-fifths "rule of thumb" is not a direct test of the practical or statistical significance of the difference between selection rates. It is an arbitrary standard because it is unrelated to sample size and provides no means of estimating how much confidence may be placed in the observed difference in selection rates (i.e., to what extent the differences may have occurred by chance alone). It is also a biased and inconsistent standard, since differences in selection rates vary directly with the selection rates of the majority group. If the majority group's selection rate is 100 percent, a difference of 20 percent is tolerated; if the majority group's selection rate is 10 percent (a not uncommon rate when the entire selection process is under consideration), a difference of 2 percent is tolerated. In effect, especially as selection rates drop below 50 percent, the 80 percent rule will identify trivial differences which have a high probability of occurring by chance alone as indicating adverse impact. Since selection rates above 50 percent are unusual, rates of 20 percent-30 percent are common, and rates of 10 percent are not unheard of, this has been a frequent occurrence.

As indicated, the acceptable professional method for determining whether or not an observed difference in selection rates constitutes adverse impact is a test of the statistical significance of the difference.

Recommendation:

While the four-fifths standard may remain as a general rule, the third sentence of 4D should be revised as follows:

> Greater differences in selection rate may not constitute adverse impact where the differences are based on small numbers *or* are not statistically significant . . .

2. Discounting smaller differences in selection rates ". . . where a user's actions have discouraged applicants disproportionately on racial, sex, or ethnic grounds" permits enforcement agency personnel to draw conclusions where adequate supporting proof typically is not possible. They would be free to cite utilization and/or applicant flow statistics inappropriately as evidence that discouraging user actions were somehow present. In short, the phrase represents a license to compliance agencies to violate the "smaller differences" standard at will.

Recommendation:

Delete the phrase cited.

3. The use of "evidence concerning the impact which the selection pro-

cedure had when used in the same manner in similar circumstances elsewhere "to determine adverse impact where the sample size in question is too small to be reliable" is analogous to generalizing the results of validity studies across situations which the guidelines prohibit unless specific conditions are met. Given what this draft proposes in other sections, agencies wishing to legitimately generalize from the administration of a selection procedure elsewhere, will have to provide evidence that (a) the jobs and populations are demonstrably the same, (b) the procedures are similarly administered, and (c) the subparts of the selection procedures are given the same weights and require the same minimum qualification levels.

Recommendation:

Unless the guidelines specifically require compliance agencies to meet (a), (b), and (c) above, the use of data generated elsewhere cannot be permitted.

Section 5H—Selection for Higher Level Jobs

As presently written, and so long as a majority of those *hired* do progress, this section permits a user to continue to use a procedure on a pre-hire basis to select for higher level jobs, even though post-hire procedures are systematically screening out a disproportionate number of any racial, sex, or ethnic group. Nothing is said about a validation requirement for post-hire procedures.

It is also not clear whether the "employment practices" described could be construed to include the procedure originally used to select for the higher level jobs. If such were the case, then any evidence of adverse impact resulting from the procedure, even though valid, could result in a compliance agency insisting on the more stringent "majority of those hired" standard.

Simply stated, the FEA standard should remain unchanged. Users should be permitted to select for a higher level job if it can be shown that a majority of those remaining employed progress to that job within a reasonable time. Users should be advised separately that if employment practices other than the procedure used for such selection are subsequently and systematically screening out a disproportionate number of any racial, sex, or ethnic group, then those procedures must be validated in accordance with the guidelines.

Recommendation:

Revise § 5H to include the following language:

> Evaluation for a higher level job would not be appropriate (1) if the majority of those remaining employed do not progress to the higher level job; (2) if there is reason to doubt that the higher level job will

continue to require essentially similar skills during the progression period; or (3) if knowledge, skills, or abilities required for advancement would be expected to develop principally from the training or experience on the job. If employment practices other than the procedure used for such selection are subsequently and systematically screening out a disproportionate number of any racial sex, or ethnic group, users also will be expected to either modify these procedures or show their validity in accordance with these guidelines.

Section 6B

In its present form, this section is not in accord with other guideline sections in that it presents an incomplete list of the options available to a professional or a user when validation techniques are not feasible or appropriate.

Recommendation:

Revise 6B as follows:

(i) When an unstandardized, informal, or unscored selection procedure which has an adverse impact is used, the user should (1) seek, in so far as possible, to eliminate the adverse impact or (2) demonstrate the content relatedness of the procedure, if appropriate, (3) modify the procedure, if feasible, to one which is formal and scored and then validate it in accord with these guidelines, (4) adopt a standardized selection procedure and validate it or support it (7B) in accord with these guidelines, or (5) otherwise justify continued use of the procedure in accord with Federal law.

(ii) When a standardized, formal, or scored selection procedure which has an adverse impact is used, the validation techniques contemplated by these guidelines usually should be followed, if technically feasible. Where the user cannot do so, the user should (1) modify the procedure to eliminate the adverse impact, (2) support the procedure on the basis of validity evidence obtained elsewhere (7B), (3) demonstrate the content relatedness of the procedure, if appropriate, (4) adopt another procedure which may be supported on the basis of validity evidence obtained elsewhere, or (5) otherwise justify continued use of the procedure in accord with Federal law.

Sections 7C, 7D, and 8D—Other Variables

Each of these subsections refers to "variables which are likely to affect validity significantly" in use of validity studies in situations other than that in which the original study was done. Without better definition the employer will be faced with innumerable and interminable arguments with EEOC investigators and compliance officers on factors other than predictors and criteria. In addition, if a study meets the requirements of § 14B and thus, § 7B, no additional requirements should be necessary unless they were specifically noted in the design of the original study or in the conclusions reported.

Recommendation:

Delete all reference to "variables which are likely to affect validity significantly" and permit portability upon showings of similarity of job, criterion and use.

Section 7D—Other Variables

If "other" studies are not considered applicable because they contain or do not contain "variables which are likely to affect validity significantly" the user is expected either to conduct an internal validity study or to comply with § 6. Section 6 includes a provision for use of alternative procedures which will produce "affirmative action" with no consideration of the validity of these alternative procedures. This will of necessity trigger guideline requirements since it will discriminate against any group not favored by the alternatives.

Recommendation:

Delete this reference and § 6A.

Section 14B(2)—Criterion Bias

This section leaves the impression that evidence of rating bias can be (1) identified, (2) quantified, and (3) eliminated, when none of these objectives is truly possible to achieve. It must be recognized that when there are significant differences in rating measures of job performance for different groups, the amount of difference, if any, which is attributable to true performance difference or other kinds of bias is impossible to measure. The user community and professional practices would be served better if the guidelines followed *Albemarle* and general professional opinion by advising users that while the absence of bias cannot be assured, supervisory ratings should be focused or based on specific critical or important job duties, work behaviors, work requirements, or work outcomes, and instructions to the raters should be detailed and carefully developed in order to maximize the objectivity of the procedure.

Recommendation:

Revise § 14B(2) to include the following language:

> The possibility of bias should be considered both in the selection of criterion measures and in their application. In view of the possibility of

bias in subjective evaluations and recognizing that the absence of bias cannot be assured, supervisory rating techniques should be focused on specific critical or important work behavior, work outcome, work requirements, or job duties, and instructions to the raters should be detailed and carefully developed so as to maximize rater objectivity.

Section 14B(8)—Fairness

The rationale for inclusion of 14B(8) in guidelines is stated quite clearly in its subsection (a) "When members of one ethnic, racial, or sex group characteristically obtain lower scores on a selection procedure than members of another group, and the differences are not reflected in differences in measures of job performance, use of the selection procedure may unfairly deny opportunities to members of the group that obtains the lower scores." One sentence thus describes the theory of differential prediction—that tests valid for whites might be less valid or invalid for blacks and other affected subgroups, thus unjustly handicapping them for employment consideration by predicting a lower level of job performance than they would actually achieve if hired.

At the time of its espousal in the mid-1960s, the differential theory generated an instant and hopeful reaction, particularly as it applied to blacks. It hypothesized that because of cultural differences and deprivations, test scores achieved by blacks could have a different meaning than test scores achieved by whites; that given the chance, blacks would perform better on the job than their test scores would indicate and at a higher level than whites with similar test scores would perform. If pursued to its logical conclusion through a major program of basic research, the prediction error the theory assumed to exist for blacks and other subgroups could be corrected.

Unfortunately, however, as a consequence of its extremely positive appeal and a lack of understanding that laws and regulations dealing with controversial social and political issues are exceptionally resistant to change, the theory of differential prediction was incorporated into the 1968 OFCC Testing Order. The net result of this action was to transform an *essentially untested* theory, which should have remained a subject for free scientific research with federal support, into a required pursuit with federal sanctions for non-compliance. With the unilateral issuance of the 1970 EEOC Guidelines the requirement was extended, without provision for comment, to all employers then covered by the Civil Rights Act of 1964.

Free and major research nevertheless went on and, in 1972, the findings of the first major study on the subject were released (See J. Campbell, et al., *An Investigation of Sources of Bias in the Prediction of Job Performance: A Six Year Study*). Funded by the Ford foundation and conducted jointly by Educational Testing Service and the U.S. Civil Service Commission, the study involved a variety of jobs and a variety of ethnic groups and measurement techniques and *failed to find any substantial evidence of the existence of the differential validity phenomenon.* To the contrary, the research found that minorities not only tended to score lower on the tests studied, but also tended to perform poorer on the job to at least the same degree. The results and implications of this landmark study were perhaps best summarized in the following statement by the late S. Rains Wallace, one of the most respected professionals in the field of industrial psychology:

> It appears to me to be about time for us to accept the proposition that written aptitude tests, administered correctly and evaluated against reasonably reliable, unbiased, and relevant criteria, do about the same job in one ethnic group as in another. It seems clear that people like me who expected race to act as a moderator variable for validity relationships were wrong. . . . In short, differential or single group validity is an artifact of small samples, inequalities in restrictions or their correction, or biases in criteria.

In the months which followed the Campbell report, the body of research data continued to grow, all leading to a similar conclusion: the theory of differential prediction was not supportable by the evidence. At the same time, the mathematical soundness of many of the early 1960 studies purporting to find the phenomenon was severely discredited. (See L. Humphries, *Statistical Definition of Test Validity for Minority Groups,* 58 Journal of Applied Psychology 1-4, 1973). More sophisticated analyses of earlier results additionally showed that the experimental findings purporting to support the concept could be accounted for by chance and thus proved nothing. (See F. Schmidt et al., *Racial Differences in Validity of Employment Tests: Reality or Illusion?* 58 Journal of Applied Psychology, 509, 1973; see also E. J. O'Connor et al., *Single Group Validity: Fact or Fallacy?* 60 Journal of Applied Psychology, 352-355, 1975.)

In summary, the theory of differential prediction on the basis of subgroup membership has been demonstrated to have no scientific merit and to be no better than a chance phenomenon. Test fairness considerations implied by the differential validity hypothesis have been similarly discredited. The federal agencies issuing these guidelines, including the U.S. Civil Service Commission, which participated in the first major demonstration of the non-existence of differential prediction, and the U.S. Department of Labor, which thus far has had similar results with its GATB research, are nevertheless proposing to require public and private employers to seek what they, the agencies, have not been able to find themselves, and to pursue what the vast majority of professionals now believe to be nothing more than a chance phenomenon. In short, differential validity-prediction and fairness concepts are not developing ones. They have been discredited and sample size and general feasibility considerations are therefore irrelevant. The issue is whether such a requirement in guidelines is still supportable, and the weight of evidence indicates that it is not. Further, if findings of "unfairness" are not regarded as chance occurrences and this guideline proposal is followed, the result typically will be the counterproductive establishment of *higher* cut-off scores for blacks than for whites.

Recommendation:

Remove all references to differential prediction and fairness.

Section 14C—Content Validity

The content validity section of the FEA Guidelines (12c) is the product of an extensive four-year effort to develop content validity definitions and requirements which would reflect professional opinion and practice and be understandable. What is there resulted from repeated reviews by professionals and the professional societies and was finally endorsed by these same groups.

The authors of this draft have chosen to ignore that history and endorsement, and have injected concepts and terms which are still the subject of considerable discussion and uncertainty among professionals in the field. As a consequence, this Proposal's treatment of content validity confuses rather than clarifies, and attempts to lead professional thought, rather than reflect it.

Recommendations:

Revise 14C as follows. Revise all related documentation and definition sections.

(1) Users choosing to adopt a content validity strategy should determine whether it is appropriate to do so in the particular employment context.

(2) A demonstration of the relationship between the content of a selection procedure and a content domain or domains of the job is critical to content validity. Content validity may be shown if the knowledges, skills or abilities measured by the selection procedure are substantially the same as the knowledges, skills or abilities shown to be critical or important to the job content domain(s). The closer the content of the selection procedure is to actual work samples, or behaviors, or activities required by the job, the stronger is the basis for showing content validity. The need for careful docu-

mentation of the relationship between the content of the selection procedure and the content domain of the job increases as the content of the selection procedure less resembles that of the job content domain.

(3) There should be a clear definition of the content domain(s) of the job(s) in question. Job content domains may be defined through a job analysis of the work behaviors or activities of the job and/or by the pooled judgments of persons having knowledge of the job. Job content domains should be defined on the basis of competent information about job tasks and responsibilities and include critical or important work behaviors, work products, work activities, job duties, or the knowledges, skills or abilities shown to be necessary for performance of the duties, behaviors, activities or the production of work. Where a job content domain has been defined as a knowledge, skill or ability, that knowledge, skill or ability must be used in job behavior. A selection procedure based on inferences about psychological processes cannot be supported by content validity alone. Thus content validity by itself is not an appropriate validation strategy for intelligence, aptitude, personality, leadership, spatial ability, or interest tests. Content validity also is not an appropriate strategy when the selection procedure involves knowledges, skills or abilities which an employee will be expected to learn within a short period of time on the job.

(4) A selection procedure which is a representative sample of a content domain of the job as defined in accordance with subsection (3) above is a content valid procedure for that domain. Where the domain or domains measured are critical to the job, or constitute a substantial proportion of the job, the selection procedure will be considered to be content valid for the job, and may be used operationally for that job. The reliability of selection procedures justified on the basis of content validity should be a matter of concern to the user. Whenever it is feasible to do so, appropriate statistical estimates should be made of the reliability of the selection procedures.

(5) A selection procedure designed to sample a content domain of the job may be developed specifically from the job and job analysis in question, or may have been previously developed by the user, other users, or a test publisher.

(6) If a user can show, by a job analysis or otherwise, that a higher score on a content valid selection procedure is likely to result in better job performance, the results may be used to rank persons

who score above minimum levels. Where a selection procedure supported solely or primarily by content validity is used to rank job candidates, the selection procedure should measure those aspects of performance which differentiate among levels of job performance.

(7) A requirement for specific prior training or for work experience based on content validity, including a specification of level or amount of training or experience, should be justified on the basis of the relationship between the content of the training or experience and the content of the job domain(s) for which the training or experience is to be required.

(8) Where a training program is used as a selection procedure and the content of a training program is justified on the basis of content validity, it should be justified on the relationship between the content of the training program and the content of the job domain(s).

Section 14D(1)b—Construct Validity

There is a concern that the wording of the empirical evidence requirement of this section can be construed to require a criterion-related validity study for every job for which construct validity is claimed. If such were the outcome, the recognition of construct validity as a separate and equal validation strategy becomes meaningless.

Recommendation:

Revise the last sentence of 14D(1)b to read as follows:

> The relationship between the construct measured by the procedure and the related work behavior(s) should be supported by empirical evidence from one or more criterion-related studies involving the job or a reasonable number of the group of jobs in question . . .

Section 14D(2)b—Construct Validity

This section appears to reflect a misunderstanding of construct validation. If the observable portion of two jobs is the same, jobs are likely to be the same job. Hence there is no need for construct validation. One simply does a criterion-related study on the job. Constructs by definition also are not observable. If two jobs have some observable components in common there may be evidence of commonality of constructs in work behaviors, but many jobs can involve the same constructs and have few common observable job components.

Recommendation:

Rewrite 14D(2)b as follows:

> In determining whether two or more jobs have one or more work behaviors in common, the user should compare the work behaviors in each of the jobs and the work products in each of the jobs. If neither the work behaviors nor the work products are the same, the Federal enforcement agencies will presume that the jobs are dissimilar.

Section 15B(7)—Documentation

While validity estimates of various selection procedures investigated may be known, data concerning their impact is a function of their use and will not be available in any meaningful form.

Recommendation:

Delete the impact data requirement.

Sections 15B(9), 15C(7), 15D(7)—Documentation

The use of a selection procedure in any manner other than that suggested by the available validity and/or job analysis data is inconsistent with professional standards. The impact of the recommended use of such procedures also is often not known until long after the report is prepared. Finally, any suggestion that users are required to consider or implement alternative, quota-based usage of validated procedures is inconsistent with professional standards and with what the law and *Griggs* permits or requires users to do.

Recommendation:

Delete all reference to impact data and alternative methods of use.

Section 15E(1a)—Documentation

It must be specifically stated that comparisons of jobs may be made on the basis of job duties. The present definition of the term "work behavior" creates the impression that jobs may be compared only on the basis of mental or physical activities required to perform these duties.

Recommendation:

Revise this section to permit job comparisons on the basis of job duties.

Section 15E(1c)—Documentation

Quite apart from the fact that the presence of other variables will seldom be of significant magnitude to affect validity in a transport situation, the data called for is typically not available in the literature, or in reports or manuals. Also, a subgroup comparison between the original research sample and the user's relevant labor market is not relevant in validity transport considerations. The other variables concept stems from the hypothesis that there are sample or population characteristics that are likely to moderate validity from location to location. Recent research (e.g., Zedeck, 1971; Schmidt, *et al,* 1976, 1977) indicates that the concept of moderator variables is not a viable one insofar as their effect on validity is concerned.

Recommendation:

Delete this section.

IV. The Ad Hoc Group

The Ad Hoc Group includes many organizations representing the private sector, including The Business Roundtable, National Association of Manufacturers, Labor Policy Association, National Retail Merchants Association, Edison Electric Institute, American Society for Personnel Administration, American Paper Institute, American Petroleum Institute, American Iron & Steel Institute, the College and University Placement Association, Master Printers of America, Organization Resources Counselors, National Federation of Independent Businesses and the U.S. Chamber of Commerce, as well as representatives of the following companies: AT&T, American Can, Caterpillar Tractor, Citibank, N.A., Dow Chemical, DuPont, Eastman Kodak, Exxon, Firestone Tire & Rubber, Ford Motor, General Electric, General Motors, W.R. Grace, IBM, International Paper, Marcor, Minnesota, Mining & Manufacturing, Prudential Insurance, Reynolds Metals, Sears Roebuck, Shell Oil, Travelers Insurance, and United Parcel Service. The Ad Hoc Group's Technical Subcommittee includes a substantial number of prominent industrial and measurement psychologists, many of whom have been or are in leadership positions in the American Psychological Association and its Division of Industrial-Organizational Psychology.

In addition, members of public sector groups have attended Ad Hoc working sessions and contributed to our recommendations. These include the International Personnel Management Association, and representatives of the International City Managers Association, the National Association of Counties, the Governor's Association, the National League of Cities, the Conference of Mayors, the Conference of State Legislatures and the Council of State Governments.

exhibit 7

Standard Form 100
(Rev 12-76)
Approved GAO B-180541 (R0077)
Expires 12-31-78

EQUAL EMPLOYMENT OPPORTUNITY
EMPLOYER INFORMATION REPORT EEO-1

Joint Reporting Committee

- Equal Employment Opportunity Commission
- Office of Federal Contract Compliance Programs

Section A — TYPE OF REPORT
Refer to instructions for number and types of reports to be filed.

1. Indicate by marking in the appropriate box the type of reporting unit for which this copy of the form is submitted (MARK ONLY ONE BOX).

(1) ☐ Single-establishment Employer Report

Multi-establishment Employer:
(2) ☐ Consolidated Report
(3) ☐ Headquarters Unit Report
(4) ☐ Individual Establishment Report (submit one for each establishment with 25 or more employees)
(5) ☐ Special Report

2. Total number of reports being filed by this Company (Answer on Consolidated Report only)______________

Section B — COMPANY IDENTIFICATION *(To be answered by all employers)* | OFFICE USE ONLY

1. Parent Company
   a. Name of parent company (owns or controls establishment in item 2) omit if same as label — a.

Name of receiving office				Address (Number and street)	b.
City or town	County	State	ZIP code	b. Employer Identification No.	

2. Establishment for which this report is filed. (Omit if same as label)
   a. Name of establishment — c.

Address (Number and street)	City or town	County	State	ZIP code	d.

b. Employer Identification No. (If same as label, skip.)

3. Parent company affiliation (Multi-establishment Employers: Answer on Consolidated Report only)

a. Name of parent—affiliated company			b. Employer Identification No.	
Address (Number and street)	City or town	County	State	ZIP code

Section C — EMPLOYERS WHO ARE REQUIRED TO FILE *(To be answered by all employers)*

☐ Yes ☐ No 1. Does the entire company have at least 100 employees in the payroll period for which you are reporting?

☐ Yes ☐ No 2. Is your company affiliated through common ownership and/or centralized management with other entities in an enterprise with a total employment of 100 or more?

☐ Yes ☐ No 3. Does the company or any of its establishments (a) have 50 or more employees AND (b) is not exempt as provided by 41 CFR 60-1.5, AND either (1) is a prime government contractor or first-tier subcontractor, and has a contract, subcontract, or purchase order amounting to $50,000 or more, or (2) serves as a depository of Government funds in any amount or is a financial institution which is an issuing and paying agent for U.S. Savings Bonds and Savings Notes?

NOTE: If the answer is yes to ANY of these questions, complete the entire form; otherwise skip to Section G.

Section D — EMPLOYMENT DATA

Employment at this establishment--Report all permanent, temporary, or part-time employees including apprentices and on-the-job trainees unless specifically excluded as set forth in the instructions. Enter the appropriate figures on all lines and in all columns. Blank spaces will be considered as zeros.

JOB CATEGORIES	NUMBER OF EMPLOYEES										
		MALE					FEMALE				
	OVERALL TOTALS (SUM OF COL. B THRU K) A	WHITE (NOT OF HISPANIC ORIGIN) B	BLACK (NOT OF HISPANIC ORIGIN) C	HISPANIC D	ASIAN OR PACIFIC ISLANDER E	AMERICAN INDIAN OR ALASKAN NATIVE F	WHITE (NOT OF HISPANIC ORIGIN) G	BLACK (NOT OF HISPANIC ORIGIN) H	HISPANIC I	ASIAN OR PACIFIC ISLANDER J	AMERICAN INDIAN OR ALASKAN NATIVE K
Officials and Managers											
Professionals											
Technicians											
Sales Workers											
Office and Clerical											
Craft Workers (Skilled)											
Operatives (Semi-Skilled)											
Laborers (Unskilled)											
Service Workers											
TOTAL											
Total employment reported in previous EEO-1 report											

(The trainees below should also be included in the figures for the appropriate occupational categories above)

Formal On-the-job trainees		A	B	C	D	E	F	G	H	I	J	K
	White collar											
	Production											

1. NOTE: On consolidated report, skip questions 2-5 and Section E.
2. How was information as to race or ethnic group in Section D obtained?
   1 ☐ Visual Survey
   2 ☐ Employment Record
   3 ☐ Other — Specify ....
3. Dates of payroll period used –
4. Pay period of last report submitted for this establishment
5. Does this establishment employ apprentices?
   This year? 1 ☐ Yes 2 ☐ No
   Last year? 1 ☐ Yes 2 ☐ No

Section E — ESTABLISHMENT INFORMATION

1. Is the location of the establishment the same as that reported last year?
   1 ☐ Yes 2 ☐ No 3 ☐ Did not report last year 4 ☐ Reported on combined basis
2. Is the major business activity at this establishment the same as that reported last year?
   1 ☐ Yes 2 ☐ No 3 ☐ No report last year 4 ☐ Reported on combined basis
3. What is the major activity of this establishment? (Be specific, i.e., manufacturing steel castings, retail grocer, wholesale plumbing supplies, title insurance, etc. Include the specific type of product or type of service provided, as well as the principal business or industrial activity.

OFFICE USE ONLY

e.

Section F — REMARKS

Use this item to give any identification data appearing on last report which differs from that given above, explain major changes in composition or reporting units, and other pertinent information.

Section G — CERTIFICATION (See instructions G)

Check one
1. ☐ All reports are accurate and were prepared in accordance with the instructions (check on consolidated only)
2. ☐ This report is accurate and was prepared in accordance with the instructions.

Name of Certifying Official	Title	Signature	Date

Name of person to contact regarding this report (Type or print)	Address (Number and street)				
Title	City and State	ZIP code	Telephone Area Code	Number	Extension

All reports and information obtained from individual reports will be kept confidential as required by Section 709 (e) of Title VII

WILLFULLY FALSE STATEMENTS ON THIS REPORT ARE PUNISHABLE BY LAW, U.S. CODE, TITLE 18, SECTION 1001

JOINT REPORTING COMMITTEE
- Equal Employment Opportunity Commission
- Office of Federal Contract Compliance Programs

EQUAL EMPLOYMENT OPPORTUNITY COMMISSION
WASHINGTON, D.C.

EQUAL EMPLOYMENT OPPORTUNITY

STANDARD FORM 100, EMPLOYER INFORMATION REPORT EEO-1
(RCS: GAO No. B189541—R077, Expires 12-31-78)
100-110

INSTRUCTION BOOKLET

Under Public Law 88-352, Title VII of the Civil Rights Act of 1964, as amended by the Equal Employment Opportunity Act of 1972, all employers that have 15 or more employees are required to keep records and to make such reports to the Equal Employment Opportunity Commission as are specified in the regulations of the Commission. See the Appendix for the applicable provisions of the law, Section 709(c) of Title VII and the applicable regulations, Section 1602.7-1602.14, Subpart B, Chapter XIV, Title 29 of the Code of Federal Regulations. State and local governments, school systems and educational institutions are covered by other employment surveys and are excluded from Standard Form 100, Employer Information Report EEO-1

In the interests of consistency, uniformity and economy, Standard Form 100 has been jointly developed by the Equal Employment Opportunity Commission and the Office of Federal Contract Compliance Programs of the U.S. Department of Labor, as a single form which meets the statistical needs of both programs. In addition, this form should be a valuable tool for companies to use in evaluating their own internal programs for insuring equal employment opportunity.

As stated above, the filing of Standard Form 100 is required by law; it *is not voluntary*. Under Section 709(c) of Title VII, the Equal Employment Opportunity Commission may compel an employer to file this form by obtaining an order from a United States District Court.

Under Section 209(a) of Executive Order 11246 the penalties for failure by a Federal contractor or subcontractor to comply may include termination of the Federal government contract and debarment from future Federal contracts.

1. WHO MUST FILE

Standard Form 100 must be filed by—

(A) All private employers who are: (1) subject to Title VII of the Civil Rights Act of 1964 (as amended by the Equal Employment Opportunity Act of 1972) with 100 or more employees EXCLUDING State and local governments, primary and secondary school systems, institutions of higher education, Indian tribes and tax-exempt private membership clubs other than labor organizations; OR (2) subject to Title VII who have fewer than 100 employees if the company is owned or affiliated with another company, or there is centralized ownership, control or management (such as central control of personnel policies and labor relations) so that the group legally constitutes a single enterprise, and the entire enterprise employs a total of 100 or more employees.

(B) All Federal contractors (private employers) who: (1) are not exempt as provided for by 41 CFR 60-1.5, (2) have 50 or more employees, and (a) are prime contractors or a first-tier subcontractor, and have a contract, subcontract, or purchase order amounting to $50,000 or more; or (b) serve as a depository of Government funds in any amount or, (c) is a financial institution which is an issuing and paying agent for U.S. Savings Bonds and Notes.

Only those establishments located in the District of Columbia and the 50 states are required to submit Standard Form 100. No reports should be filed for establishments in Puerto Rico, the Virgin Islands or other American Protectorates.

2. HOW TO FILE

The Standard Form 100 is a five-part snapout form. File the original and first two copies with the Joint Reporting Committee. The remaining two copies may be retained for employer records.

All single-establishment employers, i.e. employers doing business at only one establishment in one location, must complete a single Standard Form 100.

All multi-establishment employers, i.e. employers doing business at more than one establishment must file (1) a report covering the principal or headquarters office; (2) a separate report for each establishment employing 25 or more persons; and (3) a consolidated report. The consolidated report MUST include ALL employees by race, sex and job category in establishments with 25 or more employees as well as establishments with fewer than 25 employees; (4) a list, showing the name, address, total employment and major activity for each establishment employing fewer than 25 persons, must accompany the consolidated report. The total number of employees indicated on the headquarters report, the establishment reports, and the list of establishments with fewer than 25 employees, *must* equal the total number of employees shown on the consolidated report.

All forms for a multi-establishment company should be collected by the headquarters office for its establishments or by the parent corporation for its subsidiary(s) and submitted in one package.

The term **parent corporation** refers to any corporation which owns all or the majority stock of another corporation so that the latter stands in the relation to it of a subsidiary. Where a parent corporation is shown to control the operations or labor policies of its subsidiary(s), they constitute a single legal entity for employment purposes.

3. WHEN TO FILE

This annual report must be filed with the Joint Reporting Committee no later than March 31.

Employment figures from any pay period in January through March may be used. Those previously reporting year-end figures may continue to do so.

4. WHERE TO FILE

The completed report should be forwarded in one package to the address indicated in the attached memorandum.

5. REQUESTS FOR INFORMATION AND SPECIAL PROCEDURES (Formerly Section 4(C))

An employer who claims that preparation or the filing of Standard Form 100 would create undue hardship may apply to the Commission for a special reporting procedure. In such cases, the employer should submit in writing an alternative proposal for compiling and reporting information to: The EEO-1 Coordinator, 2401 E Street, NW., Washington, D.C. 20506.

Only those special procedures approved in writing by the Commission are authorized. Such authorizations remain in effect until notification of cancellation is given. All requests for information should be sent to the same address.

Computer printouts may be substituted for all types of EEO-1 reports (headquarter's, individual establishments, special reports) EXCEPT the consolidated report. The consolidated report MUST be prepared on the actual EEO-1 form. Additionally, computer printouts MUST contain ALL address label codes and COMPLETE information for each item on the printed form.

All computer printouts which do not include complete information will be returned for correction. Sample printouts may be submitted for approval prior to final submission.

6. CONFIDENTIALITY

All reports and information from individual reports will be kept confidential, as required by Section 709(e) of Title VII. Only data aggregating information by industry or area, in such a way as not to reveal any particular employer's statistics, will be made public. The prohibition against disclosure mandated by Section 709(e) does not apply to the Office of Federal Contract Compliance Programs and contracting agencies of the Federal Government which require submission of SF 100 pursuant to Executive Order 11246. Reports from prime contractors and subcontractors doing business with the Federal Government may not be confidential under Executive Order 11246.

HOW TO PREPARE STANDARD FORM 100

Definitions of Terms and Categories are Located in the Appendix

SECTION A—TYPE OF REPORT

Check one box indicating type of report.

SECTION B—COMPANY IDENTIFICATION

Item 1—Parent Company. Please provide company name, receiving office, address and employer identification number of the headquarter's office of a multi-establishment company.

Item 2—Establishment For Which This Report Is Filed. Please provide the name, address and employer identification number of each company establishment where 25 or more persons are employed; if different from the label.

Item 3—Parent Company Affiliation (consolidated report only). Please provide the name, address and employer identification number of the company which owns all or the majority stock of the company shown in Item 1 or centrally controls or manages same.

Employer Identification Number refers to the 9-digit number which an employer has been assigned by Internal Revenue for tax and business income tax reporting purposes.

SECTION C—EMPLOYERS WHO ARE REQUIRED TO FILE

Questions 1 thru 3 must be answered by all employers. If the answer is "Yes" to question 1, 2 or 3, complete the entire form. Otherwise, skip to Section G.

SECTION D—EMPLOYMENT DATA

Employment data must include ALL full-time, part-time and temporary employees who were employed during the selected payroll period, except those employees specifically excluded as indicated in the Appendix. Employees must be counted by sex, race/ethnic category for each of the nine occupational categories.

Establishments located in Hawaii will report only total employment in columns A, B, and G. All male employees should be reported in column B regardless of race/ethnic designation; and all female employees should be reported in column G regardless of race/ethnic designation.

On-the-job trainees should be reported in each column, where appropriate, as well as in the space provided at the bottom of Section D.

a. Race/Sex Data—See Appendix for detailed explanation of job categories and race/ethnic identification.

Every employee must be accounted for in one and only one of the categories in Columns B thru K.

b. Occupational Data—Employment data must be reported by job category. Report each employee in *only one* job category. In order to simplify and standardize the method of reporting, all jobs are considered as belonging in one of the broad occupations shown in the table. To assist you in determining where to place your jobs within the occupational categories, a description of job categories is in the Appendix. For further clarification, you may wish to consult the Alphabetical and Classified Indices of Industries and Occupations (1970 Census) published by the U.S. Department of Commerce, Census Bureau.

SECTION E—ESTABLISHMENT INFORMATION

All questions must be answered. Questions 2 and 3 refer to the major product or group of products manufactured or distributed, or services rendered. The major activity should be sufficiently descriptive to identify the industry and product produced or service provided. If an establishment is engaged in more than one activity, describe the activity at which the greatest number of employees work.

SECTION F—REMARKS

Include in this section any remarks, explanations, or other pertinent information regarding this report.

SECTION G—CERTIFICATION

If all reports have been completed at headquarters, the authorized official should check Item No. 1 and sign the consolidated report only.

If the reports have been completed by the individual establishments, the authorized official should check Item No. 2 and sign the establishment report.

APPENDIX

1. DEFINITIONS APPLICABLE TO ALL EMPLOYERS

a. "Commission" refers to the Equal Employment Opportunity Commission.

b. "OFCCP" refers to the Office of Federal Contract Compliance Programs, U.S. Department of Labor, established to implement Executive Order 11246 (dated September 24, 1965).

c. "Joint Reporting Committee" is the committee representing the Commission and OFCCP for the purpose of administering this report system.

d. "Employer," under Section 701(b), Title VII of the Civil Rights Act of 1964 as amended by the Equal Employment Opportunity Act of 1972 means a person engaged in an industry affecting commerce who has fifteen or more employees for each working day in each of twenty or more calendar weeks in the current or preceding calendar year, and any agent of such a person, but such term does not include the United States, a corporation wholly owned by the Government of the United States, an Indian tribe, or any department or agency of the District of Columbia subject by statute to procedures of the competitive service (as defined in section 2102 of Title 5 of the United States Code), or a bona fide private membership club (other than a labor organization) which is exempt from taxation under Section 501(c) of the Internal Revenue Code of 1954; OR any person or entity subject to Executive Order 11246 who is a Federal Government prime contractor or subcontractor at any tier (including a bank or other establishment serving as a depository of Federal Government funds, or an issuing and paying agent of U.S. Savings Bonds and Notes, or a holder of a Federal Government bill of lading) or a federally-assisted construction prime contractor or subcontractor at any tier.

e. "Employee" means any individual on the payroll of an employer who is an employee for purposes of the employer's withholding of Social Security taxes except insurance salesmen who are considered to be employees for such purposes solely because of the provisions of Section 3121(d)(3)(B) of the Internal Revenue Code. The term "employee" SHALL NOT include persons who are hired on a casual basis for a specified time, or for the duration of a specified job, and work on remote or scattered sites or locations where it is not practical or feasible for the employer to make a visual survey of the work force within the report period; for example, persons at a construction site whose employment relationship is expected to terminate with the end of the employee's work at the site; persons temporarily employed in any industry other than construction, such as seamen, longshoremen, waiters, movie extras, agricultural laborers, lumbermen, etc., who are obtained through a hiring hall or other referral arrangement, through an employee contractor or agent, or by some individual hiring arrangement; or persons on the payroll of a temporary service agency who are referred by such agency for work to be performed on the premises of another employer under that employer's direction and control.

It is the opinion of the General Counsel of the Commission that Section 702, Title VII of the Civil Rights Act of 1964, as amended, does not authorize a complete exemption of religious organizations from the coverage of the Act or of the reporting requirements of the Commission. The exemption for religious organizations applies to discrimination on the basis of religion. Therefore, since Standard Form 100 does not provide for information as to the religion of employees, religious organizations must report all information required by this form.

f. "Commerce" means trade, traffic, commerce, transportation, transmission, or communication among the several States; or between a State and any place outside thereof; or within the District of Columbia, or a possession of the United States; or between points in the same State but through a point outside thereof.

g. "Industry Affecting Commerce" means any activity, business or industry in commerce or in which a labor dispute would hinder or obstruct commerce or the free flow of commerce and includes any activity or industry "affecting commerce" within the meaning of the Labor Management Reporting and Disclosure Act of 1959. Any employer of 15 or more persons is presumed to be in an "industry affecting commerce."

h. "Employer Identification Number" is the 9-digit number which each legal entity (corporation, partnership, or sole proprietorship) has been assigned on the basis of its application (Form SS-4) to Internal Revenue Service for an identification number, and is used to identify the company on all company reports to the Social Security Administration and to the Internal Revenue Service. This number should also be used on all employer information reports and communications concerning these reports.

i. "Establishment" is an economic unit which produces goods or services, such as factory, office, store, or mine. In most instances, the establishment is at a single physical location and is engaged in one, or predominantly one, type of economic activity (definition adapted from the 1957 Standard Industrial Classification Manual).

Units at different physical locations, even though engaged in the same kind of business operation should be reported as separate establishments. For locations involving construction, transportation, communications, electric, gas, and sanitary services, oil and gas fields, and similar types of physically dispersed industrial activities, however, it is not necessary to list separately each individual site, project, field, line, etc., unless it is treated by you as a separate legal entity with a separate EI number. For these types of activities, list as establishments only those relatively permanent main or branch offices, terminals, stations, etc., which are either (a) directly responsible for supervising such dispersed activities, or (b) the base from which personnel and equipment operate to carry out these activities. (Where these dispersed activities cross State lines, at least one such "establishment" should be listed for each State involved.)

j. "Major Activity" means the major product or group of products produced or handled, or services rendered by the reporting unit (e.g., manufacturing airplane parts, retail sales of office furniture) in terms of the activity at which the greatest number of all employees work. The description includes the type of product manufactured or sold or the type of service provided.

2. DEFINITIONS APPLICABLE ONLY TO GOVERNMENT CONTRACTORS SUBJECT TO EXECUTIVE ORDER 11246

a. "Order" means Executive Order 11246, dated September 24, 1965.

b. "Contract" means any Government contract or any federally assisted construction contract.

c. "Prime Contractor" means any employer having a Government contract or any federally assisted construction contract, or any employer serving as a depositary of Federal Government funds.

d. "Subcontractor" means any employer having a contract with a prime contractor or another subcontractor calling for supplies or services required for the performance of a Government contract or federally assisted construction contract.

e. "Contracting Agency" means any department, agency and establishment in the executive branch of the Government, including any wholly owned Government corporation, which enters into contracts.

f. "Administering Agency" means any department, agency and establishment in the executive branch of the Government, including any wholly owned Government corporation, which administers a program involving federally assisted construction contracts.

g. "Compliance Agency" means the agency designated by the Director of the Office of Federal Contract Compliance Programs to conduct compliance reviews and to undertake such other responsibilities in connection with the administration of Executive Order 11246 as the Director may determine to be appropriate.

3. RESPONSIBILITIES OF PRIME CONTRACTORS

a. At the time of an award of a subcontract subject to these reporting requirements, the prime contractor shall inform the subcontractor of its responsibility to submit annual information reports in accordance with these instructions and, where necessary, provide the subcontractor with copies of Standard Form 100 which it shall obtain from its compliance agency.

b. If prime contractors are required by their compliance agencies, or subcontractors by their prime contractors, to submit notification of filing, they shall do so by ordinary correspondence. However, such notification is not required by and should not be sent to the Joint Reporting Committee.

4. RACE/ETHNIC IDENTIFICATION

You may acquire the race/ethnic information necessary for this report either by visual surveys of the work force, or from post-employment records as to the identity of employees. Eliciting information on the race/ethnic identity of an employee by direct inquiry is not encouraged.

Where records are maintained, it is recommended that they be kept separately from the employee's basic personnel file or other records available to those responsible for personnel decisions.

Since visual surveys are permitted, the fact that race/ethnic identifications are not present on employment records is not an excuse for failure to provide the data called for.

Moreover, the fact that employees may be located at different addresses does not provide an acceptable reason for failure to comply with the reporting requirements. In such cases, it is recommended that visual surveys be conducted for the employer by persons such as supervisors who are responsible for the work of the employees or to whom the employees report for instructions or otherwise.

Please note that conducting a visual survey and keeping post-employment records of the race/ethnic identity of employees is legal in all jurisdictions and under all Federal and State laws. State laws prohibiting inquiries and recordkeeping as to race, etc., relate only to applicants for jobs, not to employees.

Race/Ethnic designations as used by the Equal Employment Opportunity Commission do not denote scientific definitions of anthropological origins. For the purposes of this report, an employee may be included in the group to which he or she appears to belong, identifies with, or is regarded in the community as belonging. However, no person should be counted in more than *one* race/ethnic group. The race/ethnic categories used for this survey are:

White (Not of Hispanic origin)—All persons having origins in any of the original peoples of Europe, North Africa, the Middle East, or the Indian subcontinent.

Black (Not of Hispanic origin)—All persons having origins in any of the black racial groups.

Hispanic—All persons of Mexican, Puerto Rican, Cuban, Central or South American, or other Spanish culture or origin, regardless of race.

Asian or Pacific Islander—All persons having origins in any of the original peoples of the Far East, Southeast Asia, or the Pacific Islands. This area includes, for example, China, Japan, Korea, the Philippine Islands, and Samoa.

American Indian or Alaskan Native—All persons having origins in any of the original peoples of North America.

5. DESCRIPTION OF JOB CATEGORIES

Officials and managers.—Occupations requiring administrative personnel who set broad policies, exercise overall responsibility for execution of these policies, and direct individual departments or special phases of a firm's operations. Includes: officials, executives, middle management, plant managers, department managers, and superintendents, salaried foremen who are members of management, purchasing agents and buyers, and kindred workers.

Professional.—Occupations requiring either college graduation or experience of such kind and amount as to provide a comparable background. Includes: accountants and auditors, airplane pilots, and navigators, architects, artists, chemists, designers, dietitians, editors, engineers, lawyers, librarians, mathematicians, natural scientists, registered professional nurses, personnel and labor relations workers, physical scientists, physicians, social scientists, teachers, and kindred workers.

Technicians.—Occupations requiring a combination of basic scientific knowledge and manual skill which can be obtained through about 2 years of post high school education, such as is offered in many technical institutes and junior colleges, or through equivalent on-the-job training. Includes: computer programmers and operators, drafters, engineering aides, junior engineers, mathematical aides, licensed, practical or vocational nurses, photographers, radio operators, scientific assistants, surveyors, technical illustrators, technicians (medical, dental, electronic, physical science), and kindred workers.

Sales.—Occupations engaging wholly or primarily in direct selling. Includes: advertising agents and salesworkers, insurance agents and brokers, real estate agents and brokers, stock and bond salesworkers, demonstrators, salesworkers and sales clerks, grocery clerks and cashier-checkers, and kindred workers.

Office and clerical.—Includes all clerical-type work regardless of level of difficulty, where the activities are predominantly nonmanual though some manual work not directly involved with altering or transporting the products is included. Includes: bookkeepers, cashiers, collectors (bills and accounts), messengers and office helpers, office machine operators, shipping and receiving clerks, stenographers, typists and secretaries, telegraph and telephone operators, and kindred workers.

Craft Worker (skilled).—Manual workers of relatively high skill level having a thorough and comprehensive knowledge of the processes involved in their work. Exercise considerable independent judgment and usually receive an extensive period of training. Includes: the building trades, hourly paid supervisors and lead operators who are not members of management, mechanics and repairers, skilled machining occupations, compositors and typesetters, electricians, engravers, job setters (metal), motion picture projectionists, pattern and model makers, stationary engineers, tailors and tailoresses, and kindred workers.

Operatives (semiskilled).—Workers who operate machine or processing equipment or perform other factory-type duties of intermediate skill level which can be mastered in a few weeks and require only limited training. Includes: apprentices (auto mechanics, plumbers, bricklayers, carpenters, electricians, machinists, mechanics building trades, metalworking trades, printing trades, etc.), operatives, attendants (auto service and parking), blasters, chauffeurs, delivery workers, dressmakers and seamstresses (except factory), dryers, furnace workers, heaters (metal), laundry and dry cleaning operatives, milliners, mine operatives and laborers, motor operators, oilers and greasers (except auto), painters (except construction and maintenance), photographic process workers, stationary firefighters, truck and tractor drivers, weavers (textile), welders, and flamecutters, and kindred workers.

Laborers (unskilled).—Workers in manual occupations which generally require no special training perform elementary duties that may be learned in a few days and require the application of little or no independent judgment. Includes: garage laborers, car washers and greasers, gardeners (except farm) and groundskeepers, stevedores, wood choppers, laborers performing lifting, digging, mixing, loading and pulling operations, and kindred workers.

Service workers.—Workers in both protective and nonprotective service occupations. Includes: attendants (hospital and other institutions, professional and personal service, including nurses aides, and orderlies), barbers, charworkers and cleaners, cooks (except household), counter and fountain workers, elevator operators, firefighters and fire protection, guards, doorkeepers, stewards, janitors, police officers and detectives, porters, waiters and waitresses, and kindred workers.

On-the-job trainees:

Production.—Persons engaged in formal training for craft worker—when not trained under apprentice programs—operative, laborer and service occupations.

White collar.—Persons engaged in formal training, for official, managerial, professional, technical, sales, office and clerical occupations.

6. LEGAL BASIS FOR REQUIREMENTS

SECTION 709(c), TITLE VII, CIVIL RIGHTS ACT OF 1964

(As Amended by the Equal Employment Opportunity Act of 1972)

Recordkeeping; reports

Every employer, employment agency, and labor organization subject to this title shall (1) make and keep such records relevant to the determinations of whether unlawful employment practices have been or are being committed, (2) preserve such records for such periods, and (3) make such reports therefrom as the Commission shall prescribe by regulation or order, after public hearing, as reasonable, necessary, or appropriate for the enforcement of this title or the regulations or orders thereunder. The Commission shall, by regulation, require each employer, labor organization, and joint labor-management committee subject to this title which controls an apprenticeship or other training program to maintain such records as are reasonably necessary to carry out the purposes of this title, including, but not limited to, a list of applicants who wish to participate in such program, including the chronological order in which applications were received, and to furnish to the Commission upon request, a detailed description of the manner in which persons are selected to participate in the apprenticeship or other training program. Any employer, employment agency, labor organization, or joint labor-management committee which believes that the application to it of any regulation or order issued under this section would result in undue hardship may apply to the Commission for an exemption from the application of such regulation or order, and, if such application for an exemption is denied, bring a civil action in the United States district court for the district where such records are kept. If the Commission or the court, as the case may be, finds that the application of the regulation or order to the employer, employment agency, or labor organization in question would impose an undue hardship, the Commission or the court, as the case may be, may grant appropriate relief. If any person required to comply with the provisions of this subsection fails or refuses to do so, the United States district court for the district in which such person is found, resides, or transacts business, shall, upon application of the Commission, or the Attorney General in a case involving a government, governmental agency or political subdivision, have jurisdiction to issue to such person an order requiring him to comply.

TITLE 29, CHAPTER XIV, CODE OF FEDERAL REGULATIONS

Subpart B—Employer Information Report

§ 1602.7 Requirement for filing of report.

On or before March 31, 1967, and annually thereafter, every employer subject to Title VII of the Civil Rights Act of 1964 which meets the 100-employee test set forth in Section 701(b) thereof shall file with the Commission or its delegate executed copies of Standard Form 100, as revised (otherwise known as "Employer Information Report EEO–1") in conformity with the directions set forth in the form and accompanying instructions. Notwithstanding the provisions of Section 1602.14, every such employer shall retain at all times at each reporting unit, or at company or divisional headquarters, a copy of the most recent report filed for each such unit and shall make the same available if requested by an officer, agent or employee of the Commission under the authority of section 710(a) of Title VII. Appropriate copies of Standard Form 100 in blank will be supplied to every employer known to the Commission to be subject to the reporting requirements, but it is the responsibility of all such employers to obtain necessary supplies of same prior to the filing date from the Joint Reporting Committee, Federal Depot, 1201 East 10th Street, Jeffersonville, Indiana 47130.

§ 1602.8 Penalty for making of willfully false statements on report.

The making of willfully false statements on Report EEO–1 is a violation of the United States Code, Title 18, section 1001, and is punishable by fine or imprisonment as set forth therein.

§ 1602.9 Commission's remedy for employer's failure to file report.

Any employer failing or refusing to file Report EEO–1 when required to do so may be compelled to file by order of a U.S. District Court, upon application of the Commission.

§ 1602.10 Employer's exemption from reporting requirements.

If an employer is engaged in activities for which the reporting unit criteria described in section 4(c) of the Instructions are not readily adaptable, special reporting procedures may be required. In such case, the employer should so advise by submitting to the Commission or its delegate a specific proposal for an alternative reporting system prior to the date on which the report is due. If it is claimed the preparation or filing of the report would create undue hardship, the employer may apply to the Commission for an exemption from the requirements set forth in this part.

§ 1602.11 Additional reporting requirements.

The Commission reserves the right to require reports other than that designated as the Employer Information Report EEO–1, about the employment practices of individual employers or groups of employers whenever, in its judgment, special or supplemental reports are necessary to accomplish the purposes of Title VII. Any system for the requirement of such reports will be established in accordance with the procedures referred to in section 709(c) of Title VII and as otherwise prescribed by law.

Subpart C—Recordkeeping by Employers

§ 1602.12 Records to be made or kept.

The Commission has not adopted any requirement, generally applicable to employers, that records be made or kept. It reserves the right to impose recordkeeping requirements upon individual employers or groups of employers subject to its jurisdiction whenever, in its judgment, such records (a) are necessary for the effective operation of the EEO–1 reporting system or of any special or supplemental reporting system as described above; or (b) are further required to accomplish the purposes of Title VII. Such recordkeeping requirements will be adopted in accordance with the procedures referred to in section 709(c), and as otherwise prescribed by law.

§ 1602.13 Records as to racial or ethnic identity of employees.

Employers may acquire the information necessary for completion of Items 5 and 6 of Report EEO–1 either by visual surveys of the work force, or at their option, by the maintenance of post-employment records as to the identity of employees where the same is permitted by State law. In the latter case, however, the Commission recommends the maintenance of a permanent record as to the racial or ethnic identity of an individual for purpose of completing the report form only where the employer keeps such records separately from the employee's basic personnel form or other records available to those responsible for personnel decisions, e.g., as part of an automatic data processing system in the payroll department.

§ 1602.14 Preservation of records made or kept.

(a) Unless the employer is subject to a State or local fair employment practice law or regulation governing the preservation of records and containing requirements inconsistent with those stated in this part, any personnel or employment record made or kept by an employer (including but not necessarily limited to application forms submitted by applicants and other records having to do with hiring, promotion, demotion, transfer, lay-off or termination, rates of pay or other terms of compensation, and selection for training or apprenticeship) shall be preserved by the employer for a period of 6 months from the date of the making of the record or the personnel action involved, whichever occurs later. In the case of involuntary termination of an employee, the personnel records of the individual terminated shall be kept for a period of 6 months from the date of termination. Where a charge of discrimination has been filed, or an action brought by the Attorney General, against an employer under Title VII, the respondent employer shall preserve all personnel records relevant to the charge or action until final disposition of the charge or the action. The term "personnel records relevant to the charge," for example, would include personnel or employment records relating to the charging party and to all other employees holding positions similar to that held or sought by the charging party; and application forms or test papers completed by an unsuccessful applicant and by all other candidates for the same position as that for which the charging party applied and was rejected. The date of "final disposition of the charge or the action" means the date of expiration of the statutory period within which a charging party may bring an action in a U.S. District Court or, where an action is brought against an employer either by a charging party or by the Attorney General, the date on which such litigation is terminated.

(b) The requirements of this section shall not apply to application forms and other pre-employment records of applicants for positions known to applicants to be of a temporary or seasonal nature.

exhibit 8

survey of current employment*

(This survey should be prepared by each organizational unit and job categories should indicate those in same line of progression)

		TOTAL EMPLOYEES			MINORITY GROUP EMPLOYEES							
					MALE				FEMALE			
JOB CATEGORIES	Wage/Salary or Grade	Total Employees	Total Male	Total Female	N	SSA	O	AI	N	SSA	O	AI
OFFICIALS AND MANAGERS Total												
PROFESSIONALS Total												

* This and other sample forms are examples only. They are not officially required forms. This Chart is similar to the EEO-1 Reporting Form which must be filed annually by all employers of more than 100 persons and by government contractors [See Exhibit 7]. For internal affirmative action audits, more detailed information is needed to identify levels of jobs and compensation. This chart suggests subdivisions under each major job category, which may indicate common job classifications, skill groupings and/or salary range. Note: Government contractors are required to conduct separate utilization analyses for minorities and females. Many employers thus find it useful to record detailed data separately for these groups. However, this is not required. It is necessary that data indicate breakdowns by race and sex, as above.

survey of current employment—*Contd.*

JOB CATEGORIES	Wage/Salary or Grade	TOTAL EMPLOYEES Total Employees	Total Male	Total Female	MINORITY GROUP EMPLOYEES MALE N	SSA	O	AI	FEMALE N	SSA	O	AI	
OPERATIVES (SEMI-SKILLED) Total													
LABORERS (UNSKILLED) Total													
SERVICE WORKERS Total													

TOTALS

survey of current employment—*Contd.*

JOB CATEGORIES	Wage/Salary or Grade	TOTAL EMPLOYEES: Total Employees	Total Male	Total Female	MINORITY GROUP EMPLOYEES: MALE				FEMALE			
					N	SSA	O	AI	N	SSA	O	AI
SALES WORKERS Total ___												
OFFICE & CLERICAL Total ___												
CRAFTSMEN (SKILLED) Total ___												

Source: U.S. Equal Employment Opportunity Commission, *Affirmative Action and Equal Employment: A Guidebook for Employers,* (Vol. 1) (Washington, D.C.: U.S. Government Printing Office, January 1974), pp. 24-A through 24-C.

exhibit 9

affirmative action program analysis of relevant work area

FORM Y

	MALE							FEMALE					
	Non-minority	Negro	SSA	Oriental	American Indian	TOTAL MALE		Non-minority	Negro	SSA	Oriental	American Indian	TOTAL FEMALE
% of population labor area surrounding facility													
% of present work-force at facility													
unemployment of labor area surrounding facility (%)													
availability of those with requisite skills in reasonable recruiting area (%)	SEE FORM 2 →												
availability of women seeking employment in recruitment area # %	X						# / %						
availability of promotable or transferable women from within the organization	X												

Organizational Unit __________

Location __________

Name of Person Preparing Data __________

Date __________

SAMPLE

Training institutions capable of training persons in the requisite skills.

Training which organizational unit is able to undertake as a means of making all job classes available to women.

Source: U.S. Equal Employment Opportunity Commission, *Affirmative Action and Equal Employment: A Guidebook for Employers* (Vol. 2) (Washington, D.C.: U.S. Government Printing Office, January 1974), pp. A-22, A-23.

FORM Z

affirmative action program—*Contd.*
availability of requisite skill persons by job category in reasonable recruiting area

	RELEVANT LABOR AREA*	MALE							FEMALE					
		Non-Minority	Negro	SSA	Oriental	American Indian	TOTAL MALE		Non-Minority	Negro	SSA	Oriental	American Indian	TOTAL FEMALE
Officials & Managers														
Professionals														
Technicians														
Sales														
Office & Clerical														
Craftsmen (Skilled)														
Operatives (Semi-skilled)														
Laborers (Unskilled)														
Service Workers														

SAMPLE

*Relevant Labor Area Codes

N National
R Regional
S State
A SMSA
C County
L City

exhibit 10

data sources for utilization analysis and developing affirmative action goals*

Much data on various minorities and females in the population and workforce of relevant labor areas and their general or specific skills can be obtained from national, state and local sources. You may find it difficult to get exact numerical information on females or minorities with specific skills who are available in your area. The following resources should be helpful. However, excessive data collection is not necessary if your own employment survey reveals absence or serious underrepresentation of any group. Affirmative efforts to locate and/or train females and minorities for jobs where they are not represented will be more productive than intensive effort to locate data justifying their underutilization.

I. Census Bureau, U.S. Department of Commerce, Washington, D.C. 20233.

Basic data on population, education, employment and occupational status may be obtained from the following publications:

A. *1970 Census of Population: General Social and Economic Characteristics PC (1)-C Series.* Separate reports for each State, with data on age, race, sex, Spanish heritage, mother tongue, years of school completed, vocational training, employment status, occupation, industry, and other factors. Data is presented for Counties, Standard Metropolitan Statistical Areas (SMSA's), Urban Areas, and Places of 2500 Inhabitants or More. Total cost of 53 reports: $121.75 Individual state report costs vary. Order from Superintendent of Documents, U.S. Government Printing Office, Washington, D.C. 20402, or U.S. Commerce Department Field Offices.

Source: U.S. Equal Employment Opportunity Commission, *Affirmative Action and Equal Employment: A Guidebook for Employers* (Vol. 2) (Washington, D.C.: U.S. Government Printing Office, January 1974), pp. B-1 through B-5.

*Publications are free unless otherwise noted. See page [505] for new Affirmative Action data "package" prepared by U.S. Department of Labor.

B. *1970 Census of Population, Detailed Characteristics PC (1) D Series.* More detailed breakdowns of educational, vocational training and occupations cross-classified by sex, age and race. Information available for nation, states, SMSA's and large urban areas. For details and prices write: Publications Distribution Section, Bureau of Census, U.S. Department of Commerce, Washington, D.C. 20233, or Superintendent of Documents (see above).

C. *U.S. Census of Population 1970, Final Report PC (2) 7 (C) Occupation by Industry.* Breakdowns by race, national origin and sex. $7.25 (from Superintendent of Documents, address above).

D. *U.S. Census of Population Final Report PC (2) 8 (B). Earnings by Occupation and Education.* Detailed breakdowns by industry, race, sex, national origin. $4.50 from Superintendent of Documents (address above).

E. *Maps—Number of Indians by Counties of the United States:* 1970 (GE-50 No. 549); *Number of Negro Persons by Counties of the United States:* 1970 (GE-50 No. 47); and *Negro Population As Percentage of Total Population by Counties of the United States:* 1970 (GE-50 No. 48)—may be obtained for 50 cents each from the Superintendent of Documents, U.S. Government Printing Office, Washington, D.C. 20402, or from Commerce Department District Offices in major cities.

II. Women's Bureau, Employment Standards Administration, U.S. Department of Labor, Washington, D.C. 20210.

A. *A Guide to Sources of Data on Women and Women Workers for the United States and for Regions, States and Local Areas.*

This comprehensive guide lists major data sources on population, education, civilian labor force, employment, unemployment, occupation, industry and labor reserve, indicating in each case whether data is available by region, state, or SMSA. It includes basic data sources on minorities as well as women. Cited are: materials from Census Bureau, U.S. Department of Health, Education & Welfare, and extensive materials from U.S. Department of Labor's Bureau of Labor Statistics and Employment Standards Administration.

Also available from the Women's Bureau:

B. *Women Workers in Regional Areas and in Large States and Metropolitan Areas. (1971).*

C. *Facts on Women Workers of Minority Races. (1972).*

The Women's Bureau regularly prepares tabulations by State of selected data on women workers. Request data on particular states from the Bureau.

III. Equal Employment Opportunity Commission,
Office of Research, 2121 K St., N.W., Washington, D.C. 20506.

Job Patterns for Minorities and Women in Private Industry, 1970, Volumes I and II.

Numbers employed in companies filing EEO-1 reports, by industry, industry group, major occupation group, sex and minority group; for the nation, states and SMSA's. (More recent data is available on microfilm). Data on minority and female participation in Joint Apprenticeship Programs also is available.

IV. Bureau of Labor Statistics, U.S. Department of Labor,
Washington, D.C. 20210.

A. *Geographic Profile of Employment and Unemployment* (Annual). Data on labor Force, employment, unemployment, by race and sex, for the nation, states and for SMSA's.

The Bureau of Labor Statistics (BLS) also has other useful publications, such as:

B. *Occupational Outlook Handbook,* (1972-73 edition). Estimates, among other data, the number and proportion of women to total employed in selected occupations. National data. $6.25.*

C. *Employment and Earnings* (monthly). Major occupation groups and selected subgroups of employed persons by race and sex. Race and sex breakdowns on national data only. Single copies $1.00, annual subscription $10.00.*

D. *Industry Wage Surveys.* Data for selected occupations within individual industries by sex. Areas covered vary. Write Bureau of Labor Statistics for list and cost of individual reports.

V. Educational Data Sources

A. *Statistics Concerning Doctorates Awarded to Women.* Available from Association of American Colleges, Project on the Status and Education of Women, 1818 R St., N.W., Washington, D.C. 20009. A compilation of three (3) studies indicating percentage of doctorates awarded to women in various disciplines, and by specific institutions for the period 1953-1969.

*Publications marked * are available from Superintendent of Documents, Government Printing Office, Washington, D.C. 20402, at price indicated.

B. *Earned Degrees Conferred 1969-70: Part A. Summary Data; Part B. Institutional Data.* National Center for Educational Statistics, Office of Education, U.S. Department of Health, Education and Welfare. (annual). Part B provides details on degrees conferred by sex, field and level at individual institutions, grouped by state. Part A. $.50; Part B. $5.00 from Government Printing Office, Washington, D.C. 20402. *1970-71 Edition available:* Write Government Printing Office for price.

C. *Students Enrolled for Advanced Degrees, Part A. Summary Data; Part B. Detailed Data by Institution.* Enrollment by sex, full-time and part-time attendance, nationally, and by institution. (Annual) Part A $.55, Part B $2.25. Available from Government Printing Office, address above.

D. *Fall Enrollment in Higher Education.* Enrollment by Sex, full-time and part-time attendance, nationally, and by institution. (Annual) Available from Government Printing Office, address above. $2.00.

E. *American Science Manpower 1970.* National Science Foundation. Available from Superintendent of Documents, Government Printing Office, Washington, D.C. 20402. $2.00. Detailed data by sex on numbers, specialties, employment status, earnings, etc.

F. *Summary Reports, Doctorate Recipients from U.S. Universities.* (Annual Reports from 1969-1972). National Research Council, National Academy of Science, 2101 Constitution Ave., N.W., Washington, D.C. 20418. Field of doctorate, present area of employment and other data by sex. 1973 survey will include race.

G. *Equal Employment Opportunity for Minority Graduates* [see Exhibit 14, p. 539] is also a good information source on minority graduates.

VI. State and local data sources

In addition to sources already listed, the following sources can provide useful detailed local data:

A. *State and Local Employment Services.* Basic data and special studies on employment and unemployment. Many State Services prepare special skill employment and unemployment surveys, market studies, etc. Contact Offices of Research, Employer Relations or Labor Market staff at state level.

B. *State and City Department of Human Resources, and Departments of Industry, Labor or Commerce* also prepare employment, unemployment and skill surveys. A listing of major state (as well as Federal) agencies concerned with manpower, employment, industrial relations and fair employment practices that can provide data and information on training programs and recruitment sources is: *Labor Offices in the United States and Canada,* Employment Standards Administration, U.S. Department of Labor, Washington, D.C. 20210.

C. *Local and State Chambers of Commerce.* (Consult telephone directory).

D. *Regional Offices, Equal Employment Opportunity Commission.* Further assistance on data and recruitment sources.

E. *Regional Offices, Manpower Administration, U.S. Department of Labor.* Information on employment, training and job programs.

F. *Regional Offices, Women's Bureau, U.S. Department of Labor.*

G. Local offices of Urban League, Urban Coalition, and other minority organizations.

New data "package" for affirmative action from U.S. Department of Labor.

The Labor Department has announced availability of standardized "packets" of local work force statistics, including minimum data needed to analyze "underutilization" of minorities and women for Affirmative Action Plans. Data "packets" will be available at State Employment Security Offices for some areas starting in November, 1973, and are expected to be available for all areas by Spring 1973. The packets will include recent information by sex and minority status on: population and labor force, employment status, occupations of employed persons, last occupations of experienced unemployed workers and occupational characteristics of job applicants at public employment offices.

exhibit 11

FORM XX

SAMPLE

—affirmative action program

goals & timetables analysis

* N = Nation
R = Regional
S = State
A = SMSA
C = County
L = City

Page 1 of 2

					CURRENT EQUAL OPPORTUNITY STATUS																														
			Total by Sex		FEMALE EMPLOYEES					MALE EMPLOYEES						RELEVANT LABOR AREA										UNDERUTILIZATION									
																FEMALE					MALE					FEMALE					MALE				
																										NM	N	SSA	O	AI	NM	N	SSA	O	AI
JOB FAMILY	Salary Grade	Total Employees as of (date)	Male	Female	Non-Minority	Negro	SSA	Oriental	American Indian	Non-Minority	Negro	SSA	Oriental	American Indian	Natl., Reg., State, SMSA*, City, County	Non-Minority	Negro	SSA	Oriental	American Indian	Non-Minority	Negro	SSA	Oriental	American Indian	Col. 17X(3-6)	Col. 18X(3-7)	Col. 19X(3-8)	Col. 20X(3-9)	Col. 21X(3-10)	Col. 22X(3-11)	Col. 23X(3-12)	Col. 24X(3-13)	Col. 25X(3-14)	Col. 26X(3-15)
			No.	No.												%	%	%	%																
Column # 1	2	3	4	5	6	7	8	9	10	11	12	13	14	15	16	17	18	19	20	21	22	23	24	25	26	27	28	29	30	31	32	33	34	35	36

Source: U.S. Equal Employment Opportunity Commission, *Affirmative Action and Equal Employment: A Guidebook for Employers* (Vol. 2) (Washington, D.C.: U.S. Government Printing Office, January 1974), pp. A-24 through A-28.

FORM XX

goals and timetables analysis

Page 2 of 2

Location ______________
Organizational Unit ______________
Name of Person filling out form ______________
Date ______________

PROJECTED EQUAL OPPORTUNITY STATUS																															
5 YEAR GOAL (Net Change)										Projected Total Employees Next 12 Months	Projected Turnover Next 12 Months	Net Job Openings	Promotables Next 12 Months									GOAL NEXT 12 MONTHS Period Covered ______									
FEMALE					MALE								MINORITY				FEMALE					FEMALES (Net Change)					MALES (Net Change)				
Non-Minority	Negro	SSA	Oriental	American Indian	Non-Minority	Negro	SSA	Oriental	American Indian				N	SSA	O	AI	NM	N	SSA	O	AI	Non-Minority	Negro	SSA	Oriental	American Indian	Non-Minority	Negro	SSA	Oriental	American Indian
Column 37	38	39	40	41	42	43	44	45	46	47	48	49	50	51	52	53	54	55	56	57	58	59	60	61	62	63	64	65	66	67	68

SAMPLE

FORM XX

Column 1

List each job family in the organizational unit having a similar level of skill and/or wage (salary) and the same relevant labor area. Since goals are to be set by the job family the relevant labor area for the job group must be the same.

Column 2

List the salary grade(s) for each job family.

Column 3

Total number of employees, male and female, minority and non-minority. Date is the last day of the month in which this form is filled out.

Column 4-5

Total male employees and female employees respectively, regardless of minority or non-minority group.

Column 6-10

Number of female employees by the groups indicated.

Columns 11-15

Number of male employees by the groups indicated.

Column 16

Since your labor market area varies with the level of the job category, indicate for each job grouping the area; e.g. U.S., Midwest, Indiana, Dallas SMSA, Bartholomew County, Columbus. Note! Where the percent of the minorities to the total population is greatly diluted by using the broader area, the unit may be required to use the smaller area. On the other hand, you may be required to extend your normal relevant labor area where a large minority community is within reasonable distance (approximately 50 miles). The recruitment area for exempt employees is usually national, although in some instances regional recruitment is acceptable.

Column 17

Percent non-minority females are represented in the labor force of your relevant labor area.

Columns 18-21

Percent each minority female group is represented in the population of your relevant labor area. This figure is applied in each job grouping as explained above.

1970 Census Series
Source material: PC(1)-B-C-D
See above information.

Column 22

Column 22 has been added for two reasons: (1) non-minority males are typically underutilized in the Office and Clerical category and in job categories and/or departments having a disproportionate high concentration of minorities, and (2) you can show the percent change of non-minority males as you add minorities and women to the job category. You need not obtain statistics on non-minority males from census reports. Merely arrive at this figure by subtracting total percent of all other groups (all women and all minorities) from 100 percent.

Columns 23-26

Percent each male minority group is represented in the population of your relevant labor area. Apply percent figure same as explained above.

> Note! The same percent figure is used in each job grouping having the same relevant labor area. For example, if the relevant labor area for supervisors, craftsmen and below is the same, then the same percent figure is used.
>
> Source material: Same as for minority females.

Columns 27-36

Note computation formula at the top of each column; e.g., to obtain underutilization on non-minority (NM) females, multiply column 17 by column 3 and subtract column 6.*

Columns 37-46

Both 12 month and 5 year goals are required. You are asked to insert figures you believe you can reach based on existing availability of qualified and qualifiable people; anticipated availability of people, projected manpower needs; amount of training you can conduct; extent to which your organization can actively work with training and educational institutions to encourage minorities and women to prepare themselves for work in your industry, etc. In many categories you will be expected to reach minority (male and female) population and labor force (non-minority female) parity within the five years depending on the skill level, education required, experience necessary, seniority system, and so on. For those job groups in which you do not set the parity

*The "computation formula" typed at the top of columns 27-36 reads 17 x (3-6). The parenthesis is wrongly placed. It should read (17 x 3)-6 and similarly for each of the columns following. (EEOC Memo, June 26, 1974.)

figure (i.e., the same figure as in the "underutilization" column), you should state specifically the reasons for a smaller figure. In short, the figures inserted in columns 37-46 should be the same as columns 27-36 but if they are not the same, please explain.

Note! The numbers of employees shown in Columns 37-46 are net figures, therefore, they are not total employees you should have in five years, but total additions to your present workforce.

Column 47

Reflect expected expansion or contractions of each job grouping.

Column 48

As used here turnover means replacement of people who terminate either voluntarily or involuntarily. Insert net turnover; i.e., do not include those openings that will be filled by employees with recall rights, by promotions and by transfers. Also, where you reduce your work force and you do not replace people who quit or are terminated, this will affect your turnover.

Column 49

Number of vacancies you intend to fill once you have accounted for expansion or contraction and turnover. For example:

Column 47 = 50 employees represents increase of 2 employees where present workforce is 48.
Column 48 = 3 employees quit and you intend to replace them.
Column 49 = 5 (2 new jobs + 3 replacements)

Column 50-58

Number of minorities (male and female) and non-minority females you expect to promote within the next 12 months. As used here promotables means those people whom you have identified as having the qualifications (or will have within the next 12 months) to fill a higher job and such higher job(s) will be open within the next 12 months. If you have more qualified minorities and/or women than you have job openings, so indicate on the comment sheet. (Attach separate list of promotables where no jobs are open in the next 12 months.)

Columns 59-68

Number of each group you plan to add or subtract to each job group the next 12 months. Do not insert a figure representing present employees plus additions.

Please total all your figures and insert dates.

FORM P

exhibit 12

affirmative action plan applicant flow data

(Organization Unit) ____________________

(Location) ____________________

(Time Period) ____________________

Person Preparing Report ____________________

DATE	NAME	RACE	SEX	POSITION APPLYING FOR	REFERRAL SOURCE	EED CATEGORY OF JOB	DISPOSITION *	Complete only if hire: JOB TITLE	DATE OF HIRE	RATE OF PAY	ORG. UNIT WHO HIRED

1 - Interviewed, no offer
2 - Interviewed, offer extended, & hired
3 - Interviewed, offer extended, but rejected

Source: U.S. Equal Employment Opportunity Commission, *Affirmative Action and Equal Employment: A Guidebook for Employers* (Vol. 2) (Washington, D.C.: U.S. Government Printing Office, January 1974), A-16.

exhibit 13

principles for the validation and use of personnel selection procedures

Division of Industrial Organizational Psychology, American Psychological Association (1975)

Foreword

Because of growing concern over professional standards for employee selection research, I was instructed by the Division 14 Executive Committee at its August, 1974, meeting to appoint an ad hoc committee to develop an appropriate set of principles for the validation and use of personnel selection procedures. This document resulted. Its objective is to provide Division 14 members with professionally developed guidelines which they can follow in conducting validation research.

Robert M. Guion was appointed chairperson of the committee and Mary L. Tenopyr was named to work with him in drafting the document. Twenty-six Division members were appointed to review the various drafts and to advise on the content and style of the document. In addition, the April, 1975, issue of *The Industrial-Organizational Psychologist* announced the availability of the third draft of the *Principles* to members of the Division who might wish to review and comment on the document. A number of Division members took advantage of this opportunity. Furthermore, comments and suggestions regarding the *Principles* were solicited and obtained from the Committee on Psychological Tests and Assessment of the American Psychological Association.

Dr. Guion's qualifications as chairperson of the ad hoc committee are innumerable. Among many that could be cited are his roles as principal author of *Standards for Educational and Psychological Tests,* published by APA, and as a former member of the advisory committee on testing to the Office of Federal Contract Compliance. Dr. Tenopyr also served on the OFCC advisory committee and is widely recognized by the profession for her many contributions to psychological testing and its applications to employee selection.

At its May, 1975, meeting the Executive Committee of Division 14 reviewed the final draft of the *Principles* and authorized its publication. This is, therefore, an official document of the Division of Industrial and Organizational Psychology.

I extend the gratitude of our Division to Drs. Guion and Tenopyr for their effective efforts in writing the *Principles,* to the members of the ad hoc committee who advised on the document, to the Division 14 members who offered many useful comments and suggestions, to the members of the APA Committee on Psychological Tests and Assessment for their help, and to Dr. Arthur C. MacKinney who arranged for its publication.

DONALD L. GRANT
President

Principles for the Validation and Use of Personnel Selection Procedures

Statement of Purpose

This statement of principles has been adopted by the Executive Committee of the Division of Industrial—Organizational Psychology, American Psychological Association, as the official statement of the Division concerning procedures for validation research, personnel selection, and promotion. The purpose is to outline principles of good practice in the choice, development, and evaluation of personnel selection procedures. When using standardized tests or other selection procedures, the essential principle is that evidence be accumulated to show a relationship between decisions based on assessments made by a given procedure and subsequent criteria, such as job performance, training performance, permanence, advancement, and other job behavior.

This statement intends to provide:

(1) principles upon which personnel research may be based,
(2) guidance for practitioners conducting validation,
(3) principles of use of valid selection procedures, and
(4) information which may be interpreted for personnel managers and

others who may be responsible for authorizing or implementing validation efforts.

The interests of some people will not be addressed by this statement. These principles are not intended to:

(1) be a technical translation of existing or anticipated legislation,

(2) substitute for textbooks outlining validation procedures,

(3) be exhaustive (they cover some of the more important aspects of validation), or

(4) freeze the field to prescribed practices, nor to limit creative endeavors.

The last point deserves emphasis. Traditional technology calls for a showing that (a) assessments made by a particular method (or combination of methods) are useful for predicting behavior in some aspect of employment and (b) that the predictions can be made within an acceptable allowance for error (usually expressed in terms of percentage of misclassification or correlation coefficients). Principles presented here are stated in the context of the traditional approach. Other approaches are not explicitly addressed here, e.g., the use of formal decision theory (Cronbach & Gleser, 1965; Dunnette, 1974) or various forms of synthetic validity (Guion, 1965; McCormick, 1959, in press; Primoff, 1959). The traditional approach is emphasized because its principles have been established through a long history. Other approaches may be equally good or even superior, but it seems premature to try to articulate formally the principles of their use.

These principles are meant to be consistent with the *Standards for Educational and Psychological Tests* (APA, 1974). They are intended to clarify the applicability of the *Standards* (written for measurement problems in general) to the specific problems of employee selection, placement, and promotion. Like the *Standards,* these guidelines present ideals toward which the members of this Division and other psychologists are expected to strive. Circumstances in any individual study will affect the applicability of any given principle. Psychologists should, however, consider very carefully any factors suggesting that a general principle is inapplicable or that its implementation is not feasible. It is appropriate to bear in mind the following statement from the *Standards:*

> A final caveat is necessary in the view of the prominence of testing issues in litigation. This document is prepared as a technical guide for those within the sponsoring professions; it is not written as law. What is intended is a set of standards to be used, in part, for self-evaluation by test developers and test users. An evaluation of their competence does not rest on the literal satisfaction of every relevant provision of this

document. The individual standards are statements of ideals or goals, some having priority over others. Instead, an evaluation of competence depends on the degree to which the intent of this document has been satisfied by the test developer or user (APA, 1974, p. 8).

Unlike the *Standards,* these guidelines will contain references for further reading. References to individual standards themselves will be by number.

There are many legitimate uses of tests within organizations which are not covered by these guidelines. For example, tests might be used solely for organizational analysis or for evaluation of training programs; these uses, although necessarily consistent with the *Standards,* are not covered here.

A comment on "fairness"

Social and legal influences have led to a concern, shared by psychologists, for fairness or equality in employment opportunity. A basic assumption of this statement of the principles of good practice is that those who follow them will also further the principle of fair employment. The interests of employers, applicants, and the public at large are best served when selection is made by the most valid means available. Bias in the use of employment procedures is ineffective for reaching both employer and job applicant objectives.

There are technical problems associated with the detection and reduction of bias. A simple difference between groups, whether in selection ratios, mean scores, or correlation coefficients, is not adequate evidence of bias in the use of an assessment procedure; bias is detected in reliable differences between groups in predictions or in the accuracy of predictions. This statement of principles does not choose between different statistical definitions of bias, some of which are essentially incompatible and have generated scientific controversy (Cleary, 1968; Cole, 1973; Darlington, 1971; Guion, 1966; Petersen & Novick, in press; Thorndike, 1971). The choice of a statistical definition depends on the psychologist's objectives.

These guidelines are technical in focus. They are principally concerned with validity. The maximization of opportunities for sub-group members can be most effective where validity enables one to attain the highest level of accuracy in prediction or assessment of qualifications.

Application of principles

It is not likely that anyone will completely satisfy the ideal of every applicable principle. This probability raises the question of relative levels of stringency in adhering to the individual principles. The importance of a principle depends on the consequences of error. Will errors result in physical, psychological, or economical injury to people? Will the operating efficiency of the organization be impaired because of selection errors? If so, then the principles may need to be followed more rigorously than in less crucial situations.

Three axioms underlie the application of all these principles:

(1) Individuals differ in many ways.

(2) Individual differences in personal characteristics and backgrounds are often related to individual differences in behavior and satisfaction on the job.

(3) It is in the best interests of organizations and employees that information about relevant differences between people be developed and used in assigning people to jobs.

Definition of Purposes

Before any assessment procedure is considered or any validation effort planned, one should have a clear idea of what the assessment or validation is for. Any such statement of purpose logically must come from an understanding of the needs of the employing organization and of its present and prospective employees. As a general matter, a psychologist should develop clear objectives for an assessment procedure and design the validation effort to determine how well they have been achieved; those objectives should be consistent with professional, ethical, and legal responsibilities.

Ideally, all aspects of the decision-making process should make a valid contribution to achieving those purposes. Psychologists should demonstrate the validity of as many aspects of the decision-making process as feasible; generally, all assessment methods should be shown to be valid. When it is impossible or infeasible to apply validation methods to a given part of the decision-making process, that part should have a relationship, discernible by a reasonable person, to appropriate purposes of the employer.

The three aspects of validity described in the *Standards* are criterion-related validity (predictive or concurrent), construct validity, and content validity. Any of these may be emphasized in showing a relationship between various parts of the selection process and the objectives of the organization.

Criterion-Related Validity

In general, the purpose of employee testing is to predict future behavior, measured by a "criterion." The success or failure of the validation effort depends in large part on the adequacy of the criteria. The choice of measures to predict, and of measures to predict from, must be made thoughtfully and with great care.

In this section, the word "predictor" will be used in preference to "test." The competently developed and standardized ability test or personality inventory may be assumed as a mode. The term "predictor" should not be limited to such measures but should include, for example, biographical data and interview ratings as well. Insofar as technology and ingenuity permit, predictors should be standardized and should yield quantified "scores" or scale values amenable to psychometric analysis. The principles in this section apply to all predictors, although more easily to those most thoroughly standardized.

A. Criterion Development

1. *All criteria should be clearly related to the psychologist's purposes.* Criteria should be chosen, not on the basis of availability, but on the basis of importance and relevance. This implies that (a) the purposes are clear, (b) they are acceptable in the social and legal context in which the employing organization functions, and (c) are appropriate to the employing organization's purposes.

2. *All criteria should represent important work behaviors or work outputs, on the job or in training, as indicated by an appropriate review of information about the job.* Criteria need not be all-inclusive, but there should be clear documentation of the reasoning determining what is and what is not included in a criterion. Criteria need not reflect actual job performance. Depending on the purpose of the test user, various criteria such as overall proficiency, training time, sales records, number of prospects called, and turnover may be used (Wallace, 1965).

3. *If a criterion construct is not being satisfactorily measured, then substitute attempts to find another criterion measure should continue to focus on measurement of the same construct;* it is not acceptable practice to use substitutes measuring constructs not related to the psychologist's purposes. For example, if work output records prove unreliable or otherwise unsatisfactory, one should seek other measures of productivity and not shift to measures of employee conduct (such as absenteeism). One's purposes may, of course, call for the prediction of several constructs. However, one does not choose a construct irrelevant to those purposes simply because it is predictable.

4. *The possibility of bias or other contamination should be considered.* Ethnic or sex bias, correlations between ratings and the length of acquaintance of the rater and ratee, or differences between day and night shifts are

among variables which may bias the criterion measure. There is no clear path to truth in this matter. A difference between ethnic or sexual groups, older or younger employees, or day and night shifts may reflect bias in raters, equipment, or conditions—but it may also reflect genuine differences in performance. What is required is that the psychologist consider the possibility of bias, gather information relevant to that consideration, use his best judgment in evaluating the data, and be able to explain that judgment.

5. *If several criteria are combined to obtain a single measure, there should be a rationale to support the rules for combination.*

6. *Criterion measures should be reliable.* The reliability of a criterion measure should be estimated where feasible; estimates should be based on appropriate methods (Stanley, 1971). Reliability of a criterion measure need not be high, but there must be some reliability (Thorndike, 1949). Obviously, nothing will correlate with an unreliable criterion.

B. Choice of Predictor

1. *Predictor constructs should be chosen for which there is an empirical or logical foundation* (cf. Std. H1, H1.2). This principle does not call for elegance in the reasoning behind the choice of predictors so much as for having some reasoning; there should be some reason to suppose that a relationship exists between a predictor chosen and the behavior it is supposed to predict. For example, the research literature or the logic of development may provide the reason. One should consider alternative predictors for people of differing experience levels or probable approaches to the job (cf. Std. H1.2). This principle does not intend to rule out application of serendipitous findings, although such findings usually need verification.

2. *An investigator must be flexible in considering options in the choice of predictors,* i.e., not wedded to any favorite measurement technique nor prejudiced against any. No predictor should be ruled out at the stage of preliminary consideration except, of course, for technical or practical inadequacies or for legal or ethical reasons.

3. *Among predictors relevant to the purposes, those which minimize the effects of testers or testing situations should be chosen* (cf. Std. H4). The assessment of a candidate should not depend on who did the assessing. This is one reason why interviews are ordinarily less desirable than tests as predictors. Where non-test predictors are chosen, care should be taken to develop procedures which will minimize variance due to different users.

4. *Outcomes of decision strategies should be recognized as predictors.* Whether elements entering a decision have been quantified or not, the predictor having the effect is the decision reached. This fact applies to a range of decision strategies from test score composites to interviewers' judgments.

If the decision strategy is to combine test and non-test data (reference checks, medical data, etc.) into a subjective judgment, the predictor in the final analysis is the judgment reached by the person who weighs all the information.

C. Design of Validation Research

1. *The feasibility of studying criterion-related validity should be considered carefully.* The ideal is that only predictors validated in well-designed studies should be used in making employment decisions. It is not always possible to do a well-designed or even reasonably competent study; a poor study is not better than none at all. Several questions must be considered in deciding whether a study of criterion-related validity is feasible (cf. Stds., pp. 26-28).

First, one must consider the rate of change of job characteristics. The logic of validation research assumes that it is done under conditions representative of those in which the predictor will eventually be used. If technology, product, management practice, applicant populations, or other conditions are especially likely to change in ways that might affect validity, then a single criterion-related study is probably not useful, and one should consider alternative strategies, including a continuing program of research.

Second, a reasonably valid, uncontaminated, and reliable criterion is assumed in criterion-related validation. If such a criterion measure cannot be developed, criterion-related validation is not feasible. "Criterion-related validity studies based on the 'criterion at hand,' chosen more for availability than for a place in a carefully reasoned hypothesis, are to be deplored" (APA, 1974, p. 27).

Third, a competent criterion-related validation is based on a sample representative of the population of people and jobs to which the results are to be generalized. A wide variety of influences may distort actual samples: restriction of range, the use of existing employees rather than applicants, attrition, or population changes over time. Severe distortion from any source may render criterion-related validation infeasible.

Fourth, it is not useful to do a study where reliable results cannot be obtained. Of necessity, many employment test validations are done with numbers of cases too small to do the job as reliably as desired. There is a point in any practical situation where one says flatly that the N is too small. No firm minimun N, applicable to all situations, can be recommended, although a procedure can be. For example, the psychologist might, in a bivariate study, estimate the minimum validity coefficient he would accept in that situation. Then, on the basis of conventional statistics, he can determine the minimum N at which the validity coefficient would have a sufficiently narrow confidence interval. At the very least, the confidence interval should be narrow enough to exclude a value of zero.

If the above requirements cannot be met, the situation does not lend itself to the use of criterion-related validity for the evaluation of assessment, and the psychologist should so advise the client or employer.

2. *The appropriate validation model should be used.* Three methods have had some use for criterion-related validation: predictive, concurrent, and classificatory methods. Each of these is designed to answer a different research question; therefore, they are not ordinarily interchangeable. Moreover, any inferences the test user makes from a criterion-related study using a given method should be clearly stated within the context of the questions that method is designed to answer.

a. The predictive model, in which predictor information is obtained prior to placement of employees on a job and criterion information is obtained later, answers the most common employment question: whether the predictor does indeed have predictive value with respect to later job behavior. As such, the predictive model is, from the standpoint of scientific merit, to be preferred in most employee selection research. Its use properly begins with job candidates, not incumbents.

b. The concurrent method, in which both predictor and criterion information are obtained for present employees at approximately the same time, cannot be expected to answer questions of prediction. The concurrent method can only answer questions about the relationships of a given characteristic of preselected employees at a designated time. Often, the psychologist must choose between a concurrent study and no study at all. If concurrent validation is used, the psychologist should be particularly aware of restriction in range which may have occurred in criterion or predictor variables, effect of learning on the job on performance on these measures, and differences between the employee sample and the job candidate population on other relevant variables such as age or motivation. If any of these three considerations suggests that the results of a concurrent study would differ markedly from those of a predictive study, the psychologist is advised to use the predictive method or to declare criterion-related research infeasible.

c. The classificatory method (e.g., classifying scores as more like those either of people on a certain job or of people in general) is useful for answering questions about the degree to which persons not in a job compare with those holding the job. When answers to questions concerning probable performance or competence of job candidates are called for, the classificatory method is rarely appropriate.

3. *The sample upon which validation research is based should be reasonably representative of the population to which the predictor will be applied.* Because of the difficulty in defining the candidate population, this principle is difficult to follow, despite its importance. Among other things, it implies the superiority of predictive over concurrent designs, or, more accurately, of the use of an applicant sample rather than a presently employed sample in gathering predictor data.

When there is a substantial restriction of range in performance in the sample, a statistical correction for the effects of the restriction may be applied to a validity coefficient. However, it should be recognized that these apparently simple corrections may not be justified. Unless specific conditions exist, the results of such correction are subject to considerable error (Brewer & Hills, 1969). Any such correction should, of course, be based on data from the appropriate job candidate population.

4. *Validation research should ordinarily be directed to entry jobs, immediate promotions, or jobs likely to be attained.* Where a selection procedure is designed for a higher level job than that for which candidates are initially selected, that job may be considered an appropriate target job if the majority of the individuals who remain employed and available for advancement progress to the higher level within a reasonable period of time (cf. Std. E7.4.2). The point here is that predictability often diminishes over long time spans because of changes that occur in jobs and many other variables.

5. *Validation research should, in general, be based on samples large enough to yield reliable results.* However, the combination of data from dissimilar groups, e.g., persons in different job levels, for the sake of obtaining a large sample size is to be avoided. Moreover, if the sample size is extremely large, results may be statistically significant but of little practical use. An extremely large sample or cross validation is required before any credence can be placed in unusual findings, including but not limited to suppressor effects, moderator effects, nonlinear regression, results of configural scoring, or any other result which is likely to be affected by capitalization on chance effects. Partial and multiple correlation, in particular, require careful preplanning of data collection.

6. *Where traditional criterion-related validation is not feasible, the psychologist should consider alternative research strategies.* These may involve techniques not yet well understood or sufficiently studied. Examples might include the use of assessment centers, personal appraisals, or other judgments based on both person and job characteristics in which the predictor to be validated is a "final judgment." Other examples include "synthetic" validation or cooperative research plans such as industry-wide vali-

dation, consortia of small users, or generalization of validity. Such activities call for some pioneering research work, and they are not to be undertaken lightly.

7. *Procedures for test administration and scoring in validation research should be standardized and should be consistent with the standardization planned for operational use* (cf. Std. C1). Any operational characteristics (such as time limits, oral instructions, practice problems, answer sheets, scoring formulas, and physical conditions in the testing area) should be clearly defined and followed in validation research. Failure to follow the same standard procedures in operational use would suggest that validity of the predictor as used is in fact unknown, despite the prior research. The point of this principle is that the research should be consistent with procedures that will actually be used.

8. *Procedures of data collection should be consistent with the purposes of the study* (cf. Std. E7). If possible, predictors should be validated prior to the proposed use (cf. Std. E7.1). Some employers consider this principle difficult to follow because of the need to get on with the business of making employment decisions. Where there is external evidence which supports the probability of valid prediction (such as evidence of construct validity and of the appropriateness of the construct, carefully reasoned inferences from job descriptions, records of success of the same predictor in apparently similar situations, etc.), it may be feasible to utilize the predictors immediately. However, the psychologist must avoid situations that make it impossible or difficult to detect validity. For example, decisions should not be so highly selective that severe restriction of range results.

There is often no firm basis for the presumption of validity. In such cases, the psychologist must carefully judge whether the dangers of postponing the use of the predictor are greater or less than the dangers of using it prematurely.

9. *The collection of predictor data and collection of criterion measures should be operationally independent* (cf. Stds. E4.11, E7.3). A common example of non-independence is the collection of criterion ratings from supervisors who know the test scores. If a significant validity coefficient is obtained, it may be due either to a valid relationship or to manipulation of ratings to conform to scores. Such ambiguity should be avoided.

D. Data Analysis

1. *The type of statistical analysis to be used should be specified in planning the research.* The kinds of decisions to be made, and the way in which predictor variables are to be used in determining those decisions, should be considered in determining the method of analysis to be used. Al-

though any standard method of analysis may be used, any new or unusual method should be clearly explained in the research report. (It is understood that conditions may arise requiring changes in plans.)

2. *Data analysis should yield complete information about the relationship between predictor and criterion measures* (cf. Stds. E8, E6.2). The analysis should provide information about the statistical significance of the relationship. Traditionally, a validity coefficient or similar statistic which has a probability of less than one in twenty of having occurred by chance may be considered valid for typical purposes. There may be exceptions to this rule; professional standards have never insisted on a specific level of confidence. However, departures from this traditional convention should be based on reasons which can be stated in advance (such as power functions, utility, economic necessity, etc.).

The analysis should provide information about the strength of the relationship. This is usually expressed in terms of correlation coefficients, but other methods (such as per cent of misclassification) are acceptable and even preferable in many situations. The analysis should also give information about the nature of the relationship and how it might be used in prediction. Regression equations or expectancy tables may be appropriate.

Complete information includes numbers of cases and measures of central value and variability of both predictor and criterion variables.

3. *Statistical corrections of correlations should be made when required for appropriate inferences about populations from which the samples are drawn* (cf. Stds. E6.2.2; E8.2). It is important to note that traditionally-developed confidence intervals appropriate for uncorrected coefficients of correlation do not apply to coefficients adjusted for the effects of restriction of range or unreliability. Usually, the corrected coefficient can serve only as a basis for a point estimate (not an interval) of the population coefficient.

If corrections are made, uncorrected r's should, of course, also be reported.

4. *The analysis should, when reasonable and feasible, investigate the possibility of moderating effects.* If the candidate sample can be divided into sub-groups where prior research or logical considerations (such as indications of gross differences in job duties) suggest different relationships between predictors and criteria, the analyses should be done separately for the sub-groups if technical and situational considerations permit (cf. Std. E9). The implementation of this principle may be approached through an investigation of such moderator variables as ethnic group, socio-economic status, age, sex, cognitive styles, etc., although this approach has generally

not been found to improve validity appreciably. There are many difficulties in research with moderator variables. Technical and situational considerations often preclude the proper conduct of such studies. The moderator variable adds a variate and a multiplicative term to the regression model, and cross validation is therefore essential before the moderator can be used for selection decisions. Again, a poorly conducted study is not better than no study at all (cf. Std. E10.2).

5. *If a validity coefficient is to be adjusted for the unreliability of the criterion, the method of estimating criterion reliability should avoid spuriously low estimates.* A spuriously low estimate of criterion reliability produces a spuriously high estimate of the adjusted validity coefficient. Particularly inappropriate is the use of internal consistency reliability with a heterogeneous measure. No adjustment of a validity coefficient for unreliability of a predictor should be reported unless one clearly states that the resultant coefficient is purely theoretical and unachievable with the actual predictor involved.

Any estimates of reliability should be presented in reports in such a way that an employer or other reader will not confuse the reliability statement with a validity coefficient (cf. Std. J3).

6. *Where predictors are used in combination, the combination of intended use should be validated and the method of combination cross-validated or replicated where technically feasible* (cf. Stds. E8.4, E8.5, E10, E10.1, E10.11, E10.2). Simple linear combinations are generally more reliable than complex non-linear combinations, simple weights are more reliable than complex weights, and confirming evidence from more than one sample is more reliable than evidence from a single sample. (This may be a useful place to reiterate the caveat that these principles are ideals. Clearly, one does not cross validate a regression equation where the N barely permits the original computation of regression weights. One does not divide a group of merely acceptable size into two small groups, from which only unreliable statistics may be derived, and call it replication. One does, however, make some judgments about the costs of using data that have not been cross validated relative to the cost of alternatives—which might be limited essentially to random selection. In short, one does the best one can.)

7. *Any method of analysis should be chosen with due consideration of the characteristics of the data and of the assumptions involved in the development of the method* (cf. Std. E8.1.3). Some violation of assumptions may usually be tolerated with few ill effects; others may be grossly misleading. It is the responsibility of the investigator to know the assumptions of the method chosen and the consequences of violations of them.

8. *Data should be free from clerical error.* Coding and computational work should be checked carefully and thoroughly.

Construct Validity

The notion of construct validity, with its many optional procedures, may be extended to the point where it may be used to justify selection procedures. That justification requires that the construct be well defined, that the selection procedure considered is a measure of that construct, and that an appropriate criterion of job behavior involves that construct to more than a tangential degree.

In view of the lack of a substantial literature extending the concept of construct validity to employment practice, no principles for its use are presented here. Psychologists should, however, be aware that obtaining support for the relevance of a construct to a particular job, and of the validity with which a particular selection procedure measures that construct, is both an extensive and arduous undertaking, involving more than a single criterion-related validity study. It is, however, an undertaking that may pay great dividends in improving the scientific foundations for employment decisions.

Content Validity
(Content-Oriented Test Development and Use)

The content validity of a test is the degree to which scores on a test may be accepted as representative of performance within a specifically defined content domain of which the test is a sample. If the test is to be used for employment decisions, the relevant content domain is performance (or the knowledge or skill necessary for performance) on the job or on specified aspects of it. A test may be highly valid as a sample of a given content domain, but if that domain is not an important part of the job, the value of the test for employment purposes is negligible.

The distinction between a content domain and a psychological construct is not always a clean one. A useful distinction between content validity and construct validity can be made, however, in terms of the methodology associated with each. Construct validation is essentially an empirical, statistical process, involving more than a single validity coefficient. On the other hand, content validation has been primarily a judgmental process concerned with the adequacy of a test as a sample of specified activities. (Efforts to quantify such judgments have been proposed but have not yet had extensive trials.)

Content sampling is properly involved in any test construction, whether scores are to be interpreted as measures of achievement or as measures of an abstract construct. This discussion is limited, however, to situations where the assessment is evaluated solely in terms of content sampling. It is to be noted that content sampling is as useful in the construction and evaluation of criterion measures as it is for tests used for employment decisions.

In content sampling, any inferences about the usefulness of a score must be preceded by a set of inferences about the instrument itself based on the method of its construction (Messick, 1974). For that reason, the emphasis of this section and of its title is on the development of content-oriented assessment instruments rather than on the inferences from scores. Any evaluation of existing tests in terms of the adequacy of content sampling might follow parallel considerations.

A. *The job content domain to be sampled should be defined.* That definition should be based on an understanding of the job, organizational needs, labor markets, and other considerations leading to personnel specifications and relevant to the organization's purposes. The domain need not be inclusive insofar as any larger domain is concerned. By this we mean that it does not have to cover the entire universe of duties of a particular job or of topics covered in a training course. In fact, there may be many domains in the total content universe for any given job. For what it does include, a job content domain should be completely defined and thoroughly described.

The Standards (p. 29) discuss the question of domain definition for employment tests. The following statements are intended to clarify that discussion:

1. Job content domains should be developed and defined by job analysis, which may be a formal investigation, or the pooled judgments of informed persons such as production engineers, job incumbents, their supervisors, or personnel specialists. The domain should be defined on the basis of competent information about job tasks and responsibilities.

2. Job content domains should be defined in terms of those things an employee is expected to do without training or experience on the job, i.e., the content should not cover knowledge or skills the employee will be expected to learn after placement on the job or in training for the job.

3. The definition may be restricted to "critical, most frequent, or prerequisite work behaviors" (p. 29). There is no virtue in measuring ability to handle trivial aspects of the work.

4. A test content domain may likewise be defined. Essentially, the content validity of an employment test should be seen as the degree to which a

sample of elements from a test content domain matches the elements of a job content domain.

5. Once a specific job content domain has been defined, subject to the above constraints, an employer can justify the use of an employment test on the grounds of content validity if he can demonstrate that the content of the test is reasonably representative of important aspects of the job domain.

B. *A content domain should ordinarily be defined in terms of tasks, activities, or responsibilities.*

The principle here is that the domain be defined principally in terms of activities or consequences of activities which can either be observed or be reported by the job incumbent. One can add to this nucleus, without straining credulity, statements of specific items of knowledge, or specific job skills, prerequisite to effective activity. It is a much larger "inferential leap," however, to move from observation to inferences concerning underlying psychological constructs such as empathy, dominance, dexterity, leadership skill, spatial ability, etc. Such constructs suggest hypotheses to be tested in criterion-related or other empirical research. It is therefore inappropriate to define job domains in such terms if one's purpose is to develop and justify a test solely on the basis of that domain.

It follows that many tests developed for general use in a variety of situations are not representative samples of an appropriately defined domain of job content. Most such tests tap general constructs, not samples of specific knowledge or behavior required in a specific setting.

C. *Sampling of a job content domain should assure the inclusion in a measure of the major elements of the defined domain. Random sampling is probably inappropriate unless done within systematically sample areas or "subdomains."*

Sampling the job content domain is the process of constructing the selection procedure. The selection procedure should be developed according to accepted professional practices; however, once the domain and sampling procedure are defined, the actual construction of a test may not require the services of a psychologist.

Consider, for example, the content validity of assessments of performance during a new employee's probationary period. If random assignments include many trivial activities and exclude many crucial ones, the probationary period lacks adequate content validity. Probationary tasks should be systematically designed to include crucial assignments or assignments to activities which must be competently carried out before the worker is ready for further training.

D. *Panels of experts used in any aspect of the development of tests defended on grounds of content validity should be clearly qualified.* In developing evidence of content validity, the psychologist should document carefully every step of the procedure. Panels of experts (i.e., people with thorough knowledge of the job) may be used in defining domains, in writing test items, in developing simulation exercises, and in evaluating items or total tests. An important part of the documentation is a thorough statement of the qualifications and job knowledge of the people on such panels.

Implementation

Validation, discussed in the preceding sections, is the investigatory phase in the development of selection procedures. Whatever the outcome of such research, the psychologist should prepare a report of the findings; the importance of documentation in the form of such a report is especially great if the assessment procedure is to be adopted for operational use. Many valid testing programs fail at the point of their implementation. The following principles are intended to assure effective and proper use of measures found valid.

A. Research Reports and Procedures Manuals

1. *Whenever an assessment procedure is made available for use in employment decisions, one or more documents should be prepared to describe validation research and the standard procedures to be followed in using the results of that research* (cf. Std. A1). Reports of validation research should include enough detail to enable a competent fellow psychologist to know precisely what was done to draw independent conclusions in evaluating the work. A basic principle in the preparation of such reports is that they should not be misleading. For example, studies which result in negative findings should not be omitted or buried since they may influence overall conclusions.

2. *Informational material distributed within the organization should be accurate, complete for its purposes, and written in language that is not misleading* (cf. Std. A1.2.3). Memoranda should be worded to communicate as clearly and accurately as possible the information that readers need to know to carry out their responsibilities competently and faithfully. Care must be taken in preparing such memoranda to avoid giving others within the organization an impression that an assessment program is more useful than it really is. Too often such memoranda serve as sales documents; persuasion may be necessary to get cooperation, but it should not be misleading.

3. *Research reports and procedures manuals should be reviewed periodically and revised as needed; any changes in use or in research data that*

would make any statement in such documents incorrect or misleading should result in revision.

4. *Research reports or procedures manuals should help readers make correct interpretations of test data and should warn them against common misuses of tests and test information* (cf. Std. B1).

5. *The reasoning underlying an assessment program should be clearly stated in a research report or procedures manual* (cf. Std. A2). The selection of criteria may involve certain inferences about the nature of the job. The kinds of traits considered predictive of such criteria were determined by some sort of reasoning. Measures of criteria and predictors have been chosen and may have been empirically or logically evaluated. The reasoning in all of these processes should be stated clearly enough for readers to evaluate that reasoning from their own perspectives. The point of these illustrations is that another psychologist should be able to evaluate the research reported not only in terms of statistical evidence but in terms of how well it fits whatever psychological insights he may have (cf. Std. B3).

6. *Any special qualifications required to administer a test or to interpret the scores should be clearly stated in the research report and/or procedures manual.*

7. *Any claim made for any selection procedure should be supported in documentation with all available research evidence, including evidence that may be unfavorable to the conclusion* (cf. Stds. B5, B5.1, B5.2, B5.3, B5.4, B5.5 and sections C and E above).

8. *Any procedures manual for people who administer tests (or use other predictors) should specify the procedures to be followed and emphasize the necessity for standardization; these instructions should be clear enough that all persons concerned know precisely what they are supposed to do* (cf. Stds. C1, C1.1, C1.11). In one unit of one organization, a timed arithmetic test was given with no time limits because "we weren't getting enough people to qualify." One must be both insistent and persuasive to get people to understand both the nature of and the need for standardization. Where the psychologist cannot supervise directly the administration of tests or the use of other procedures, periodic seminars may be needed to reinforce the written instructions; observational checks or other quality control mechanisms should be built into the system. It should be made clear to everyone that failure to follow standardized procedures renders the research report irrelevant to some degree. There may be situations where research is based on data from operational studies where non-standardized procedures may have been used and where the results show no serious impairment of validity. In such situations the degree of standardization is shown to be rela-

tively unimportant; this, however, should not be assumed without investigation.

9. *Any scoring or scaling procedures should be presented in the procedures manual with as much detail and clarity as possible to reduce clerical errors in scoring and to increase the reliability of any judgments required.* When the keys must be kept confidential, this material should be made available *only* to people who do the actual scoring or scaling of responses.

10. *A research report should contain clear and prominent descriptions of the samples used in the research; such information should also be summarized on any accompanying report forms in which scores are given with normative interpretations such as centiles or expectancies of success.*

Too many people do not know that normative interpretations and estimates of validity and reliability are specific in the study that produced them. Almost magical properties are sometimes attributed to test scores.

Ordinarily, norm tables are less useful than expectancy charts for employment decisions. One should recognize, of course, that the expectancy chart is a normative interpretation of test scores; i.e., it indicates the proportion of a specific sample of candidates who reach a standard level of success. Norm tables may, therefore, be useful in identifying the effects of a cutting score, even if not in interpreting individual employment test scores.

11. *Any normative reporting should include measures of central tendency and variability and should clearly establish the nature of the normative data given,* i.e., centiles, standard scores, expectancies, predicted levels of attainment, etc. (cf. Std. D3).

12. *Any derived scale used for reporting scores should be carefully described in the research report or procedures manual.* Whether using standard derived scores (such as those described in general textbooks on measurement) or "home-grown" scales (such as "qualified," "marginal," or "unqualified"), the psychologist should make clear their logical and psychometric foundations.

B. Validity Generalization

1. *Validity evidence obtained in one unit of a multiunit organization or in a consortium may be applied to other units where jobs and job settings are essentially similar.* Validity coefficients are obtained in specific situations. They apply only to those situations. A situation is defined by characteristics of the samples of people, of settings, of criteria, etc. Careful job and situational analyses are needed to determine whether characteristics of the site of the original research and those of other sites are sufficiently similar to make the inference of generalizability reasonable.

A pressing problem in employment psychology is that of determining how to generalize validities. Psychologists are strongly urged to engage in cooperative research ventures such as industry-wide validation studies, consortia of civil service jurisdictions, and the like. Until such time as such cooperative research results in an understanding of the limits of generalization, there will be few principles to observe in this area. The principle that one may apply validity evidence to essentially similar job units is an interim principle; it is not intended to discourage continued research to determine whether such application exceeds the legitimate boundaries of validity generalization.

2. *Assumptions of validity generalized from promotional literature, testimonial statements, or empirical studies in unrelated settings may not be used as evidence of the validity of the procedure in a specific situation.*

C. Use of Research Results

1. *It is the responsibility of the psychologist to recommend specific methods of score interpretation to the employer.* Although the employer usually reserves the final decision on whether to use a specific selection procedure, it is the responsibility of the psychologist to make recommendations on this question and on questions of how the procedure is to be used. The recommended use should be consistent with procedures with which validity was established.

2. *Validity of selection procedures should be assumed only for jobs for which validity has been situationally determined or for comparable jobs involving the same criteria to which validity may generalize.*

3. *The utility of a selection procedure should be considered in deciding whether to apply it operationally.* In reaching the decision, consideration should be given to relative costs and benefits to both the organization and its employees. It is not recommended that procedures with minimal usefulness be applied, but a procedure with at least some demonstrated usefulness is ordinarily preferable to one of unknown validity or usefulness.

4. *Selection standards may be set as high or as low as the purposes of the employer require, if they are based on valid predictors.* As in principle A.1 under criterion-related validity, this implies that (a) the purposes of selection are clear and (b) they are acceptable in the social and legal context in which the employing organization functions.

5. *Employers should provide reasonable opportunities for reconsidering candidates whenever alternative forms exist and reconsideration is technically feasible* (cf. Std. J7.2). Under at least some circumstances, employers should allow candidates to reapply. There might be any of several reasons for questioning the validity of prior assessment for any given per-

son. Where there has been opportunity for new learning, retesting is usually a desirable practice.

In some situations, validity information does not generalize to the retest situation. In cases where biographical data or scored interview forms are the predictors, the validity of the retest is usually unknown; it may be negligible. The test user is expected to balance these opposing considerations.

6. *The use of a predictor should be accompanied by systematic procedures for developing additional data for continued research.* Changing social, economic, technical, or other factors may operate over time to alter or eliminate validity; continuing (or periodic) research is therefore necessary. A serious problem is that the operational use of a valid predictor may result in such severe restriction of range that its validity cannot be demonstrated in subsequent research (Peterson & Wallace, 1966). There is no well-established technology for checking validity of instruments in use; however, psychologists are urged to exercise their ingenuity to observe the principle that validity once demonstrated cannot be assumed to be eternal.

7. *All persons within the organization who have responsibilities related to the use of employment tests and related predictors should be qualified through appropriate training to carry out their responsibilities.* The psychologist or other person in charge of any testing program should know measurement principles and the limitations on the validities of interpretations of assessments (cf. Std. D1). That person should understand the literature relevant to the test use or employment problems. Other people in the organization may have some responsibilities related to the testing program. It is the psychologist's responsibility to see to it that such people have the training necessary to carry out those responsibilities competently (cf. Stds. G3, G3.1).

These considerations suggest the need for workshops, seminars, or other planned approaches to training technicians and managers involved in assessment procedures and in the interpretation of assessments.

8. *Psychologists should seek to avoid bias in choosing, administering, and interpreting tests; they should try to avoid even the appearance of discriminatory practice* (cf. Std. G4). This is another principle difficult to apply; it goes beyond data analysis. The appearance of bias may interfere with the effective performance of a candidate in the assessment situation. At the very least, a test user can create an environment that is responsive to the feelings of all candidates, insuring the dignity of persons.

9. *Psychologists should periodically review test use* (cf. Std. G5). Departures from established procedures often develop over time. New findings

in psychological or psychometric theory, or new social criticisms, may be relevant to one or more of the assessment procedures in use. The principle is that it should not be left to chance to find examples of misuse or of obsolete data; some systematic plan for review should be followed.

10. *The psychologist is responsible for clerical accuracy in scoring, checking, coding, or recoding test results* (cf. Std. 13). This principle applies to the psychologist and to any agent to whom he has delegated responsibility; the responsibility cannot be abandoned by purchasing services from an outside scoring service (cf. Std. I3.1).

11. *If cutting scores are used as a basis for decision (i.e., as rigid pass-fail points), the rationale or justification should be known to all users* (cf. Std. 14). This principle does not recommend cutting scores. Rather, "The intent is to recommend that test users avoid the practice of designating purely arbitrary cutting scores they can neither explain nor defend" (APA, 1974, p. 67). If cutting scores are to be established, some consideration should be given to the different effects of different cutting scores; e.g., the effects of the two kinds of error: selecting people who later prove unsatisfactory as opposed to rejecting people who would have been satisfactory if hired.

12. *The psychologist must make considered recommendations for the operational use of a predictor for which differential prediction is established.* A finding of differential prediction should not automatically lead to differences in predictor use for different groups. For example, if the study were based upon an extremely large sample, a finding of statistically significant differential prediction may have little practical impact. For another example, data apparently indicating differential prediction may be due to statistical artifacts or may suggest courses of action inconsistent with societal goals. In such situations, the reasonable course of action would be to recommend uniform operational use of the predictor for the different groups (or perhaps conduct further research).

Should a finding of differential prediction be compelling enough to warrant other action, possible approaches to dealing with it are (1) revising or replacing the tests involved, or (2) using the test operationally taking into account the differences in prediction systems.

Action under the second alternative should be in accordance with the definition of fairness upon which the study indicating differential prediction was based. (See "A Comment on Fairness," above.)

13. *The psychologist or other test user is responsible for maintaining test security* (cf. Std. 15). This means that all reasonable precautions should be taken to safeguard test materials and that decision makers should beware of basing decisions on scores obtained from insecure tests.

This principle is difficult to apply to non-test predictors such as judgments reached in an employment interview; nevertheless, the principle of security as a means for standardization may be applied to other variables as well. Reference checks, for example, should be held confidential as an illustration of the extension of this principle.

14. *In making interpretations of test scores the psychologist should be aware of situational variables introducing error* (cf. Std. J1). An individual test score may lead to invalid inferences because of unusual features of the testing situation (e.g., uncommon distractions), exceptional characteristics of the individual (e.g., a physical handicap) or the passage of time (e.g., new learning since testing occurred). Sometimes these may form a basis for retesting; they may suggest the consideration of other information. The principle is that some degree of judgment be retained in the interpretation of test scores obtained in circumstances differing from those in the validation research. Perhaps a better statement of the principle is that some degree of judgment should not be ruled out automatically in all situations.

15. *Test score information should not be available for use in personnel decisions when it is no longer valid.* It is recognized that some traits are more stable than others, but as a general principle, it is poor practice to retain test scores in personnel files long after the scores were obtained. Files should be purged of data, rendered invalid by new experience, aging, maturation, or other personal change—or by changes in jobs or in organizations—so that no one will base decisions on such invalid scores.

16. *When reporting test results, the psychologist should consider the level of knowledge of the person receiving the report; the report should be in terms likely to be interpreted correctly by persons at that level of knowledge.* Ordinarily, actual test scores should not be reported to candidates or to managerial personnel. If for any reason scores are reported, they should be explained carefully to be sure that interpretations are correct. In particular, one should not report actual scores to people who may later be asked to provide criterion ratings for validation.

17. *Scores on many tests developed for educational use are sometimes given in derived score form as I.Q.'s, grade-equivalent scores, or other terms not likely to be meaningful in the employment context; such terms are to be avoided* (cf. Std. D5.25; J4.2). Such terms are psychometrically and logically questionable as well as inappropriate for employment use. Even where they had legitimate psychometric significance historically, they have been so encrusted with spurious meaning that they lend themselves to misinterpretation.

Glossary

Assessment procedure: any method used to evaluate characteristics of persons.

Bias: any constant error; any systematic influence on measures or on statistical results irrelevant to the purpose of measurement.

Centile: commonly percentile; a point on a distribution. Centile rank or percentile rank refers to the percentage of all scores falling at or below a particular value.

Central value: an average of a set of measurements; e.g., mean, median.

Coefficient of correlation: an index number, which may be positive or negative, ranging from 0.00 to 1.00, indicating the extent to which two variables covary.

Construct: a formally articulated concept of a trait, i.e., an hypothesized property of people, objects, or events inferred from data.

Construct validity: the degree to which scores obtained through a specified test or other assessment procedure may be interpreted as measuring or reflecting a specified construct.

Content domain: a body of knowledge and/or a set of tasks or other behaviors defined so that given facts or behaviors may be classified as included or excluded. (See Job content domain, Job content universe.)

Content validity: the degree to which scores on a test may be accepted as representative of performance within a specifically defined content domain of which the test is a sample.

Correlation: the degree to which two or more sets of measurements vary together; e.g., a positive correlation exists when high values on one scale are associated with high values on another.

Criterion (pl., *criteria*): the behavior, performance level, or result of behavior, on the job or in training, to be predicted.

Criterion-related validity: the statistical statement of the existence of a relationship between scores on a predictor and scores on a criterion measure.

Cross validation: the application of a scoring system or set of weights empirically derived in one sample to a different sample (drawn from the same population) to investigate the stability of relationships based on the original weights.

Cutting score: a specified point in a predictor distribution below which candidates are rejected.

Derived scale: a scale of measurement using a system of standard units (based perhaps on standard deviations or centiles), to which obtained scores on any original scale may be transformed by appropriate numerical manipulation.

Expectancy table: a table or chart used for making convenient predictions of levels of criterion performance for specified intervals of predictor scores.

Feasible: capable of being done successfully; i.e., in criterion-related research, economically practical and technically possible without misleading or uninterpretable results.

Grade-equivalent score: a derived score which interprets a person's test performance in school grade norms; usually inappropriate for employment testing.

I.Q.: a derived score with a mean of 100 and, usually, a standard deviation of 15 or 16; used only with general mental ability or scholastic aptitute test; generally inappropriate for employment use.

Internal consistency: degree to which performance on a part of a test or other assessment procedure correlates with performance on other parts.

Job content domain: a defined segment or aspect of the job content universe regarding which inferences are to be made.

Job content universe: the total job; everything, known and unknown, which the incumbent does and must know in order to do it.

Linear combination: the sum of scores (whether weighted differentially or not) on different assessments to form a single composite score; distinguished from nonlinear combinations in which the different scores may, for example, be multiplied instead of added.

Moderator variable: theoretically, a variable which is related to the amount and type of relationship between two other variables; in practice, it is usually a basis for subdividing a sample into subgroups for independent analyses of the correlations of interest.

Normative: pertaining to norm groups, i.e., the sample of subjects from which were obtained descriptive statistics (e.g., measure of central tendency, variability, or correlation) or score interpretations (e.g., centiles or expectancies).

Objective: verifiable; in measurement, pertaining to scores obtained in a way that minimizes bias due to different observers or scorers.

Operational independence: gathering of data by methods that are different in procedure or source so that measurement of one variable, such as a criterion, is not influenced by the process of measuring another variable.

Predictor: a measurable characteristic used to predict criterion performance, e.g., scores on a test, judgments of interviewers, etc.

Psychometric: pertaining to the measurement of psychological characteristics such as aptitudes, personality traits, achievement, skill, knowledge, etc.

Regression equation: an algebraic equation which may be used to predict criterion performance from specific predictor scores.

Reliable: consistent or dependable; repeatable; reliability refers to the consistency of measurement.

Replication: a repetition of a research study designed to investigate the generality or stability of the results.

Restriction of range: a situation, varying in degree, in which the variability of data in a sample is less than the variability in the population from which the sample has been drawn.

Score: any specific number in a range of possible values describing the assessment of an individual; a generic term applied for convenience to such diverse kinds of measurement as tests, production counts, absence records, course grades, or ratings.

Standard deviation: a statistic used to describe the variability within a set of measurements, based on the differences between individual scores and the mean.

Standard score: a score which describes the location of a person's score within a set of scores in terms of distance from the mean in standard deviation units; may include scores on certain derived scales.

Synthetic validation: an approach to validation in which the validity of a test battery put together for a specific use may be inferred from prior research relating predictors to specified and relevant criterion elements.

Target job: the job in which performance is to be predicted at the time of the employment decision; not necessarily the initial job assignment.

Tester effect: bias in assessments attributable to differences between test administrators, test scorers, or others involved in the assessment procedure.

Validation: the process of investigation (i.e., research) through which the degree of validity of a predictor can be estimated. [Note: laymen often misinterpret the term as if it implied giving a stamp of approval; they should recognize that the result of the research might be zero validity.]

Validity: the degree to which certain specified inferences from scores on tests or other assessments may be considered justified or supported by research or by the method of test construction.

Validity coefficient: a correlation coefficient showing the strength of relationship between predictor and criterion.

Variability: the extent of individual differences in a particular variable.

Variance: a measure of variability; the square of the standard deviation.

References

American Psychological Association, American Educational Research Association, and National Council on Measurement in Education. *Stan-*

dards for Educational and Psychological Tests. Washington: American Psychological Association, 1974, 76 pages.

Brewer, J. K. and Hills, J. R. Univariate selection: The effects of size of correlation, degree of skew, and degree of restriction. *Psychometrika*, 1969, *34*, 347-361.

Cleary, T. A. Test bias: Prediction of grades of Negro and white students in integrated colleges. *Journal of Educational Measurement*, 1968, *5*, 115-124.

Cole, N. S. Bias in selection. *Journal of Educational Measurement*, 1973, *10*, 237-255.

Cronbach, L. J. and Gleser, G. C. *Psychological tests and personnel decisions* (2nd ed.). Urbana: University of Illinois Press, 1965.

Darlington, R. B. Another look at "cultural fairness." *Journal of Educational Measurement*, 1971, *8*, 71-82.

Dunnette, M. D. Personnel selection and job placement of disadvantaged and minority persons: Problems, issues, and suggestions. In H. L. Fromkin and J. J. Sherwood (Eds.), *Integrating the organizations.* New York: Free Press, 1974, 55-74.

Guion, R. M. Employment tests and discriminatory hiring. *Industrial Relations*, 1966, *5*, 20-37.

Guion, R. M. Synthetic validity in a small company: A demonstration. *Personnel Psychology*, 1965, *18*, 49-63. (b)

McCormick, E. J. Application of job analysis to indirect validity. *Personnel Psychology*, 1959, *12*, 402-413.

McCormick, E. J. Job and task analysis. In Dunnette, M. D. (Ed.), *Handbook of industrial and organizational psychology.* Chicago: Rand McNally [1976].

Messick, S. Meaning and values in measurement and evaluation. Address delivered at meeting of American Psychological Association, New Orleans, August, 1974.

Petersen, N. S. and Novick, M. R. An evaluation of some models for culture-fair selection. *Journal of Educational Measurement,* in press.

Peterson, D. A. and Wallace, S. R. Validation and revision of a test in use. *Journal of Applied Psychology*, 1966, *50*, 13-17.

Primoff, E. S. Empirical validations of the J-coefficient. *Personnel Psychology*, 1959, *12*, 413-418.

Stanley, J. C. Reliability. In Thorndike, R. L. (Ed.), *Educational Measurement* (2nd ed.). Washington: American Council on Education, 1971.

Thorndike, R. L. Concepts of culture-fairness. *Journal of Educational Measurement*, 1971, *8*, 63-70.

Wallace, S. R. Criteria for what? *American Psychologist*, 1965, *20*, 411-417.

exhibit 14

some resources for recruitment

I. The Office of Voluntary Programs, EEOC, 1800 G St., N.W., Washington, D.C. 20506, offers the following services:

A. *The Educational Programs Division* (address above) (202) 343-7908, has available a detailed listing of "talent banks" and specialized referral sources throughout the country.

B. *The Talent Search Skills Bank* (address above) (202) 343-6286, maintains a file of minority and female applicants with professional skills and can refer qualified individuals to employers.

C. *Regional Voluntary Programs Officers* can provide further information on local referral sources.

II. Directories and Professional Rosters*

A. *Equal Employment Opportunity for Minority Group College Graduates: Locating, Recruiting, Employing* (1972). Compiled by Robert Calvert, Jr., $4.95 (prepaid) $5.95 (if billed). Garrett Park Press, Garrett Park, Md. 20766.

A comprehensive and useful directory. Specific listings include: names, addresses, and enrollment by degree level and field of specialization of predominantly black colleges and universities, and of institutions with substantial number (numbers listed) of Spanish-surnamed, American Indian and Oriental American students; numbers of identified minorities at all other higher educational institutions; names and addresses of media (newspapers, periodicals, broadcast) serving each minority group; a comprehensive listing of

Source: U.S. Equal Employment Opportunity Commission, *Affirmative Action and Equal Employment: A Guidebook for Employers* (Vol. 2) (Washington, D.C.: U.S. Government Printing Office, January 1974), pp. C-1 through C-6.

*Unless otherwise noted, publications are available without charge.

minority organizations and consulting firms, Human Rights Commissions and other agencies. The publication also has many specific suggestions on methods and techniques of recruiting and retaining minorities.

B. *A Directory of Predominantly Black Colleges and Universities in the U.S.,* National Alliance of Businessmen, 1730 K St., N.W., Washington, D.C. 20006. (Revised Edition 1973). Enrollment, types of degrees offered and numbers granted.

C. *Directory of Minority College Graduates 1971-72.* Prepared by Manpower Administration, U.S. Department of Labor. Identifies black, Spanish-surnamed and other minority graduates of 1971 and '72 by name, address, degree earned and major discipline. Available from Superintendent of Documents, Government Printing Office, Washington, D.C. 20402. $8.00.

Computer listings of these graduates by specific educational disciplines are available from: Office of Equal Employment Opportunity, Office of Assistant Secretary for Manpower, U.S. Department of Labor, Washington, D.C. 20210. Cost, if any depends on amount of computer work required.

D. *Spanish-Surnamed College Graduates.* Cabinet Committee on Opportunity for the Spanish Speaking, 1707 H St., N.W. Washington, D.C. 20506. Updated annually. Includes names, addresses, college and major discipline of juniors, seniors, and graduates with Spanish surnames. Listing includes schools and graduating students by state and by discipline. *The Cabinet Committee also makes job referrals.*

E. *1971-72 Accredited Institutions of Higher Education.* Federation of Regional Accrediting Commissions, American Council on Education, 1 Dupont Circle, N.W., Washington, D.C. 20036. Lists all accredited institutions, by state, with number of male and female students.

F. *Women's Caucuses, Committees and Professional Associations and Supplements: Recruiting Aids #1 and #2;* and *Recruiting Minority Women.* Available from Association of American Colleges, Project on the Status and Education of Women, 1818 R St., N.W. Washington, D.C. 20009.

Comprehensive listings include many professional registries of women in specific fields, and caucuses in professional societies which provide formal or informal referral services. Also included: organizations representing male and female minority professionals.

G. *Civil Rights Directory.* Office of Information, U.S. Commission on Civil Rights, 1121 Vermont Ave., N.W., Washington, D.C. 20225. (Revised edition available Fall, 1973.) Lists major national and local civil rights, educational, women's, religious and fraternal organizations, and public agencies (local, state and federal) responsible for enforcing civil rights laws.

H. *Directory of Labor Offices in the United States.* Lists all federal and state agencies concerned with manpower and training information.

I. *Directory of Spanish-Surnamed and Native Americans in Science and Engineering.* Dr. Joseph Martinez, Foundation for Promoting Advanced Studies, 464 Furnace Road, Ontario, N.Y. 14519. $15.00.

J. *Women's Organizations and Leaders: 1973 Directory of Women's Organizations.* Today Publications, National Press Building, Washington, D.C. 20004. $25.00. Comprehensive listing indexed geographically (by state) and by subject of major activity. Includes national, state and local organizations.

K. *Engineering and Technician Enrollments, Fall 1971.* Engineer's Joint Council, Engineering Manpower Commission, 345 E. 45th St., New York, N.Y. 10017. $20.00. Lists number of women and Negroes, by institution, in 1st through 5th year of Bachelor's, Masters' and Doctor's degree programs.

III. Organizational Resources

Following are some major national organizations prepared to make referrals or to direct the employer to their local units which can refer minorities and females at various skills levels.

A. General Resources

1. *Local Employment Services Offices* are important referral sources. (Consult local telephone directory). Urban areas have professional listings.
2. *City and State Human Resources Departments and Human Rights Commissions* may be helpful referral sources.
3. Regional Offices of Manpower Administration, U.S. Department of Labor.

B. Some National Organizational Referral Sources for Minorities (Male and Female) at Various Skill Levels.

1. Americans for Indian Opportunity
   1820 Jefferson Place, N.W.
   Washington, D.C. 20036

2. American G.I. Forum
   P.O. Box 336
   Beeville, Texas
   (512) 358-2535

3. Bureau of Indian Affairs
   Indian Federal Employment
   Referral Program
   Albuquerque, New Mexico 87103

4. Commonwealth of Puerto Rico
   Department of Labor—Migration Division
   322 West 45th Street
   New York, N.Y. 10036
   (212) 245-0700

5. League of United Latin American Citizens (LULAC)
   10966 LeCont Ave.
   Los Angeles, California 90024
   (213) 679-8225

6. National Alliance of Businessmen
   1730 K St., N.W.
   Washington, D.C. 20006
   (202) 254-7105

   Local units in 150 cities provide referrals and funds for training.

7. National Association for the Advancement of Colored People (NAACP)
   1790 Broadway
   New York, N.Y. 10019
   (212) 751-0300

8. National Puerto Rican Forum, Inc.
   214 Mercer Street
   New York, N.Y. 10012
   (212) 533-0100

9. National Spanish Speaking Management Association
   1625 Eye St., N.W.
   Washington, D.C. 20006
   (202) 785-3500

10. National Urban League
    National Skills Bank
    477 Madison Avenue
    18th Floor

New York, N.Y. 10022
(212) 751-6077

11. Opportunities Industrialization Centers (OIC)
(Headquarters)
100 West Coulter St.
Philadelphia, Pa. 19144
(215) VI9-3010

Local OIC's provide job training and referrals.

12. Puerto Rican Research & Resource Center
1519 Connecticut Ave., N.W.
Washington, D.C. 20036
(202) 677-7940

13. Service Employment Rehabilitation (SER)
9841 Airport Blvd. Rm. 1020
Tishman Bldg.
Los Angeles, California 90045
(213) 649-1511

C. Some National Referral Sources for Women with Specific Skills

1. American Association of University Women
2401 Virginia Avenue, N.W.
Washington, D.C. 20037
(202) 785-7750

Compiles lists of professional registries in all major fields.

2. National Federation of Business & Professional Women's Clubs
Talent Bank
2012 Massachusetts Avenue, N.W.
Washington, D.C. 20036
(202) 293-1100

In cooperation with more than 20 women's professional organizations, maintains a file of professional women's resumes which are matched to employer requests.

3. National Organization for Women (NOW)
1957 East 73rd Street
Chicago, Illinois 60649
(312) 324-3067

Local units may provide some referrals.

4. National Association of College Women
4620 Kossuth Avenue
St. Louis, Mo. 63115

An association of black college graduates. Provides some informal referral services.

5. Negro Sororities and Service groups. (Can provide some referrals).

   Alpha Kappa Alpha
   1751 New Hampshire Avenue, N.W.
   Washington, D.C. 20009
   (202) 387-3103

   Delta Sigma Theta
   1814 M Street, N.W.
   Washington, D.C. 20036
   (202) 338-7727

   Zeta Phi Beta
   1734 New Hampshire Avenue, N.W.
   Washington, D.C. 20009
   (202) 387-3103

6. Professional Women's Caucus
   P.O. Box 1057
   Radio City Station
   New York, N.Y. 10019

7. Women's Equity Action League (WEAL)
   538 National Press Building
   Washington, D.C. 20004
   (202) 638-4560

   Units of this organization in 30 states provide informal referrals of professional women.

8. Federation of Organizations for Professional Women
   1346 Connecticut Ave., N.W.
   Washington, D.C. 20036 (202) 833-1998
   Report on Registries. Lists 36 women's organizations with professional registries. $5.00. (1973.)

   Additional Reference. A 214 page *Directory for Reaching Minority Groups,* issued by the Bureau of Apprenticeship and Training, U.S. Department of Labor, in August, 1973, lists Federal, state and local governmental units, community action agencies, educational institutions, fraternities, sororities, press-broadcast media and religious and minority organizations by State and city, with addresses and telephone numbers. Single copies may be obtained without cost from Office of Information, Manpower Administration, U.S. Department of Labor, Washington, D.C. 20210.

exhibit 15

management development course no. 117 human awareness in modern management

Gail Lum-King

I **Method**

Course lasts 8 hours.

Methods used include: films, overhead slides, case studies, group discussion.

A booklet including history, culture, and current problems of different ethnic groups is distributed after class.

II **Objectives**

Part I—To provide an increased awareness of how prejudicial thinking and behavior can negatively affect management decisions and actions.

Part II—To provide an increased understanding of today's multi-ethnic work force through discussion of the history, culture, and current problems of various ethnic groups in America, today.

III **Part I**

Slides of optical illusions and trick pictures lead group members to recognize that human perceptions can often be erroneous. These erroneous perceptions often lead to assumptions about other people which in turn can lead to stereotyping. By developing the results of stereotyping, the group experiences the "creation of prejudice" and demonstrates its effect in open discussion. The understanding of these effects lead to the recognition that management must base its decisions and actions on the objective qualifications of each individual rather than on subjective feelings and opinions.

"The Eye of the Storm" (film—30 minutes) demonstrates the "Pygmalion Effect" or the self-fulfilling prophecy. This film demonstrates

Source: Used with permission of Blue Shield of California.

how a teacher's expectations of her pupils actually affects their learning ability and classroom performance. Class discussion after the film relates this concept to how erroneous expectations based on stereotypes can negatively affect employees' performance in a work situation.

Through discussion of four case studies, group members experience simulated work situations which involve prejudice. The interchange of ideas on why each problem exists and how each should be solved allows members to experience others' sensitivities in dealing with problems of prejudice in a work environment.

IV **Part II**

"The Prejudice Film" (film—30 minutes) further explores the nature of prejudice, and introduces the historical causes and effects of prejudice on various ethnic groups in America.

This is further emphasized through discussion of the history and culture of various minority ethnic groups, particularly those which have largely settled in the San Francisco Bay Area. These groups include Native Americans, Blacks, Chicanos, Chinese, Japanese and Filipinos. Emphasis is put on the reasons for each group's entry into the United States, their frustrations during their early years in this country and a review of current problems faced by many today.

Discussion begins by tracing the route by which the *Native Americans* travelled to America, and their gradual evolution into the many North American tribal cultures. The destruction of the people and the land which came as a result of the European settlers is then reviewed, leading up to current problems of today. Discussion centers around problems in employment, alcoholism, mental health, and living standards of Native Americans in the Bay Area.

The ancestry of *Black Americans* is traced back to West Africa, and their civilization on the African continent is described. The "justification" behind the widespread importation of Black slaves, leading to emancipation, Jim Crow Laws, the Civil Rights Movement and current problems of today are discussed. In particular, the impact of today's inflationary economy on Black employment is emphasized.

Discussion on *Mexican Americans* begins with the definition and origin of the term "Chicano". Historical aspects emphasize the loss of Mexican territory to the United States after the Mexican-American War, leading to the dispossession of the people living in that area (now the American Southwest). The current problems of today's Mexican American community, particularly in the areas of employment, education, income, language, and living conditions are explored.

The history of the Bay Area's *Chinese Americans* is traced back to the time of the first Chinese immigrants. Understanding is gained regarding the conditions in both China and California which prompted their immigration, and their fate during their early years here. Discussion of the problems of the Chinese community center around statistics regarding housing, income, employment and education.

A comparison of the population densities of Japan and California reveals the major reason for *Japanese* immigration to this country. The fate of Japanese Americans during World War II is covered, including the "justification" for their internment, the economic losses faced after internment, and post-war prejudice. Discussion of current problems centers around the urban housing crisis faced by many elderly Japanese Americans in San Francisco.

A history of immigrant groups in the Philippines creates a better understanding of the many aspects which are reflected in today's Filipino culture. Reasons for immigration into the United States, both past and present, are explored. In particular, conditions in the Philippines in relation to education, employment, income, politics gives a basis for understanding problems faced by Filipinos immigrating to America today.

V Conclusion

Concluding discussion summarizes the responsibility of management to base its decisions and actions on the objective qualifications of each individual rather than on subjective feelings and opinions.

A discussion of the goals of Affirmative Action reveals management's responsibility toward obtaining these goals.

The poem "The New Colossus" from the Statue of Liberty serves as a reminder that everyone living in America today was once an immigrant. Group members recognize that when we discriminate against newcomers or those who are different from ourselves, we are perpetuating prejudice.

"Is It Always Right To Be Right?" (film—8 minutes) is an Academy Award winning film which concludes the program by emphasizing the destructive effects due to group polarization and the constructive effects of group understanding and cooperation.

references

suggested sources of additional information

The Legal Framework

Ash, P. "The Implications of the Civil Rights Act of 1964 for Psychological Assessment in Industry," *American Psychologist,* Vol. 21 (1966), 797-803.

Ash, P. and L. P. Kroeker. "Personnel Selection, Classification, and Placement," *Annual Review of Psychology,* Vol. 26 (1975), 481-507.

ASPA. "Test Justification and Title VII," *Personnel Administrator,* Vol. 21, No. 1 (1976), 46-51.

Baxter, B. "Review of Selected Federal and Professional Positions on the Use of Tests in Employment," *American Psychological Association Journal Supplement Abstract Service Document,* Ms. No. 802, 1974.

Bureau of National Affairs, Inc. *The Civil Rights Act of 1964.* Washington, D.C.: BNA, Inc., 1964.

Byham, W. C. and M. E. Spitzer. *The Law and Personnel Testing.* New York: American Management Association, 1971.

Edwards, K. J. *Fair Employment and Legal Requirements and Practical Guidelines.* Rosemead, Calif.: Rosemead Graduate School of Psychology, 1976.

Equal Employment Opportunity Commission. *Tenth Annual Report.* Washington, D.C.: the Commission, 1976.

Gastwirth, L. and S. E. Haber. "Defining the Labor Market for Equal Employment Standards," *Monthly Labor Review,* Vol. 99, No. 3 (1976), 32-35.

Harvard Law Review. "Developments in the Law—Employment Discrimination and Title VII of the Civil Rights Act of 1964," Vol. 84 (1971), 1109-1316.

Hunt, T. "Civil Service Testing and Affirmative Action: A Psychologist's Perspective." *University of Cincinnati Law Review,* Vol. 44 (1975), 690-697.

Lopatka, K. T. "Developing Concepts in Title VII Law," in L. J. Hansman et al. (eds.), *Equal Rights and Industrial Relations.* Madison, Wis.: Industrial Relations Research Association, 1977, pp. 31-69.

Peterson, D. J. "The Impact of Duke Power on Testing," *Personnel,* Vol. 51, No. 2 (1974), 30-37.

Ringler, L. J. "EEO Agreements and Consent Decrees May Be Booby-Traps!" *Personnel Administrator,* Vol. 22, No. 2 (1977), 16-21.

Schlei, B. L. and P. Grossman. *Employment Discrimination Law.* Washington, D.C.: BNA Books, 1976.

Shaeffer, R. G. *Nondiscrimination in Employment: Changing Perspectives, 1963-1972.* New York: The Conference Board, 1973.

Shaeffer, R. G. *Nondiscrimination in Employment, 1973-75: A Broadening and Deepening National Effort.* New York: The Conference Board, 1975.

U.S. Department of Justice, Office of the Deputy Attorney General, *Questions and Answers on the Federal Executive Agency Guidelines on Employee Selection Procedures.* Washington, D.C., 1977.

U.S. Equal Employment Opportunity Commission. *A Decade of Equal Employment Opportunity; 1965-1973; Tenth Annual Report.* Washington, D.C.: U.S. Government Printing Office, 1977.

Wallace, P.A. *Equal Employment Opportunity and the AT&T Case.* Cambridge, Mass.: MIT Press, 1976.

Wood, N. J. "Equal Employment Opportunity and Seniority: Rights in Conflict," *Labor Law Journal,* Vol. 26 (1975), 345-349.

Validation Research

American Psychological Association. *Standards for Educational and Psychological Testing.* Washington, D.C.: APA, 1974.

American Psychological Association, Division of Industrial-Organizational Psychology, *Principles for the Validation and Use of Personnel Selection Procedures.* Washington, D.C.: APA, 1975.

Anastasi, A. *Psychological Testing.* New York: Macmillian, 1976.

Anderson, C. and A. Nash. "Statistical Methods for PAIR," in D. Yoder and H. G. Heneman Jr. (eds.), *ASPA Handbook of Personnel and In-*

dustrial Relations, Volume IV: Planning and Auditing PAIR. Washington, D.C.: The Bureau of National Affairs, Inc. 1976, 129-183.

Arvey, R. D. and S. J. Mussio. "Determining the Existence of Unfair Test Discrimination for Female Clerical Workers," *Personnel Psychology,* Vol. 26 (1973), 559-568.

Asher, J. J. and J. A. Sciarrino. "Realistic Work Sample Tests: A Review," *Personnel Psychology,* Vol. 27 (1974), 519-533.

Baehr, M. E. *A Practitioner's View of EEOC Requirements with Special Reference to Job Analysis.* Occasional Paper 37. Chicago: University of Chicago Industrial Relations Center, 1976.

Barrett, R. S. *Performance Rating.* Chicago: Science Research Associates, 1966.

Bartlett, C. J. and B. S. O'Leary. "A Different Prediction Model to Moderate the Effects of Heterogeneous Groups in Personnel Selection and Classification." *Personnel Psychology,* Vol. 22 (1969), 1-17.

Bartlett, C. J. and I. L. Goldstein. *A Validity Study of the Reference Check for Support Personnel.* College Park: University of Maryland Psychology Department, 1976.

Bass, A. R. and J. N. Turner. "Ethnic Group Differences in Relationships Among Criteria of Job Performance," *Journal of Applied Psychology,* Vol. 57 (1973), 101-109.

Baylie, T. N., C. J. Kujawski, and D. M. Young. "Appraisals of People Resources," in D. Yoder and H. G. Heneman (eds.), *Staffing Policies and Strategies.* Washington, D.C.: Bureau of National Affairs, Inc., 1974, 4-159-201.

Berwitz, C. J. *The Job Analysis Approach to Affirmative Action.* New York: Wiley, 1975.

Boehm, V. R. "Negro-White Differences in Validity of Employment and Training Selection Procedures: Summary of Research Evidence," *Journal of Applied Psychology,* Vol. 56 (1972), 33-39

Campbell, J. P. "Psychometric Theory." in M. D. Dunnette (ed.), *Handbook of Industrial and Organizational Psychology.* Chicago: Rand McNally, 1976, pp. 185-222.

Campbell, J. T. "Tests Are Valid for Minority Groups Too." *Public Personnel Management,* Vol. 2 (1973), 70-73.

Cascio, W. F. "Turnover, Biographical Data, and Fair Employment Practice." *Journal of Applied Psychology,* Vol. 61 (1976), 576-580.

Cummings, L. L. and D. P. Schwab. *Performance in Organizations: Determinants and Appraisal.* Glenview, Ill.: Scott, Foresman, 1973.

Edwards, A. L. *Statistical Analysis.* New York: Holt, Rinehart, and Winston, 1974.

Einhorn, N. J. and A. R. Bass. "Methodological Considerations Relevant to Discrimination in Employment Testing." *Psychological Bulletin,* Vol. 75 (1971), 261-269.

Farr, J., B. S. O'Leary, and C. J. Bartlett. "Ethnic Group Membership as a Moderator of the Prediction of Job Performance." *Personnel Psychology,* Vol. 24 (1971), 609-636.

Fincher, C. "Differential Validity and Test Bias." *Personnel Psychology,* Vol. 28 (1975), 481-500.

Ghiselli, E. E. *The Validity of Occupational Aptitude Tests.* New York: Wiley, 1966.

Gross, A. L. and W. Su. "Defining a Fair or Unbiased Selection Model: A Question of Utilities." *Journal of Applied Psychology,* Vol. 60 (1975), 345-351.

Guion, R. M. *Personnel Testing.* New York: McGraw-Hill, 1965.

Hiestand, D. L. *Discrimination in Employment: An Appraisal of the Research.* Ann Arbor: Institute of Labor and Industrial Relations, University of Michigan, 1970.

Hunter, J. E. and F. L. Schmidt. "Critical Analysis of the Statistical and Ethical Implications of Various Definitions of Test Bias." *Psychological Bulletin,* Vol. 83 (1976), 1053-1071.

Kerlinger, F. N. *Foundations of Behavioral Research.* New York: Holt, Rinehart and Winston, 1974.

Lazer, R. I. "The Discrimination Danger in Performance Appraisal." *Conference Board Record,* Vol. 13, No. 3 (1976), 60-64.

Ledvinka, J. "Technical Implications of Equal Employment Law for Manpower Planning," *Personnel Psychology,* Vol. 28 (1975), 299-323.

McCormick, E. J. "Job Information: Its Development and Applications," in D. Yoder and H. G. Heneman (eds.), *Staffing Policies and Strategies.* Washington, D.C.: The Bureau of National Affairs, Inc. 1974, pp. 35-83.

McNemar, Q. *Psychological Statistics.* New York: Wiley, 1969.

Miner, J. B. "Management Appraisal: A Capsule Review and Current References," *Business Horizons,* Vol. 11, No. 5 (1968), 83-96.

Moore, C. L., J. F. MacNaughton, and H. G. Osburn. "Ethnic Differences

Within an Industrial Selection Battery,'' *Personnel Psychology,* Vol. 22 (1969), 473-482.

O'Connor, E. J., K. N. Wexley, and R. A. Alexander. "Single Group Validity: Fact or Fallacy?'' *Journal of Applied Psychology,* Vol. 60 (1975), 352-355.

Osburn, H. G. and W. R. Manese. *How to Install and Validate Employee Selection Techniques.* Washington, D.C.: American Petroleum Institute, 1972.

O'Toole, D. L., J. F. Gavin, L. B. Murdy, and S. B. Sells. "The Differential Validity of Personality, Personal History, and Aptitude Data for Minority and Nonminority Employees,'' *Personnel Psychology,* Vol. 25 (1972), 661-672.

Prien, E. P., and W. W. Ronan. "Job Analysis: A Review of Research Findings,'' *Personnel Psychology,* Vol. 24 (1971), 371-396.

Rouleau, E. J. and B. F. Krain. "Using Job Analysis to Design Selection Procedures,'' *Public Personnel Management,* Vol. 4 (1975), 300-304.

Ruda, E. and L. E. Albright. "Racial Differences on Selection Instruments Related to Subsequent Job Performance,'' *Personnel Psychology,* Vol. 21 (1968), 31-41.

Schmidt, F. L., J. E. Hunter, and V. W. Urry. "Statistical Power in Criterion-Related Validation Studies,'' *Journal of Applied Psychology,* Vol. 61 (1976), 473-485.

Schneider, B. *Staffing Organizations.* Pacific Palisades, Calif.: Goodyear, 1976.

Schwab, D. P., H. Heneman, III, and T. A. DeCotiis. "Behaviorally Anchored Rating Scales: A Review of the Literature,'' *Academy of Management Proceedings,* 1975, pp. 222-224.

Sharf, J. C. "How Validated Testing Eases the Pressures of Minority Recruitment,'' *Personnel,* Vol. 52, No. 3 (1975), 53-59.

Smith, R. D. "Models for Personnel Selection Decisions,'' *Personnel Journal,* Vol. 52 (1973), 688-695.

Tenopyr, M. L. "Content-Construct Confusion,'' *Personnel Psychology,* Vol. 30 (1977), 47-54.

Thorndike, R. L. "Concepts of Culture Fairness,'' *Journal of Educational Measurement,* Vol. 8 (1971), 63-70.

United States Department of Labor. *Handbook for Analyzing Jobs.* Washington, D.C.: Government Printing Office, 1972.

United States Department of Labor. *Productive Employment of the Disadvantaged: Guidelines for Action.* Washington, D.C.: Government Printing Office, 1973.

United States Department of Labor. *Task Analysis Inventories.* Washington, D.C.: Government Printing Office, 1973.

United States Department of Labor. *Job Analysis for Human Resource Management: A Review of Selected Research and Development.* Manpower Research Monograph No. 36. Washington, D.C.: Government Printing Office, 1974.

Zedeck, S. and M. R. Blood. *Foundations of Behavioral Science Research in Organizations.* Monterey, Calif.: Brooks/Cole, 1974.

Zedeck, S. and M. L. Tenopyr. "Issues in Selection, Testing, and the Law," in L. J. Hansman et al. (eds.), *Equal Rights and Industrial Relations.* Madison, Wis.: Industrial Relations Research Association, 1977.

Affirmative Action

Alper, S. W. "Racial Differences in Job and Work Environment Priorities Among Newly Hired College Graduates,"*Journal of Applied Psychology,* Vol. 60 (1975), 132-134.

Bassford, G. L. "Job Testing—Alternatives to Employment Quotas," *Business Horizons,* Vol. 17, No. 1 (1974), 37-47.

Beaumont, A. G. *Handbook for Recruiting at the Traditionally Black Colleges.* Bethlehem, Pa.: College Placement Services, Inc., 1973.

Bureau of National Affairs, Inc. *Equal Employment Opportunity: Programs & Results.* Personnel Policies Forum Survey No. 112, February 1976.

Bureau of National Affairs, Inc. *Selection Procedures and Personnel Records,* Personnel Policies Forum Survey No. 114, August 1976.

Churchill, N. and J. Shank. "Affirmative Action and Guilt-Edged Goals," *Harvard Business Review,* Vol. 54, No. 2 (1976), 111-116.

Crane, D. P. "How Blacks Become Managers in Atlanta, Georgia Companies," *Training in Business and Industry,* Vol. 8, No. 6 (1971), 21-26. 21-26.

Evans, V. M. "Unisex Jobs and Nontraditional Employment," *Personnel,* Vol. 52, No. 6 (1975), 31-37.

Fernandez, J. P. *Black Managers in White Corporations.* New York: Wiley, 1975.

Gery, G. J. "Hiring Minorities and Women: The Selection Process," *Personnel Journal,* Vol. 53, No. 12 (1974), 906-909.

Gruenfeld, E. F. *Promotion: Practices, Policies, and Affirmative Action.* Ithaca, N.Y.: New York State School of Industrial and Labor Relations, Cornell University, 1975.

Hedges, J. N. and S. E. Bemis. "Sex Stereotyping: Its Decline in Skilled Trades," *Monthly Labor Review,* Vol. 97, No. 5 (1974), 14-22.

Higgins, J. M. "The Complicated Process of Establishing Goals for Equal Employment," *Personnel Journal,* Vol. 54 (1975), 631-637.

Iacobelli, J. L., and J. P. Muczyk. "Overlooked Talent Sources and Corporate Strategies for Affirmative Action," *Personnel Journal,* Vol. 54 (1975), 532-535, 549, 575-577, 587.

Koff, L. A. and J. H. Hanlon. "Women in Management: Keys to Success and Failure," *Personnel Administrator,* Vol. 20, No. 2 (1975), 24-28.

Kraut, A. I. "The Entrance of Black Employees into Traditionally White Jobs," *Academy of Management Journal,* Vol. 18 (1975), 610-615.

Ledvinka, J., and R. D. Gatewood. "EEO Issues with Pre-employment Inquiries," *Personnel Administrator,* Vol. 22, No. 2 (1977), 22-26.

Lockwood, H. C. "Equal Employment Opportunities," in D. Yoder and H. G. Heneman (eds.), *Staffing Policies and Strategies.* Washington, D.C.: Bureau of National Affairs, Inc., 1974, pp. 245-287.

Miner, J. B. *Studies in Management Education.* Atlanta, Ga.: Organizational Measurement Systems Press, 1965.

Miner, J. B. *Motivation to Manage: A Ten Year Update on the "Studies in Management Education" Research.* Atlanta, Ga.: Organizational Measurement Systems Press, 1977.

Miner, J. B. and M. G. Miner. *Personnel and Industrial Relations: A Managerial Approach.* New York: MacMillan, 1977.

Purcell, T. V. "How GE Measures Managers in Fair Employment," *Harvard Business Review,* Vol. 52, No. 6 (1974), 99-104.

Purcell, T. V. "Management and Affirmative Action in the Late Seventies," in L. J. Hansam et al. (eds.), *Equal Rights and Industrial Relations.* Madison, Wisc.: Industrial Relations Research Association, 1977.

Purcell, T. V. and G. F. Cavanagh. *Blacks in the Industrial World: Issues for the Manager.* New York: Free Press, 1972.

Quinn, R. P. "Differences Between Those Who Do and Do Not Use Nonability Factors in Decisions to Hire or Promote Managers,'' In B. M. Bass, R. Cooper, and J. A. Haas (eds), *Managing for Accomplishment.* Lexington, Mass.: Heath, 1970, 26-42.

Richards, S. A. and C. L. Jaffee. ''Blacks Supervising Whites: A Study of Interracial Difficulties in Working Together in a Simulated Organization,'' *Journal of Applied Psychology,* Vol. 56 (1972), 234-240.

Rosen, B. and T. H. Jerdee. ''Sex Stereotyping in the Executive Suite,'' *Harvard Business Review,* Vol. 52, No. 2 (1974), 45-58.

Salipante, P. and P. Goodman. ''Training, Counseling, and Retention of the Hard-Core Unemployed'' and ''Organizational Rewards and Retention of the Hard-Core Unemployed,'' *Journal of Applied Psychology,* Vol. 61 (1976), 1-21.

Schmidt, F. L. and R. H. Johnson. ''Effect of Race on Peer Ratings in an Industrial Situation,'' *Journal of Applied Psychology,* Vol. 57 (1973), 237-241.

Sharf, J. C. ''How Validated Testing Eases the Pressures of Minority Recruitment,'' *Personnel,* Vol. 52, No. 3 (1975), 53-59.

Stanton, E. S. *Successful Personnel Recruiting and Selection.* New York: AMACOM, 1977.

Stone, C. H. and F. L. Ruch. ''Selection, Interviewing, and Testing.'' In D. Yoder and H. G. Heneman (eds.), *ASPA Handbook of Personnel and Industrial Relations: Staffing Policies and Strategies.* Washington, D.C.: Bureau of National Affairs, Inc., 1974, pp. 117-158.

Weaver, C. N. ''Black-White Differences in Attitudes Toward Job Characteristics,'' *Journal of Applied Psychology,* Vol. 60 (1975), 438-441.

Wells, J. A. *Counseling Women for Careers in Business.* Washington, D.C.: U.S. Women's Bureau, 1973.

Wisner, R. W. ''The Kirkland Case—Its Implications for Personnel Selection,'' *Public Personnel Management,* Vol. 4 (1975), 263-267.

index of authors cited

G

H

I

J

K

L

M

N

O

P

subject index

T